Through Darkest Seas

Through Darkest Seas

The untold story of how Duyfken, *Australia's first ship, was recreated and sailed into history ... again.*

Graeme Cocks

Through Darkest Seas
The untold story of how Duyfken, Australia's first ship, was recreated and sailed into history ... again

www.duyfkenbook.com

First published in Australia in July 2023, Revised
Motoring Past Vintage Publishing
Astuto Pty Ltd
PO Box 297, Inglewood WA 6052, Australia

ISBN
Hardcover :   978-0-9925078-3-1
Paperback: 978-0-9925078-1-7
Ebook: 978-0-9925078-2-4

Email: gacocks@iinet.net.au
Facebook: Duyfken Book "Through Darkest Seas"
Copyright © Graeme Cocks 2023

Front Cover Photograph: Thanks to Robert Garvey, taken near Banda Neira, Indonesia, June 2000.

Graeme Cocks asserts the moral right to be identified as the author of this work. All rights reserved. Except for short extracts for the purpose of review, no part of this book may be reproduced, stored in a retrieval system or transmitted in any form or by any means, whether electronic, mechanical, photocopying, recording or otherwise, without prior written permission of the publisher.

'Life is either a daring adventure or nothing'

Helen Keller

For Cathy, Louise and Daniel
Who gave more for the ship than anyone else,
and to all the crazy souls who shared the Duyfken *dream*

Drying the sails. Duyfken *at Banda, Indonesia, June 2000.*

CONTENTS

INTRODUCTION		17
PROLOGUE		20
CHAPTER 1	IT SEEMED LIKE A GOOD IDEA AT THE TIME	22
CHAPTER 2	WHAT'S A *DUYFKEN*?	30
CHAPTER 3	GLORIOUS, ENTHRALLING NAIVETY	38
CHAPTER 4	GIVE ME JUST 10 HOURS OF YOUR TIME	59
CHAPTER 5	ROMANCE VERSUS REALITY	70
CHAPTER 6	AN IDEA WHOSE TIME HAS COME	84
CHAPTER 7	FROM LITTLE ACORN TO MIGHTY OAK	95
CHAPTER 8	MR I SAY I SAY	129
CHAPTER 9	FREMANTLE IS THE CENTRE OF THE UNIVERSE	133
CHAPTER 10	THE LITTLE DOVE SPREADS HER WINGS	149
CHAPTER 11	TRAGEDY AND TRIUMPH	163
CHAPTER 12	STORM CLOUDS OVER INDONESIA	172
CHAPTER 13	CYCLONES AND SAILORS	184
CHAPTER 14	LEAVING THE NEST	198
CHAPTER 15	FOUR RUBBER STAMPS AND SIGNATURES	218
CHAPTER 16	NO TURNING BACK	230
CHAPTER 18	SUGAR AND SPICE AND ALL THINGS NICE	246
CHAPTER 19	LEARNING NOTHING FROM HISTORY	277
CHAPTER 20	HELL	283
CHAPTER 21	IN SEARCH FOR MEANING	297
CHAPTER 22	EPIC OR EXPLOITATION	312
CHAPTER 23	WHERE TO NEXT?	333
CHAPTER 24	MOUNTAIN SCALED	345
CHAPTER 25	THE BIG ONE	353
CHAPTER 26	INTO THE INDIAN OCEAN AGAIN	370
CHAPTER 27	LEAVE NOTHING BUT FOOTPRINTS	385
CHAPTER 28	A FRESH START	428
EPILOGUE		451
LIFE AND TIMES: A *DUYFKEN* ALBUM		467
ACKNOWLEDGEMENTS		506
GLOSSARY		508
INDEX		514

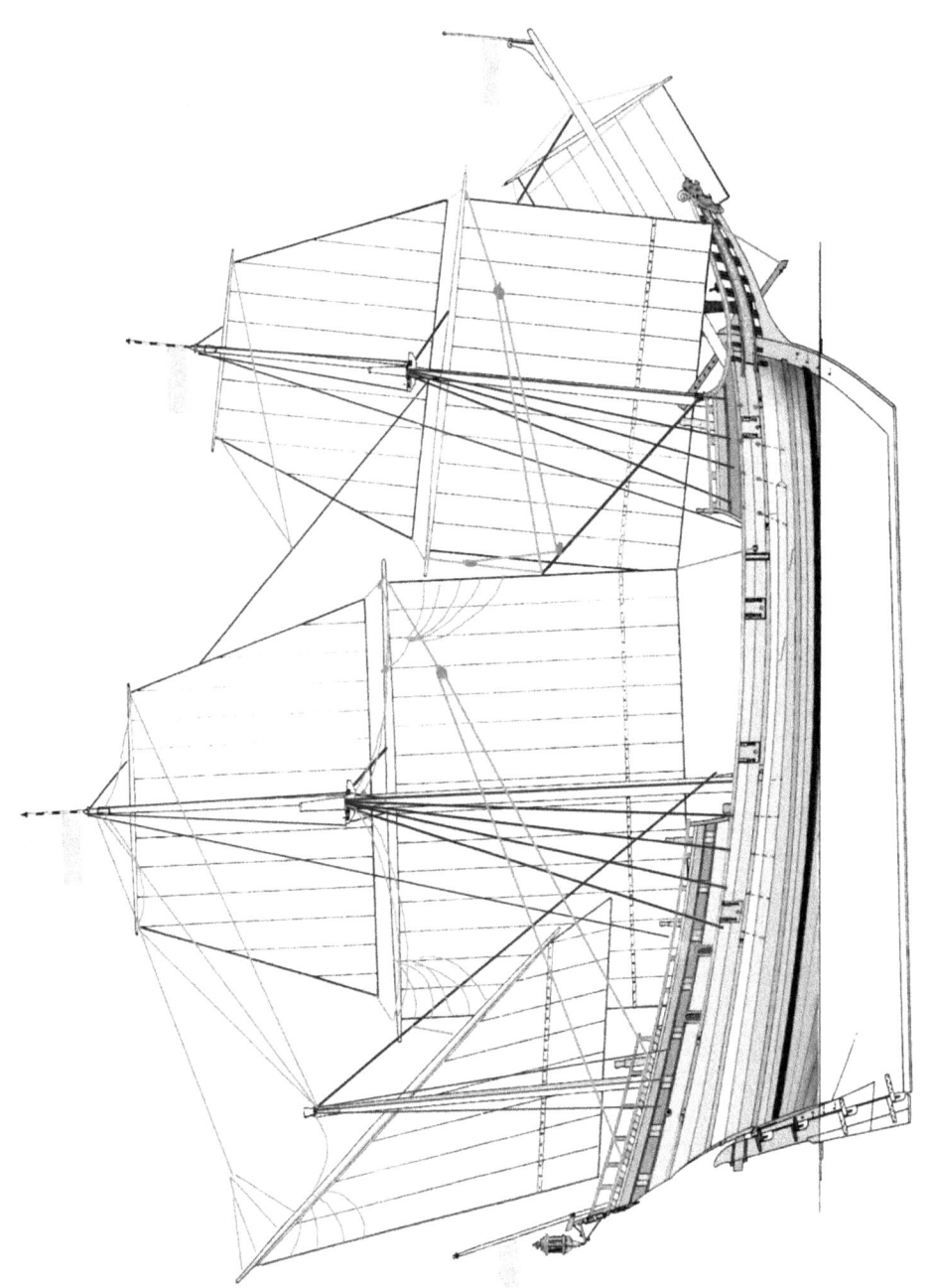

Duyfken Replica Specifications

Project Announced	26 February 1995
Keel laid	11 January 1997
Launched	24 January 1999
First Sail	10 July 1999
Rig	Three masted, square rigged fore and main masts, lateen rigged mizzen, spritsail
Planking below waterline	60mm oak
Planking above waterline	40 to 50mm oak
Framing timbers	approx. 400 mm
Length at keel	16.8 m
Length between stem and sternpost	19.94 m
Length overall (between beak head and taffrail)	25.2 m
Rope	3.5 km of rope used for standing and running rigging
Engines	Two 82 kw Hino diesel marine engines
Maximum beam	6.01 m
Freeboard midships	1.8 m
Height at stern (above the waterline)	5.5 m
Draft, deep laden	2.4 m
Depth in hold	2.2 m
Displacement at nominal draft	98.493 tonnes (fully laden - 110 tonnes)
Sail area	290 m²

Drawings by Adriaan de Jong with Nick

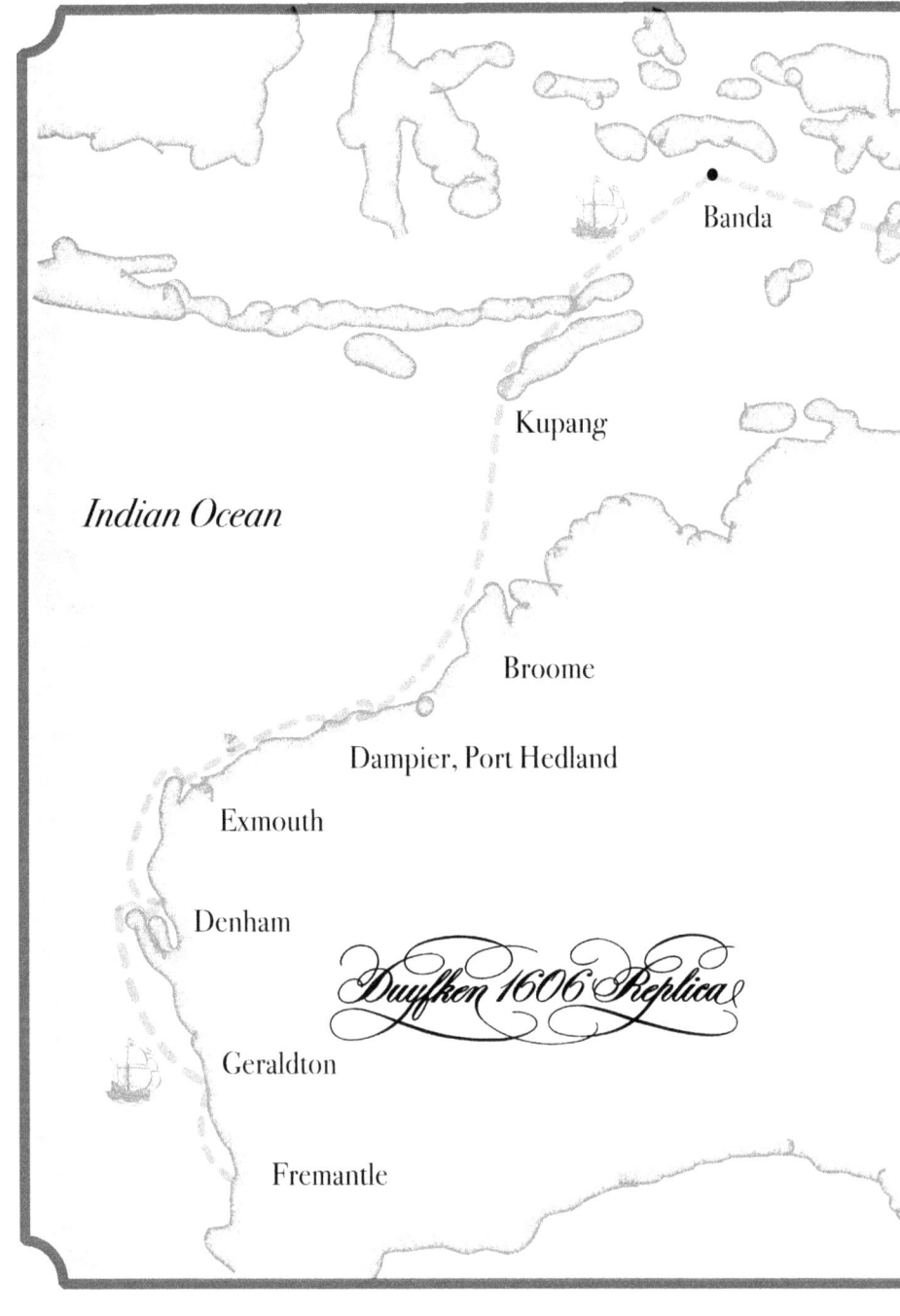

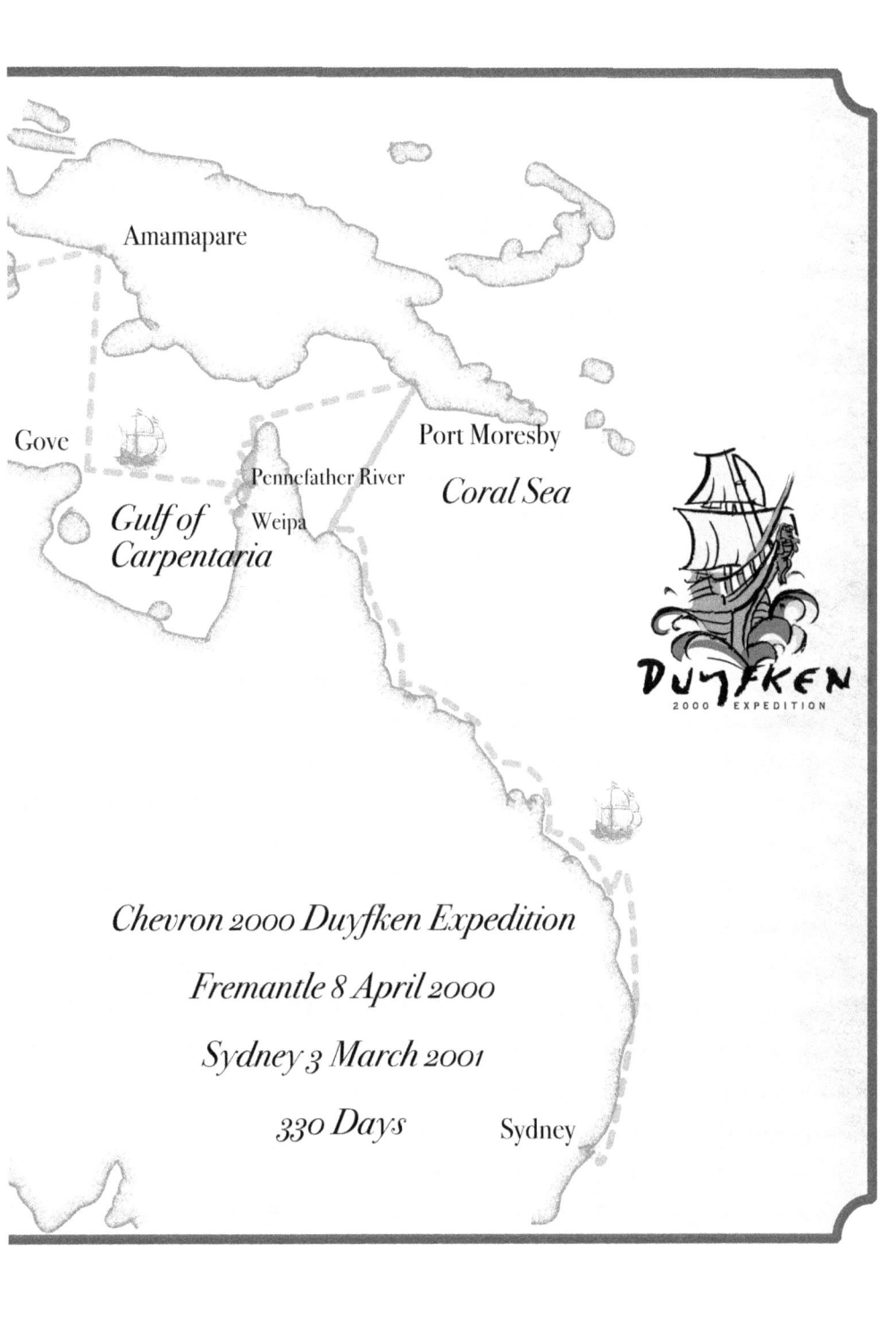

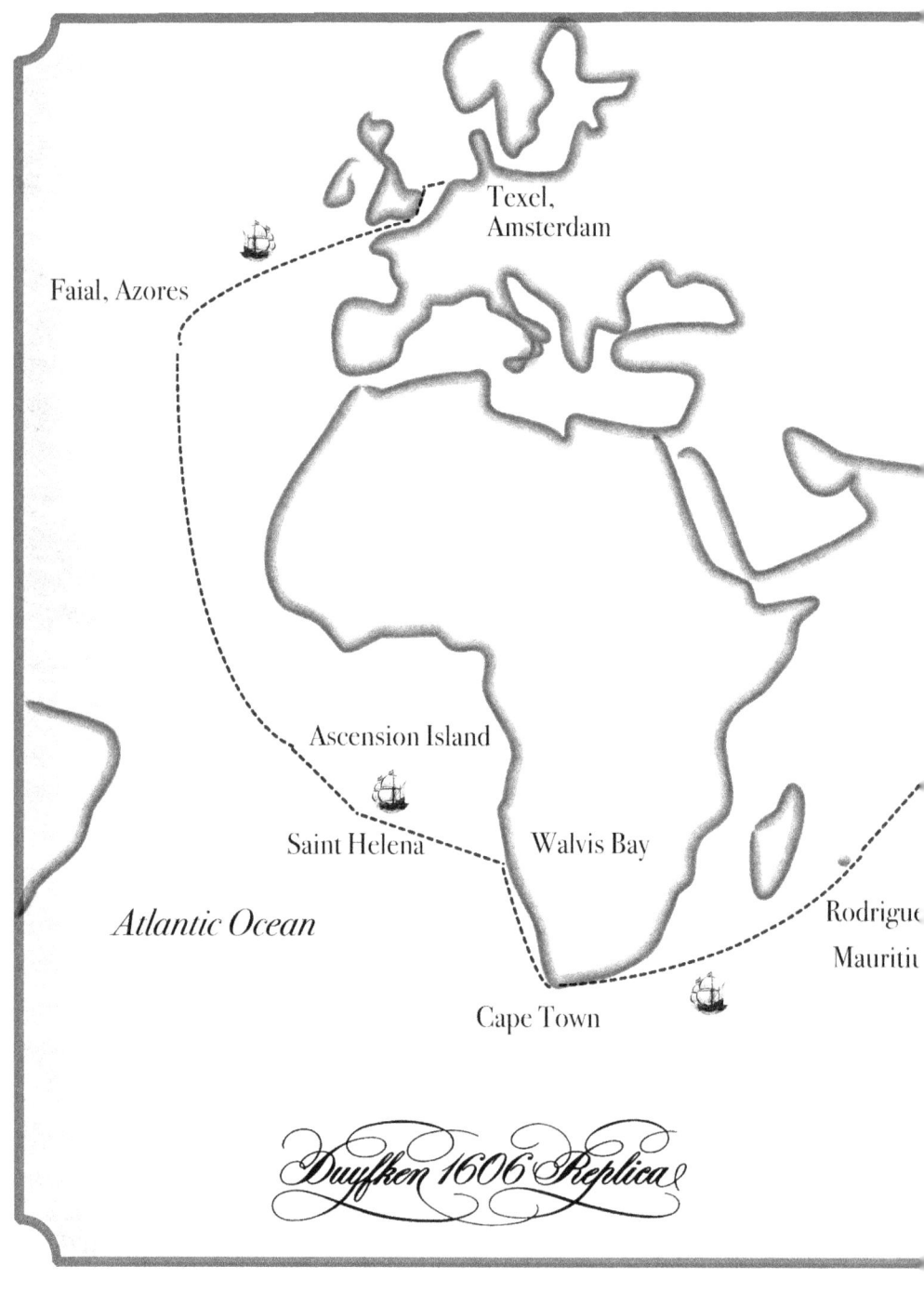

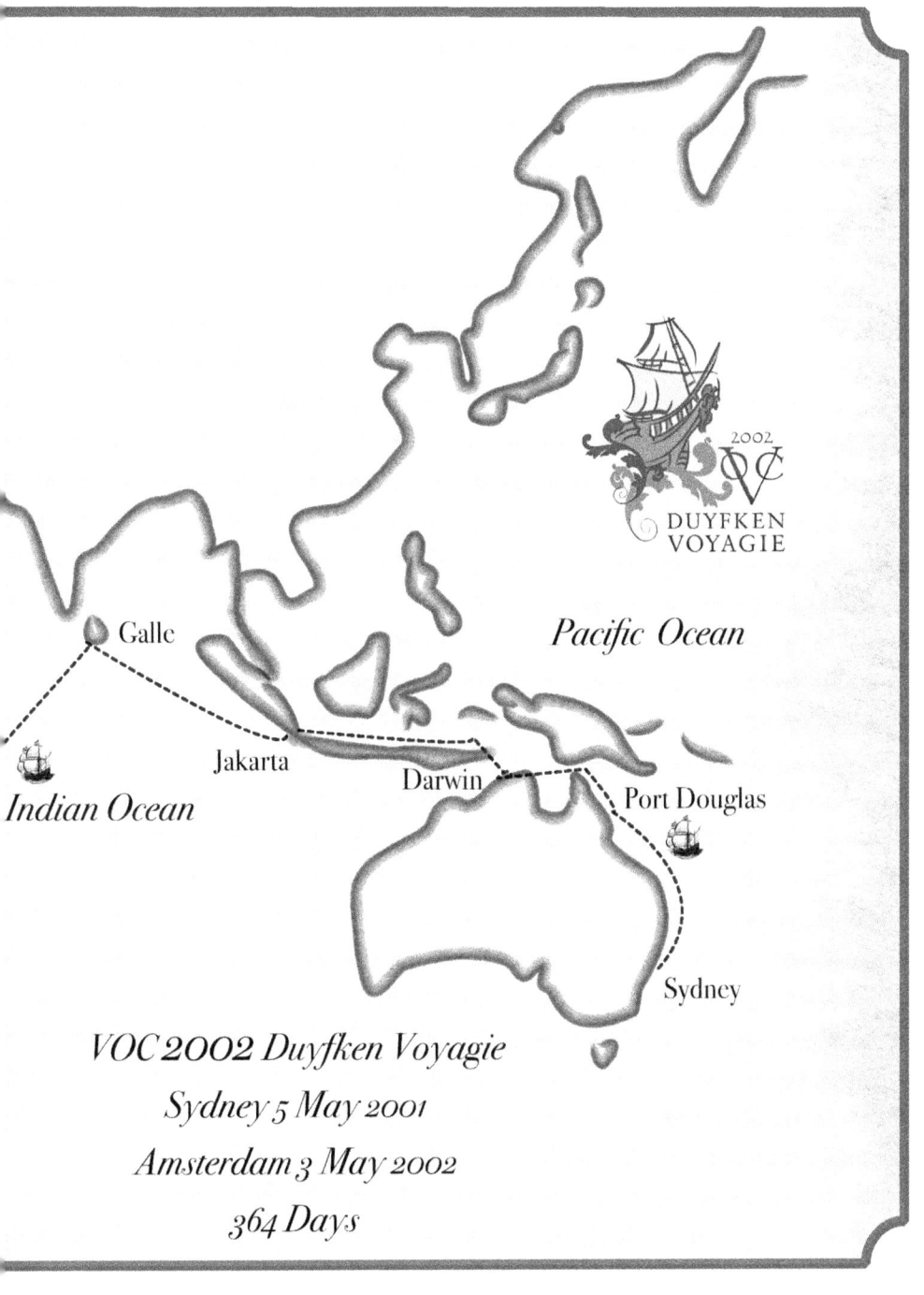

I'm getting old and before my memory fades
Let me tell you a tale of a little ship,
The remarkable people who built and sailed her,
The stormy seas she encountered,
The triumphs and the pain

Graeme Cocks, 2023

Introduction

It's bumper-to-bumper peak hour traffic on the Mitchell Freeway in Perth. I'd hitched a ride with two old friends, Tracy McCullough and David Kerbey, and we were heading to the final meeting of the *Duyfken* 1606 Replica Foundation in Fremantle. We'd be late but it didn't matter. The Foundation was to be dissolved and our ship permanently re-located from the western coast of Australia to the bright lights of Sydney.

Tracy had been my able lieutenant during the great years of voyaging the *Duyfken* replica sailing ship, while her husband David also caught the *Duyfken* disease and was Chairman for a number of tough years when funds were non-existent and it was a struggle to stay afloat — and we had a few years like that. We wanted to be there at the end although it gave us little pleasure to see the slow decline of the *Duyfken* Foundation. We felt we had to pay our respects to the Project in some way.

Tracy and David told me that they'd spent a night ship-keeping on *Duyfken* a few days before the ship was stripped of its component parts and shipped as a bare hull aboard another ship to Sydney. Ship-keeping was a *Duyfken* ritual where people slept aboard to make sure nothing went amiss during the hours of darkness. Since her launch 22 years before, she had never been alone. Tracy and David took their teenage daughter Zoe with them that night. She wasn't born when we were voyaging the ship. Another *Duyfken* veteran, Michael 'Barney' Barnett, also slept aboard to spend one final night with the ship for old time's sake. He amazed his fellow ship-keepers, regaling them with his knowledge: Barney seemed to know everything there was to know about *Duyfken*, his passion undiminished. He was a musician, the son of a chimney-sweeper, and a chimney-sweep himself in his youth, who came down to the shipyard looking for work and helped fire-bend the planks which formed the oak hull. He could tell a story about every last piece of that little ship. Barney wrote a song which became our own anthem, 'The Ballad of the *Duyfken*'. We could sing it by heart and he even performed the song in The Netherlands when he crewed on our wildly-successful summer tour. Barney didn't bring his guitar to keep ship, but Zoe did, and she played and sang him his own song. For the first time, someone played it for Barney. He was touched. *Duyfken* passions run deep.

"You know, Graeme, I still think about that day at the Pennefather River," said Tracy while we were stuck in the traffic. "It makes me very emotional."

I had to agree with her, I get a lump in my throat whenever I talk about it and it was 20 years ago for Christ's sake. "We did something good, didn't we?" I said, still seeking the affirmation, the recognition that achievement longs for. "Yes. Do you remember the journalist from the Courier Mail who was aboard?" said Tracy. "He said afterwards that it may have been the most important story he would ever write."

"It was the Sydney Morning Herald, wasn't it?" I said. And yes, I did remember that story now she mentioned it.

I told Tracy that I still struggled to find meaning in those *Duyfken* events of 20 years ago. I had been in touch with a few crew members from our voyages and they, too, were still coming to grips with what had happened. Contacting them had opened up old wounds. *Duyfken*'s designer Nick Burningham once said that the three months he spent sailing *Duyfken* were a highlight of his life. "I even enjoyed the bits that weren't enjoyable (though I might have seemed unusually grumpy and irritable at the time)," he once said, as if to turn attention away from the lows of the experience. Ben Manthorpe told me: "It took me a very long time to eat dahl again, and now when I have it, most of the time it isn't good enough."

Our ship's artist from the first voyage, Robert Jefferson, grappled for 20 years with the questions raised by the voyage. The burden to produce something tangible from the experience became too much. It took him three months to burn his boxes of archives, drawings and woodblocks. He sent me the remnants of his work. It revealed his inner torment. Some things stuck in my mind. He said in one of his musings: "To grow is to constantly question and review our belief systems, to constantly review and rearrange our views, our thoughts and attitudes and so make clear … to resolve our state of mind."

I have kept my distance from the ship in recent years, preferring to look to the future rather than the past. I didn't want to be the tedious "you're doing it wrong, we did it this way" critic. I also felt that the Project had somehow lost its way, but I'd had my chance and it was now in others' hands.

Time has taken many of the people who turned the dream of *Duyfken* into a reality. I often thought I should document my years with the Project so that the glorious folly of those days was not forgotten. Of course, as it often does, life got in my way. The sad demise of the Foundation spurred me into action.

What began with a desire to record the history of the replica ship Project as a personal memoir has become my journey into the soul of the *Duyfken*. Sometimes small things take me back. Every time I attend a function and I hear a half-hearted, tokenistic acknowledgement of past owners of the land I cringe and think about our time at the Pennefather River in Queensland when we passionately thought that what we were doing was important. It has been estimated that, from an Aboriginal population of about 300,000 people prior to European settlement, between 10,000 and 20,000 Aboriginal people died as a direct consequence of the European assumption that they had a God-given right to this land. The original *Duyfken* was a tool of the Dutch East India Company which wrought misery on millions of people. The *Duyfken* replica poked both these blisters. The big question I now ask is why we built a replica of *Duyfken* at all? Were we that naive? Does time on this earth give us wisdom? Not always. For sure, it gives us hindsight. It gives us the opportunity to reflect on what has gone and where we have been.

Damn that traffic. We arrived late to the meeting as the sun was setting and the strong sea breeze was cooling the air. We had to sneak into the room and find stools to perch on at the back of the room. I looked around and there mustn't have been more than a few dozen people to hear the last rites of the *Duyfken* Foundation being performed. I could only see a handful of people I knew from the early days. Do the others know what they are giving away? Like the ship itself, I was a relic from another era. There were a few speeches, painting defeat as victory, seeking Trumpian affirmation that they had acted in the best interests of the ship. Should I say something? No, let it go Graeme. They wouldn't understand.

The *Duyfken* 1606 Replica Foundation was wound up with a few hundred dollars left in the bank. Not a bad result considering we started with nothing in 1994, I suppose.

This is not a book about the romance of sailing ships. No, this book is about the completely crazy adventure of building a ship and embarking on voyages into the unknown — and how it changed a lot of us.

Prologue

What sort of hell is this? I am on my back in a bunk in the tiny Captain's Cabin of *Duyfken*. It is barely wide enough to fit my shoulders. I am staring straight up like an Egyptian mummy, hemmed in and unable to move from one side to another, a wall of oak planking on one side and a side rail on the other There is a tiny glassless window behind my head. I try not to move, fearing that I may roll down onto the floor of the cabin when we hit the next wave. Above me, a droplet of water grows like a stalactite, larger and larger on the mouldy pinaster pine plank ceiling. It forms a bulb which rocks from side to side as the ship slides across two metre swells. The droplet gives way, liberated, and drops right into the middle of my forehead, then explodes. It's cold. I don't bother to wipe it away. My face stays wet. I no longer have the energy to move, every bone in my body aches, the nausea overwhelms me. I close my eyes, hoping that this will all end soon. I know that another droplet is bulging. In a few minutes it will be free and gravity will send it toward me. I don't care. I haven't the energy to resist this torture any more.

My thoughts wander and I curse that leaking deck above. It shouldn't leak. It's barely two years old. I remember the squabble that those wrongly sawn deck planks caused during the construction of the ship — the frustration of the shipwrights who had no control over what they were told they must use — even though they knew the deck would never seal. Those bloody planks are one of the reasons fate brought me here, I remind myself. "Graeme, it was your decision. You've got no-one else to blame." I doze off once again.

I've been laid low on my back like this for the past 24 hours. We left Newcastle in New South Wales on 1 March 2001, with only a short hop left in the great voyage from Fremantle to the spice islands of Indonesia. We were heading for Sydney, Australia's largest city, to proclaim that we had accomplished what we had set out to do. Just two more days and the 330 day voyage would be over. I wasn't about to miss the chance to be aboard as we sailed triumphantly through the heads into Sydney Harbour, under the famed harbour bridge and into Cockle Bay Wharf at Darling Harbour to berth at the Australian National Maritime Museum.

It had been an eventful departure from Newcastle the day before. Near gale force winds from the south delayed our departure for several hours until they moderated to the south east. We set sail on a gloomy grey day into strong winds and a stormy sea, pounding into a big swell and riding down the waves. We picked our way through a line of iron ore ships waiting at sea before coming into port to unload their cargo. The *Duyfken* crew quickly got into their regular pattern, splitting into two watches, with half disappearing below deck to rest and the others following the orders of the Ship's Master, Gary Wilson. I climbed to my favourite position onboard, wedged way up in the stern of the poop deck, where I could see everything happening on the main deck and I could enjoy a brilliant view of those great steel bulk carriers as we sailed past.

Of course, this was a mistake. As *Duyfken* wallows, the movement is magnified so far from the keel. The ship swings rhythmically from side to side and then climbs up and over another wave, a constantly repeating cycle which confounds everything my brain and body expect. Once again, the landlubber has succumbed to seasickness. I'm overwhelmed with nausea.

I ask myself why I keep doing this? I don't even like the ocean. The dark green wallowing mass stretching from one horizon to another is like a desert to me.

My journey began 12 years before.

Chapter 1

It Seemed Like a Good Idea at the Time

The *Endeavour* replica's hull sat precariously atop the sharply angled, greased ways which would send it into Fremantle Fishing Boat Harbour to float for the first time. The shipbuilding team led by master shipwright Bill Leonard had its last great job to do — to set the hull free from an existence on land to life at sea. Every vantage point inside the building was taken with special guests and VIPs, friends and family of the team. Thousands of people were gathered outside to witness the moment. Everyone loves the spectacle of a launching. The media throng I coordinated was in place around the ship and ringed the harbour outside. My job was done and I snuck up to a point on one of the staircases which hugged the stern. I would be able to almost touch the ship when she slid past. I was happy to be so high in the building. I chose this spot carefully. If something went wrong and the worst happened, I had no intention of being crushed by a wayward hull toppling over and crushing the people crammed behind barriers far below. With a nod to Sir Joseph Banks, the Australian botanist and Chairman of the CSIRO, Professor Adrienne Clarke, did the honours, smashing a bottle of Grange Hermitage wine on the hull. The speech was shorter than expected and the tide had peaked earlier than forecast. It was critical to send the ship away on the high tide but it was already ebbing. Bill Leonard told John Longley that it was the optimal time. They were seven minutes before the scheduled launch window but why wait any longer? Endeavour was set free with hefty swings of axes, severing the ropes which held surprisingly small levers for such a large hull in place. I needn't have worried. The hull slid past me, gathering speed. Surely I could touch her if I could lean out just a little further? I did not tempt fate. The hull glided into the water, floated without any fuss, then slewed sideways just enough for everyone to take a deep breath. She decelerated without drama, feeling water on her hull for the first time. Then the tugs took control as she settled into her new aquatic home. Three cheers for *Endeavour*!

There is something overwhelmingly sad about an empty shipyard the day after a ship has been launched. Only 12 hours before, at 5.23pm on 9 December 1993, the *Endeavour* shed had been full of energy and anticipation. The next day, the hull, or should I now say *Endeavour* for she had become a ship, was safely tied up at Victoria Quay to receive more ballast. A few of us went back to the shed because we didn't quite know what to do next. All our efforts had been focussed on the launch. I'd forgotten just how large the shed was without a hull inside. On the greased ways, the last reminders of the great event of the day before were now just rubbish to be cleaned up — smashed glass from the Grange bottle which had sent her on her way was all that was left. A couple of people grabbed the shards for old time's sake. Soon they, too, were gone. And soon *Endeavour* would also be gone. Eventually, she would be home-ported at Darling Harbour in Sydney under a deal with the Federal Government which agreed to help finish what Alan Bond had started in 1987 with the rhyme 'A Gift to the Nation from the Bond Corporation'. It was hard to find anyone in Fremantle who was happy with this outcome.

The idea of building a replica was proposed by the journalist and historian Bruce Stannard. Invited by the Royal Historical Society of Queensland to write about his contribution he later wrote that he had "been deeply conscious always of the profound debt that we (Australians) all owe to the genius of Captain James Cook, and to his extraordinary exploits as seaman, navigator, explorer, meticulous cartographer, and courageous and compassionate commander. As a Fellow of the Royal Society and one of the central figures in the European Enlightenment, Cook understood the inevitable consequences of his discoveries for the peoples of the Pacific. Cook was the man who 'gave us a Hemisphere' and in so doing played the seminal role in the gestation of our nation." Bruce Stannard successfully approached Alan Bond to support the replica idea as a generous gesture to the country in which he had become a national hero. However, when a run of bad business deals and a recession knocked him off his vulnerable pedestal, his pet project went broke — but not rudderless. A charitable foundation, The HM Bark *Endeavour* Foundation, was created in August 1991 from the ashes of the Bond Corporation and it secured the asset.

Meanwhile, the construction of the replica of Lieutenant James Cook's ship had become part of the fabric of Fremantle. Everyone knew someone who worked at the yard or who had supplied some service to the team. John Longley managed the project. A keen yachtie, he had been on Bond's winning America's Cup team, headed Bond's unsuccessful defence campaign and, above all, he was a local lad. Along with his marketing manager, Vern Reid, they had an instinct for attracting publicity by always keeping the media informed of every storm they faced. It was a publicist's dream. John Longley's stature in the Perth community grew when he battled on against the odds to get *Endeavour* funded and completed after Bond fell from grace. He and others worked for months without pay to save the project. Volunteer guides kept the shipyard open for visitors when there was no money. Margaret Rapanaro, who ran the *Endeavour* souvenir shop, said that the volunteers were the project's saviours: "The guides were amazing and tireless in their loyalty during the most bleak times."

Bill Leonard, the master shipwright appointed to build the ship, also stuck with *Endeavour* during the highs and lows when the cash flow was reduced to a trickle. They had a very loyal team working for them, too. The shipyard ran as an excellent tourist attraction with a stylish video presentation, visitor access to all areas of the yard to see every element of the construction of the Whitby collier, a contingent of voluntary guides led by the ever-enthusiastic John Lancaster, an education program run by ex-teacher and children's author, Mike Lefroy, a highly-polished marketing effort by Vern Reid, and a shop run by Margaret Rapanaro with stylish, quality souvenirs. Tourism was the lifeline which gave the Project a public face and kept the construction going through the good times and the bad.

Together with the WA Maritime Museum's shipwreck galleries and their treasured exhibits from Dutch shipwrecks including the *Batavia*; and the 'Cappuccino Strip' with its cafes and restaurants, the *Endeavour* shipyard became one of the primary attractions at the old port city. And this was where I came in. Returning home in 1984 after a year backpacking the world, and South and Central America in particular, with my girlfriend Cathy (whom I later married) I thought that travel journalism would be just the ticket to get me out of provincial Perth. The West Australian capital city seemed awfully small and parochial after a year seeing the wonders of the world. An old university friend, Bob Johns, helped me get a job working with him as a journalist on tourism trade magazines. The wages weren't great but the travel perks made up for the relentless grind of three magazines a month.

We enjoyed breaking news stories and we were sometimes regarded as a pest by the government of the day. After I wrote a series of articles in 1988 which were seen as negative towards the State Government tourism marketing body, the Western Australian Tourism Commission, I was encouraged to apply for a job at the very organisation which I had criticised. It came with a big boost in salary, and I guess they thought they could shut me up. It worked. I jumped at the opportunity. From pumping out the column inches at the travel magazines, I was now relentlessly pumping out media releases and vacuous ministerial speeches. Thankfully, the Tourism Commission had an extensive program of hosting media visits which got me out of the office and to every corner of the State from Cape Londonderry to Cape Leeuwin. I often guided media groups to Fremantle and because I enjoyed visiting the *Endeavour* shipyard so much, my groups would invariably end up at Mews Road. John Longley would beguile the journalists with a guided tour of the latest developments in the construction of the ship and stories from Cook's voyages. He had an entertaining spiel. The travel journalists loved it and lapped it up. I began to know the patter off by heart until one day John said to me: "You know what to tell them, why don't you give the tour and I can continue with my work?" And so it was that I would regularly breeze into the shipyard with the latest media group from Japan, Europe or the USA. It was fun getting to know everyone in the yard and sharing their latest news and gossip.

Bruce Stannard continued to attract major private backers to help fund the completion of the ship. The breakthrough for the floundering *Endeavour* Project came when a foundation was formed by Sir Arthur Weller and several Sydney identities with some support from the Federal and New South Wales Governments. The support came with a condition that one day the ship would be home-ported at the Commonwealth Government's new Australian National Maritime Museum in Sydney. It was a bold move by the Government as Alan Bond was no longer a national hero and the long-suffering taxpayer was being called upon to fix the problem of the multimillionaire's half-built ship. There was also an emerging reappraisal of Australian history and the effects of colonisation on indigenous Australians. It was the early days of an increasing Aboriginal assertiveness which was beginning to challenge the traditional mainstream narrative surrounding old schoolboy heroes such as Cook. *Endeavour* had been symbolic of the 'heroic' British colonisation of the Australian continent. Despite these negatives, with the Federal money and donations from a handful of wealthy backers, John Longley, Bill Leonard and the shipbuilding team could finish the job which had begun with the laying of the keel in January 1988 at the start of the Bicentennial Year. A launch date in December 1993 was set. Such was the enormous public and media interest in the event that John Longley went to meet with the Chairman of the WA Tourism Commission, Kevin Harrison, with a plea for help. Media interest in the Project was overwhelming and he spent too much time talking to the media and not concentrating on the launch. He needed someone to manage the flood of media requests. He asked whether I could be seconded to the *HM Bark Endeavour* Foundation for the months leading up to the launch. Kevin Harrison agreed. Of course, I agreed, too!

The HM *Bark Endeavour* Foundation had virtually no advertising budget and yet constant media coverage helped make the shipyard a leading tourist attraction. From October 1988 to October 1994, the *Endeavour* shipyard and the ship placed on exhibition attracted more than half-a-million visitors and netted $10,000 a month. I learned a lot during this exciting time at *Endeavour* — particularly the power of media publicity when an engaging narrative is created. It was crafted as an inspiring tale of the underdog succeeding against all odds and the media lapped it up.

Alan Bond's Nine Network was a willing partner and there was nothing like television in those days to get the message out. It wasn't always easy, balancing the negativity surrounding Alan Bond's involvement and the enormous sense of ownership of the ship felt by the Perth public. Our erstwhile national hero had a bad 18 months. First he was declared bankrupt and then sentenced to prison time after being found guilty of charges arising from the collapse of the Bond Corporation. He was subsequently acquitted but his fall from grace was complete. Alan Bond had no plans to attend the launch but it was arranged for him to visit the shipyard in the lead-up to the event to acknowledge his role in founding the Project. The up-and-coming Nine Network journalist Liam Bartlett was tasked with interviewing him as a national exclusive. The journalist had to choose between a 'puff piece' or to ask some tough questions.

Alan Bond however had just come out of hospital and was just a little, shall we say, vague? As Shakespeare wrote: "All the world's a stage, And all the men and women merely players; They have their exits and their entrances, And one man in his time plays many parts." And so it was with Alan Bond. He arrived driving his Range Rover rather erratically, jumped a kerb, pushed past the media throng from other media outlets who were not allowed into the yard, and entered the building. Puffing his way up a series of steps overlooking the ship and looking like he was about to expire, he gave a pointless interview which he cut short when the questions became a bit tough. He was like a zombie when he left. I was disappointed that he appeared to have no interest in *Endeavour* or the people who had worked so hard for six years to finish his Project. It was just a piece of theatre. Alan Bond exited, stage left.

On the other hand, politicians loved to be associated with the ship now the hard work had been done. Whilst Federal Labor had provided some funding to enable the completion of the vessel, all politicians were welcome to bask in the glory. Sometimes they just did not get it. Dr John Hewson was opposition leader with a good shot at beating Prime Minister Paul Keating in the polls. He arrived in the shipyard dressed in the mandatory dark blue suit, white shirt and tie and shiny black business shoes — the hallmark of a Liberal politician. The deck of *Endeavour* was finished and there was a strict 'no black soles' policy for walking on the pristine white wooden deck before the launch. A populist politician would have turned this into a winning national media image, laughing and joking as he took his shoes off, but not Dr Hewson. It was embarrassing as he acted with surprise at the prospect and shyly removed his shoes while the cameras were rolling. He lost the 1993 election.

Days later, I was standing on the balcony in the *Endeavour* shed watching her slip by and feeling a great deal of satisfaction with the small part I had played in the Project. I returned to my job at the Tourism Commission soon after, once more churning out interminable media releases and ministerial speeches. Meanwhile, *Endeavour* was rigged and in April 1994, she completed her first sail in the waters of Gage Roads. She was a fine ship, a museum-standard replica of the highest quality. She completed six months of sea trials and day sails before leaving for an extensive exhibition tour and, ultimately, her new home in Sydney.

On 23 December 1993, a short letter to the editor, titled "A new *Endeavour*?" was published in the *Fremantle Herald* owned by the firebrand newspaper proprietor Andrew Smith. His newspaper was fiercely independent and he loved stirring up local issues. The letter writer lamented the impending loss of *Endeavour* to Sydney and proposed that a new ship should be built to preserve the traditional shipbuilding skills nurtured by the *Endeavour* Project. The writer proposed that the first ship in Australia's history should be built. That 'tiny' ship was *Duyfken*, a small Dutch jacht a fraction of the size of *Endeavour*. It would be comparatively cheap to build (*Endeavour* cost $17 million) and it could stay in Fremantle. Its upkeep would be considerably less than the replica of Cook's ship. On 8 January, 1994, the letter also got a run in The West Australian newspaper. The publicist in me thought it was good work by someone to get two runs for the same letter — especially as it was for a ship I had never heard of.

1994 was a watershed year for me. I was geting restless. I needed to get away from the predictable grind of the tourism job. It was time to move on from the Tourism Commission. I resigned and chanced my hand as a public relations consultant. I immediately picked up a number of contracts including a local PR consultancy role with Qantas which led to a major public relations campaign to promote the new Qantas subsidiary Airlink launching in Western Australia. John Longley also asked me to help out with the promotion of *Endeavour* on a paid basis. My brief career as a public servant was over.

I was aboard the ship for a breakfast sail in mid 1994, prior to her maiden voyage in October of that year. What a perfect morning! The sea was flat, the horizon above the Darling Scarp turned orange, and then the sun came up, turning the cream-coloured sails a soft yellow. The volunteer crew were busy aloft setting sail. John Longley and I retired below decks to the 'modern' part of the ship to enjoy a cooked breakfast from the well-appointed galley. Like most people in Perth I wasn't very happy about *Endeavour* leaving Fremantle. It was 'our ship' after all. "What do you think about the idea of building another replica in Fremantle?" I asked John. "I think it's a great idea," I said. He groaned and then laughed. I wasn't the first person to ask the question. He made it very clear to me that the last thing he needed in his life was another ship project. I didn't know that at the time he had been diagnosed with a terminal illness (from which he subsequently recovered). He said that he had talked to the people involved and he thought they were on the right track. He'd told them that they could always come to him for advice but he made it clear that this was to be his only involvement. He had great plans for sailing *Endeavour* to Britain and the United States and he planned to spend a good deal of time away from Fremantle. He told me that the small group was incredibly enthusiastic but they had absolutely no appreciation of the magnitude of the task they had set themselves. He agreed with them that it would be easier to raise the funds for a small ship and a Dutch vessel would make sense for the West Australian coast with its long Dutch maritime history.

Then he said something which would change my life: "You know, Graeme, you should get in touch with them and offer your services. They really have no idea of marketing and public relations and they could really do with someone with your skills."

I thought about what he said. Mark Twain once wrote: "Twenty years from now, you will be more disappointed by the things you didn't do than those you did. So throw off the bowlines. Sail away from safe harbour. Catch the wind in your sails. Explore. Dream. Discover."

Yep, at that moment I thought that maybe I should put my money where my mouth was and offer to help. "John, do you have a phone number for that guy who wrote the letter?"

Chapter 2

What's a Duyfken?

"The first Europeans who are known to have seen Australia were Dutchmen. In November, 1605, the yacht Duyfken sailed from the new Dutch settlements in Java. The plan was to explore New Guinea, where the Dutch hoped to find a 'great store of gold.' The Duyfken *explored part of the south coast of New Guinea, and sailed past the strait soon afterwards discovered by Torres. Her commander guessed there might be a passage there, but was not sure. Then, in March, 1606, the* Duyfken *sailed part way down the western coast of what we call Cape York Peninsula. Her crew were the first Europeans whom we know to have seen Australia. They were not pleased with what they saw. Nowhere was there any sign of gold, or any promise of trade. For the most part the land was a desert, and the natives were wild and primitive savages. Much the same report was made by the* Pera *and the* Arnhem, *which followed in the* Duyfken's *tracks in 1623. They, too, missed Torres Strait: indeed, the passage is narrow and dangerous and easy to miss among the shallows. The men of the* Pera *and* Arnhem *drew maps of a large part of the Gulf of Carpentaria but they, like the men of the* Duyfken, *said that the country was wild and terrible.* "We found nothing," said the Dutchmen, "but wild coasts, barren land, and extremely cruel, savage and barbarous natives." A Concise History of Australia by FLW Wood.

I'd never heard of *Duyfken* and this is all I could find in my books when I returned home after the morning sail. It was in my father's old school text book from 1944. It wasn't much to base a new shipbuilding project upon and there didn't appear to be any good news in the story. "Extremely cruel, savage and barbarous natives"? Who would have thought? As the years progressed, we would also find that this accepted history of *Duyfken* was wrong in so many ways, and the real story of *Duyfken* was more nuanced and far more interesting than this story of savages in a barren land.

As a Western Australian child of the sixties, I was aware of the early Dutch maritime stories which were part of local folklore. Hugh Edwards' book *Islands of Angry Ghosts* was on the high school reading list and its epic story of the shipwreck of the *Batavia* in 1629 and the subsequent bloodthirsty mutiny was entrancing and encouraged teenagers like me to take an interest in local maritime history. It was a counterpoint to the stories of Captain Cook which were part of the mythology of the European colonisation of eastern Australia. James Cook was a noble figure in our history books while the Dutch explorers seemed to have a rough and wild edge which appealed to young Australian males from the suburbs like me. Sure, Cook was a great navigator but how about a real mutiny, a rescue mission on the high seas and the mutineers being hung and quartered!

I must admit that I thought the first European to set foot on the Australian continent was Captain Dirk Hartog in October 1616. He came ashore from his ship *Eendracht* at Cape Inscription on today's Dirk Hartog Island (called Wirruwana by the local people) and planted a pewter plate on a pole — incontrovertible evidence that he was there (This historical truth would later be used against us). The Dutch ships wrecked along the western coast had great exotic names. There was the *Zuytdorp*, the *Zeewijk*, and the *Vergulden Draak* to name just three. And who could not be intrigued by the English buccaneer William Dampier who buried a treasure chest somewhere along the coast? And there was the voyage of the Spaniards Pedro Fernandes de Queirós and Luís Vaz de Torres which departed from Callao in Peru in December 1605 and sailed through Torres Strait five months after *Duyfken*'s voyage, missing Australia completely. How did they get that so wrong?

There was a logic to building the replica of *Endeavour* for the Sydney-centric Australian Bicentennial celebrations as it was the ship which charted the last quarter of the continent's coastline. This led to the convict settlement at Sydney Cove and the Australia we know today. Compared with *Endeavour*, *Duyfken* was seen as a footnote in the history of eastern Australia. It grated with many West Australians, including me, that there were 164 years of Dutch exploration of the rest of the Australian coastline before Cook and it was largely ignored outside of Western Australia.

So, the idea of building the first of these Dutch ships had some merit — if only it had explored the West Australian coast. This has always been a stumbling block for *Duyfken* boosters and it often required some careful word juggling in descriptions of the Project. *Duyfken* was the first ship recorded in history to visit Australia. Yes, it marked the beginning of the European exploration of the Australian coastline; and that was about where the story met a dead end. It was a ship which appeared to have no backstory apart from being the first. When the captain of *Duyfken*, Willem Jansz, landed at the Pennefather River on Cape York Peninsula, Queensland in 1606, it also marked the first time recorded in history that Aboriginal people met people from the outside world. Even the word *Duyfken* (often spelt *Duiijfken*) was the subject of considerable debate. The 'ken on the end of the word is the diminutive used in old Dutch. Today the diminutive commonly used is 'je'. A Duif in modern Dutch generally refers to a pigeon, but a small pigeon is a dove so a *Duyfken* would be a *Duifje* today. Therefore, the reasoning has it that the meaning of *Duyfken* is a small pigeon not a small dove, or simply a dove (because a dove is a small pigeon anyway). The translation *Little Dove* eventually stuck, probably because doves are cute, and little ones, more so. It pleased most people although 'Little Pigeon' or 'Dove' would be more accurate.

While it had a name (which most Australians had trouble pronouncing) *Duyfken* undoubtedly had size on its side. While *Endeavour* was about 550 tonnes displacement and about 44 metres long, *Duyfken* was thought to be about 100 tonnes and about 20 metres long. It was obvious that *Duyfken* could be built for a fraction of *Endeavour*'s $18m construction bill.

Michael Young was the letter-writer proposing to build a replica of this ship which never came to Western Australia. He was not alone in proposing new historic ship projects. Lots of people had big ideas and grappled with which ship would be the best to continue the nascent historic shipbuilding industry in Fremantle after *Endeavour*. The trials and tribulations of the construction of Cook's ship and its tourism benefits had been at the forefront of the positive side of the *Endeavour* replica story but it also had brought together a team of artisans with rare skills. This could be the real legacy of the Project. Fremantle was regarded at the time as the cultural hub of the Perth metropolitan area and it was felt that the traditional skills would be dissipated if another project was not found to utilise them. If

Fremantle could build another ship then the old port could perhaps gain a reputation as a historic shipbuilding centre and it could attract other wooden shipbuilding projects. This has turned out to be a pipe dream — communities tend to want to build their own historic vessels in their own backyards — Lelystad has *Batavia*, Bristol has the *Matthew*, and Melbourne has the *Enterprize*. We (and the State Government) believed in the validity of this flawed argument at the time.

Before the *Endeavour* launch and in the months after the ship was rigged and trialled at Gage Roads off Fremantle, the prospect of another ship was an increasingly popular topic of conversation. Western Australia did not have a particularly good record of fostering historic and large sailing vessels. In the 1980s, an enthusiastic boatbuilder Royce Carrigg constructed a viking longboat called the *Jorgen Jorgensen* and tried without luck to find a home for it on the Swan River. In frustration and with a large dose of desperation he phoned the Premier of Queensland, the inimitable Sir Joh Bjelke-Petersen. Incredibly, he got put through to the man himself who listened to his plight and invited him to take the ship to the Gold Coast instead. A keen local yachtie and Member of Parliament for Nedlands, Richard Court, spoke out about Mr Carrigg's plight but the Minister for Tourism in the Labor Government, Pam Beggs, would not help the modern day Viking and the ship was lost to Queensland. Richard Court also spoke out about the controversial sale in 1984 of Alan Bond's winning America's Cup yacht *Australia II* to the Commonwealth Government for display at its new Australian National Maritime Museum. The WA Government was offered the historic yacht for $2 million and turned it down. It irked Richard Court but his time would come.

The barquentine sail training ship *Leeuwin* was the dream of the irrepressible orthopaedic surgeon, Malcolm Hay, who began fundraising to build the vessel in 1974. The 45m hull was launched in 1986 and although *Leeuwin* was a fine craft, it also constantly struggled to get adequate funding. Did Western Australia need another sailing ship problem?

Michael Young's letter generated great debate. The accomplished wooden boat builder and rigger, Robin Hicks, put up a sound argument that instead of planning a new replica, more energy should be put into restoring the WA Museum's decrepit heritage vessels. The vessel *HMS Beagle* which took Charles Darwin through Patagonia to the Galapagos Islands where he formed many of his ideas on the theory of evolution was talked about by the staff at *Endeavour*. It had Western Australian history. Under the command of John Stokes, it visited in 1840, just after the formation of the Swan River Colony. It was estimated that it would cost about the same as the Cook replica and its hull would fit nicely into the *Endeavour* shipyard building. They could just switch from one vessel to another in the same yard. A smaller vessel was also proposed. It was HM *Cutter Mermaid*, the ship commanded by Lt Phillip Parker King for his surveying work along the West Australian coast. At 84 tonnes she would be cheap to build, too. The speedy craft appealed to some members of the yachting fraternity as well as members of the Maritime Heritage Association including one of its leading lights, Nick Burningham. A group of ex-submariners put their case. They were keen to get one of the Royal Australian Navy's decommissioned Oberon-class submarines to Fremantle and they were also knocking on doors seeking funds.

The most vocal and persuasive rival push to build a different replica vessel came from the Swan River and Rottnest Island Tricentennial Committee. The committee was formed to look at ways to mark the 300th anniversary of Willem de Vlamingh's expedition to find out what became of the Dutch East India Company ship, the *Ridderschap van Holland*, which had been lost while bound for Batavia in Indonesia, and to see whether anyone had survived the loss of the *Vergulden Draak* in 1656. The high-powered committee of historians and Dutch community members had an executive officer based at Eventscorp, the events branch of my old employer, the WA Tourism Commission. Eventscorp was formed within the WA Development Corporation during the 1980s when the Brian Burke state government developed unhealthy links with some smart operators in the local business community. When deals began falling apart, the term 'WA Inc' was used to describe the mess. Although it had been used as a tool of the Labor Government, Eventscorp re-emerged under the Tourism Commission structure as the Government's events organisation. It had the remit of maximising the tourism industry benefit of special events. Governments of both political persuasions recognised its usefulness. With the warm glow of the Australian Bicentenary year still present, the Tricentennial year celebrating the 300th anniversary of the visit of the Dutch mariner could be used as a way to promote tourism. Vlamingh named both Rottnest Island and the Swan River. The usual run of dull activities for this type of anniversary was planned: commemorative events, art exhibitions, sporting team visits from The Netherlands and books. It was even suggested that the *Batavia* replica could be shipped from The

Netherlands to Fremantle after she was launched. This did not eventuate and the Committee still wanted something exciting to focus upon. It raised the idea of building Vlamingh's frigate the *Geelvinck*. Vlamingh's small fleet of ships also included a three-masted hooker, the *Nijptangh*, and a galliot, the *Weseltje*. In May 1994, *Endeavour*'s master shipwright, Bill Leonard, was asked by Graeme Henderson, the Director of the WA Maritime Museum to look at how much one of these vessels and *Duyfken* would cost to build. Graeme's Museum housed the world's finest collection of Dutch shipwreck artefacts including the hull fragments from the *Batavia* found at the Abrolhos Islands. Bill estimated that the *Geelvinck* and the *Weseltje* would cost about the same as *Endeavour*, however, the *Nijptangh* would cost about the same as a *Duyfken* to construct. His estimate based on displacement was about $3.2 million. He was asked to weigh up the advantages of each vessel and report back to the tricentennial committee. *Duyfken* scored well for its national significance and its small size but he cautioned that, like *Endeavour*, it could be lost to another state after it was built as it did not have a history binding it to Western Australia. That was a prophetic call.

We also had other critics who used the growing public interest in *Duyfken* to get a few centimetres in the print media. In November 1995, Perth historian Associate Professor Leslie Marchant was shown an ancient map by a Perth map dealer, Steven Marcuson, which purported to show an outline of Western Australia in 1581. The German cartographer Heinrich Bunting produced the map. Although it had been discounted as wildly inaccurate, its 'discovery' got the Australian media into a frenzy. "Who was Australia's Christopher Columbus?" Professor Marchant asked. Maritime historian Nick Burningham who was by then working for *Duyfken*, responded with a letter headed "Old Crap Muddies State's History" which identified the claims and said that it muddied the waters for serious researchers.

It didn't rest there. The Portuguese community (a powerful lobby group in Fremantle thanks to its fishing roots) and some amateur historians began telling us that we'd got it all completely wrong. How could we ignore the Portuguese seafarers? The Portuguese community in Fremantle felt slighted that we hadn't chosen to build a Portuguese ship. They said that the Dutch weren't the first Europeans to come to Australia. It was the Portuguese and the proof was in the maps of the cartographer Manuel Godinho de Erédia. They said he had drawn maps including Bathurst and Melville islands in the Northern Territory in about 1602. The theories were given some weight in

1996 when the Emeritus Professor of Geography at Flinders University, Murray McCaskill, publicly supported its proponents, although serious cartographers gave no weight to the theories. The issue bubbled away until 1997 when the WA Arts Minister, Peter Foss, unveiled a monument in Fremantle marking the 500th anniversary of Vasco da Gama's voyage around the Cape of Good Hope and across the Indian Ocean to India, even though there was no direct link with the Portuguese navigator and Australia's western coast, let alone Fremantle. Justice was seen to be done and things settled down. Manuel Godinho de Erédia's maps of Northern Australia have never been recognised as proof that the Portuguese visited Australia before the Dutch but don't tell that to someone from the Portuguese community.

Even though the State had a rich and colourful maritime history, funding for the research and display of that history was always in short supply. It was often a battle for the coterie of maritime archaeologists to get their pet projects funded. Replica ships were a means of highlighting maritime history but they were also seen as massively expensive ventures which were like a vacuum cleaner, sucking up potential sources of funding while less public but more historically significant undertakings were left penniless. Overlaying this was the understandable self-interest of the historians themselves who, not surprisingly, preferred their personal projects which represented their life's work to have the priority.

The eminent geologist and maritime archaeologist, Dr Phillip Playford, was one such critic who enjoyed a high public profile in Western Australia as the discoverer of the wreck of the Dutch East Indiaman, the *Zuytdorp*. The ship carried a hoard of 250,000 guilders in silver coins and came to grief on the western coast in 1712. He was a local legend and he argued for many years that the pretext for building *Duyfken* was wrong — that, in fact, there was no proof that the Captain Willem Jansz came ashore in Australia. Sailing along the Gulf coast was not the same as coming ashore, he said. He was a strong proponent of building a vessel with Western Australian history. He stoked this fire and the issue simmered for several years. In February 1997, when the Dutch ambassador Roelof Smit attended the unveiling of a replica of Vlamingh's plate at Cape Inscription on Dirk Hartog Island in Shark Bay (Vlamingh took the plate left by Dirk Hartog and replaced it with one of his own in 1697), the outspoken Shark Bay shire President, Les Moss, put a shot across the bows of the WA Premier Richard Court (yes, the Member for Nedlands was now the Premier of the State). He said there was no proof that Willem Jansz landed on Cape York in 1606 and one of Vlamingh's small boats should be built instead of *Duyfken*. He said that the support of *Duyfken* was undermining the marketing of Shark Bay as the site of the first European landing. Shame on the *Duyfken* promoters!

Clearly there was work to be done to substantiate *Duyfken*'s claim as the most worthy ship to build — but everyone underestimated the redoubtable letter writer from East Fremantle.

Chapter 3

Glorious, Enthralling Naivety

It was late afternoon on a warm summer day in early 1994 with the fresh sea breeze blowing from the south west to cool Fremantle. I must've been sitting on the doorstep for half an hour wondering what I had gotten myself into. I'd called the phone number John Longley gave me. Michael Young, the guy who wrote the letter to the Fremantle Herald, answered and invited me to a meeting at 3pm the next Sunday at his home in Fortescue Street in East Fremantle. I was at the right house and right on time but there was nobody home so I sat on the front step and waited. If I hadn't waited and I'd just gone home to enjoy the rest of the weekend then the next 20 years of my life would have been vastly different.

The verandah step was a pleasant enough place to pass some time so I thought I'd give him another few minutes. Michael and his wife Janine had converted the front yard into a native garden with Eucalyptus trees and bush plants and, unlike most Perth front yards, no grass. It was just a little avant-garde for conservative Perth in those days and it was relaxing to sit in the shade with the cool sea breeze blowing through the trees and the sweet scent of eucalyptus in the air. Finally, a car pulled up and a tall and lean, slightly balding middle-aged guy wearing a loose white cheese-cloth shirt jumped out with a bundle of papers under his arm. He looked like a typical Freo local — just a little alternative, a bit hippy but not short of a dollar, either. It was Michael. He smiled, duly apologised for giving me the wrong starting time for the meeting, and invited me in. Little did I know that I was about to get aboard an out-of-control roller coaster!

Soon others began arriving and we sat down to coffee and traditional Dutch cinnamon speculaas biscuits. Michael passed around piles of photocopies he'd made using the photocopier at the office of the state government department where he worked. It was an interesting mix of people at my first meeting of the *Duyfken* replica group. There were the Dutch, including Gonnie Bonda and Nell Ottenhoff, Gloria Jackson, Ria and Nanne Sjerp, and Peter Becu. They were incredibly energetic, optimistic and sometimes forceful in a way that I would come to admire in the post-war Dutch migrants who'd made Western Australia their home, but was a little off-putting at the time. They were passionate and excited to tell the story of the Dutch exploration of the Australian coastline and they were proud to be involved. They were Australians now, but Michael had given them something which brought together their Dutch and Australian heritage. Bill Leonard agreed to attend some of the meetings to offer advice. Another who joined the group was Charlie Welker who was a senior executive at the State Government's Environmental Protection Authority before a change of Government found him needing a new job. He didn't have a Dutch connection but Michael had roped him in for his planning expertise. There was blind enthusiasm and a spirit in this disparate group which was quite intoxicating. They had absolutely no idea what they were getting themselves into, but that wouldn't stop them.

Michael moved around the room like a primary school teacher handing out a test. Everyone tried to look at what he'd just given them and make sense of the reams of paper building up on their laps. He told us that the maritime history of the Spice Islands of Indonesia ranked with the Silk Road from China as one of the most romantic chapters of human history. One photocopy caught my eye. It was photograph which had been copied so many times that there were no mid tones left but the subject was fascinating. It was a small ship called the *Halve Maen* in Dutch (in English, the *Half Moon*). Six figures with stovepipe hats stood on the foredeck and with its large crow's nests, which looked out of proportion to the rest of the ship, it resembled a fantasy sailing ship from a children's book. Michael said that it was a replica of a ship similar to *Duyfken* which was sailed by English mariner, Henry Hudson, up the Hudson River near New York in 1609. It was built in The Netherlands for the tercentenary of the voyage in 1909, transported across the Atlantic and gifted to the United States. Michael proclaimed that our ship would look like the *Half Moon* and it would only cost abut $1.8 million to build. We were excited. We later found out that the 1909 replica had a sad end. After the commemoration festivities, she became a tourist attraction but visitor numbers dwindled and maintenance slipped. By the 1930s, she was a derelict hulk and a fire finally destroyed her.

There was a big lesson in that end story. It is fine to build a replica ship but from the outset it must be accompanied by a long term plan for its use and a practical business model. We were, however, more fired up by the romanticism of building a ship than caring about the distant future of what we wanted to build – and $1.8 million didn't sound like much.

Then Michael began to list all the people he'd talked to in the past few weeks. It was a mind-boggling list of media, public servants, politicians and diplomats extending from Australia to New Zealand and The Netherlands. Anyone who showed the slightest interest was hailed as a fervent advocate of the Project. It was tremendously exciting to be talking about building a wooden sailing ship from scratch. This informal group became the *Duyfken* Replica Project Committee.

One of the people at the meeting was the accomplished artist Gillian Kaye-Peebles. She was the official artist for the Kookaburra Syndicate during the America's Cup defence in Fremantle and a guest artist aboard Jacque Cousteau's turbo-sailed research vessel, *Alcyone*, for his voyage along the West Australian coast. She was accredited with the Royal Academy of Arts in London. Gillian had a personal interest in the *Endeavour* Project as one of her ancestors was the half-brother of Zachary Hicks who sailed on Cook's *Endeavour* (Point Hicks is named after him). She met Michael while giving art classes. One of her pupils was Michael's wife Janine. She recalls the evening when Michael Young probably began the campaign to build the ship. "I really believe that the history of the *Duyfken* Replica commenced in Janine and Michael Young's lounge room," she said. "I had been invited to their home for dinner. When I arrived, Michael was lounged over a chair reading a small thin book about the original *Duyfken*. Over the meal we spoke about how sad it was going to be to lose all the skilled craftsmen and women who had been working on the *Endeavour* Project. Michael said that the original *Duyfken* was the first to record the coastline of Australia, not Captain James Cook, and he declared that he would try and get people interested in building a replica of her. On that night, we made an extensive list of people that should be contacted and approached. I believe this was the true beginning. I have a very good photograph of Michael taken that night in the armchair reading that book."

Michael knew Fremantle architect Richard Longley and he asked him whether he could introduce him to his brother John. After the introduction,

Michael called John several times to discuss *Duyfken* and to sound him out on whether he would like to help build the ship. John was always non-committal.

Michael was a skilful networker. Casual meetings would become personal endorsements of the Project and the impression was created that support was coming from a wide variety of sources. When John Longley said that the *Endeavour* shipwrights could build a ship like *Duyfken*, Michael latched onto it, and put it in his briefing documents. When John said that the Western Australian coastline should be called the 'Dutch coast' because of its long Dutch maritime history, he began using that phrase, too.

John told Michael that he had been told about a *Duyfken* ship's model being built in the suburb of Applecross near Fremantle but he did not follow it up. He suggested Michael might care to follow it up.

The retired journalist, James Henderson, who was constantly taking notes at that first meeting I attended, was also aware of the model. When Michael wrote to the Fremantle Herald, James was one of the first to respond. He, too, had been interested in the story of the first ship recorded in history to visit Australia and a friend of his, Dr Cornelis (Cees) De Heer was building the model. He'd been working on it for four years. Coincidentally, James was actively researching the history of the original *Duyfken* and he planned to make it his fifth book on West Australian maritime history. His son was Museum Director Graeme Henderson.

Bill Leonard remembers the first time he heard about *Duyfken*. He was working in the *Endeavour* shipyard. John Longley's office was a glass box on the mezzanine floor. "I saw John out of the side of my eye, waving at me in panic gesturing for me to come up to his office," said Bill. "He had a meeting with James Henderson and he wanted some back-up." James arranged for Michael, John Longley, Bill Leonard and Honorary Dutch Consul Jan Gunnick to visit Dr De Heer's home in the suburb of Applecross to view the partially completed ship's model in February 1994. John recounted this meeting when we were aboard *Endeavour*. At the meeting, John politely told Michael once again that he was happy to provide advice from a distance but *Endeavour* was his number one priority — sea trials of the Cook replica were due to start in the following month. John knew that without a big chunk of money the Project would never happen and after years of knocking on doors for Cook's ship, he had no appetite to help raise funds for another one. He knew that all replica projects begin as a dream in someone's mind — and sometimes dreams become reality — but only when lots of cash is found. John subsequently agreed to be the *Duyfken* group's first patron. It was another respected name to add to Michael's growing list of supporters.

Dr De Heer's interest was not in building a full-scale replica of *Duyfken*. He was in poor health and he was quite happy to continue building his ship model with no involvement in the events which would unfold. As the research on *Duyfken* progressed, the ultimate design of the *Duyfken* replica evolved until the final ship only had a passing resemblance to his model. Ultimately the model was sold to the WA Maritime Museum for permanent display at the Shipwreck Galleries in Fremantle, and it is now a reminder of the origins of the Project.

I couldn't help but feel that James Henderson was a little indifferent to my presence at the early meetings. He came from the old school of journalists which regarded public relations and marketing people with cynicism — the enemy of the truth-seeking, hard-bitten news hound. I had gone over to the dark side. PR people were there to keep journalists away from the truth, not to help them find it. In the coming years, James' hostility softened and he came to accept the value of my contribution and we became friends. James Henderson and Michael Young were motivated in vastly different ways. James had aspirations to trace the original voyage of discovery from Banda in Indonesia to Queensland with a yacht supplied by Chris Hansen from the Fremantle Sailing Club, and later a pearling vessel supplied by the MG Kailis Group. It would coincide with the 400th anniversary in 1995 of the construction of the original *Duyfken*. It was later proven that the first *Duyfken* to sail to the East Indies in 1595 was not the *Duyfken* which visited Australia in 1606 but we had very little awareness of the true history of the ship as we proceeded headlong into our planning.

The monthly gatherings at Michael and Janine's home in 1994 became formalised as the Friends of the *Duyfken* community support group and ultimately, the *Duyfken* 1606 Replica Foundation, which would fund and oversee the construction of the vessel. It became clear why Michael had been so keen for me to attend the meeting. The group had virtually no money. Actually, it wasn't virtually no money, it was absolutely no money. The Project was being underwritten by the Department of Commerce and Trade which was unwittingly paying for hundreds upon hundreds of photocopies being churned out by Michael every week and being sent through the department's mailing system to anyone whom he thought should know about his fascinating scheme. Years later, he boasted that he'd mailed 1,000 letters in that first year. It was clear that nothing concrete could be achieved without a costed business plan and Charlie Welker had the skills to put a document together. The business plan incorporated the first fundraising strategy. It was fortunate that Charlie was at a loose end until he found work. Charlie later set up one of Western Australia's most successful environmental consultancies but kept his association with *Duyfken* until 2003. I was able to help Charlie with marketing input in the months that followed. He tabled the first business plan for the construction of the ship at an interim boaarding meeting on 27 November 1994, arriving at an initial costing with Bill Leonard based on length and displacement. It was a simple volumetric analysis which turned out to have accuracy within 10 per cent.

Our initial aspirations were modest. "Once the replica is finished the intention is to home port it in Fremantle and to undertake local sailing trips along the Western Australian coast and possibly voyage to the rest of Australia," said the first business plan. "The extent to which the *Duyfken* replica will be used in this way will depend upon the final design (for example whether it will contain a motor(s) to propel the ship and be capable of housing a crew for long voyages) of the vessel."

I came back from that first meeting, telling my wife Cathy that I couldn't quite believe what I had just experienced. Having come from the big-spending *Endeavour* Project, I'd just spent two hours with a group of people who had absolutely no plans for the ship, didn't even know precisely how long the hull had to be, had no money, and thought they could hold raffles to raise the millions of dollar required to build it. But their enthusiasm was infectious and I told her that I would offer my skills and see how it went. I knew how to put together a decent sponsorship proposal and at least I could help them with that. I signed up as member number eight. When I left the Tourism Commission and set up a small communications consultancy on my own, *Duyfken* became my biggest client — unfortunately it was all unpaid work.

Seeing himself as something of a modern day Indiana Jones, Michael travelled to Indonesia in May 1994 and came back with more ideas and even more energy, if that was possible. I enjoyed being part of Michael's obsessive passion. We all did. He was a wizard casting his *Duyfken* spell over everyone he met. At times, it was like being in a cult. He knew how to network. Everyone who showed the slightest interest received a wad of papers telling the story. Michael was sometimes infuriating, ringing at all hours, constantly sending emails, making suggestions, pushing and prodding but always relentlessly moving the Project along. We were all given titles and responsibilities and then contact lists were distributed so we could all network within the group. This was community action at its best. We all had jobs to do. Michael Young was obsessed. He was not to be denied. A spare bedroom was transformed into the Project's first working office and Michael said that this became his 'cell' for nearly two years.

Janine Young later said that he would keep working until 2 or 3am, forgetting that he hadn't eaten. "It was just him, one man, in the beginning. It was incredibly courageous of him never to give up or lose heart. I think he should get heaps of credit," she said. Dr de Heer's model was coopted as the design of the ship which was to be built and Michael sent photos of the model to any media outlet or community group around Australia which showed the slightest interest in the Project. Michael enlisted the help of a talented artist, Adriaan de Jong. He came to Australia from The Netherlands in 1982 with a Diploma in Applied Science and Chemistry to work as a chemist. His passion, however, was Dutch maritime history, building ship models and painting maritime art. His attention to detail and artistic ability was just what the *Duyfken* Committee needed to bring the *Duyfken* story to life. He painted a romanticised picture of *Duyfken* arriving at the Pennefather River and visual representations of a Dutch shipyard we planned to recreate in Fremantle. Adriaan's talent for translating early Dutch manuscripts became a huge asset to the Project in its early days. Later, Nick Burningham obtained a microfilm copy of the *Gelderland* ship's log. The *Gelderland* led the 1601 Dutch fleet including *Duyfken* to the Indies and Adriaan took on the mammoth task of translating the old handwriting. He went at it like a man possessed, immersing himself in the old Dutch used at the time, piece by piece reconstructing the log and finding out fresh aspects of the *Duyfken* story which had not previously been unearthed.

Soon Michael had 'committee members' (anyone who showed any interest found themselves appointed to a committee) in The Netherlands and New Zealand. If you had a Dutch connection then you were likely to be tapped on the shoulder. The Dutch consul in Melbourne, David van Iterson, was conscripted. So was Perth accountant Rinze Brandsma who was chair of the Rottnest Island Foundation and the son of Dutch immigrants. His firm of Brandsma and Crockett in West Perth had a blue-chip client list. He pledged to help with articles of incorporation and approached the law firm, Kott Gunning, to help. The trust deed of the HM Bark *Endeavour* Foundation was used to draft a new document. He also obtained recognition for the ship as a 'floating museum' with the Taxation department allowing full tax deductibility for donations. Almost without knowing it, Rinze was drawn into Michael Young's obsession.

Michael's own story, often recounted, became part of *Duyfken* replica folklore. Born Jacob Jong on 26 February 1947 in the famous tulip growing centre of Hillegom in The Netherlands, he was the youngest of three children. His parents were established business owners, but when he was just three years of age, his parents decided to start a new life in Australia. Their first taste of Australian life was at a migrant hostel at Nelson Bay north of Newcastle. They eventually settled on a remote northern NSW farm station, working for the Livingston family. His mother once said that Michael was not very interested in his home schooling, but he would sneak out of bed at night and delve into the Livingston's home library where he read anything he could get his hands on. He was fascinated by the world outside the confines of the farm and at eight years of age, he told his mother that his history lesson that day was wrong: the Dutch, not the English, were the first Europeans to visit Australia. That historic truth, and an annoyance that the Dutch seafarers were not given proper recognition, stayed with him as life took many turns.

Tired of the constant mispronunciation of his name, Jacob Jong changed his name to Michael Young. He studied for an economics degree at Sydney University, left to work at a bank, joined the Army Reserve, married Janine, bought a home in Surry Hills, returned to university to study and completed a social science degree – and restored three heritage homes along the way. With a life-long love of art, he restored a two-storey horse stable at the rear of their Annandale home and he made it into an artists' studio. He invited artists to stay and work at the studio.

"My love affair with *Duyfken* began in Sydney in 1979 after I read and later obtained a donation of 300 copies of Priscilla Murdoch's 1974 book on the ship from the publisher (she must've had a hard time selling them)," he said. He was also influenced by his Dutch background and his family's involvement in maritime history. In 1985, he and his family moved from Sydney to Perth so he could take a position in the Premier's Department of the WA Government. He developed a keen interest in social justice and he was always on the move. In 1989 and 1990, he managed one of the oldest Aboriginal art centres, Tiwi Designs, on Bathurst Island, 80 km north of

Darwin. He discovered many Dutch names around the islands and it stimulated an interest in the indigenous connections with Dutch explorers. He was fascinated by the stories of Bathurst Islander descendants living in Sulawesi.

In 1990, he visited his sister in Tamworth, NSW and she showed him her family history research which showed the Jansz surname in its family tree and he fantasised that he was descended from the master of *Duyfken*, Captain Willem Jansz and another great name in history. "My mother is also a de Ruyter," he would say. "Michael de Ruyter is the most famous Dutch naval hero." He told the story that by the time he moved to Fremantle from Sydney in 1987 he had only two battered copies of the Priscilla Murdoch books left and no real support for a replica project. "On discovering the *Endeavour* Project I felt strongly that Fremantle had the best chance of successfully building the ship, especially if we could keep it there. My second last copy (the least worn) I gave to Pat Baker (a photographer working at the WA Maritime Museum) after a *Batavia* lecture he gave at the Museum," he said.

The WA Maritime Museum in Fremantle was the most powerful and respected organisation engaged in the study of Dutch maritime history in Australia, and respected around the world. The Museum had barely been involved with the *Endeavour* Project, however, if our plans to build a replica of a Dutch ship were to succeed, then it was critical for us to tap into the Museum's expertise and to have the tacit endorsement of its two most internationally respected experts. As Director of the Museum, Graeme Henderson had a long and distinguished career in maritime archaeology. He discovered the wreck of the VOC ship *Gilt Dragon* when he was only 16 years of age and he became one of the founders of maritime archaeology as a scientific discipline in Australia. The head of the Department of Maritime Archaeology was Jeremy Green. He came from Oxford University to the Museum in Fremantle in 1971. His pioneering work on the *Batavia* shipwreck (which became his life work) attracted world wide attention and since 1994, the WA Maritime Museum had been granted the honour as the Australian Centre of Excellence for Maritime Archaeology. Jeremy Green contacted Michael Young independently of the Hendersons and offered to help. Both Jeremy and Graeme Henderson agreed to form a Technical Committee to determine the design of the vessel. This close association with the WA Maritime Museum continued right through the construction years and was vital to the Project's credibility.

Nick Burningham, who was well known for his work as part of the WA Maritime Heritage Association and had been constructing a large scale model of *Batavia* in the Shipwrecks Gallery at the WA Maritime Museum, also joined the committee. Nick was often seen wearing a tweed jacket and with his grey beard he had the look of an English country gentleman. He had a passion for Indonesian shipbuilding traditions and he was part of the *Hati Marege* Project. A replica of a 19th century Makassan perahu, it was built and sailed from Indonesia to Arnhem Land in 1987/88. The ship did not have an engine but it did have a support vessel and it was towed in and out of port if the conditions didn't favour it. In these early days of the *Duyfken* Project, he was quite open about the need for engines and he took the view that they could be retro fitted to *Duyfken* if required. Little did we know at the time that the abstract debate over the need for engines would come back to haunt us later.

Nick had a lot of experience with Indonesian shipyards. Many Indonesian sailing vessels still employed plank-first construction used by the Dutch four centuries before. They did not build ships from plans, but rather fire bent planks to create the hull shape. In December 1994, he was asked to look at the options for shipwrights to come from Indonesia to assist with fire-bending and he recommended finding shipwrights from the island of Madura in the province of East Java to come to Fremantle and help with the construction. He was an early backer of the proposal to build a replica of the Captain Phillip Parker King's *Mermaid* but he became a great enthusiast for the *Duyfken* Project when it gathered momentum and he became one of the key people in the construction of the vessel.

A lot of encouragement came from the *Batavia* Project in The Netherlands. *Batavia* is a most magnificent replica of a ship from what was called the Dutch 'Golden Age' when Dutch traders ruled the eastern seas and the wealth they generated encouraged the flourishing of science and art. It was being built by the shipwright Willem Vos at Lelystad in The Netherlands. The vessel was huge but unmanageable because it was not built to sail. It displaced 1200 tonnes and its mizzen mast was taller than the overall length of the whole ship we planned to build. The cleverly-designed Bataviawerf shipyard was a major tourist attraction in Lelystad and our inspiration for the yard in Fremantle. *Batavia* was only months away from being launched (Queen Beatrix smashed a clay bottle with seawater from the Abrolhos Islands over her bow on 7 April 1995). There was no plan to ever sail this massive wooden ship. It was always to be a static attraction and the shipyard planned to switch to an even bigger vessel called the *Seven Provinces* to exploit the public fascination with wooden shipbuilding.

A maritime historian who worked for *Batavia*, Robert Parthesius, visited Fremantle in December 1994. He inspected the *Batavia* hull model Nick was building for the WA Maritime Museum and he generously endorsed the "enthusiasm and expertise" in the *Duyfken* committee. He and Jeremy Green got together and publicly proposed building a replica of Willem de Vlamingh's sloop which he used to explore the Swan River during his 1696/97 voyage as a test project for the bigger *Duyfken* task — but it required funding of a further $237,000 — and it was never built.

A young Dutch researcher, Marit van Huystee, arrived in Western Australia from The Netherlands in 1993 with her husband Willem ,who was studying for his PHD at the University of WA, and her three year old son Wouter. Marit needed to find work and when Willem arrived early to begin his studies he contacted Jeremy Green. He explained that Marit had a masters degree in Dutch linguistics and perhaps her skills could be put to use at the museum. Marit was welcomed with open arms and two weeks after she arrived she began translating sections of the *Batavia* Log from the old Dutch and other more technical translations from a book about shipbuilding written by Nicolaes Witsen in the seventeenth century.

"One afternoon in 1995, Michael Young and James Henderson and their wives came to visit our house unexpectedly in Ord Street in Nedlands," she said. "They told me about *Duyfken* and the plan they had to build a replica and asked me if I was interested in participating and doing some research." Marit agreed and she began to delve into the history of *Duyfken* as very little had ever been written about the ship. It turned out most of it was wrong, or misleading.

On a visit to The Netherlands, she undertook extensive research at the Rijksarchief in Den Haag and she found the only drawings of *Duyfken* sketched from life. They revealed enough information to build a faithful replica. She also found mentions of the ship in the ship's logs of others ships and the *Duyfken* story began to come to life. With her knowledge of the Dutch archives, she painted a new and more accurate picture of *Duyfken*'s history.

Marit became a wonderful addition to the *Duyfken* Project team, later working closely with Adriaan de Jong and Nick Burningham.

The *Duyfken* Project had an obsessive commitment to authenticity right from the beginning and we felt that this was necessary to provide our ship with a point of difference from *Endeavour*. The WA Maritime Museum was only interested in collaborating on a ship which would use original techniques and materials, and provide valuable insights into the way Dutch ships were constructed.

The archaeologists at the WA Maritime Museum could see little point in a replica vessel like *Endeavour* which they saw as deeply compromised. The replica of Cook's ship was conceived in 1987 as a working museum vessel to be berthed at the Australian National Maritime Museum in Darling Harbour. The original *Endeavour* (*Earl of Pembroke*) was built without plans, but she was measured several times after the Admiralty took her over and the plans, called 'drafts', were held at the National Maritime Museum in Greenwich. They formed the basis of the replica which was conceived with no great ambition beyond being tied up and placed on public exhibition at the Australian National Maritime Museum in Darling Harbour, Sydney. Alan Bond was more enterprising and agreed to fund the construction of a seaworthy ship which could be sailed from Fremantle to Sydney for a delivery voyage. This presented a raft of design compromises to achieve a modern survey. There were many differences between the original ship and the replica. Instead of the traditional elm, oak or spruce, the replica was built mainly from jarrah, a native Western Australian hardwood which would ensure a long life for the ship. Old growth Oregon, (Douglas Fir), imported from the USA was used for the masts, spars, topsides and decks. The larger masts and yards were of laminated. Whilst having a commitment to authenticity externally, the ship had modern engines and a modern lower deck with an electric galley, a desalination plant, modern toilets and services. To prevent rotting, and for crew comfort, the replica had better ventilation than the original ship and both modern and traditional wood preservatives were used on the timbers. Iron fastenings were galvanised. The running rigging was polyester; the standing rigging was manila (but still made on a 140 year old rope walk to the exact specifications of the original rope), rather than hemp which was used on the original ship. The sails were made of Duradon, a synthetic which looks and handles like flax canvas. *Endeavour* was a sensible compromise for the modern world and a very practical vessel.

To satisfy the scientific aims of the museum curators, *Duyfken* presented a fundamental challenge. Unlike the English shipyards of the eighteenth century, the Dutch shipyards of the late sixteenth century did not work from precisely drawn plans. They simply modified an existing design and used their on-the-job experience accumulated over generations of shipbuilding to create the final product. The oak could only be shaped to a certain extent so the process of fire-bending timber planks for the hull informed the shipwrights of the hull shape. Without original plans, *Duyfken* would rely on careful research to build a ship in the likeness of the original ship. It would be our best guess on what the original ship looked like. In that sense, it was not a replica in the meaning of a precise copy or a duplicate. It made sense to build the ship this way but only if we could source original materials. For our shipwrights to achieve a similar sweep of the hull, European Oak would have to be used as it was only oak species that would bend in precisely the way we wanted. Compared with *Endeavour*, *Duyfken*'s construction would be experimental or reconstruction archaeology with few concessions to the modern world. It was thought that just as much could be learnt about these vessels as they were built as could be learned once they were completed and sailed. After all, this would not be a ship which would have to sail from Fremantle to Sydney after she was completed.

Duyfken was to be Fremantle's little ship, telling the story of 164 years of Dutch exploration along the Australian coast before *Endeavour* sailed up the east coast of the continent. She could be sailed every now and again, placed on public display and add to the vibe of the historic port. She would have no modern conveniences because there was no need. She would not have synthetic Duradon sails and manila ropes like *Endeavour*. The sails would be cut from material woven using twine made from flax ,and the ropes made from hemp fibre. This commitment to authenticity and traditional methods of shipbuilding from the sixteenth century, and the close working relationship between the shipbuilders and the WA Maritime Museum's archaeologists and historians, became a major plus for promoting and fundraising to build the ship. *Duyfken* was to be no 'mini-*Endeavour*'. In our promotional materials we proclaimed that our ship was to be the most authentic 'Age of Discovery' replica in the world. Although we used this phrase 'Age of Discovery' at the time, I now use it with a little hesitation. It is, of course, heavily charged with western ideas that there was a world waiting for them to discover. It refers to the European 'Age of Discovery' when Europeans sailed the world encountering other civilisations and land masses. From the perspective of the rest of the world, it is the age of European invasion and colonisation. The Dutch hardly 'discovered' Australia as people lived on the continent for tens of thousands of years before their mariners arrived. Similarly, we would come to question how appropriate is was to refer to the Dutch 'Golden Age', but that was all in the future.

Lively discussion took place in the early days about where in Fremantle to build the ship. Our Project was 14,000 km away from the original ship's home, and the modern shipyards of Henderson, a few minutes south of Fremantle, were more used to building massive aluminium fast catamaran ferries than anachronistic wooden boats. The *Endeavour* Shed was built on land in Fremantle Fishing Boat Harbour leased from the State Government by prominent Italian fisherman Joe Rotondella. Upon the completion of *Endeavour*, the superb covered shipyard building reverted to Joe and when Michael Young approached him to see whether *Duyfken* could be built in the shed, Joe was very agreeable to the idea and said that for $100,000 a year he could have it. That wasn't quite the deal we were hoping for and we looked around for other options including the heritage-listed Swan Dock at Victoria Quay. Swan Dock was completed in 1942 to accommodate submarines and small cargo vessels. The open area near the Fremantle Fishermen's Co-op building at Bathers Beach was also identified and the forecourt of the WA Maritime Museum on Cliff Street had several advantages. Lots of ideas were explored. The Department of Training was contacted to see whether the ship could be built as a training ground for young marine apprentices. The idea was not enthusiastically embraced. It was thought that the skills would not be transferrable to the modern shipbuilding industry.

Enthusiasm was not being converted into cash and we struggled to raise funds. Early sponsorship approaches went nowhere. The obvious targets were disinterested. The multinational Dutch brewing company, Heineken, gave a flat out no to sponsorship and the Export Director said he could see no commercial value in it. Similar responses came back from KLM and Shell. Perhaps *Endeavour* could donate some of its shipbuilding equipment to the new Project? Even that was refused as *Endeavour* needed all the money it could raise from selling the gear to fund its voyages (a massive shipbuilders' band saw was eventually loaned to the Project).

There were enough positive responses, however, to give us hope that the private sector would eventually support the Project. When Michael contacted Harold Clough from the Clough Engineering Group with the idea of supporting an expedition to find the original *Duyfken* in Indonesia, he offered to help raise the ship from the seabed if it was possible. He constructed the greased ways which were used to launch *Endeavour*. An early sponsor was one of the world's biggest surveying companies from The Netherlands. Fugro Survey, through its West Australian manager, Grey Roughan, was keen to help and James Henderson locked him in to fund his book project. This enabled him to enthusiastically carry on with his research and writing while we explored more avenues for funding the actual ship. Similarly, David van Iterson, the Dutch Consul-General, offered to help fund the translation of original Dutch manuscripts. While small donations such as this were welcome, much more money would be required if we were to build our ship.

The drive for *Duyfken* to be more than just another replica ship venture but a conduit for telling new stories began to coalesce almost from day one. The first Project plan included James Henderson's desire to sit down with Aboriginal elders of Cape York Peninsula and to talk to them about their oral history relating to *Duyfken*'s visit to Australia — simply, to get their side of the story. As well as forming part of his book, it became one of the main elements of our story-telling for years to come. It was encapsulated in the first plan. "The Project embraces the multicultural nature of Australian society. It can become a genuine symbol of pride for all Australians, blending the historical and international heritage of the Dutch, Indonesian and all Australian people. Approaching a new century, it is desirable for the national reconciliation that historical research should be focused on the true events in 1606, especially the Dutch first contact with and subsequent clash with the Aboriginal Wik people of northern Queensland. Aboriginal elders will be invited to be part of the Project, to give their oral version of the *Duyfken*'s 1606 visit and the important place it deserves in early Australian history."

As a white Australian living in the city, I had limited involvement with Aboriginal people but I had some awareness of the raw deal they had endured since European colonisation. In August 1980, I was a journalist in training when I drove my battered Morris Minor from Perth to Eneabba with another journalism student, Deryn Thorpe, to report on what became known as the Noonkanbah Convoy. An oil exploration company pegged ground at Noonkanbah Station in the Kimberley region of WA in 1976, to drill for oil. The Yungngora people protested that the drilling would desecrate several important sacred sites. The issue was unresolved until 1980 when the West Australian Premier, Charles Court (father of later Premier Richard Court), decreed that the drilling should go ahead despite the will of the traditional owners. We camped with the Police at their camp on a lonely bush track to report on the departure of the drilling rigs from the company's previous exploration base near Eneabba. It was a surreal and sobering sight: Police cars and blue lights in the early morning light ahead of massive trucks towing drilling machinery. The Yungngora people and their supporters could do little to halt the convoy when it arrived at Noonkanbah. The drillers desecrated the sacred sites, found no oil and moved on, leaving a broken community.

Fortunately, Australia seemed to be coming to grips with its past. Fourteen years later, for the first time in the construction of a replica sailing ship, the richness of the indigenous story was at least as important, if not, more important than the heroic European story of exploration which was the usual motivating factor in building replicas. It was exciting that I could be part of this new way of looking at our history.

The ability of the ship to strengthen relations between Australia, Indonesia and The Netherlands was also recognised as a key feature of our Project. Even with these ideas swirling about, our sights were not set far beyond Fremantle — she would be able to visit other ports along the coast but there was no long term plan for any transoceanic voyages.

By June 1994, the *Duyfken* Project group had expanded to a membership of 100, but it was clear that our circle lacked the horsepower to raise the big funds to build the ship. It was a tough task to raise large chunks of money for a dream. Doors kept closing.

Perhaps financial support could be found in Queensland? Michael Young asked his brother, John, to approach his state member in the Queensland seat of Albert, John Szczerbanik, to ask the Queensland Minister for the Arts, Dean Wells, for support. Dean Wells approached the curator for maritime archaeology at the Queensland Museum, Peter Gesner, for advice. We were stunned when he slammed the Project saying that the Queensland Government should not support a project based in another state and that if it was to be built it should be built in Queensland. If a replica ship was supported, he said it should be HMS *Mermaid* which was used by John Oxley on a voyage of discovery to Moreton Bay and the Brisbane River and was wrecked off Cairns in 1828. He said it would be smaller and cheaper to build. Boosting the *Mermaid,* he said it had more significance to Australians because it circumnavigated the continent three times. With the benefit of hindsight, maritime archaeology in Queensland was starved of funds and the response from the Queensland Museum could be seen as simply safeguarding its share of meagre state government funding from a high profile interloper. I guess if we had done our homework, the response wouldn't have come as a complete surprise. However, it was exactly this attitude which prompted the push to build a replica of the first ship in Australia's history. Inconveniently for some, it was Dutch. The Dutch exploration of the Australian coastline was well accepted in Western Australia but the Anglocentric attitude coming out of the Queensland Museum was quite a setback. Peter Gesner also condemned the "historically inaccurate and ambiguous assumptions" about first contact with the Wik people of Cape York fuelled largely by a drawing Michael circulated showing a dramatised confrontation between the Dutch and Aboriginal people on the original voyage. It was a mistake for us to use that imagery — a rookie mistake — and it was quietly deleted from our promotional materials. Clearly, the Project had to do more than just talk about embracing the Aboriginal communities in Cape York. James Henderson would lead the way.

There were many lessons to be learned from the *Endeavour* Project. In June 1990 when the Bond Corporation had to abandon funding of the construction, there was a brief dalliance with a Japanese firm, the Yoshiya Corporation. It was short-lived and the Project was virtually moth-balled until 1991 when a philanthropic Englishman, Arthur Weller, stepped in and formed a new entity, the HM Bark *Endeavour* Foundation, to complete the job which had begun four years before. *Duyfken* needed a champion like this, someone with the credibility and the financial muscle to get the right people to come aboard to find the funds we needed. The obvious choice was an Australian of Dutch descent who would have an emotional link with the Dutch exploration story and his or her Australian home. Nobody came to mind. Michael Young asked John Longley who he thought would be best to approach and he thought Michael (MG) Kailis would be worth approaching. A Greek?

Michael George Kailis was one of the most impressive and charismatic figures in the Western Australian business community. Like many West Australians of Greek descent, his family came from the island of Castellorizo near the marine border with Turkey. Michael was descended from sea captains who traded in the eastern Mediterranean. His father came to Australia after the Great War, initially working in Darwin and finally settling down in Perth. Michael Kailis was born in 1929 and like many Castellorizians in the Perth community, he grew up with drive and determination. He went to school on the wrong side of the tracks, in

Highgate, just across the railway line from the Perth city centre and he had a larrikin streak. His family returned to Darwin and in 1942, when the Japanese attacks began, he was evacuated with his mother, Mary, and two sisters, Kathie and Angie, from Darwin back to Perth on the *MV Koolinda*. From age 13 he had to work to help support his family. He gained his matriculation as an adult student and he studied mine management in Broken Hill. After some aimless years, he began fishing for lobster in his mid-twenties. He saw an inefficient, small-scale industry but also great opportunities. He designed a processing plant which drastically increased the recovery of lobster tail flesh. It led to a thriving lobster tail export industry. He never sat still for long. He pioneered the prawn fishing industry at Exmouth Gulf in 1963 and in 1966, he did the same in the Gulf of Carpentaria, basing a fleet at Groote Eylandt. Over 40 years of hard work by Michael and his wife, Dr Patricia Kailis, the company was transformed into the MG Kailis Group of Companies exporting lobster, fish and prawns to Japan, Europe, South East Asia and the United States.

Michael Kailis was a classic entrepreneur. He knew he could build better fishing craft so he built a few for his own use. His Engineering Division ended up manufacturing more than 100 'K Class' trawlers which operated in Australia, Indonesia, Myanmar, Papua New Guinea, India and West Africa. It built a further 300 vessels of various kinds. His domestic fleets operated in Exmouth Gulf and in the Gulf of Carpentaria. He saw opportunities in the pearling business, too, and he established the first cultured pearl farm in Roebuck Bay near Broome. With Patricia's medical expertise, Kailis Broome Pearls was the first company to train Australian pearl technicians to culture the pearls in innovative hospital-like environments. His cultured pearling operation was the second largest in Australia. Michael Kailis also had Indonesian connections. He pioneered a prawn fishery in southern Maluku and he provided humanitarian support for the fishing communities of Roti Island when the Australian Government began to enforce its legal fishing zone in the north which excluded the fisherman from their traditional fishing areas.

Michael had an engaging charm but his happy go lucky demeanour masked a fierce determination and an incredible business mind. He once told me that ideas were easy to come up with and he had a lot of them. If only one out of every 10 of his ideas worked, then he was ahead and he didn't mind writing off the time and expense of the others. His staff loved him and he loved nothing more than mixing with them at work and socially.

Clearly, Michael Kailis could make a great leader of the our Project. The only challenge was for Michael Young to get a foot in the door. Michael Kailis operated from an office overlooking his engineering yard in Mews Road and he didn't have time for meetings not related to his business interests. His staff were his protectors, fending off wild ideas from outsiders and keeping him focused on the main business at hand. Someone had to provide an entré to penetrate the inner sanctum. John Longley suggested that Michael could ring Michael Kailis' cousin, Victor, who owned the successful Kailis Fish Market & Cafe next door to Michael's office building. He could talk to 'MG' and encourage him to meet. It was a typical small town plan (John and Victor were in the same class at primary school) and the way Fremantle worked. Anything could be achieved if you just spoke to the right person. Victor called Michael Kailis and asked him to meet with Michael Young. Michael Kailis then arranged for Michael Young and James Henderson to have an initial meeting with the MG Kailis Chief Engineer, Terry Hewitt. He was asked to hear what they had to say and to prepare a report.

Why should a Greek-Australian fishing magnate be interested in a Dutch ship? It was the obvious question. The *Duyfken* Project came at a perfect time for Michael Kailis. He was in his mid-sixties. His business empire was thriving. His sons, George and Alex, were taking an increasing role in the family's business affairs. He was a highly respected member of the community. *Duyfken* was something he could latch onto which combined his marine interests and his strong sense of giving something back after a long and successful business career. It didn't matter to him that it was a Dutch ship and he was Greek. It was a part of Australian history, a history which we all shared; and to add a personal perspective, he had a connection with most of the islands in Indonesia where *Duyfken* had sailed. Like most cray fishers, he also had gathered an artefact or two from Dutch shipwrecks along the coast. He dived on many of the wrecks and loved the stories.

He was fully briefed by Terry Hewitt when Michael and James arrived at his office. Michael Young made his presentation. The Project had grown into a bewildering array of interlocking activities overseen by the ever-enthusiastic Michael Young. There was the ship model, a 're-enactment' voyage planned to re-trace the *Duyfken* route of 1606 from Indonesia to Australia, the plan to dive on where the wreck may have been located at Ternate in the Spice Islands and the research for the book James was writing which would take him to Cape York. Michael Young asked Michael Kailis whether he could support the search for *Duyfken* with one of his steel fishing boats and he tentatively agreed. Michael Young sold the big picture — a grab bag of opportunities — they could transport the replica to the 1998 Tall Ships Festival in Sydney, the 2000 Olympic Games in Sydney, and it could be involved in the Australian Centenary of Federation events in 2001. He said that the Royal Netherlands Embassy was backing the Project and volunteers from all over Australia and the world were offering to help. Michael, however, was more interested in the fundamental questions any shipbuilder would ask. What would she look like, how and where would she be built and exactly how much would she cost? Michael Kailis listened to all Michael's plans and ideas and whittled it down to something he could understand — a shipbuilding project — something which he knew a lot about.

In the back of Michael Young's mind was a grand plan for his own future. He envisaged leaving the State Government and working on the Project full time from an office in Fremantle. He would travel the world in the wake of the original *Duyfken*. He would research the history of the ship in the Dutch archives and explore Indonesia. He'd be able to find the last resting place of the original *Duyfken*. He was absolutely immersed in the history of the ship but perhaps not the practical challenge of building a wooden sailing ship on budget and on time.

He told Michael Kailis that the Project's Technical Committee was still grappling with the fundamental philosophy of the vessel's construction and whether it would have an engine. It would take years and great angst until this issue was finally resolved. Would it be a museum piece without compromise or a more versatile vessel? Michael Young summed up his thinking in a letter he wrote to Graeme Henderson on 22 November 1994, after he met with Michael Kailis:

> *I am now keen on a pure 1A classification for the replica which would mean no engine. I have heard of real problems in putting an engine in a replica re cost effectiveness and damage to rigging etc. It seems that tall square-rigged ships were not designed to be motored and real (expensive) damage can occur. The* Leeuwin *people have information on this. But I still would like to be able to sail the vessel within limits, as the* Batavia *(pure) replica will be. Limited sailing is also far less expensive re crew and other costs and the* Duyfken *can still be shipped to long distant venues. I understand that the*

> *Museum staff are also keen for a full historical replica. The Duyfken Foundation Board, when incorporated, will need to consider this carefully.*

Michael Young came out of the meeting optimistic that Michael Kailis would join the Project, and he would get an answer in a couple of weeks — the answer came in a week. Michael Young did not know that Michael Kailis had already made up his mind. A few years later, Michael Kailis told James Henderson that he'd asked his Executive Assistant, Kathryn Cartwright, afterwards what she thought of the idea. She'd been in the meeting taking notes. She replied: "Well, it's an Australian project and it's right here; I'd support it". Michael's mind was probably already made up. He would be the Chairman of a new Board which he would constitute and he would select the people he wanted to help achieve the goal of building the ship. He wanted to start straight away — it wasn't in his makeup to let grass grow under the idea. He launched into it with all the energy and enthusiasm for which he was renowned. In the months ahead, the community project was transformed. And it went from what had just been a good idea to a juggernaut. While Michael Young had taken it to this point, Michael Kailis saw a much bigger picture. The community activist and the entrepreneur came together.

The first meeting of an interim *Duyfken* Board was held in the MG Kailis Boardroom on 26 November 1994. Michael Kailis chaired the meeting, Rinze Brandsma was asked to be treasurer and Michael Young agreed to take the role of secretary. Another meeting was held only two weeks later and all the elements of the *Duyfken* 1606 Replica Foundation took shape. Michael Kailis made a quick decision on the preferred location for the shipyard, adamant that he was not about to pay a fellow fisherman, Joe Rotondella, the princely sum of $100,000 a year for his shed. He also didn't like the way the yard could be tucked away among old buildings near the decaying Swan Dock on the other side of town. He loved the idea of the shipyard being built in the prized location on the grass concourse outside the Maritime Museum. It was only a two minute walk from his office and adjacent to the old port's most visited tourist attraction. Nobody could miss it. Decision made.

Chapter 4

Give Me Just Ten Hours of Your Time

I didn't know quite what to expect when I was summoned to Michael Kailis' office for the first time. Michael was Fremantle royalty. His sharp new offices at the Fremantle Fishing Boat Harbour were opened by his friend, the WA Premier Richard Court. They were very slick even for the new harbour which had been enlarged for the America's Cup defence. His receptionist was very formal and his Executive Assistant, Kathryn Cartwright, was welcoming and polite. I sat down in the reception area with a cup of coffee waiting to be called. What a difference to a few months before when I was sitting on a doorstep in East Fremantle waiting for the other Michael to arrive.

Kathryn ushered me into Michael's office through the Boardroom. I noticed a slew of business awards on shelves and a very nice model of a white square-rigged sailing ship, a model of a Kailis captain's ship from the Castellorizo time. Michael bounded out. He was in his mid-sixties, short and his face was tanned and lined like someone who had spent his whole life outside rather than in an office. His white business shirt was unbuttoned at the neck and barely tucked in, his tie was loosened and had been pulled out from the collar, both sleeves were carelessly rolled up and he gave me one of his smiles which made you feel instantly at ease. We got on well straight away. His office looked out over the engineering wharf and he could see everything that was going on below. His in-tray was piled up and as we talked, Kathryn would come into the office and put something else in it. Michael wanted to know everything about me, my family and my world. He was genuinely interested and he made me feel important. He asked me what I thought of *Duyfken* and what it needed. Money was my obvious answer. He knew that, too. A plan was forming in Michael's mind and in the coming months we would all see it implemented.

Michael Kailis was soon joined by two men initially recommended to Michael Young and Charlie Welker by Vern Reid from *Endeavour*. They were well known in Perth as business leaders and super fundraisers: Sir James Cruthers and Syd Corser.

Sir James began his working life as a cadet journalist and when The West Australian newspaper won a licence to operate the first local television station, he was asked to build it from the ground up. As Managing Director of TVW Seven, he was a pioneer of television in Australia. After Rupert Murdoch opened his News Corporation office in New York, Sir James was his principal adviser and the legend went that to reach Murdoch's office you had to get through Sir James' office first. In 1967, with fellow business executive Brian Treasure, he created a live to air fundraising weekend on TVW Seven called Telethon with the funds raised going to research at the Princess Margaret Hospital for Children. The eminent medical researcher Dr Fiona Stanley was able to study many aspects of children's health thanks to his fundraising efforts. As a journalist, Sir James was part of the Daily News newspaper expedition (under the nom de plume Jay Winter) to the wreck site of the *Zuytdorp* organised by Dr Phillip Playford in 1954 so he, too, had a long interest in Australia's Dutch maritime history. In 1994, he was, effectively, retired but he maintained an office at the Murdoch-owned Sunday Times newspaper and he was Chairman of the Board. His wife Sheila was prominent in the art world. She assembled Australia's best collection of artworks by Australian women artists when mainstream collections had little interest in the works. Philanthropy was Sir James' passion and he saw the Project as a worthy cause and an interesting fundraising challenge. He had connections he wasn't afraid to use.

Syd Corser was a successful home builder whose companies included Pacesetter Homes which pioneered the concept of building houses cheaply and efficiently on concrete slabs. He was a keen yachtsman with many national titles to his credit and in later years he enjoyed the spirit of the fundraising chase. Always dressed impeccably and appropriately for every occasion, Syd was suave and oozed confidence. He had charm and donors found it hard to say no. Like Sir James, his fundraising accomplishments were legendary. When he contracted prostate cancer, he decided that Western Australia required more expertise than what was available so he began a fundraising push which created the Urological Research Foundation at the University of WA.

Michael Kailis formed a small Executive Committee with Syd and Sir James which worked above the Foundation Board. I was co-opted to the group of three as their assistant. They did not want to be constrained by a large group of Board members with competing interests. These three men knew that big decisions were best made by small teams. Sir James' Board at the Sunday Times was three people — the Chairman, the Managing Director and the Company Secretary. Unsurprisingly, the Chairman's view always prevailed. Michael Kailis immediately put $15,000 in a bank account, primarily to pay for stationary expenses and to pay me as a consultant to the Executive Committee. Syd Corser also wrote a cheque to support the group. My role was to provide the written materials they required for their fundraising push. Never was it ever a question whether they would fail to raise the funds. They were all self-made people with total self-belief. They were the most optimistic people I had ever met. The first meeting was a revelation. The obvious question was: how were they going to raise the funds? They agreed they needed a fundraising plan. Syd had an idea. He was going to ask several of his friends for only 10 hours of their time to be provided free of charge to attend a series of meetings over a couple of months. They would help to develop the plan. Those friends included the up-and-coming media and machinery entrepreneur Kerry Stokes, entrepreneur Dennis Horgan of Leeuwin Estate Winery fame, and the successful insurance broker Gary Pierce. They all caught up for lunch once a month so it wasn't going to be too difficult to persuade them to help him out. Syd could be very persuasive. His pitch was along the lines of: "How much do you make an hour? $10,000? Well, give me 10 hours of your time and it is like giving us $100,000 worth of your expertise!" The meetings were great fun. For the first time I began to understand how the fundraising game worked at the highest levels. Syd was a sly old fox. By the time the committee was dissolved with its work done, the 10 hours of time stretched to over 30 hours — everyone knew it was a bit of a con, but they didn't mind. They would do anything for Syd. The meetings resulted in a broad fundraising plan which was based upon first obtaining State Government support, then obtaining Commonwealth Government backing to match the State money. This gave credibility to go to the private sector to secure the additional funds required.

A charitable foundation would be created to administer the funding to build the ship. This was the *Duyfken* 1606 Replica Foundation Inc. Michael Kailis looked over the constitution prepared by Rinze Brandsma and Kott

Gunning solicitors and suggested major changes. The Foundation would not be a democracy — more a benevolent dictatorship. Everyone had to place their trust in Michael's business acumen, and be aware that he didn't want anyone, or anything, to get in the way of completing the task. Michael Kailis was the Chairman of the Board and eminent members of the community would be invited to join the Board. The Executive Committee with the addition of Rinze Brandsma would still run the show.

I developed a proposal to incorporate the *Duyfken* Replica Project Committee formed by Michael Young and James Henderson into a new organisation called the Friends of the *Duyfken* which would operate at arm's length from the Board. This organisation would invite membership, run social events and raise money from the community. It would also enable people from all over the world who didn't or couldn't participate in Fremantle functions to still be engaged in the Project through newsletter updates. The Friends would also provide volunteer guides for the shipyard. The chair of the Friends would be invited to sit on the Board of the Foundation. Gloria Jackson from the Australia-Netherlands Chamber of Commerce agreed to chair the group in December 1994 and I agreed to take on the role of deputy. Jan Hough, James Henderson, Peter Becu, Michael's wife Janine, Nell Ottenhoff, Ria Sjerp and Gonnie Bonda were all part of the original group. Our first fundraising function was a great success with 300 people enjoying Dutch food and music. The Friends brought everyone together. Gonnie remembers the first function held at the MG Kailis Shipyard. It showed her that Michael Kailis was a great leader of the Project. The organising team had been allocated a small room to cut up a mountain of donated watermelons. It was a hot day (42°C) and the room wasn't air-conditioned. "Mr Kailis came in to see how we were going (nobody else did) and he offered his office area upstairs with kitchen and air conditioning. He donated big bowls of prawns on ice and sardines to barbecue," said Gonnie. "He was amazing: anything I wanted for functions, he provided. I don't think anyone was aware of that!"

The Technical Committee formed by Michael Young would continue to provide advice to the Board. The Board could address broader planning issues which were beyond the immediate fundraising goals of the executive. For example, Peter Becu prepared a discussion paper in February 1995 on the burning question of what we would do with *Duyfken* when she was completed. His paper suggested that the ship should remain in Fremantle to become an attraction for visitors and to sail only occasionally. He recommended that the ship should not be built with engines. The report was accepted but that issue of engines was always deferred and it would not be resolved for three years.

I began working for Michael Kailis and Sir James. They saw something in me they liked and they took me under their wing. They became my greatest mentors. It was a fabulous learning experience. These guys were good. Sir James' favourite phrase was: "Don't waste money with chook raffles, always go for the big lick." By this he meant that it took just as much time and effort to ask someone for $1,000 as it did for $250,000 so it was more efficient to focus on the big sponsors. As soon as someone showed the slightest interest after a contact had been made, he said that it was important to get to meet them personally. In the years to come I would fly across Australia and South East Asia many times at short notice hunting down sponsorship leads. Sir James understood people. He believed that big sponsorships were not necessarily secured by rational proposals and carefully structured arguments. Personal relationships were way more important. He didn't waste time putting a sponsorship proposal together until after the target had agreed in principle to the sponsorship and how much they were going to give. The sponsorship proposal was just to tidy things up and to take to their Board for endorsement if required.

We had friends in high places. Premier Richard Court, agreed to launch the *Duyfken* 1606 Replica Foundation and I set to work putting together a high profile function which would make people sit up and take notice. Unfortunately, he was overseas on the scheduled day — 26 February 1995. In his place, the Minister for Resources Development and Energy, Colin Barnett, represented him. We planned a spectacular launch in the *Batavia* Gallery of the WA Maritime Museum in Fremantle. The stage was placed under the stone portico found at the *Batavia* wreck site. The magnificent stone structure was in *Batavia's* hold bound for the port at Batavia as one of the fortress gates before the ship hit the reef at the Abrolhos Islands. The *Batavia* stern fragments rose up as an impressive wall of black timber to half fill the room. An old actor friend of mine, James Sollis, dressed as the Dutch sea captain Willem Jansz, gate-crashed the event, telling his own story and regaling the audience with anecdotes. It was a brilliant performance and it helped set the historical tone for the Project. I was asked to write speech notes for the Minister; something which I had done hundreds of times before. I thought my notes were fine, short and to the point. I hadn't taken into account Colin Barnett's photographic memory. He launched into a speech which included the whole maritime history of Western Australia, speaking it perfectly and without referring to any notes, including mine. I was stunned but especially pleased when people told me how much they had enjoyed the speech I had prepared for him. I had to tell them that most of it was not my work.

Mr Barnett said a special foundation, the *Duyfken* 1606 Replica Foundation, had been formed to oversee the Project, which was expected to take about two and a half years at a total cost of $3 million. In fact, the *Duyfken* Replica Committee used a sum of $3.5 million and had a 36 month timeline including a six month research period. The Minister said it would "involve about 20 specialist shipwrights and, while authenticity of the Dutch ship would be key, local services and suppliers would play a pivotal role. A special shipyard would also be constructed at Fremantle as a part of the Project." With great optimism, he said that the Replica Project would be followed with several similar ventures and it would establish WA's expertise internationally both in historic and modern boat building. "Importantly, the ship will stay in WA after being built and she will become an ongoing tourist drawcard for the old port," he said. "The *Duyfken* will also be a perfect addition to plans to develop the historic maritime precinct." A logo designed by Perth graphic designer, John Barnett, was unveiled and a new flag unfurled. The tagline was "Building our History". The community project now had a sharp, professional aura to it and a new-found confidence and self-belief.

In the afterglow of the launch, the Dutch Consul-General from Melbourne, David van Iterson, arranged an invitation for Michael Kailis and his wife, Dr Patricia Kailis, to attend the launch of the *Batavia* Replica by Queen Beatrix at Lelystad in The Netherlands in April 1995.

The modest thinking of building a simple replica of Australia's first ship was to be transformed. Michael Kailis later said that the Dutch treated them like royalty. He was introduced to the Queen and every major dignitary. Behind the sizzle of the launch, Michael Kailis saw the epic struggle of Willem Vos to build a replica ship. It took the determined shipwright 25 gruelling years to recreate the 1200 tonne *Batavia* which was almost eight times the capacity of *Duyfken*. From small beginnings his shipyard expanded and it became the biggest tourist attraction in The Netherlands outside of Amsterdam. It was a European centre for historic shipbuilding. A massive range of skills were revived and the public saw traditional shipbuilding in action. Willem Vos was sometimes seen as gruff and cantankerous, but it was probably more about frustration. He had a constant struggle for funds to build the ship and he tapped into any government resource he could exploit — he used the unemployed, volunteers and anyone he could find off the street who was prepared to work on the job. The lengthy construction phase also presented challenges. The ship was built in the open and the shipbuilders had to cope with the changing seasons and the deterioration of the timber from the elements. Michael Kailis suspected that Willem Vos would have been quite happy if the ship had never been completed, but that wasn't Michael's way. He returned to Fremantle resolving to build our ship under cover and to build the ship quickly. He wasn't interested in a project which took as long as *Batavia* — or even as long as *Endeavour*. He also believed that the *Batavia* Project was fundamentally flawed. His trawlers were used as far away as Africa, India and Burma and they were capable of traversing the world's oceans. Willem Vos built the *Batavia* replica with no great ambition to sail her. It was enough for him to recreate the 'Golden Age' of sail with a static museum ship. He often said that his aim was simply to be able to step aboard a Dutch East Indiaman to experience what it was like to stroll the decks. Michael was adamant that he was not going to be involved in building a ship like *Batavia* to be tied up at a dock and to be ignominiously towed into and out of harbour. He was bursting with enthusiasm and with a bold idea to reenact *Duyfken*'s original voyage beginning in Amsterdam, then to Banda in Indonesia and then south east to the Pennefather River on Cape York Peninsula. His ultimate destination was to be the Sydney Olympic Games.

The Technical Committee, which Michael Young formed to guide the design and construction of the vessel, began to look more seriously at a shipbuilding location. Joe Rotondella wasn't budging on his fee to use the *Endeavour* shed and the committee quite rightly agreed with Michael Kailis that the ship should be built under cover to protect it from the harsh Australian summer. It was feared that the European Oak timber would shrink and split in the heat and the low humidity. Michael Young asked Adriaan de Jong to visualise the ship being built in the staff car park of the WA Maritime Museum. We all thought it was a great idea but the Museum staff were dead against it. Where would they park their cars? A more practical consideration was that the yard would not be covered during construction. Finally, it was decided to build a shed on a vacant grassed area in front of the Museum. Negotiations soon began to structure a memorandum of understanding with the Museum. Learning from the *Endeavour* experience just down the road, the shed had sufficient length and height to build the ship's hull completely under cover. Visitors would walk through a shop selling souvenirs before coming to a viewing platform. An outdoor area where a fire could be maintained to bend the oak hull planks was part of the plan. At one end of the building there would be a three storey high mural depicting a Dutch shipyard. It would be the largest painted mural in the State.

In May 1995, Michael Young and Graeme Henderson travelled to Indonesia to look at traditional shipbuilding at Madura Island following Nick Burningham's recommendation on 'shell-first' shipbuilders and to explore the possible location of the wreck of the original *Duyfken*. They saw how the shipwrights bent the timber hull planks using fire and how the planks were formed into the hull shape before internal framing was added. They found that the highest levels of craftsmanship were seen at Pasean and Ambunten, and came back with a recommendation that a couple of Madurese shipwrights could perhaps be hosted in Fremantle to help build the hull, establishing a tangible link with Indonesia. From Madura Island, they travelled to the Maluku Islands, the centre of the trade in nutmeg, cloves and mace which brought the Dutch to the East Indies. They planned to find the original resting place of *Duyfken*, visiting the island of Makian and then moving onto Ternate Island where it was thought that the ship was careened in poor condition and broken up in 1608. Graeme Henderson dived several times in the harbour near Fort Oranje and Michael looked for remains of oak hull timbers in the old buildings in the town. Their search was inconclusive with the landscape greatly changed from the *Duyfken* days but it was a tantalising trip, raising more questions than answers. They returned to Fremantle and Michael made many presentations on what they'd found, giving great impetus to the Project and energising everyone involved.

It was agreed that nothing could happen to begin construction until State Government sponsorship was secured. Once this hurdle was overcome, all the other doors would open up. Importantly, a big chunk of State Government money would enable a keel to be laid. That would be a sign of confidence and something tangible to persuade everyone else to come aboard. Leveraging the State Government contribution to the task would then enable us to put together a strong submission to the WA Lotteries Commission to fund the shipyard building. Lotteries would enjoy naming rights to what became known as the Lotteries *Duyfken* Village.

Duyfken's Finance Committee met with Colin Barnett in May 1995 and put to him a proposal for the State Government to loan the Project $1 million to be repaid after five years. Michael Kailis followed up with a letter which stated: "It is expected that after the *Duyfken* Foundation has completed the construction of the replica, it will be gifted to the people of Western Australia through the State Government so that it permanently becomes a part of the Maritime Museum's collection and an ongoing tourist attraction." An executive summary stated: "Integral to the Foundation's Mission is for the ship to be permanently home-ported in Fremantle." These words would become powerful levers in the troubled years ahead. The intention was to appeal to Premier Richard Court's WA-first attitude which returned the winning America's Cup yacht *Australia II* to Western Australia from the Australian National Maritime Museum after a successful, high profile public campaign. It had been a bugbear for him since 1984. The Premier pledged to make the famous yacht the centrepiece of a grand new maritime museum and to create a maritime heritage precinct. *Duyfken* fitted into this master plan for Fremantle. The old port city enjoyed over 900,000 visitors a year and the new projects would make it the number one destination outside of Perth and Kings Park.

The State Government proposal was moving too slowly through the bureaucracy for anyone's liking, so it was resolved that Michael Kailis and Kerry Stokes would meet directly with the Premier and ask him for $500,000 in cash, rather than a loan, to get the ball rolling. Michael and Kerry's connections with the Court family went back a long way. They both knew the Premier and his father, Sir Charles Court (who Sir James Cruthers always referred to as 'Big Charlie'). He was a local hero credited with enabling the West Australian mining boom which transformed the State. The Court family respected Michael Kailis' business ability and his merry band of fund-raisers. Kerry Stokes and Richard Court were firm friends so a meeting was easily arranged.

Michael drove up from Fremantle and picked up Kerry from his West Perth office. They drove down the hill along St Georges Terrace to the Premier's office, parking in the street outside. They both reached into their pockets to get some coins to feed the parking meter. The two millionaires were penniless and they couldn't help but laugh that they were heading into a meeting to ask for half a million dollars and they didn't even have any money for a meter. The meeting went well. Richard Court, a keen yachtsman, was very positive about the prospect of building the first ship in Australia's history in Fremantle. His main concern was that if they didn't complete the construction of the ship, the State would lose its money and the opposition would come after him. His solution was simple and took them a little by surprise. He asked Michael and Kerry whether they would guarantee that if the ship was not built, they would give the State's money back. A little surprised, they glanced at each other and nodded. The deal was done. Michael and Kerry both provided a written guarantee to the Premier that they would refund $250,000 each if the ship was not built, and Michael followed up with a letter to the Director General of Finance at State Treasury on 20 September 1995, confirming the commitment.

The simple handshake agreement turned into months of negotiations with Treasury. A lot of work had to be done behind the scenes to secure the funds. Syd Corser asked an old friend and former Mayor of Canning, Eelco Tacoma, to assist with the detailed submission to Treasury. Nick Burningham provided a supporting document on the construction of the vessel and it was becoming clear that he would be a vital part of the team if the ship went ahead. I provided a marketing budget.

With State funding committed, Syd Corser then approached the Federal member for the seat of Swan, Kim Beazley, who was the Deputy Prime Minister under Paul Keating (and Charlie Welker's neighbour in South Perth), for assistance. Kim Beazley asked one of his staffers, Mike Megaw, to look into the possibilities for Commonwealth funding of the Project. On 14 September 1995, Paul Keating's personal adviser wrote to Michael Kailis saying that the Prime Minister had no interest in funding the ship. It was a blow. We thought Kim Beazley would lobby harder for us. If anything, however, it made the fundraising trio more determined than ever. Syd Corser and Sir James Cruthers always joked that it would take three 'no' replies before they accepted a funding refusal. "People always say no the first time," they said. Undeterred, Michael Kailis then approached his old friend Simon Crean who was the Federal Minister for Employment, Education and Training, suggesting a training scheme for young apprentices. No luck there, either. Once again, the political winds were blowing against us.

Despite the knock-backs, planning to build the ship continued. One of the most pressing tasks was to obtain the correct timber to build the hull. The ship required European Oak (Quercus robur) which was the timber of choice for Dutch shipyards. The ancient oak forests of Europe have been decimated for centuries and either replaced with farmland or managed forests of quick growing timber. Oak trees were rarely found in plantations, and even by the sixteenth century, the Dutch were looking to the Baltic for timber supplies. Tony Trilling from the timber importer, Unimark Associates, suggested that he could supply oak from Latvia in the sizes required for the hull and he made enquiries when he visited there in September 1995. Latvia was an emerging nation which was granted independence from the crumbling Soviet Union in 1991 after two million people linked hands across Estonia, Latvia and Lithuania demanding independence. It was still finding its feet in the post-communist world. About half of the land area of Latvia was forested, and timber was an important part of the economy. Oak was not widely used except by barrel makers. Even though the very old oak trees of Latvia were regarded as national treasures, it was possible to buy large planks of oak and the weird shapes required to cut the hull formers (the floors, the futtocks and the knees) for the ship. Nick Burningham with the assistance of the accomplished maritime historian, Tom Vosmer, estimated the ship would require 95m³ of oak at a cost of $300,000.

Even though there were no funds available to make an order of oak, 1995 had been a year to celebrate. *Duyfken* seemed to be an idea whose time had come. The Friends of the *Duyfken* group was wildly successful. The functions had become so much fun that 300 members joined and had been drawn into the *Duyfken* dream. The funds being raised were vital to the first year of the Project. The *Duyfken* 1606 Replica Foundation was up and running with regular Board meetings and the Executive Committee was working through a fund raising plan. Michael Kailis topped up the coffers many times and money was always available to prepare marketing materials to help with the push for funding. Failure was never considered. The Technical Committee was getting a very good idea of what our ship would look like thanks to the work of Michael Young, Marit van Huystee, Adriaan de Jong and Nick Burningham. The Executive Committee had become the Finance Committee and while it had not yet secured the first major sponsor, plans were well advanced and we were confident that the State Government funding would create a wave of new funders. 1996 was set to be a great year.

Chapter 5

Romance Versus Reality

Imagine a flavour that was so exotic and enticing, so fragrant and so expensive that only a wealthy few ever had the pleasure of tasting it. For Europeans in the Middle Ages, the flavour of cloves, nutmeg and mace (the outer protective covering of the nutmeg seed) came from beyond the outer reaches of the known world. During the Renaissance, ships arrived in Venice from Alexandria in Egypt or Tyre in Lebanon with spice cargos more valuable, ounce for ounce, than gold. The ultimate indulgence of wealth was to eat what nobody else could afford and to be surrounded by the most exclusive aromas. The Holy Roman Emperor, Henry VI, was reputed to have arrived in Rome with the streets made fragrant by burning nutmeg. Spices were traded across Europe. It was a transcontinental business with a lot of hands from many countries carrying the spices over sea and land. The trade, extending to Africa, the Middle East and Europe in the west and to China in the east, had been underway for several thousand years. Cloves from Maluku have been found in a Mesopotamian pantry in the ancient city of Terqa in Syria dated 1700BC. In China, they were placed in the mouth of supplicants to freshen their breath during the Han Dynasty 2,000 years ago.

The spices treasured in mediaeval Europe were obtained by the Mamelukes of Egypt from the Gujarati traders of northwest India via the Red Sea. The Gujaratis obtained them from traders further east. Everyone added a little to the price of the commodity. The Maluku Islands of Indonesia were the original source of cloves and nutmeg. The nine metre tall clove tree was only found on the small volcanic islands of Ternate, Tidore, Moti, Makian and Bacan between Sulawesi and West Papua in Indonesia. Nutmeg and mace was endemic to the tiny islands of the Banda Archipelago further south beyond Seram and Ambon.

Researchers have attempted to estimate the volume of spices which arrived in Europe every year from the Maluku Islands. It was probably less than 50 tonnes in the year 1400. When the Portuguese found a way around the Cape of Good Hope and then to India and beyond, the traditional spice trading routes across Asia and the Middle East were supplanted. The Portuguese followed the trading ships from the Indian sub-continent to the Muslim kingdom of Melaka in today's Malaysia and then ventured to the Maluku Islands themselves to monopolise the spice trade through the sixteenth century. They eventually began to trade with East Asia as well. Boundless riches could be had if the spice supply could be controlled and the prices in Europe maintained. When the intermediaries were eliminated from the trade, profits of 1,000 per cent were possible. Compared with the old trading routes across land and sea, one small ship the size of *Duyfken* could transport enough spice in its hold to provide a year's supply of the prized flavourings to Europe.

In his 'Discours of Voyages into ye Easte & West Indies', the Dutch merchant and trader, Jan Huygen van Linschoten, described the many uses of the spices of Maluku, and he inspired the Dutch to venture on their own. He said the clove trees had 'the pleasantest smell in the world':

> *When they are green, they use to salt them with salt and vinegar in Maluco (Maluku), and some they put in sugar, which are very pleasant to be eaten. The water of green cloves distilled is very pleasant of smell, and strengthens the heart, likewise they procure sweating in men that have the pox; with cloves, nutmeg, mace, long and black pepper; some lay the poulder (poultice?) of cloves upon a man's head that hath a pain in it, that proceedeth of cold. They strengthen the liver, the maw (jaw) and the heart, they further digestions, they procure evacuation of the urine and stop laxativeness, and being put into the eyes, preserved the sight, and four drammes (a very small quantity) being drunk with milk, do procure the lust ... (Nutmeg) comforteth the brain, sharpeneth the memory, warmeth and strengthen the maw, driveth wind out of the body, maketh a sweet breath, driveth down urine, stopperth the laske (diarrhoea), and to conclude, is good against all cold diseases in the heads, in the brain, the maw, the liver and the matrice (womb)."*

Was there anything that these incredible spices could not do? They were miraculous foods and it was a tantalising prospect that bringing them to Europe would lead to almost instant wealth. The Dutch wanted a piece of this action. They were a nation of traders, perfectly located in the heart of Europe and they had the tools — big trading ships which could carry large cargoes. The Dutch built a new generation of ocean-going vessels which were a technological advance on their European competitors. While the Portuguese galleons of the sixteenth century were large and heavily armed, with bulbous hulls and great windage, they were slow and difficult to manoeuvre. The Dutch East Indiamen of the seventeenth century were comparatively strong, fast in even light airs, seaworthy and well-armed. They could out-run the galleons if required. This enabled them to project power across the seas and, like the Portuguese before them, their cannon were superior to anything else in the eastern world at the time.

It was one thing to research and build the first ship recorded in history to visit Australia but we were also strongly motivated to delve deeper into the *Duyfken* story and to understand how the voyage fitted into the broader brush of history. We had only the vaguest idea of *Duyfken* and her place in historical events but as more information came to light, we came to realise that *Duyfken* and her crew participated in one of the pivotal eras in world affairs. What began to emerge was more than just the story of a short voyage to northern Australia, but a story of global trade rivalries and European trade dominance. *Duyfken* would never have sailed to Australia without the European lust for spices and the rise of The Netherlands as a European economic and military power.

With such large and impressive ships in the Dutch fleets, scant attention had been paid to the smallest ships which accompanied the large cargo ships: the jachts. Barely 25 metres long, they were easy to ignore. *Duyfken* was one of these unpretentious vessels. Jacht means to hunt or to hurry in Dutch. Jachts were the 'eyes of the fleet', or the scout ships, heavily armed for their size but with relatively small cargo capacity. *Duyfken* boasted two bronze, longer range guns and six smaller cast iron, media range cannon on conventional wooden carriages. All fired a three pound ball. The ship also had four small, breech loaded, wrought iron, swivel guns mounted on the deck rail. It was a formidable array of weapons for such a small vessel.

These ships were directed to sail ahead of the main fleets to investigate safe anchorages and to determine whether the locals were friendly. They carried messages and important people between trading outposts. Jachts were expendable. Compared with the great Dutch East Indiamen such as *Batavia*, *Duyfken* was assumed to be a minor vessel in the story of the Dutch East India Company. Research would reveal that she had a vital role: communicating between trading outposts, skirmishing if needed and gathering supplies.

Spurred on by Michael Young's initial research, Marit van Huystee scoured original Dutch records and found out more about the history of the scout ship of the fleet. Up to this time, most historical research had focused on the large ships which were grandiosely decorated and bristling with cannon. She worked with historian Frank Broeze from the University of Western Australia; the head of maritime archaeology at the WA Maritime Museum Jeremy Green; Nick Burningham and Adriaan de Jong from the *Duyfken* Project; and Robert Parthesius and Philippe Lach de Bere in The Netherlands. As Marit delved further and she and Adriaan translated more texts, we began to learn a lot more about *Duyfken*, or rather, the three ships named *Duyfken* which straddled the years around that first recorded voyage to Australia. It became clear that *Duyfken* should not just be left in the footnotes of history.

The *Duyfken* story began when a Dutch consortium, the Compagnie van Verre (Company from Far), put together the first fleet to the Indies in 1595 under the command of Cornelisz de Houtman to grab a piece of the spice trade from their trading rivals, the Portuguese. One of the ships named in that fleet was *Duyfken* and it was always assumed that the ship which sailed to Australia in 1606 was the *Duyfken* from this first fleet. Marit soon established that our *Duyfken* could not have been that ship as the *Duyfken* of the first fleet was renamed the *Overijssel* in Jacob Cornelius van Neck's second fleet in 1598 and returned in 1599. She wrote: "The *Overijssel* departed the Texel roadstead on 21 December 1599 on her third and last voyage. She arrived at Bantam on 1 September 1600. After sailing in the Indies, the *Overijssel* left for The Netherlands on 9 September 1601, arriving in the roads of Texel again in June 1602. However, more than a year earlier, on 23 April 1601, another yacht named *Duyfken* departed from Texel arriving at Bantam on 26 December 1601. This is almost certainly the *Duyfken* that was to sail to Australia in 1606." She then found yet another *Duyfken* in the records: "A third *Duyfken* left the Netherlands on 29 December 1611 (she ran aground and was lost near Surat in 1617), but the second *Duyfken* had already been lost in 1608 off Ternate, one of the Molucca's Spice Islands."

Marit was then able to zero in on the second ship and *Duyfken*'s part in the spice trade began to be revealed. The 1601 fleet of Admiral Jacob van Heemskerck gathered at the Texel roadstead in the spring. With 13 ships all being provisioned for the voyage to the edge of the known world, it must have been a magnificent sight. The Dutch invested heavily in this spice fleet, spurred on by the successful but barely profitable return of the first fleet. Five ships were under the command of Admiral Wolfert Harmensz. These were the *Gelderland*, *Utrecht*, *Wachter*, *Zeelandia*, and *Duyfken*. The captain of *Duyfken* was the 34 year old seafarer, Willem Cornelisz Schouten. Although he made three voyages to the Indies, he might have been forgotten in maritime history if it wasn't for his later voyage in 1616 with Isaäc Le Maire which was planned to find an alternate route to the Indies and to undermine the, by then, VOC monopoly of the spice trade. Willem Schouten rounded the cape at the southernmost tip of South America and called it Cape Horn, after the ship *Hoorn* which was, in turn, named after his birthplace of Hoorn. He named the strait itself 'Le Maire Strait'. Willem Schouten came from a family of seafarers. He was born at Hoorn in 1577 and his father, Cornelisz Jansz Schouts, owned his own ship and sailed to the Indies as captain of Admiral Steven van der Haghen's flagship *De Zon* in the Old East India Company fleet of 1599. His uncle, Cornelis Jansz Melcknap, also sailed as a captain in the fleet.

Admiral Wolfert Harmensz' ships were called the Maluku Fleet of the Oude Oost-Indische Compagnie (Old East India Company) as the VOC had not yet been formed. They had one specific mission: to sail to the spice islands and to fill the cargo holds with spices so a substantial profit could be made upon their return. Cornelisz de Houtman's first fleet to the Indies had successfully returned to The Netherlands but without a massive cargo of spices. Admirals van Heemskerck and Harmensz were intent on making the huge investment in the fleet pay off with full cargo holds. The ships *Zeelandia* and *Utrecht* were to sail to Ambon and Banda and "Concerning the jacht called the *Duyffgen* (sic), [she] should stay with those (two) ships from which she could sail in the easiest way to the other (two) ships in order to bring news and to sail to Banda, and if there is apparently more cargo or nuts than the ships are able to take in, and to sail with it to Ternate. And if possible the same yacht should sail back from Ternate to Banda to bring the news on the Ternate trade to Banda in this way. And in case at Ternate for some reason there won't be enough (crop), the same jacht should go to Ternate with the cargo of nuts."

The Maluku group of the fleet sailed to Mauritius and stayed for three weeks. A drawing by crew member, Jouris Joostenz, showed *Duyfken* at anchor. It is one of only a couple of drawings of *Duyfken* taken from life.

This fleet left Mauritius and was sailing through the Sunda Strait on 24 December 1601 when they encountered a Chinese merchant in a Javanese vessel who told them that a fleet of ships commanded by the Portuguese admiral Andrea Furtado de Mendoça was at Bantam. The Portuguese sailed from Goa in India to reaffirm Portuguese domination of the spice trade. They were laying siege to Bantam, about 100 km west of Sunda Kelapa in Java. Bantam was controlled by the Sundanese monarch Abdul Kadir. He controlled the trade of pepper grown in western Java and Sumatra, as well as maintaining an entrepôt for goods coming from the east and the west. Merchants from as far away as Abyssinia and China lived and traded within the town walls. The Dutch made the decision to fight the Portuguese fleet and Admiral Harmensz ordered the cannons which had been stowed for the long voyage to be brought back on deck. With eight galleons, 22 galleys and 30 Fusta (small galleys) at his disposal, de Mendoça was well-equipped but he was surprised when the smaller Dutch force attacked.

An unsigned letter written on board *Duyfken* was published in an 1864 book entitled 'The summary of the Dutch authority in the East Indies' and was translated by Adriaan de Jong:

> ... *everything being prepared accordingly have in the morning of 25 December 1601 two hours before dawn hoisted the sails and about sunrise had approached the Portuguese fleet and within range shooting with all guns and muskets aimed at them demonstrating all possible hostility, sailing through and again through the Portuguese fleet who were surprised un-expecting, weighed their anchors, made sail, hoisting the blood flag to fight back at us. And after the battle had lasted considerable time, the Portuguese settled their ships under an island, named Poelopenzang [Pulau Panjang], and ours under a certain other high island, repairing the damage the ships had suffered from the fighting, amongst it also our Admiral, due to the bursting of a half cannon (that had been cast at Utrecht).*
>
> *The 26th it was bad weather, such that the ships could not utilise sail nor guns.*
>
> *The 27th being good weather, we again made sail and sailing in at*

> the Portuguese fleet our admiral engaged and boarded the Portuguese Admiral. *The ship* Seelant *another large carrack and the ship* Utrecht *and the ship* Wachter *a galley each, the small yacht too another galley, have taken-on the large ships bravely, the two galleys were boarded, captured, plundered and destroyed, the Portuguese having the advantage of wind and current set three of their galleys on fire and to cause us damage let them drift, but were evaded by our ships, and so drifting the battle lasted by day and night when the lay of the land and the current permitted such until the Portuguese resolved to leave from Bantam, with us being free of damage and feared, in pursuit until the first of January 1602, having put the Portuguese to rout, let them go.*

The Battle of Bantam was perhaps the first major sea battle between European powers outside Europe. It marked the end of the Portuguese monopoly in the East Asian trade. The galley which the captain of *Duyfken*, Willem Schouten, would have plundered was probably a large Javanese vessel rowed by slaves which had a single mast and sail. It carried soldiers and once contact was made with other ships, the soldiers would rush onto the other vessel and engage in combat. William Schouten would have taken anything of value from the war galley before sinking it. *Duyfken* was not quite the humble ship of exploration we thought!

We learnt a lot about *Duyfken's* activities within the Indonesian archipelago from the journals of the administrators. Having beaten the Portuguese and their local allies, the Dutch fleet sailed east to Maluku. The ships spread out to obtain trading goods. The seas of Indonesia were like roads connecting towns. After the long voyages from Europe, sailing between the trading posts was accomplished in days or maybe weeks, not months. *Duyfken* was sent to Seram to load provisions of sago. Whilst farmers in western Indonesia grew rice in flooded fields, in the eastern islands, it was more common to grow sago palms for the starchy pith in the heart of the plant. The dried cakes made from the plant were popular as food aboard the ships undertaking long ocean voyages.

Duyfken's Captain Willem Schouten was also given a wider artikelbrief (the ship's orders from the admiral of the fleet): "Secondly, whether there is anything to be had there besides sago, their way of doing business and in what places, what commodities had best be sent there, and to what limits their further navigation extends, also, whether they have any knowledge of

Nova Guinea, whether they have sent ships there, or whether ships from Nova Guinea have ever come to Ceram. In the island of Banda, actum April the 10th, A.D. 1602, on board the ship *Gelderland*. God send his blessing unto salvation. Amen."

There is no record of what Willem Schouten found out about Nova Guinea on his visit to the Ternate sultanate at Ceram, but the Dutch desire to explore further eastwards did not abate.

On 25 August 1602, with holds full of spices, *Duyfken*, *Gelderland* and *Zeeland* sailed from Bantam for The Netherlands. At Cape Agulhas, the southernmost tip of the African continent, *Duyfken* lost touch with the other two ships during an overnight storm and arrived in Vlissingen on 17 February 1603. The other ships arrived two months later after resting at St Helena in the South Atlantic while the crews recovered from scurvy. The financial result was a return on investment estimated at about 300 per cent.

While the fleets to the Indies had been away, the United Dutch East India Company (VOC) was created on 20 March 1602 to bring together the trading companies which were rivals when raising capital for the East Indies fleets. The States-General of the United Provinces arbitrarily assigned a monopoly for the new company over a trading zone from the Cape of Good Hope in southern Africa to the Straits of Magellan on the southernmost tip of South America. The new VOC was granted extensive rights over this zone. A new commercial empire was created with almost unlimited rights of exploitation. The VOC was given the power to appoint governors, raise armies, make laws and enforce justice. The newly-formed VOC purchased the ship *Duyfken* in the months before October 1603 for 2,200 guilders and on 18 December 1603 the ship departed Texel as part of the 12 ship fleet of Admiral Steven van der Haghen. *Duyfken* now was under the command of Willem Jansz. This was the first fleet sent to the Indies by the newly-formed VOC. Van der Haghen opened secret orders from the company once his fleet was at sea. The orders were aggressive — as well as engaging in trade, he was instructed to attack the Portuguese whenever he had the opportunity and to burn the ships of the enemy.

Marit's research described how the fleet stayed from 10 January to 12 February 1604 in the friendly English port of Plymouth and from 10 March to 30 May at Maio Island in the Cape Verde group. With 1,200 crew aboard the ships of the fleet, supplies of fresh water as well as coconuts, plantains, figs and grapes were vital to provision for the long voyage ahead. The fleet reached Mozambique on 17 June 1604 where they found the Portuguese

Fort São Sebastião barely defended as the garrison had left to quell an uprising elsewhere. A Portuguese carrack lay at anchor near the fort and despite shelling from the fort it was captured and yielded some ivory as plunder. Another smaller ship arrived which they also boarded and renamed *Mosambique*. The carrack would have been an important prize. The most famous carrack of this era was captured by Walter Raleigh when the British attacked a Portuguese fleet returning from the Indies in 1592. In its hold, the ship contained 425 tons of pepper, 45 tons of cloves, 35 tons of cinnamon, three tons of mace and three tons of nutmeg. *Duyfken* would have run rings around a carrack which was a product of medieval seafaring tradition with its large castles at the bow and stern and heavy masts. While seaworthy enough, carracks were slow and cumbersome to sail and difficult to manoeuvre in battle.

The Dutch set the carrack alight and then Willem Jansz and *Duyfken* remained with two other ships to continue attacking local shipping in the area. Intending to remain in the area for five weeks to continue the blockade, the three ships could find no opponents to engage so they rejoined the others at the Comoro islands near Madagascar and 'harassed' the Portuguese near Goa in India until November 1604. *Duyfken* was then involved in the successful siege of the Portuguese fort at Ambon before sailing to Banda. In September 1605, Willem Jansz sailed *Duyfken* to Bantam and prepared for her voyage beyond the known world. Admiral Steven van der Haghen appointed Houtman as governor before departing for The Netherlands and it was Houtman who assigned Willem Jansz and his supercargo, the merchant Jan Lodewijkszoon van Roosengijn, to sail *Duyfken* on an expedition to the unknown southern lands.

Imagine that meeting for a moment. Bantam is the meeting place of traders from all over the world. In the bustle of the port there are Portuguese, Chinese, Arabs, Indians from all the sub-continent's trading ports and even traders from the lands of the Abyssinian empire. The Dutch trading fleet would be like the US Sixth Fleet arriving today. It oozed power. The previous Dutch fleet had carried all before it to arrive triumphantly at Bantam a few years before. The fleet soon fanned out to gather cargo from islands across the archipelago for the return voyage to Europe. Still they wanted more and they could gain the upper hand over their trading rivals if they had the courage. There was rumour of a great source of gold beyond the world they knew. All three men — Houtman, Jansz and van Roosengijn — knew that their Dutch compatriots had developed comprehensive knowledge of the spice islands and that knowledge was encased in secret maps — but they had no maps of the land to the east. They knew that it was over the summer months that the winds blew to the south east. Houtman probably told his two capable lieutenants that there was a greater prize awaiting them all over the horizon and he wanted them to take one of the smallest, most expendable ships to see whether they could find it. No, he didn't want to risk one of the large VOC vessels. *Duyfken* was a nimble craft which could use its speed to get out of trouble if that is what they found. They were to search for the fabled land of gold and to report back without telling another soul. It was standard practice to make a map of the area they visited so that subsequent Dutch ships would know where to sail if they needed to return.

A log of Jansz' voyage to Cape York no longer exists but some elements of the voyage can be pieced together with fragments of information from other sources, including records from their English trading rivals. The East India Company was formed by the English to trade in the Indies. Compared with the Dutch it was a minor participant in the spice trade. The ships from the company's second voyage to the Indies arrived in Bantam three months after the Dutch VOC fleet. The small English contingent split up. Several ships remained in Bantam loading pepper and two others headed for Maluku to buy more spices. A 25 year old Yorkshireman, John Saris, from the English company was in Bantam later in the year. One mention has him receiving a sable (later called a sabre) sword cut on his forefinger during a brawl with a Dutchman. He noted all the comings and goings of ships in the harbour.

On 26 October 1605 he wrote in his diary: "The sixe and twentieth, Admiral Vanhangen (sic) of Utricke departed for Holland, with two ships more in company, by whom we advised the Company of all matters at large." A month later he added: "The eighteenth (November), heere departed a small pinnasse of the Flemmings, for the discovery of the Island called Nova ginnea, which, as it is said, affordeth great store of Gold." The voyage was clearly not a complete secret!

The search for gold was just as motivating for the Dutch as the search for spices. While the voyage of Christopher Columbus in 1492 opened up the New World for Spain, it was Hernan Cortes who plundered the gold of Mexico in 1519. It was easy pickings. The Central and South Americans had already won the gold and silver from the ground, and refined it. All the Spanish had to do was conquer them with their superior weaponry, transport it across the seas and melt it down. Spain became the wealthiest country in Europe thanks to its new colonies. The Treaty of Tordesillas in 1494 divided the world between the rival Spanish and Portuguese monarchs with a line which went north and south in the Atlantic Ocean. The Spanish went west while the Portuguese were free to exploit trade to the east. The myth of King Solomon's mines from the Bible persisted. Ferdinand Magellan's 1522 voyage of circumnavigation was probably motivated more by gold than spices. In 1568, the Spanish explorer Álvaro de Mendaña sailed across the Pacific from east to west and named the Solomon Islands after King Solomon because he thought that he had discovered Ophir, the biblical source of the Biblical king's gold. The Dutch were just as keen to find this mythical 'El Dorado' which was speculated to be east beyond the known world of the Indies.

Six months later, Captain Saris wrote: "The fifteenth of June (1606) have arrived Nockhoda Tingall a Cling-man from Banda, in a Java Junk, laden with mace and nutmeg, the which he sold to the Guzerats; he told me that the Flemmings Pinnasse which went upon discovery for Nova Ginny, was returned to Banda, having found the Island: but in sending their men on shoare to intreate of Trade, there were nine of them killed by the Heathens, which are men-eaters: so they were constrained to returne, finding no good to be doene there." The "cling-man" or "Keling man" to whom Saris was referring was probably an Indian trader.

And from this short diary note, the first recorded voyage to Australia was immortalised. Captain Saris then slips from *Duyfken* history (he subsequently rose through the East India Company ranks to become the chief factor or intermediary for the British enterprise before returning to England in 1609).

Using the Saris dates (which have been shown to be somewhat unreliable) the exploratory voyage can be assumed to have begun on about 18 November 1605, returning during May or June 1606. After this time, *Duyfken* continued to be used as part of the VOC presence in Indonesia. The heat and humidity of the tropics was a harsh environment for a ship built of European Oak, and it was also probably battle-scarred. On 17 September 1607, *Duyfken* was repaired in Bantam and sent to Ternate with supplies of rice and arrack.

Trouble was brewing for the Dutch on the islands of Tidore and Ternate. Dutch Admiral Matelieff gathered together a fleet of eight ships including *Duyfken* to impose his presence on the local rulers. A Spanish expedition had arrived from Manila in The Phillipines and the Portuguese constructed two new fortresses to protect their interests. In turn, the Dutch Admiral established his own fortress. Jan Lodewijkszoon van Roosengijn who had been supercargo or 'chief merchant' aboard *Duyfken* on the voyage to Cape York was placed in charge of a fleet of four ships of 170 men (including *Duyfken* with 20 crew) while Admiral Matelieff sailed for China to pursue further trade. The enemy attacked the partially built fortress and *Duyfken* was ordered to sail to Bantam to get food supplies and obtain help for the beleaguered garrison.

Departing Bantam on 6 November 1607, *Duyfken* sailed to Maluku to resupply Ternate. Jan Roossengijn wrote that on 20 January 1608: "..the jacht *Duyjken (sic)* arrived off Ternate coming from Bantam and was loaded with rice, beans and a bit of arrack, which brought much joy amongst our people and gave courage to the Ternatens as well, because we are greatly lacking in these things; (29 January). I sailed off with the aforesaid jacht: and captured a prahu, which came from the island Makian and was on its way to Ternate, with about 2.5 last (about five tonnes) of cloves, about which we came to blows with the enemy the next day with two galleys and a small frigate (a smaller type of galley), about five hours, and they fired more than 80 shots to us, but God be praised no injury was done to us."

When Portuguese reinforcements arrived from Manila, the Dutch were undermanned and unable to attack. *Duyfken* and another ship, the *Kleine Son* (*Little Son*), attempted to lure the Portuguese ships from under the cover of the fortress but they cold not tempt them out.

In May 1608 Admiral Paulus van Caerden wrote:

> *On 18 do., saw three galleys and some junks of the Portuguese laying off Ternate, and arrived towards evening under Ternate, and caste anchor off Malayo, we found there the ships* Gelderland, *the* Kleine Son *and the* Duyfken, *and the frigate which had been taken at Celebes ...*
> *On 24 do. we saw two sails offshore, assumed that they were Spanish ships, therefore the* Duyfken *and the* Kleine Son *and the frigate went there to reconnoitre, they came back the 25th with the tiding that the galleys had brought in a Spanish ship with victuals ...*
> *On 28 do. arrived on the roads the ship* China *and the yacht* Jager *... the same day the* Duyfken *and the frigate sailed to Gilolo and Sebue, to pick up the blacks, who were out on a trip. On 30 do. the*

> *frigate arrived with some corecore (Kora Kora - Indonesian paddle boats or canoes) and about 300 blacks ... On 3 do. (June) the* Duyfken *came back accompanied by several corecores with blacks who were mustered, found them about 400 strong...*
> *On 7 do. the males set sail on the frigate, and the Admiral coming aboard, appointed the commissioner Jan Rosegein (Roossengijn) for captain ... towards evening resolved to sail to the town of Ternate.*

Duyfken had taken a beating during the repeated missions to exert dominance over the spice trade in Maluku with an iron fist. Paulus van Caerden left Makian on 20 July and sailed to the town of Malaya on Ternate where he arrived the following day. According to Van Caerden, much work had to be carried out there, including repair to the *Duyfken*:

> *We have brought the* Duyfken *here inside the recyff (reef) having made great efforts and having done much work, found that her whole body had broken down/gave way, and because of her old age could not sail again, the knees have completely come loose, caused by putting her ashore, two beams are burst in the hold, and the sides have bulged out totally, therefore there is nothing we can do for her and she must remain as a wreck.*

Another source that mentions problems with the *Duyfken* is a letter from Jacque I'Hermite, who was upper merchant at Bantam, to the directors of the Amsterdam Chamber in November 1608. Ships meant to sail to the Indies were built with double planking below the waterline as protection from the teredo worm:

> *The* Duyfgen *is burst in the doubling (in't verdubbelen — lining of extra planks), so that it is necessary to send some ships thither with food and other things.*

And that was the last Marit van Hustee could find in the records for *Duyfken* in 1995. Her careful research, however, had expanded our knowledge of Australia's first ship. A picture of *Duyfken* was now emerging. Willem Jansz and Jan van Roosengijn were battle hardened when they set sail for the fabled land of gold. They were not genteel merchants but 'hard-core' and quite mercenary fortune-seekers in an age in which commerce and war were bound together. We now knew we were recreating a vessel which was intimately associated with the fierce rivalry for the spice trade. *Duyfken*'s role in the Indies stretched from relieving garrisons, to attacking shipping and gathering trading good to be transferred to the larger East Indiamen. And when she was not engaged in these activities, the *Little Dove* was sent in search of new lands and new people with whom trade could be conducted. She was no cuddly little dove.

Chapter 6

An Idea Whose Time Has Come

This was the big announcement we'd worked so hard to achieve. On 21 February 1996, Premier Richard Court stood at a lectern on the grass in front of the WA Maritime Museum and announced to a small group of media that the State Government would contribute $500,000 towards the construction of a *Duyfken* replica and provide other in-kind support to help make it happen. He said *Duyfken* would be a tangible symbol of the European exploration of Australia, an attraction for visitors and all Western Australians, and an important educational tool. After months of negotiations with Graeme Rolfe and Andy Rose from State Treasury an agreement was now in place. The Project was no longer an abstract idea, it was a reality.

The nature of the relationship between the Maritime Museum and the Project was actively discussed as a memorandum of understanding took form to secure the grassed forecourt of the Museum for our shipyard. It gave us great credibility to be associated with a team of scientists of such world renown. In turn, the archaeologists led by Jeremy Green, had their reputations to protect. They did not want to be associated with anything that did not aspire to the highest standards of authenticity. We knew that there was a great deal of cynicism about replica ship projects in the academic community around the world. Many replicas only vaguely mimicked famous ships from the past. The Maritime Museum displayed the remains of Dutch shipwrecks, expertly conserved and beautifully displayed — national treasures — a lifetime's work for many archaeologists. For them to endorse it, they wanted the Project to become a case study for experimental archaeology in the purest sense (in their view, engines were superfluous, of course). Jeremy Green once joked to me that the best thing to do after

Duyfken was completed was for her to be scuttled so that they could also study her deterioration as she sat on the sea bed. Serious or a perverse joke? I couldn't tell.

The funding announcement came at just the right time. We had to maintain the momentum we'd generated in the initial phase of the Project — to stop talking about building a ship and to begin construction. Nobody ever saw the months of work which went on behind the scenes to raise money and design shipyards. People were getting restless and rivalries developed. Gloria Jackson, as coordinator of the Friends of the *Duyfken*, had been replaced by Rod Murfitt and the retired Dutch businessman, Con Smit, later took the role. Michael Young, who aspired to be the paid professional manager of the whole *Duyfken* Project, was also side-lined while still retaining his seat on the Board.

Fortunately, the State Government announcement unleashed a flurry of activity. It enabled the Executive Committee to fund raise in earnest, order timber and hire staff. Syd Corser had a person in mind to guide the Project. He was the gifted yachtsman, Noel Robins, who worked for many years as a school teacher whilst pursuing a dazzling career sailing yachts. He had many Australian championship trophies on his mantelpiece and he'd competed in significant international events including the America's Cup. He had known Syd Corser through yachting since they were both young men. Unlike Syd, who had great business acumen, Noel dabbled unsuccessfully in property development and he was probably only a few years away from retirement. Rinze Brandsma and I were asked by Michael Kailis to interview Syd's nominee but we couldn't find a time which suited us both so we arranged separate meetings. I met Noel at the trendy Ted's Cafe in Northbridge. He oozed self-confidence and he regaled me with yachting stories from the 1980s. Rinze also met with him, and we reported back to Michael that we thought he could handle the job. We were, however, both never in doubt that he would be appointed. We were simply the rubber stamps. Noel accepted on the condition that he employed his own personal assistant, Peggy Rogers, who was a highly experienced and capable office manager with whom he had worked at the Royal Perth Yacht Club. He also brought a friend from yachting, Alan Knight, into the Project to handle the accounts.

From his appointment in March 1996, Noel had a lot to contribute but he had trouble adapting to Michael Kailis' charismatic management style. Michael saw everyone as part of a team with himself as the team leader. He wanted that recognition. He didn't want to interfere in day-to-day activities but all the major decisions had to go through him. He liked to spend time on the factory floor, to chat with the staff and to get to know them. Noel's management style represented the anti-thesis of this approach. He was stubborn and he wanted to keep everything close, to take charge and get on with the job without interference. He wanted to make the big decisions himself, and to enjoy his fair share of the media acclaim. The pair first came into conflict when Noel signed the Memorandum of Understanding with the Maritime Museum while Michael was away on business. Michael was not happy when he returned and he let Noel know it. Another conflict arose when Eelco Tacoma pushed for the *Endeavour* Project's storeman, Brian Ewens, to be appointed to handle the same job at *Duyfken*. Noel pushed back because he had not chosen him. Eelco went to the top. Brian got the job but Noel determined that Eelco would not have a future at the Project. Eelco also became increasingly agitated by Michael Young's eccentricity and saw ulterior motives in just about everything that was being done. Eelco left the Project soon after.

With money in the Project bank account, Nick Burningham was engaged to work in a professional capacity to design the ship. His experience in Indonesia and his knowledge of ship design was essential in coming up with the best design.

As we had State Government funding and local community support we could approach the Lotteries Commission of WA for a grant to build the shipyard in the Museum grounds. Sir James had no doubt he could obtain what we wanted from Lotteries. He was highly respected at the institution. A Colorbond-clad industrial shed within an enclosed yard was designed for the Maritime Museum forecourt. We didn't have the time or the budget to create a building in the style of the old limestone Customs House buildings but a temporary design was proposed which had a similar roofline and colours that would not clash too badly with the heritage buildings. Adriaan de Jong put together some colourful visualisations to persuade Lotteries to fund the steel-framed building with a $250,000 grant. Like just about every new development in Fremantle, the newly-named Lotteries *Duyfken* Village had its detractors. South Ward Association convenor, David Utting, and Fremantle Society President, Ralph Hoare, both got the boots in saying that the City of Fremantle and the Heritage Council had made a major mistake in approving the temporary building. Their myopic view was not supported by most people in Fremantle who looked beyond the temporary structure and saw the tremendous opportunity for the old port to continue the historic shipbuilding activity in partnership with the Museum. We were the talk of the town before the first footing had been poured.

Construction of the building began in late 1996. Harold Clough, whom Michael Young had approached several years before, allocated several staff at his engineering firm, Entact Clough, to oversee the construction and many suppliers provided goods and services for free or at cost. The building bolted together very quickly and the roof went on in December of the same year. Highly-regarded Perth interior designer Susan Griffiths created a design for a shop and a public entrance in the style of a rustic store room. A massive mural was painted on one inside wall of the building depicting a curtain held by Amphitrite, the wife of Poseidon, being opened to reveal a Dutch shipbuilder's yard from the 1600s. Amphitrite was like an angel looking over *Duyfken* as the ship took shape below. Three artists: Robyn Gaines, Gaetan Nemorin and Rick Wymer spent more than three months creating and painting the mural. It was a stunning addition to the working shipyard. We loved it and everyone who came to see it loved it. There was one person in Australia who didn't. The artists needed the face of a classic woman for Amphitrite. They found one in a New Idea women's magazine. It so happened that it was Nicole Kidman. After the mural was completed, and always on the hunt for positive publicity, I naively wrote to Kidman's agent to let her know that her client's face adorned the painting. I thought she'd be delighted and flattered, or at least, amused. It was an easy play to get some publicity. I subsequently received a legal letter warning me that we had not asked Kidman's permission to use her image and that we should not ever claim any connection with Nicole Kidman. If we did we would face legal action. My media instincts told me to give the letter to the media and to sit back and wait for the controversy it would generate. However, I also feared what would happen if Nicole Kidman's agent did go after us. I chose to keep quiet. For the next three years, anyone visiting the shipyard would look aloft and immediately spot the likeness of the Australian actor. "Look. It's Nicole Kidman!" but it was never acknowledged in any of our printed material.

Our fundraising committee was continuing to work on a grand financing scheme. Now that the State Government funds were locked in, we needed to secure some decent Commonwealth support. One week after the State Government funding announcement in early 1996, John Howard beat Paul Keating in the Federal Election and Australia had a new Liberal

Prime Minister. It was time to re-start negotiations with a fresh batch of ministers in Canberra. This time, it was through the new Minister for the Arts, Senator Richard Alston, and the new Minister for Finance, John Fahey. The latter was the former Premier of New South Wales who had narrowly lost the State election the year before and switched to Federal politics, immediately scoring a key job in the new Ministry. There was something about Michael Kailis and politicians. Outwardly, Michael was neither a Labor nor Liberal supporter. He made modest donations to both parties and he could move seamlessly between the two. They loved his cheerful, knockabout demeanour and he could ring anyone on any side of politics and they would take the call. When his old friend, the senior Liberal politician, Billy Snedden, passed away, the pall-bearers at the funeral were Andrew Peacock, John Howard and Bob Hawke on one side and Michael and two other old friends on the other. He also had international standing. He was an invitee to the prestigious World Economic Forum in Davos, Switzerland for many years before it became fashionable for Australian politicians to spend a few days at the ski resort, hobnobbing with the rich and powerful.

It was no problem to target the Liberals. Behind the scenes, Sir James, the great fundraising strategist, quickly worked out a new plan of attack. Watch out Canberra, Michael and Sir James were coming!

We had to find a way to unlock funding from the Dutch Government too. Even though Australia and The Netherlands sold about $500m worth of goods to each other, we had no big point of leverage. The Dutch Government had a range of maritime heritage projects in The Netherlands all begging for support, and the Dutch Embassy did not have the clout to obtain significant funding from Den Haag. The third nation of our three nations plan was Indonesia. This presented an even bigger problem. Grant money flowed from Australia to Indonesia, not the other way around. Nevertheless, Sir James and Michael Kailis had a big private Indonesian donor in mind.

In Australia, the Seven Network was our prime target as a large corporate sponsor and for months Sir James pursued the Network Chairman, Kerry Stokes, and his executives for a $1.5m commitment to the Project. We offered exclusive broadcasting opportunities: the sizzle of the re-enactment voyage from Amsterdam to Queensland then to Sydney for the Olympic Games. We compared it with Thor Heyerdahl's balsa raft voyage across the Pacific and the Columbus re-enactment voyage of 1992. Our voyage would eclipse both, but even though Kerry Stokes had supported the initial idea with a funding guarantee, he was not interested in contributing any cash. That attitude filtered through the staff at head office in Sydney. *Duyfken* simply didn't excite him and we needed people with passion to support this unusual enterprise. Michael Kailis had lunch with the head of Westpac, Bob Joss, and popped the question but he didn't take the bait either.

On a lesser scale, we were being quite successful with in-kind sponsors such as the Danish paint manufacturer, Hempel, which was approached by Nick Burningham. Noel Robins was also quite successful with similar small but important donors, but we urgently needed cold, hard cash.

The pathways to obtaining sponsorship and fund raising are sometimes not direct. Usually, they depend on following leads from friends, business colleagues and acquaintances. Sometimes it seems like people are just waiting to be asked and then they give more than you could have possibly imagined. Julius Tahija is a case in point. He was born in the Maluku Province of Indonesia. He was dark-skinned with Melanesian ethnicity and when his father moved to Surabaya in Java he was obviously not a Javanese and he stood out. His father was a herbalist and this helped him gain admission into a Dutch elementary school — a rarity for the colonial days. He learnt to speak Dutch and he came to understand the techniques used by the adminstrators to rule their East Indian colony. He had a passion for language, taking a bus to language school in the evening to study English and later German. At 18 years of age, he began his own haberdashery delivery business which was a great success. At age 21, he joined the Dutch East Indies Army, following on from his father who had also served in the colonial army. He was sent to Aceh to join a special group of Acehnese jungle fighters, one of the most elite forces in the colonial army. By the time the Dutch Government in exile, which still controlled Indonesia, declared war on Japan following the Pearl Harbour raid in 1941, Julius Tahija had risen to the rank of sergeant. His ability to speak English, a rarity in the colonial armed forces, found him escorting a shipload of Japanese to Fremantle to be taken to internment camps in Australia. After unloading the prisoners, the ship headed back to Java. Before it reached the archipelago, the Dutch army surrendered to the Japanese and his ship was hastily turned around. They were soon back in Fremantle. The Dutch army in exile directed its troops in Fremantle to relocate to Camp Pell in Melbourne and it was there that Julius met a young Australian dentist, Jean Walters, and they fell in love. They were soon parted by war with Julius being selected to learn the techniques of what was called guerrilla warfare at a training camp in northern Australia. In July 1942, his small team of Indonesian soldiers was sent to the island of Yamdena in the Tanimbar Archipelago, 500 km from Darwin. Their task was to protect the town of Saumlaki from a Japanese takeover. The Tanimbar Islands were uncomfortably close to the Australian mainland. The 13 soldiers put up a stout and clever resistance, killing an estimated 200 Japanese soldiers, but when faced with overwhelming force they had no option but to retreat or be captured. Led by Julius Tahija, seven surviving soldiers devised a remarkable escape and after five days at sea, the group made landfall at Bathurst Island where the local Aboriginal people greeted them and gave them supplies.

Julius Tahija was hailed a hero in the Australian media for inflicting heavy losses on the Japanese force, facing almost certain death, and yet escaping to fight another day. He received the highest Dutch military honour, the Militaire Willems Orde, but he suffered nightmares from that fateful night for the rest of his life. A soldier of his calibre was soon recruited for the Australian elite secret army group called Z Force. He conducted many missions into Indonesia by submarine. Upon his return to Indonesia after the war, he found that he had earned the respect of his former Dutch colonial masters. His time in Australia had given him an international outlook. He joined the nationalist movement for independence, becoming a politician for a short time. He was elected to the East Indonesian Parliament and appointed Minister of Social Affairs and Information, before returning to business. His big break came when he joined Caltex (he was CEO of PT Caltex Pacific Indonesia from 1966 to 1977). Thanks to his influence, the American oil company escaped nationalisation of its Indonesian oil assets in 1971. His business acumen found him owning and operating an enormous array of companies.

Jean and Julius had two sons, George and Sjakon. While George was clearly destined for a career running the family's business empire, Sjakon followed medicine like his mother and became an ophthalmologist. In 1993, he moved to Perth to study vitreo retinology at the world renowned Lions Eye Institute. The institute was founded by Dr Ian Constable who was regarded as a leader in the field. Sjakon Tahija enjoyed a great friendship with Dr Constable and his wife Elizabeth. She was an independent local Parliamentarian at a time when it was regarded as almost impossible to be elected as an independent in State Parliament. The Constables were well known amongst the Perth charity fundraisers — Michael Kailis, Sir James Cruthers and Syd Corser.

Through Dr Constable, Michael Kailis invited Julius Tahija to visit Perth for a chat about the *Duyfken* Project. Julius was suffering poor health and it took a year before he could fly from Jakarta. The *Endeavour* replica was completed in April 1994 and I was still working on special projects for the HM Bark *Endeavour* Foundation helping to arrange the media for her departure from Fremantle in October. It was a bittersweet day and some media commentators estimated that 100,000 people turned out to see her sail away. After a successful tour of the east coast during the southern winter, she travelled to New Zealand and then back to Fremantle for a refit at the MG Kailis dock. I was working on the promotion of the next leg of her international voyage. *Endeavour* would be visiting several ports in South Africa before heading to the United Kingdom and ultimately Whitby where the original collier had been built and called the *Earl of Pembroke*. After her refit she was back in Victoria Quay for a short stay before yet another grand departure from Fremantle. We asked John Longley whether *Duyfken* could host a dinner in the Great Cabin on 4 October 1996.

The Great Cabin was an attractive room in the stern of the ship where Lieutenant James Cook and Sir Joseph Banks lived during their Pacific voyage. Cook would have laid out his charts on the great table, as it was called, and conducted his day-to-day affairs in the room. Banks would have sorted out his specimens on the table. A small but powerful group was invited to dinner aboard including Colin Barnett and our fundraising team. I was a minnow amongst these elite individuals. Julius Tahija was urbane and sophisticated, a raconteur of the highest order. Ships and the sea were discussed in the convivial atmosphere. Not once was sponsorship discussed.

After dinner I was standing with Julius Tahija on the aft deck waiting for his car to arrive. We were alone and the lights of the port were reflected on the still water. He was pensively looking out to North and South Mole and Gage Roads beyond. "Mr Tahija," I asked formally. "It has been a privilege to meet you but I have one question. Why would you want to sponsor the construction of a ship in Fremantle?" He replied, looking at me directly, "This ship will help bring the people of Indonesia, Australia and The Netherlands together." Then he paused, and took a breath and pointed out to sea. "You know, Graeme, when we came back from our missions and the submarine broke the surface and we came on deck, I looked out and saw Fremantle. I knew I had survived and I will always associate Fremantle with my survival." I will never forget that moment, the emotion and the power of his statement. The real reason for funding *Duyfken* in Fremantle.

Next morning, I went down to Noel Robins' office at the Maritime Museum. It was our job to find out from Julius how much he would contribute to the Project. We didn't know what we should ask for; too much and it might embarrass him, and too little and we had wasted a great opportunity. We agreed that Noel would slip him a piece of paper which included construction costs for specific parts of the ship ranging from $20,000 or $30,000 to a million dollars. Julius arrived and we sat down for a coffee. Eventually it was time to pop the question. Noel slipped the small piece of paper across the table and said to Julius that there was a range of costs and he might like to choose one level to support. He looked at the list and pointed to $300,000 for the oak timber and $200,00 for the rigging to build the ship. "This is what I will contribute," he said. "It is the same as your State Government and a ship cannot be built without timber and it can't come to Indonesia without sails. It will be from the people of Indonesia as equals." When the money arrived in the *Duyfken* bank account it came from an account in the United States. It was $620,000 Australian dollars — Julius naturally thought we were talking about $500,000 US dollars!

This sponsorship by one of the most respected business magnates in Indonesia who was married to an Australian with children who easily moved between the western world and Indonesian life would prove to be a powerful asset for us and our little ship — but we had no idea just how significant Julius Tahija's support would be in the years ahead.

Every December, Michael and Patricia Kailis gathered together their employees, family and friends for a massive Christmas party in their Fremantle Fishing Boat Harbour shipyard. We were newcomers but we felt right at home and part of the MG Kailis family. Business was going well for thr MG Kailis Group. 1996 had been a good year. Hundreds of people mixed in an ambience of celebration. The Kailis fishing fleet from the north always returned to Fremantle to shelter from the cyclone season and to refit for another winter season. The harbour was lined with blue and white striped trawlers sporting the distinctive capital 'K' inside a blue ring on their superstructure. It was a wonderful sight. 1996 had been a great year for the *Duyfken* Project, too. We had the funding to build a shipyard and most of the money we needed to build a ship. Michael Kailis was now looking well beyond the launch of the vessel but he knew that he would have to build the ship quickly if it was to be able to fit into his grand voyage plan. Not for want of trying but we still hadn't made any progress in Canberra or Den Haag.

It took another year to obtain any significant funds from the Dutch Government. It came about in a convoluted way. The Dutch Prime Minister, Wim Kok, was visiting Australia to launch the Vlamingh Tricentennial year and to foster trade between the two countries. It was the first visit to Australia by a serving Dutch Prime Minister. Michael and Patricia Kailis were invited to attend a State Dinner hosted by our Prime Minister John Howard in Canberra on 10 November 1997. A few months before, in May 1997, Don Randall, the local member for Swan in the House of Representatives, arranged for the Minister for Finance, John Fahey, to visit the shipyard. A year long celebration of the Centenary of Australian Federation had been announced in the recent Federal budget and we were hoping that we could secure some funds from this $400 million national slush fund. Our three years of lobbying various governments and politicians in Canberra yielded nothing, but we thought we had a good chance to get some money from this new avenue. Unfortunately, the Centenary of Federation did not see us as a good fit. We weren't aware, however, that a lot was happening behind the scenes to prepare for the Dutch Prime Minister's visit. Without us knowing, the stars were starting to align and our work was about to pay off. In the months leading up to Wim Kok's arrival, we'd lobbied both the Minister for Foreign Affairs, Alexander Downer, and the WA Liberal senator, Ian Campbell, for help. John Howard needed something significant, a Dutch/Australian 'initiative' to announce. John Fahey hastily approached Michael Kailis with a proposal for the Australian Government to provide a $500,000 grant towards building the replica. There was no budget allocation for such a grant so there was a lot of juggling within government to make it happen at short notice. The obvious opportunity was for the Dutch Government to reciprocate. Mr Kok agreed and he announced that the Dutch Government would provide a similar amount in recognition of Australia's important historic ties with the Netherlands. The dinner in Canberra was a great success. John Howard made his grand announcement and then Wim Kok announced that he, too, would match the funding with $500,000. We thought we had $1 million in the bank. Michael Kailis was very excited and came out of the dinner to ring me with the news. Wim Kok's office was later to point out that he had, indeed, promised to match the funds announced by John Howard — but in Dutch dollars — guilders! The European Monetary Union had not yet happened and the Dutch guilder was much less than our dollar. You win some, and you lose some, but in one evening we had added over $800,000 to the sponsorship account. With a lot of persistence and a little luck we now had enough funding to build most of the ship.

Michel Kailis wasn't reluctant to ask his major suppliers to support the Project, too. His seafood factories used an enormous number of cardboard boxes and his supplier, Amcor Fibre Packaging, agreed to donate $100,000. We joked that it was a wise business decision on Amcor's part. By the end of 1997, more than $2.5 million in promises had been raised, and if the support provided in-kind and at cost was added then *Duyfken* had raised more than $3 million since 1994. Still more money was required and every last dollar counted. The Friends of the *Duyfken* ran social functions, quiz nights and raffles to generate funds. It was small compared with the big government and corporate donors but still vital to the Project. Sir James Cruthers came up with another concept to top up his considerable fundraising achievements and to link the ship into the business community. It was called the *Duyfken* 1606 Club and its aim was to raise $160,600 from 100 business people who would be 'tapped on the shoulder' to each donate $1606 to the cause and in return they would be invited to exclusive functions associated with the ship. He enlisted insurance broker, Graham Reynolds, an old family friend of the Kailis' to head the club, and my wife, Cathy, and her business partner, Lorna Barnett, agreed to coordinate the Club. Graham Reynolds was a member of the WA Club and had his own excellent connections in the business community. It was a very successful concept as few business people would say no to an invitation to join when they only had to find $1606. Membership would include people who are now household names in business including Gina Rinehart and Andrew Forrest.

The Lotteries *Duyfken* Village was very successful, attracting 22,000 visitors and dozens of school groups in the first eight months of 1997 when there was very little to see in the yard except the keel. In October 1997, *Endeavour* completed her 137 day British tour with 215,000 people boarding the ship in 17 ports. An average of 1,559 visitors per day boarded the ship. John Longley bullishly claimed it was Australia's most successful ever cultural export. He planned to sail the ship to the east coast of the USA and visit another 15 ports along the eastern seaboard before sailing through the Panama Canal to the west coast. It got us thinking about looking seriously at doing the same with *Duyfken* on Australia's eastern seaboard. With Michael Kailis' leadership, we were encouraged to think big.

Chapter 7

From Little Acorn to Mighty Oak

Build me straight, O worthy Master!
Stanch and strong, a goodly vessel,
That shall laugh at all disaster,
And with wave and whirlwind wrestle!

Henry Wadsworth Longfellow (1849)

To his consternation, as Michael Kailis swung the shipwright's adze down on the long oak plank, the tool bounced straight back at him, hardly piercing the surface. It was still green and full of sap. He balked, grimaced and a bead of perspiration appeared on his forehead. Then he chopped at it again, and again, not giving up until fragments of oak were eventually dislodged and we all cheered. He did the honours of being the first to hew a piece of *Duyfken* timber and to symbolically begin the task of constructing the ship.

It was 27 November 1996, two years to the day after the first meeting of the *Duyfken* board, and our first load of 25 tonnes of European Oak had arrived at last from Riga in Latvia. In front of a small group of staff, Michael Kailis sensed the importance of the occasion but he hadn't prepared anything to say. He stumbled for a moment then spoke briefly, talking about the pride he felt that for generations to come, our children and grandchildren would see the *Little Dove* sail off the coast of Fremantle and we could all be proud that we were there when the construction of *Duyfken* began. The words came from the heart.

The freshly felled oak was four centuries younger than the hull planks of *Batavia* only metres away in the shipwreck galleries of the Maritime

Museum but it was essentially the same timber from the same forests. Recent research has revealed that the hull timbers of *Batavia* below the waterline came from the Baltic in about 1625. The arrival of the shipment from Latvia brought great satisfaction and a degree of relief to Nick Burningham who had selected the timber in Latvia months before. He placed his trust in Unimark, the timber supplier, and he was assured that the oak would be first class. It had survived six weeks from Riga on the container vessel *Pegasus Bay* but Nick wasn't overly confident that the timber would be fine once it had been felled and milled. It had been a difficult mission for him to select every single piece.

Nick arrived in Latvia in early October. It was autumn and the ground was covered in frost. The daytime maximum temperature was sometimes as low as minus five degrees. His first visit to the sawmill at Smiltene, which would prepare the *Duyfken* oak, was disappointing. The timber he viewed was poor, riddled with fungal disease, and he couldn't see that much of it could be used to build the ship. The Government of Latvia, however, saw a great future in its timber industry. In the post-Soviet era it could sell timber to world markets rather than just within the Soviet bloc. *Duyfken* was the sort of prestigious customer the timber industry needed to help find new markets. The next day, Nick was introduced to the Minister for Forests, Arvids Ozols, who assured him that Latvia wanted to provide the best possible timber to the *Duyfken* Foundation and he would personally take an interest to make sure it happened. He said that timber from forests in the South West of the country would be better quality and this timber would be shipped to the sawmill. The selection of timber over the coming days became a feat of endurance for Nick with timber selection during the day and compulsory sessions of beer and whiskey drinking with the millers during the evening. Eventually Nick was comfortable that the timber he had selected would do the job and he could return to Australia with his liver intact.

Nick Burningham straddled the two interest groups who came together for the *Duyfken* Project. There was Michael Young and the community of people who wished to see a sailing replica of the first ship recorded in Australia's history, and the archaeologists and historians who wanted to explore every fine detail of how the Dutch ships were constructed. They were interested in the academic process of experimental archaeology where the construction would enable people to understand how a Dutch ship of four centuries ago was built. The final design was important to both groups.

Michael Kailis was more pragmatic. He decided quite early on that he wanted a ship to sail on a grand voyage. It had to look right but he was keen to see the Project completed without, as he said, too much 'navel-gazing'. He was happy to accept compromises along the way. He learned a lot from Nick Burningham and Bill Leonard as the ship was researched and built and he came to realise that *Duyfken* was going to be more than he had envisaged when he agreed to take on the role as leader of the *Duyfken* Foundation. The interaction between all the interest groups created an exciting environment, and sometimes passionate debates, but the Project benefited from so many people from different backgrounds being part of the team.

The task of designing *Duyfken* came down to a joint effort between Nick Burningham and Adriaan de Jong. At the beginning, we had scant knowledge of Dutch jachts from 1600. Little research had ever been done. Through her research, Marit determined that our jacht was built in late 1600 and early 1601 in The Netherlands, probably at one of the many shipyards near Amsterdam. Marit's research also showed that the ship had a strong association with Middleburg which is the capital of the Dutch province of Zeeland. Clearly, our *Duyfken* would have to be a tough little ship if she could emulate her namesake's achievements. The original *Duyfken* sailed to the Indies twice and it was only after surviving several sea battles with Portuguese and Spanish forces, that she was condemned on the beach at the island of Ternate in July 1608. The design of the *Duyfken* which made the historic voyage to Australia in 1606 would have to embody other qualities, too. Jachts were typically fast and manoeuvrable ships. They were selected for long, exploratory voyages to be the scouts, or eyes, of the Dutch fleets. They were fast and relatively expendable. They would be sent ahead to sound for shallow water and suitable anchorages and if they were fatally damaged it was not a great loss. They carried small cargo or troops and when required could be heavily-armed with light cannon. Evidence from contemporary log books supported the view that the original *Duyfken* was true to her class of vessel. She was relatively fast and she could beat to windward more efficiently than most vessels of her time.

Nick was often called upon to explain how he designed the ship and he gave many talks as the hull was taking shape in the Lotteries *Duyfken* Village. He would begin by explaining that the objective of our research was to design a reconstruction that would sail well enough to emulate the achievements of the original. However, performance alone was not enough as the ship had to look like a Dutch jacht of 1600. He studied shipbuilders' contracts specifying the dimensions and arrangements of timbers used in ships' construction, contemporary artwork showing sailing ships and the remains of contemporary Dutch ships discovered by archaeologists. Logbooks and other documents confirmed the performance of *Duyfken* and other similarly employed jachts. Computer models were made of the proposed designs to assess performance and stability. The world experts on Dutch ships of the period Femme Gaastra, Thijs Maarleveld, Robert Parthesius and Ab Hoving, were consulted. Marit van Huystee and Adriaan de Jong delved into the archives held at the Maritime Museum in Fremantle. Marit also accessed archives in The Netherlands.

"One of the first objectives in the research was to learn to draw ships with the right external style and appearance," said Nick. "This was prompted by feedback from Ab Hoving at the Rijksmuseum (Amsterdam), who commented about a sketch plan I produced early in the research. He said that it 'looked too English', and he was quite right."

Nick compiled a catalogue of Dutch marine art from the time of *Duyfken*. He then measured each drawing to find typical forms and ratios of proportions. He noticed that some proportions consistently indicated a hull form radically different from ships of half a century later. "There had been a number of theoretical (on paper) reconstructions of Dutch ships of *Duyfken's* time," he said. "In the absence of any original plans there was a tendency to assume the relatively narrow and box-like hull form of the later seventeenth century when plans were available. Combining this with the high stern and large, billowing sails of the late sixteenth-century galleon could be disastrous if tried at full size."

"Initially we took the same approach, adding a bit of beam to confer better stability but using the boxy shape with broad bluff bows. In retrospect, it appears that this was not a conscious strategy but an untested assumption," he said. "Following clues in the iconography, we began to take tentative steps towards a design with more beam, and with longer and sharper bow and stern. The iconography very consistently showed that the beam at the forward end of the forecastle is half, or less, of the beam at the forward end of the aftercastle, which is approximately amidships. I was slow to accept the implications of the clear evidence from the iconography. And even when I did draw lines with the much longer entry and narrower bows that the iconography implied, it was done without questioning a flat-bottomed, cross-sectional shape that was assumed to be a Dutch tradition."

As a design began to emerge from the research, reports were sent to experts in The Netherlands for comments and criticism. Thijs Maarleveld, Head of Underwater Archaeology at the Centre for Archeological Soil Research in The Netherlands, provided confidential drawings from an ongoing undersea investigation of a shipwreck in the muddy tidal waters of the Wadden Sea, known by its site location as SO1. It was a fluyt ship designed by shipbuilders in Hoorn for trade rather than combat. It was carrying a cargo of wheat when it sank on Christmas night in 1593. The drawings were a revelation as they showed a long and relatively sharp bow and stern that Nick had hypothesised based on his analysis of art of the period. "It provided evidence for an unexpectedly sharp cross-section shape (hollow garboards) — a surprisingly 'un-Dutch' shape when compared with many later hull forms. The investigation of SO1 also seems to show that there is no reverse curve to the tumblehome (the way the upper part of the hull slopes inwards). We had been drawing all our proposed designs with the reverse curve seen in later Dutch and English ships. Yet, when one is prompted to question it, the iconography is remarkably consistent in showing that the reverse curve in the tumblehome was not a normal feature of Dutch ships of the Duyfken's time. It is the solid evidence of archaeology that has shown what other evidence hints at, if you are looking for it."

Nick was keen to accept the evidence of SO1's midsection shape and sharp hollow lines below the waterline in the bow and stern because they would improve the ship's sailing characteristics but he was not sure whether the SO1 hull was typical of the period. There are no ship plans from the time as ships were built by eye and the plans were in the shipwrights' heads. He looked at other references and found some evidence in the form of Dutch and Flemish ship models from circa 1600. "These 'church models' cannot be regarded as anything like scale models," he said. "The modelmakers have concentrated on the richly ornamented topsides." He said that a researcher, Werner Jaeger, argued that because the models were always displayed hung at above eye-level, the model-makers exaggerated the proportions of the topsides and diminished the underwater body to produce something that would look right in the odd 'fish-eye view' from which the models would be seen. "We had to accept that all of these models are grossly distorted representations but allowing that, they all show the same kind of hull form." Nick noted that none of them were anything like flat-bottomed. In every case the model-maker assumed that the vessel he represented has considerable deadrise (the v-shaped angle on the hull cross-section), and also that it had a fairly long and relatively sharp bow below the waterline. Regarding this as more than coincidence, Nick decided to adopt this kind of moderately sharp-bottomed hull form in his reconstruction of *Duyfken*.

Nick's proposed design, a broad-beamed but sleek design, was tested using a Western Australian software called Maxsurf. *Duyfken* was the first historic ship to be designed using this state-of-the-art computer design software. The Maxsurf software was developed by Formation Design Systems in Fremantle during the America's Cup but it was new to the market (it's now used around the world in ship design) and was provided to the Foundation at no cost. Using the software, Nick was able to analyse the hull's movement in the water, resistance and propulsion, and sailing performance. It showed that the design had good stability and it would be able to maintain good average speeds even in light conditions, in keeping with the historical evidence.

Nick and Adriaan's research efforts yielded a Dutch jacht with a keel 16.8 metres long and a beam of six metres. Her overall length from beak (at the bow) to taffrail (the high stern of the ship) was a little over 25m. She could carry 50 to 60 tonnes of cargo and displaced about 110 tonnes. She was three-masted and carried a square rig on the fore and main masts and a lateen-rigged mizzen. Her hull planking was 60mm thick oak, and thinner above the waterline. She carried about 20 crew and eight to 10 cannon. Of course, we had no idea whether the theoretical design would perform on the high seas in full scale. We would simply have to wait and see.

Meanwhile, work was well underway to build the shipyard. *Duyfken* would require every skill of the ancient shipwright's trade to be reproduced in a hastily constructed yard. Bill Leonard, Nick Trulove, Don Cockrell and Josh McLernon were the first to be employed. Bill Leonard was appointed Master Shipwright and he was responsible for the construction of *Duyfken*. He was the son of a boat-builder and followed his father into the famous Clydeside Fairlie Yacht Yard in Scotland where he started a five-year apprenticeship building wooden yachts. After three years at Fairlie, he moved to South Shields in England's north-east where he spent a year building clinker dinghies. For the final year of his apprenticeship he moved to Wallsend and Swan Hunter's yard where he helped to build super-tankers. By then, Bill had a thorough grounding in ship and boat building and fate must have had a hand in his next move to the south of England to complete a course in yacht and boat-yard management.

He worked for a time for Port Hamble Ltd, which builds yachts and power boats, before taking a six-year sabbatical, sailing other people's yachts over half the world. During this time he visited boat-building yards throughout the Mediterranean and in the United States. Marriage led to a relatively settled period of three years in Bermuda restoring wooden yachts. Bill's older two children were born in Bermuda. Then it was back to the south of England to work on the reconstruction of two major yachts, *Crusade* and Tommy Sopwith's celebrated J-class *Endeavour*. *Crusade* and *Endeavour* had been narrowly beaten, four races to three, in the 1934 America's Cup challenge.

Bill migrated to Australia in 1986 and he worked with local boatbuilder, Steve Ward, building 12-metre yachts. It was a new experience for him working in aluminium. With Steve, Bill then became involved in the lofting of the *Endeavour* replica and never left. From 1988, Bill stuck with the *Endeavour* through thick and thin, serving as Technical Manager and Master Shipwright to bring the Project to its successful conclusion. Bill was working for the WA Maritime Museum when Graeme Henderson approached him to be seconded to the *Duyfken* Foundation to lead the construction team.

When Michael Kailis welcomed Bill Leonard to the *Duyfken* Project, he described him as a boat-building genius and the self-effacing Bill was very embarrassed whenever he said it at functions. After the first shipment of oak timber arrived and it was unwrapped, the enormous challenge of building *Duyfken* came home to all of us, but Bill saw the raw material he would craft into a ship. I can't disagree with Michael's assessment of Bill, and I can't do justice to the knowledge which was brought to the task of building *Duyfken* other than by reproducing the text of a speech he gave in 2000. Speaking in his strong Scottish brogue, he entranced the audience. Bill Leonard was not just a shipwright, he was immersed in the mind of a sixteenth century master shipwright.

Talk by Bill Leonard
Building a ship of 1606

On seeing the title of this talk, I really didn't know whether to laugh or cry.

Cry, because of the lack of information available, and laugh because the entire substance of this talk may last all of two minutes. Shipbuilding before the early seventeenth century is the question the *professors of maritime archaeology don't like to be asked. It is also the trick question that students of maritime archaeology see in their exam papers and tremble.*

We probably know more about the construction techniques of the Roman shipwrights than those of the nuts and bolts of the everyday ship construction that took place in the early seventeenth century Dutch shipyard. Hopefully, Duyfken *will answer the many questions that the sometime abstract world of maritime archaeology asks.*

What clues do we have? A few notes, some drawings, books of formulae, a few interesting contracts and, of course, those magnificent fragments of the early Dutch shipwrights — the most famous in the southern hemisphere being our own Batavia. *It's always wonderful to watch people walking into the* Batavia *Gallery. They wander in to be confronted by a wall of wood, with interesting little openings near the top. They walk around to the foreside or look down from the gallery. What do they see? A confusion of random shapes, shambles of wood piled upon each other. What they are viewing is the art of the ancient shipwright's trade. To modern day shipwrights like myself, these magnificent relics give the answer to how. These ships were built by Master Shipwrights. Master Shipwrights in those days were people of substance, highly educated and organised. As an example, let's take the famous sixteenth century English shipwright Phineas Pett. Born in 1570, he started boarding school at Rochester and later in his teens studied at Greenwich before completing his four year degree course in 1590 at Emmanuel College, Cambridge. He then was fortunate to acquire a shipwright apprenticeship at Deptford, eventually falling in with Matthew Baker in 1595. This is the famous Matthew Baker whose ancient ships' drafts are available for all to see in Greenwich Maritime Museum.*

How did they start?

To reiterate, Master Shipwrights of the sixteenth century were bright, professional people (unlike some of their modern brethren). So how did they start to build a ship? By first of all having in their hand, the contract. Let's firstly set the scene. A knock on the door and there before the shipwright stands a wealthy merchant of Amsterdam.

"Master Shipwright, I need a ship of great burden. Of course it will be grander than that old hooker, that 'so and so' just returned from the East Indies. This ship will reflect my position at Court. So I intend to make my fame and fortune in the East Indies."

The shipwright, reaching down for a piece of parchment, writes down the price and hands it over to the merchant. On recovering, the merchant in his best double Dutch exclaims: "Sir, you charge like a wounded bull!!"

The shipwright, of course, acts most indignantly and states "Sir, I care not for fame, however I intend to make my fortune right here!!"

Centuries have come and gone but some things never change! The next question asked by the now sheepish merchant is the "big" one: "What do I get for my money?"

Contracts are a really important clue for the building process of early ships, because they often describe in sequence the events of the construction. (The scantlings of materials, how they were joined, fastenings to be used.)

There are four or five of these sixteenth century contracts available for viewing, all you need to know is how to speak sixteenth century Dutch! Personally I really wish there was more documentation available on sixteenth century ship production. I am given to believe that *Batavia* took nine months to launch: that shows very real organisational skills, not a confused process of construction, not a haphazard shambles of wood, but an amazing degree of pre-planning, a complete understanding of the shipbuilding process, a well organised and controlled labour force.

They knew exactly what they were doing — and knew that mistakes cost money. With his contract in hand, the builder would meet with other important people — suppliers of wood, sparmakers, blockmakers, sailmakers, riggers, blacksmiths, suppliers of tallow, tar and oils. He would get things organised and moving.

Finally, his thoughts would settle on the keel, or probably the number of keel blocks required, or possibly the condition of the stocks (the slipway foundations) that the keel blocks secure to.

At this stage, surprisingly, a launching procedure is clarified in his mind.

His previous experiences and intuition are coming to the fore. No point in building it if he cannot get it into the water!

Soon the sawyers in the pits would start sawing timber for the keel, *the dimensions of which were given by the shipwright from his book of proportions and formula. Perhaps these dimensions were passed down from his father, however personal experience would have been his judge.*

Passing the keel pieces over to the shipwrights, comments like "How do they do it?" are heard in the yard. Perfect straight cuts reflect the sawyer's skill.

The shipwright joining these pieces together with a tapering scarf joint then proceeds to cut out the rabbet, which is the recess in the keel that takes the lowest plank, the garboard strake. The bevels and angles are known to the shipwright, the final trimming of which is determined by the twist of the plank itself as it reaches the stem and sternpost. The shipwright's concerns could revolve around the supply of good compass timber. He certainly cannot build the ship without it, and having to select it himself, will find it a time consuming process. You see he needs it by the cartload!!

The first major piece of compass timber required is the stem, and its shape was determined by a couple of sweeps of a line, or in many cases, by the curvature of the stem itself. On larger ships, the stem would have been built up of three or four pieces. Down at the other end of the keel, the shipwrights will have started the sternpost framing. Consisting of the sternpost itself and compass timber in the form of fashion pieces, wing transoms, transoms, lighter pieces of wood in the form of stanchions and the long narrow top timbers that extend this pre-fabrication right up to the stanchions on the upper deck. This massive structure is not only a major structural element but also defines the shape of the stern, and like the stem, is secured to the keel with the help of large knees that are fastened in place with bolts. And with the stem, this being set up on the keel, completes the ship's major centre line structure.

During this period, ships constructed in Holland were built shell first. That is, she was planked out to the rung-heads — the turn of bilge, prior to the floors etcetera being installed. The garboard strake at the bow tends to be sharply twisted and bent, and would have been formed with the help of an adze from homegrown curved timber and then steamed or at least baked over a fire. To make it bend to its final curve, the shipwrights used a klass, an iron device, a sort of adjustable fork that they engaged over the edge of the plank to twist it.

The timbers may have been thoroughly soaked in water, the end would have been secured to the end of a bending frame and while a fire was ignited beneath it, men using klasses would force it into the designed shape.

The garboard would then be nailed to the rabbet on the keel and the stem and sternpost, while cleat like blocks on the keel ensure a correct angle between it and the strake. Steamed over fire, the planking continued with the next strake being fastened with temporary cleats to the garboard, props in the form of short shores were also employed to help create the proper shape.

As the planking extended outboard, clamps and chains were used to pull the planking together and this method of construction if applied by skilful shipwrights could produce wholly satisfactory results. The question of symmetry would often arise and this would be checked constantly by the use of a long plank and a string level extending over both sides of the ships.

Having reached out to the turn of the bilge, the shipwright would then install perhaps three sets of floors (I say perhaps because each Master Shipwright in each yard had their own procedure, their own secrets for building their vessel.

Hopefully Duyfken will let us explore these construction pathways and secrets won't be secrets any more.

From these initial floors, frames would extend upward to the full height of the ship's sheer. They would then be interconnected fore and aft by a series of ribbands that extend from the fashion piece top-timbers in way of the sternpost, to the stem itself. What we have now is something that looks like a ship.

At this stage the rest of the floors are installed, as well as the remaining frames, hawespieces (framing around the bow), counter framing, 'tween chocking and port transoms. After fairing, the planking can continue apace to the top of the sheer, the only constraint being that the external planking is through fastened to the internal planking. The fastenings used are trunnels, being lengths of dowelling with wedges driven in each end. The remaining centreline structural members can also be installed, keelson (an internal keel that sits on top of the floors), apron, various breasthooks, deck hooks, transom, knees, mast straps etc.

As the internal planking (ceiling) extends up so it meets the clamps *that are in effect heavier planks that support the deck beams and, depending on the width of the ship, these beams may in fact have pillars and knees for support between these beams, there are also installed what are called carlines and ledges that provide support to the beams and deck above. The deck would then have been laid, possibly starting with the heavier waterways and tying strakes. On being laid, the completed structure would have been caulked with oakum, the seam being finally payed with pitch.*

The ceiling would then be through fastened to the external planking as it extended up towards the upper decks and again a similar process continues with clamps, beams, carlines ledges, hanging knees, waterways, tie-strakes, caulking, pitching seams.

In the meantime other important components are being made for the ship prior to being installed. The rudder, whipstaff, windlass, capstan if she had one, beakhead, tree pumps, hatch, gratings, etc.

The internal fit out starts to loom. The owners possibly taking a special interest in the accommodation. The yard blacksmith and his team of helpers have been busy during the construction process with the supplying of fastenings, ringbolts, hinges, hoops for carriages, rings for spars, forelocks bolts, perhaps even the ship's anchors.

The sparmakers have converted the trees into spars, the sailmakers have completed the sails, and the riggers, having completed as much preparation as possible, wait in anticipation of a successful launch. Then they can step the spars and rig her for her working life, the hull having been caulked perhaps with calf hair and pitch.

Before the launch, the underwater parts of the hull would have been perhaps dressed with a mixture of tar and white lead to prevent and lessen fouling. The stocks would have been greased with tallow or whale oil, the ship could have been eased over to her bilge and with the use of tackles finally launched.

Looking at it, the Master Shipwright would be considering his final fit out or perhaps looking, observed, that wooden sailing ships are the finest things that dreams have ever made.

Bill Leonard knew the type of people he wanted on his team. They all had passion and pride. Second-in-charge was Nick Trulove, a highly experienced woodworker. He built the magnificent Great Cabin and 'Gentlemen's Quarters' on *Endeavour*. Don Cockrell came from the Department of

Marine and Harbours where he worked as a shipwright before joining Bill Leonard for two years when he was retained by the Maritime Museum to help restore its wooden boat collection. Josh McLernon joined *Endeavour* straight out of school at 15 and gained his experience building the replica Whitby collier, then he went to sea with the ship learning the sailor's trade.

Once the timber arrived in Fremantle there was a clear pathway to the construction of the vessel. Nick Burningham presented a hull design and Bill Leonard was keen to get stuck into the shipbuilding phase of the Project and lay a keel. This is a celebratory moment in the construction of any ship through the ages. Crown Prince Willem-Alexander was invited to perform the ceremonial task while he was in Australia representing The Netherlands at the Vlamingh Tricentennial events and a date was set: 11 January 1997. We'd been talking for some time about the importance of blessing the keel, a solemn tradition of shipbuilders who believe that the Mighty One will protect the shipwrights as the ship is constructed and then the crew and passengers who sail in her. With so many details of the ceremonial keel laying event to be finalised, the actual blessing slipped between the cracks. Michael Kailis was miffed when he asked about it and nothing had been arranged. He was particularly keen on following the custom. He respected nautical tradition and he didn't want any ill fortune to fall on our ship. He believed that it would definitely have to happen before the keel-laying ceremony on the Saturday morning. Father Vincent Conroy from the Stella Maris Seafarers Centre arrived at late notice on the eve of the keel laying ceremony to perform the solemn duty. He stood next to the large timber balks which had been cut to form the keel. He made a splendid prayer and poured holy water onto the timber from a Bellarmine jug like the ones found at many Dutch shipwreck sites along the coast. Similar jugs were certainly carried onboard *Duyfken*. Ceramic jugs were the standard container for most liquids in homes and onboard ships of the fifteenth to eighteenth centuries. They were clay jugs with a rough salt glaze which provided a shiny and sometimes speckled finish to the natural clay colour. It was, of course, an appropriate historic vessel to hold the holy water but also somewhat ironic. Ballarmine jugs were made in Germany and had the image of the Jesuit cardinal and theologian, Saint Roberto Bellarmino, on the neck. His image was a disrespectful reference to his opposition to the Protestant reformation. He frowned upon the hard drinking Protestants of the Low Countries where the Bellarmine jugs were made, so it is not surprising that a caricature of his face should appear on the popular drinking jugs of the era. Bill Leonard watched as the pale surface of the keel was splotched with dark colouring for a few minutes "until the dampness was absorbed or evaporated — leaving only the enduring sense of goodwill." It was a relief to get it done before the big day. *Duyfken* has always been a blessed ship.

Even at this early stage in the Project passions ran high. Many people in the Dutch community felt a strong sense of ownership of *Duyfken*. A member of the Friends of the *Duyfken* felt marginalised when we said it was inappropriate to present an Admiralty model of *Duyfken* to Prince Willem-Alexander at the ceremony. It had taken many months to work through the correct royal protocols and gifting a model at the keel laying ceremony at the last minute was not appropriate. He complained to the national media and roundly condemned the 'terrible people' in charge. His outburst caught us by surprise. The defining moment of the Project so far was in danger of going off the rails in the lead-up to the visit. Some last minute damage control was required to appease him. The show did, however, go on.

Prince Willem-Alexander was about to turn 30 when he arrived in Australia. He was serving his royal apprenticeship. His destiny was to replace his mother, Queen Beatrix. Sixteen years later he was crowned King Willem-Alexander. He had a strong interest in ships and the sea and served in the Dutch navy for three years before becoming a navy reservist and studying history at Leiden University. It was a typical sunny summer morning in Fremantle — a bright blue sky, a gentle cooling sea breeze beginning to form off the coast and a buzz of excitement in the new shipyard as we waited for the arrival of our special guest. Bill Leonard and his shipwrights reluctantly donned traditional Dutch working clothes and seventeenth century conical felt hats made by the Friends of the Duyfken. The Crown Prince arrived and formalities were soon underway. Michael Kailis told the 200 assembled guests, including the honorary Dutch Consul from Queensland, Kasper Kuiper (who would later play a big part in the *Duyfken* story), that laying the keel was the moment of conception for a ship. Then, referencing a recent news story, he took a swipe at our detractors: "Don't believe what anyone says about fake coins found in sand dunes — all the evidence points to *Duyfken* as the first ship in Australia's modern history." He said that *Duyfken* would be the finest 'Age of Discovery' replica ever constructed and that the Foundation planned to complete the ship in just two years and ship her to The Netherlands. *Duyfken* would then embark on the longest re-enactment voyage ever contemplated for a museum standard replica. With gravitas he announced:

"We will sail *Duyfken* from The Netherlands to Indonesia and Australia, echoing the voyages of Captain Willem Jansz 400 years ago. It will be done without the assistance of modern engines," he said. "Our plan is to sail as far as Sydney in time for the 2000 Olympic Games." He said that the ship would join the replica ships *Batavia* and *Endeavour* in Sydney for the Olympics.

Julius Tahija's shorter speech pointed to a greater significance of the *Duyfken* Project: "Today's ceremony is symbolic of thinking of the past and planning for the future. In a world of conflicts, let us not dwell only on matters of controversy but specifically focus our wisdom on matters and subjects of mutual interest between our three countries — Australia, Holland and Indonesia. In fact, for the first time 400 years ago, the voyage of the *Duyfken* linked the histories of The Netherlands, Australia and Indonesia. The *Duyfken* was in Indonesia during the many encounters between the colonial powers which were vying for control of the rich spice trade. Looking into the future, the *Duyfken* has a contemporary purpose. Australia and Indonesia are developing a close relationship based on strong business and government links. The *Duyfken* is a symbol of these developing relations, as traditional Indonesian shipwrights will offer their expertise in the unique 'plank first' style of ship construction. When the *Duyfken* sails into Indonesian waters during her re-enactment voyage and in later voyages she will have Australians and Indonesians onboard. With Australians and Indonesians working together on this great project, the voyage will be the catalyst for greater understanding of the past and a shared future."

Julius Tahija's heartfelt speech was a reminder that *Duyfken* would be viewed through many different lenses. In Indonesia, she was a reminder of colonial rivalries for the riches of the islands. In Western Australia, *Duyfken* was seen as the ship which began the European maritime exploration of the continent. In The Netherlands, *Duyfken* was seen as symbolic of the Dutch 'Golden Age' of commerce, trade and technology. The shipyard was on land close to Bathers Beach where a family of Aboriginal people lived prior to settlement but no Aboriginal people had been invited to share the moment, and we didn't think of even inviting Aboriginal representatives. Missing from the ceremony was the perspective of the Aboriginal people of Cape York Peninsula. It was only as the ship took shape and the significance of those first contacts emerged, that the profound importance of what we were creating became apparent.

Prince Willem-Alexander responded without the bullishness of Michael

Kailis or the philosophical view of Julius Tahija, saying that the ship was good for Dutch-Australian relations and he hoped it would sail well. Fair enough. Short and simple. We couldn't disagree with his sentiments. The Prince put on a pair of brand new work gloves and he used a block and tackle to lower the first two tonne timber balk to form the keel. He had one last task to perform, throwing the first orange streamer over the keel. It was the signal for hundreds of streamers to be thrown by guests — a moment of joy and celebration. It was time to build a ship.

Prince Willem-Alexander continued his royal duties after laying the keel, meeting members of the Friends of the *Duyfken* and launching the Hartog to De Vlamingh exhibition at the Maritime Museum next door. Michael Young had unsuccessfully tried to get the name of the exhibition changed from 'Hartog to De Vlamingh' to Jansz or '*Duyfken* to De Vlamingh'. He had a good point but the entrenched WA view was that their world started with Dirk Hartog and *Duyfken* was less important. After the opening, the Prince was taken to the Burswood Park to unveil a statue commemorating Willem De Vlamingh's exploration of the Swan River. The slightly subversive statue has a surprised De Vlamingh resplendent in his seventeenth century garb and a startled black swan rising up in a defensive gesture. I see it as a striking and symbolic statue of the moment when Europeans first arrive in a foreign land. The Friends of the *Duyfken* had a food stall nearby. Nell Ottenhofff, Else Bernstein, Janine Young and Ria Sjerp baked 1500 smoutballen, traditional Dutch sweet dumplings, for the occasion. They offered one to the Prince but he was training to run a marathon and he politely declined. Michael Young cheekily arranged for him to be offered a *Duyfken* t-shirt and he gladly accepted it, later asking whether he could buy another 10 for the Royal party. I had come to enjoy the forthright approach of the Dutch. The Admiralty model which had caused such grief in Fremantle was handed to the Prince and I think it now resides somewhere in the Australian National Maritime Museum. Prince Willem enjoyed scuba diving and he was invited to dive on the wreck of the *Batavia* at the Abrolhos Islands after the formalities of the Perth visit. Graeme Henderson and several staff of the Maritime Museum hosted the trip. Michael Kailis was a keen diver and he joined the group. It wasn't the first time he had dived on the *Batavia* and the convivial atmosphere of the dive trip bode well for our planned voyage from The Netherlands and our relationship with The Netherlands.

Back in Fremantle, we were planning to open the Lotteries *Duyfken*

Village to the public on 1 March 1997. Bill Leonard now had a team of six including three apprentices and, with the keel in place, they set to work to cut the sternpost which would help define the ultimate shape of the ship. It was raised onto the keel in time for the opening day.

The construction of *Duyfken* was based on the three-to-two-to-one principle that 300 cubic metres of oak from trees in Latvia was required to produce 200 cubic metres of rough sawn timber which was then turned into about 95 to 100 cubic metres of timber used in the ship. Sweeping the floors was no small task: wooden shipbuilding creates mountains of wood shavings and sawdust. One of the great characters to join the team came from the *Endeavour* shipyard. He was Jimmy 'Sunny Jim' Mottram who wandered into the *Duyfken* shipyard with his friend Val and volunteered to sweep the floors. The 'broomers' as they were called soon became part of the *Duyfken* family. He and Val regularly caught the bus from their caravan park homes in Kwinana south of Fremantle. A navy veteran who had served in Vietnam, it was good for Jim's mental health to be part of a team and he added good humour and a cheerful atmosphere to the *Duyfken* yard. It was a happy place. Smaller pieces of wood were kept for use in items such as blocks and trunnels. Then the broomers would collect up all the chips and shavings to be used in the fire pit for bending of the planks or as souvenirs in the shop. Nothing was wasted.

The shipyard was not just a place to build the ship, it was designed to tell the story of Dutch exploration of the Australian coastline and to be a visitor attraction. In the first few months of building a ship there is little to see so we developed interactive displays. One showed how pulleys worked with only human muscles on a ship, challenging visitors to lift their own weight using a bosun's chair. Children could life their parents. We had two globes: one from today and one with the European knowledge of the world in 1600. Visitors were asked to see whether they could find where Fremantle was on the 1600 globe. There was also a display of tools used to build ships by hand in Indonesia today. A balcony enabled visitors to look down into the hull. The shipwrights got quite used to working in the fishbowl atmosphere.

A volunteer guides group was formed from the Friends of the *Duyfken* and Barbara den Hartog took the role of the first volunteer guide coordinator. Weekly training lectures were given to get the guides up to speed on Dutch shipbuilding practices. Margaret Rapanaro joined the staff to run the shop. She had run the very successful *Endeavour* shop and she was a great addition to the team. The rustic wooden shop fittings had been made by our shipwrights while they were waiting for our oak to arrive from Latvia. The shop and everything for sale in it reflected the quality ethic of the Project. Margaret's friend, Nina Pope, also joined to help manage the seven-days-a-week operation. The shop got off to a great start when word got out that Prince Willem-Alexander had bought a bunch of t-shirts and now everyone wanted one!

Our first open day was a massive success. Crowds packed the yard and we feared that the newly constructed observation deck might not take the weight of thousands of people flowing through the building. Dutch music filled the air and displays overflowed into the passageway between the Maritime Museum and the shipyard. Even with very little to see, visitor numbers constantly increased. Between 1,800 and 2,000 visitors per month streamed in. By year's end, we had attracted about 35,000 visitors since we opened. Up to a third of these visitors were schoolchildren as *Duyfken* integrated with the primary school curriculum and the shipyard complemented the displays inside the Museum. Visitors could buy the 'Big Ticket' which gave them entry to the Hartog to de Vlamingh exhibition as well as the Lotteries *Duyfken* Village. As visitor numbers increased, it was clear that the guiding required a separate organisation more closely linked to the management of the shipyard rather than the Friends of the *Duyfken*. Jenny Gibbs and the Museum's guide coordinator, George Trotter, took over the day-to-day organisation of more than 30 volunteer guides. The Lotteries *Duyfken* Village was soon one of Fremantle's top visitor attractions.

Following the keel being laid in January, the stem was attached permanently. Its shape was defined by the curvature of the oak tree trunk and, prior to it being installed, the rebates for the planking were cut into the sides. The sternpost was also installed with its knees, transoms and top-timbers. For the first time, visitors could see the height of the ship — it seemed to reach the roof! It was a slower start for the shipwrights. Bill Leonard and his team were coming to grips with the challenge of fire bending massive planks of European Oak. It entailed heating the hull planks to the point where the cellulose in the timber became malleable, without raising the temperature high enough to damage the wood or cause the bending to be uncontrollable. A long hearth was set up in the open behind the shipyard building. Upright stanchions were erected either side of the hearth. Holes were drilled through them at regular intervals to accept a two inch steel pipe. The pipes crossed the hearth to create a trestle over which the planks were toasted and bent. The fires were normally concentrated under the trestles. Each plank was bent with a large fork (the 'klass') which provided the leverage to create.

Josh McLernon was placed in charge of fire bending the planks. "After using steam to bend the hull planks at *Endeavour*, fire bending the *Duyfken* planks was brutal," he said. "We arrived early in the morning to light the fire in the hearth and to get it to a temperature for bending. Then, we put the plank onto the trestle and heated it up. When the timber was hot enough, we could start bending. The oak was always green and I could hear the planks crying, almost bleeding — creaking and cracking — as we bent them more and more. If I felt the grain opening up, I had to stop, leave the plank alone and give it a rest for a while. Then I would return to it and try again. I became so in tune with the timber, I thought that I was almost talking to the planks as I bent them."

When the plank had taken on the required shape and cooled, it was moved onto the ship where it was clamped in place. The first plank, (the 'garboard strake' in shipbuilding parlance) was fitted into the rebate on the side of the keel in May 1997. It took a week to install it because it was required to twist from about 10° amidships to 90° (vertical) at the stem and sternpost.

Bill Leonard jokingly said at the time that he feared that unless the process could be speeded up it would take six years to bend the 300 planks required for the hull! "The oak from Latvia was good timber to use. The challenge was that wood is never perfect," said Bill. "The annular growth rings determine which way the plank will twist and bend and, generally speaking, it will only twist in one direction. There were about 90 pieces of planking per side and almost every plank required a different bend and twist." Josh did speed up, having two, and then three or four planks, on the trestles at one time, all being heated and prepared for bending. The hard-working trade assistant, Steve Edwards, took on the full-time role of fireman, keeping the heat up to the 60mm thick oak planks and assisting with the twisting and bending over the hearth. Josh and his assistants bent all the planks up to the waterline, then he went to other tasks.

It was after the hull had risen, strake by strake, that the floors, futtocks and knees were placed inside the hull and everything was attached with trunnels or 'tree nails' which were pegs nailed into each plank. It was a great challenge for all the shipwrights who had come from the later tradition of shipbuilding where the skeleton of the hull is erected and then planks are attached to the frames. The shipwrights soon began to master the techniques involved in building the hull 'shell first'.

One of the trade assistants was the musician, Michael Barnett. He recalls the challenge of bending the planks. "The most challenging to bend was one of the wales, a running strake, it was about 250mm square. We spent two and a half days bending it then as we attached it to the ship it cracked. That meant another two and a half days of painstaking work to bend another," he said. When the first anniversary of laying the keel was celebrated in January 1998, the planking was beyond the turn of the bilge and the lower wale was in place.

Many of the shipwrights and trade assistants that came to work on *Duyfken* soon became part of a close team and the work provided some with purpose, fellowship and a sense of real achievement. Josh said that Bill Leonard was the wise grandfather who could always provide advice on how to do any job. He said that the ship building team was like a family with a single goal.

Our ambition had always been to create the most authentic replica of a late sixteenth/early seventeenth century Dutch jacht. The question of what 'authentic' meant in practice was vexed. In the last 400 years, we have found better ways to do things. Shipbuilding has progressed in this time but newer isn't always better. Some replica ships opted for modern screws and bolts to attach the hull planks but there were reports that the modern fasteners worked loose. We opted for trunnels, the traditional method which proved to be the best, and they never worked loose.

One of the most experienced shipwrights, Ray Miller, was responsible for the trunnels. At 70 years of age there was little that he couldn't turn his hands to. He made thousands of them as well as belaying pins and wooden blocks for the rig. His most obvious contribution was the bilge pumps. He made up a jig and used a massive Bosch drill to gouge a 40mm hole through the core of a five metre Elm tree trunk. Then, when that was done, he did another and then made a larger hole at one end for the piston. These pumps have been used on the ship for 20 years.

In other areas, there were compromises and some were more successful than others. Our shipwrights wanted to create a beautifully finished ship. As Bill Leonard explained in his treatise, the original *Duyfken* was a workhorse which would have been built in months, not years. There was no time for finessing. The hull planks would have been finished with hand tools and the surface would have retained the marks from the tools. Time was money in those days, too. Modern power tools were used to provide a smooth, carefully planed finish — far better than the original ship. Bill was proud of what they achieved and he opted to varnish the completed hull rather than oil it in the traditional manner. Modern sealants were used to seal the hull planks instead of oakum and tar. This was successful below the waterline but would prove problematic above the waterline where shrinkage was an issue for our European timber in the harsh Australian climate. Hempel Paints provided us with modern marine paint which was far more durable than the paint which would have been used on the original ship. Coach bolts with nuts were sometimes used rather than spikes with wedges or large rivets. The nuts were hidden with wooden plugs so that the cover could be taken off and the nut tightened. Every compromise between authenticity and practicality was discussed and sometimes debated for months.

Others were a very simple choice. The notorious but tiny mollusc called *teredo navalis*, more commonly known as the teredo worm, loves eating unprotected European Oak timber. It is particularly prevalent in tropical waters and it was one of the reasons why Dutch East India Company ships had such short lives. For centuries, shipbuilders tried all sorts of ways of preventing the infestation of teredo. There was copper sheathing with animal hair underneath as a barrier and many other alternatives such as lead. The original *Duyfken* probably had a layer of felt soaked with tar resin between the doubling and the main hull planking. They had no means to keep the teredo at bay once it got in. The hulls ended up like Swiss cheese when they were damaged and it was one of the things which defined the lifespan of a VOC ship. It was an easy decision to use modern anti-fouling supplied by Hempels to seal the hull from teredo invasion. Even with modern anti-fouling, however, the slightest loss of the coating would result in an infestation. It was a constant battle to keep the wood worms at bay.

Michael Kailis enjoyed nothing more than wandering down Mews Road from his office and dropping in to see how construction was progressing. He would stand on the observation deck, looking across at the hull taking shape, and wave to Bill Leonard to come over for a chat. Bill thought that Michael would have loved to be the shipyard manager. He wanted to be more involved but he was constantly being kept at arm's length by Noel. One day he leaned over to Bill and said quietly: "It should have an engine." Bill replied that it wouldn't — that was not in the plan. "It won't be insurable!" said Michael. Bill agreed with him but his job was to build the ship to the plans he had been given. "I privately agreed with Michael. I was almost banished from the Museum and regarded as some sort of philistine for wanting an engine," said Bill. Nothing more was said.

A highly-decorated ex US Marine Colonel who had served in Vietnam, Jim Lucas, came into the yard one day and offered his services. He became the chief driller and hammerer of the thousands of trunnels made by Ray Miller. For many months, his job was to drill a 25mm hole, then hammer the trunnel home. About 3,500 trunnels were required to build the ship and many of them had the signatures of school groups written along the shaft. They were then hammered like massive nails into the hull for perpetuity and the 'bitter end', which was cut off after the trunnels were hammered home, was presented to the students.

It wasn't just trunnels which had hidden messages. The shipwrights had fun leaving messages hidden in places where they couldn't be seen — a gift for a future maritime archaeologist to interpret. Hidden on one of the futtocks was the ditty: "There was a young shipwright named Lyall, Who said that he built ships with style, The truth is they stunk – and most of them sunk, So now he builds junks on the Nile."

A timely supply of quality timber was a major issue. Nick Burningham flew to Latvia in March 1997 to choose more logs and baulks of oak. This time it was bitterly cold during his visit with wind coming off the Baltic Sea and snow covering the timber yards. Once again, he had to battle the language barrier and the difficulty of explaining the unusual timber needs of a sixteenth century Dutch jacht. He found it a challenge to get enough good timber and he was concerned that some of the good timber that was felled for our order had been sold to other buyers. When the last shipment of timber arrived from Latvia many months later, a high percentage of it was unusable and much of it seemed to have just been thrown on top of the shipment to make up the volume. It was badly diseased and the shapes were not what he described. Some of the timber, which seemed fine when it was chosen, twisted badly as it dried out in the heat of a Fremantle summer. After the ship was launched, Rinze Brandsma and I had the unenviable job of negotiating a fair last payment with the supplier. It was a long and spirited discussion!

Some timber we needed was simply unobtainable from the Latvian forests at the time we needed it. Delays would add to our costs. The hanging knees, which attach the beams across the ship to the inside frames called the futtocks, were usually cut from the root boles of oak trees but the Latvian foresters did not have access to heavy equipment to dig them out of the frozen ground. We looked closer to home for a solution. Western Australian tuart trees from the South West of the State supplied these shapes. The honey-coloured tuart looks so similar to oak when it is roughly hewn that few people could identify the gum tree hanging knees on the ship after she was launched.

Noel Robins used his contacts at the Department of Conservation and Land Management to obtain maritime pine (*pinus pinaster*) tree trunks to make the masts and yards. Even though the timber was grown in Western Australia, seeds for the trees came from Portugal and the Spanish and Portuguese sourced shipbuilding timber from the same Iberian forests. It was not favoured for anything but structural use in Western Australia as, unlike *pinus radiata,* which was also grown in plantations near Perth, it took up the minerals from the sandy coastal soil and had streaks of grey in the grain. We didn't mind, especially as it was donated and it meant that the ship wouldn't have unsightly laminated masts. Josh McLernon and a team of enthusiastic volunteers had the task of shaping the masts and yards. The tree trunks came from the Gnangara Pine Plantation and they were unloaded at the MG Kailis Wharf. The team set parallel railway tracks close to the logs. Josh used his Datsun 200B family car to drag the logs around the yard and line up them up. A chainsaw was connected to the railway tracks by an ingenious home made jig using skateboard bearings. They then ran the chainsaw down the track and cut four square sides on the round logs. The square sided logs were then put onto trestles and eight sides were cut using a suspended band saw designed by Ray Miller. The logs were then finished off with planes and spokeshaves until they had a circular cross section.

Duyfken attracted the best craftspeople in Western Australia. One of them was the accomplished wood carver, Jenny Scrayen. She was born in Belgium, from the Flemish part of the country, and learned her craft from her artist father, who taught her the basics of drawing early in her life. When Jenny's father retired from full time work he decided to concentrate his efforts on sculpture in wood. Producing major wood carvings is more than a one-person job so Jenny was co-opted into wood carving. Fortunately Jenny's training went much further than merely carving wood and her father taught her the basics of wood working. This was to prove invaluable when the recently divorced Jenny arrived in Perth in the late 1980s needing work to support herself and her children. She found that the flexibility permitted by her father's thorough training enabled her to work in the furniture industry and in the field of design. Wood carving by itself would not keep food on the table. Teaching at TAFE and conducting workshops for the University of WA and the School of Wood at Dwellingup provided Jenny with satisfying employment. However, it was her 12 months working with the *Endeavour* team on woodcarving for that replica that led directly to her work for the *Duyfken* Project.

It was inspiring to watch Jenny at work on the beautifully carved reliefs of the *Little Dove* and the Coat of Arms of Fremantle which were placed prominently on the stern of the *Duyfken*. Wood carving is a team enterprise with the master craftsman, Jenny in this case, marking out the wood and providing supervision for large volumes of the wood to be removed before she executed the fine details needed to complete the work. Decorative reliefs to embellish the bow of the ship and two sculpted heads of Mercury were also on her work list. Her *pièce de résistance* was carving the lion of Amsterdam figurehead at the point of the beakhead. This was completed and installed after the ship was launched. Jenny was a perfectionist and she wanted the carvings to be finely finished. There were many animated discussions on how rustic her carvings should be. Relics from the period show that the carvings were not sanded to perfection like marble statues and she had to accept that the carvings would still have the chisel marks upon them when they were painted.

Nick Trulove was entrusted with one of the most dramatic parts of the build. The beakhead was ahead of the bow of the ship. It was a useful place to handle the spritsail but this beautiful structure also had another less savoury use. It was used as a latrine for the crew, and this is where the term 'heads' on a ship comes from. Nick Trulove would have to interpret Nick and Adriaan's drawings to create a three dimensional object. It was his tour-de-force, topped off with Jenny's superb lion!

The skilled rigger, Igor Bjorksten, could turn his hand to just about any job in the yard. He worked as a general shipwright until it came time to construct the ship's rig. He learned his trade from an old Welshman, George Herbert, who sailed on square riggers around Cape Horn and spent two years passing his knowledge onto his young pupil. The informal apprenticeship stretched over the restoration of two old schooners in Melbourne. He loved wooden boats. Igor once told me that "if the Good Lord had meant us to sail fibreglass boats, he would have created fibreglass trees!" Rigging is the final step in the preparation of a newly-built ship for sea and Igor found himself working as a shipwright on *Endeavour* before helping to rig her. From there, he went to Sydney to work on the *Bounty* replica, regularly overhauling the rigging. He also worked on the *Enterprize* replica ship in Melbourne for two and a half years and after it was completed, he took a year off shipbuilding for a working holiday, sailing in European waters, particularly the Baltic Sea. During the construction of the *Duyfken* hull he collected hundreds of oak offcuts. He needed about 100 blocks (wooden pulleys) and 50 dead-eyes of all shapes for the ship and when it came time to start on the rig he had all the timber he needed.

The shipyard also became a venue after the shipwrights finished for the day. Perth's resident Court Jester, Jonathon De Hadleigh, who provided entertainment at the launch of the Foundation in February 1995, returned to Fremantle after 11 months performing in many venues across Europe. He played for five months at London's new Shakespeare Globe Theatre, the reconstruction of the famous theatre (constructed using oak just like *Duyfken*!) built in 1599. He performed his own one-man show, 'The Sailmaker's Tale' in the shipyard over summer. It blended history and theatre.

Artists were attracted to the once-in-a-generation undertaking. The Maritime Museum's education officer, Mike Lefroy, wrote, and one of the *Duyfken*'s talented trades assistants, Rick Martin, illustrated, a children's book entitled 'The Trees that Went to Sea' which was launched at the Fremantle Children's Literature Centre in March 1998. It was just one example of the great creative surge *Duyfken* gave to Fremantle. The book was enormously successful with gentle watercolour illustrations telling the story of the original voyage and the construction of the replica.

On 10 January 1998, as the hull was taking shape and visits to the shipyard were increasing, a special Executive Committee meeting was held in the MG Kailis Boardroom to consider a new timetable for the future of the Project. It was clear that the ship would not be constructed in the two years originally planned. Michael Kailis loved to see the progress of the ship but he was impatient. Costs were rising. He said that he thought the Project was six months behind schedule and he asked John Longley to attend the meeting to talk about his experience completing *Endeavour* and conducting an exhibition tour of the east coast. It was agreed to launch the ship during January 1999 and Noel Robins was told he had 12 months to complete the hull to floating stage. Although we had raised several million dollars in promises, more would be required to complete the task. We were spending $50,000 a month and we had $550,000 in the bank. To increase the pace of construction so that we could meet the original two year construction timeline would require more shipwrights and therefore more cost. It was not until April that the Dutch Ambassador Roelof Smit arrived with a cheque for $350,000 covering the money promised by the Dutch Prime Minister. In May, Senator Alston disbursed the Commonwealth Government grant. Sir James put together a list of more than 20 major corporations to approach and we were once again on the sponsorship trail. We had some high level advocates in this period. The WA Premier Richard Court wrote to Queensland Premier Rob Borbidge to ask him to support the re-enactment voyage from The Netherlands to Sydney and the arrival in Sydney for the Olympic Games. Unfortunately, our timing was poor. The Queensland Premier was about to contest an election. He lost, and our focus had to be turned to the rambunctious new Labor Premier Peter Beattie.

Michael Kailis thought it was important that the ship lived up to our claim of building the most exacting 'Age of Discovery' replica ever constructed and he wanted Nick Burningham and Adriaan De Jong's design work and the craftsmanship of Bill Leonard and his team to be recognised. I arranged for another client of mine, Qantas, to sponsor the visit by Ab Hoving from the Rijksmuseum in Amsterdam, regarded as a leading authority on Dutch sailing ships of the 'Golden Age', to visit Fremantle. Ab Hoving left Fremantle positive that the Australians were on the right track. The peer group support would pay dividends when we arrived in Texel three years later. At the practical level, we had the first informal visit by the local team from the Australian Maritime Safety Authority to view the construction process. There was no thought of the ship being used to take passengers to sea on a regular basis. We said the ship would be a 'floating exhibition' but they insisted that she would still have to comply with basic stability requirements.

At the next Executive Committee meeting in March 1998, Sir James Cruthers voiced his concern that the Project's operating costs had increased to $100,00 a month and we would run out of cash by August. We would need another $400,000 to finish the bare ship. He proposed pre-selling the Lotteries *Duyfken* Village shed which had cost about $374,000 all up to build and equip, to a local businessman, Warren Jones, for $120,000. He thought that Noel Robins could do this deal. He also suggested that Michael Kailis' contribution be capped at $250,000 rather than Michael occasionally topping up the coffers when needed. He also suggested pushing the Dutch Ambassador Roelof Smit hard to source some large Dutch companies to make substantial contributions to the Project. They had been notably absent from the sponsorship lists. A close look was taken at our operating costs. The shop and entry income was substantial but the commercial operation had run at a loss of $3,000 a month for seven months. Although it was seen as important to contain costs, it was also accepted that the shop and visitors were an important part of achieving the goal of promoting *Duyfken* in the community. The time was fast approaching when an overdraft facility put in place by Michael Kailis and Kerry Stokes would need to be drawn down. It would cost more to stop construction and then crank it up again later, rather than take the job through to completion at the current pace of work.

Sir James was at his best during a financial crisis and he relished the challenge of finding clever solutions. He concocted a plan. When the Dutch Ambassador and his wife Traute arrived in Perth, Syd Corser invited them for a river cruise aboard his launch, the *Compass Rose*. Sir James was intent on getting some sort of commitment from the Ambassador to help him lock down some major Dutch corporate support. We would discuss it during a quiet cruise down the Swan River, and gain a commitment from the Ambassador to help us. However, we sadly misjudged where we sat in the pecking order of Dutch cultural projects. It was clear that *Duyfken* was a sideshow for the Dutch Government. The tactful ambassador side-stepped the issue. It was clear the Dutch wanted the *Batavia* replica to become the biggest attraction in Sydney Harbour for the Olympic Games. Shipping the 57 metre long VOC ship to Australia aboard a semi-submersible vessel for the 2000 Olympics was to be an expensive undertaking and it would become the entire focus of the support group for the Dutch Olympic Games Team. It was planned for the ship to be a virtual clubhouse for the team and its sponsors. It was to be moored at the Australian National Maritime Museum which had invested in the visit expecting to enjoy a big rise in visitors. They expected to achieve visitor numbers comparable with the 350,000 visitors a year which the ship attracted in Lelystad. While the ship had not sailed in The Netherlands, it was bravely planned to sail the vessel off Sydney for the first time, attracting global media attention. Dutch multinationals such as Phillips, ABN Amro, Rabo Bank and ING Bank believed the numbers being thrown around and agreed to underwrite the Project. Like a massive vacuum cleaner, *Batavia* had sucked up all the sponsorship money we could potentially get from The Netherlands to complete the ship and to conduct a re-enactment voyage from Amsterdam to the Sydney Olympics. One after another our sponsorship prospects fell away. It was heart-breaking and very frustrating.

Both Michael Kailis and Sir James Cruthers were ill and unable to attend the critical April 1998 Board meeting which would map out the Project's future. Michael had been admitted to Sir Charles Gairdner Hospital and he was undergoing therapy for a rare form of leukaemia. Syd Corser chaired the meeting and the financial problems of the Foundation were discussed in detail. Sir James and our fundraising committee had been unable to attract any more big corporates. Seemingly oblivious to the funding crisis, it came as a surprise when Noel Robins announced that *Duyfken* would be registered as a yacht with the Royal Perth Yacht Club. He said that for voyages the ship would have navigation equipment, ablution and cooking facilities installed on removable pallets. He said that the ship could be made unsinkable by equipping her with large fireproof floats disguised as spice bales which would provide buoyancy if the ship went down. He said that the naval architect Len Randall had been asked to provide some input and suggested that engines could be retro-fitted if required. Noel had also followed up the sale of the shed. He had approached the City of Albany to buy it for a whaleboat building project. They wanted exclusivity which meant that Warren Jones could not be approached. He asked approval to send a letter to the City of Albany and the Board approved it. It transpired that the City of Albany had no intention of buying a shed which had been funded by the WA Lotteries Commission. They simply asked for Lotteries to arrange for the *Duyfken* Foundation to gift the shed to them and for Lotteries to fund the re-erection of the shed on the Albany waterfront. It was made more complicated as Sir James and I had been negotiating with the Lotteries Commission for an additional shipbuilding grant which would help with the completion of the ship. We had been outmanoeuvred while Michael Kailis and Sir James had been absent. We were confident that we could have both sold the shed to a third-party and obtained an additional grant, raising a total of $370,000. When Sir James returned to good health, he went into damage control and raised the dilemma with the Lotteries Commission. He asked whether we could be compensated for the loss of income from the 're-gifting' of the shed. Thanks to his credibility with the Lotteries Board, the *Duyfken* Foundation received a $350,00 grant in July to create the 'Lotteries Sailmaking Loft' and to employ a team to hand sew a suit of sails for the ship using traditional flax cloth. The Board meeting was a turning point in the fragile peace which existed between the General Manager of the Project and the Executive Committee.

A measure of Michael Kailis' national standing in the community was seen when, although still unwell, he hosted a function in the Lotteries *Duyfken* Village for the entire Federal Labor Shadow Cabinet which was in Perth for a meeting on 14 June 1998. The Leader of the Opposition, Kim Beazley, spoke effusively about Michael and his achievements, and thanked him for hosting the function. It was noted privately that Mr Beazley had not secured any funding a few years before when we had desperately needed it.

In June 1998, reality started to set in at *Duyfken*. Hosting high profile cocktail functions was one thing, but completing the task of building a ship was another. Some Board Members were beginning to feel uncomfortable that with funds running low, and the overdraft activated, that they might carry liability for the $500,000 State Government contribution if the Project folded. At the June Board meeting, Michael Kailis assured them that he would cover all the liability carried by he and Kerry Stokes if the ship was not completed. A new set of budgets were sought, covering hull completion (prior to being launched and rigged), launching the vessel, fitting out and rigging, and trialling. The grand plan of sailing the ship from The Netherlands to Sydney was now being tempered by the reluctance of Dutch companies to support the Project and future sponsorship documents would delete this voyage from the sales pitch. A more modest voyage was now being discussed from Ambon to Queensland and Syd Corser was concerned that even that may be impractical without a tender vessel to accompany the engineless ship. Michael Kailis offered his motor launch *Manitoba* whilst privately thinking about how to install engines and discussing the issue with his engineering staff. It was also becoming clear that Fremantle was not exactly bending over backwards to home port the ship. Despite lobbying by the *Duyfken* Foundation and some informal promises, a new maritime precinct announced by the State Government in the Swan Dock area of Fremantle harbour adjacent to the new Maritime Museum did not include a wharf for *Duyfken*. As it turned out, this project, called Stage Two of the development of Victoria Quay never happened but it held great promise to revive the area which has languished ever since.

Even though funds were tight, the *Duyfken* Executive Committee's fundraising program to this point had been very successful. To July 1998, we had secured $2.6 million to build the ship and a further $550,000 was due within the next few months. It was, however, quite clear that no full budget had been prepared to complete the vessel to sailing trim and another $290,000 would be required above the budget to get the ship launched and to reach this stage of completion. There was never a budget allowance or a plan if the ship was to be equipped with engines and voyaging equipment. Early estimates suggested that installing engines could add 20 to 30 per cent to the cost of the build. Michael Kailis was becoming increasingly frustrated about being kept in the dark by Noel Robins who was doing little to hide his view that Michael's questions were a hindrance and he should let him get on with it without any interference. It was a clash of big personalities and it affected everyone working at the Project.

The matter came to a head in June 1998 when I was invited by Michael for a coffee at Kastello, his magnificent limestone home overlooking the Swan River in Mosman Park, on a Monday afternoon. This was highly unusual. Our meetings had always been in his office at the MG Kailis yard. I knew something was up. I walked up to his front door. On one side was a Lantaka cannon from Indonesia which he'd obtained whilst on a trip to one of the outlying islands. They were rare artefacts. Japanese scrap metal merchants scoured the archipelago for anything they could melt down, and villagers had sold most of the cannon. Patricia showed me through the house to Michael's office. It was an atmospheric man's den which was a little intimidating. While his boardroom had a selection of trinkets from his years as a fishing entrepreneur, his office was packed with awards and presentation gifts from far and wide — honours from Brazil and Taiwan, swords and framed photographs. Soon Sir James arrived and we sat down for a cup of coffee and a chat. Michael talked about his frustration working with Noel and asked me what I thought. I said I found Noel difficult to work with but once I came to understand the way he worked it was possible to get things done. I always worked for Michael and the Executive Committee rather than for Noel, and anyway, I was only a lowly consultant in the hierarchy. Sir James expressed his concern that the Board still did not have a plan for the future beyond building the ship. Sir James rolled his eyes during one of the Board meetings when Noel proclaimed that any event, even a ship's launch, only needed six weeks to organise. This rankled Sir James. Charlie Welker had produced a report outlining the challenges involved with launching the vessel from its location but time was running out to make it an event of national significance befitting our achievement in building the ship. It was clearly a huge job and Noel had his hands full to coordinate the completion of the hull to launching stage. Sir James was concerned that there was no plan for fit out and conducting sea trials. Michael was dismissive and incredulous of the proposal to make removable pods of modern equipment and ballast for the ship. He was annoyed that it had been presented as a fait accompli at the Board meeting which he could not attend. With his boat-building and experience running ships, he couldn't see how it was at all practical. He laughed at the idea of buoyancy bales. On top of all this, he suspected Noel was deliberately slowing down the build to extend his term of employment.

We talked about how to solve the problems. Michael and Patricia were planning on visiting Europe in September and it was an excellent opportunity to arrange to see Queen Beatrix or Prince Willem-Alexander and prospective donors in The Netherlands and London. The scaled-back voyage from Indonesia to Queensland was then the best option for the future if funds could not be raised from The Netherlands. Sir James had been instrumental in arranging a visit to the shipyard by all the Australian State Governors while they were in Perth for a conference and he thought that we would be able to have a meeting with the new Premier of Queensland, Peter Beattie, via the Governor of Queensland, Peter Arnison. He thought that Peter Beattie was more open to fresh ideas than his predecessor who had shown little interest in the Project. Sir James and I had been working on getting the support of News Ltd and the Seven Network for the launch and the voyage. Sir James even mentioned the possibility of Rolf Harris getting involved in a documentary. In hindsight, perhaps it was a good thing that the documentary never eventuated!

I had an inkling of what was coming. I'd talked about it with Cathy before I left for the meeting. Once, when Michael was annoyed about something at the shipyard, he casually asked me, almost as a passing remark, whether I would take over the Project? I laughed it off, saying that I was too busy and I had more clients than just *Duyfken* and things were going pretty well for me. After all, I knew nothing about building ships or arranging voyages. Michael's remarks were never as casual as they first appeared. He was smarter than that. I reflected, however, upon a statement made to me 15 years before by Chris Hurd, the owner of the publishing company where I worked. He would always come into the office and blurt out a comment about one thing or another. This day he came into the office and announced that if we didn't achieve our life ambitions by the time we were 40 then we would never achieve them. After 40 it was all over! I was only in my mid-twenties at the time and this revelation came as a complete shock to me. I was writing copy and editing travel trade magazines. It was a lot of fun travelling around and being wined and dined by hotels and resorts. I'd left university with a whole life in front of me and now I only had 15 years to do something useful. At 40 it would be all over! I always had that comment in the back of my mind. I was now 38 years of age. That damned clock was ticking. I'd helped the *Endeavour* with promotion of the ship's contentious departure from Fremantle, then the tour of South African ports beginning in Durban. Cathy and I, and our young children, Louise and Daniel, flew to London for the ship's arrival and the visit of the Queen in 1997. We all stood as part of an honour guard on the wharf. I had the privilege of travelling down the Thames to the National Maritime Museum at Greenwich aboard the ship. I had been part of the *Endeavour* Project but always on the periphery. It was a great experience but I had come to understand what worked and what didn't with these projects. I knew that they required basic business management skills and sometimes people got carried away with the emotion of the romantic task of building and sailing a historic ship. I was aware of the old adage told to me by Cathy that you don't employ librarians who like to read as they will just sit and read books all day. John had done a great job with *Endeavour* and I could see where the *Duyfken* Project offered an opportunity to do something completely different and new. I thought if John could do it with *Endeavour*, then I was up to the job with *Duyfken*. OK. I know now that I actually had no idea what I was in for.

I must give credit to Michael and Sir James for the excellent way they constructed the meeting. These guys were good. We talked at length about all the problems with the Project, then of their great vision for the future. I agreed that the construction was in danger of dragging on way beyond the original timeframe and there was no sense of urgency about meeting deadlines. There was no question that a fine ship was taking shape, but we would fail if we ran out of money along the way. They finally got to the point: Noel would only be retained up to the launch of the ship. They wanted me to take over as CEO immediately, planning the launch of the vessel and everything after that. For the next six months I would work with Noel, then I would be entirely responsible for the ship.

Before I left for the coffee, Cathy and I discussed what I would say if Michael did, indeed, ask me to take over the management of the Project. It would entail giving up my other clients, and losing the independence which comes from not having to manage staff. I said to Cathy that I had turned

Michael down once, and if I did it again, then I should just walk away from the Project. I could not stand by and criticise from within. It was a case of "put up, or shut up".

I said to Michael and Sir James that I knew this day was coming and, yes, I would accept their offer. From that point on, the transition was not handled well. In retrospect, with the big egos involved, the situation was bound to end badly. The Executive Committee was informed of the outcome of the discussions and appointed me as head of the Project. Syd Corser had championed Noel Robins from the early days of the Foundation and he was caught between supporting his old friend and making an important decision for the future of the *Duyfken* Foundation. He chose not to attend the meeting. There was a lot of discussion about the impracticality of having a Project Director and a Chief Executive Officer at the same time but the will of the Chairman prevailed. When the minutes of the meeting were circulated to Board members for ratification at the next Board meeting, I found I had been demoted. "It was agreed that Graeme Cocks be appointed the Director of Promotion and Publicity and Press for the ship's launching, and that he should form a committee to assist him." Even though he was still unwell, Michael Kailis attended the Board meeting and asked Rinze Brandsma to chair it. The minutes were immediately amended. It was disturbing and a little sad that Noel had deliberately tried to change the record of the meeting. It was uncomfortable for everyone. Noel was angry and hurt. Unsurprisingly, he thought that he had been stabbed in the back. A few days later, I suggested that we have a coffee to discuss the situation. We sat down and almost immediately, he pulled out a management chart which placed him reporting to the Board and me reporting to him. He would just not accept the decision and he was pushing me too far. I angrily grabbed the piece of paper and scrawled the correct set-up. From that day on, Noel did everything possible to make life hard for me — even in petty ways like leaving me off staff lists!

In the following months, I was regarded with suspicion by some and as a confidante by others. If there was a problem which couldn't be resolved by meeting with Noel, then they came to me. For me, the line of demarkation, however, was clear. I was to arrange the launch and beyond and if they had a problem with Noel then it was up to them to sort it out. I could bide my time. Sir James reported to the Board in September 1998 that as far as he was concerned the Fundraising Committee's work was done. The Committee had raised $3.45m and the target of $3.7m would shortly be reached. It was a sign that it was fast approaching the time when he would move on, saying that future funding would largely be a matter of financial management once the ship was launched. Charlie Welker prepared the outline of a launch plan. Two new committees were formed to manage the future: a Launch Committee and a Re-enactment Voyage and Queensland Committee, both chaired by Charlie. Alan Knight retired from the accounting role and my Dutch/Australian friend, Michiel van Doorn, joined as financial controller. He became a great asset to the Foundation and he set to work on accurate budgets for the launch and completion of the vessel. We quickly concluded that we were about $300,000 short of funds to complete the ship.

There was a lot of work to be done in a short time. Fremantle naval architect Ken McAlpine had to measure *Duyfken*'s hull and come up with a ballasting plan for the launch. He was just down the road from the shipyard and a highly credentialed professional who was the measurer for the America's Cup class of yachts as well as a designer of commercial vessels. We had our own concern that the stern castle seemed a long way above the waterline and we wanted to be sure that *Duyfken* wouldn't roll over as she sat in the water immediately after the launch. Ballast was one of the biggest costs which was not listed in any budget. The Dutch East India Company ships did not have ballast like a modern ship. The cargo was stowed to create stability. Often clay bricks were stacked deep in the hold to be used for construction work when the ships arrived in the Indies. They returned with holds full of spices and other exotic goods. *Duyfken* would require lots of ballast. Graeme Henderson was still on the *Duyfken* Board. He offered 20 tonnes of ballast – pig iron ingots from the recently-slipped submarine HMAS *Ovens* which would probably never have sea water on its hull again. We were invited to take a look before we agreed and a few of us clambered into the buoyancy tanks on the submarine to inspect the booty. The triangular ingots, weighing 15 kg each, were perfect and a team from the shipyard was sent down for the difficult job of extracting them. They crawled through the hull openings of the submarine to cut off the ballast tie down straps and remove the ingots one-by-one. The laborious process took three days. Perth businessman, Peter Briggs, also donated spare lead ingots from his Admiral's Cup yacht, Hitchhiker. They were fitted in November 1998. Initially, 30 tonnes of cast iron and lead ballast was placed inside the hull temporarily for the launch.

Chapter 8

Mr I Say I Say

Even as the ship was nearing completion and the yard was being inundated with excited visitors, we still had our detractors. Our success with the construction of *Duyfken* and the national and international publicity we enjoyed still rankled with people who were welded-on to the important story of Dirk Hartog arriving at Cape Inscription in 1616.

We saw that *Duyfken* was a way of talking about all the Dutch voyages to the Australian coastline but the Shark Bay Shire President, Les Moss, found a platform in The Australian newspaper and told the reporter, Natalie O'Brien, that the 'claims' that Willem Jansz's crew came ashore on Cape York Peninsula were ruining the tourism industry in Denham and embarrassing the locals. He said that the "ridiculous kerfuffle" was caused by publicity-seeking by those building the replica. "They want to re-write history," he told the reporter. "This is very serious to us — we are horrified at what the consequences will be. We are defending Australian history." Les Moss found an ally in author Hugh Edwards. As an ex-journalist with an ability to communicate without academic verbosity, his views were always sought by the media. He said that the theory about the *Duyfken* landing was "not only unsubstantiated, but also unlikely." He based his view on the story of half the crew being massacred in New Guinea before Jansz sailed south to Australia, questioning why the depleted crew would risk more lives by coming ashore. Once again, we had to defend our Project and explain the more likely chronology of events.

Beginning with Michael Young's energetic pursuit of everything about *Duyfken* then the creation of his design committee at the Maritime Museum, and then James Henderson's work to distill the story into book form, we had a much clearer idea about what had happened at the

Pennefather River in the Gulf of Carpentaria in 1606. Marit van Huystee and Adriaan de Jong did a great deal of work with the archived records of the Dutch East India Company and tracked our *Duyfken* through the various ship's logs, memoranda and journals. *Duyfken*'s original ship's log did not exist and the burning issue of whether the crew came ashore came down to the 1623 journal of Jan Carstensz who commanded the jacht *Pera*. In company with the *Arnhem,* Carstensz headed out on a voyage to take another look at the lands recorded by Willem Jansz in 1606. Marit translated the record of 11 May 1623: "...and in the afternoon sailed past a large river which the men of the *Duyfken* went up in 1606 and where one of them was killed by the throwing (of arrows or spears) of the savages." The journal then covers the next day: "...in their...huts on the beach we have found nothing except...a piece of metal which the wounded (Aboriginal) man had in his net and which he possibly received from the *Duyfken*." The clincher was the 15 May 1623 record which said: "...they have also knowledge of muskets, which terrible effects they seem to have learned in the year 1606 from those of the *Duyfken* who landed here." She also referred to the instructions written by directors of the Dutch East India Company which specifically mentioned that the purposes of the voyages to the South Land were to pursue trading opportunities. It made no sense that they would not go ashore. James Henderson and Nick Burningham backed up Marit's view. When we began sailing the *Duyfken* replica, we decided that it was inconceivable that you wouldn't want to come ashore from the ship after spending even only a few weeks at sea!

"Marit's reading of the *Duyfken* chart was very important," said Nick Burningham. "Everyone from Matthew Flinders on thought that *Duyfken* coasted along the southern coast of New Guinea before turning south and exploring the west coast of Cape York Peninsula. Few had spotted that the chart has outward and return courses marked and that *Duyfken* sailed east-south-east in the middle of the Arafura Sea to the landfall at Pennefather River. If nine of the crew were killed then most of them probably met their fate after the exploration of the Cape York Peninsula."

Rather than discouraging everyone associated with the Project, the debate energised us to tell the story. It reinforced the whole reason for building *Duyfken*.

While the day-to-day activities during *Duyfken*'s voyage were uncertain, we had just as much trouble putting some flesh on the bones of *Duyfken*'s captain, Willem Jansz. His logbook also has never been found. There were three people at the time in the employ of the VOC who had the same name. We think our William Jansz was the man boringly described by one of his contemporaries as "by nature a moderate, simple man who acquitted himself excellently in his task." Certainly, any Ship's Master who agreed to sail from Europe to the Spice islands, and then to go even further, into uncharted waters beyond the known world, must have been exceptional.

Willem Jansz was born in about 1570 and he was recorded as a ship's officer on the *Hollandia* on 21 December 1599 for the second Dutch fleet to the Indies under Jacob Cornelius van Neck. The first fleet barely covered costs but van Neck came back with massive profits of several hundred per cent for the Dutch investors. They were pleased that their money was well spent. Surviving the voyage and returning to Amsterdam, Jansz did not stay long, and he was appointed Master of the ship *Lam*. He is mentioned in the records as a fine cartographer. He was then appointed as Mate on the *Ram* and directed to make maps of the Malayan coast.

He did not emerge from history as a towering figure like other 'Age of Discovery' explorers such as Christopher Columbus. He has not had hundreds of books written about him like James Cook. There were, however, a couple of things which gave an insight into Jansz's character and unique foibles.

Francois Valentijn, a VOC historian and chronicler from the seventeenth century, wrote about Willem Jansz's time as a Governor of Banda. Valentijn said that he was an Amsterdam foundling who worked his way up in the company hierarchy but never lost his slum accent and his excitable way of inserting 'Ik zeg, ik zeg' (I say, I say) into all his conversations. He was commonly known in Banda as 'Mijnheer Ikzegikzeg' (Mr I Say I Say). Other historians, however, disagree whether he was a foundling at all, citing his parents as Volckert Jansz and Elisabeth Claessen. When he returned to Amsterdam as a wealthy man at the end of his career (to die less than a year later), Valentijn said he spurned a woman who purported to be his mother. "When he came to Amsterdam he met two women, one who pretended to be his mother, and the other who claimed to have been his wet nurse. To the first he said: 'I say, I say, if thou art my mother, thou art a great harlot, and thou hast been most unmerciful in laying me in the street (which he well knew); and therefore, I say, I say, did you not want to know me then for a son, when I have gone out, and had nothing, neither do I know you now for my mother. To the other he said, I say, I say, hast thou nursed me, thou hast dealt with me as a good mother, and thou shalt find that I will deal with thee as a good son.'" As he verily did." Wouldn't the gossip columnists have had a field day in Amsterdam that year!

Valentijn tells another story from Banda:

> At one time he had dressed himself very handsomely, and asked his chief councillors, who were also well attired; to take him on a leisure trip to one of the islands. The day before he had ordered the shipyard master to tar the boat he intended to use, and all the benches well, but he did not tell them. He then walked with them to where the boat lay, in which there were no quartermaster to steer, nor sailors to row. He did not make many outward courtesies to wait for them or make them call, but first jumped in, and, however wet the benches were with tar, sat down at the helm, and said to them: 'I say, I say, where a governor sits at the helm, the chief merchant, fiscal and the other councillors may each take an oar in his hand and row.' They looked to their noses, having no thought of having come from there, to row, and much they murmured against those frail benches, but whether they murmured this or that, they must go on those benches with their fine garments, sit down and row obediently; but they so fondly remembered this little pleasure (while he laughed in his fist at their rotten clothes and soft hands) that they no longer had any desire to go on a leisure trip with him.

There was, however, another story by Valentijn which was deeply disturbing: "While serving in Banda, he kept a few mardijkers (freed, mostly Christian slaves) with 20 kora kora on Pulau Ai for a long time to look after the runaway Bandanese, and thus captured many of them, whom he firstly had hanged or beheaded without any plea, of which many heads can still be found in a certain well on Pulau Ai. This frightened them so much that there and elsewhere on the mountain they no longer knew how to hide themselves, after that time (they) chiefly consented to leave Banda and to the islands of Kei Besar and Kei Kecil, Aru, Goram, East Ceram, Macassar, etc." Willard Hanna in his book Indonesian Banda said that the expedition returned with hundreds of heads. "These were dropped into a deep well on Lonthor from which, half a century later, skulls were still being dredged up."

It was something which didn't suit our narrative of Willem Jansz — our great explorer and spice trade adventurer. We continued building a ship.

Chapter 9

Fremantle is the Centre of the Universe

In the second half of 1998, the shipyard was a scene of intense activity. Everyone had to work to a fixed deadline for the ship to be launched. Initially, the date was to be Australia Day, 26 January 1999 but we moved to 24 January to avoid competing with the Australia Day Fireworks in Perth. Our plan was to have the ship launched by then and to anchor in Perth Water for the evening of the fireworks display.

The launch of *Duyfken* was my first chance to show everyone associated with *Duyfken* that we could be far more than just shipbuilders. With my skills and more freedom to get things done, I would be able to elevate the Project to a greater height of public recognition. I always believed in putting on a good show and providing entertainment. The launch of the ship was our big chance to say that we had done something fantastic and now it was time for the whole world to know. We aspired to a launch festival which was fresh and different in the slightly oddball spirit of Fremantle.

We initially thought that the logical way to launch *Duyfken* was to place her on a platform, transport her across the railway line between the Maritime Museum and the Fremantle Fishermen's Co-op building and run her down into the Indian Ocean at Bather's Beach. Yep, straight into the surf. It sounded simple. It was not so simple when we started to look into the practicality of manoeuvring *Duyfken* and trailer with an all up weight estimated at 64 tonnes, a height of nine metres, and a width of seven metres. She would have to be moved sideways, fences dropped, we'd have to make sure that there weren't any National Rail trains coming and then we'd have to build a slipway into the ocean on a beach which can get a good walloping from the sou'wester. Maybe we could take her down to Swan Dock and use the old slipway which was barely used? Once again, it was not so easy.

A master at moving big things, Bill Fletcher from local firm, Global Hire, suggested taking the greased ways out of the *Endeavour* shed and relocating them to near the Sardine Jetty for a clear run into Fishing Boat Harbour. Our first thinking was that a spectacular launch for the ship down the greased ways built for *Endeavour* into the harbour would provide a great spectacle. They were all grand ideas but funds were flying out of the *Duyfken* bank account at a rate of knots and we weren't about to spend too much on a launch when we had a ship to finish. In the end, we thought a simple parade down Marine Terrace on the back of a large jinker-like trailer, past the Esplanade Hotel, then a right turn across the Railway Line into Mews Road and Fremantle Boatlifters would be the most practical solution. We could then lower the hull into the harbour using a Tami lifter (a large wheeled crane where the vessel was slung between two uprights). Michael Kailis owned Fremantle Boatlifters so the price would be right. The only trouble was the magnificent old Moreton Bay fig tree in the Esplanade Park which overhung the road. We'd have to trim some branches to get past, but the Council said 'no way' could we damage the heritage-listed tree.

The planning for the launch of *Duyfken* began in earnest in August 1998. I enlisted the help of an old friend from the Fremantle Sailing Club, Ian Gillon, who headed the Fremantle hosting team for the first Whitbread Round the World Race in 1989. He jumped into the launching job with great enthusiasm. Peter Becu also joined the launch planning team, as did the Mayor of Fremantle, Richard Utting, and Con Smit from the Friends of the *Duyfken*. There was a massive amount of work which had to be done to move the vessel. Bill Fletcher thought quite the opposite. He did not think lifting the ship and placing it on the trailer to be towed by a Brambles Manford truck presented much of a challenge — they had lifted and moved much heavier objects. His confidence was comforting. The challenge was getting the ship through Fremantle.

The end result of all the discussions was a radically expanded and more spectacular route: an epic drive through Fremantle. The journey was to begin at the Lotteries *Duyfken* Village then take a left turn north along Cliff Street, right at Phillimore Street, all the way east to turn right at the Pioneer Reserve outside the railway station and along Market Street and then into South Terrace and the popular Cappuccino Strip of coffee shops and restaurants. At Suffolk Street, *Duyfken* would again turn right and link up with Mews Road to arrive at her final land destination of Fremantle Boatlifters. She would then be placed into a shed for final preparations until the day of the launch. What could possibly go wrong except having to negotiate eight street corners, light poles, roundabouts and a railway line? The general agreement with the haulage company, Brambles Manford, and Bill Fletcher was that it could be done but it would require dozens of large plates of steel to cover the intersections where the big rig had to turn and mount kerbs to run along footpaths. These areas were soft underneath and the rig could easily rip up the slabs and grind to a halt. The bonus for us was that instead of a slow move through the backstreets of Fremantle we were now planning to take the ship down the most popular street in Western Australia. Western Power and the Main Roads Department agreed to move power lines and temporarily remove traffic lights for no charge. It would normally cost $35,000. The Water Corporation sponsored the street parade to the tune of $50,000 and the all up sponsorship support and donations amounted to well over $150,000. Our actual out-of-pocket amounted to approximately $20,000 so I could generate a handy profit to be put back into the cost of completing the vessel and making her seaworthy. It was a small ship but when she was squeezed down the Cappuccino Strip she would look monstrous.

While heavily involved in planning the launch, we also had our chance to get the re-enactment voyage to Queensland locked away. We secured a meeting with the new Premier of Queensland, Peter Beattie, at his office in Brisbane in October 1998. It was the culmination of months of discussions. Michael Kailis, Sir James Cruthers and I flew to Brisbane in early October to do a deal. In the week before we left Perth, we carefully concocted a plan for the meeting and I produced a comprehensive presentation document. We couldn't show the Premier around the shipyard in Fremantle so we needed a prop; something he could touch and feel. Adriaan de Jong had crafted a superb model of the ship's boat after spending months researching the design. We planned to place the model on his desk. Then Michael would do his short speech which had been so successful in the past. It went along the lines that he was a Greek-Australian and the sea had been his life etc. Although *Duyfken* was a Dutch ship, it told the beginning of the maritime history of Australia and it was important that all our children knew these stories and how we came to be Australians. Appealing to the Premier's parochialism, he would say that few people knew that the first European visitors to Australia arrived in Queensland. He would then say that he had personally put in $150,000 to build the ship. I was then to swing into the discussion and talk about the proposed re-enactment voyage and how good it would be for Queensland. Sir James was then going to close the deal. He would talk about how millions had been raised but nothing from Queensland even though *Duyfken* was the first ship recorded in history to sail there, how we still needed money to finish the vessel and conduct the voyage and how he could help us build the ship's boat which would have carried Willem Jansz ashore at the Pennefather River. Then Sir James would say he could get all this for $500,000. Shake hands. With our work done, we'd then fly back to Western Australia.

Flying to Queensland and travelling across Brisbane with a fragile balsa wood model of a boat without breaking it was quite a challenge but we made it to the Premier's office on the fifteenth floor of the executive building. With its dark wood panelling, I found it rather palatial compared with the more modest WA Premier's pad. We sat down in large armchairs with the boat model on the coffee table in front of us. Peter Beattie bounded into the room full of energy with his trademark beaming smile and he was introduced to all of us by his adviser. We could see he was in a bit of a rush and after the usual light-hearted banter about the advantages of WA versus Queensland, Michael was about to launch into his introduction. The Premier was distracted and pointed to the boat model. "What's that?" he said and laughed. "You brought that all the way from WA?" Michael then started on his speech which always went down well. Michael then asked me to explain the voyage. As soon as I started Peter Beattie cut in, laughing at my formality. "OK. So what do you want?" He had obviously read the briefing notes and he didn't have time for me to explain it all again. Michael mumbled and threw to Sir James. "Jim?" he said, encouraging him to jump in. And without the blink of an eye Sir James said, "$500,000 to finish *Duyfken*, and you get a ship's boat and a re-enactment voyage." Peter Beattie replied, " OK, but I don't need that ship's boat and you must bring the ship to Queensland." Handshakes and beaming smiles all round, the unwanted ship's boat tucked under my arm in a box, and away we went with another $500,000 in the kitty. It turned out that we would need every last cent of that money before we even left Western Australia.

Even with regular trips to Brisbane, it took another four months of negotiations with the Premier's staff to finalise the sponsorship. It came with 12 conditions including having the ship on exhibition in Brisbane after the voyage, educational visits to all the major ports along the Queensland coast and the option to winter the ship every year in Queensland. Surprisingly, we also agreed to build two ship's boats with one to stay in a museum in

Queensland — but that never happened!

In the early hours of Tuesday 22 December 1998, two Police officers noticed smoke coming from the *Duyfken* Village. Constables Bragg and Gill looked into the yard and a fire was burning out of control in the fire-bending area of the yard. With the assistance of cleaning staff from Cicerello's Seafood Restaurant in Fishing Boat Harbour they managed to extinguish the blaze before the fire brigade arrived. Fortunately, the fire did not spread to the ship and only minor damage was done. Local media ran hot with the story. It was a timely warning that only when bending the hull planks did fire and timber mix, and without the local Police officers and Cicerello's cleaners, the *Duyfken* story may have ended there and then.

Whilst planning was underway for the launch, fundraising was continuing and we were under siege from our historical critics, the shipbuilding team also had problems. They were finding it increasingly difficult to complete the bare hull to meet the launch schedule. More and more labour was thrown at the task from November 1998. Over 40 staff were employed to finish the ship and then more and more contractors, volunteers and shipwrights were engaged to help get the job done. In the New Year, with only weeks to the launch, the shipyard had a frenetic atmosphere and every day there were workers swarming over the hull. I would later find that the labour budget had blown out by $70,000 in the three months up to the January 1999 launch. It was money I needed to finish the ship for sailing and it had just been reduced to piles of sawdust.

Our pre-launch publicity was kicking-in and visitors were pouring into the shipyard to get a glimpse of the ship and to buy souvenirs. The public identification with *Duyfken* as a ship built by West Australians for the benefit of the West Australian community was very strong. We enjoyed enormous public support. The donation box in the shipyard received $1000 a month in coins and notes. Michael Young remembers receiving a note from a pensioner which said "Here is $5 to help you with *Duyfken*. It is all I can afford but I want to help finish our little ship." Yes, we had the big corporate and personal sponsors, and big government support, but she was always the people's ship.

After six months of planning, a milestone was reached only days before the launch. It was time for the shed to be removed so that the hull could be prepared for the street parade and its relocation to Fremantle Boatlifters. The roofing sheets were removed on 5 January and from the hull jammed into the shipyard, we could now see how *Duyfken* looked. For the first time, the ship was showered in Australian summer sun. There was no doubt that Bill Leonard and his team had done a fine job with Nick Burningham and Adriaan de Jong's design. The sweep of the hull, her sleek lines and the towering stern-castle were simply beautiful. The beakhead or beak (the sweeping decorative section forward of the bow – looking just like the beak of a bird) was magnificent. There was little time for the shipwrights to ponder what they achieved. Work was continuing day and night to get the ship ready for launch.

I will treasure a memory of sitting high up in the stern late one afternoon at what became my favourite spot on the ship, looking forward, as the deck widened and then curved gently towards the bow of the ship. Beyond the beautiful beak was Gage Roads, Rottnest Island and the Indian Ocean. The sun was setting and only a handful of people were still in the yard. Nick Trulove, as always, was one of the last to leave. He was still working on the beak. This had been his creation and he had worked closely with Nick and Adriaan to create a three-dimensional sculptural form in oak which, I thought, attached like magic to the bow. He called it a day as the setting sun was low on the horizon, put away his tools and came up with a beer to join me. It was a beautiful view which would be gone in a few days time and never repeated. We both knew it. This was a moment to savour. I will always value chatting with Nick on that summer's evening as the sun dropped below the horizon. It dawned on me for the first time that the dream of building a ship would soon be accomplished and what had been created was more wonderful than any of us could have imagined when we sat around at Michael and Janine Young's kitchen table eating cinnamon biscuits and drinking coffee five years before.

Amidst the frantic work to complete the ship, the hype we were creating to promote the launch was cranking up. The *Duyfken* summer in Fremantle began in December with the launch of a new beer, *Duyfken* Ale, by the Sail & Anchor Pub in Market Street. The pub's upstairs Brasserie Bar was renamed the *Duyfken* Bar. The Sail & Anchor Pub Brewery grew out of Brewtech, later to become the Matilda Bay Brewery, which created the Sail & Anchor from the old Freemasons Hotel during the America's Cup. The micro brewery just off the main bar was soon too small for the Matilda Bay Brewery which moved to bigger premises, but the small tanks were ideal for producing hand-crafted beers such as *Duyfken* Ale. Part proceeds from sale of the beer contributed to the construction of the ship and *Duyfken* Ale t-shirts became a popular item at the shipyard and in the Sail & Anchor bottle shop. The bar was decorated with a *Duyfken* theme, featuring shipbuilding and nautical paraphernalia from the shipyard.

The brewing team of Peter Nolin and, appropriately, his friend Dutchman, Bill Hoedemaker, used hops grown in the Willamette Valley, Oregon USA to brew the beer. Peter compared the brewing of traditional ales with the building of *Duyfken*. We were always keen to make a link between other crafts and building the ship and in this case it was a long bow to connect beer with *Duyfken*, but we had fun with it. At the launch of the beer, Peter Nolin said: "As *Duyfken* was built using the age old technique of skin first construction using fire bent planks, so *Duyfken* Ale is brewed using the time honoured ingredients of water, malt, hops and yeast plus the skill of the brewer."

Thanks to research by Nick Burningham, Michael Kailis proclaimed that beer was an indispensable cargo on *Duyfken* when she set sail from the Netherlands for the East Indies. He said that she carried approximately 5250 litres of beer for her crew of 20 — and sailors were also permitted to bring their own personal supply! Potable water was hard to come by and even though it was stored in casks for long periods, it was often fit only for cooking. The journal of the second Moluccas Fleet to sail from the Netherlands noted after five and a half months at sea that: "We have drunk the last of our beer and have had our first allowance of water." The water was mixed with wine or spirits. The stronger the wine or spirits, the more water was mixed with it. Complaints from the crew were long and loud if the wine and spirits ran short, requiring more water in the mix.

All the events associated with the launch were grandly packaged up as the Festival of the *Little Dove*. I asked an old work colleague from my Tourism Commission days, Tracy McCullough, to join me to help with the mammoth task of staging the events. She was soon hooked on *Duyfken*, too. In the years to come, she became an important organiser in our shore team and a great fan of the ship. The Festival kicked off with the launch of an exhibition of Bellarmine jugs at the Kailis Pearls gallery called Artisans of the Sea in Fremantle. The Kailis family was closely involved with the University of Notre Dame Australia which opened in the West End of Fremantle in 1992 and the Vice-Chancellor, Dr Peter Tannock, supported our Project. We arranged a series of lectures on Dutch maritime exploration and *Duyfken* in the lead up to the launch to establish a link between the study of the history associated with the original voyage and the University. Professor Geoffrey Bolton was the keynote speaker and Marit van Huystee and Nick Burningham also spoke. The lectures were a great success, selling out for every session with 300 people attending the talks and validating the research aims of the Foundation.

On Thursday 21 January 1999, just a little over five years after Michael Young wrote his letter to the Fremantle Herald, the team from Global Hire installed hydraulic jacks underneath *Duyfken* and the process of lifting her high enough to be slipped onto the Brambles trailer began. *Duyfken* for the next few hours was no longer the responsibility of Noel Robins, Bill Leonard and his team. We all stood quietly as the ship was slowly lifted up by six 100-tonne hydraulic jacks and then lowered onto six stools so that the 64-wheeled self-levelling trailer could be backed underneath the ship. It seemed incredible that the trailer could then be lined up with Cliff Street but it was soon done and *Duyfken* was on her way without any fuss. The stern was taller than the two storey buildings in the West End. The Brambles Manford prime mover team made easy work of getting the ship to Fremantle Railway Station where they were joined by hundreds of people who were forming the street parade. Court Jester, Jonathan de Hadleigh, *Duyfken* volunteer guides, dancers, the Freo Samba percussionists which are such a feature of Fremantle festivals, a papier mache sea dragon provided by our guides coordinator Jenny Gibbs, mounted police and a pipe band created a Festival of the *Little Dove* on Market Street. Long lengths of blue cloth on either side of the ship lifted up and down mimicking waves. By this time, thousands of people were waiting for the ship to arrive in South Terrace where we had arranged for the parade to take a short interlude. Brian Mitchell from The Fremantle Herald came over to me and asked what I thought about the day. I replied that it was Michael Young's relentless enthusiasm and dogged determination which had got us to this point. It was lamentable that Michael was, by this time, just another face in the crowd with no formal role — but many of us knew that he was the founder of this whole crazy project.

The parade halted in South Terrace and a scissor lift serving as a stage was pushed over to the stern of the ship. South Terrace is lined with buildings from the Goldrush era of the 1890s. It was a visage of old and very old. I felt very satisfied with myself that we had pulled it off and got this far — perhaps the only time a ship had sailed down the Cappuccino Strip. The steel sheets on every corner had done their job and we had not destroyed the roads and footpaths of Fremantle or crushed any water or sewerage pipes! We only had the sweet smell of success.

It was here that the Mayor of Fremantle, Richard Utting, would present Michael Kailis with the Fremantle Coat of Arms carved by Jenny Scrayen and painted by Adriaan de Jong to be attached to the stern of the ship. This shield was a departure from the historical authenticity which had guided the Project. *Duyfken* would probably have had the crest of the City of Amsterdam or one of the seven chambers of the VOC on her stern. Nobody knows for sure, but what we did know was that the *Duyfken* replica was Fremantle's ship and she should forever carry the symbol of her home port. Michael Kailis happily accepted the Coat of Arms from the Mayor and presented him with a large glass container sitting on an oak base. It was filled with wood shavings of oak and pinaster from the ship. Nick Burningham suggested that it was appropriate to follow a South East Asian custom that the shavings are symbolic of the ship's navel and they are traditionally kept at the ship owner's home so that it knows where to return. The shavings in the jar were kept at the Fremantle Town Hall for many years — I hope they are still there.

With Bill Leonard at the controls, Michael Kailis and Richard Utting ascended to the stern on the scissor lift to place the crest just above the rudder. Bill later admitted that he was nervous as it was the first time he'd driven one! Now Richard Utting always had a feel for the media and he knew what was needed to get a headline. Amongst cheering and applause he said: "This proves once and for all, that Fremantle really is the centre of the Universe!" And nobody disagreed!

There was more to be done before the day was over. The Dutch choir began singing and once again *Duyfken* was connected to the prime mover. Away she went, past the Sail & Anchor Pub, the Fremantle Markets, across the railway line and into Fremantle Boatlifters. She was backed into one of the large painting sheds where she would stay for the next three days before the Sunday launch. Large orange plastic curtains were hung across the shed opening, hiding the ship from public view, and enabling a big reveal on Sunday before the launch. Only the majestic beakhead of the ship could be seen poking out from behind the orange drapes.

The Rijst Tafel at Notre Dame University on the Saturday evening before the launch was a grand affair. The invitation set the scene:

> She starts, — She moves, — She seems to feel
> The thrill of life along her keel,
> And, spurning with her foot the ground,

> *With one exulting, joyous bound,*
> *She leaps into the ocean's arms.*

> *The Rijst Tafel will be held in the romantic surrounds of the courtyard of the University of Notre Dame Australia, 19 Mouat Street, Fremantle at 7.00pm on Saturday 23 January 1999.*

> *Your Rijst Tafel will include 17 main course dishes featuring the spices of the Spice Islands of Indonesia laid on several long tables. Our very own* Duyfken *Ale will be specially brewed for the evening and you will have a choice of fine Western Australian wines. The night will be completed with* Duyfken *Port.*

> *The night will feature Dutch, Australian and Indonesian entertainment.*

For the first time we had everyone involved with the *Duyfken* Project together — the shipbuilding team and staff, the Friends of the *Duyfken*, volunteer guides, the 1606 Club members and sponsors. It was a memorable night with all the emotion which comes with launching any ship, the end of one phase and the beginning of another. Nick Burningham felt the drama more than most. The team of the last three years was to be broken up and on Monday he would have a new boss, me! I thought he felt that Noel had been wronged by my appointment and an injustice had been perpetrated. He later said that he was actually annoyed that Noel had not been mentioned in the speeches and that my appointment had been accepted by the staff. In any case, he let me have it. His passion was understandable. I had nothing to say, except that if he didn't like it, he could walk. We could discuss it next week after the launch. Now it was time for us all to go to bed.

The next morning was hot with a predicted top of more than 35ºC. Fortunately the ship was to be launched early in the morning. We wanted the launch to be broadcast nationally on the Seven Network but the Australian Open Tennis was underway and nothing was more important for the television station than the tennis. We were given the slot before the matches in Melbourne began. *Duyfken* would touch the water after 7.30am.

Pleasure boats began arriving in the late afternoon of the day before the launch to get the best positions in the harbour. Before sunrise, people started streaming into Fremantle and taking positions along the shore. Activities began with the Army band playing for half an hour and then a gamelan band following up with rhythmic Angklung Banyuwangi Indonesian music. The TVW Seven weather presenter Geoff Newman was our urbane master of ceremonies and the Premier's daughter, Billie Court, sang the national anthem.

Bill Leonard climbed aboard *Duyfken* to place olive branches in her beak. They had been pruned by Benedictine Monk, Dom Christopher Powers, from the 100 year old olive grove at the Benedictine monastery in New Norcia north west of Perth and brought down to Fremantle especially for the launch. James Henderson went to New Norcia to select them. The branches had great symbolism for the ship which was named after Noah's dove. As the Old Testament story says, when the great flood abated Noah first sent out a raven to search for dry land. The raven had no luck so he sent a dove to search. The dove went out twice and found land on the second occasion, returning with an olive twig in its beak. James Henderson's book was titled *Sent Forth a Dove*.

Early Greeks used olive branches in harvest festivals and Medieval Christians believed that the twig carried by Noah's dove was carried from the olive tree in the first orchard in the Garden of Eden. With such great symbolism of venturing forth and returning after finding land, the Dutch merchants of the late sixteenth and seventeenth century often named the small scout ship of their fleets the *Little Dove* or *Duyfken*. Today, the image of a white dove with an olive branch in its beak is a universal symbol of peace and reconciliation. We thought that *Duyfken* was an appropriate name for a ship which was built to help all Australians understand the events which surrounded the nation's early modern history. We were keen to downplay *Duyfken*'s aggressive scout ship role. How naive we were.

The *Duyfken* 1606 Replica Foundation's search to find an appropriate beverage for the Premier's wife, Jo Court, to smash against the hull was another chance for us to do something more akin to the era than simply exploding a bottle of champagne and we didn't want to use a bottle of Grange like *Endeavour*. We knew that Dom Perignon, a French monk, invented the bubbly drop in 1697 and the English claimed to have made sparking wine about 30 years before. *Duyfken* predated champagne! Naturally, we deferred to our resident historian, Nick Burningham, to give us some advice. He told us that the launching of ships with wine had obvious associations with birth and bringing to life. The washing of the bow to open the eyes with wine is done in several parts of Asia and he thought that it may explain the very similar use of wine in European traditions — in effect, wetting the baby's head. He said that early European traditions of using red wine to launch ships also had associations with the 'blood and toil' of the shipwrights and in all traditions it was designed to give good luck to the ship and crew. This was obviously a very important aspect of the launch and we would all need to give it some serious thought. Our launch bottle had to have a West Australian flavour and what better than a fine Western Australian Cabernet Sauvignon wine? Michael Kailis had an association with a noted French-Australian wine maker, François Jacquard. One of Michael's less successful schemes had been importing cheap wine from eastern Europe (Bulgaria in particular) and François had helped him with marketing it (The wine was, shall we say, cheeky, and didn't sell and Cathy and I ended up with as many cases as we could consume). François studied initially at the acclaimed University of Dijon in Burgundy where he graduated in Oenology and Viticulture in 1983. His skills had taken him to vineyards such as Domaine Dujac in Burgundy, Adelsheim vineyards in Oregon, Bannockburn vineyards in Victoria and Chittering Estate in Western Australia. He migrated to Australia after a visit to the Chittering Valley in 1989 where he met his wife, Carolyn, in a vineyard. He finally established his own company Jacwine in Perth.

François had vintaged some wine in 1995, so the wine was as old as the ship. He used high quality grapes in a selected low yielding vineyard applying what he called "a more European approach than Cabernet Sauvignon wines usually produced in Western Australia." This special wine had never been released onto the local market and was soon to be shipped to Europe. For the record, it had a fresh flavoursome berry flavour, some subtle oak flavours (European, of course) with a great complexity and balance. From the Foundation's viewpoint, a European-style Australian wine was an excellent choice for the launch and we could secure the whole vintage of 3000 bottles to be sold as the launch collection of the *Duyfken*. It was yet another fundraising opportunity. François agreed and held some back to sell to restaurants around town. Bottle number one was a magnum to be used for the launch and the rest were numbered from three to be sold to benefit the Foundation. Number two was another magnum kept just in case something went wrong with number one before the critical moment.

We had to make sure that the bottle would break appropriately on the day. Igor Bjorksten made up a very nice rope cradle for the bottle and we cheated just a little bit by grinding a weak spot into the glass on the neck. We didn't want it to bounce off the ship to our total embarrassment.

The gates to Fremantle Boatlifters had to open early as many of the 1,800 invited guests packed the street outside. They streamed in and no small number of uninvited gusts also managed to slip past the security guards in the rush. Seated close to the ship was the Premier Richard Court and his wife Jo, the Dutch Ambassador Albert Nooij and his wife Gisella, the Indonesian Ambassador Wiryono Sastrohandojo, and eight local and national politicians who all came to see Michael Kailis' latest accomplishment. With about 200 uninvited guests, every space was filled. Fremantle Fishing Boat Harbour was packed with boats and people lined every possible spot on the jetty. I was impressed when people in the spectator area told me after the event that the harbour-side was more packed than when *Endeavour* was launched. Believe it or not — I chose, of course, to believe it. Every major media organisation was in attendance including international organisations such as Reuters. The launch received media coverage across Asia and across the rest of the world with CNN. Naturally, it became big news in The Netherlands.

An old friend from my days at the WA Tourism Commission who also left government employ, Vaughan Emery, was hired to stage the launch. We had a surprise in store. After everyone was in place, the harbour went quiet and the booming, ethereal, low-pitched sound of a lone didgeridoo player, James Webb from the Wadumbah dance group, caused a tingle down everyone's spine. Then the orange curtains, which were symbolic of The Netherlands, opened to reveal the majestic bow of *Duyfken* with the olive branches in her freshly painted beak and the magnum of wine hanging below.

The Tami lift edged across the yard, then lined up with the launching dock where it waited until the ceremony could begin.

The *Duyfken* team had many talents. Michael Barnett from the plank bending team was a musician. His night job was as a rock and folk artist and a leading member of the five-piece group, Mockonajar, which played at venues all around Perth and in the south west. The group also appeared for six weeks in 1997 on the ABC television program Rage. Being a full time musician was not always as rewarding financially as it might be, and when in February 1998 his girlfriend mentioned that there was work available on the *Duyfken* Project, Barney jumped at the chance. He simply wandered into the yard one day and asked for a job and Bill Leonard put him to work tending the fires used to bend the planks for the ship. He graduated to bending the planks. As he stood beside the planks, stoking the fire and helping to gently curve them to the correct shape, the tune of a song began forming in his mind. That tune was 'The Ballad of the *Duyfken*'. It took about two weeks to write and he began to perform it at schools around Fremantle as part of educational shows designed to teach school children the story of the *Little Dove*.

Now he was on the stage in front of thousands of people, guitar in hand. His song stirred the heart of anyone who loved the romance of the sea and the ancient craft of wooden shipbuilding. 'The Ballad of the *Duyfken*' told the story of the original *Duyfken* and her recreation.

Father Vincent Conroy, who blessed the keel, was now in residence at Santa Maria College. He agreed to follow up the keel blessing with the blessing of the launch. He was pleased that his previous blessing led to a smooth construction phase. Indeed, the only major injury I can remember was when a shipwright was working on the outside of the hull and drilled through the hull planking into the foot of another shipwright who was working inside the hull.

It was always fascinating to me that although few of us associated with the ship had strong religious beliefs, we were always prepared to accept blessings when they were offered. And Father Conroy began:

> IN THE WORDS OF THE 60TH CHAPTER OF THE
> PROPHET ISAIAH,
>
> *What are these ships that skim along like clouds*
> *Like doves returning home?*
> *They are ships coming from distant lands*
> *Bringing God's people home.*
>
> *We pray you Lord to look down on this ship* — Duyfken, *which began as 'a noble vision of building history'. Through the drive and support of many and the skills of the craftsmen, God-given talents have enabled this beautiful ship to be built to honour explorers of old and unite the three nations of Holland, Indonesia and Australia in a common purpose.*
>
> *We are grateful, Lord, that no harm has befallen us in this Project and for the joy and hope that has filled the hearts of all in its construction.*
>
> *May you extend your blessing upon the new* Duyfken *and give her safe passage.*

As you protected Noah from harm and helped him find safe harbour through the scouting of a dove, we pray that those who sail on the Duyfken *may always find safe harbour through your guiding hand.*

Amen.

It was then Premier Richard Court's turn to praise the *Duyfken* Project.

"Many of us have watched with pride and awe as *Duyfken* has taken shape at the Fremantle Museum site and we have marvelled at the ancient skills that have been used by the craftsmen and women in faithfully recreating a wooden Dutch sailing ship. WA has a proud maritime tradition from the early explorers and settlers to the America's Cup challenges and defence, the feats of yachtsmen Jon Sanders and David Dicks, and the building of wonderful boats such as *Endeavour* and now *Duyfken*," he said. "This ship will be a floating advertisement to the skills and dedication of the Western Australians who have built her."

It was, indeed, a proud moment for all associated with the Project. When Michael Kailis rose to speak, he was very emotional. Australian born of Greek parents, his link with *Duyfken* wasn't obvious but he was passionate about Australia's history and he couldn't ignore the lure of building a replica of Australia's first ship. He knew Indonesia through his shipbuilding interests and he'd visited the Spice Islands in 1972 to deliver the ship he'd built, *K Djartama*. Oddly enough, Djartarma means 'I shall return'. He supported a charity on the Indonesian island of Roti which helped fishing villages which lost access to traditional fishing grounds when Australia imposed a broad economic zone. He always talked about his first encounter with the word *Duyfken* from his school history book, 'Australia since 1606' by GV Portus, which described *Duyfken*'s visit. Now a ship with that name was about to be launched. Since he was recruited to the *Duyfken* Project by Michael Young and maritime author James Henderson, he had sometimes been frustrated and sometimes angry with some decisions, but he was always enthusiastic and driven to complete the Project. His health problems in the last year must have been weighing on his mind as he sat on the stage in the heat of the morning.

At approximately 7.45am, Mrs Court said the immortal words, "I name the ship *Duyfken* and God bless all who sail in her", before breaking the magnum of *Duyfken* wine on the ship's bow. *Duyfken* was gently lowered into the water and the harbour erupted with the joy of a ship touching water for the first time. The RAAF Roulettes aerobatic team performed overhead to most people's complete surprise and the Fremantle class patrol boat HMAS *Geraldton* skippered by Lieutenant Commander Phil Orchard fired her cannon. The Defence Department had proudly announced that the navigator on *Geraldton* would be Lieutenant Michael de Ruyter, "a descendant of the famous Admiral Michiel de Ruyter who in 1667 commanded the Dutch Fleet and gave the English Navy a bloody nose on the River Thames." Michael Young was pleased with the Dutch maritime connection, another illustrious de Ruyter!

Lest I be accused of glossing over the negatives of the *Duyfken* story let me mention just one more thing. Yes, it was true that Jo Court's dress was sprayed with hydraulic fluid when the Tami lifter sprang a leak.

Granted, the *Duyfken* launch didn't have the spectacle of a slightly hazardous slipway launch where the ship ploughs into the water, but for us, it was just as sweet.

The next part of the *Duyfken* odyssey was about to begin.

Chapter 10

The Little Dove Spreads Her Wings

The Festival of the *Little Dove* had one more performance before we settled down to the final stage of completing the ship.

The fireworks display in Perth for Australia Day, called Lotto Skyworks, was on the Tuesday evening after the Sunday launch. We planned to tow the bare hull 20 km up the Swan River from Fremantle to Perth. We called it the *Duyfken* River Parade. It was a great opportunity to expose the ship to a massive audience of people who had not visited the *Duyfken* Shipyard. My objective in the months ahead was to make the ship's name a household word — *Duyfken* was a tricky one to get into the Australian mind. Some people said Dove-ken, others Dive-ken and Duff-ken. Our Dutch friends tended to pronounce it as Dive-ken so that is what I preferred. We played around with also referring to the ship as the *Little Dove* interchangeably with *Duyfken* but a ship needs one name and we persisted with *Duyfken*.

Thanks to Andrew Walton from our sponsor, the Lotteries Commission, *Duyfken* was integrated into the Australia Day event. The fireworks synced with a Perth radio station, PMFM, and in the two hour lead up to the fireworks a crew from the station was to broadcast from the ship. As the event was scheduled only two days after the launch, we had no time for procrastination. Six months of preparation by Ian Gillon delivered a very good plan. The ship was re-ballasted after the launch and stowed with radio broadcast equipment, bilge pumps, fire-fighting gear and three brass ceremonial cannon built for the America's Cup by Army technicians at Midland. The cannon were to be fired regularly by two armourers and a munitions expert from the Army.

We were placed under tow by two tugs from Stirling Marine and *Duyfken* was escorted from Fremantle Fishing Boat Harbour by HMAS

Geraldton. Michael Kailis' motor cruiser *Manitoba* carried the Freo Samba drummers to provide a musical accompaniment as we headed 20 km upriver. We timed our tow at low tide to give ourselves the best chance of slipping under the bridges. We were confident we'd make it but there was always a little apprehension. Did we get our calculations right? Our big test was to fit under the Fremantle Railway Bridge and then the old Fremantle traffic bridge and the new one further upriver. The lowest of the three bridges was the old wooden traffic bridge and we snuck though with a half metre to spare. There was visible relief from everyone aboard.

We made our way up stream through a part of the river I knew very well. I learned to row at Fremantle Rowing Club and a good part of my teenage years and early twenties was spent paddling boats around this part of the Swan. Twenty-five years before I would have been rowing a racing shell where I was now on the deck of a seventeenth century sailing ship with music blasting out and cannon being cheekily fired at the spectators on the river bank. *Duyfken* passed Michael Kailis' house on the limestone cliff at Mosman Park and then Sir James' house along Blackwall Reach where the cliffs closed up and the river narrowed. The drumming echoed off the cliffs, heralding our passing. Then from Point Walter the river opened out. *Duyfken* edged forward escorted by the *Manitoba* with the drums pounding away and a fleet of historic wooden yachts following. It was satisfying to see the great joy and curiosity of people in parks and lookout points along the banks.

The next challenge was the bridge at the Narrows leading into the large lagoon called Perth Water. Hundreds of power boats were already gathering in Melville Water and Perth Water as we approached the Narrows. If we got this one wrong, the whole world would know. Fortunately we scraped through with what seemed like only centimetres to spare and we moored *Duyfken* between four barges supplied by Ian Gillon's company, Kulin Industries. Vaughan Emery from Corporate Theatre had lights powered by generators on the barges so that the ship could be lit for the evening. The artillery squad secured their cannon and left the ship and we all had a few moments to take in the scene around us. Hundreds of thousands of people were streaming down to the foreshore, everyone with their radios tuned to the radio broadcast which had live crosses from the PMFM people aboard. Not far from us, large barges carried the fireworks. The lanky TVW Seven newsreader, Rick Ardon, climbed aboard to do a live cross to the 6pm evening news and by 7.30pm everyone except our *Duyfken* crew and a few friends and family were off the ship. All the fire extinguishers were checked and it was time for us to lay back and enjoy the fireworks. We had the best seat in town as the fireworks exploded above us. Sometimes residue floated down to the deck and we pondered how we'd react if a really large glowing chunk of firework hailed down on us. *Duyfken*'s first voyage was completed with a tow back to Fremantle the following morning. We deemed it a great success. The tow had worked but we couldn't imagine operating the ship having to get a tow every time we wanted to leave port.

The reality of my circumstances soon dawned on me. I was sitting in the manager's office the next morning and I was now fully in charge. I had the total responsibility for a sailing ship project. The last few months had been particularly difficult for both Noel Robins and me. Noel had done a good job getting the Project to this stage. He'd been forced to work to a launch deadline while he had expectations that he could spend another six or nine months in 1999 to complete the hull, with more money raised in the interim to fund the completion of the vessel. Unfortunately, Michael Kailis had lost patience with him and placed me in charge of the completion of the ship after the launch and the subsequent re-enactment voyage. Two cooks in one kitchen was a recipe for conflict and it was never a happy arrangement. Noel's resentment was palpable and he continued to undermine my authority right up to the day he left. Perhaps the worst example was when he 'gifted' plant and equipment from the shipyard to the Albany whaleboat project. We came to blows on that one.

Noel never formally handed over the Project to me. He was embittered and he didn't even turn up for his own staff send-off. It was left to Con Smit, Nick Burningham, Peggy Rogers, Alan Knight and Bill Leonard to brief me on the state of play. I had three weeks to get together a comprehensive status report for the Board. The finances weren't rosy, to say the least. Workers were interviewed by Noel without consulting Bill who had to find jobs for them that matched their skills. Labour was thrown at the ship in the final months to achieve the launch schedule. This ate into the revised post-launch budgets I had prepared with Michiel van Doorn. We still hadn't funded the re-enactment voyage or the shakedown trip we planned to Shark Bay. It was clear that we would not be able to reach Sydney in time for the Olympic Games (and we thought that the ship would be overshadowed by *Endeavour* and *Batavia* in any case). We considered accepting an offer from New Zealand and bypassing the Olympics all together, sailing to Cape York and Cairns and then to New Zealand to highlight the 1642 voyage of Abel

Tasman — but everything was dependent upon completing the ship and getting more and more funding.

My revised plan slashed expenditure as we sought to contain expenses. With the vessel now afloat, our staffing costs were significantly reduced. Peggy Rogers and Nick Burningham agreed to stay and their professionalism was a great asset to the Project. Bill Leonard and Don Cockrell kept working for a few months and eventually returned to the Maritime Museum. Danny McDermott, who was one of the most hard-working shipwrights, worked with Nick Trulove to complete the myriad jobs still required with the ship after Bill and Don left. Igor Bjorksten stayed as Master Attendant for the ship, effectively in charge of the floating vessel. Another excellent rigger, Gavin Reid, worked with him to complete the rig. Sailmakers Rick Mitchell from Melbourne and Andrea Cicholas completed the suit of sails. Mike Rowe worked on the completion of the masts in C-Shed on Victoria Quay. Our volunteer shipwrights and cleaners (we called them broomers) always helped out. Margaret Rapanaro continued to run the shop. Jenny Gibbs and her 40 volunteer guides were required more than ever as visitors were now welcome aboard the ship which they had previously only seen from a distance. I was grateful for Con Smit's wise counsel as I worked my way into the new responsibilities. He was just a boy when the Germans invaded The Netherlands, and he survived the terrible famine of 1944-45 called the Hongerwinter by the Dutch. Behind his tough exterior borne from his early life experiences was a kind man who was passionate about our little ship.

Nick Burningham initially took on the onerous and time-consuming task of maintaining a schedule of shipkeepers. We now required people to be aboard 24 hours a day to keep an eye on the mooring lines and to make sure that the ship and her contents were secure. From the day *Duyfken* was launched she was never unattended. We expanded our range of functions with the aim of generating revenue all day and, if possible, all night with school group and corporate sleepovers — any way to 'make a buck'.

Our days headquartered at the WA Maritime Museum were numbered. The shed was completely dismantled, the shop removed (many of the shop fittings eventually went to the *Leeuwin* sail training office) and the office vacated. Within months, new grass was laid and there was nothing to indicate what great things had happened on that unassuming patch of beach sand and limestone. I was approached by Bob Maher, who was the uncrowned 'night club king' of Perth. He created a string of late night venues including Pinocchios, Beethoven's and Gobbles and his latest venture was The Zanzibar in the old Lombardo's building in the Fishing Boat Harbour. The Lombardo's building was part of the redevelopment of an area called Fisherman's Wharf. It was created for the America's Cup defence in 1987. It never quite worked as a multi-restaurant and bar attraction and the Lombardo family sold it to Singaporean investors. Bob was a charmer but he could also be a little intimidating. He and his staff were always dressed in black and he drove a black car with black window tinting. I guess they reminded me of the local gangs in Fremantle during the 1970s: black t-shirts with a pack of cigarettes under the sleeve, black Levis and black ripple-sole desert boots! The Lombardo's building was not suitable to be rented commercially because of its shape and he persuaded the Singaporean owners to agree to our use of the building on a temporary basis at no charge. Less than one month after the launch, the *Duyfken* office and Ship Shop were re-located to Fisherman's Wharf and the ship was moored alongside for her final fit-out. The facility included a reception room and we offered tours of the ship combined with dockside functions. We planned to run all three parts of the operation within one area for the rest of the year. A dockside display including boardwalk reading panels added to the visitor experience and provided customers with greater value-for-money. It was the beginning of an exhibition concept for every port we visited in future years.

Some of the unusable timber from Latvia was given to Bob for his interior decorator to use in The Zanzibar and our tenancy seemed to be a happy arrangement. Bob had another interest in developing a relationship with us. One of his good friends was John Cornell. Born in Kalgoorlie, John performed with Paul Hogan asthe character 'Strop' in their television comedy show. He was one of the people behind World Series Cricket and the Crocodile Dundee movies. Bob and John were working on a new film idea. In 1876, six Irish Fenian prisoners escaped from Fremantle Prison aboard the converted New Bedford whaler, the *Catalpa*. The bold escape made headlines around the world and it became a heroic story of triumph over injustice. The movie needed a replica of the *Catalpa* and he asked us whether we could build it in Fremantle. Of course we could! *Catalpa's* hull would fit in the *Endeavour* shed. Nothing came of the movie concept and our tenancy at Lombardo's building was short-lived. Within months we were asked to move as the owners had found paying tenants. It was frustrating but we found a new office above Cattalini's Chemist in the High Street and I began talking to Henry Laicos and Tony Unmack from

Cicerello's Fish Restaurant about docking the ship at their landing. This angered Victor Kailis who thought that the ship should be at his wharf. We had a fine line to navigate when it came to the competing interests in the little harbour. Tony Unmack spent $30,000 to dredge the lagoon so we could use it but a large lump of limestone which couldn't easily be removed made it a difficult berth. Three days before we were due to leave on the voyage to Indonesia we hit that pesky old lump of reef and we had to lift the ship to repair the slight damage. It was also difficult to attract paying visitors when they could see the ship for free from the restaurant tables.

Michael Kailis celebrated his 70th birthday on 14 February 1999. It was a memorable night of celebration at Kastello with politicians flying in from all over Australia to mingle with the Perth glitterati. The Castellorizians and other members of the Greek community were out in force and it was a Who's Who of Perth business leaders. *Duyfken* was now part of the Kailis success story. Michael's bullish enthusiasm and his ability to push through problems had delivered an excellent ship and I had every expectation that his dreams for *Duyfken* would be fulfilled. Sadly, behind the happy exterior he showed that night, he was battling a serious illness.

Duyfken never had a suitable wharf in her home port. Clearly, the ship needed a permanent berth after her voyaging was over. The new harbour development beside the Maritime Museum which was under construction at Victoria Quay was in the distant 'Stage 2' of the Project. Even in 1999, it was doubtful whether it would ever be funded. A permanent berth had not been allocated to *Duyfken* in the final plan even though Premier Richard Court showed a lot of initial interest. The new Museum should have included an all-weather marina, wooden and historic boat building facilities and space for visiting vessels such as ocean-going yachts and sailing ships but it never happened.

The blistering summer sun and heat were causing us some problems aboard the ship. The oak from the frozen forests of Latvia had been gently ageing in the covered shipyard but now it was fully exposed to the elements. There was cracking beyond the normal level of shrinkage we expected from European Oak. The deck was also beginning to leak. The issue of the deck timber had been one of the few things which had caused Bill Leonard to get into a heated verbal disagreement with Noel. The low-grade timber we used was donated to the Project and Noel simply went ahead and had it sawn and dried without asking Bill how he wanted it cut. When the timber arrived at the yard, Bill rejected it. Not only was the timber sawn incorrectly but it was also of poor quality. Noel would not hear any criticism of the timber and insisted that Bill use it. The planks began to warp from the day they were installed. After 12 months of daily deck washes and thousands of visitors, the planks began to get furry on the surface, too. On top of that, Noel was persuaded to use modern caulking compound in the deck seams rather than traditional oakum and tar. This method was fine on a modern yacht deck with narrow planks but on a traditional ship with wide planks the rubbery sealant could not stretch enough when the green planks shrank. It was a problem which haunted the ship for years.

One of the pleasures of this time when the hull became a ship was my regular management meetings with Michael Kailis. They usually took the form of a quick chat in his office and then a short stroll down to the boardwalk outside Cicerello's seafood restaurant where we would eat some fish and chips out of paper and then have an ice-cream. I must have put on about 10 kg in weight in a few months while Michael stayed as trim as ever. I don't know how he did it. Our chats often turned to the need for a permanent home for the ship and ways of reducing the heavy future maintenance costs. In Fremantle's post-America's Cup malaise, harbour properties were regularly offered for sale. The Fremantle Crocodile Park was adjacent to our mooring at Lombardo's. It had been a grand idea by Wyndham crocodile farmer, Don Wieringa, to breed and show crocodiles to the public in one of the America's Cup sheds. The park was not successful and the harbour lease and building were for sale for about $650,000. It was right next door to Fremantle Boatlifters which Michael also owned. We talked about buying the building and creating a floating dock inside. *Duyfken* would be out of the weather. We envisaged the interior decorated as a sixteenth century Dutch or Indonesian port with bars, restaurants and shipbuilding displays. The end of the building would be openable so *Duyfken* could sail out whenever needed. We were inspired in part by the Manitoba Museum in Canada which had a replica of the Hudson Bay Company ship *Nonsuch* dry-docked in a gallery surrounded by a set mimicking the London Docks. It was a brilliant concept and with *Duyfken* afloat rather than static we were sure it could work. We would be able to create income from the attraction to pay for the long term maintenance of the ship. Michael was a hard negotiator. In principle, he wasn't going to pay the asking price. He thought that Fremantle Fishing Boat Harbour was struggling with commercial tenancies. As he was the only potential buyer he could afford to hang out for a good price. His initial low offer to begin discussions was rejected outright and he decided to play the waiting game. Circumstances in the ensuing year scuttled this idea. Some time later, the Sail & Anchor brewers, Peter Nolin and Bill Hoedemaker, came to us with a similar idea for the *Endeavour* shed but it was not adequately funded and it did not have the grand scope of our ambitious development at the Crocodile Park. Today, the Crocodile Park is the micro-brewery Little Creatures and the *Endeavour* shed has government offices in it.

Our more immediate problem was that we didn't have enough timber to complete the ship. *Duyfken* did not have crows nests on its masts like larger ships but some cross pieces called cross-trees and trestle-trees. The last shipment of timber from Latvia had some timber selected for these structures but it proved unusable. We had to source more oak from eastern Australia to complete the job. I was exasperated to find that substantial parts of the ship still to be completed were unfunded. There was still a lot of work to do. Four shipwrights were needed to complete the hull. Nick Trulove built the Captain's cabin bulkhead and door using laminates of timber because we simply ran out of oak planks. Windlass hawser pipes had to be made in sections rather than from a single piece. Bill Leonard battled to fill and repair new cracks caused by the hull timber shrinkage. Jenny Scrayen finished carving the Lion of Amsterdam for the beakhead, as well as the door frame and the colonnades leading into the hutch. Meanwhile, lots of other detail work was being done. Hatch covers meeting modern regulations were made. Another volunteer, Rupert Weller, set about constructing a ship's lantern to be placed above the stern. The biggest challenge was making the lantern's translucent panes. Con Smit visited the abattoirs south of Fremantle and wangled donations of cow horn. Rupert cut them into slices and boiled them for a week until they were soft and he could flatten them out. The black outer layer of the horn was scraped off the sheets to make them translucent. The final lantern was an absolute masterpiece.

Duyfken's sail loft was in A-Shed on Victoria Quay. Igor was in charge of a small team: sailmakers Rick Mitchell and Andrea Cicholas along with the rigger Gavin Reid. *Duyfken* has three masts. The main lower mast extends 15 metres from its heel to where the topmast adds another seven metres to the total height. The foremast, again in two parts, is slightly shorter and the mizzenmast shorter again with no topmast. The main and foremasts each carry two square sails, the course and topsail, while the mizzen carries a single, lateen sail. There is also a spritsail set on the bowsprit.

We were intent on creating a rig using authentic materials. *Duyfken*'s standing rigging (the ropes which hold the masts in place) was made using tarred hemp rope, rather than a more modern substitute such as manila fibre, with more Stockholm tar applied after the rigging was complete. The hemp rope was sourced from a Dutch company, Touwfabriek Langman, in Nijkerk which has been making rope since 1638. It was owned by the Langman family for more than a century. The hemp rope proved popular with the crew as it was soft to the touch. We also opted for authenticity over a modern substitute for the sails. Rather than more durable Duradon polyester sails, hundreds of metres of flax canvas was purchased from the British Millerain Company in Rochdale, England to make the sails. It was made 76 cm wide just as the sails were from the seventeenth century but with anti-rot and waterproofing chemicals added (which proved ineffective).

I was impatient to see the ship finished and under sail. I regularly dropped in to see how Igor and his team were progressing. Every sail was hand-stitched. It was an incredibly slow process and I couldn't speed them up. Igor was always non-committal on when the rig and sails would be competed. At times I felt like the Pope asking Michelangelo when the ceiling of the Sistine Chapel would be finished. Igor had the power in his hands. Once the rig and sails were completed, there was a month of frantic activity for the rigging team getting masts, spars, standing and running rigging ready for *Duyfken*'s planned sea trials.

The ship did not yet have some of the basics such as anchors. The Kailis yard had a heap of anchors and we could take our pick but we wanted period correct examples on our ship. Nick Burningham did not have to go far to research an accurate design. One of the things which last longest on shipwrecks are the anchors. The WA coast had a lot of Dutch shipwrecks — and a lot of anchors. He scaled down the enormous anchors discovered at the *Batavia* shipwreck site. Lawrence Bielken, an amateur blacksmith from South Fremantle, put a team together and they struck the anchor flukes, arms and shanks at the Shire of Kalamunda's forge at Forrestfield. With the two anchors weighing 175 kg and 240 kg, it was an enormous challenge to forge the arms to the shank. Each anchor required perfect forge welds on all the joins and an experienced German blacksmith came to Fremantle from Esperance to complete the fabrication before final finishing was completed by a voluntary blacksmithing group.

The shipwreck galleries at the WA Maritime Museum have expertly conserved paraphernalia from shipboard life which was recovered from Dutch wrecks. We wanted the experience of stepping aboard *Duyfken* to be similar to stepping aboard the ship in 1606. Community craft groups were approached by my brother Rodney to try fabricating the day-to-day items used by the crew. Timber was supplied to the Wandi and Melville woodturning groups to make the wooden bowls and other small items such as wooden spoons. Bob Malacari made stave tankards. George Walker helped with the carving. Gerald Young made large sea chests for food storage. Every week something new turned up at the ship, including Bellarmine jugs made in Geraldton. Metalwork students from Safety Bay High School made spoons and cannon balls.

In the quest for authenticity we wanted to have guns (cannon) aboard but we were concerned that having 12 guns on the deck would make the ship too unstable. *HMS Victory* in Portsmouth has fibreglass guns which look fine until you give them a tap and realise they are hollow. I thought we could make ours from aluminium so at least they had a metallic ring to them. Allan Vaughan from Casting Supplies Foundry in East Fremantle agreed to cast the gun barrels using scrap from chopped-up old cray boat hulls. We decided that we would make one bronze gun just in case we ever thought of firing it. I soon went off this idea as the *Little Dove,* a ship of peace and reconciliation, should not blast off a cannon shot when it arrives in port. It was altogether the wrong image and we were told that an unsupervised teenager had lost his arm when firing a swivel gun on the *Bounty* replica. We had the casting patterns for the guns made by a young pattern maker from the Czech Republic, Jiri Zmitko. He worked as an engineering pattern maker and a puppet carver in his home country before migrating to Western Australia. He worked for Mike Rowe, who made the cannon trucks in C-Shed, after he finished work on the masts. My brother, Rodney, also made patterns for the small 'murderer' swivel guns which were attached to the poop rail. The *Little Dove* must have been a fearsome hawk when she was in battle mode.

While our small team was working as hard as ever to complete the ship as an early seventeenth century vessel, plans were also taking shape to gain a marine survey so she could operate in the modern world. When I contacted the Australian Maritime Safety Authority (the Commonwealth Government's organisation in charge of administering international shipping regulations) they were dismayed that nobody contacted them during the years it took to fabricate the hull. As soon as we had one paying customer aboard, *Duyfken* became a commercial vessel. They weren't able to certify the vessel as the hull had not been inspected during the construction phase. The issue went all the way to head office in Canberra to be resolved but AMSA was reluctant to certify our vessel under its jurisdiction for any type of international commercial activities. The State Government Department of Transport, however, agreed to work with us to obtain 2D certification under the Uniform Shipping Laws code which guided the design and construction and then the operation of commercial vessels in Australian waters. This classification meant that we could take 12 passengers in local waters. A helpful naval architect working at the Department of Transport, Frank Jarosek, was assigned to take us through the certification process. We soon knew that we'd require a lot of work to be done by Ken McAlpine and Nick Burningham to meet the 2D regulations. The ship required two heads (toilets) and showers, a galley, generator, pumps, life rafts and safety gear, fire detectors and a long list of other items — and of course, engines.

Once the need for engines was agreed, just how the power was to be transmitted to the propellors was discussed at length. There were several options. Michael Kailis had been open to any ideas but he favoured simplicity using traditional solid shafts connecting the props to the engines. It was hardly new technology and there was concern over the modifications we'd have to do to the hull to retrofit the stern tubes. We were encouraged by the technocrats to fit a hydraulic system with a powerful motor driving a hydraulic pump connecting to pods outside the hull. These pods would hold bronze propellors which were driven by the hydraulic pump. The pods could be moved to any angle making it easy to berth the vessel. They were bolted to the hull and hydraulic lines were all that would breach the hull. It was an expensive option but it sounded quite clever. We went a long way down this design path before abandoning the idea. The replica of John Cabot's caravel, *Matthew*, built at Bristol in the United Kingdom had problems with similar technology and replaced it. The hydraulics caused uncomfortable vibration in the wooden hull and excruciating noise. We decided to go for the tried and trusted old-school technology, which was cheap, instead.

Safety regulations required the ship to have sealable bulkheads so that the hull was divided into watertight compartments. There was, however, no way we would compromise the historic integrity of the ship below decks. We wanted visitors to experience an authentic environment. According to modern regulations, the coaming on the hatches was also too low. The ship could be swamped if large quantities of water weighing many tons flooded the deck above the level of the coaming and it breached the hatch covers. Because of our small size, we were given an exemption on the bulkheads but not the height of the coaming. Rather than compromising the design of the deck, we opted for large aluminium hatch covers shaped like a large box. They gave a coaming which complied with the regulations applying to the freeing ports (which on *Duyfken* were the gun ports: the windows on deck which were opened for the cannon to fire) and the scuppers. The hatch covers could be installed for use at sea and then taken off when the ship was in port and the ship was placed on exhibition. They were ugly and bulky, but a practical solution to the problem.

With the ship moored at Fremantle Fishing Boat Harbour and the specialist team working on the final details of the fit out, Bill Leonard took a break before heading back to his position at the Maritime Museum. The *Duyfken* Project owed a debt of gratitude to the unassuming Scot. At his departure from the Project, it was left to Nick Trulove, his loyal second-in-charge, to pay tribute to the man who had harnessed the team of tradespeople to build the ship. "I still feel that Bill Leonard was the vital factor in the excellent development of our ship," he said. "Bill's cheery enthusiasm, determination and vision, as well as his never-ending encouragement, were always there to help all of us in the Project. Without Bill, I'm sure the standard of excellence for which Fremantle is now admired worldwide could not have been achieved. Bill Leonard is so talented in so many aspects of shipbuilding, and he has the energy and skills to make the dream a reality." Bill is probably the only Master Shipwright in the world who has constructed both an eighteenth century pre-industrial revolution ship (*Endeavour*) and an early seventeenth century 'Age of Discovery' ship (*Duyfken*). Both are masterful examples of the shipbuilder's craft.

Michael Kailis was not well. His illness returned more strongly than before and it was taking its toll. He was admitted to Sir Charles Gairdner Hospital for treatment in March 1999. He made a special effort to accompany Julius Tahija on Wednesday 19 May at Fremantle Boatlifters to step the masts. Placing coins under the masts of a ship was a tradition which went back to Roman times and ensured that the ship and crew were blessed with good luck on their journeys. After stepping the masts, the standing rigging which held the masts up could be attached and then the running rigging which held the yards and the sails could be hung. There was then nothing to stop us taking her to sea for the first time.

Julius was to place an Indonesian coin under the foremast and Michael to place an Australian coin under the mainmast. The Australian Minister for Finance, John Fahey, was planning to visit the ship later in the morning and then to have lunch with the dignitaries. Igor Bjorksten and his team lined the step into which the heel of the mast was inserted with pitch so water would not sit in the hole and rot the timber. The coins had to be gently placed in the black gunk. Michael and Julius both had trouble getting below to lay their respective coins. Sadly, Michael was so sick that he could not lean down to place the coin himself and he handed it to his Executive Assistant, Kathryn Cartwright, and asked her to place it on the heel for him. It was a telling moment but we thought nothing of it at the time. Michael always bounced back. Nothing could keep him down for long.

It was to be Michael's last symbolic contribution to the ship. *Duyfken* was now only six weeks from her first sail scheduled for 10 July 1999. His health deteriorated rapidly in the following weeks and it got to the point that his wife Patricia suggested that I should visit him at Sir Charles Gairdner Hospital. He had lost a lot of the spark I so admired. We talked about the ship for a few minutes. We always talked about the ship. He was getting tired and then he said: "Look after our little ship for me, won't ya?" I nodded, and I remember walking alone down the long, empty hall in the hospital as I left for the last time.

Michael George Kailis AM CBE passed away on Friday 25 June 1999. *Duyfken* was sitting majestically in Fremantle Fishing Boat Harbour, the standing rigging transforming our hull into a ship and the final fit-out almost complete. Ken Palmer, Michael's second in charge at the MG Kailis Group, asked me to come down to his office that day. The few staff who were there made no noise and the lights seemed dimmer than usual. Ken and I met in his office. He wished to make it clear that it was Michael's intention that the MG Kailis Engineering Department would continue to work with me to complete the 20th century fit out of the ship and that the MG Kailis Group would cover the costs and continue to support the Project. This was Michael's wish. He said that the repayment of the expenditure would be a discussion to be had in the future but Michael wanted to see the ship completed and for it to undertake the voyages we had planned. He emphasised that the Kailis family would support me to get the job done.

In Fremantle Fishing Boat Harbour, only metres from Michael's office, on Tuesday 29 June 1999, *Duyfken*'s magnificent new flags fluttered at half mast. Many hundreds of people from all walks of life, from fishermen to heads of government, arrived at the Greek Orthodox Cathedral in Northbridge. Mourners spilled out into the surrounding streets. Michael was laid to rest.

Chapter 11

Tragedy and Triumph

When the Little Dove's *sails feel the wind,*
And the ocean moves beneath her keel for the first time,
We know that you'll be watching over us,
Duyfken *will always sail with your dreams and inspiration*
(Memorial Notice from the Duyfken 1606 Replica Foundation, June 1999)

Duyfken sailed for the first time on Saturday 10 July 1999. If only Michael Kailis had survived another 11 days he would have seen the fulfilment of his dream.

Outwardly we were oozing optimism, but inwardly we were filled with trepidation. We'd be relying on Ken McAlpine's stability calculations to be comfortable that the ship wouldn't tip over. "We don't know for sure how this Dutch jacht will sail," I said when asked the obvious question by a journalist. "This will be the first time in 350 years that a Dutch ship of this kind has sailed in the Indian Ocean, or any ocean, for that matter. The first sail of the 24 metre oak replica will be the ultimate test of the experimental archaeology applied to the construction of the ship." Yes, I was nervous.

The first sail of *Duyfken* had none of the jubilation associated with the launch. The mood was solemn. The Greek tradition of 40 days of mourning was being observed by the Greek community, the Kailis family and friends. Patricia Kailis was keen for us to go ahead with our plans, saying that Michael, the shipbuilder, would have approved. Maybe he was keeping an eye on us anyway.

The ship, however, had lost perhaps her greatest champion. While Michael Young created the *Duyfken* dream, it was Michael Kailis who had the skills and bullish drive necessary to get the ship built. Behind the scenes,

Sir James was asked and agreed to take over as Chairman of the *Duyfken* Foundation whilst a replacement was found. It was unnecessary to find a leader immediately. We all knew what we had to do.

Firstly, we had to obtain approval to sail our engineless craft in Gage Roads without a tether. Frank Jarosek inspected *Duyfken* during the afternoon before the first sail and gave us clearance to be towed out of the harbour by two tugs before being set free. With one day to go, Nick Trulove and his team affixed the Lion of Orange figurehead carved by Jenny Scrayen and her assistants to the beak of the ship. It was the final finishing touch and it looked magnificent. Igor Bjorksten tested the sails and the rig while the ship was tied up at the wharf. The ship strained at the lines as puffs of wind filled the sails and there was no question that she was itching to be set free. I called a staff meeting in the late afternoon on the eve of the first sail to run through our sailing plan. We appointed the Chief Executive of the *Leeuwin* Sail Training Foundation, Captain Greg Tonnison, to be Ship's Master for the momentous first voyage. The crew was a mix of our shipbuilding team and Fremantle's best square rig sailors who'd sailed aboard *Leeuwin* and *Endeavour*. Everyone was aware of the importance of the first sail. The world would be watching.

Pictures of ships of *Duyfken*'s era invariably show them dressed with flags and pennants flying from every conceivable place during ceremonial departures or arrival celebrations. We were inspired by the famous painting by Hendrick Cornelisz Vroom of the return of the second fleet to the Indies in 1599. The first *Duyfken* (renamed the *Overijssel*) is fully-dressed and resplendent in the right of this painting now at the Rijksmuseum in Amsterdam. What a sight it must have been. The owner of Perth flag maker Pennant House, Stewart van Raalte, offered to make us a wardrobe of flags appropriate for the significance of our day. With a name like van Raalte, I thought he'd be a shoe-in to help. It turned out that his grandfather, Henri van Raalte, who brought the name to Australia, was a Londoner and not Dutch at all. Never mind, Stewart was a walking treasure trove of vexillology, the science of flags: how to make them, protocol, geography and history. He researched and designed a full wardrobe of flags for the ship. The flags used in The Netherlands at the turn of the seventeenth century used the colours of the national tricolour which was thought to have been adopted in 1579 when the Dutch were revolting against the Spaniards under the Prince of Orange. Originally the flag was orange, white and blue, the livery colours of the House of Orange. About 1630, the orange band was replaced by one in red which was more recognisable at sea. The blue was quite light originally so it was changed to a dark blue (subsequently replaced by cobalt blue in 1937). The Dutch flag was defaced (as the vexillologists say) with the company logo of the United Dutch East India Company or VOC. It was magnificent: it had a three metre hoist and measured six metres long. In a departure from contemporary practise, *Duyfken* flew the Dutch flag at the stern in port rather than the Australian flag because, in the words of Rear-Admiral Phillip G N Kennedy AO, RAN Retd, whom we consulted: "In such cases we believe history overcomes protocol." But the Australian red ensign was flown at sea. Four small swallow-tailed pennants with a 75 cm hoist and two long tricolour pennants with the same hoist but about five metres long completed the magnificent array of decoration for the first sail. These flags hung from the ends of the yards like enormous streamers or kites.

Duyfken was tied up at the MG Kailis Wharf southern extension jetty. Hundreds of people deserved to be aboard for her first sale but we had to limit our numbers. The Friends of the *Duyfken* and our volunteers packed two ferries hired for the occasion. Our conservative plan was for the ship to be towed into Gage Roads and then to be carefully prepared for sailing. Greg Tonnison had other ideas. We left the dock right on time. There was only a light breeze and little swell. He asked Igor and his crew to set the fore course immediately and directed the stern towline to drop away. *Duyfken* was under sail and she had not yet left the harbour! As soon as she was clear of the harbour entrance he cast off the bow towline, too, then set the main course and mizzen and, without further ado, *Duyfken* simply sailed. Igor and Greg had a brief, affirming chat with a nod and smile as the ship passed South Mole at the main harbour entrance. Yep, more sail! The main and fore top sail were also hoisted and our marvellous, beautiful, wondrous ship was away. My first thought was: "please don't roll over now" but it was soon replaced with a deep feeling of satisfaction.

Reflecting on the audacious decision years later, Greg Tonnison said: "We had Igor onboard with a good team of people, so I felt confident to get her sailing as soon as possible. It was like venturing into the unknown — we had no idea how she would sail and how accurate the replica was. We were all very eager to get those sails up and see if we could get this 400 year old design going. To our surprise she sailed like a dream! The other surprise was she could sail very close to the wind for an old design, although it was flat water. I believe history tells us that these vessels were the smaller more manoeuvrable scout vessels so could point much higher than the much larger vessels. And, history was proven by the *Duyfken* replica that day!"

The public crammed every vantage point on North and South Mole to catch a glimpse of *Duyfken* under sail for the first time. Our volunteers and supporters were close by in the ferries cheering their lungs out. A helicopter was buzzing overhead, light aircraft circled the informal fleet. Dozens of spectator craft of every description jostled in the foaming sea to get a better look. The rich honey coloured oak gleamed with fresh varnish. The creamy white of the sails reflected the occasional patches of sun through the overcast day.

The ship's crew comprised 18 staff of the *Duyfken* Foundation who had helped build the ship, and representatives of the Friends of the *Duyfken*, *Duyfken* volunteer guides, ship-keepers and several of the team from the *Duyfken* souvenir shop. Included in the crew was Mark Payne from the mining town of Weipa in Queensland's Gulf of Carpentaria near where *Duyfken*'s crew came ashore 393 years before. Mark was hoping to sail on the 2000 *Duyfken* Expedition and he represented the people of Queensland on that first sail. Special VIP guests were onboard including Western Australian Premier Richard Court and representatives from BankWest who agreed to help us out with sponsorship of the first sail, providing some more much-needed funds to help complete the ship.

The first sail had special meaning for everyone knowing that Michael Kailis would have loved to have been there with us. Patricia Kailis had a wreath of olive leaves and when the ship was moving gracefully through the water and the spectator craft had moved away, she tossed it into the sea. We paused for a few minutes to think about Michael's loss and the years of work which had got us to this point. Patricia was stoic, and she put on a brave face, but she was shattered.

The day also had its lighter moments with the Premier Richard Court being handed a line by Igor and cheekily told to help pull the yards up the mainmast. A yachtsman at heart, the Premier took the line without hesitation and gave it a good heave.

For Bill Leonard and his team, it was also a very satisfying morning. "There was a solid group of people who built the ship and we were incredibly proud of our achievement that day," he said. "It is always wonderful to see the happiness the ship gave to other people." It was a time of reflection for him, too. "We'd overcome a lot of problems and I thought that our difficulties with staff and materials were just the same as those of the seventeenth century shipwrights who built the original ship. Nothing much had changed in 400 years."

Nick Burningham took detailed measurements of *Duyfken*'s performance on that first day and then again on another two test sails in the following weeks. We were keen to get some data on how she performed compared with the original *Duyfken* before the modern equipment such as the motors were installed and propellors would influence the flow along the hull. The data also was essential for us to plan the re-enactment voyage and the final fit-out for survey. In an eight to 12 knot breeze, the ship made four knots, and six or seven knots in more favourable conditions. *Duyfken* was able to make about 70° to the wind. All in all, she was a very able, fast and seaworthy vessel. I'm sure Willem Jansz would have been happy to take command of such a fine ship.

The Engineering Department of the MG Kailis Group had been working with a sense of urgency to plan and implement the fit-out. Retrofitting the engines was a challenge. Normally, the ship would be designed around the engines, but *Duyfken* would have to be modified to take the engines and the stern tubes. The job was made a little easier as Bill Leonard had quietly placed extra timber mounts in the stern during construction to allow for the addition of engines. The work was scheduled to take place during the winter when the trawling fleet returned to the northern fishing grounds after refit and the yard wasn't so busy. It was critical for us to have everything on hand once the ship was out of the water. Delays would be costly. There were no new Hino marine engines available locally, so on the day before Michael passed away, Kailis engineer Brad Gillam had arranged for two 82 kw Hino marine engines to be taken off the production line in Yokohama, Japan and sent to Australia. Hino supplied all the diesel engines to power the refrigeration units on the Kailis trawlers so the Kailis team was well acquainted with installing them. It would save time and money. Through my contacts at Qantas, they were air-freighted directly to Perth — a total of 440 kg of air-freight as a contribution to the Foundation. The ship was lifted out of the water on 10 August. Terry Hewitt and his team had a comprehensive work plan to transform the ship into a 2D surveyed vessel. Nick Burningham, Ken McAlpine and the Engineering team designed a permanent installation of the modern equipment which required minimal changes to the fabric of the vessel. Time is money, and there would be no stopping once the ship was out of the water at Fremantle Boatlifters. The ship was slipped on 10 August 1999 and then returned to the water on 4 September. The team went hard at it for seven days a week to get the job done. They were on a mission, and the work had to be signed off in less than four weeks.

Normally, the stern tubes were installed in the hull as the ship was under construction (stern tubes encase the shafts which transfer the rotation from the engine to the propellors at the stern) and they were integral to the hull. Nick Trulove had the difficult task of retrofitting stern tubes. It required great precision to drill at an angle from inside the hull to reach a specific point outside the hull. It was a revelation that Nick did it with such precision — a highly skilled effort. He also learnt that plank first construction meant that the two sides of the hull were not exactly the same. All the measuring had to be done twice.

Meeting modern stability requirements was key to obtaining a survey. Marine architect, Ken McAlpine, and his team used drums filled with 220 litres of water which were positioned across the deck in different places to obtain raw data. Under Australian shipping standards of the time, *Duyfken* was fine in smooth water. She had to be self-righting at 70° and she could self right at 66°. In open water, that extended to 90°. The preliminary estimates of *Duyfken's* stability were now able to be calculated:

Smooth water	70° required
	66° *Duyfken*
Open water	90° required
	66° *Duyfken*

An extra seven tonnes of lead was later used for the steel encased lead shoe which was placed under the hull to meet the regulations. The ship required 11 tonnes of ballast overall to meet this regulation. The result, however, was that *Duyfken* was said to feel 'over-ballasted' and extremely 'stiff' compared to a ship of the sixteenth century which historians believe would have tended to roll more smoothly in big seas. It is thought that the original *Duyfken* would have been more comfortable to sail in heavy seas. However, as with many aspects of the replica, there are many different views. Gary Wilson who sailed the ship on many of her great voyages had a different perspective: "Yes, she rolled heavily at times, especially downwind, but this tends to be a factor in all square riggers," he said. "*Duyfken* doesn't have the staysails (triangular sails rigged along the centre line of a ship) which can be sheeted flat to help mitigate the roll a little." It became a talking point which was debated for many years.

While the ship was out of the water, a template was made for the shoe to be fitted along the keel. Ken McAlpine speculated that if the ship had been only half a metre wider in the waist then it would not have been required. Lead was melted in large crucibles and poured inside the shoe to a depth of 150mm, then the shoe was offered up and bolted along the length of the keel. A sacrificial keel of jarrah was attached underneath the false keel to prevent minor damage should the ship run aground. Meanwhile, inside the hull, fuel tanks were fitted and then the engines and gearboxes installed. A bewildering array of equipment was then added in under four weeks: showers, toilets, fridge, hot water system, a desalination plant, generator, an electrical system, bilge pumps, strainers, grey and fresh water tanks. Over 1,000 hours of work was required to complete the ship so she could be placed back in the water. The *Duyfken* Foundation now had ship to survey and a debt of $270,000 to the MG Kailis Group.

Rubbing down the whole ship, varnishing and painting it was a tortuous episode. We applied for funds from the Commonwealth Government's Work for the Dole scheme. The funding enabled us to employ Michael 'Barney' Barnett to supervise the participants in the scheme and to teach them the fundamentals required to get the job done. Under the scheme, we had workers at the ship every day. A great result, or so we thought. The Kailis yard provided pontoons to be tied up alongside for the painters. Some days we'd have four or five people, some days none. Barney had to ring them to get them out of bed. He compiled an amusing list of sometimes bizarre excuses they gave for not turning up. To be fair, several of the young people were great and loved the work environment but these more driven individuals soon got paying jobs and moved on. We were constantly stuck with the unmotivated ones who had an array of difficult personal problems. It was very frustrating. One day I came down to the ship and Barney was above deck sanding an area for varnishing. This meant that he didn't have enough workers and he was doing the work himself rather than supervising others. This always made me cranky. I looked over the side and there was a big guy we called 'The Bear' tucked up asleep on a pontoon. I said to Barney: "Come on! He should be working!" Barney whispered to me quietly: "Ssh. Don't prod The Bear. He gets very angry when he is woken up."

The Work for the Dole participants also helped with one of the dirtiest jobs. *Duyfken* had ballast secured in the bilge of the hull but the original ship would have been ballasted with cargo in the hold. In the shipwrecks along the coast, mounds of ballast bricks were a sign that a Dutch ship may have come to grief in the vicinity. The clay bricks were loaded in The Netherlands to be used in civic buildings in the East Indies. The ships returned to Europe with cargoes of spice. I had the scathingly brilliant idea that we could line the hold with a layer of ballast bricks from the *Batavia* as a kind of false floor. I got the idea from the display in the *Batavia* Gallery at the Maritime Museum. So I approached Graeme Henderson with the idea. I knew that they had a pile of them on pallets behind the Museum and they didn't really have any use for so many bricks. I thought we could have authentic, original ballast bricks on the ship making a nice link with the past. Graeme, to his credit, liked the idea but under the State Shipwrecks Act they were the property of the Museum and they couldn't easily be given away. I was annoyed. For years, people had come into the shipyard telling us that they had a few ballast bricks at home which they had found washed up along the beaches of the Abrolhos Islands. They'd grabbed them as souvenirs. I asked Graeme whether we could just have one brick and he said no. Oh well, we'd have to make our own replica bricks for our replica ship. When I asked the brickworks in Perth whether they could produce some bricks for me of the old size common in The Netherlands, they asked me how many hundred thousand I wanted. In the end, we purchased some red-coloured Perth house bricks and rented a brick saw. The Work for the Dole participants had to slice every brick in half to fit to the floor. It was a horribly messy job. The bricks were so perfect and regular that they looked terribly out of place on our rustic ship and I hated them.

In November 1999, engine covers were completed. Nick Burningham sourced some Indonesian baskets of the style still used today across the archipelago to transport goods. They were sliced into squares and glued to the engine covers so that they looked like a stack of cargo. We needed 16 sea chests, one for each crew member living below to stow their personal belongings for the Expedition. I found what I was looking for at the Community Aid Abroad shop in Fremantle. The crude chests made in India were perfect, with hand forged hinges and hasps. There weren't enough in stock in Western Australia so they were hunted down in CAA shops all over Australia to fill our order. We knew that sea chests were often rustically carved by sailors with their name and symbols from home so we gave them to Jenny Scrayen and she got students in her woodcarving classes to take one sea chest each and to carve something from the era which related to their personal cultural background. They came back with some marvellous designs and they aged beautifully on the subsequent expeditions. She also got them to carve linstocks. These are wooden handles which hold the smouldering priming cord (which was soaked in saltpetre) to light the gunpowder when firing cannons. The gunner would light the cord and use the linstock to keep a safe distance from the guns. We were inspired by the ornate linstocks founds on the wreck of the *Mary Rose*. Our linstocks were all carved with different mythical sea creatures. The acclaimed Margaret River winemaker, Bob Cartwright, from Leeuwin Estate Winery donated wine barrels so that the ship's hold looked more original. Unfortunately they didn't have his award-winning chardonnay inside. It was fun fitting out a sixteenth century ship.

Chapter 12

Storm Clouds Over Indonesia

I was sitting in the palatial lobby of my Jakarta hotel waiting for a car arranged for me by Julius Tahija. I was to be collected and taken to his home in South Jakarta. I nonchalantly flipped through the English-language Jakarta Post newspaper. I had no idea who would be coming to collect me, so I kept one eye towards the entrance to see whether I could spot a taxi driver or one of Julius' aides looking for me. I needn't have bothered. A luxurious black Mercedes drove up to the entrance. Julius had sent his own driver and car to collect his Australian visitor. The hustle and bustle in the foyer stopped. Everything went quiet and everyone in the foyer looked around as the driver walked in and spoke to the concierge. Then the concierge quietly walked across to the lounge and told me that my car was waiting. I was sure that every set of eyes in that foyer followed me as I walked to the car. It was at that moment I realised that there was more to the charming Julius Tahija than I appreciated. I was now in his town.

It was a short drive to his home at Jalan Patra Kuningan. As we rounded the corner, the street looked more like an army camp than a residential street in an up-market neighbourhood. "President Habibie!" exclaimed the driver as he saw me peering out of the car looking at the soldiers having a smoke and chatting to each other. They were casually standing around armoured personnel carriers and light tanks which lined both sides of the street.

I was ushered into Julius and Jean Tahija's house and shown to his study. It was a modest home compared with the ostentatious modern houses surrounding it. It looked like a classic colonial residence. Unlike everywhere else I had been in Jakarta, the air-conditioning wasn't turned on and what little breeze there was could flow through the house. It was comfortably cool and dark inside. Julius soon came in and welcomed me with a big smile like an old friend. He invited me to his study where we sat in lounge chairs. He offered me a glass of water and we began to chat.

My mission to meet Julius in Jakarta was precipitated by a letter he'd sent to Michael Kailis expressing his reservations about the wisdom of the re-enactment voyage. It was April 1999 and Michael couldn't travel so I was to be his envoy. My first question was the most obvious: "Why all the tanks in the street?" Julius chuckled and rolled his eyes, grinning slightly. One of his neighbours was Bacharuddin Jusuf (BJ) Habibie, the controversial President of Indonesia. The new President was very concerned about his personal safety, he said with a laugh. It made the quiet street very busy, he said. Ever the diplomat!

I began to outline our voyage plans and Julius listened quietly to what I had to say. Then he responded. I did not really appreciate that we were planning to sail a replica of a Dutch colonial ship to Indonesia during the most volatile period in its recent history. The nation had been ruled with an iron fist by President Suharto for three decades, and every aspect of the daily lives of its citizens was controlled by the Jakarta military/political establishment. Even the toll road I took from Hatta Airport the day before was owned by one of the Suharto siblings. Indonesians looked at the economic miracles of the rest of South East Asia and wondered why their country, with its enormous population and richness, was stumbling along with low economic growth. The cronyism of the Suharto family was one of the root causes of the weak economy. Corruption had been endemic. Then an economic debt crisis swept across the whole of South East Asia and Suharto had no option but to call on the International Monetary Fund to bail out his nation before it went broke. The world was watching in early 1998 as violent protests broke out in Jakarta and many cities across the archipelago. There were fears that the island nation would descend into civil war. As outrage grew over the austerity measures imposed by the government, clashes in Jakarta directed mainly at Chinese businesses cost 1,000 lives. In May 1998, President Suharto resigned and his crony, BJ Habibie, who had been Vice-President for only two months, was appointed to the foremost job in the nation. His presidency marked a transition to more democratic institutions. Under pressure from within and from the international community, he promised to hold the first free and fair elections since 1955. They were due to be held in two months time and it was hoped that they could be conducted without the country descending into chaos.

BJ Habibie was a close family friend of Suharto. A loyal servant of the previous President, he was known for his eccentricity and his ambitious and sometimes bizarre national projects. As an Aeronautical Engineer who received his degree in Germany, he wanted to establish a national aircraft construction industry on the European model. He spent more than US$2 billion on the plan before becoming President. It was clear to the ruling elite that President Habibie would only be an interim leader and he would not be suitable as a long term President of Indonesia. Habibie had a volatile and sometimes erratic personality. The problems of the old Portuguese colony of East Timor, which had been incorporated into Indonesia since independence, was one of the pressing issues for the new President. Unshackled from Suharto, the independence movement in East Timor had grown in strength and the Australian Prime Minister, John Howard, had suggested in a letter to his Indonesian counterpart that a referendum should be held to determine whether the people wanted autonomy from Jakarta. Indonesians were upset by what they saw as interference in their domestic affairs and when the President announced that a referendum would be held in August 1999, Australia was blamed for the troubles and accused of trying to break up the nation. The violence was ongoing. While Julius and I were meeting in Jakarta on Friday 16 April, pro-integration militias supported by the Indonesian military were preparing to 'cleanse' Dili of pro-independence leaders prior to the referendum. The weekend raids resulted in more than 20 dead. It was feared that far worse was to come if the Timorese voted for independence and the Indonesian military did not accept the result.

There was a feeling that Indonesia was teetering on the edge of a precipice. Questions were being asked about the viability of the nation. There were many local conflicts which required strong leadership from Jakarta to control, and often that leadership was found wanting. Some made headlines around the world, largely because of their savagery, whilst others were not reported in any detail. In Borneo, racial conflict between the local Dayaks and transmigration workers from the island of Madura was accompanied by ghastly accounts of head-hunting, mutilation of bodies and cannibalism. Then there was a flare-up between Malays and Madurese with the Dayaks supporting the Malays. Thousands died and perhaps 100,000 people were displaced by the ongoing violence.

In Ambon, the capital of Maluku Province, violence broke out between Muslim and Christian groups. Several hundred people died and the intensity of the clashes was increasing. Christians and Muslims were also fighting at Poso in Sulawesi. There was continuing violence in the province of Aceh in West Sumatra where a hardline Muslim independence movement was very active. In Irian Jaya (West Papua), the Free Papua Movement which had conducted a guerrilla war against the Indonesian Government was energised by President Habibie's referendum in East Timor. I kept a close eye on these events, hoping that things would settle down by the time we sailed to Maluku.

Julius was circumspect about the voyage. He said that the violence was localised and we could avoid the trouble spots. He thought that the voyage should go ahead but he emphasised that it was definitely a bad time to consider *Duyfken* visiting Jakarta. He thought that the symbolism of a Dutch colonial ship sailed by Australians arriving in the old Dutch capital while Indonesia was struggling through this painful period transitioning to a new democratic government sent all the wrong messages. I couldn't disagree. We seemed to have immersed ourselves in the VOC history of the seventeenth century and our ambitious journey, rather than looking at the modern affairs of the country and the lives of its current citizens. The Indonesia through which we planned to sail was not the romanticised tourist paradise of Bali. Julius thought that Singapore would be a better option for us, and then perhaps to visit Melaka in Malaysia because of its VOC significance. After conquering the Portuguese garrison, the Dutch ruled Melaka for 184 years and the trading community prospered under VOC rule. It was a story we could tell. We could then sail through the Indonesian archipelago to Ambon, and on to Banda to begin the re-enactment voyage. Julius told me that a visit to Jakarta would have to wait. Once things had settled down it would be possible, he said, but not now.

Julius Tahija's family came from Ambon and he was enthusiastic about the ship visiting the island. He told me at our meeting in Jakarta that he thought it was important for us to visit the capital of Maluku. Australians and Indonesians fought the Japanese in a bloody battle on the island during the war and hundreds of Australians were massacred by the Japanese after they surrendered. He thought it was essential that *Duyfken*'s visit was used to help recognise the sacrifice of the Australians and Indonesians during the war. He also wanted the ship to visit Saumlaki in the Tanimbar Islands where he defended the islands from Japanese attack. He thought the ship should visit Komodo Island, famous for its large lizards — the Komodo dragons — to help publicise the environmental issues facing the country. I left the meeting feeling that Julius would quietly work away in Jakarta to facilitate the re-enactment voyage. He was determined about the ship being seen as a way of bringing Indonesia and Australia together.

My next appointment in Jakarta was at the Australian Embassy with our Ambassador to Indonesia, John McCarthy. He was one of Australia's 'star' diplomats. He'd been senior private secretary to the Australian Minister for Foreign Affairs, Andrew Peacock, and a rising star through four Ambassadorial posts before landing the plum role of Australian Ambassador in Washington. John Howard then gave him what was seen as the toughest job of all: Ambassador to Indonesia during the nation's political crisis. My interview was arranged via the Cultural Attache, Gregson Edwards, my primary contact. I found John McCarthy to be good listener as I explained the motivation for the voyage and our link to Julius Tahija. The Ambassador visited the Australian and Indonesian war graves in Ambon with Julius. He assured me that the Embassy staff would provide any help they could. Julius Tahija was a great friend of Australia, he said. While we were chatting, I kept getting distracted by the large plate glass windows behind his desk. In particular, there was a single hole in the window about the size of a ten cent piece. Finally, I couldn't help myself and asked him, "What's the story with the hole?" Without emotion, and almost matter-of-factly, he replied that someone had taken a shot at him from somewhere across the street. They had obviously missed. He said that what was more annoying was that someone else had poisoned the ponds in the garden around the Embassy and killed all their ornamental fish. It was a disconcerting reminder that diplomats faced a range of everyday risks quite unlike the average office worker. In 2004, only two days before the third anniversary of the 11 September attacks on New York and Washington, a suicide car bomb was detonated outside the Embassy killing nine people and injuring 150 with the terrorist group Jemaah Islamiyah claiming responsibility. The friendly local security guards at the main entrance, who were a joy to meet when I visited the Embassy, died in the attack (not one person inside the building was killed). The Australian Government subsequently moved the Embassy to a new secure location. At the time, it was the most expensive cluster of buildings ever constructed by Australia overseas.

The dream of a pleasant voyage across the Indonesian archipelago was turning into a nightmare. The more we delved into the history of the region, and the current state of affairs, the more we asked ourselves whether it was correct for us to take *Duyfken* back to places where her history was tied to misunderstanding, oppression, murder and bloodshed. The mere fact that *Duyfken* had been created made a statement about the importance of the events in which she was involved. Sailing the ship to the places where it influenced history also offered a value judgement on the ship's importance to that history, or highlighted the Dutch colonial story. And then there was the recurring civil strife which was plaguing Indonesia and Julius Tahija's reservations which we had to consider.

I flew back to Perth to present a new plan based on Julius' advice and my meetings with the Embassy staff. The *Duyfken* Board listened to my report and debated whether we should just sail directly from Fremantle to Queensland completely avoiding Indonesia. Perhaps this was not the time to take a symbol of colonialism into the fringes of a power struggle. Finally, the Board agreed to support the Expedition because they realised that the constant funding difficulties of the Foundation meant that the opportunity may never arise again. It was a brave, perhaps foolhardy, decision which I completely supported.

Shortly afterwards, I was on a plane to South East Asia again to follow up on Julius Tahija's suggestions. I used my tourism contacts to arrange a meeting with the management of the tourist island of Sentosa in Singapore. I could construct a voyage plan which avoided Jakarta and included Singapore and Malaysia. Melaka used its long Dutch colonial history to promote tourism so it seemed like we could gain some local support. It was close to Singapore, too, making it simpler to sail across Indonesia to the spice islands (Maluku).

My meetings in Singapore were very productive. Sentosa was keen to find new ways to attract visitors and wanted to lay out the red carpet. I was greeted with great enthusiasm and big ideas. The Singapore Convention Centre wanted us to lift the ship and take her from the harbour across Singapore to the Convention Centre for display at a major trade show for two weeks during the visit. No problem they said, telling me that they saw on the news when we did it in Fremantle. We knew how to take the ship overland. Singapore could do it, too. What a spectacle that would be. Fortunately, taking the 100 tonne ship across the roofs of underground car parks put an end to that idea but the authorities at Sentosa Island were still keen for us to visit and offered a $50,000 inducement and a share of visitor and day sail revenue. It could work, if we could obtain similar funds from the Malaysian Government. I hired a driver and headed up the Malayan Peninsula to meet the Head of the Malaccan (Melaka) Tourist Authority.

The colonial quarter of the city was beautifully renovated. The meetings were very positive but cash was simply not available in Malaysia to defray our voyage expenses and I couldn't see that the local community would provide us with enough income across the gangway. Without both sources of funds we could not pay for the extra time required to sail into the Malacca Strait and then backtrack across the Java Sea. Another factor which worried my Board was difficult to overcome. Piracy in the sea lanes between Malaysia and the Indonesian island of Sumatra had become a major problem for international shipping with about 90 attacks in the previous year. 1999 was shaping up to be a new record year for piracy in the region. Raids varied from local villagers using knives and pistols to hold-up vessels and demanding small ransoms, to very organised criminal networks even hijacking and 'disappearing' large ships. Unsupported private yachts were often assaulted and a slow-moving, small wooden vessel like ours would be very vulnerable to the gun-toting, high speed raiders. We would need a military escort of some kind to safely traverse the route. Reluctantly, I had to decline Singapore's generous offer to visit Sentosa. I constructed a clipped itinerary which took us to the Spice Islands by the quickest route directly from Australia, avoiding Java, Singapore and Malaysia altogether.

As voyage planning was underway, it was still not clear whether we'd have enough money to conduct the re-enactment. The fit-out was costing more than my initial budget estimates and I had to call on funds from our overdraft to get the ship finished. The MG Kailis Group was spending hundreds of thousands of dollars installing the modern equipment and at some stage we would have to reimburse the company. Thanks to Michiel van Doorn crunching the figures, I now had a clearer idea of the daily costs of the voyage. The estimates were depressing. We needed a lot more money.

It came through an unlikely source: Peter Jones. An old friend of Sir James Cruthers, Peter Jones was an ex-farmer and State Government Minister under the current Premier Richard Court's father, Sir Charles Court, during the years of the resources boom of the 1970s and 80s. Peter Jones was a renowned backroom negotiator with mining and resources companies and he led the State's strategic push into China when other governments in Australia were still focused on more traditional trading partners. During his career, he held 13 state government ministries, served four years as President of the WA Liberal Party and as a Federal Vice-President for six years. The North West Shelf Gas Project was one of his main portfolio areas and he was known as the architect of the energy industry in Western Australia. He was now enjoying the quiet life as a retired politician but still kept active as the Chairman of the WA Water Authority. Sir James rang and asked me to go and see Peter at his home. I rang him and he cheerfully invited me over for a cuppa. I soon put two and two together. We received sponsorship for the launch of *Duyfken* from the Water Authority and here I was speaking to its Chairman who just happened to be one of Sir James' good friends. That's how it works! Peter Jones was a charming man and extremely straight forward. He asked me how much money we needed and he said that he could help me by writing a couple of letters. He thought that Chevron Petroleum should assist with the Project. Chevron, through its associated company WAPET, made the first oil discovery in Australia in the 1950s, coincidentally on North West Cape, where the Master of *Duyfken* charted the coastline some 10 years after the historic Cape York expedition. It was a major partner in the North West Shelf Project with Shell and Woodside. Through Caltex, Chevron was also at the forefront of exploration in the Indonesian archipelago, and in Papua New Guinea, where the company developed the first commercial oil fields. His contacts were at the highest level and he knew Julius Tahija through Chevron, too. He also wrote to Sir Leo Hielscher who was Chairman of the Queensland Treasury Corporation for advice. Sir Leo was one of the heavy hitters in Queensland and his influence straddled both the government and the private sector. Peter Jones was an excellent man to have on our side.

It is no exaggeration to say that the letters he sent worked like magic. Soon our cause was on the desk of the Chief Executive Officer of Chevron Overseas, Peter Robertson, at Chevron head office in San Ramon, California and with the Australian Chief Executive of Chevron Petroleum, John Gass.

From the appropriately named John Gass, the letter was forwarded to Dr John Powell, who was Project Director of a huge development concept called the PNG Gas Project. This was Chevron's plan to build a $2 billion pipeline from the oil and gas rich highlands of Papua New Guinea, down to the coast, and then across the sea bed of Torres Strait to Cape York Peninsula — a 650 km long underwater tube of steel. It would then snake down to supply gas to the industries of northern Queensland with extensions possible to the Northern Territory and even Southern Australia in the long term. The 3,800 km pipeline project was headed by Chevron as the lead investor with other international investors and support from the Queensland Government. The project was certainly ambitious and it would bring great benefits to Papua New Guinea and Queensland if it went ahead. As with all these projects, it got down to how much the gas would cost.

Meanwhile, I think I must have spoken to, presented at, or contacted in one way or another, just about every major company in Queensland. Even though I had used some other excellent introductions, there was no money in Queensland aside from Premier Beattie's support for the voyage. Chevron was our last chance. I received a call from the External Affairs Manager of PNG Gas, Cliff Leggoe, in October 1999. He asked me to come over to Brisbane for a chat so I rearranged some sponsor presentations in Sydney and once again headed across the Nullarbor chasing funds. Sometimes the planets align and you find a person who completely understands what you are doing and why. This was the case in meeting Cliff Leggoe. He was an expatriate son of Perth and he used any opportunity he could to return to his home town. He had a great fondness for WA although Queensland was now his home. We met for breakfast at the Polo Club in Brisbane and we had a long chat about mutual acquaintances. His cousin was the Australia Post Public Relations Manager in Perth, Ian Leggoe, who helped us with a fundraiser using first day covers.

It would have been easy for Cliff to meet with me, write a short memo to say that he couldn't see how the *Duyfken* voyage would benefit Chevron and recommend that a small donation could be made to keep us happy. Compared with some of the other presentations I had made, this would have been a good outcome. However, Cliff Leggoe was not that kind of company man. The PNG Gas Project was a massive, risky venture for a global oil company to take on. It was dealing with a nation which had many levels of corruption and complex political alliances. Chevron was offering a product, gas, which was abundant around the world. There were massive environmental and native title issues to overcome in both countries, customers to be locked away and joint venture partners to be persuaded to invest in the infrastructure. The kind of people who worked on these projects were the ones who didn't want the quiet life in head office. They were motivated individuals and Dr John Powell and Cliff Leggoe led a team of go-getters. For them, getting the Project up was a long-shot but a gamble worth taking. At Chevron, I always got the feeling that the PNG Gas Project team was regarded as slightly crazy and all eccentric outsiders — just our kind of people!

Cliff was very interested in the *Endeavour* replica. His family history connected him to the botanist, Sir Joseph Banks. He dressed up as Banks in several Cooktown festivals over the years and thought all this ship stuff was good fun. When the *Endeavour* replica was in Cooktown he thought it would be good to get Chevron involved with the ship in some way. It had never come about because the HM Bark Endeavour Foundation did not take on sponsors. *Endeavour*'s loss was our gain. If he couldn't get involved with *Endeavour*, then why not *Duyfken*? Being from Perth, he knew all about Dutch maritime explorers but like everyone else, very little about *Duyfken*. Cliff did not let slip at that time that there was a network beavering away behind the scenes to make it all happen, and if the truth be known, the deal had probably already been done. Finally, Cliff asked me how much money I needed. I said $300,000 should do it, and he nodded his head. In classic Sir James Cruthers style, it was agreed that I would put together a sponsorship proposal asking for the exact amount and including the following points as agreed: giving naming rights to the voyage which would now be known as the Chevron *Duyfken* Expedition, and committing to visit Port Moresby and PNG Gas Chevron operations. An exhibition explaining the PNG Gas Project would follow the ship and be erected dockside at every port. The proposal should say that the ship would be used as a mobile meeting and hospitality venue for VIPs in every port, and that it would be linked to community and education opportunities, as well as having an environmental theme. This would be acceptable to his upper management. I left the breakfast thinking that the fundraising task was done. We were off to Indonesia for sure. Many years later, I was shown a letter from Chevron head office in San Ramon. There was a note written on it: "Give the Indonesian **** what he wants." Julius Tahija had come through again.

Michael Kailis was the leader who had kept the *Duyfken* Foundation surging forward like a juggernaut. With his loss, the Project was not exactly rudderless but there was nobody who had his dynamism and ambition for our ship. Michael had been a charismatic leader and Board members went along with just about everything he proposed — most of the big decisions were made by the Executive Committee, anyway. There was also an element of fatigue coming from the Board, particularly the fundraising group. At first the plan was to simply build a ship to be tied up in Fremantle virtually as a floating museum like the ships at the Australian National Maritime Museum in Sydney where most of the exhibits never moved and a few made an occasional foray onto Sydney Harbour. Then Michael Kailis expanded the vision to include a grand re-enactment voyage from The Netherlands to Sydney for the Olympic Games. We spent an enormous amount of energy to plan and get this funded but it was a step too far. Then there was the funds-sapping push to have the ship launched on schedule and the realisation that there had been little planning to make the ship able to be used commercially. The re-enactment voyage morphed into the Chevron 2000 *Duyfken* Expedition combining a voyage to Indonesia and an extensive exhibition tour of Queensland. A re-enactment voyage from The Netherlands was shelved for the time being.

Sir James chaired the first few Board meetings after Michael passed away and Rinze Brandsma, who had been on the Executive Committee for some time, was his deputy. The first Board member to leave was Peter Becu who resigned from the Board in October 1999. He had been seconded to the Iron Ore Company of Canada in Labrador. Syd Corser also resigned the same month. He'd been drawn into the *Duyfken* juggernaut four years before and he thought that with the ship funded and built it was time for new people to carry on with the Project. He regarded *Duyfken* as a management challenge rather than a fundraising job. Sir James shared his view but I think there was another reason, too. It was just not as much fun without Michael. A few weeks later, Patricia Kailis who attended a couple of meetings during the year also resigned from Board membership, citing the pressures of running the MG Kailis Group. *Duyfken* was always Michael's Project and she never had the same passion. Her continued moral support, however, would be vital in the coming years. In November, James Henderson also resigned from the Board. He said that the ship was completed and his book was written. Michael Young had been sidelined from a direct paid role with the Project after the *Duyfken* 1606 Replica Foundation was formed and Noel Robins was appointed to the main role. He was now looking to a future living and working in Indonesia dealing in Ikats and wooden artefacts. He soon asked for leave of absence from the Board. It was granted and Michael's interest in the *Duyfken* Foundation began to wane.

The experienced insurance manager, Graham Reynolds, who was prominent in the *Duyfken* 1606 Club, and Ian Gillon, who helped with the ship's launch, joined the Board briefly. In January 2000, with the ship built and the Expedition funded, Sir James also resigned citing health reasons. However, he also knew that his work was done and it was time for him to move onto other projects. In the years to follow, he became my mentor. I occasionally rang him or visited his home and asked his advice. His clear thinking and amazing contacts around Australia and overseas were always a great help. Despite all the changes at the board level, the Friends of the

Duyfken was as strong as ever and now we had real, live sailors joining our Project. They brought fresh energy and a lot of youthful vigour to the ship.

Rinze Brandsma agreed to chair the new Board which took on a different character. There was no real Executive Committee and all the working committees were eliminated with one Board meeting monthly. The Board was now operated in a more conventional way, receiving my reports, checking finances and leaving me to get on with the Project. It was a massive change. Previously I had implemented the grand plan. Now I was generating the grand plan. I can see today, that was somewhere in this maelstrom of activity to finish the ship, the resignation of Board members and hiring a crew for the Expedition (with input from others) that, for better or worse, the Project began to become a reflection of my own personal vision. Sometimes, I brought a lot of experience to the job. With my tourism industry knowledge, I had a clear view of how the ship would operate in each port as a tourist attraction. As I was the Project Director and Publicist for the voyage, I was adept at controlling the marketing message. On the other hand, there was nobody left on the Board, and I certainly did not have the contacts, to pick up a phone and call State Premiers or business leaders and be granted an audience.

In the last months of 1999, we worked hard to find a long term business model for the ship. We wanted to create a unique product which could work on a 24 hour clock, generating revenue all day and night if possible. During the day, we wanted to create the most interesting display possible with the seventeenth century artefacts onboard and display panels dockside telling the story of the ship. The ship as a floating exhibition was a big positive as it gave a reason for people to visit. I was fascinated by recreating shipboard life and I loved researching all this with Nick Burningham and then commissioning the artefacts. The display worked brilliantly when we were visiting other ports but we were constantly hampered by the lack of a suitable location in Fremantle. The Cicerello's wharf didn't work because it was too open to the public gaze. Eventually, all we could generate from the location was gold coin donations. To have the ship working after hours, we put a lot of energy into setting up a formal dining environment below decks using a table which could be knocked down and stowed. Period crockery and cutlery graced the table. We held a Board meeting aboard in October 1999 to test the product and the hold had a cosy atmosphere with small lanterns providing mood lighting and the constant splashing of water against the hull. We certainly felt it could work. It would soon be time to put our floating museum to the test.

Chapter 13

Cyclones and Sailors

1 January 2000 always had a nice ring about it when we talked about the re-enactment voyage. Yes, there was the millenium bug waiting to attack our computers, but the world was also enchanted by the romantic idea of a fresh start. It would be a good time to begin the voyage and, with the right publicity, we could ensure that the whole world was watching. It seemed to have everything going for it.

It was possible for Captain Willem Jansz and his crew to sail south east towards Australia because he did it during the summer with the prevailing north west monsoon winds. In winter, the south east trade winds made it difficult for a square-rigged sailing ship to make headway from Maluku to Queensland. Yes, if we were to accurately re-enact the voyage of discovery from Banda then it was best to leave at about the same time as the original *Duyfken*. There was one small problem — the cyclone season only gave us a small window during the winter months. It took time to sail north from Fremantle to Indonesia before the re-enactment could begin. The tropical cyclone season in Western Australia runs from November to April. If we were to leave in January then the ship would have an easy run north on the south east trades but sailing towards Indonesia from the Indian Ocean across the Timor Sea would put us in the highest risk area of the cyclone belt.

Our Board member, Graham Reynolds, hailed from the insurance industry and he agreed to negotiate insurance cover for the ship and her voyage. Often issues were inter-related. Many a heroic adventurer who built replica vessels in the past for great re-enactments had a laissez-faire attitude towards risk. They often put all their personal possessions on the line to accomplish the feat and if it was all to fail then they had nothing more left to lose. Their fellow crew members understood the risks and many of them lived with a carefree attitude to life which was at odds with most people's ordinary day to day existence. They didn't mind the risk. If our ship was a private vessel she could be insured but she could not take passengers or receive any commercial income. It went back to our original debate about building the ship as an exercise in experimental archaeology and our initial plans to tow her in and out of harbour when needed. When we decided to use the vessel as more than simply a museum piece to show off on small trips from Fremantle, then it was obvious that she would require some kind of survey. The survey which we pursued over many months of work in 1999 was 2D under the USL Code. This registered *Duyfken* as a 'sheltered waters non-passenger vessel for operations in smooth and partially-smooth waters only.' Under 2D, the vessel was registered to carry 12 berthed passengers and 30 crew for what would effectively be day sails. This enabled us to make some people temporary crew who paid for the privilege. Every little bit helped.

With a survey, we could then obtain insurance cover for the voyage. The original voyage took place during the wet season. As the Australian continent heats over summer, the warm, moist air is drawn south and the South East trade winds reverse. Willem Jansz and his crew were blown to Australia by these monsoonal winds. This weather pattern is, of course, accompanied by the threat of cyclones. Nick Burningham consulted with Sam Cleland from the Bureau of Meteorology in Darwin and he put together a very good paper showing that it would be possible for us to sail north during the summer cyclone season, avoiding the high risk area off the Kimberley coast for all but 300nm. From Banda, the risk was small until the ship reached the Arafura Sea and the Ship's Master would have to be more prudent to avoid any risk. The cyclone season in Queensland could not be avoided but we had options to find safe harbour. In the end, all this cyclone planning came to naught. No insurer would cover a vessel going north of the Tropic of Capricorn during the tropical cyclone season, even with Nick's compelling arguments balancing risk.

If tropical cyclone worries were not enough, the political situation in Indonesia continued to deteriorate and Australia was deeply embroiled in a developing crisis. On 30 August 1999, four out of every five voters in East Timor cast their vote in favour of independence from Indonesia. The fears that it would lead to independence movements across the archipelago and the ultimate disintegration of Indonesia were real. President Habibie, and the Australian Government led by John Howard, were blamed by many elements in the nation for creating the crisis. In Timor, paramilitary groups, often under the command of Indonesian military officers, began to take revenge on the Timorese people, razing villages and towns and causing tens of thousands of people to flee into the mountains to escape the savagery. It is now believed that 2,600 people died in that violence, 30,000 were displaced and 250,000 were moved to West Timor after the ballot. Under massive international pressure, in September 1999 President Habibie announced that the Indonesian military would leave East Timor and an international peace-keeping force from the United Nations led by Australia would restore peace and security to the newly-independent nation.

Clearly, the *Duyfken* Foundation would need yet another plan. Charlie Welker headed the voyage planning group and we spent many nights at his house in South Perth looking at options. It still had all the makings of a grand, but risky, adventure. The Chevron 2000 *Duyfken* Expedition (or expedisi in Bahasa) would leave Fremantle in April 2000, thus ensuring that the ship avoided any possibility of cyclones and the insurance industry was able to provide us with adequate cover. Any thoughts of a shakedown voyage to Shark Bay and return to placate the good burghers of Denham was out of the question. The ship had taken months for the final fit-out to achieve 2D survey and we had a small window to get into Indonesia and then back into Australia before the next round of cyclones. Instead, *Duyfken* would sail from port to port along the West Australian coast at the start of the voyage as the shakedown and then, barring mishaps or hold-ups, leave Australian shores for Indonesia from Broome. I looked at departing Australia from Darwin but I wanted the Northern Territory Chief Minister to pay for our visit and he could not see any value in it. Sorry Darwin, maybe next time. As we were sailing extremely close to the financial wind, our rule had to be: "No Pay. No Visit". Jakarta was also out of the itinerary. Bali was 1,000km to the west of Timor and we concluded the best port to make landfall in Indonesia was Kupang in West Timor. It was only about 880 km almost due north of Broome, and then we had only a short sail of 900 km through the Banda Sea to Ambon in the Maluku Province. Kupang was a controversial choice at that time, but we were assured that it was tranquil. We did not know that while we were discussing the advantages of a Kupang landfall, the city was being ringed by makeshift refugee camps and the volatile security situation was deteriorating.

Ever since Michael Young visited the Maluku Province, to learn more about *Duyfken*, we had all been energised by the romance of the famous Spice Islands. Few ideas took hold of our collective imagination like a Spice Islands voyage. It was history on a grand scale. Ambon was the main trading island for the Dutch. Cloves were harvested from the islands of Ternate, Tidore, Makian and Bacan, and nutmeg and mace from the Banda Islands. *Duyfken* was part of the Dutch East India Company which existed to trade in spices for the European market. The ship departed from the nutmeg island of Banda on her 1606 voyage of discovery. We planned to sail to Ternate where the original *Duyfken* was broken up in 1608 after a battle with the Portuguese. We saw the re-enactment voyage as a fresh opportunity to tell the story of the Dutch spice trade which was rarely studied outside The Netherlands. *Duyfken* would then sail on the original route to the Pennefather River in the Gulf of Carpentaria, and then over the top of Cape York before the next cyclone season. We'd conduct an extensive exhibition tour culminating in a grand arrival up the Brisbane River. With the sponsorship by Chevron approved, we slipped another country into the itinerary. *Duyfken* would also sail to Port Moresby in Papua New Guinea as part of our mission to tell the PNG Gas story.

A ship needs a crew, and her survey and insurance dictated high levels of competency from the senior team. The Australian Maritime Safety Authority advised what qualifications we needed in our crew when we sailed beyond Australian territorial limits. We set our sights not simply on a competent crew, we wanted the best square-rig sailors in Australia. Our national promotional campaign highlighted that this would be no ordinary voyage. It was a voyage of international significance. We sought a hard core team of credentialed professionals: a Ship's Master, a First Mate and a Second Mate/Bosun (both would serve as watch keepers); as well as an Engineer to maintain and operate the 20th century equipment. We also required a Ship's Cook who was prepared to work in woeful conditions in a galley about the size of a small wardrobe. Alongside them would be about a dozen crew including three leading hands with certificates and experience. Finally, a couple of spaces were set aside for a film crew. We wanted crew who could bring other skills to the ship. They did not all necessarily have to be hard-core sailors. We looked for a carpenter, as well as ship's artist and a naturalist — and a mix of youth and experience.

For months I had been in discussions with Firelight Productions, a relatively new Sydney-based production company specialising in documentary films. Firelight had recently completed a four part series called

'Afrika — Cape Town to Cairo' which screened on ABC TV in 1998. It was sold to seven countries including the United States, The Netherlands and the United Kingdom. Firelight had the ability to put together a voyage documentary which could reach an international audience. Firelight was run by partners Marcus Gillezeau and Ellenor Cox. The conditions in Indonesia did not faze them. They'd just returned from shooting a one hour documentary 'Disunity in Diversity' in Indonesia. Marcus was supremely confident about everything. He had all the bravado and swagger of a film maker and the confidence which comes from rising above the pack in the cut-throat Sydney television business. Marcus' persuasiveness got him sales agreements and funding of $400,000 from the Seven Network, ZDF in Germany, AVRO in The Netherlands and Granada Media in the UK. That was topped up by some Government funding. Making documentaries was obviously more expensive than running expeditions! His partner, Ellenor Cox, produced the documentary.

Margaret Papst, a human resources consultant who was a good friend of Patricia Kailis, helped with assessing resumes for the top jobs on board. By July 1999, we thinned the pile of applications down to two people who stood out as possible masters of the vessel: Peter Manthorpe from South Australia and Gary Wilson who was currently working out of Hong Kong. Both were regarded as being amongst the finest square-rig sailors Australia had produced. I was stunned at their depth of experience.

Peter Manthorpe flew into Perth in August 1999 to discuss the challenge of leading a crew on the Expedition. I found him a calm and confident man with a reassuring manner. He was within months of completing a degree in English Literature. I liked that. When I took him down to the ship he almost floated aboard, skipping from place to place, looking at the rig and eyeing the ship from every angle. I could tell he was excited. He said that his love of the sea began when he was only a very small boy and the salt water had been in his veins ever since. He began his seagoing career with the Australian National Line in 1979 and, through experience, training and study, gained his Master Class 1 (Limited) Certificate of Competency in 1986. He said our ship was beautiful. "Thanks Peter, we think so too!"

Peter had experience under sail aboard the *Moongara*, a 10-metre timber sloop in which he travelled over 7000 nautical miles between 1968 and 1998. On what he described as a romantic whim, he sailed on the *Bounty*, a replica of the eighteenth century ship that was made infamous by the mutiny against Captain Bligh. It was his first square-rigged sailing ship. For

15 months in 1987 and 1988 as a part of the Australian Bicentennial First Fleet Re-enactment, he was First Mate. In 1988 be obtained his unlimited Certificate of Competency and he became involved in sail training with the brigantine *One & All* in South Australia. He was hooked on square-rigged sail and served as master on six different sailing ships. He also spent five years in the offshore oil and gas industry.

Peter had sailed the world's oceans and visited every continent in sailing vessels. He also enjoyed working on the repair and maintenance of sailing ships. "When I was on *Bounty* I wondered why the old time sailors' way of thinking was so different from ours," he said. "I realised that they didn't worry about speed. Reliability was paramount. It was most important to get there and this philosophy resulted in some astounding voyages." He struck us as ideal for the job of taking the *Little Dove* to Indonesia. He returned to Fremantle in September 1999 to sign a contract. On 20 January 2000, he arrived back in the West to formally take over the vessel and to begin preparing for the departure.

Gary Wilson was equally qualified to master *Duyfken* on her first expedition. He was the classic Aussie bloke, proud as hell of his home town of Sydney which I always came to disparagingly refer to as the Convict Colony when I spoke to him. He arrived at our first meeting wearing his trademark dark blue work shirt and trousers and a well worn-in brown Akubra hat. He was much taller than I expected of a sailor and when he delivered orders he did it with a clear, deep, commanding voice. He had a presence about him and a terrific sense of humour — but he had no time for slackers.

He was a sailor through and through, going to sea in 1981 and gaining a cadetship with BHP in 1983 where he stayed until 1987. He could proudly list over 50 different ships he had sailed aboard including nine square-rigged sailing vessels, identifying the ship's owner and master, Anthony 'Tiger' Timbs, from the famous brigantine *Eye of the Wind* as one of his heroes. He was one of the few people in modern times, certainly one of the few under 80 years of age, who had rounded Cape Horn under square sail when he did it as a crew member on *Eye of the Wind*. He also served aboard the world's last seagoing paddle steamer, *Waverley*, and the *Endeavour* replica. Like Peter Manthorpe, Gary relished the idea of sailing an early seventeenth century Dutch jacht. He was up for the challenge.

Gary accepted the position as First Mate for the voyage but there was no questioning his ability to command *Duyfken* whenever required. The two men had vastly different personalities. Peter was the sailor philosopher while

Gary was the consummate professional seaman. Both men could handle *Duyfken*. There was no doubt about that. Historians tend to want to study the history and design of ships and the events in which ships and crews were involved. Sailors simply want to sail a ship. In Peter and Gary we were pleased that we had found two people who had diverse interests which formed a bridge between the two.

In the 1950s, the legendary sea captain, Alan Villiers, had a strict policy of no women aboard the *Mayflower II* on the first re-enactment voyage of modern times across the Atlantic. He famously said: "They talk back and you can't handle them. No! No women." Fortunately, we live in slightly more enlightened times. Andrea Cicholas had spent 12 months on square riggers including several ocean crossings and she had a quiet confidence as well as an ability to lead by example when jobs had to get done. She was hand stitching the hammocks for our crew when she applied for the job as Bosun/Second Mate. The bosun organised the day work teams aboard, and as second mate, commanded her own watch. As part of the small team of sailmakers and riggers who finished the vessel in the last 18 months before the Expedition she was a great asset when we were at sea.

Greg O'Byrne was a leading hand on the Expedition. He had been at sea for about a decade working on *One & All*. He was young and confident and aspired to sail *Duyfken* as the last section of his own personal circumnavigation of the continent under sail. Coxswain/leading hand was 'Long' John Colvin (he was tall like Gary) who had been around yachts as a teenager and then progressed to a variety of ocean craft. He was voyage crew aboard *Endeavour* from Fremantle to South Africa and to London a few years before and knew his way around the Australian coast from Fremantle to Queensland. He was a very good sailor, too.

The 19 year old 'pocket dynamo' Nicole Gardner was the youngest and most feisty member of our crew. "It started on the sixth of July, 1988," she said. "Piper Alpha, an oil and gas platform in the North Sea, blew up and 167 men were killed. I was seven years old at the time, happily doing normal seven-year-old things at our family home in Staffordshire. I barely noticed the news, but my parents definitely did: my dad worked on the rigs. After Piper Alpha, he didn't want to go back to the North Sea, so my family moved to Australia."

"Compared to the West Midlands, living near the beach in Western Australia provided never-ending opportunities for a girl to develop a love of the ocean. As I grew older, my Scout troop gave me a chance to learn, explore and try new things. One of those new things was a day-trip on the *STS Leeuwin* in 1995. I discovered that I preferred being at sea to being in the sea. The physical challenges, the teamwork, and the giant rope climbing frame caught me in their web. I found a part-time job, saved my money, and in 1996, I completed a ten-day voyage as a trainee. Volunteering on a ship part-time while completing high school was an interesting balancing act, complicated by my decision to study vessel operations by correspondence on top of my normal studies," said Nicole. She was captivated by the sea and completed 20 voyages on *Leeuwin*. She lived and worked aboard while studying for her tertiary entrance exams in 1997. She had an insatiable desire to learn and become better at everything she did. She wasn't short of an opinion. As we got to know each other, if I ever wanted the honest truth about something, I could rely on Nicole to tell me. She didn't have an off button.

We all agreed that the most difficult job aboard was the Ship's Cook. Cooking three meals a day for 18 people while jammed into a small cupboard required someone with patience and fortitude. Jane Doepel was a physiotherapist from Armidale in New South Wales and she spent time at sea as voyage crew aboard the *Enterprize* replica in Melbourne. She was calm and confident and we didn't want to give her time to change her mind — we signed her up as Ship's Cook immediately! Rupert Weller was appointed ship's carpenter. Born in Geraldton, he'd been a teacher all his life and when he retired he joined as a volunteer at the shipyard where he was willing to take on any task assigned to him. He was extremely competent with a calm, purposeful manner. Michael Hemsley from Geraldton was appointed the Ship's Engineer with experience working on Kailis fishing vessels and fuel barges.

Peter Manthorpe had his first chance as ship's master to conduct sea trials in Gage Roads during early December. The day trips gave him a feel for the speed of the vessel and he began working on the Expedition timing using a daily average of 36nm. He planned an easy voyage north without a great deal of trouble but the biggest problem he saw was working south along the Queensland coast after passing through Torres Strait. He was up against the South East trade winds which blow reliably from April to September and make it difficult sail a square-rig vessel south. He couldn't find a model where we could visit Port Moresby and still make it south before the cyclone season was once again upon us. If we sailed to Port Moresby and lost too much time, then we'd have to remain in Papua New

Guinea until after the following cyclone season. There was so much we wanted to do in the Spice Islands that we could easily have stayed in Indonesia for a year. I loved the idea but I simply couldn't fund such a long voyage straddling two winter seasons. And finally, the Expedition could not begin on a Friday. If Michaeil Kailis was still with us, he would have insisted that *Duyfken* would never start a major voyage on a Friday – it was simply bad luck.

Crew training got underway when the crew began signing on in early February 2000. *Duyfken* was scheduled to depart on the Expedition on 8 April 2000. With six weeks to go before departure, we called the first of many crew meetings. The crew were told about the uncertainties of our passage through Indonesia and some began to doubt whether it was a good idea to be part of this grand, and perhaps foolish, adventure. We put a lot of thought into our crew selection and I had great faith in all my staff and crew but everything about the Expedition was new to us and we really had no idea how it would pan out once we left Fremantle. Outwardly, I exuded confidence but inside I knew that we had only the barest idea of how the ship would perform for months on end and whether the Indonesian part of the voyage could even be achieved during the tropical dry season when we were heading south west against the South East Trades.

My self doubt was constantly being challenged by the crew and sometimes decisions which I saw as minor became a big deal for some of them. One of the younger crew members wanted to wear the garb of a seventeenth century sailor and pushed back hard when I said that he couldn't. He had it in his mind's eye that he was virtually an actor in a period drama. He wanted to live the fantasy of the 'Age of Discovery'. I thought that this Hollywood idea (the 'Pirates of the Caribbean' film series was still two years away) was all wrong for us. It became complicated when Marcus Gillezeau told our crew that they had to prepare to dress like seventeenth century sailors for dramatisations of scenes they wanted to film aboard. The reality of life at sea in the seventeenth century was not something that I wanted the crew to re-live. It was ridiculous to think that by simply dressing like a seventeenth century sailor it would help us understand what they went through. I saw us as modern people recreating a voyage in a professional manner. I could just imagine our crew arriving in an Indonesian port with dirty, smelly clothes hanging off them in tatters like they had just left the set of Les Miserable. Instead, we asked the more experienced what uniform would work best on a ship without modern washing machines. They said that cotton rotted at sea but hemp would last. I approached the Hemp Shop in Fremantle to help and they supplied heavy-duty hemp shorts for our crew. Margaret Rapanaro from our souvenir shop arranged t-shirts and polos in cotton and when we departed Fremantle our crew looked terrific in their casual dark blue gear. The colour helped to hide the blackened tar which got on their clothes whenever they touched the rig.

With the shakedown voyage to Shark Bay off the agenda, we planned a much more modest outing for *Duyfken* in early March, but the weather kept conspiring against us. A very unusual tropical cyclone called Steve created a lot of interest as it travelled across from Queensland to the Northern Territory then down through Western Australia finally petering out in the Great Australian Bight. It was the first cyclone recorded to have had such a long and unusual track. The last thing we wanted was to get caught up in a cyclone. We kept an eye on the weather until it settled down to the usual summer pattern with light easterlies in the morning and fresh afternoon sea breezes. Apart from day sails, the ship still hadn't ventured far from her Fremantle home so we thought it was time to test her and the new crew in ocean conditions. We thought a short sail in the late afternoon to Rottnest Island, setting the anchors in Thompson Bay for the night, then an early start the next day out into the Indian Ocean beyond Rottnest would try them out.

It was important that we developed a routine to secure, set and haul the new anchors. They were one of the essential pieces of safety equipment aboard and when they were needed they had to be unlashed and set quickly without harming any crew members in the process. The crew spent a day trying to work out the best way to secure the anchors along the beak and the bow, and then a procedure for using the windlass to control the anchor cable. They had to be able to recover the anchors quickly. It was new territory for everyone.

Being in the ocean swells off the continental shelf overnight would be a good test before returning to Fremantle and preparing for a weekend on exhibition at the Mindarie Quays marina. The short cruise to the northern suburbs of Perth was an opportunity to work up some systems for setting up the exhibition aboard and at the berth. We were only about three weeks from departure with so much to do.

I chose not to sail on the sea trial. It was an opportunity for Peter Manthorpe to work with his new crew and to take full charge of the vessel without me looking over his shoulder. It was also Cathy and my wedding anniversary and, of course, bashing about in big Indian Ocean swells was not my cup of tea. I leave it up to you to choose whichever of these excuses is most credible.

Outwardly, everything was going well, but behind the scenes departure day for the sea trials was chaotic. The freshwater tanks were only half full, gear wasn't lashed down and the crew wasn't yet working as a unit. We gathered everyone together at Cicerello's Landing in Fremantle Fishing Boat Harbour for a pep talk and I wished them well before they headed off.

There was a minor piece of history we were making in this mini-voyage. It was our first sail to Rottnest Island and it had been 300 years since the first Dutch anchor had hooked itself into the 'Rotto' seabed. In December 1696, Captain Willem de Vlamingh was the first recorded European visitor to Rottnest when he anchored the *Nyptang*, the *Geelvink* and the *Weseltje* nearby. It was uninhabited when he arrived although Aboriginal people walked to the island when the sea retreated during the last ice age until the sea levels levels rose again. The Nyoongar people call it Wadjemup or "the place across the water where the spirits are" and it had been a place to perform ceremonies. Willem de Vlamingh knew nothing of this but he did see the small marsupial Quokkas on the island and called it 'Rats' Nest' or Rottnest Island. The unfortunate Dutch name stuck.

Thomson's Bay was sheltered from the sou' westerlies and the crew could sort out their anchoring technique in a calm location. *Duyfken* was put to anchor north of Bathurst Point. Most of the crew were willing to sleep aboard in the style of the original crew who virtually camped. The Dutch crews often found any place they could to sleep and there are descriptions of them stretching animal skins between cannon to use as shelters. The original crew would usually only be allowed to go below under supervision and they certainly weren't permitted to sleep amongst the cargo or the provisions. Our crew had no such limitation and they slept on mats on the deck to enjoy the cool summer air, or down below if they preferred it. Many of the crew found that the thin mats we supplied were too uncomfortable. Andrea Cicholas sewed enough hammocks or 'hangmats' as the Dutch call them so that the crew could find a more comfortable way to sleep in the hold if they wanted to. They wouldn't have been part of *Duyfken's* original equipment. Christopher Columbus introduced the hammock to Europe a century before *Duyfken's* voyage, but they were only used on some English ships by 1606. She used the British design adopted by *Endeavour* and they were extremely practical for our ship.

Preparing breakfast for the first time next morning, Jane Doepel came to grips with the impossibly small galley which was located in what may have been the bread storage room in the original jacht. Our crew got a good workout weighing anchor. There were no motors to substitute for good old-fashioned crew power. The crew sat in a long line on the deck as the anchor cable was hauled through the windlass and a spike inserted into the drum to give mechanical advantage for the windlass rotation. A primitive ratchet prevented the cable from unwinding. (One crew member on our voyage to Indonesia described it like having a tug-of-war with the sea-bed.) It took an hour to secure the anchors and Peter and Gary once again discussed at length the best place to stow several hundred kilograms of dead weight.

The bonnets were set on the mainsails. These were extensions to the lower side of the sail to add more surface area. They worked well and Igor Bjorksten, Andrea Cicholas and Karim Kouniali, who had all worked on the rig, were aboard and happy with the way the ship's rig was performing as she sailed at six knots in a fresh 15 knot breeze. Then the sea breeze strengthened to about 25 to 30 knots. It made for a rip-roaring sail north and the crew shortened sail. While the ship was tossing about, some of the crew noticed an unusually large amount of water in the hold so the bilge pumps were turned on. To make matters worse, the Ship's Engineer Michael 'Mick' Hemsley started the main engines only to find that the propellors were fouled with craypot lines. It is a square rig sailor's worst nightmare — stranded off a lee shore in rough weather with no power backup. In a foaming sea, with the ship heaving, Mick drew the short straw to dive overboard with a knife to cut the poly rope clear of the props — an extremely dangerous manoeuvre in heavy seas. He managed to free the prop but then the craypot line fouled the safety line tied around his waist and he was pulled under. He and the craypot (with no crayfish inside!) were recovered but it was a near miss which reminded the crew of the ever-present dangers of life at sea.

I was at home in the evening when the phone rang. There was a lot of background noise. It was Peter Manthorpe calling from the ship. "Graeme. We're sinking," he said in a low, calm voice. He knew that would get my attention and I suspect he enjoyed uttering those words. He then went on to explain that the sailing was magnificent, and they were about 35 km west of Hillarys Boat Harbour as the wind speed increased to 27 knots, sailing with the wind, when he decided to tack, and then things began to go wrong. Water began gushing through the topside seams in the hold above the waterline. It was clear what had happened. The planks had shrunk on the port side of the ship in the hot summer sun. The ship's modern bilge pumps were failing. Alarmingly, the modern pump filters regularly clogged with wood shavings floating in the bulge since the ship's construction. The crew were pressed into service to begin pumping the original lever operated bilge pumps. First they primed the pump with a bucket of water and then they began lifting and lowering the large wooden lever. They sucked the water up with a plunger within a hollow elm tree tube. The pump discharge ran down into a channel called the pump dale. With the modern pumps not keeping up with the ingress of water, Peter Manthorpe was heartened that the replica pumps "just sucked up the gunk and spat it out!" However, with all the pumps at work, there was still more water coming in than being pumped out. Yes, strictly speaking, *Duyfken* was sinking but there was no immediate danger as Fremantle was quite close and if the ship was kept upright then the topside seams were above the level of the waves.

Peter Manthorpe brought the ship back to Fremantle and tied up at Cicerello's Landing a few minutes shy of midnight. It was the first of many times in the next few years when I felt totally helpless. Once the ship is at sea, the crew is in the hands of the Ship's Master and there is nothing to be done except wait for updates. I went to bed at midnight. We had dodged our first bullet. The seams were caulked again first thing in the morning and the ship was in good order to depart for Mindarie Quays for a weekend on exhibition and day sails.

With two weeks until departure and long hours being put in by everyone to get ready, the crew of *Duyfken* undertook a sea survival training course at the IFAP Survival Training Centre at Rous Head in Fremantle. There were no complaints from the crew about this sojourn after the alarming voyage off Rottnest. The IFAP Survival Training Centre was one of only a handful of marine survival training centres around the world. It was established to service the oil industry and a feature of the Centre was an indoor heated pool specially designed for survival training. Our crew was trained on the use of 16 person self-inflating life rafts, correct procedures for abandoning ship, rescuing in 'sailor overboard' situations, techniques to minimise energy loss while floating in the sea and fire extinguisher drills.

It was a busy time and we did not have the luxury of being able to stop our public programs. A limited number of half-day sails was still undertaken by the ship's new professional crew for $200 per person. The Foundation also offered a few voyage crew positions for people who would like to join the Expedition as crew for a daily fee of $200. Every dollar counted.

There was a great sense of anticipation in Fremantle. More than 26,500 people visited the ship from January to her departure on 8 April 2000 and they were all keen to get one last look at the ship before her grand voyage. With one week to go and still chasing funds, we arranged a dinner on the grass concourse of the Fremantle Sailing Club with the ship moored nearby. Many local artists contributed over 40 original works of art for a fundraising auction which raised thousands more dollars for the ship. It was a wonderful, happy night of cameraderie for all the true believers. Although we did not realise the significance of this event, *Duyfken* 1606 Club members and Friends of the *Duyfken* gathered as a group for what would be the last time. Like a ship ploughing through the ocean, the relentless drive to build *Duyfken* had been successful but little thought had been given to what we had left in its wake. We were about to leave these people behind to pursue a new dream.

With only three days to go before departure, *Duyfken* was lifted again for a last minute touch-up to her hull. The 250 tonne Tami shiplifter at Fremantle Boatlifters in Mews Road, Fremantle Fishing Boat Harbour — the same lifter which launched the ship on 24 January 1999 — gingerly placed her on the hard-standing. We had repeatedly kissed the limestone outcrop near our tight berth at Cicerello's Landing and every time we scraped more anti-fouling from the keel. It was an unwanted distraction but we had to make sure that the ship's hull was well covered with protective paint before she headed into the tropical waters of northern Australia and Indonesia.

Chapter 14

Leaving the Nest

Duyfken was her name but it means little dove
The eyes of the fleet was her very first job
In a battle one Christmas 1601
Victory was theirs and the spice trade was won ...

Chorus:
Now the Little Dove's *spreading her wings again,*
400 years have gone by,
Fremantle town is a bird's nest,
that'll make this fledgling fly ...

Captain Janszoon, his orders were clear
Take your fair men, and sail from here
South bound Willem, foreign sand
So he took a right turn into the Great Southern Land

A brave little ship the battles she's won,
The fortress they took, the barrels of rum
Small in length, but big in heart
She charted our coastline, this was the start ...

Battle scarred Duyfken *was hauled on her side*
Both her wings broken, left there to die...
But the Little Dove's *spreading her wings again ...*

And so, Michael 'Barney' Barnett led the South Thornlie Primary School choir to the most emotional performance of *The Ballad of the Duyfken* as the ship left Fremantle on the Chevron 2000 *Duyfken* Expedition. Saturday 8 April 2000.

The pressure had been building for days. On the eve of departure, as last minute equipment was being stowed, we had the Kailis wharf to ourselves. All the Kailis engineering staff had left work for the day. It should have been a time of great excitement but I think we all felt the fatigue from months of work to get the voyage underway. Syd Corser arrived at the wharf, totally unannounced, driving his ritzy 1960s two-door Mercedes (one of the more stylish cars in Perth) and wearing his trademark blue blazer, impeccably pressed white trousers, matching white shirt and boat shoes. He asked me whether he could speak to the crew for a moment. Everyone gathered around. Syd spoke about the early days, how we had crafted a fundraising project which raised almost $4 million. He mentioned the enormous public support from West Australians — 185,000 people visited the ship while she was under construction and another 23,500 while she was on exhibition at the wharf. He spoke about the work of the shipbuilding team and the other staff, and of the Friends of the *Duyfken* who gave so much to create the ship which the crew were about to take on a great expedition. He told the crew that they were now her custodians and they had a great responsibility to look after the *Little Dove* and to do justice to the effort of all of those people who had come before and made it possible. He said that they were ambassadors for Australia. He referred directly to Michael Kailis and the great loss we all felt. He closed by wishing the crew good luck: "fair winds and following seas." It was a humbling speech, and I felt that he summed up everything that I felt which I had never expressed to the crew in the hurly burly of preparing for the Expedition. I wished I could make speeches like that. We were about to embark into the great unknown and Syd grasped the importance of what we were about to do.

Without a doubt, the voyage was underfunded. Patricia Kailis agreed to fund my salary as we clicked into overdraft and activated the guarantees provided by Michael Kailis and Kerry Stokes all those years before. This was on top of the $300,000 debt she now held within the MG Kailis Group for the completion of the ship with its modern equipment. The crew conducted day sails in the month leading up to the departure, and this raised $20,000 to help fund the voyage. I was still chasing funds wherever I could find them. Nothing about this Expedition made financial sense. Sir James' favourite phrase "Don't waste money with chook raffles, always go for the big lick," had been replaced with "let's raise the funds from wherever we can find them!"

We still didn't have the treasured piece of paper which would allow us to sail into Indonesian waters — the sailing permit — but we had to get moving. We did not want to be stranded in Indonesia, unable to return to Australia before the cyclone season.

Crowds began gathering as the crew were having breakfast aboard. Volunteer guides and Friends of the *Duyfken*, former employees and anyone with an appreciation of the great challenge ahead gathered at the wharf. The media put the number at 2,000 with another 90 boats waiting in the harbour to escort *Duyfken* along the coast. The newly-elected Chairman of the *Duyfken* 1606 Replica Foundation, Rinze Brandsma, presented the Ship's Master Peter Manthorpe with an 'Artikelbrief', inspired by the list of instructions presented by the Dutch East India Company to their departing skippers before they left the Texel Roadstead for the Indies. My father, Jack, produced an impressive document worthy of the occasion using a chiseled calligraphy pen on parchment.

Duyfken's Artikelbrief contained a summary of what the 2000 Chevron *Duyfken* Expedition was aiming to achieve in northern Western Australia, Indonesia, Papua New Guinea and Queensland in the next nine months. It also included a rather vague line about building bonds of friendship between the people of Australia, Indonesia and The Netherlands.

In April 2000, before the ship was scheduled to begin the Expedition, a very special cargo was placed aboard which came to symbolise what we thought was a new approach to the re-enactment voyage paradigm. Michael Young was determined that we should acknowledge the Aboriginal community. In 1989 and 1990, he managed one of the oldest Aboriginal art centres, Tiwi Designs, on Bathurst Island, 80 km north of Darwin. He was surprised to find so many Dutch place names around the islands and it stimulated his interest in the indigenous connections with Dutch explorers. He was fascinated by the stories of Bathurst Islander descendants living in Sulawesi. Their ancestors probably sailed with the Makassan trepangers back in the 1700s. He saw them commemorated in Arnhem Land ceremonies. He used to joke: "I have always maintained that the first Australian homestay visitors to Bali were Aboriginal." We were keen to involve *Duyfken* with the Aboriginal community wherever we could do so. Under Michael's guidance I contacted Gail Hodgekiss who was the Aboriginal Liaison Officer with the nearby City of Melville. Fremantle was called Walyalup by the local Whadjuk people who were part of the larger Noongar language group of Australia's South West. She approached Ashley

Haywood from the Noongar community who consulted with other members of the community and came back with an idea for young Aboriginal people to make traditional Boorn Wongkiny (stick talking) or message sticks with messages written in Noongar to go with the ship. Our crew would give the Boorn Wongkiny to Aboriginal children from the Aurukun, Napranum and Mapoon communities of Cape York when we arrived. The painted message sticks, which were about 40cm long, were the traditional way that messages were relayed between Aboriginal groups. They were also used as invitations to feasts, initiations and funerals.

Ashley Haywood presented the Ship's Master with a spear and the message sticks. When he presented them to us, he said that the indigenous community of Melville was glad to be involved and it was very proud to be part of "this momentous event".

We all resolved that there were to be no men in white tights planting Union Jacks and firing off muskets on this voyage. We knew so little about what we were about to embark upon but a new approach was beginning to emerge in our thinking. We said that in 1606, Captain Jansz would not have asked for permission to land. We would, in a small way, correct this mistake of history and ask for permission via the messages contained on the message sticks. It was all very vague, but instead of just carrying Dutch history we would also carry history from Aboriginal Australia.

I was pleased with myself that we had shown appropriate recognition to the Aboriginal history of *Duyfken* and that we would work with the Aboriginal community in future. This was no time for reflection, but looking back today, I can see how ignorant I really was at that moment. The ship was about to leave from near Bathers Beach. The local Whadjuck tribal group comprised about 30 people who occasionally had feasted on beached whales at that beach before colonial settlement. The mouth of the Swan River nearby was where tracks from all over the area converged so the river could be crossed at the limestone bar. The Aboriginal resistance leader Yagan had been gaoled at the Round House adjacent to Bathers Beach before he was sent to Rottnest Island for incarceration. The Whadjuck was one of about a dozen tribal groups and there were probably 450 people living in the area before settlement pushed them away. Our standard response to the question of whether the ship was a symbol of white invasion was that the Dutch only ever came to Australia for trade on the mantra that: "God is good, but trade is better", and that they had no intention to be colonisers. It was a good line but we would see as the voyages unfolded that this was a superficial view. Perhaps we were just playing with the glitter of history rather than exploring the underlying symbolism of a European ship. Once again, we were inadvertently telling a Eurocentric version of Australian history because we didn't know any better.

Of course, we also had objects emblematic of our own culture. The ship had olive branches in her beak as a symbol of the spirit in which the voyage would be conducted. "The *Little Dove* was named after Noah's dove which went out to search for land and came back the second time with an olive branch — that symbol of dove with olive branch is a symbol of peace," I said to the crowd. Fremantle Mayor, Richard Utting, farewelled *Duyfken* on behalf of the people of the ship's home port who had adopted the vessel as their own: "*Duyfken* will always return to Fremantle," he proclaimed to wide applause.

And then it was time to leave. As the volunteer guides threw hundreds of multi-coloured streamers from the wharf onto the deck, it was like they were making one last effort to pull her back, to stop her from leaving home. And then the crew responded with water-bombs lobbed onto the wharf in a joyous and cheeky gesture of defiance. That wasn't in the script but who cared? I just shook my head and laughed. I was so happy.

Peter Manthorpe ordered the crew to set the topsails as soon as the ship was clear of the Kailis wharf. When he glimpsed the open ocean beyond Fremantle Fishing Boat Harbour, he ordered the rest of the sails to be set and the engines switched off.

To the port side of the ship was the slim outline of Rottnest Island. Our destination was a tiny group of islands a little more than five times the land area of Rottnest. At about 104 square kilometres, the islands of Banda are barely a speck on any map of Indonesia, let alone the globe, but we were soon to discover that they have had a disproportionate influence on our world.

The sea breeze was our friend as the ship's sails filled and *STS Leeuwin* joined the long parade of vessels wishing us well. The shoreline was dotted with colour all the way north to City Beach. There must have been tens of thousands of people farewelling us. Peter Manthorpe ran perilously close to the shore and I asked him whether he was sure it was deep enough. I almost thought he was sailing into the swimmers in the breakers at Cottesloe, but he was keen to give the people of Perth one last glimpse of their *Little Dove*. The crew were carefully trimming the sails and she was continually picking up speed, easily achieving seven knots. It was time for Rinze Brandsma, the

Channel Seven crew and me to leave *Duyfken* while we could — next stop could be 400 km north. Peter gave the order to heave to and the ship stalled so we could disembark. I wished everyone well, as my fellow landlubbers and I clambered over the gunwale into a speed boat. We watched the ship pick up speed immediately and charge off to Scarborough Beach before striking north west. For the first time the ship was no longer ours. The next time I would see the ship and crew was in Geraldton.

Peter Manthorpe and his crew were now the temporary custodians of our treasured jacht. Crew members were divided into watches with a watch leader who was a senior crew member and then a number of hands. While a watch was working the ship, other crew were resting or sleeping. The crew of 16 down below was now living and sleeping in an area hardly larger than a double car garage. Master and Mate, Peter Manthorpe and Gary Wilson, were in the captain's cabin on the main deck at the stern which also had the chart table. "Rank hath its privileges" as they say and in this case they had windows and narrow cots. The disadvantage of the cabin, however, was that day and night crew came into the room to consult the sailing charts, plot a route and write in the ship's log. The Master and Mate of a ship like *Duyfken* are never in a truly deep sleep anyway, and they always seem to have one ear receptive to unusual movements in the ship, changes in wind noise or activity aboard. Life below decks presented its own challenges. Spare rope and blocks were stored for'ard toward the bow. It was sometimes referred to as the 'love nest' as it was the only place on the ship where couples could have some privacy. At the stern was the tiller flat where two cannon were directed out of two rear hatches and the tiller attached to the rudder swept across to connect with the whipstaff or kolderstok (which was the lever which steered the vessel on the deck above). With no headroom, crew had to crawl through the tiller flat almost on hands and knees to go below and although it was a flat comfortable deck and a prized location for sleeping, it could also be inconvenient. The galley was on the port side and two heads and showers to the starboard side. With water always at a premium, the showers were rarely used on longer voyages. Two large engine boxes covered with woven baskets were on either side of the passageway which went down the centreline of the hold. Every crew member had one of the small carved sea chests for personal belongings. These were lashed to the inside of the hull and an array of barrels, food supplies, boxes and storage containers made it important for the crew who slept in the hold to be clean and organised. Most of the regular crew preferred the hammocks and others the mats. My favourite spot was on the starboard engine cover.

After the first 24 hours, *Duyfken* was already more than 150 nautical miles north of Fremantle, and Peter Manthorpe averaged 6.5 knots in the first day — at this rate, he was set to complete the first leg three days ahead of schedule.

Peter reported that they were sailing in "near perfect conditions with a moderate easterly breeze and long Indian Ocean swells." He assured me that the ship was holding together well with no breakages. The crew were now on regular shifts to hand pump the bilge. A flying fish landed on deck in the early hours of the morning — a good omen for some seafarers beginning a voyage.

I should list the first crew of *Duyfken* on the Chevron 2000 *Duyfken* Expedition. Peter Manthorpe, Gary Wilson and Andrea Cicholas each had a watch with John Colvin, Greg O'Byrne and Nicole Gardner all leading hands. Igor Bjorksten and Karim Kouniali from the shipbuilding team were aboard for the first part of the voyage to help the crew during the shakedown. Jane Doepel was cook and Rupert Weller was ship's carpenter. Mick Hemsley was Engineer. One of our keen sailor/shipyard volunteers was the farmer John Harcourt Smith who joined the first leg of the Expedition as voyage crew. Journalist John Carey and photographer Richard Polden from The Sunday Times newspaper also joined for the passage north. Marcus Gillezeau and Chris Watson were aboard to film their documentary. Peter's father, Pep Manthorpe, joined as voyage crew. He was an experienced sailor and he could pull his weight when required.

The final crew member was the Fremantle printmaker, Robert Jefferson, who agreed to join the ship for the first passage to see whether he could cope with life under sail. I was keen for the crew to reflect a voyage of exploration from the 'Age of Discovery'. In those days, the crew often had a chronicler who drew illustrations of the places the ship visited. Robert soon fell in love with the ship and wrote:

> *The difference between* Duyfken *and other ships like, say Endeavour, is the conscious intention of the voyage. A week aboard was enough for me to understand that it was the charter, the values, and the intentions that are the real cargo of the* Duyfken. *As an artist, my task aboard is not only to record, but to demonstrate the values of the Chevron* Duyfken *Expedition. Values that are quintessentially different from the first* Duyfken *that they need to*

be captured by a medium that is not literal but is reflective of these values. The Duyfken *as I see it is already a work of art: a resounding piece of dramatic art. My role I see would initially be to capture the values which surround the idea of this voyage of goodwill and of all the people involved. The shared memory, the living memory and confirming these memories, what remains after this maiden voyage is over. And giving those who did not sail a new sense of wonder.*

He talked about the cultural messages the ship carried and Aboriginal dreaming. "A ship sailing out of the context of its own time is definitely symbolic of our dreaming. I hope to capture what is the *Duyfken* Dreaming."

Robert Jefferson immediately grasped the symbolic significance of *Duyfken*. Having him aboard appealed to my desire to constantly find new ways of interpreting the well-worn re-enactment voyage concept. Unfortunately, his voyage didn't end up quite like we planned. We did not have space for passengers and he was placed in a watch every day. It stifled his creative ability, and it became a massive lost opportunity which I regret to this day. Despite his frustration, he stayed with the ship all the way to Cairns.

Our intention was for the Expedition to tell not just the story of *Duyfken* but to recognise all the Dutch seafarers who came to Australia by visiting some of the significant places along the coast with Dutch maritime history. *Duyfken's* voyage to Cape York was the first of these voyages. The most famous of the west coastal encounters was *Batavia's* tragic shipwreck in 1629, and we planned a small diversion to her resting place at the Abrolhos Islands. *Duyfken* was well ahead of schedule. She arrived in the Abrolhos group after only two days. The ship was proving to be surprisingly fast downwind. In 49.5 hours, *Duyfken* covered 219nm averaging an impressive 4.4 knots. Peter hove to in sight of Half Moon Reef. In 1727, the Dutch East India Company ship *Zeewijk* came to grief on this reef, and 96 survivors from over 200 passengers and crew made it to nearby Gun Island. Another 30 people stayed on the wreck. A small team took one of the ship's longboats with the aim of making it to Batavia and were never seen again. A seaworthy boat was later built from wreckage of the *Zeewijk* by those marooned and 82 people were saved. Clearly, these were waters not to be messed with. The crew spent an hour swimming nearby before Greg O'Byrne spotted a shark and it was all aboard once again.

Peter aimed the ship toward the Zeewijk Channel from the open ocean, planning to pass through Wooded Island Passage from the south. He asked his father Pep to climb the mainmast as a lookout, then proceeded at two knots, with crew members calling soundings all the way. He safely passed through the channel to the anchorage, but just north of Morley Island, the worst happened. The ship grounded on an uncharted coral head. The sickening noise of coral against oak which had been heard 371 years before when the *Batavia* met her fate and 273 years before when the same noise was heard aboard *Zeewijk* was being repeated. He immediately sent a crew member below to check for any sign that the coral had pierced the hull. It hadn't, so he started the engines and reversed off the outcrop. Peter aimed to dive into the water to inspect the hull from the outside but with more sharks cruising nearby he waited until the next morning. An inspection showed that the grounding had put a 600mm scrape, about 10mm deep, down the starboard side of the ship's stem. It was not a fatal blow. The damage was minimal but embarrassing so early in the Expedition.

With a newspaper crew aboard, I was faced with a dilemma. Should we ignore the grounding and almost certainly wait for John Carey to tell the story in *The Sunday Times* newspaper or should I get on the front foot and announce it to the world? On the one hand, it could enhance the romance and peril of the voyage, but on the other hand, it could make us look reckless. It was an easy choice for me. I wanted a publicity coup. I put out a media release with the headline: '*Duyfken* Crew Finds Abrolhos Just As Treacherous 371 Years Later.' I said that the grounding was a stark reminder of the challenges faced by Dutch seafarers who charted the West Australian coastline. "The aim of the Chevron 2000 *Duyfken* Expedition's WA leg is to explore the maritime history of our coast — but we didn't want to do it quite so closely as this," I said. The media release went on to say that the crew were reminded of the events of 4 June, 1629 when *Batavia* ran aground on the Abrolhos Islands two hours before daybreak. While *Duyfken* sailed on, the news media picked up the story and it was carried far and wide.

Twenty-four hours later, *Duyfken* sailed past Traitors Island in the Wallabi Group and in memory of the *Batavia* disaster, Peter threw overboard the olive branches which they carried from Fremantle. The ship's skipper sailed a rescue boat to *Batavia*, but 125 survivors were massacred by a group of rebel sailors while he was away and the bloody events which unfolded became one of the great shipwreck stories of the world. Our crew paused and drank a toast to all the seafarers who had perished on the 'Dutch coast' over the centuries. Gary Wilson poured a little red wine into the ocean for the 'angry ghosts'. "Not too much," he said. "We don't want to get them drunk." The crew were quite happy to see off those olive branches — the olives were clogging up the strainers in the bilge pumps.

Duyfken anchored overnight at Turtle Bay, East Wallabi Island in company with *STS Leeuwin*. The crew explored West Wallabi Island to find the fort erected by the VOC loyalists led by Webbi Hayes during the *Batavia* mutiny. It is reputed to be the first European 'building' erected on Australian soil.

I wanted a way we could make it possible for anyone who opened our website to see where we were and what we were doing. Grey Roughan, the Australian manager with the Dutch multinational surveying company, Fugro Survey, assisted us with modern navigational and communication gear which we installed. The equipment was supplied by its subsidiary called Omnistar. We simply didn't have the space to erect a large antenna used by large ships for communication. The solution was Inmarsat 'Satcom C', a telex format which converted text written on the ship's 'Toughbook' laptop computer to an email. It was an extraordinarily expensive way of communicating with every keystroke costing a cent. By the end of the voyage, daily emails had cost us $12,000.

Web developer Marjolein Towler, via her company, Consultas, created a visually striking website, but like most websites at the time, it was largely static. The concept of social media with a product called Facebook was four years away — Mark Zuckerberg was still a teenager in high school. I asked Marjolein whether it was possible to run a daily ship's log which we could publish every day. She set up a system where we could upload emails from the ship and we could put them into a constantly updating database which could be read by anyone with a computer. Scott Ludlum, who later became a very successful senator for The Greens party, worked on the graphic design. The Captain's Log was born and it was quite revolutionary. *Duyfken* broke new ground with the ability of a small vessel to communicate daily and effectively run its own news service to the outside world. Marcus Gillezeau and Chris Watson from Firelight Productions, also produced 'mini-movies' or 'micro-docs' as they called them which were edited onboard the ship and uploaded to the web when the ship reached port. Today it is ho-hum but in 2000 we were the only people experimenting with these concepts. In later voyages, we managed to reduce the extortionate cost of Sat C thanks to two amateur sailors at Palo Alto in San Francisco Bay. Jim Corenman and Stan Honey invented an email communication link with HF radio in 1996 called SailMail. By connecting our laptop computer aboard the ship with the radio via a modem, we were able to send 10kb messages which worked out at about 1,500 words at most, once a day. They were transmitted by special earth stations around the world. It only cost a few hundred dollars for an annual subscription to the service compared with the thousands of dollars a year we were paying for the satellite service.

The romance of a life under sail and the traditional image of the captain of a ship which accompanied it held great curiosity for the media and the public. I could use this to our advantage. From very early on I had the view that the Ship's Master would be the conduit for our media profile and it was he who would speak for the Expedition and the *Duyfken* Foundation during the voyages. It worked extremely well and we enjoyed positive publicity everywhere we went.

As everyone knows, content is king and without good content every news service fails. We didn't realise it at the time, but we were about to find a literary star: Peter Manthorpe. After a few teething problems and a lot of more pressing jobs, he came out with his first log on day five while at anchor near East Wallabi Island in the Houtman Abrolhos on 12 April 2000:

> *Work is Love*
> *Our emotion-charged departure from Fremantle seems like a long time ago as we lie to anchor at East Wallabi Island in the Houtman Abrolhos. After the frantic rush to prepare the ship for her maiden voyage, settling into the normal shipboard routines over the last few days has been quite a relief for us seafarers. As we busied ourselves with rigging maintenance, stitching up bags for storage, and various carpentry jobs, I noticed the crew becoming infused with a relaxed contentment. We are remembering how it feels to be sailors, self contained on our ship, our own little world which we must care for as if our lives depended on her because, of course, they do.*
> *I heard there were lots of tears as we left Fremantle and I can understand it. Spending time working on such a beautiful ship is to fall a little bit in love with her. You grow to love the smell of the timber and tar and to enjoy the feel of the natural fibres in the rig.*

> *The crew were smiling at their work today and we are all developing a bond with the ship that will become stronger over the coming voyage. We look after her so that she might return the favour in the next gale. Love is never based purely on aesthetics after all. That's just the lure. Mutual trust is the real foundation.*

Duyfken sailed into Geraldton a few days later. Gary Wilson was keen to meet his old friend, David Murgatroyd, who was now the Harbour Master. He had arranged for the port to donate a much-needed rubber rescue boat to the ship. With due ceremony it was handed over. Peter was tetchy about my crass efforts to gain some publicity at his expense when he started getting asked about the 'disaster' near Half Moon Reef. The last thing any Ship's Master wants on his record is a grounding. It can be a blot which remains with you for your whole career. I didn't appreciate this and I thought that it was good publicity for the voyage as it had ricocheted around the world and for the first time *Duyfken* was big news. Even if it was just a fleeting moment, this awareness would help us in the future. The Daily Telegraph in the United Kingdom ran with a story 'Replica of historic ship hits trouble' carrying a magnificent image of the ship under full sail probably taken by Richard Polden. The exaggerated story said that the £1.5 million replica had hit a reef, that the skipper had blamed a local fisherman for giving him false directions and the ship had to call into Geraldton for repairs. Not much of this was true. It was point taken. If Peter had been less forgiving, then this could have been a disaster for our relationship but I now understood his annoyance and perhaps he began to understand the dynamics of how I played the media game, a high profile voyage and our need for publicity. It proved to be an unstable marriage at times.

The first indication that we were really onto something with the Captain's Log came a few days later. The next log on Day 10 was posted as *Duyfken* sailed past the infamous Zuytdorp Cliffs named after another VOC ship which came to grief at this lee shore in 1712 on its way to Batavia. However, it wasn't history which got people's attention:

> '...And the Scuppers Ran with Blood'
> *Duyfken was made very welcome in Geraldton and thousands of people came down to the wharf to see over the ship. This level of interest in the first port of our voyage was gratifying — a good omen for the future perhaps.*

> Last night, just as the sun was setting, we set the fore and main topsails and the foresail and sailed out of Geraldton Harbour into the Indian Ocean swells again. There was a big crowd lining the wharf to see us off, not to mention a number of yachts.
>
> As soon as we were clear of the harbour limits we started to roll in the following sea and we have been rolling ever since. At times Duyfken *lurches over 30 degrees one way before rolling back 30 degrees the other way. Anything not secured down goes sailing 'schooner rigged' across the deck, and this includes the crew if they don't hang on to something.*
>
> This afternoon we caught the first fish of the voyage: a small striped tuna. As I hauled it in we had a strike on the other line and Greg pulled in another stripey, bigger than the first. My mouth always starts watering when a tuna comes aboard. Raw tuna, straight from the sea, is sensational. I bled the fish as it seems to make them taste better, although because of the rolling the decks became quite messy. I filleted them and cut some strips of sashimi. We even have a tube of wasabi, Japanese horseradish, onboard. I noticed this treat is not everyone's taste, and some of the 'green hands' went a shade greener at the sight of the raw fish slithering down the throats of those of us who think there is nothing on earth as yummy as sashimi.
>
> It's hard enough to make a cup of tea with the ship rolling like this, so imagine my surprise when Greg came in the cabin with a tray of sushi (raw tuna, carrot, cucumber and rice rolled up in a layer of seaweed). I feel especially sorry tonight for those in the crew who have lost their appetite on account of the rolling.
>
> We are making such good time that we should be in Shark Bay tomorrow.

This log captured the fantasy of the adventurous life our crew were experiencing better than any media release I could write and Peter was on his way to becoming an online celebrity. We began not just putting the logs onto the website. Tracy McCullough, who was our voyage coordinator based in Perth, and I started sending them out to anyone who was interested. More and more people began emailing us wanting to be on the distribution list so that they didn't have to wait for it to be put online. Our email lists got longer and longer as the public's hunger for their daily fix of *Duyfken* news grew. People wanted to be able to log in and get an update during breakfast or as soon as they got to work. From hundreds of readers a day, it went to thousands of readers a day, and then more.

While Peter was enjoying the sailing on deck, the experience was not shared by the ship's cook, Jane Doepel, down below. It was almost impossible to cook in the heavy swell. All the pots were lashed off to shelf rails. "I kept being burned on the back of my legs from hitting the stove when getting food from the fridge," she said. "I was constantly thrown sideways into the heads on the other side of the passageway. Eventually Andrea made me a strap to secure me to the sink – who knew I'd be grateful to be tied to the sink."

Now, I must make an admission before we sail too far into this story of the Expedition. I don't understand the mind of a sailor. I'm a landlubber through and through. Give me the city life or the inland of Australia any day, rather than the dark seas beyond the horizon. Again and again, I would come unstuck when my land-based values came up against the life views of our crew. I was too busy trying to work six weeks or even 12 months ahead of the ship, coming up with new ways to fund the Expedition and, with Tracy's help, to arrange port visits or approvals. I didn't have time to resolve crew disputes, so when things aboard got a little bit heated between the Ship's Master and the First Mate as we sailed north along the west coast, I wasn't the best listener. As far as I could tell there was a clash of personalities between the relaxed Master and the more strict First Mate. There was an issue of a sarong being worn aboard by the Master. I was wrong. Some of the crew thought Gary was behaving too much like a martinet and told him so in no uncertain terms. Peter had to step in as the peacemaker. They both wanted to talk to me about their feelings and so the phone calls began. I was still in Fremantle and not in the mood to listen. Once again, I was packing up our office. This time we were moving from digs above Cattalini's Chemist in the High Street into home offices as we couldn't afford to keep a dedicated office running. I was so preoccupied with other problems I thought: "Shit, I've just appointed them and we are a few weeks into a six month voyage. Why do I need this!" I told them both in separate calls just to sort it out between themselves. I wasn't going to get involved. Maybe it was an act of genius because they did sort it out and they parted many months later with a healthy dose of mutual respect and are still friends today.

Duyfken's crew departed Denham bound for Cape Inscription on the northern tip of Dirk Hartog Island at Shark Bay. The limestone crag is unremarkable except that Dutch seafarers encountered it several times in the seventeenth century. Dirk Hartog placed his pewter plate on a pole to record his presence at the spot in 1616. Willem de Vlamingh found the plate in 1697, took it down, replaced it with his own and carried the original to Batavia. Another century elapsed. Napoleon Bonaparte directed Nicolas Baudin to chart the land known as New Holland. In 1801, Captain Jacques Hamelin of the corvette *Naturaliste* was separated from Baudin's ship *Géographe* and arrived in Shark Bay. One of the crew, Louis de Freycinet, found de Vlamingh's plate. Nicolas Hamelin had his own plate made (although this one has never been found) and erected it. In 1818, Louis de Freycinet sailed to Shark Bay on *Uranie* and took de Vlamingh's plate back to France. There were a lot of plates left at Cape Inscription but none for 200 years so we thought we should follow the same maritime tradition and put up our own.

As *Duyfken* sailed across Shark Bay, Rupert Weller spent hours tapping the names of all the crew on a large copper disk formed into a plate using only a hammer and a punch. When the ship arrived at Cape Inscription, the newly-named *Port of Geraldton* rescue boat was launched with Peter Manthorpe and Rachelle Walker, the film crew and the Sunday Times team. The Manthorpe plate was duly erected near the replicas of the other plates. We had followed the European maritime tradition.

The inscription read:

> THE 22 APRIL IS HERE ARRIVED THE JACHT
> *DUYFKEN* OF FREMANTLE
> THE MASTER PETER MANTHORPE THE CREW
> GARY WILSON ANDREA CICHOLAS NICOLE
> GARDNER JOHN COLVIN GREG O'BYRNE
> MICHAEL HEMSLEY JANE DOEPEL RUPERT
> WELLER RACHELLE WALKER CHRIS WATSON
> JOHN CAREY RICHARD POLDEN JANITA
> BELLOTTIE ADAM JOHNSTON LEE BEST
> SHEREE CARRUTHERS MICHELLE PLUME
> TRACY BEALES RENETTE HILDER. THE SAME
> DAY MADE SAIL FOR REGIONS NORTH,
> HISTORY FURTHER TO EXPLORE AND BOUND
> FOR BANDA THEN PENNEFATHER RIVER THE
> MEETING OF CULTURES ALSO TO EXPLORE.
> -ANNO 2000-

It was a bit of irreverent fun and another chance to tell a story from history and link *Duyfken* to the western coast. It was also making a point to Shark Bay Shire President Les Moss. We saw *Duyfken* as helping tell all the stories of Dutch exploration not just the Cape York story. *Duyfken* Ship's Master, Willem Jansz, did have a connection with this coast. He sailed as upper-merchant on the VOC ship *Mauritius* skippered by Lenaert Jacobszoon who named a river on North West Cape, Willems River, in 1618. It is likely Jansz came ashore. His river is now called Yardie Creek.

Duyfken visited Carnarvon and Exmouth and the crew were settling into a routine for port visits, stowing the day-to-day equipment and replacing it with a display of seventeenth century shipboard life. On shore, we had a mobile shop on a trailer and a large number of display panels telling the *Duyfken* story. We were a fully-fledged travelling exhibition in port and an expedition at sea. At each port, new voyage crew joined the ship, paying a fee for the privilege of sailing on the Expedition and providing much-needed funds to keep our ship relentlessly sailing north.

The romance of life aboard wasn't necessarily matched by the reality. John Carey from The Sunday Times newspaper published his own log of the first weeks of the voyage after he arrived in Dampier. The ship's log described the ship rolling moderately and 'sailing free' as they ventured out of Exmouth Gulf past Vlaming Head and into the Indian Ocean at 6.45pm. Here's what John Carey said:

> *6.45pm "Sometimes I just cry," says the Ship's Cook Jane Doepel as she prepares the next meal. Turbulent seas make her job hell — it's like cooking in a cupboard tied to a bungee rope. And Jane has the cuts, burns and bruises to prove it. With only two bar fridges, fresh food supplies rapidly decline, and pasta and rice become our staples."*

The next day he writes in the diary:

> *12.30pm "It's your fault," a crew member blurts at me. I've just steered the ship right off course. The ship has to make a 180-degree turn and skipper Peter Manthorpe is less than impressed. I've also set the ship back three hours in sailing time."*
>
> *2.34pm The toilet has broken down. Engineer Mick Hemsley has pulled it apart and cleaned it out overboard. Just an "average day at the office" declares Mick. "You've got to have a sense of humour,"*

> he adds. A laid-back approach that can irritate other crew members. Day 24, 3.45pm The confined living space continues to cause subtle tensions among the crew — and fuels personality clashes. With John (Colvin) and four others, I escape in our small rescue boat and make course for Great Sandy Island."

On 30 April, still only three weeks out from Fremantle, *Duyfken* sailed toward Barrow Island in the wake of two of the most famous explorers in Australian history: William Dampier and Abel Tasman. A Dutchman, Tasman's 1644 voyage sailed Western Australia's north western seas and he is credited with establishing the continuity of the coast from North West Cape to Cape York.

William Dampier, the first Englishman to visit Australia (if we accept that there were no English sailors aboard the Dutch ships which explored the Australian coastline before 1686) made two voyages to Australia in 1686/91 and again in 1699. Barrow Island also has a more contemporary link: it was the first oilfield in Western Australia established by WAPET, now part of Chevron. Oil was discovered at Barrow Island in 1964 and the company began operating an oilfield in 1967. The North West is now one of the world's major gas regions. Chevron arranged a photographer in a helicopter to meet the ship off Barrow Island. The company wanted a spectacular image of the ship sailing past the island for its Annual Report and to hang in the Perth boardroom. To get the shot in the white-cap seas, the crew repeatedly wore ship (turned away from the wind) and turned around for another run with the island in the background. They cursed the photographer in that chopper who wanted to impose the outside world on their shipboard life.

As *Duyfken* made passage north the crew enjoyed following winds and a sailing schedule which was easy to accomplish. It gave time for reflection. *Duyfken* was changing people, or at least, giving them a new perspective. Our youngest crew member, Nicole Gardner, wrote in her diary during an early morning watch while the ship was anchored at Great Sandy Island, a deserted and isolated dot on the map between Onslow and Dampier:

> *Tuesday 2 May 2000 0240 hrs. I'm on anchor watch, and what a beautiful night. The wind is quite fresh, F2-F3 and backing, the sky is clear and the anchor is holding well. I have seen several shooting stars, some bright enough to leave a trail. I find it amazing*

> how much a part of the universe I feel on this ship — part of nature, part of history. Yesterday morning, standing on the anchor stock to stop it hitting the ship, everything felt right, as it was meant to be; we look after our ship, she looks after us. There are only a few people who have felt the 'one-ness' of a small square-rigger at sea, the power of the wind lifting the ship over each crest, then down into the valley. The feeling that we are here to serve a greater power, that nature is testing us, toying with us. We are here at her convenience, us and our ship. Every movement, the creaking of the wood, the feel of the deck planks shifting, water lapping. The breathing, snores and grunts of the off-duty watch…it feels as if we are caught in an endless moment, that this will never end. All is as it should be.

The euphoric sailing did not last. *Duyfken*'s crew met consistent headwinds for the first time since leaving Fremantle. The narrative I expected to come from the voyage was a romantic sailing adventure, re-visiting Dutch seafaring stories and gaining an insight into life aboard the original jacht. What we found sometimes, however, were uncomfortable truths. The Captain's Log was becoming a portal for telling these stories. During the visit to Dampier, the local manager of the Department of Conservation and Land Management (which went by the acronym CALM) took Peter and any crew members who wanted to join them to the rock art on the Burrup Peninsula. From the Captain's Log:

> Chris took us to a canyon where artwork appeared wherever we looked. Weathered boulders coloured in that classic Pilbara red lay in great unruly piles among the spinifex covered hills and nearly every second boulder carried an image. We identified wallabies and kangaroos, turtles and dugong, emus and snakes all painstakingly chipped into the rock. To my untrained eye most of the works had a disarming delicacy about them. They were clearly made with a great deal of care and the strokes of the stone chisel that made them must have been aimed with precision and skill.
> We saw plenty of images of humans among the rocks. Some may have a special relevance to what we are doing. Chris took us to a small gully where there are several representations, clearly more recent than the oldest images, of what look like groups of figures one above the other clinging to vertical lines. Some researchers have

speculated they may represent sailors climbing the rigging of European ships. The more I looked the more I saw how feasible it is. The vertical lines converge at the top just like Duyfken's *shrouds. Also the artist would only have had to take a step up the rocks to be able to gaze over the top of the ridge and out over Mermaid Sound, a fine anchorage for a sailing ship. It is easy to imagine these pictures being made while their unwitting models went about their furling unaware they were being recorded in the most permanent way imaginable.*

This story has a tragic and shameful end. A plaque on the peninsula reads:

"Hereabouts in February 1868 a party of settlers from Roebourne shot and killed as many as 60 Yapurarra people in response to the killing of a policeman in Nickol Bay. This incident has been known as the Flying Foam Massacre."

What isn't mentioned on the plaque is that the policeman was speared because he raped a Yapurarra woman. So the Yapurarra, who have been chiselling these rocks into works of art for thousands of years, have no living descendants. An ancient community who had persevered for millennia in this harshest of environments was cut dead in the blink of an eye; in the short time since the coming of the colonisers. No amount of apologising will ever reconcile us with these aggrieved artistic spirits.

Sometimes as they sailed north, *Duyfken* and her crew seemed to be in a parallel universe to the world in which I was working. I addressed a crew meeting in Dampier on 4 May 2000 to give them an update on how our plans for Indonesia were progressing. Considering we'd soon be heading out of Australian waters and into the Indonesian archipelago, I wanted everyone to be aware of the challenges I was confronting every day. We still did not have a sailing permit to enter Indonesian waters and after I left Dampier, I planned to fly to Jakarta to secure the important piece of paper. Without that piece of paper, we would not leave Australia. The situation in Indonesia was difficult. I said that a group, the Laskar Jihad, had called for a holy war against the Christians in Maluku Province. The capital city of the province of West Timor, Kupang, was to be our 'safe' entry point to Indonesia since Jakarta was ruled out. In West Timor, some estimates indicated that there were up to 100,000 refugees from East Timor in 200 refugee camps. We were monitoring the unfolding events very closely with advice from the

Australian Embassy in Jakarta. There was also the issue of piracy which was troubling some of the crew. What if the ship was held up and crew members were taken hostage? What if they wanted to take our female crew? So many questions and not too many satisfactory answers.

At Port Hedland, the ship was lifted at the BHP Transport slipway at Stingray Creek to inspect the hull. The crew had to repaint the scrape from the Abrolhos Islands with anti-fouling before we headed into the tropics where the dreaded teredo worm would play havoc with our oak hull if it got half a chance.

We budgeted on having paying voyage crew on each leg as we sailed north as a way of supplementing the income of the ship, but on some legs our full complement was only 13 crew compared with the 18 crew we could accommodate. It was placing more pressure on the voyage budget. The nature of the Board had now changed. Rinze Brandsma was still Chairman and Charlie Welker his deputy. They were joined by Captain Chris Bourne from the Fremantle Port Authority and another sea captain, Wim Alebeek, who ran his own freight company. Michiel van Doorn was the Minutes Secretary, Con Smit continued representing the Friends and Michael Young attended when he was in town. It was like we were back in the early days of the *Duyfken* Committee at Michael's home without anyone from the big end of town bringing their business and political influence. Rinze was understandably risk averse. The financial situation was grim. It looked as if I needed another $200,000 to complete the voyage and we had gambled on engaging a marketing company in Queensland to help us raise sponsorship funds. They were good talkers but they hadn't raised a cent and it was a reminder that fundraising required passion and total commitment more than simply a good cause. We had an outstanding debt of $296,000 with the MG Kailis Group hanging over every decision the Board made. I was asked to look at a range of options including continuing the voyage around Australia and back to Fremantle, decommissioning the ship and placing her on static display; creating an enclosed tourist attraction for the ship in Fremantle along the lines of the building Michael and I had discussed before, or sailing the ship to The Netherlands. We had become the custodians of a dream which sometimes was more like a nightmare. Sure, we had a magnificent asset but we were sailing towards an uncertain future in more ways than one.

Chapter 15

Four Rubber Stamps and Signatures

While the crew were sailing to Port Hedland, their penultimate port visit in Western Australia before heading into the Timor Sea and landfall at Kupang, I was on another mission in Jakarta.

Staff at the Australian Embassy had been working hard for 11 months using all their diplomatic powers of persuasion to secure a sailing permit so that we could enter the Indonesian archipelago. There were two people in Jakarta who would be able to make an impossible voyage possible. The first was Captain David Ramsay who had a glittering career in the Australian Navy before taking on the diplomatically challenging job of Naval Attaché to Indonesia. He was fluent in Bahasa and he'd worked in Indonesia for so long that he was a trusted intermediary during a time when Australia needed to be nimble and smart in its dealings with the young democracy. Geoff Leach had taken over from Gregson Edwards as the Cultural Attaché and he was also an excellent operator. He was a hard-bitten old ABC journo with a soft heart who had seen it all and knew how Asia worked. Australia needed to engage with Indonesia in a positive way at a person-to-person level, and his experience as a foreign correspondent gave him an ability to get on with people from vastly different backgrounds. He saw *Duyfken* as a great national asset and he appreciated the cultural and symbolic value of the ship. Between the two of them, there didn't seem to be anyone in Jakarta they didn't know.

Captain Ramsay was very well-connected in the Indonesian defence forces. His best contact was Navy Colonel Aji Sularso who was a graduate of the Joint Services College in Canberra and Secretary General of the Indonesian Sail Training Federation. He arranged participation for two vessels in the Sydney to Hobart Yacht Race in 1999. Our initial discussions swirled around the possibility of the Indonesian Navy's 39m cadet training schooner *Arung Samudera* and *Duyfken* sailing in company through Indonesia and exchanging crew as the voyage progressed. Ramsay wrote to Admiral Achmad Sutjipto, the Tentara Nasional Indonesia (TNI) Chief of Navy (who went with the acronym KASAL), requesting his support for the voyage. The Indonesians had been in no rush to provide approval as the security situation had been very volatile and changed from week to week.

With only six days to go until the ship's departure from Fremantle, the pressure was mounting and I did still not have approval. On 3 April, David Ramsay had emailed me to say that he'd visited Aji Sarwono, the Minister for Sea Exploration and Fisheries, several times to discuss our permit.

To Graeme Cocks Cc Geoffrey Leach.
Subject: Re 2000 Duyfken *Chevron Expedition*
Date Monday, 3 April 2000

Dear Graeme
I have seen quite a bit of Aji Sularso recently. He rang this morning just after I opened your email to say that the Security Assistant to KASAL had contacted him to advise against the Duyfken *going to Ternate on the grounds of the recent upswing in violence there. He had no problem with Banda or Kupang and was only concerned with the onshore situation in Ternate, which I take to mean Tidore and Makian as well. Solor and Bacan were not mentioned, but I shall check as Bacan pops up in the news from time to time.*
In a similar vein, I understand from Geoff Leach that DFAT have drafted a letter for their Minister pointing out that the Travel Advisory still applies to most areas of Maluku Province and recommending different port calls or postponement. I am not surprised that they are taking a conservative line because they have a Consular responsibility to assist Australians in trouble and prefer to see people avoiding all risk. I detected that same sense of responsibility in Aji's tone after his call from the Assistant for Security, as they near signing up to the Sailing Permit. It is not clear yet whether the formal response from the Indonesian Navy will forbid proceeding to Ternate or merely advise against it. However given that circumstances have not changed for the better in North Maluku and you are being cautioned against it by both sides of the

> house, I suspect the time has come to invoke Plan B.
> I told Aji that Banda was the most significant part of the re-enactment voyage and that you had a more southern route as a backup. I suggest you forward the details of that route to him and to me and he can incorporate it in the Sailing Permit.
> I asked Aji about Arung Samudera. He said he would check but he thought that he had heard mention that KASAL had received the letter and passed it to the relevant authorities within TNI AL. In this case the Military Sea Lift Commander apparently has the Arung Samudera on his books so he will be asked to authorise its participation. Again, it would help to advise the revised routing for their planning purposes.

My heart sank. Plan B was to avoid Maluku Province altogether which would mean no visit to *Duyfken*'s last resting place and the historic chain of spice islands including Banda. Later in the day, David Ramsay was back in touch:

> From David Ramsay
> To Graeme Cocks
> Subject: Re 2000 Duyfken Chevron Expedition
> Date. Monday, 3 April 2000 13:23
> . . . I just spoke to Aji on his handphone. He has not yet had a chance to follow up on Arung Samudera because shortly after we spoke this morning he was called away to the funeral of the father of the skipper of Dewaruci which is enroute to the US at the moment for a Tall Ships race and Independence Day celebrations. He is currently in a car enroute to Rangkasbitung, 100+ km from Jakarta, and will be back Wed and will chase up then. Time is short, I know, so I will try separate enquiries, but I don't want to give rise to suspicions of great Defence interest in the Project as they are paranoid enough about Aust intentions in Eastern Indonesia.
> Sorry for the confusion
> Cheers
> David Ramsay

Ever since John Howard pushed for a vote of self-determination in East Timor, the Indonesia press and politicians had been hammering Australia.

East Timor was linked to the push for independence by elements in Irian Jaya (West Papua) and the accusation was made that Australia was in favour of the break-up of Indonesia. Aji Sularso returned a few days later. With only three days until *Duyfken* departed Fremantle, David Ramsay once again made contact with him:

> From David Ramsay
> To Graeme Cocks. Cc Geoffrey Leach
> Subject: Re[2] Re:2000 Duyfken *Chevron Expedition*
> Date: Wednesday, 5 April 2000 6:58
>
> Dear Graeme
> *Aji has just rung in a state of some agitation. He has heard that the Assistant for Security to KASAL, who is processing the Sailing Permit, has been told by the Foreign Ministry not to permit any foreign vessels to enter the waters around trouble spots. Aji says this now means all of Maluku and includes Banda (and although he did not mention them, the Tanimbar and Aru Islands as well by my reading of the map). He also said the decision appears to have followed a debate between the Foreign Ministry and the Intelligence Agency (BAIS). We have encountered a lot of obstruction from both agencies in recent months due to paranoia over Australian intentions wrt [with regard to - ed.] Eastern Indonesia.*
> *Aji went on to say that this would mean that* Arung Samudera *would not be made available. He expects that we should receive a formal letter from KASAL in response to yours.*
> *It sounds pretty grim and you may need to be thinking of Plan C, but I am endeavouring to confirm through other sources*
>
> Cheers
> David Ramsay

Meanwhile, the feared letter from Alexander Downer, the Minister for Foreign Affairs arrived at our office in Fremantle, dated 4 April 2000:

> Dear Mr ~~Cocks~~ Graeme
> *Thank you for your letter dated 12 March 2000 concerning the 2000* Duyfken *Expedition and the schedule of intended ports of call.*

Your Project is an interesting and worthwhile one and I realise that much planning has gone into organising the Duyfken *Expedition thus far. It had been our hope that the security situation in the parts of Indonesia, to which you planned to travel, would have settled by now. Unfortunately, this has not been the case. My Department's travel advisory remains much as it was since December last year, when it was first drawn to your attention. It states that,*

"The situation in many islands in Maluku province and North Maluku province, including Ambon, Seram, Halmahera, Ternate and Tidore remains very unstable due to the continuing Christian-Muslim conflict. Until the situation improves, Australians are advised to avoid all travel to the area."

I am aware that you are not scheduled to enter Indonesian waters until 25 May and that your travel to Ternate, Banda and Ambon will not take place until late June. I would urge you strongly to have alternative plans should there be no marked improvement in the security situation in the region or, indeed, if the security situation should deteriorate further.

At the moment officers of the Embassy are largely prevented by the Indonesian Government from visiting Ambon because of security concerns.

I am aware that the Embassy has been liaising with the Indonesian navy about the possibility of providing an escort for your visit. I am aware, too, of the interest of the Dutch Government in this enterprise. While the Indonesian navy appears to have been very helpful to this stage it may be that a navy escort might not be forthcoming. This, too, would provide another reason for reconsidering your itinerary

It is my wish that the Project be successful and safe and would therefore stress the importance of avoiding areas and situations that are dangerous. I am grateful for your invitation to launch the Duyfken, *but regret to say that I will be unable to do so…*

Yours sincerely
Alexander
Alexander Downer

We now had the Australian Government 'I told you so' escape letter which protected its arse in case we got into trouble. The letter was, however, clearly at odds with the enormous effort by the Embassy to use every diplomatic tool at its disposal and to work all its contacts to help make our visit happen. Two days after *Duyfken* departed Fremantle, I sent Geoff Leach our Plan B. That evening Charlie Welker chaired a Board meeting and it was agreed that *Duyfken* would not leave Australian waters until a sailing permit to enter Indonesia had been granted. If the permit had still not been received by the time the ship left Broome, Peter Manthorpe would be instructed to sail to Darwin, and sit, as long as required in harbour, until we either had the voyage permit, or we had to swing over to Plan C, which was to avoid Indonesia altogether and sail directly to Queensland. Publicly, we were only saying that we planned to sail from Broome to Banda and the approvals were in place. The *Duyfken* Board later got into lock step with the Australian Government and resolved that the ship would leave Australian waters only if Canberra said it was safe to do so. Somehow I would need to find a way.

When I spoke to the crew in Dampier, I still did not have a sailing permit. Although I had received indications that it had been prepared, the volatile situation in Indonesia had meant that it still had not been approved. It was agreed that when I flew back to Perth I would get on another plane to Jakarta. Once again I would try to obtain the valuable piece of paper.

I was sitting in the foyer at my hotel in Jakarta on 9 May 2000. *Duyfken* was due in Port Hedland in the next couple of days. Time was running out. Geoff Leach arrived and apologised. He said that David Ramsay would be along soon. He just had to sort out a few things with the permit at the Minister's office. As if the violence in Maluku wasn't bad enough, there had been a sharp escalation in piracy in Indonesian waters as a result of the crumbling economy and the deteriorating political situation, and the Embassy was getting very jittery about sailing anywhere near eastern Indonesia without a naval escort. Eventually, David Ramsay arrived with an Indonesian representative from Aji Sularso's office. We all sat down. I ordered refreshments all round and we had a chat. During the protracted negotiations, Geoff, David and I had become friends and we joked about the problems of the last few months. Even simple things like paying Aji Sularso for the voyage permit became bureaucratic mountains to overcome.

Geoff and David said that despite the highlighted difficulties, there were signs that the security situation was improving. The Indonesian President, Abdurrahman Wahid, also known as Gus Dur, who replaced Julius Tahija's neighbour, President BJ Habibie, knew Australia well and he had been a frequent visitor to Melbourne before he became President. He was now leading the nation in another turbulent presidency and working hard to fix the domestic problems in the country. It was genuinely feared that the Free Aceh Movement in Sumatra's Aceh province would be successful and another part of Indonesia would become independent. He was negotiating behind the scenes to bring peace to the province. According to some reports, tensions were easing in Timor. Refugees were being encouraged to return home, and the first land border crossing had been opened in Batugade between Kupang and Dili. David said that it was about time we got to the point of my visit. He pulled out a document from his folder of papers. It was the clearance number 001676, listing the ports of Kupang, Solor, Bacan, Ternate, Ambon, Banda, Saumlaki and Aru. I couldn't believe my eyes. Every port we had requested was on the permit. My excitement was short-lived. David Ramsay got out his felt pen and struck out Ternate and Ambon, smiled and handed me the permit. "Welcome to Indonesia," he said.

I was elated — the last piece of the jigsaw was in place. Then I looked at the fine print. This important piece of paper listed the owner of the vessel as Geoff Leach! There was no doubting the significance of that inclusion. *Duyfken* represented Australia and this approval gave us Indonesian Government approval and the tacit endorsement of the Australian Government.

The day after I obtained the permit, the Australian Embassy in Jakarta issued a modified advisory: "The situation in Maluku and North Maluku provinces (in particular, Ambon and northern Halmahera Island) has stabilised over the past two months, although outbreaks of violence are still occurring. Australians should defer non-essential travel to Maluku and North Maluku provinces. . . The situation for Australians in the area of Nusa Tenggara Timur (West Timor) has eased considerably since the problems experienced in late 1999. Australians still need to exercise caution however if working in or travelling near Displaced Persons camps in West Timor, particularly in the border regions of Belu and TTT district." It seemed like things were looking up.

With permit in hand, I made the best of my short visit to Jakarta, calling on Julius Tahija, Australian Ambassador John McCarthy and the Dutch Ambassador, Baron Schelto van Heemstra.

My visit to Jakarta concluded with a meeting which would determine the future of *Duyfken* after the Expedition. In 1998, the Dutch Consul

General in Sydney, David van Iterson, suggested that we should make an approach to the Dutch Government to be involved with celebrations to mark the 400th anniversary of the founding of the United Dutch East India Company in 2002. Enric Hessing, a Dutch Member of Parliament, became one of the prime movers and he headed the Stichting 400 Jaar VOC (VOC 400 Year Anniversary Foundation). He was visiting Jakarta for a trade conference and he wanted to sit down and have a chat about *Duyfken*'s possible visit to The Netherlands as part of the VOC year. I met him in the foyer of his hotel which was just across the road from the Australian Embassy. He was well dressed and urbane — a smooth operator.

Indonesians were freer to express their views than they had ever been since independence and Enric Hessing told me that he found that Indonesia wasn't quite as ready to celebrate this Dutch part of its history as he had anticipated. The Dutch East India Company story in the young nation of Indonesia was a touchy subject. The VOC represented colonialism and all the ills which came with being ruled by a foreign power. Indonesians fought the Dutch to win their independence. He came well prepared for our meeting and he was fully aware of the past history of the *Duyfken* Foundation. He knew that the Project enjoyed the tacit endorsement of Crown Prince Willem-Alexander as he had laid the keel.

It is easy to see why the Indonesians were so reluctant to embrace the VOC 2002 celebrations. The opening page of the briefing paper of Enric Hessing's committee proclaimed:

> *Celebration of 400 Years VOC. The 'Vereenigde Oost-Indische Compagnie' (VOC, Dutch United East India Company) was founded on March 20, 1602. This was the result of a decision by the 'Staten Generaal' (the equivalent of a parliament in those days). It marked the start of the international orientation of the Netherlands, and of a period of great economic and cultural growth. In 2002 this will be 400 years ago. This calls for a celebration!"*

It finished with:

> "The importance of the VOC lies not only in the past, but also in the present and future. As such, in this celebration ample attention will be given to the importance of an international orientation,

entrepreneurship, craftsmanship and innovation for the future of The Netherlands.

Nothing was said about what would later be called the 'Dark Shadows' of the story. Indeed, the briefing document made no mention of the Indonesians at all:

What was the VOC?

VOC is short for 'Vereenigde Oost-Indische Compagnie' (Dutch United East India Company). In the seventeenth and eighteenth centuries the VOC was the largest commercial enterprise in the world, with a fleet of more than a hundred ships, thousands of employees, dozens of offices in Asia, and six establishments in the Netherlands. These were the VOC chambers in Amsterdam, Enkhuizen, Hoorn, Rotterdam, Delft and Middelburg.
After Dutch merchants were excluded from the lucrative trade in Asia by the Portuguese around 1590, several Amsterdam merchants decided to break the Portuguese monopoly. In 1595 they organised the so-called 'First Shipping' to Asia. Other merchants followed suit. In the next five years 15 fleets comprising 65 ships sailed to the Far East, resulting in extensive competition amongst the Dutch. The 'Staten Generaal' (the equivalent of the parliament) decided to act, and persuaded the merchants to join forces and co-operate. This resulted in the establishment of the Dutch United East India Company (VOC). On March 20, 1602 the Staten Generaal gave a license to the VOC, granting them a Dutch monopoly for the trade in the Far East. The VOC was governed by the 'Lords XVII'. These were representatives from the six VOC chambers. They decreed general policy, and divided the tasks among their chambers. The chambers carried out the work. They built their own ships and warehouses, and traded their goods. In the period between 1595 and 1795 almost 4800 voyages to the Far East were made. Though the risks were great, less than four per cent of the vessels were lost. The Lords XVII provided the captains with elaborate information on sea routes, prevailing winds, sea currents, shallows and orientation points. The VOC made its own sea charts, and various navigation instruments were made in their own workshops.

> On the voyages to the Far East both trade goods and utilities were taken along, including textiles, wines, paints, food, water, tools, spare parts and ammunition. However, the most important part of the cargo was gold and silver that were to be used for purchases in the Far East. The voyage to the Far East took an average of eight months.
> Batavia, now known as Jakarta, was the main settlement of the VOC in the Far East, and the centre of an extensive trade network. Indeed, the VOC undertook extensive local and regional trade. For instance, silk was bought in China and traded in Japan for copper and gold. This went to India and was exchanged for textiles that were in turn traded for spices in the Moluccas. Later, coffee, tea and sugar became important trade goods. From Batavia goods were shipped to the Netherlands. On the way back, cinnamon was bought in Ceylon.
> This enormous commercial enterprise lasted two centuries. Toward the end of the eighteenth century trade was declining. The reasons for this deterioration were tough competition, and the war with England. In 1795 the VOC was disbanded.

No 'Dark Shadow' there! I must admit that I wasn't too worried about the implications of a Dutch celebration that seemed to exclude any reference to the thousands of deaths and the pain inflicted on Indonesians by the company. *Duyfken* was yet to visit Indonesia, and all I knew about Banda was what Michael Young had shown me. We were soon to come face to face with that pain and experience the 'Dark Shadows' for ourselves.

I had received a letter in March 2000 while we were conducting sailing excursions into Gage Roads every day and preparing *Duyfken* for the Expedition. It was from the Director of the Maritiem & Jutters Museum at Oudeschild in The Netherlands. His name was Benno van Tilburg. I had no idea where Oudeschild was and when I looked up the name of the Museum it said that Jutters meant beachcombers. My first thought was that maybe it had something to do with Spike Milligan's 'World of Beachcomber' comedy show which I watched as a child. Spike was surrounded by junk washed up on a beach. When I did a quick online search, all I could find were pictures of a Dutch windmill along with a heap of rusty old ship's anchors next to a black weatherboard house. Oudeschild was the principal town on Texel Island. I looked that up, too, and found that Texel was one of the string of islands which protected the Ijsselmeer from the North Sea. It was on the sheltered roadstead near Texel where the VOC fleets were gathered at anchor before they set off for the Indies. Mr van Tilburg wanted us to take our ship to The Netherlands. *Duyfken* could sail to Texel, the place from where she left The Netherlands twice (the second time never to return). Mr van Tilburg had formed a working group called VOC-Texel 2002. I didn't think much more about it because we received many letters asking for our ship to visit various ports — there was never a cheque attached.

I asked Enric Hessing whether he knew of Mr van Tilburg and he assured me he did and the approach was serious. Indeed, they had been in communication for some months. Benno had a plan to make Texel the starting point for VOC2002 year events. He'd been Director of the Maritiem & Jutters Museum since 1995 and he had great plans. Some time later, Benno explained how he reached the conclusion that a ship on the other side of the world should visit his island.

"My Museum was overlooking the former roadstead but the VOC ships were long gone and now there were only small fishing boats," he said. "Of course, in the Museum we had lots of interesting exhibitions — period paintings and objects like cannons found on the bottom of the roadstead in the influential period of Texel in the seventeenth and eighteenth century — but nothing large like a replica ship. Around 1999 I was looking forward to the coming festivities in 2002. I also wanted to contribute to the festivities and to recover the greatness of the former Texel roadstead. We needed ships — big ships! But original VOC ships didn't exist anymore — unless you count the ones laying on the seabed in the roadstead."

"So I was looking in The Netherlands at the so-called replicas. The replica *Amsterdam* moored at the Maritime Museum in Amsterdam couldn't sail and it was supposed to stay in Amsterdam during the festivities, anyway. That other ship — *Batavia* — was more likely to come over to the Texel roadstead. But this was a complicated Project and the Foundation taking care of this well-built replica decided to go to Australia for the Olympics.

"So no replicas in The Netherlands. What to do? Then I read an article in the newspaper of the launching of *Duyfken*. This was interesting. A relatively small ship — 24 metres — and even better a former Dutch ship (bought by the VOC in the beginning of the seventeenth century and sailed in 1606 to the shores of Australia. Willem-Alexander laid the keel of the *Duyfken* in 1997 so this ship really was a Dutch-Australian combined

Project. This was the ship I needed in 2002!" So he sent a letter.

Enric Hessing wasn't at all convinced that *Duyfken* could sail to The Netherlands but Benno was persuasive. He told the VOC2002 group that *Duyfken* was big, but not too big so it could go everywhere they needed including all the former Dutch VOC cities of Amsterdam, Hoorn, Enkhuizen, Rotterdam, Delft and Middelburg. My meeting with Enric Hessing became a gentle interrogation. He asked lots of questions. I said that compared with a certain Dutch built replica, *Duyfken* could sail! Enric pointed out that the replica of the *Batavia* at Lelystad couldn't even leave the Ijsselmeer so what made Australians think they could do it? Maybe it would be easier if we shipped *Duyfken* to Amsterdam? I told him that *Duyfken* was a sailing ship and she would sail to Europe. Why not? The original *Duyfken* sailed to and from The Netherlands twice without any trouble. I said he should trust the Dutch ship designers of four centuries ago. They knew what they were doing. Enric found the whole idea slightly outrageous but he would discuss it with his committee members in Den Haag and we agreed to keep in touch.

"The committee members were not daredevils and more or less afraid that during the sailing trip a member of the crew went (would be lost - Ed.) overboard or accidents would happen," said Benno later. "I countered that critic by saying that we (the Dutch) did this kind of sailing on a daily basis in the VOC period and I would guarantee the safety of the crew which was the responsibility of the Australian partners." The Committee resolved that Benno would make a fact-finding mission to Australia and talk to the Board of the *Duyfken* Foundation.

Chapter 16

No Turning Back

I flew back to Perth, our sailing permit tucked safely away in my briefcase. I spent the weekend at home, before getting on yet another flight first thing on Monday morning. Although fully supportive of my new role at *Duyfken*, there was a growing annoyance from Cathy, and our two children Louise (12) and Daniel (9) that I was spending so long away from home, and when I was home I was ensconced in my office on my computer. I didn't see it. I was running on adrenalin. For me it was exciting. This time I was headed to Broome to hand over the precious document to the Ship's Master before he left Australian waters.

The crew found it hard going getting into Broome. Heavy seas constantly splashed over the deck. They couldn't make headway for two days against a 35 knot offshore wind and things got hairy on one occasion when Peter decided to wear ship (turn away from the wind). Rupert Weller caught hold of a line which carried him off the deck. Then another part of the rig came away in the fierce breeze and the Ship's Engineer, Mick Hemsley, didn't see an unrestrained wooden block flailing about and it crashed into him causing a big gash on his forehead and a puddle of blood on deck. Many of the crew were battered and bruised from the rough weather. Peter called time on the torture. Without making any headway and already a day behind our informal schedule, he turned the engines on and plugged on for 65nm to get *Duyfken* to port. It was only the second time that the engines had been used in this way. We were reluctant to use them for many reasons. We expected the pitching and yawing caused by the engines pumping into the wind to place a lot of stress on the rig which was not designed to take these loads. The engines were never designed to replace sailing, only to assist in emergencies or to enable manoeuvring into and out of port. They used a lot of diesel fuel working into a headwind. I always emphasised with our Ship's Masters that *Duyfken* was a sailing ship and she would sail wherever possible. I would always support the Master's judgement to sail. Peter weighed up whether to wait it out for maybe a week or two until he had a window to sail into Broome or to go for the engine option. Twenty hours later, *Duyfken* dropped anchor and one of the most unpleasant episodes in *Duyfken*'s short history was over. "These incidents reminded us, if we needed reminding, that sailing a ship like this is fraught with potential hazards. Out here in a gale, the public tours of the ship in port, the revisiting of historical events, the receptions and the speeches are all far from mind. Our task out here is not much different from our early Dutch counterparts: we must get from one place to another without falling victim to the sea," said Peter.

The use of the engines to meet port deadlines had been constantly debated since *Duyfken* was built. She was built and sailed for the first time without engines. If she had been without engines on the passage to Broome, Peter would probably have had to wait it out at sea or head north west until he found winds which could take him back to Broome. It could easily have taken weeks. We always put together a busy program in port which usually comprised a civic welcome, visits by local school children and the general public, and functions aboard. The port visits were important to tell the *Duyfken* story and to generate revenue but were they more important than sailing the ship as she was intended to be sailed? I sat somewhere between the two viewpoints. *Endeavour* was known for setting arrival times down to the minute and arriving dead on time, under engines if needed. We planned our voyages with a lot of extra sea time so the crew were under less pressure to constantly log average sea miles. However, Broome showed that even a few days leeway was sometimes not enough. I preferred to keep our arrival times open and schedule civic receptions in the evening or the following day so that we had much more flexibility. It was made clear to the Masters that only in exceptional circumstances were the engines to be used. I also viewed this as a marketing advantage. People in port never knew quite when *Duyfken* would appear over the horizon. It gave the broadcast media something to talk about, too. It made us different to the sail training ships and *Endeavour* with her authenticity above the waterline as a floating museum but powerful Caterpillar diesels working away in the engine room. They arrived on time; we were on expeditions or grand voyages!

In this case, the crew had, indeed, done it tough. When the ship arrived in Broome, Michael Hemsley emerged from below with a big bandage around his head. It was punishing enough that he had to endure working in the cramped engine rooms below while the ship was pitching in the ocean swell but now he was being attacked on deck! The crew were a bedraggled, salt-encrusted and smelly mess from the constant salt spray washing over the decks. Despite the frustrations of the previous 24 hours they had enjoyed an impressive five weeks under sail. They covered 1,674nm at 4.1 knots. *Duyfken* was, indeed, the fastest ship in the VOC fleet.

The ship also looked weather-beaten and worn. She was no longer the showpiece which had left Fremantle. Bill Leonard wanted the hull to be varnished to show off the fine craftsmanship of his team and when she began the voyage, the hull shined with a deep honey colour. A combination of warmer conditions, greater exposure and heavy seas caused the glossy coating to break down. Large areas of varnish on the hull planking were now gone and parts of the topsides were bare wood once again. Gary Wilson had never been a big fan of varnishing the ship, and he had an ally in Nick Burningham. The old Dutch marine art from the 'Age of Discovery' shows the ship as a dark blue-black from repeated applications of pine tar and oil to the timbers. Over time, the timber would get darker and darker. Nick thought that our ship just looked too new when it was varnished and I agreed with him. Gary's view was that we had a crew whose job it was to maintain their home every single day while they were at sea. Oil was easy to apply. They had to tar the rig to prevent it from rotting so they should treat the hull in the same way. I agreed with Gary. The crew began the long and tedious process of scraping off the residual varnish in Dampier. Initially, they replaced it with Hempels teak oil. That soon washed off — and Hempels said that they could not supply more coatings for us now we were on the voyage and out of sight of their warehouse! And so it was that Gary Wilson began experimenting with wood oil. He used boiled linseed oil, beeswax, pure turpentine, Stockholm tar and thinners in varying quantities. He would heat the bees wax and add gum turpentine and Stockholm tar to the mix. It made a concoction with would stick to the timber. Eventually it washed off, but it was easy for the crew to slap on another coat. Gary took it as his calling, and therefore, the crew's job during the Expedition was to progressively remove varnish and replace it with oil.

Broome was very welcoming. The town had been through a tough time. The most severe tropical cyclone to hit the pearling town in 90 years had passed 20 km south a month before. Wind gusts of 290kph were recorded at sea. Miraculously, nobody was hurt but it was a timely reminder of the dangers of the cyclone season.

Rupert Weller was one of the champions of the *Duyfken* story. Originally from Geraldton, he was a trades teacher who offered his skills to the shipyard during his retirement and fell in love with the ship. He quietly worked away at any task he was given. He had absolutely no experience of sailing, but when he said he would like to come aboard for the Expedition, we were keen to have him as part of the crew. He could turn his hand at any repair to anything mechanical. He also constructed the magnificent ship's lantern. Most sailors get seasick at times (even if they won't admit it) and tell you that most people will get their sea legs after four or five days at sea. I don't believe this story as I have never emerged through that haze of pain to reach the other side. Neither did Rupert. In the five weeks sailing north from Fremantle, he constantly battled the scourge of seasickness. By the time the ship arrived in Broome, he was an absolute mess. Peter Manthorpe had serious concerns for his health if he continued on the next long hop to Kupang. I felt particularly sad that Peter would have to have the 'big chat.' Only two people were aboard who had been involved with the construction of the ship. Andrea Cicholas was the other. I supported Peter's decision and Rupert took it hard. I spoke to him afterwards but he knew that it was the right thing to do. He tried his darnedest to overcome the mal de mer but it beat him down. He was quite prepared to give it another go but I said that we had to look after his best interests, too. There was not a dry eye on deck when the crew said farewell to Rupert. But he was irrepressible and he selflessly offered to tow the *Duyfken* shop trailer over the Top End to Queensland. We also loaded four cannon onto his trailer — we wouldn't need them in Indonesia.

I rang Nick Burningham who had left our employ when *Duyfken* set sail from Fremantle. I explained that Rupert had left the ship and we were short one hand. Would he like to sail to Indonesia? Of course he would! Nick would once again turn out to be a great asset. He became a sounding board for both Peter and Gary as he'd sailed the waters of the archipelago many times before.

The last addition to our Expedition crew was a marine biologist. It had been made clear by the Australian Embassy in Jakarta that an environmental theme for the voyage through Indonesia would be helpful when we were applying for permits. Julius Tahija also suggested that we should promote an environmental angle so we began looking for a marine biologist. His view was that a scientist aboard would help allay Indonesian fears that we had some kind of ulterior motive for visiting eastern Indonesia. We thought it was a good idea, too. We put out the feelers and Paul Hough from the Great Barrier Reef Marine Parks Authority in Townsville was very keen to join us. He was the principal research scientist at the Great Barrier Reef Aquarium (Reef HQ) in Townsville. He supervised 10 biologists and five post-graduate interns. His special interest was the growth, reproduction and survival of hard corals. He put out the right messages when he said that he was inspired by the works of the famous English naturalist and wildlife collector from the 19th century, Alfred Wallace, who studied the plant and animal species of Indonesia and laid the ground work for Charles Darwin's *On the Origin of the Species*.

It was not uncommon for the VOC voyages of exploration to carry a person onboard to describe the plants and animals encountered in new lands. The pre-eminent naturalist of the seventeenth century in the East Indies was Georgius Rumphius who worked for the VOC in Ambon and published many descriptions of local flora and fauna. We now had our own Georgius Rumphius. He arrived at the jetty in Broome with an enormous stash of equipment. Besides diving gear, he had specimen gathering nets and all kinds of receptacles to safely preserve his samples. "As a coral biologist, I am particularly interested in the diversity of the corals found in these seas," he said in a media release announcing his appointment. "There are over 400 described species of coral in these waters. Indonesia is 75 per cent sea and these waters are home to 800 species of seaweed, 12 species of sea grass, 90 species of mangroves and six species of turtle. There are also 155 species of seabird, 25 species of whale and dolphin and the richest diversity of fish on earth." Hopefully he wouldn't collect one of each.

Duyfken sailed out of Australian waters for the first time on 19 May 2000. Her destination: Kupang in West Timor. Once again, I left a port before the ship was due to leave. My daughter Louise was singing in the Australian Youth Choir at the Perth Concert Hall, and I didn't want to miss that — I'd missed too much already — so I went home for a couple of days and then got onto another plane bound for Queensland to brief Dale Ryder at the Premier's Office in Brisbane. I reported that all was going well with the voyage so far and if everything went according to plan we would be in Queensland in three months time. The lack of an all-weather berthing facility in Broome forced our crew to anchor the ship over night at Gantheaume Point. *Duyfken* departed from Cable Beach, Broome at

11.00am on 18 May. The crew took last minute provisions off the beach before the anchor was weighed and sails set. The ship slipped out from Australian waters, carried north by a southerly just like the ships of four centuries before.

Duyfken's crew were at sea for 10 days without a break, the first time the crew had been at sea for such a stretch. Compared with future voyages, it was just a short hop. They were heading into *Duyfken*'s home waters where the original ship spent most of her life. Our 'new' crew member, Nick Burningham, was enjoying his time aboard and he and the crew were learning the singular skills of Dutch seafarers from four centuries ago. In his diary he wrote:

> *21st May I don't know how to write about this. It is, in many ways, a dream come true. Here we are charging across a blue sea with 15 - 20 knots of breeze in mild tropical conditions, on a beautiful, indeed exceptionally beautiful, replica sailing ship — and I designed it myself. I was involved all through the construction too. This morning we were able to put some of my historical research into practice. We were more or less hard on the wind and the breeze piping up to the point where the topmasts were perceptibly bowing to leeward. It was deemed time to get the topsails off, but that would have made the ship a bit under-canvassed and left her wallowing and slipping to leeward. So, I asked could we try leaving the topsails braced up and slack the halliards until the yards were about half-mast. The practice is suggested by Dutch marine art of* Duyfken's *time. Sails are often depicted setting in great billows even on ships beating to windward: it might be artistic license, but it might be a genuine observation.*
>
> *Before trying the topsails half mast we rehearsed several reasons why it wouldn't work, but the truth is that it works fine. The topsails are de-powered, the topmasts are standing straight and safe, but the topsails are still drawing and the main course is still luffing before the topsails. It's a fairly important contribution to sailing the ship; it gives us a sail area choice between all working sail and lowers only. The ship is romping along beautifully.*

I arrived in Kupang in West Timor, the capital of the province of East Nusa Tenggara, on 25 May and I was met at the airport by Michael Young's friend Bertie. He apologised that Michael was otherwise engaged. He offered to take me to the Kristal Hotel and I could meet Michael there. After the disappointment of being overlooked for a management position and every other paid job at the *Duyfken* Replica Project and marginalised during the construction phase by Noel, Michael got the message and made new plans. He retired from the WA public service and moved on to live a dream he'd cherished for many years. He saw himself as something of a modern day Alfred Wallace, who funded his expeditions by scouring the Indonesian archipelago for rare animals and plants to be sold to collectors across Europe. Rather than being a collector of rare animals and plants, Michael pursued his long held passion for Indonesian woven fabric called Ikat, which used a particular dying technique resulting in vivid patterns. He had an encyclopaedic knowledge of the variations in Ikat design. European and American collectors were keen on the traditional Ikat fabric which was peculiar to the far flung islands and Michael had many contacts to source them from local villages. He knew what was old and valuable and he could easily spot the junky fabric made for the tourist trade. He also knew that collectors would pay for traditional wood carvings. The craft was disappearing but he knew where to find the best antique pieces — and people who could reproduce them! Michael's life after *Duyfken* saw him owning an art gallery in Bali and regularly travelling through Indonesia on buying expeditions. Kupang was just the start.

It was serendipitous that Michael was living at our first port-of-call in Indonesia as his experience would help guide me through my first encounters with Indonesian officialdom. *Duyfken* was still in the Savu Sea with another four days until she made port. I think I was becoming the most obsessive watcher of travel advisories. The Australian Embassy put out a new warning saying that the situation in Maluku had deteriorated once again and Australians should completely avoid travelling to the region. Hopes of any short term improvement in security were dashed. In Jakarta, there were big demonstrations against the Government for its perceived reluctance to investigate former President Suharto. But I felt like I was in another country in Kupang. By Indonesian standards it was a small city — only about 400,000 people. It is mostly known in the English speaking world for its historical connection with Captain William Bligh of the *Bounty*, who was set adrift in the ship's boat after the notorious mutiny in 1789. His epic 6,000km voyage in a seven metre open boat carrying 18 crew members ended in Kupang. Bligh came ashore to the surprise of the local VOC outpost and wrote of his bedraggled crew: "perhaps a more miserable set of beings were never seen". I hoped my *Duyfken* crew would spruce themselves up before they arrived.

The Kristal Hotel was strangely deserted. I was told at reception that Michael was in a hotel room having a shower. He knew I was coming but he would be indisposed for some time and not to be disturbed, so I sat down for lunch by the pool, a solitary figure ordering one of my favourite dishes — nasi goreng special — always better than plain nasi goreng which doesn't have the egg on top! Without great natural resources to boost the local economy, I knew that Kupang was a backwater, but this didn't explain the lack of guests. Most sensible people were steering clear of the province because, as I was later to discover, it was now a cross between an Indonesian military outpost and a refugee camp.

Michael Young arrived at the pool with a smile on his face and a spring in his step, giving me a big welcoming hug. He explained his local living arrangements. He paid rent for a house in Kupang which he shared with a local civil engineer, Summi, and her family. I was welcome to stay with them if I preferred to live local rather than stay at the hotel. Either way, he would love me to meet his new Indonesian family and enjoy dinner at his new home. Our ship's artist, Robert Jefferson, had arrived a few days before and he was ensconced at Bertie's hotel nearby. There was still some time left in the day to get to work so Michael and I went down to Kupang's Port of Tenau to visit the Kantor Syahbandar (harbour-master's office) and check out where *Duyfken* would berth. When we arrived, I couldn't believe my eyes. It was a sad sight. The only jetty where we could tie up was a mess with piles of rubbish strewn across it. Scattered across the bay was a flotilla of large navy ships which looked to be slowly rusting away, the grey hulls streaked with rust. One was a very large landing ship which looked like it hadn't moved in years and was on the verge of sinking. When President Habibie was Minister for Research and Technology, he spent the whole navy budget on 39 warships, including 16 corvettes, from the former East German navy. It was a bargain, he said. His plan was to refit the ships at yards in Surabaya and create a new shipbuilding industry in the process. It was a blunder of epic proportions, as the unwanted ships were in poor condition and only suited to operating in the cold, relatively flat seas of the Baltic rather than the humid tropics. Australian Defence Minister Kim Beazley had a point when he described them in Parliament as "short-range, low-capability rust buckets". An apt description of the floating scrapyard in front of me. Six years after the ships were purchased, many were slowly deteriorating while at anchor, un-crewed and abandoned by the navy.

After an entertaining evening at Michael's residence, meeting Summi's family, chatting with Robert Jefferson and sampling local delicacies, downing Bintangs and then duty-free Drambuie, I returned to the hotel to prepare for a day of meetings. Michael knew all the local movers and shakers and we did the round of formal audiences with the Governor, the Deputy Governor and the local Police Chief (who was splendidly dressed in a shiny nylon track-suit for this important occasion!). This meant going to the local government offices, smiling broadly, shaking many hands and handing over some documents. I knew the drill in Indonesia. I had lots of documents on impressive letterhead with ink stamps and signatures. One of the officials looked closely at the document and then handed it back. He'd been holding it upside down. It always struck me that the offices were often empty of anything except a desk and a chair. We were told we could have a ceremonial welcome attended by Governor Sarwono for the princely sum of 3 million rupiah or about $300. Gifts would be provided and local media would attend. I was assured that the fee would deliver a very special occasion. It sounded like a splendid deal to me. The jetty would be cleaned up for us as part of the arrangement. We were warned to stay well clear of the Bajau Laut or 'sea gypsy' villages. They were nomadic sea people and their villages were seen as centres for criminal activity in the area. The locals lived in fear of the sea gypsies much like Europeans fear the Romani.

Thanks to Michael's work beforehand, everything was arranged in just a couple of days. With the ship yet to arrive at Kupang and nothing more to do than wait, he suggested that I join him on a buying trip into the mountains in the centre of the island. He wanted to visit the town of Soe to buy some special wood carvings from one or two local artefact dealers. It was rich buying territory for Michael as they still had traditional carvings. Large scale tourism had not yet penetrated the mountain areas. Michael had a list of European and Australian buyers looking to buy genuine traditional carvings rather than the tourist knock-offs.

Kupang had the makings of another Bali for Darwin residents before the violence on the island kept the tourists away. Watching the sunsets at the palm-frond covered beach bar, Teddy's, was an institution. Owned by a Chinese taxi-driver from Sydney, it was the watering hole for the few remaining expats still in town. Michael used the bar like his office and artefact dealers dropped by to see whether they could interest him in their latest offerings. They knew that their artefacts and Ikats had to be authentic as Michael could easily spot a fake. One of them, Onkie, had animist spirit masks from villages in East Timor. The masks were placed on buildings to encourage the spirit of dead relatives back to the family home and to deter evil spirits from taking over. Michael and Robert each bought a mask.

I'd had enough of watching sunsets at Teddy's so I agreed to join Michael, Summi and Robert for what I thought would be a leisurely 120 km drive to hunt for traditional artefacts. I quite looked forward to an overnight stay in the cool mountain air — Soe was about 800m above sea level. We headed east from Kupang past roadside factories making carved chairs and tables. Their recent production was stacked up along the roadside like a continuous street market. Everything had large hand-written price tags. We drove straight through the refugee camp at Tuapukan. At first it looked like a typical local village but then it became more of a shanty town. The newest estimate was that as many as 260,000 East Timorese, or a quarter of the population, either fled or were forcibly removed from East Timor by the Indonesian military after the independence vote. Half that number had returned to East Timor, however, there were 25,000 refugees in the three camps near Kupang. The camps were controlled by pro-Indonesian militiamen who sought out pro-independence East Timorese for retribution or to intimidate and discourage others from returning home. Now the big problem was extracting the refugees who wanted to return to East Timor and re-settling the others elsewhere in Indonesia. It was mid-morning and we didn't give the refugee camp a second thought. Suddenly a young man, with blood down his bare chest, staggered past our car carrying a machete. He was obviously on a mission of revenge. Fortunately we weren't part of his plan. We soon left the refugee camp behind and began climbing on a serpentine mountain road. Besides the occasional truck and car, we saw few people and it was a surprisingly quiet country drive. It was much greener in the mountains and the vistas were superb.

While we were ascending a mountain pass there was a sudden thrashing overhead and a Russian-made Indonesian military transport helicopter landed at a field near the road. How strange, I thought. Our driver didn't find it at all unusual and he continued to drive on, climbing ever upwards. We were soon in the clouds and we didn't arrive at Soe until after nightfall. After driving along a lonely, unlit road, the town had a magical, mysterious quality with the only light streaming through the doorways of small shops. It wasn't like the usual bustling Indonesian town after dark. We booked into a guest house but it was a struggle to find anywhere to eat. Everywhere was closed and it was surprisingly cold and windy. A pickup truck raced past us loaded with teenage boys wearing pro-Jakarta t-shirts and carrying guns. I felt like we could have been arriving in a wild west town and everyone except us knew that there was to be a gun-fight at dawn. The next morning, we took a good look around. It was a very neat little town, so typical of many towns at altitude in the tropics but with few people in the streets. Michael visited a couple of local artefact dealers that looked like they hadn't had a customer for years. Everything had thick coatings of dust over it — but it all appeared genuine and very interesting. I found out later why it was so quiet. The mountainous area in the centre of the island was where militiamen opposed to East Timorese independence and Indonesian military 'advisers' crossed over the border. These groups, numbering about 150 fighters, aimed to disrupt the United Nations peacekeeping program. It was certainly tense in the mountains and I did not like the eerie atmosphere. I was quite happy to leave. I told Michael, Robert and Summi that I would catch a bus back to Kupang in the morning.

My return to Kupang in a local bus was perilous. Military transports loaded with troops rumbled up from the coast. The trucks bounced around every corner, oblivious to anyone heading in the opposite direction. It was a battle for my bus driver to stay on the road. Then the rain started and didn't stop. Unlike the previous afternoon, it was gridlock coming into Tuapukan. We moved at a crawl until finally stopping completely in a long line of traffic right in the middle of the refugee camp area. "Check your doors are locked and wind up your windows," said the driver. It was dark. Single low wattage globes lit up individual food stalls. The road was almost underwater and young men were running up and down in the shadows alongside the cars and trucks. A couple of other men carrying knives peered through the windows of our mini-bus and took a long look at me, demanding that our driver get money from the 'Belanda' (a word for a Dutch person but now referring to any Caucasian) before he would let us pass. Our driver and his bodyguard just sat tight as the other passengers and I moved our backpacks away from the windows and out of sight. We were hemmed in. If someone wanted to attack us there was nothing we could do about it. Our driver saw a gap in the long line of cars and trucks and he went for it; careering through the traffic on the wrong side of the road. It was a skilful and opportunistic getaway. I was very happy to return to my hotel room at the Hotel Kristal that night. It emphasised to me just how volatile the situation was. Violence, including stabbings, was rampant in the refugee camps and there were many unreported revenge killings. Many former TNI soldiers from East Timor were in the camps awaiting resettlement to other parts of Indonesia. Old scores were being settled between the soldiers, the militia and East Timorese sympathisers and nationalists. I learnt later that the refugee camp was probably controlled by the notorious militia leader, Eurico Guterres, who coordinated the militia in Dili which went on a rampage after the independence referendum and murdered more than a thousand pro-independence activists and their family members. The drive into the mountains gave me an appreciation of the instability that was challenging the new democracy. Life was cheap, and the Indonesian government was struggling to impose order at a local level in many provinces. When Michael, Summi and Robert returned to the coast the following day, they were caught in the middle of a protest at the same camp. Barricades were set on fire and the military tried to regain control of the road. A man holding a machete pressed it through an open window and onto their driver's throat, demanding money to let them pass. They didn't panic or react and he withdrew the blade. They eventually made it back to Kupang.

These dramas were all unknown to the crew of *Duyfken* as they made their way across the warm Savu Sea. Faced with fickle winds and currents working against him for four days, Peter eventually tired of bobbing about on a flat ocean and started the engines for the last 49nm into the Port of Tenau arriving at the harbour on 29 May 2000. Our youngest crew member, Nicole Gardner, recalled many years later her vivid memory of her first arrival at an Indonesian port. "On the way in, I was on lookout and reported a buoy on the starboard bow. It wasn't charted. As we approached, we realised it was a dead body. When Greg went ashore in the rubber duck to pick up the officials, the guard with the gun refused to sit down, and kept the gun pointed at Greg, who drove very, very carefully," she said.

Governor Sarwono of the Province of Nusa Tenggara Timur was true to his word and put on a glorious welcome. A band was playing as the ship pulled up to the wharf and the crew came ashore. Four young women performed a Rotinese Ketupat dance swirling their Ikat shawls through the air. Peter and Gary were presented with Ikats and then the crew were delighted as they were each presented with their own gift shawls. The most significant gift was presented to Peter. It was a carved wooden crocodile. Timorese legend had it that a young boy saved a dehydrated crocodile washed up on a beach and returned him to the water. The crocodile took the boy on a long tour until he died of old age and transformed himself into the island of Timor. The presentation of the carving symbolically representing Timor was to be carried aboard the ship to protect the crew as they travelled in local waters. It is still on the ship today. Peter was particularly pleased to be given one of the local straw hats made with a lontar palm frond worn by the dancers. It was thought to be inspired by the sixteenth century headgear of Portuguese ship's officers. The ceremony finished with local dancers and crew joining in a joyful dance on the jetty.

The locals were now calling *Duyfken* 'Kapal VOC' meaning VOC ship. The word replica (also replika in Bahasa) wasn't used. Perhaps this was the return of the VOC. We planned to only spend a few days in Kupang – finalising formalities, servicing equipment and resting. Rachelle Walker rejoined the ship from Fremantle as the Ship's Carpenter, replacing Rupert Weller. The crew were bolstered with Susan Trathen from Calgary in Canada and Peter Weissenekker from The Netherlands. Peter's nephew, Ben Manthorpe, also joined the ship. Peter thought that the voyage would help "sort him out" after a run of strife in his personal life. I think shanghaied might be a word to use in this instance.

Before we left Australia, we had loaded enough supplies of the new anti-malarial drug Larium (Mefloquine) for all the crew and they were issued with their first tablets as they approached Kupang. Only John Colvin refused the preventative medication. He didn't like the side effects. He opted for Chloroquine instead. Larium was being supplied to the United States military and it was recommended to us as the answer to the inadequacy of Chloroquine. What we didn't know at the time was that it had a disturbing range of side-effects. Robert Jefferson struggled with the medication. He remembered his head feelng like it was spinning and feeling like he was hallucinating when he stepped ashore at Kupang. Some crew members felt like they were still on a rolling deck aboard the ship when they were walking on land. Others were finding them downright dangerous. Many of the crew gave the tablets away to villagers en-route. "We'd even given half our malaria tablets away on one island: they needed them more than us. That was the official reason, but if I'm honest, most of us just wanted an excuse to stop taking the tablets: one of the side-effects was hallucinations. Do you have any idea how difficult it is to focus on your work when you can see monkeys with rifles hiding around the ship? Even though I knew they weren't real, they were impossible to ignore, and I was far better off than the crew member who kept seeing snakes: at least I was fairly sure the monkeys weren't real!" said Nicole afterwards.

Many of the crew had not yet grasped the delicacy of our presence in Indonesia. Geoff Leach flew in from the Australian Embassy in Jakarta and we discussed the security situation at length. We considered the offer of a couple of Indonesian marines to join the ship as protection in case we became caught up in the internecine warfare between the rival political groups. We concluded that we would attract more attention with Indonesian military aboard than we would if we were unarmed. It was ironic that the Australian diplomatic corps was with us all the way, supporting our voyage, making things happen and keeping us informed of the latest developments. They had been fantastic. At the same time, the Australian Foreign Minister, Alexander Downer, had written to me distancing himself from the enterprise.

There was a disturbing undercurrent of danger. One day, Nicole Gardner decided to walk about 10 kilometres on her own from Kupang to the port to grab her camera which she had forgotten to take with her. I hit the roof when I heard what she had done. It was such a dangerous escapade which included being chased by a pack of monkeys and walking for hours with another young Indonesian woman who commented that if they were stabbed they would go to heaven together. Concerned for her safety, several local women escorted her through the unsavoury village where the Bajau Laut lived. Australians were perhaps the least popular people in the village since the Australian Government decreed an exclusive economic zone and began confiscating and burning boats used by trepang fishers, and imprisoning their crews. The following morning, Nicole was held in a police station for an hour so they could procure her hat and sunglasses. A small payment got her out of the station. I asked Peter to get our crew together for a meeting. I said that some crew members were becoming lax about even our basic non-negotiable rules such as when to carry their knives on belts around their waist. I reiterated that crew members were never to carry their knives on them when they were away from the ship — it was simply asking for trouble. I issued an edict that our female crew members were never to travel on their own and they must always be with another crew member. It wasn't a popular decree.

Soon it was departure day. In the glorious chaos which can typify Indonesian bureaucracy, Peter criss-crossed the port all day getting paperwork signed and stamped. Michael Young and I knew that we had to pay all the port fees before the ship left. As the day wore on, I was with Peter at the Harbour Master's office on the hill overlooking the port. I paid the fee to ensure we could leave the jetty. We thought that all the paperwork was in place so I left Peter to clear up the last loose ends and I went down to the ship at the jetty. I cheerfully said to Michael that it was all good, I'd paid the unusual fee and the ship was free to leave. Michael then told me that while I was at the Harbour Master's office, he was on the jetty paying another official exactly the same fee. They'd pulled a fast one on us. We both shrugged. That's Indonesia! Peter wasn't done with the bureaucracy and it wasn't until late in the evening that he got back to the ship and he could instruct the crew to throw off the lines.

The next island of Solor brought us into contact with the working life of Willem Jansz for the first time. The sailor had a successful career as an administrator with the VOC after his exploratory voyage to Cape York. The VOC evolved into a colonial organisation ruling over local communities rather than solely trading with them. Jansz returned to the East Indies in November 1612 and served as an upper-merchant and for a time as governor or commandeur of Fort Henricus on Solor. In 1616, he was sent by the Dutch Governor of the Indies to put down a rebellion instigated by the Portuguese and local forces on the island. After quelling the insurrection he was instructed to maintain order as Governor. Jansz obeyed orders and stayed on the island for the year. At the end of 1616 he went home with the status of upper-merchant.

Expecting a very short sea passage, our ship was becalmed for a day until an easterly took her through the Lewotobi Strait between the islands of Solor and Flores. Against a stunning backdrop of volcanic peaks and with dozens of fishing boats with small yellow lights adding to the enchanting scene, the ship set the port anchor for the night. Next morning, the ship was relocated to the village of Menanga and several of the crew visited the ruins of a fort at Lahuyong.

Our marine biologist was excited to dive around such inaccessible islands. He explored near Solor, Adonara and Lambata and encountered more than 50 coral species — including one which he believed was new to science. He found a flourishing reef growing on volcanic rock near the whaling village of Lamakera. He reported back, "From the deck of *Duyfken* I have dived in waters 5000m deep where cooler nutrient rich waters reach the warm sunlit surface and make these tropical waters among the most productive on earth." During the short time the ship had been in Indonesia, he logged six species of turtles and 155 species of sea bird. He was excited to see many pods of pilot whale, two species of dolphin and one humpback whale in the Flores Strait. Our ship was becoming part of the local sea world. Barnacles were beginning to affix themselves to the ani-fouling on the hull and getting a free ride.

Since leaving Fremantle, Gary Wilson worked the crew every day on the ship. If they weren't incessantly scraping lifting varnish or tarring the rig with Stockholm tar, they were making minor adjustments to the rig. Perhaps the most inconvenient piece of the equipment on the ship was the whipstaff or kolderstok. It is the lever attached to the tiller (which connects to the rudder). The crew member who is steering the ship turns the two metre long lever in the direction which he or she wants the ship to go. Marks carved into the deck beam above the kolderstok give a guide to where the rudder is angled. The steering on *Duyfken* is agreeably light, but the kolderstok was too short and some of the crew liked to wrap their leg around it when there wasn't much concentration required. It was agreed that if a new kolderstock could be made then it would make a sailor's life easier. At Menanga, Nick Burningham made a drawing of a modified kolderstok with just the right amount of curve in the shaft. He asked a local man, Danni, whether he could acquire an ironwood sapling of the right shape and diameter. Within an hour, he came back with a piece of tree with just the right curve for the job compared with the straight kolderstok which had done its duty since Fremantle.

Peter takes up the story: "The original one is too short, so we have a piece of local timber approximately the right size and shape, still with its bark on and with stubs of branches sticking out. It was growing in the ground yesterday. I shaped the pole with a Balinese belakas, a small side-axe, which we carry as part of our exhibition of old tools. These are said to be very similar to tools used by the Dutch shipbuilders in *Duyfken*'s era. The local boys lounging around *Duyfken*'s deck help me by holding the wood steady while I shape it. Using a tool like this in Australia would attract attention, but not here. This is how every piece of wood is shaped for all the boats that are built in these villages. I start sandpapering the shaped pole, but Gary stops me. 'Watch this,' he says. He gives each boy, there are about 15 of them, a piece of sandpaper and says 'Go!' The pole, the boys and the deck of *Duyfken* disappear under a cloud of wood dust. In about two minutes the boys, yelling and laughing, have sanded the pole smooth. Gary and I are laughing so much there are tears rolling down my face." That piece of Indonesia is still on the ship today performing yeoman service with the crocodile carving from Kupang on the ledge above.

Chapter 18

Sugar and Spice and All Things Nice

As *Duyfken* began her voyage through the Indonesian archipelago, I flew to Jakarta to put the next stage of the Expedition together. My meeting this time was with Tanya Alwi, who had been recommended by Geoff Leach at the Embassy. She was known in the film world as a 'fixer'. As opposed to the dubious operators in horse racing, a fixer in the film business is someone who can do the local groundwork for visiting film crews or any type of media. A skilled local fixer has good contacts and can arrange things ahead of time without any fuss. Tanya lived in Jakarta but she hosted visits across the archipelago by the BBC, ABC and numerous independent film crews. The success of our Expedition hinged on being able to visit Banda. It was where the re-enactment would begin. With the Maluku Islands of Ternate, Tidore, Bacan and Makian, as well as Ambon, now off limits for *Duyfken*, it was even more important for us and the crew from Firelight Productions for everything to run smoothly in Banda. There was no question that Tanya would get things done. Her father was Des Alwi, the uncrowned and self-titled 'King of Banda' whose ancestry was a marvellous mix of Arabian, Chinese and Buginese. The media savvy entrepreneur made himself the face of Banda to the outside world. I was looking forward to having lunch with both of them.

To use the phrase 'a larger than life character' to describe Des Alwi would be an understatement. He was tall and stocky and he had a commanding presence. He swaggered into our meeting, pushed himself back in his chair and proceeded to spout forth his view of the world. He'd been living in the Indonesian capital for some time, unable and unprepared to return to Banda because of the violence in the region. All air connections had been cancelled or made impossibly unreliable. His hotel on the island depended largely on dive tourism and it was not doing so well. His son, Ramon, was left to run it as best he could while it was in a moth-balled state and visitors were discouraged from visiting the province. When I told Julius Tahija about my encounter with Des, he found it very amusing that we would employ Tanya Alwi and deal with his compatriot. I think he thought that Des was a wheeler dealer, a likeable larrikin, as Australians would think of him. He was known fondly in Jakarta as 'the boy from Banda'. With lashings of self-interest thrown into the mix, he was Banda's best promoter. Des liked *Duyfken*. We'd be good for business.

Fractured reports were coming out of Maluku. I read that the Christian businesses at Ternate were all closed and shuttered up. Christians who could get out were overloading the ferries heading south. Des was full of bravado when I raised the subject. He made it clear that as far as he was concerned there was no violence in Banda and that the islands had been insulated from the ethnic conflict in the rest of Maluku. Banda was "peaceful", he said nonchalantly. He insisted that we were to be his guests when we got to Banda and this meant staying at his hotel and having dinner at his restaurant near the main jetty at the main town of Banda Neira. He would make certain that the crew would be safe during their stay. I need not worry. The Alwis would handle our every need from transfers between islands to cultural events — and we would pay a modest sum for their trouble, of course.

It was easy to see how Des Alwi Abubakar became 'Mr Banda' or 'Pak Des' as the locals reverently called him. Born in 1927, his grandfather was a successful pearl and nutmeg dealer across the islands. He told me that he met Indonesia's first prime minister, Sutan Sjahrir, and the former vice President Mohammad Hatta when he was eight years old while they were exiled to Banda by the Dutch colonial government. As a teenager, he marched with compatriots in the 1945 Battle for Surabaya in East Java. It was the fiercest of the independence battles. He later moved to Yogyakarta where he worked at the Voice of Indonesia radio station. He was proud to say that he studied at King's College in London. He served as a diplomat in several Indonesian embassies before becoming disillusioned with President Sukarno's authoritarian rule and moved to Malaysia to set up a radio station voicing opposition to his policies. Returning to Indonesia, he reinvented himself as a film-maker, writer and host to the rich and famous at his hotel at Banda Neira. Like Julius Tahija, Des was an internationalist who looked beyond the confines of his home islands in one of the most isolated parts of

Indonesia, and took a punt in the big wide world beyond.

His daughter, Tanya, also had the entrepreneurial flair of her father. After receiving a degree in the United States, she forged a career promoting environmentalism. It was a tough assignment in Indonesia but she enjoyed a high profile in the environmental movement. Public relations and hosting film crews were part of Tanya's broad portfolio of ways to make a living. She had a great sense of humour and it was fun working with her. I didn't mind paying her invoices because she had access to the halls of power which I could only dream about. If she told me to write a letter to a certain Governor or a Minister, I would do it, knowing that it was just a formality after she had already laid the groundwork for the approval we required.

As a demonstration of Tanya's great connections, while I was in Jakarta she arranged a media conference hosted by Gede Ardika, the new Indonesian Minister for Culture and Tourism, to announce the *Duyfken* Expedition. And yes, he found it only mildly amusing that Australians found his given name funny because it sounded like the Australian shortening of 'good day' to g'day. I was warned not to mention it. I was surprised when Tanya asked for money to put into an envelope in each of the press packs handed out at the announcement. My first response was "you're joking." She then proceeded to give me a stern talk about how the media game worked differently in Jakarta. The journalists were poorly paid and there were any number of stories they could file for their newspapers every day. They were frequently asked to attend media conferences which would entail them travelling across the traffic-clogged city and spending a lot of hours away from the office. She told me that if I wanted coverage, then I had to give the journalists a small payment. Unsure of whether I was being set up, I told Geoff Leach about the conversation and he assured me that it was common practice and it was done all the time. Dare I say that the Embassy probably did it, too. So I paid up, and our Expedition was covered in all the national newspapers. Tanya even arranged for the hugely popular Tempo news magazine to put a journalist aboard for one leg of the Expedition. Gede was apologetic that he couldn't host *Duyfken* to Jakarta. "There are many difficulties," was a polite way of saying that the last thing Jakarta needed at the moment was a Dutch colonial ship adding to the crisis. I responded that, one day, when things settled down, I hoped that *Duyfken* would enthusiastically visit the national capital.

Trusting Tanya to put our Banda arrangements in place, I returned to Perth. My next opportunity to meet the ship and her crew would be in Banda and it was less than a fortnight away. The first problem was getting there. All travel to Banda was via Ambon and I couldn't fly to Ambon as no foreign nationals were allowed onto the island. It was impossible to fly from Ambon to Banda anyway as the local light aircraft flight had been cancelled for months. I planned to travel with Ellenor Cox from Firelight Productions and the accomplished Perth photographer, Robert Garvey, who was completing his coffee table book on the ship and needed shots at Banda for his final chapter. I asked Tanya Alwi to find any way for us to get there. She came back with an option to rent a nine-seat twin-engine Beechcraft aircraft for $25,000. Easily fixed — just fly over the troubles. A nice idea but with our parlous financial situation there was no way I was about to spend the money. She said that there was only one other way, apart from sailing an early seventeenth century Dutch jacht, to Banda. We could fly from Jakarta to Ujung Pandang (Makassar) near the southern tip of Sulawasi, then take a weekly Pelni ferry via Ambon to Banda. The Pelni ferries were like the passenger trains of continental countries and, as expected with BJ Habibie's influence, were built in Germany. It sounded simple enough. The ferries were massive and carried several thousand passengers. We could travel in what was described as first class for a small additional cost. Most travellers slept on benches in the hold. Being pampered in the luxury of the first class cabins, we didn't anticipate any problem. Tanya warned us not to expect the standards of a cross-channel ferry in Europe.

Robert and I met Ellenor in Ujung Padang. The ferry did not arrive in the morning as scheduled so we had to fill in some time.

"I had time to kill and wandered over to the seventeenth century Dutch Fort called Ford Rotterdam," said Robert. "Suddenly the call went out. The ship was here! Hurry! If we missed the boat, no-one could say exactly when the next one would arrive. The empty wharf was now dominated by a massive ship, which rendered the dock a flimsy jetty. Where there had been calm, chaos ensued as crowds swarmed, hauling baggage and carting baskets, animals and cages."

The *Bukit Siguntang* arrived from Ambon and thousands of people streamed down the gangways as cranes unloaded all the cargo which they didn't carry off themselves. On the dock, people swarmed over the piles of freight to grab their belongings. The ferry was packed with Muslim refugees escaping from the violence in Maluku. Then the tide reversed and our departure was equally crowded with people returning to the eastern province to take a chance that it would be safe enough for them to return to their homes. This was no time to be shrinking violets as we unloaded our gear from the taxi.

"I observed the scene with dismay. How was I to fight my way through that sea of bodies with multiple cases of photographic equipment, personal effects and boxes of food supplies?" said Robert. " We had first-class tickets, which, in that panicky moment, didn't seem to account for much. Then, like a miracle, a team of porters descended, heaved our bags aloft and cut a swathe through the crowd. With the ship's horn honking imminent departure, we knew we couldn't lose those porters. Like something out of a movie, we belted after the rapidly disappearing luggage. Held above the crowd, at least we had something to aim for. Winding our way through the throng, up the gang plank, through hectic fourth-class and up, through second, and third, where we lost sight of them. Arriving at the top deck, our first class tickets were checked and we were ushered to our cabins. There was all our gear: cameras, food, clothing, neatly stacked, as it should be. Relief!" Robert recounted.

When I pulled back the covers of my bunk, I found that I was sharing it with hundreds of small cockroaches. They scattered in all directions. When it came to time to leave the cabin for lunch, we opened the door to find that the whole passageway was packed with people sitting on the floor who had claimed their spot to camp for the next couple of days. "Permisi, permisi" we said as we pushed our way down the passageway. Every single corridor of the ferry was bursting with passengers when we pushed, and shoved, and clambered over and around people every time we wanted to get in and out of our room. We squeezed past other passengers just to be able to open our door and collapse into the cabin — our peaceful retreat from the mayhem outside. I thought to myself it was time to make my peace. If this ship went down, there is no way we would make it out alive. Even if we could make it out of the passageway, there was no escape from the sinking ship. All the lifeboat pulley mechanisms had been painted over so many times that they would never move in case of emergency. I also noticed that many of them had been raided for the rations and anything else which could be exchanged for cash. There were even people sleeping in one of the lifeboats, its cover rotted to pieces in the tropical sun.

Apart from the cabin, the only respite from the hustle and bustle of the public areas of the ship was the first class dining room and the bar. We were the only ones to eat in the dining room. There were two possible reasons for this. Either, everyone brought their own food aboard, or the food was so bad that people preferred to starve. After our first meal aboard, we gave serious thought to the latter and survived mostly on dried biscuits and soft drink.

I was surprised to find a couple of booksellers aboard and, ever the optimist, I thought maybe I could find something in English to read. No chance. They weren't selling romance novels or pulp fiction but paperbacks espousing the virtues of Islamic jihad and other religious topics. The books had shocking, violent images on the covers. So with few options, the best place to while away the two days at sea was in the bar. Scrappy and worn out music videos flickering on the television screen, with the sound turned up so high that the distortion was painful, limited how many hours we could endure in one stint. At least it was a social atmosphere. There was one guy who often loitered in the bar with a couple of other young men. Occasionally he would say hello and want a short chat and we would happily oblige. There was nothing to be gained from being unfriendly and suspicious of strangers when there were maybe three thousand people on a ferry made for 2,000 passengers and we were the only foreigners.

Meanwhile, *Duyfken* was enjoying a dream run through the Flores and Banda Sea, stopping at far-flung villages on rarely visited islands and enjoying local hospitality. All the crew except Mick moved from the hold to sleep on the deck during the warm tropical nights. The old Dutch crews had the right idea after all. Peter wrote in his log: "We are living an exotic dream, sailing around a strange and beautiful tropical country in a magnificent sailing ship straight out of the pages of a child's picture book. Our task is to investigate history and to make friends wherever we go. It's a wonderful dream and we don't want it to stop."

However, things weren't totally rosy. Most of the food stowed onto the ship in Australia was running out. It was replaced by Indonesian staples such as rice — palatable to some crew members but less so to others. Ship's Cook, Jane Doepel, went ashore whenever possible to bring back whatever she could: bananas, green-leaf vegetables, limes and sometimes even honey. The crew had no choice but to adapt to an Indonesian diet. Meanwhile, on the ferry neither Ellenor, Robert or I could sometimes tell what the reddish mound was in the middle of our plates.

Eventually, the *Bukit Siguntang* slowed and crawled from the Ambon Sea into Ambon Bay. We were nervous and so was everyone else aboard. Two weeks before, gunmen in speedboats had strafed the ferry we were now aboard. They killed one passenger and wounded 50 others. I had sent that depressing news as a warning to Peter to keep right away from this trouble spot. I was aware of the deepening crisis in Maluku and it concerned me that the crew may be targeted by one of the factions involved in the fighting.

Banda was only about 200 km by sea from Ambon.

A few days before, Peter Manthorpe had come on deck in the early hours of the morning. He was surprised that he could see the beam of the Nusanive Lighthouse at the southern tip of Ambon island. Surely not? Overnight, however, there had been a wind change which wasn't spotted by the watch and the ship had veered on a more northerly heading from her planned north easterly track to Banda. She was closing on Ambon. He knew they were too close to the trouble spot and he reacted immediately, calling for a tack. He made as much distance from Ambon as he could, tacking to the south and getting under power.

Looking out from our ferry, the water was like green glass. The 20 km long bay is skinny and both sides rise up to mountainous peaks covered in jungle. There was a narrow band of houses close to the water. The ferry was only moving at a few knots, hardly splashing the water from her bow. It was disturbingly quiet. Everyone aboard was apprehensive. People shuffled about on deck, quietly getting organised with their gear and speaking in hushed voices. There was none of the noise and bustle we saw in Ujung Pandang. Everyone was waiting to see Ambon city.

The three men who had been spending as much time as us in the bar came out onto the deck. Two were now dressed in military gear. The third was dressed in an impressive Kopassus military uniform with campaign stripes and decorations — and the distinctive red beret which struck certain fear into many Indonesians. We didn't expect that. Kopassus is the Indonesian equivalent of the SAS except that they had been busier putting down separatist rebellions within Indonesia than dealing with foreign threats. They are mostly known, rather infamously in Australia, for the murder of five Australian journalists leading up to the Indonesian invasion of East Timor in 1975. They were currently heavily engaged in Timor, coordinating militias operating across the border. Kopassus also was operating in Ambon in a confusing situation which had the terrorist group Laskar Jihad fighting against the Christian groups. I heard that both police and military troopers were taking off their uniforms and fighting on either side according to their religious beliefs.

The city of Ambon slowly came into view and it looked like what I imagined Beirut would have looked like during Lebanon's civil war. The city rose from the port up a series of hills. I was told that the Christians were on one side of the town and the Muslims were on the other. There was a no man's land in the middle. Smoke rose up from a handful of smouldering buildings and many other buildings were gutted shells. Earlier in the month, more than 30 explosions across the city had broken a 12-day lull in the fighting. It was unsafe to move anywhere in the city, with snipers from both sides occasionally picking off targets. All the United Nations aid agencies left during May after they were fired upon. It was estimated that 3,000 to 4,000 people had died from the violence in in the Maluku Islands in 12 months. The wharf was packed with soldiers waiting for the ferry to dock. We would be in port for only a couple of hours while people and cargo was unloaded. We were told quite forcefully that we were not to go ashore under any circumstances. I used the opportunity to try my mobile phone. It worked spasmodically for the first time since Ujung Pandang so I called home. I didn't tell Cathy what I was seeing in front of me. No point in alarming anyone. Our Kopassus acquaintance and the two soldiers threw their packs over their shoulders and prepared to disembark. He gave us a cheeky half grin as he walked past to head down the gangway. I must have looked surprised.

On the wharf, the soldiers began talking to groups of young men who followed them from the ferry. They all piled into a truck and left. Then it occurred to me that there was an inordinate number of young men on this ship. Most of the passengers were young males. We had probably been on a jihadists' delivery ferry, bringing people from other islands coming to join the fight. I later learned that the Pelni ferries from Ujung Pandang to Ambon were used by the Muslim population during the conflict. Christians escaping Maluku went aboard the Pelni ferry which operated from Ambon to Kupang. It also emerged that Des Alwi wasn't being exactly frank with us when he told me that I had nothing to worry about because, unlike the rest of Maluku, there had been no religious violence in Banda. He said that is had been because there had been no Christians living on the islands. In fact, there had been a significant Christian population on Banda for hundreds of years since the Dutch depopulated the islands of Bandanese and replaced them with more compliant workers. When the violence began in Ambon, several thousand refugees, including Christians, fled to several of the 11 islands which form part of the Banda chain. Violence came to the peaceful islands in April 1999. The worst violence occurred when five members of a Christian family of Dutch/Indonesian descent were murdered and their plantation set ablaze. The TNI (Indonesian armed forces) arrived shortly after the violence and evacuated all the Christians except a handful of families who refused to leave. As we steamed back out of Ambon Bay into the open sea for the relatively short hop to Banda, I had no idea what we were about to encounter.

Duyfken had already arrived at Banda Neira. We were a little over 10 weeks out of Fremantle. The Bandanese were surprised when the ship arrived and so was Tom Goodman, an American PHD student, who was stranded on Banda. He was researching a thesis at the University of Hawaii on the trading routes of Maluku and Papu. *Duyfken's* arrival added a new perspective to his research. He was astonished when the ship appeared:

> Duyfken *sailed into Banda Neira Harbor like something out of a Hollywood movie, an entirely implausible one. I saw her from the bow of a small water taxi canoe that routinely ferried me and other passengers to and from the larger Pulau Banda Besar or Large Banda Island, home of the largest of Banda's world famous nutmeg and mace plantations.* Duyfken *came to my attention out of the corner of my eye as an unusually large object, one I assumed was a Korean or Japanese deep sea fishing trawler. They frequented the surrounding waters for schools of high value bluefin tuna. When I looked to my left I froze. There just a hundred or so yards away was a ship that I had only read about. I doubt there were more than five people on Banda Neira who knew what I was seeing. A VOC military scout vessel; a war boat. I couldn't stop staring at the sight of this ship sailing towards me. I had read about these ships in the VOC archives in The Hague and Jakarta. The boat was smaller and wider than I had imagined. It reminded me of the old canal transport boats I saw in Holland with their bulbous hulls and shallow draughts, ideal for plying shallow canals and North Sea coastlines. But* Duyfken *was far more beautiful than a pedestrian canal boat. Fully masted, she looked like her namesake, a little dove. I saw the crew and they saw me. I waved and they waved back. They may have been as amazed to see me as I them. Where were they from? Why was she in Banda? I may have read about* Duyfken *in my research but I didn't recall it when I saw this ship. I also wondered what* Duyfken *was doing in war torn Maluku. Didn't the captain know what he was sailing into? I assumed that Des Alwi, the orang kaya of Banda, reassured him of the islands' safety. Still, Australian media, like their Dutch counterparts, often published lurid accounts of the Ambon violence. But that was Ambon. Even Australians, Indonesia's close neighbors, don't know or care to know much about the little islands east of Ambon, let*

alone Papua. The only islands they seem concerned about were the ones like Roti, the source of most fish poachers in the Australian portions of the Arafura Sea off Darwin and northern Queensland. I wanted to meet the crew and the captain and I knew where best to find them—Des Alwi's Hotel Maulana, the home and office of Banda Neira's defacto harbormaster and king of the archipelago.

Peter was directed to moor *Duyfken* away from the main jetty so our ferry could come alongside. He chose a lovely spot near the Hotel Lagoona where he dropped a stern anchor and tied up to a tree with a long cable from the bow. The water was very deep in the lagoon so there was no danger of grounding.

I still had a few days aboard the *Bukit Siguntang* before we arrived at Banda. The hustle and bustle aboard the ferry had largely disappeared after many people disembarked at Ambon. The ferry would do a loop, visiting Banda and then returning to Ambon. It was most peaceful and cool on deck so I spent some time on my own, just contemplating what we'd find when we reached the legendary islands. For the first time ever, and I have never seen it since, I saw St Elmo's fire on the ship's masts. The luminous plasma was fleeting and just for me. An omen? Maybe I was just lucky. Peter Manthorpe has spent a life at sea and has never seen it. When I went down below to tell Ellenor and Robert of my good fortune, they were unimpressed. Maybe that night was just for me and St Elmo.

The first sight of Banda was the conical black silhouette of the active volcano Gunung Api (fire mountain) on the horizon. At almost 700m it has a towering presence, with its peak often masked by cloud. It had last erupted 12 years before with lava flowing into the sea. One of marine biologist Paul Hough's motivations to join the voyage had been the opportunity to dive on what he had heard was the fastest growing coral reef in the world. Coral was growing on the new mineral-rich lava beds in the sea beside the volcano, and from a few diving accounts, it was phenomenal.

When our ferry finally arrived at Banda, we slowed to enter the lagoon, and there was *Duyfken*, with just the unmistakable yellowy light from the translucent cow horn panes of Rupert Weller's stern lantern to indicate its presence. She was at anchor just like four centuries ago. The town was dimly lit and there appeared to be a busy little market at the jetty waiting for us. There was none of the chaos of Ujung Pandang. We came ashore without fuss and I asked Robert and Ellenor to wait at the wharf. I would find Peter in the throng of people. The marketplace was quite dark just like the refugee camp near Kupang and I felt a little uneasy. Each stall had a small light illuminating its goods. Peter strolled out of the darkness, looking refreshed, relaxed and cheerful. "Welcome to Banda!" he said with a smile. It was great to see him and my anxiety vanished. A couple of days in Banda had obviously agreed with him. We had a quick chat and I told him what we had seen in Ambon. "Was everything OK here?" I asked. He assured me that it was fine, if a little tense. He couldn't describe it. It was like everyone was watching everyone else. He showed us to the Maulana Hotel which was right next door to the jetty, so that I could meet Tanya's brother, Ramon. Meanwhile, the Pelni took just a handful of passengers aboard and steamed quietly out of the lagoon. The market stalls were soon packed up and gone. The wharf was quiet. Lights were turned off and Banda was plunged into darkness once again.

There were few sights ever so beguiling as that first view from the balcony of the hotel the next morning. It was like I was in a dream. The lagoon was smooth and still like a sheet of black glass reflecting the sky. Gunung Api towered less than 500m away on the other side of Banda Neira Harbour. It was so quiet that the slightest sound appeared to echo across the lagoon. Everyone seemed to speak in hushed tones almost out of respect for the tranquility. *Duyfken* was moored to the right of the hotel, sitting peacefully at anchor. When I went aboard, Nick Burningham was sitting on the main hatch writing in his journal. He had the look of a sailor now — greying beard and slightly bedraggled clothes. Michael Young joined the ship in Kupang and it was hugs and smiles all round when he appeared on deck from down below. It is an understatement to say that he had lived the dream. How extraordinary that his boyish enthusiasm many decades before had resulted in this surreal moment. We were standing on the deck of *Duyfken* at Banda where in 1606 Willem Jansz left on a voyage of discovery which would put Australia on the map for the first time! Just the three of us, drawn together five years before and now making our own story: the dreamer, the designer and me.

I saw that the ship now had a traditional Timorese house mask tied to the opening above the steering hutch. It was Michael's doing — one of the masks he had bought at Teddy's Bar in Kupang. He said that the masks were placed on houses in Timor to ward off the evil spirits who might want to make mischief inside. He said that a mask should stay on *Duyfken* to make sure that nothing ill would come to the ship or crew. It was perfect.

Hopefully it is still there.

The poetic scene around me that day was so peaceful, so incredibly beautiful, that it was like we had been transported to another world and I will never forget it. It's a cliché that for me it was like time stopped for an hour that morning.

The reality soon struck home as I went for a stroll around town. Several buildings had been gutted in the violence, their windows smashed and the walls scorched with black soot. They were boarded up and fenced. Others had signs saying 'No Christians' so they wouldn't be attacked. Nick Burningham recounted a conversation he overheard:

> *"Every ferry that arrived from Ambon brought more refugees whose terrible stories I sometimes overheard.*
> "How's the big church at Batu Gajah?"
> "Flat!"
> "Burned?"
> "Completely razed to the ground."

Walking through Banda, I saw a man strolling toward me who looked totally out of place. He was a tall, slightly dishevelled, American. He towered above the locals. I said g'day and we soon got chatting. He knew all about our arrival. It was Tom Goodman. It had been a lonely time for him. He described himself as a 'refugee'. He had been conducting historical research on an old maritime trade network called 'sosolot' in the small archipelagoes of eastern Seram and coastal communities along the south western Papuan coast for several months. It was his second visit to Maluku. He spent a couple of weeks in Ambon City to prepare for his field work, gathering oral histories from the raja royal families that still hold sway over the area. Later he wrote about what he saw:

> *When Duyfken arrived I was ending my second 'tour of duty.' I use that term because I was an eyewitness to violence in Ambon and the refugee crisis that affected the entire region, from Ambon to North Maluku to coastal West Papua. And, of course, Banda itself. When the violence threatened to destroy all public order, I had to flee Ambon on an rickety old ferry which was a converted cargo ship. The Indonesian government sent in the Marines a couple of days before I left the city. When they landed at Laha Airport they were*

> greeted by regular Indonesian Army units who promptly opened fired killing more than a few of their own countrymen. My friends and contacts from East Seram and the Christian host family where I stayed advised me to leave and arranged for my safe passage out of the city. When I asked them if I would be safe in the Islamic areas, they replied, "Why not? We've cleaned out all the Christians. As a foreigner you are our guest under the protection of the raja families." I complied since no other boats were leaving Ambon, mainly because snipers from the Christian kampungs along the long Ambon Bay coastline took shots at departing vessels suspected of carrying Muslims, and Laha Airport was closed due to the Indonesian military fire fight days before.
>
> The ferry captain allowed me to sleep in the ship's control room. Actually I had no choice. 'For my safety' I was his guest. The ship, one of the old rust buckets belonging to the Perintis line, carried hundreds of East Seramese and Papuan refugees from Ambon. I was told about 600, maybe more. On a cargo ship with two toilets, one was reserved for the captain, crew, and 'guests.' Most people on that boat did their bodily business standing in place like prisoners in a crowed jail cell, save for the lucky ones closer to the ship's edge. At least one person fell overboard that night, a common occurrence on the overcrowded refugee ferries. The ship never slowed down — it was assumed that falling overboard meant certain death. Whether they fell accidentally or 'accidentally' no one knew or would talk about. The larger trans Indonesian Pelni ferries had infamously experienced revenge killings in the deep holds of those vessels. When I visited Maluku the second time, I did so on the 'Christian' Pelni.

The amiable American said that *Duyfken* had arrived in Banda Neira at a complicated time. "Sure, the islands were peaceful now that one of the two warring groups, the Christians, had largely vanished," he said. "The Chinese were still there, but they lived in fear. Real fear. The locals still depended on the Chinese for commerce and larger boats, their only life insurance. The other non-Muslims on the island were several western tourists and one graduate student, me."

"Our funds kept us well fed and housed, but they couldn't buy us passage off Banda Neira," said Tom. "Ambon airport had already been closed once due to a bloody battle among Indonesia's armed forces and large ships, especially oil tankers, feared sniper attacks if they tried to sail out of Ambon's long narrow bay. Without guaranteed supplies of oil and safety, no airplanes or passenger ships served Banda, and the only other nearby 'city' with air and ferry travel connections was Tual in the Kai Archipelago, over 400 kilometers northeast of Banda, a roughly 20 hour boat ride as the crow flies." Clearly, Robert, Ellenor and I had been fortunate to have Tanya Alwi working on our behalf. How she got us aboard I will never know.

Tom felt trapped, unable to board a ferry. He was stranded on Banda. Normally he would have been happy to stay for months to continue his research work, but it was impossible under the present state of civil war.

> *Before* Duyfken *arrived I had spent the better part of the week waiting for a plane from Ambon, a plane that would never come. Then a Bandanese person I befriended told me about a medium sized Dutch tour boat that arrived from somewhere, I forget. Odd that a tour boat was wandering the Banda Sea while boats stayed in Ambon in fear of sniper fire. That means the tour boat may have sailed by Nusa Tenggara Timur and island hopped to Banda, thus avoiding Ambon altogether. In any case, I wanted to be aboard that ship and I, and others, were willing to pay good money for a lift. The boat's leader, an older Dutch woman, steadfastly refused. Local Bandanese knew her well as an imperious, arrogant ass with a colonial mindset. Some hated her. Des Alwi knew her well too and that probably contributed to the bad feelings toward her. Her attitude was that we chose to visit Banda without a tour guide, so we deserved what we got. She didn't say the evacuation was impossible just that it wasn't going to happen on her boat. We appealed to 'Pak Des' to intercede on our behalf as a personal favor in time of crisis. He tried but he couldn't change the woman's mind. Perhaps a contract was involved or he depended on the flow of rich Dutch tourist guilders during what amounted to wartime conditions. Finally the Dutch boat readied itself for a quick departure. Word spread around Banda Neira that the boat was about to leave and to rush down to the dock. People were really desperate. Banda is beautiful, but months in Banda was not. The lack of reliable news from Ambon and the BBC made things worse. The scene at the dock was chaotic. The boat engines fired up and several people, locals and visitors, hurled verbal abuse at the*

> woman and sympathetic crew. Not all the crew members, however, were unsympathetic. One Indonesian offered to assist a few people to stow away below deck. That attempt failed spectacularly, but I remember it like yesterday. The people were marched off the boat, down the gang plank to cheers from the small crowd. I was one of the would be stowaways. Thinking about it now, I realize how ridiculous and potentially dangerous that decision was, but it happened anyway. Such was the state of Banda Neira as Duyfken docked days later.

We were oblivious to what had happened only a few days before. I had to catch up with Des Alwi to talk about our plans. He made a special trip to Banda from Jakarta to give us his sage advice. We had a full program of activities so there wasn't going to be much chance to rest. Marcus, Ellenor Cox and Chris Watson saw Banda, quite rightly, as one of the highlights of their documentary and they were determined to make the most of it, using the ship and the stunning locations. Marcus was trying to work with the locals to get some traditional vessels into the harbour for a morning of filming *Duyfken* surrounded by local craft, but Des held all the cards.

Robert Garvey also wanted to get the closing pictures for his book. He asked us to sail *Duyfken* through the passage between Gunung Api and Banda Neira and past outlying Pulau Keraka or Crab Island into the Banda Sea for a day of shooting. He knew exactly what he wanted and how he was to do it. In his younger days, he worked on cray boats lifting pots. He quickly learned the hard way how to stand so he never lost his balance as he carried the pots and the crayfish across deck. The skill became invaluable when he worked as a professional photographer during the America's Cup Defence in Fremantle. While other photographers were seasick or holding on tight as the tender boats weaved around to observe the yachts in the strong sou' westerlies at Gage Roads, Robert was right at home jumping from side to side getting the best shots. All he had to do in the next few days at Banda was find a speedboat who could take him out to sea to follow the ship. The crew had no idea that it had been Robert who had put them through a tortuous day off Barrow Island in the North West of WA when they wore ship repeatedly so that the 'bloody photographer' in the helicopter could get the shot he wanted.

A small crew prepared the ship for sea as we didn't need a full complement for the day sail. Des Alwi joined us aboard. It was not dissimilar to most of the days we experienced in Banda with a dark overcast sky and frequent heavy showers. The cone of Gunung Api was shrouded by cloud.

"The day dawned with glowering skies, which made a dramatic backdrop to what would be the cover shot for my book," said Robert. "In brisk winds, the *Duyfken* headed quickly out to sea. I was keen to capture some hero shots of *Duyfken* under sail, with the majestic active volcano, Gunung Api, rising behind. The old dive boat I'd rustled up was struggling in the chop, but it held in there, and I kept the horizon level."

Beyond the protection of the islands, the sea livened up. On *Duyfken*, the sea was awake to us and the ship began rolling and pitching on every wave. After the tranquility of our protected anchorage, in the open ocean it was like the swell was surging from the deep and lifting the ship up and out of the water. Some of the Maluku Islands would be the highest peaks in the world if the height of the volcanoes was measured from where they leave the ocean floor. The sea floor around Banda can be 5.8 km below and without sunlight, the ocean is a deep, oily black, the darkest sea barely relieved by the white wash at the crests of the waves and our own foaming bow wave.

I noticed Des Alwi holding on tight as the motion of the ship increased. His demeanour all of a sudden became more serious. I knew what he was feeling. The crew about us calmly went about the business of sailing the ship under the Master's orders, walking across deck, taking a line here or there, adjusting the mainsail, letting out a line and then tugging another and making the line secure, coiling up excess rope on the deck. It was uncanny how they did it quietly and without fuss, immediately the order was spoken, as if they knew what was wanted down to the last inch of adjustment. The bunch of sailors which left Fremantle months before was now at one with the ship.

The Banda islands were soon just dark silhouettes which we could only glimpse when the ship crested the bigger waves. With the black sea and the dark clouds, the ocean looked like a very lonely place. Everyone spoke quietly as the ship surged through the waves. Only the flapping of our flax sails when we tacked, the sound of rope whipping in the wind and the thud of blocks knocking against timber, rose above the sound of the wind and the waves. On that day, I understood how the seafarers of the age of *Duyfken* could believe that 'there be dragons and serpents' in the ocean. In only a few minutes we had been transported from the other worldly Banda Islands through darkest seas to yet another realm. Soon Robert had the shots he needed and without fuss, we turned for home. It was the most fabulous morning of sailing I have ever experienced on *Duyfken*. His photographs captured the essence of the little ship battling this mighty, mysterious ocean. They were published in his book and for me they are the ultimate images taken of *Duyfken* by a masterful photographer.

For months before we arrived, Banda Neira was regularly plunged into darkness because its diesel power generator repeatedly broke down and there was nobody in Banda who could rehabilitate it. Banda was cut-off from the scheduled visits of a variety of service people who usually travelled to the islands carrying out regular maintenance. I discovered this when I had the brilliant idea that I might like something photocopied. Banda only had two photocopiers to serve the 7,000 inhabitants and the humidity was tough on the machines. The only surviving machine had broken down months before and a service technician never arrived to repair it. We couldn't do much to fix the photocopier, but our Ship's Engineer, Michael Hemsley, agreed to have a look at the generator in the powerhouse. After crawling around inside the *Duyfken*'s engine boxes for two months, it was above and beyond the call of duty for Mick to take on the job. All he wanted was some rest before going to sea again but to his credit he was keen to help the locals out. His expletive-laden description of working on the decrepit generator in a room thick with black oil and grease all over the floor and walls, power wires hanging loosely on hooks and caked in oil, was great entertainment. It was to his credit that he did manage to restore some power to the forgotten community and they were very grateful.

We also began to feel that we were now cut off from the outside world, too. The Indonesian national telephone company, PT Telekomunikasi Indonesia (Telkom) operated the only telephone service from Banda and the telephones at the hotel were useless. Same story: the maintenance people wouldn't travel through Maluku while the civil war was underway. The only option for me was a daily evening walk up the hill to the Telkom office after most of the locals were home in bed. There was a queue during the day. I would take my chance with a few other desperate souls to send very short emails. A 30 word email could take an hour to get away. I gave up on phone calls.

Banda's isolation was felt in many ways. The islands hadn't seen more than a handful of tourists for a year and there had been no need, and no ability or cash, for the hotel to stock-up on food to suit the Western palate. To our host Ramon's great credit, they did their best putting up local delicacies for us every night, but how I hankered for something a little less challenging on my stomach.

About two years before, I had placed Adriaan de Jong's splendid model of our ship's boat on the coffee table in Queensland Premier, Peter Beattie's, office. It was part of our big pitch for sponsorship. If he sponsored the voyage, one of the things we promised was to build a ship's boat (called a sloep in Dutch) for the arrival at the Pennefather River. It could go into a museum in Queensland afterwards. Always cash-strapped and under-resourced, we never had the time nor the money to build the boat. The cost to build it totally traditionally was estimated at more than $100,000 in one quote with a 12 month construction time (not including getting some more oak from Latvia). Every time I talked about it with the crew they tried to discourage me from building it. Once we began sailing *Duyfken* near Fremantle, they emphasised to me what a hassle it would be carrying it on board along with all the safety gear we had to stow on deck to comply with survey. With cannon, self-inflating life rafts, aluminium hatches and all the other gear, it would be almost impossible to move around the deck to trim the sails. The sloep would also be very heavy to get on and off the ship. It became the lowest priority on a long list until departure time approached. As we required a modern rescue boat to be on deck at all times, the sloep slipped from the list altogether. The Queenslanders, however, never forgot about it. Indeed, in the final contract we had to make two of them — one for the ship and one to be given to the Government. I came up with what I thought would be a brilliant solution — the best place to get a ship's boat made would be in Indonesia. I mentioned this to Des and Tanya Alwi when I was in Jakarta and Des was quite excited about it. I showed him Adriaan's drawings of a five metre sloep and with typical bravado, he said that of course it could be done. No doubt about it. There were some excellent shipwrights on Banda and they still built their boats the same way as the old Dutch — maybe they even taught the Dutch a thing or two about shipbuilding, he declared. How much would it cost? Now I can't re-call the exact amount of money we agreed upon but it was about $650. This was a great deal. So Des took the drawings to commission our ship's boat. He left our meeting and I kept asking quesions about the boat while he was walking away. He turned and looked at me. "Graeme, the boat won't be exactly the same as your drawing but it will be in the style of the ship's boat of the era. Trust me."

Fast forward five weeks at it was now time to see the finished ship's boat.

This was to be a moment where Dutch and Indonesian history came together — an Indonesian boat to be used to carry Australians ashore at the Pennefather River. A symbol of our two great nations working together. Robert Garvey came along with the Firelight film crew to film this momentous occasion. I can't better describe what happens next, so here is Peter taking up the story:

> *Des loads up the crew of the* Duyfken *onto his speed boat and takes us to the boatbuilder where our finished boat is ready and waiting to be launched. As we walk towards the boatbuilder's house my steps quicken with anticipation. What will the boat be like? The plans are for a boat that will barely fit on* Duyfken's *deck. They depict a heavily built, flat-bottomed, bluff-bowed boat about five metres long, fitted with a windlass for handling* Duyfken's *350 kg anchors. The plan shows a mast and a sprit-rigged sail, and big swinging lee-boards, one on each side, to stop the boat slipping sideways under sail. I estimate she might weigh around a tonne.*
>
> *I am a little apprehensive. What if the Indonesian boatbuilder doesn't follow the plans and we end up with a boat we cannot physically lift with our tackles or fit on the deck? If he follows the plans exactly it will be a close thing on both counts anyway. What will the boat be like?*
>
> *We arrive at the house of Sahran Abidin, the boatbuilder. Resting on chocks in his front yard is a beautiful example of an orembai. Imagine a narrow canoe, just wide enough to sit in, with deep V sections and high stem and stern posts. I make a mental note to come back and admire it when we have taken delivery of the ship's boat. I keep walking.*
>
> *Sahran stops me and beckons me back to the orembai. This is our ship's boat. I can't help laughing, delighted that this graceful little craft will be ours to use from now on, and equally delighted that our worst stowage nightmare has not come true and we will still be able to walk around on* Duyfken's *deck when the boat is stowed for sea. I shake Sahran's hand. 'Terima kasih, terima kasih (thank you, thank you).'*
>
> *It seems the whole neighbourhood has turned out for the launching. Two or three people could lift the orembai, but there must be 20 people crowding around her to carry her to the water's edge, all*

eager to be a part of her first taste of sea-water.

Des Alwi makes a speech. He says the boat represents the good relations that are being built between Australia and Banda, and that he wants us to return whenever we are able.

I say how much I love our new orembai and how beautiful she is. I mention that we are departing Banda next week to re-enact the first recorded European voyage to Australia. The original Duyfken *also departed from Banda, so it is entirely appropriate that our ship's boat is built here. This orembai will be our means of paddling ashore for our first landing in Australia at the Pennefather River, so at that moment the boat will represent the strong links that we have been building here between Banda and Australia.*

Sahran places a green coconut on a block of wood and hands me his machete. I raise the machete over my head and chop into the coconut, then sprinkle the milk over the bow of the orembai. Another coconut gets the same treatment from Graeme and he sprinkles the milk over the stern. Then, amid much joyous yelling and shouting, the boat is lifted into the water. Andrea hops in and takes the fore-most thwart (seat), Nic takes the middle and I am directed to get in at the stern. The boat is built for five orang (people), but when Sahran sees how deep the boat is sitting in the water with the three orang putih (white people) he signals that three is enough. We paddle the orembai back around to where Duyfken *is moored, attracting cheers from the children on the shore as we go. Are they just cheering us on, or are they laughing at our clumsy paddling style? We will never know.*

The wily Des Alwi gets paid.

We were in Banda to begin our re-enactment voyage and we were beginning to ask why? It's a very European idea, the 're-enactment voyage'. When we first began talking about it I was taken back to images in my mind of the *Kon Tiki* voyage of Thor Heyerdahl. Cathy and I had backpacked through South America in our twenties. We visited Lake Titicaca in the Andes and saw the reed boats near Trujillo on the coast which inspired the *Ra* voyage. What experiences he must have had! The classical re-enactment voyages set out to prove theories on unrecorded voyages or to mark great points in history. For example, to remember Christopher Columbus arriving in the New World in 1492 by sailing the *Nina*, *Pinta* and *Santa*

Maria replicas across the Atlantic in 1992. I saw one of the replicas on a visit to Barcelona in 1990 and I was struck by how primitive it looked. I had little awareness that the arrival of Columbus became 'invasion day' for many people and it was marked with protests in the Americas two years later. Closer to home, the First Fleet Re-enactment Voyage saw seven ships leaving the United Kingdom to sail to Sydney for the Australian Bicentennial Celebrations in 1988. That re-enactment was fraught with modern difficulties (read, they ran out of money) but made it to Sydney in a glorious show of sail. I remember wandering down to North Wharf in Fremantle to see the fleet when it made landfall in Western Australia. What an inspiring scene it was to see the ships lined up along the quay. By the time the fleet arrived in Sydney, the public interest was enormous. Sydney Harbour was packed with hundreds of thousands of people lining the shore and cramming onto ferries and spectator craft. Aboriginal people came from all over Australia for the biggest protest march ever seen in the city. Some journalists said that as many as 40,000 people, Aboriginal and white, joined the demonstration to make the point that indigenous people had little to celebrate. Their story was one of injustice, suffering and dispossession. I can't remember that on the news.

The tide was turning. The *Endeavour* replica celebrated Captain Cook as the great navigator and explorer, but the ship also carried the symbolism of a British voyage of exploration which led to either settlement or an invasion by a conqueror, depending upon which view you took. It was one reason why Captain Cook's navigational exploits were emphasised so strongly. We always thought that *Duyfken* could escape from the stain of invasion and colonisation by stressing that the Dutch never intended to conquer and settle in Australia. They were, we said, only interested in trade. In a sense, the Aboriginal people of Cape York repelled them. As James Henderson said, they gave Jansz and his crew a 'bloody nose' and the Dutch did not hang around. In light of this story-telling, we felt that Aboriginal people wouldn't be troubled by the *Duyfken* replica reenacting the original voyage.

Something changed in our thinking during the Expedition. We thought we knew all about the story of the great VOC — the world's first multinational trading company — how its fleets beat the Portuguese at their own game and took over the spice trade. My standard speech which I had given a hundred times began with "Now let me take you back four hundred years when the Portuguese dominated the spice trade …" at which point the crew groaned and their minds wandered. I would then grin at the crew members standing behind our guests, and launch into the yarn. It was our private joke. The *Duyfken* story as we told it was a simple one. *Duyfken* at Banda, sent off to search for the land of Nova Guinea and other east and south lands and a reputed great store of gold. No it was not the New Guinea we talk about today. They surveyed part of what they called Os Papuas. They make landfall in Cape York, sail south and the crew gets a hiding thanks to the brave indigenous people they encounter before reaching Cape Keerweer. They turn around and sail north, losing one crew member when exploring a river north of the Pennefather River. They keep exploring northwards to the top of Cape York, explore islands in Torres Strait and return to the Indies. Involved in many battles. Careened on the beach at Ternate. Jansz becomes a great servant of the VOC. *Duyfken's* voyage was the first of 42 voyages of discovery by the Dutch to the Great South Land, mapping two-thirds or three-quarters of the Australian coastline (depending upon how you feel), leaving it to Lieutenant James Cook to fill in the last part of the continental map 164 years later. Story told, context explained. Time for questions and a glass of wine. Careful with the glass on the deck, please. No, the cannon do not fire.

The initial stories we re-visited as *Duyfken* sailed north along the western coast of Australia mainly concerned romanticised stories of Dutch shipwrecks and plates being nailed onto posts. The stories we encountered in Indonesia, however, were different and none was more shocking than the story told to us in Banda. A particular mural at the museum in Banda Neira was a topic of conversation amongst the crew because it was particularly gruesome — but the caption was written in Bahasa and only Michael and Nick knew what it said. The mural showed the beheading of 44 Banda *orang kaya* or village chiefs by Japanese mercenaries in 1621.

The story was recounted by Tom Goodman. He had introduced himself to the crew and showed Peter around the island, explaining the significance of the shocking painting. Peter wrote in the Captain's Log:

> *In 1621 Jan Pieterszoon Coen, the VOC governor, rounded up 44 of the Bandanese orang kaya (chiefs or, literally, rich men) and held them in the fort. They were tried, tortured and found guilty of plotting against the Dutch. Coen then ordered his Japanese mercenaries to execute them. One at a time, and in full view of their fellow victims, they were beheaded, then quartered, and their heads were impaled on bamboo stakes for the villagers to see. This*

was part of Coen's ruthlessly successful bid to take control of the Bandas on behalf of the VOC. Not one for half measures, Coen would settle for nothing less than the total annihilation of the indigenous population, who were either murdered or driven from the islands. The Banda islands under Dutch rule were Christian. The courtyard of the fort is peaceful this afternoon. The ground is covered with green grasses and ferns with not a drop of blood or a severed body part to be seen. Yet as Tom relates the story, the crumbling walls of Fort Nassau surrounding me evoke images of the massacre with a vividness that words on the page, or a teacher talking in a room somewhere, could never achieve. Perhaps that is the whole point of this Expedition: to put historical stories in context. What have the hapless Bandanese orang kaya of 1621 got to do with me, an Australian living nearly 400 years later? I now realise that the Bandanese genocide was part of the same quest for wealth that sent Duyfken *on her voyage of discovery to Australia.*

The focus of the *Duyfken* Project had been on building the most authentic 'Age of Discovery' Dutch jacht. There was a lot of pride that we had taken a step up from the compromises of the *Endeavour* replica and built a ship in both look and materials which was closer to the original *Duyfken*. The voyage to Banda was a triumph because the ship sailed so well. The research, design and craftsmanship produced a superb replica ship. Our research was focused on the ship as an object to be studied and subsequently replicated. Unlocking the history of the ship through research also enabled us to tell the story of the voyage of discovery. We looked at Willem Jansz and his role in the story. In raising funds to build the ship, however, it was not helpful to talk about the historically and morally complex issues surrounding it. Building a ship of exploration is more palatable than building a ship representative of the ills of colonialism. We did not delve too deeply into the story of the VOC but in Indonesia we were compelled to confront it — the 'dark shadows' as the critics of the VOC called them. Coen almost certainly paced the decks of *Duyfken* with Willem Jansz. It was a chilling thought especially when I came to appreciate that when Willem Jansz was Governor of Banda, he also directed a small army of slaves to follow up on Coen's genocidal activities by attacking the survivors defending nearby Pulau Ai. Looking back now, I can only reflect on how strange it was that while Indonesia was tearing itself apart, we were sailing a ship from another age of bloody local history, carefully avoiding the modern euphemistically called 'trouble spots'. What in the hell were we thinking? In the hurly-burly of our visit to Banda, we never even touched upon Willem Jansz's campaign to liquidate the VOC's enemies.

Nick Burningham recounts a conversation he had with our local orembai boatbuilder:

> *One of his men asked about the purpose of our re-enactment. I did my best to explain about* Duyfken's *significance to Australia, Indonesia and The Netherlands, and our wish to increase awareness of that significance, and about building and sailing the ship to increase our understanding of the past.*
> *"Of course," added Sahran "if mankind attempts to progress, taking with us no appreciation of our past, there will be no advantage gained." He was able to say this much more poetically in Indonesian where the word 'kembang' contains the ideas of profit, increase, interest on an investment, development, and blossoming.*

The ghost of Jan Pieterszoon Coen, the 'Butcher of Banda', would follow us all the way to The Netherlands.

Four centuries ago, the Dutch were in Banda to secure the trade in nutmeg and mace, and kernels of the spice have even been found on Dutch shipwrecks of the period along the Western Australian coast. The Bandanese love nutmeg and it is used in a variety of foods on the islands. Des Alwi offered us nutmeg jam to eat with our meal and then asked us what we thought of the flavour. It tasted like Coca-Cola and this was the opening he needed to tell one of his favourite stories: that the American drinks company uses nutmeg oil in its secret recipe, and it was one of the world's major buyers of the spice. I said that we, as the Dutch had done, should ship out with some nutmeg and a large sack of the prized spice was duly loaded aboard. We were now spice traders, but it was ironic that the product which once was sought after by European royalty and the richest families, would now be sold to visitors to our ship for just a few dollars for a handful of kernels.

One of the most persistent memories I have of Banda is how surreal it all seemed. I arrived at night and it was like being suddenly transported into another world. During the day, our whole existence seemed to be contained in the small town of Banda Neira, Gunung Api and the lagoon in between.

Like a scene from Walt Disney's Peter Pan, the water was always dead calm at first light and almost black it was so deep. Thick cloud hemmed everything in and every day it rained for hours. Occasionally the sun came out and *Duyfken* glowed her honey colour, with her sails hanging out like clothes on a washing line so that they didn't rot in the wet and humid conditions. There were only two ways out — gaps in the islands leading to the Banda Sea. It would be easy to imagine staying here for months and simply losing track of time. One day when we had to move the ship it was like it had been permanently anchored to the lagoon and Banda had some sort of control over us. It was all hands on the anchor cable and the windlass to raise the anchor. It was a tedious process which usually took about half-an-hour if everything went well. This time, the anchor just wouldn't budge and it felt like we were pulling the ship down into the water rather than lifting the anchor. Anything that happened seemed to reverberate across the lagoon and the sound of 20 people sitting on a deck and groaning with every heave must have been heard all over Banda Neira. We were all heaving as hard as we could and it looked like we had lost the anchor for good. After much straining, we began lifting it very slowly, a few inches at a time. The pressure was enormous and then suddenly it broke free and the ship bucked, We wound it up normally the rest of the way. Gary speculated rationally that we must have been lifting an old cannon hooked onto the end of the 'pick'. There could be anything at the bottom of that lagoon after so many centuries of ships coming and going, but then again, maybe we were being sent a message.

As the days rolled on, there was a Mexican stand-off developing between the Firelight crew and Des Alwi. Marcus wanted spectacular shots of the local Kora Kora longboats welcoming *Duyfken* to Banda. It would make excellent television. Des knew that it would have to come at a cost. "Why shouldn't Marcus pay?" he said. Des was used to getting his own way.

The figures Des quoted were way over the top according to Marcus so the two were at loggerheads. I'd been trying to keep right out of this transaction, after all, I had already paid for the ceremonial welcome in Kupang. Marcus wasn't happy that Des seemed to be "ripping me off" as he said. He had already paid about US$3,000 for the hotel, food and various other 'charges' as well as a fixer fee to Tanya. Des didn't like Marcus' aggressive negotiation tactics. He thought he was just an upstart. Marcus is more circumspect about the stand-off today: "Des was trying to keep his business alive on a super remote island that was suffering badly at the time because of the political meltdown that had occurred when Suharto fell from power. He was stuck in the middle of this quasi civil war."

They had to agree at some stage. Des was as sly as a fox, like a trade union leader negotiating an award agreement. He said that the ceremonial welcome would entail maybe one hundred paddlers and they all had day jobs which they would have to forego to be part of the drama. They also had to make the materials and get the Kora Kora ready for the day and their meals had to be covered. This came at a cost which was only a few dollars per person but with the number of people it was beyond the Firelight budget. An added complication was that Des wanted to be paid in cash so that he could distribute the money directly to the participants. I expected Des to be honourable in this regard but Marcus had his suspicions. In the end, I became the middle man in the transaction. Marcus did not have enough cash. The inevitable happened. I agreed to cover the gap. Everyone was happy except the *Duyfken* Expedition bank account, and, of course, we had no idea how much of the money would filter down to the locals paddling the Kora Kora.

But that was the way things worked on so many levels. The small tourism industry in Banda was now non-existent and we were the new cash cow. For example, the local sea shell vendors saw us as potential buyers and occasionally paddled up to the ship offering the most magnificent shells. This appalled Paul Hough who knew the damage caused to reef ecosystems when large shellfish were caught and removed. A Japanese refrigeration ship was a regular visitor to Banda while we were there. We were told that local fishers caught tuna with hand lines from their small boats and sold them to the Japanese for much-needed cash. The Banda Sea was an important tuna fishery but we saw all sorts of fish being offered to the Japanese. The prized coral trout which would be maybe 400mm long in West Australian waters were almost fished out and no larger than about 150mm long. The very small coral trout only a few centimetres long were also caught live to sell to the Japanese buyers as tropical aquarium fish. Were these refrigeration ships the new colonialists, plundering local resources and depleting the ecosystem for their domestic market thousands of kilometres away? Were we any better paying for a welcome ceremony? Had anything changed in 400 years?

Meanwhile in other parts of Maluku Province, the violence was once again, to use the old media cliché, spiralling out of control. With the worsening situation, President Gus Dur declared a new civil emergency and announced a ban on all travel to the province. It was chaos. In Ambon, a police barracks was under siege and an elite police unit and sections of the TNI were taking sides. There were reports of 'provocateurs' paying local men to take up arms. Police arms and ammunition, as well as uniforms, had been stolen. Ambon was once again in full scale civil war, only this time, the local military chief General Rusdihardjo, admitted that some of his troops had become 'emotionally involved' in the conflict and he would have no option but to pull all his troops out and replace them with fresh soldiers. I thought about our friend on the Pelni ferry. Across Maluku it was estimated that 10,000 people fled their homes and they were getting on any means of transport they could to flee the violence. The Australian embassy was very concerned for our safety. On the day before our grand ceremonial welcome, Peter, Gary and I met to discuss a contingency plan if the violence returned to Banda. The Pelni ferry from Ambon was scheduled to arrive the following evening and it was feared the jihadis from Ambon could be aboard. Ironically, the provincial governor agreed to travel on the same ferry to participate in the welcome. We were warned that Banda could be overwhelmed by a flood of Ambonese refugees and we should be prepared to leave at very short notice. We resolved to take as many people as we could who felt that they had to leave Banda. This included anyone who felt that they may have been compromised by working with us during our visit including Des and Tanya Alwi and Tom Goodman. Jane Doepel said that she would load the ship with fresh supplies so that we could leave at a moment's notice. Without refrigeration, fresh food including fruit and vegetables could only last for two weeks before Jane would have to revert to pasta and beans, as well as canned food. Our crew was told not to wander too far from the town of Banda Neira in case we had to leave quickly. It was a massive relief when we got the news that the ferry had been diverted and it would not visit Banda. We had our little dreamlike paradise to ourselves for a few days more.

    I sometimes walked around the island when the pressure of work became too much and I needed some time to myself. One of my great joys was walking up the hill behind town. When the sun flooded the lagoon with light between tropical showers, I found great delight by glimpsing between the palm trees to sneak a once in a lifetime view of *Duyfken* at anchor. I was so proud that I had played a part in creating this magical scene.

    Des Alwi delivered on an epic welcome. Set against the backdrop of Gunung Api, *Duyfken* was a brilliant sight as she sailed into view and met two Kora Kora longboats. The drumming on the Kora Koras seemed to stir the soul as it carried across the lagoon. Then the 30 crew on each boat began chanting in harmony. The rhythmic splashing as paddles met the warm tropical water made it easy to think that we were back in the seventeenth century when *Duyfken* first sailed into these waters. "Racing towards us, with bright banners fluttering, and muscular crewmen paddling, chanting, and drumming, it was an awesome spectacle, which made my hairs stand on end," said Robert Garvey as he reflected on a morning spent weaving in and out of the boats taking photographs. Having some experience with the dragon boats of Hong Kong I knew that it wouldn't be long before it turned into a race. The locals could keep pace with *Duyfken* but they each wanted to be the first across the other side of the lagoon. It was fun to watch them paddling hard. After a few more runs at the behest of Marcus so he could get just the exact shots he wanted, it was obvious that the Kora Kora crews were utterly spent and they needed something to eat and drink. It was time for everyone to return to their day jobs.

The next act in the ceremonial welcome was held during the evening. We were invited to the village of Selamon on the main island of Banda Besar. We were all taken across the lagoon aboard small speedboats. We walked from the beach along a small path in the darkness to a modest building and into a dimly lit room. The ritual which was to be played out for us went to the heart of this strange idea of bringing back a symbol of years of Dutch colonial repression. It was a reminder that symbols are important in every culture. In the presence of the whole village and with people peering in through every window, men weaved palm fronds into three baskets and they were handed to several women. The women then filled the baskets with offerings to those who were slaughtered at the order of Jan Pieterszoon Coen. With the ritual completed, we are all shown into the adjoining room which had a selection of swords, morion helmets and shields as well as old Dutch colonial uniforms. The military equipment was battered and bruised and I'm amazed that they were still in one piece. I was assured that everything dated from the seventeenth century when the Dutch first came to these islands. With our ship's rigging rotting almost before our eyes in the constant dampness and humidity, it was hard to believe that the uniforms survived the centuries. They were essential items for the Cakalele dance which was to be performed for us in the morning. Once a ceremonial warrior dance, after Coen's massacre it became a commemorative ritual recalling the slaughter — or that is what we were told.

The Cakalele dance in front of *Duyfken* the following day was the sequel to the previous night's festivities. Five men dressed in the costumes performed the dance which was sometimes called a war dance but was now performed for ceremonial arrivals. After the dance Peter was made a 'son of the Bandas.' He was wrapped in a sarong and given a peci, the trademark black velvet hat worn by many Indonesians, including Presidents, in the years following independence. It was a joyful moment, if a little over-the-top.

The ceremonies immortalised the story recounted by Tom Goodman. There were enormous profits to be derived from importing the endemic nutmeg and mace from Banda into the European market. It motivated the Dutch to eliminate the Portuguese from the trade with the Bandanese. The Dutch wanted a monopoly and told the Bandanese in 1609 that they must deal exclusively with them. This was not how the trade worked in the past. The nutmeg and mace was sold to visiting traders and Banda controlled its own supply and distribution channels, and thus its own destiny. In an attempt to exert their authority in the face of the aggressive interlopers, the Bandanese ambushed and killed 46 members of the VOC. In the ensuing conflict, the Dutch subjugated the local population and built Fort Nassau on the island, in an instant wiping out centuries of traditional trading patterns. Over the next decade, the Dutch exerted total control over the other spice islands by brute force. They were, however, frustrated that local traders were constantly bypassing the Dutch East India Company and secretly selling to their more traditional customers. Other Europeans wanted a piece of the action. The English then arrived on the scene with their own English East India Company and tried to carve out their own trading network in Banda. Some Bandanese sided with the English, and new VOC Governor-General (Jan Pieterszoon Coen, of couse), waged a constant war against the small but pesky English contingent and the rebellious locals. In 1620, he arrived from Batavia to settle the matter once and for all. His invasion fleet consisted of 19 ships, 1,655 Dutch soldiers and 286 Japanese mercenaries. It was supplemented by the fort's garrison and native Kora Kora. In the resulting conflict, an estimated 2,500 Bandanese were killed and most of the 15,000 population of the Banda Islands fled or were deported to Batavia as slaves. Accounts vary, but some refer to less than 480 Bandanese remaining after the massacre. They were enslaved by the Dutch to teach them how to grow and harvest nutmeg. It represented the most murderous episode orchestrated by the Dutch East India Company. Records point to 44 orang kaya being decapitated by the

Japanese mercenaries. By 1681, it was thought that only 100 native Bandanese lived on the islands and the rest of the population were farm workers imported by the Dutch.

Such a conflicted history is difficult to tell. I learnt that truth in history, traditions and ritual, tourism and the local economy are so intertwined that it is difficult to unravel what we had seen. Whether Des Alwi cynically 'revived', 'recreated' or invented the rituals and the dance has been debated by academics over the years. He took credit for transforming the Cakalele dance into a piece of entertainment easily understood by Western visitors on island tours or cruise ships. The dance performance is a welcoming gesture with a twist. For people with European heritage travelling through a post-colonial Indonesia, the story of a terrible massacre performed on behalf of the Dutch by Japanese mercenaries in loin-cloths fits with our preconceptions of the cruelty of the Japanese. We know this from our World War II history lessons. It sidesteps the uncomfortable truth that Dutch overlords ordered and supervised the genocide. He moulded Bandanese history into a battle between good and evil. The reality of conflict is that truth, as always, is far more complex than 'goodies and baddies' but we agree to believe the tale when it is turned into an entertaining dance with colourful costumes. I did, until I began reading as much as I could about the VOC period after we returned from the Expedition. It surprised me to read that most people living in Banda today have no connection with the indigenous Bandanese who were massacred in the savage conflict. Coen re-populated the islands with a more compliant population from elsewhere. I did not know quite what to make of our welcome after that. Was it just a piece of theatre? Were they all just actors in a play which I had paid for? We were certainly entranced by the ceremonies and we thought they were done just for us. I found out later that similar ceremonies were performed for any visiting groups to Banda who wanted a cultural show.

I am still unsure about exactly how we were regarded by the Bandanese. They were very polite to us, but there was also incredible tension on the islands. Tom Goodman described it as a 'sad and strange place'. "You must understand that Des Alwi, or Pak Des as locals called him, was no ordinary local leader," he said. "He was a wealthy man who may or may not have local family connections. The leaders I interacted with in maritime Eastern Seram were rajas, little kings that intermarried with other little king families to facilitate trade connections in a largely stateless region. Pak Des was very different. He was feared by some on the islands because of his political and social connections throughout Indonesia, no different from the old inter-archipelago relationships Banda enjoyed with people along the important spice trade routes through Maluku, Nusatenggara, Bali, Surabaya, Batavia, Medan, and Banda Aceh at the tip of northern Sumatra where Indonesia meets the Indian Ocean." The Bandanese had every reason to be uncomfortable with our arrival considering the history of the islands, the recent factional fighting and our strong relationship with Pak Des.

The story of Coen's revenge is taught in the local schools and it was chilling to stand at the place outside the castle wall where the massacre occurred. But did our visit achieve anything? Did we bring Australians and Indonesians closer together?

Tom was very keen to join *Duyfken* for the next leg of the expedition. For Tom it was a chance to escape: "I wanted to travel aboard *Duyken* out of plain historical and maritime curiosity. I would have gladly paid for the privilege. As it turned out it was offered to me in exchange for working the shifts at four hour intervals like the other crew members. I said "yes" before I fully understood what working a seventeenth century VOC ship actually meant. The alternative was an untold number of days stranded on Des Alwi's wartime paradise. I would head for Tual with the crew and the sooner the better." Tom said he also vaguely remembered being told by a crew member not to mention that he would leave with *Duyfken* in order to prevent hostility from the stranded visitors. "I would have stayed silent anyway, as I felt some guilt getting free passage from an emerging nightmare. I felt the same way when I escaped Ambon on the overcrowded ferry. This refugee boat would be a trip of a lifetime," he said.

Iwan Setiawan from the prestigious magazine Tempo in Jakarta arrived to join the ship and (translated from Indonesian), he described seeing the ship for the first time: "*Duyfken* looked as if it was meditating on the surface of the sea: elegant, beautiful and mysterious. That was the first impression of seeing its figure floating in the waters of Banda Neira. Meanwhile, the thin mist that enveloped its body slowly opened up as the *Bukit Siguntang* ferry that I was aboard approached." Iwan and Tom Goodman received their induction to the ship. Our visit to Banda was drawing to a close. From here, Peter Manthorpe would take his crew on the business end of the re-enactment expedition and the next time we would meet would be in Queensland. Ellenor, Robert and I bid the crew farewell thanks to the confirmed tickets arranged by Tanya Alwi, and we re-traced our steps to Ujung Pandang and back to Australia.

Chapter 19

Learning Nothing from History

Our re-enactment voyage looked easy on a map. From Banda in Maluku to the Pennefather River in Queensland is about 1,600 km as the crow flies. The simplest way to do this had to be to sail using Jansz's chart on the precise route that he used to come to Australia.

Willem Jansz's original chart does not survive, however, a copy of the chart was made and included in the remarkable Atlas Blaeu Van der Hem, a collection of 2,400 maps in 46 volumes which was assembled by Laurens Van der Hem, a Dutch lawyer and connoisseur of the art of map making in the seventeenth century. He used as the basis for his work Joan Blaeu's majestic Atlas Blaeu Van der Hem which was the largest and most expensive book production of the seventeenth century. Laurens Van der Hem's work expanded on the Blaeu Atlas, adding a number of charts from the Dutch East India Company which were secreted away by the company so that they could not be used by competing commercial interests. Thankfully, Willem Jansz's chart was copied for the atlas, and the atlas survived. It has been in Vienna since 1730 and is now housed at the Österreichische Nationalbibliothek in the Austrian capital. The chart is both proof of Willem Jansz's voyage and contains enough detail to speculate how and why he sailed this route.

Nick Burningham had experience in Indonesian waters, having sailed seven times from Indonesia to Australia during the wet season. When the possibility of a re-enactment voyage was discussed three years before, he offered a voyage plan which used information embodied in the original *Duyfken* chart and fragments of information on the voyage revealed by Marit van Huystee and Adriaan de Jong. Patrick Baker from the WA Maritime Museum provided Nick with astronomical data from 1605 to

1606 and he tried to put the puzzle together and reconstruct the timing of the original voyage. His hypothetical description brought this voyage, about which very little is known, to life.

According to the Saris account, Willem Jansz sailed from the trading port of Bantam in West Java on 18 November 1605 to begin his voyage of exploration. Nick postulated that the departure probably coincided with local sailing practice of taking to sea five days after the new moon. "The northwest monsoon would have been approaching but had not arrived in earnest, so *Duyfken* would have made a slow passage eastwards along the north coast of Java, frustrated by stifling calms and violent squalls that could come from any direction," he wrote. Sailing across the Bali Sea and then the Flores Sea, Jansz then turned north east across the Banda Sea to Banda. Whether Jansz and his crew remained in Banda for Christmas is unknown, but Nick speculated that *Duyfken* could have sailed on the fourth day of the full moon under the monsoon which would have, by then, enabled a relatively fast two or three day passage to the Kei Islands and a further run downwind to Dobo in the Aru Islands.

"Local sailors in Eastern Indonesia prefer not to sail on long voyages during the northwest monsoon when driving rain can reduce visibility to a hundred metres or less, sometimes for hours on end, making landfall very dangerous. They especially avoid sailing at full moon and new moon when conditions are generally stormiest, and it seems quite probable that *Duyfken* would have waited for the new moon at Dobo," said Nick. This meant that Jansz may have departed Dobo around 15 or 16 January 1606. Sailing towards West Papua, Nick thought that they probably anchored at the mouth of the Digul River along a dangerous stretch of coast with strong tidal streams and shallow water. "Jansz carefully sailed past Palau Yos Sudarsa (Frederick Hendrik Island) into the Arafura Sea. Taking into account the 15° deviation evident in Jansz' compass settings, he probably sailed south west from False Cape (Cape Waios) towards Cape Wessel in Arnhem Land." Nick estimated that Jansz came within 200nm of the Australian coast before resuming his south-east passage. Sailing across the Gulf of Carpentaria would have required great vigilance as the vague maps such as Ortelius' World Map of 1570 placed Nova Guinea (not today's island of New Guinea) in this area. "We can assume that they sailed east cautiously and probably hove to at night or proceeded under short canvas sounding at regular intervals," said Nick.

After four or five days, they made landfall at the Pennefather River then proceeded southwards for 120nm to Cape Keerweer. Nick surmised that they may have sheltered in Albatross Bay (which they named Fly Bay) during the heavy weather and spring tides of the new moon, and went ashore along the coast to collect firewood and search for fresh water. They then turned north from Cape Keerweer.

"From their original landfall at Pennefather River they continued to survey northwards to the Batavia River. It appears that they went some miles upstream, presumably in the ship's boat, with *Duyfken* anchored in the mouth of the river. After this the chart shows their course very close inshore, apparently passing inside Keer Reef to the north of Batavia River, but this seems unlikely. More likely, they were obliged by the shoal water along that stretch of the coast to sail further offshore, and this explains the rather less accurate nature of the chart north of Batavia River. As they approached Endeavour Strait, currents may have been sweeping the ship north. Jansz seems to have greatly underestimated the distance from Batavia River to the islands on the western side of Endeavour Strait. That fits with the calculation that this part of the voyage took place when the northwest monsoon was still strong and the current was setting to the east through Torres and Endeavour Strait. According to my speculative reconstruction, this would have been about the 23rd February with a full moon producing strong tidal flows," said Nick.

He noted that the north-south lie of the Cape York Peninsula coast was 'fairly accurately' plotted on the *Duyfken* chart, despite the earlier appearance of a 15° unobserved deviation. The course across the western approaches to Torres Strait shows more than 15° divergence from the reality shown by a modern chart. Perhaps this reflects a combination of the apparent compass problem and the current setting to the east through the Straits. The chart shows *Duyfken* heading away from Cape York sailing north of west, but the several islands which Jansz charted show that he was set east of north to the Torres Strait islands. It seems likely that Jansz anchored in the lee of at least one of these islands and very likely went ashore. It may be that Rossengin (the supercargo) was trading with Torres Strait Islanders. The relative sizes and positions of the islands are shown with some confidence suggesting that they were circumnavigated, perhaps by men in the ship's boat, and that *Duyfken* spent some time amongst the islands. Quite likely Jansz was simply unable to work back to the west against both wind and current. *Duyfken* threaded her way north past the islands and reefs for some eighty-miles (Jansz thought it was rather more) until they met a complete barrier of shallow reef, running parallel to the coast of what we (but not Jansz) call Papua New Guinea."

It was then probably early March in 1606, the northwest monsoon was waning and winds from the south east began intermittently. It was time to return to Banda. Nick then described a difficult journey to the west in the "slow and tedious windless season" finding False Cape and probably anchoring at Tiuri village on the northwest side of Frederick Hendrik Island (today called Pulau Yos Sudarso) in West Papua. They then sailed north of the Aru Islands and named the large land mass Os Papuas. "Perhaps Jansz had been aiming for Aru, because on reaching the coast of Os Papuas he changed course by 90°. This took *Duyfken* southwest between the islands of Aru and Kei. They would not have sighted low-lying Aru, but probably caught sight of the relatively high mountains of Kei Besar which prompted them to change course, again by about 90°, and pass north of Kei. There is no sign on the chart that they stopped at Kei, rather, they went through the middle of the passage between the Tayandu off-lying islands of Kei and the Watubelu islands," he said.

According to Nick's reconstruction there would have been no moon to help them sight islands in the night. They were heading straight for Banda which he estimated they may have reached on 7 April, 1606. He noted: "After the visit to Tiuri, the style of navigation seems to change. The ship runs away to the northwest, missing Aru and almost ricochets off the Os Papuas coast: they sight Kei Besar and keep to the middle of the passage between the Kei Islands and the Watubelus, heading straight for Banda. There is no consideration of stopping at Dobo for trade. It is this last part of the voyage, as shown on the chart, that looks like a voyage made by a small ship with a significant part of the crew killed."

A voyage of the *Duyfken* replica during the wet season, the Australian summer, and utilising the winds which made the voyage possible, was practical. If Jansz did it then, why couldn't we do it now?

Then came the realisation that the powers that rule risk at sea, the insurers, would not countenance such a voyage during the cyclone season. When Peter Manthorpe visited Fremantle to begin planning the route we had in mind that we'd make a slight detour to Port Moresby to satisfy our sponsor, Chevron. Peter couldn't come up with a voyage plan which enabled us to sail north during the dry, before the cyclone season was declared in November, sail through Indonesia to Banda, and then arrive at the

Pennefather River, sail through Torres Strait, drop into Port Moresby, and make it below the Tropic of Capricorn before the next cyclone season was called. We removed Port Moresby from our planning before Pennefather and added it to the route after Cape York. We knew that the voyage we were planning ran counter to the whole idea of reenacting Jansz's actual voyage and plotting ourselves precisely on his chart. How could we reenact a voyage in the wrong season? Jansz was blown to Australia. It made perfect sense for him to explore new lands by hitching a ride on the north west winds, and discovering where they would take him.

Everyone involved with the Project grappled with the idea of authenticity at one time or another. It was a constant debate from the very start when we were sitting around at Michael and Janine Young's house and discussing building the ship. Of course, we were proud that people like Ab Hoving and Robert Parthesius in The Netherlands praised the ship for its authenticity but there was a continuing discussion about how many modern solutions to age old problems would be incorporated into the ship. Some were no brainers — such as using modern Hempels anti-fouling on the hull. Dutch ships to the Indies were lucky to reach their teenage years because of the dreaded teredo worm and they found no adequate solution to the twin problems of humidity and therefore rot from within and attack by teredo from the outside. Modern 3M sealant had been used on the hull rather than oakum and tar. The authenticity debate was just as real with the Expedition. How could it be a re-enactment voyage if the engines were used? The simple answer was that we had no choice. Insurance requirements dictated the time of the year that presented the lowest risk for ship and crew.

Duyfken was about to embark on a voyage which would pit the crew against the prevailing winds and make them fight their way across the Banda and Arafura Seas, before dropping into the Gulf of Carpentaria. With northern Australia to the south and West Irian and Papua New Guinea to the north, Peter Manthorpe would be boxed in with no sea room to search for favourable breezes. No Dutch sea captain of 1606 would even remotely consider such folly. Fortunately, without the northern Maluku Islands and Ambon now in the itinerary, we had more time — and two Hino diesel engines. Peter and Gary Wilson agreed that the voyage out of season was possible if the ship could use its engines when required but it would also entail strapping fuel drums on deck. The diesel tanks on the ship were only designed to supply enough fuel to power the ship for a few hundred nautical miles into a headwind. None of us liked to revert to the engines, and it meant abandoning our ambition of following Jansz's chart to Australia.

The need to keep to some sort of schedule was a modern idea for seafarers. It was only made possible when ships could defy the winds and engines could replace sail. The voyage under sail was certainly possible if time was no object. We set an Expedition schedule which was very broad with a lot of leeway for the Ship's Master to sail all the route, but even this schedule was thrown out when the winds conspired against us. Already on the West Australian leg of the Expedition, where we planned to have a reliable following wind, it didn't always work out and Peter turned on the engines a few times. The 'steel sails' which were designed to get *Duyfken* into and out of port and to prevent her from coming to grief on a lee shore enabled him to substitute days of tacking for a few hours of motoring. The Dutch seafarers who found the reefs and cliffs of Australia's west coast would have been happy to use engines, too, if they had been available. However, even if Jansz had engines, I am sure that he wouldn't have contemplated what our crew were about to do.

The next section of the Expedition was to be the greatest test of whether it was possible to defy thousands of years of sailing wisdom or whether it was a folly. If *Duyfken* could not make headway from Banda to Cape York, then the Expedition would halt somewhere in eastern Indonesia and we'd have to sit it out until the weather made it possible to sail back to Australia. Any thoughts of a purist re-enactment were replaced by pragmatism.

Chapter 20

Hell

"It was like a nightmare when Nicole Gardner, one of the crew, woke me around midnight. Until dawn, it was our group that has to be on duty. Above the deck, at first my eyes could see nothing but the shadows of people milling about, because there were no lights at all. The feeling of wet and cold piercing into my bones. I saw that the two team-mates were already in their respective positions, namely on the front platform and at the wheel. Whereas I was only able to curl up in the right corner of the ship enduring the cold and the drowsiness. Eventually, I fell asleep on top of the box, in the right corner of the wheelhouse for a few moments. Finally, I had to be a 'watcher' for the last hour. Actually, the watcher's task is simple, namely to observe whether there are ships, islands, or obstacles ahead. But the waves hitting the bridge were so fierce that even standing up was difficult. I can understand why the fishermen in the waters of Banda and Maluku at certain times offer sacrifices to the sea. They believe that the Banda Sea has a very strong guard." Only hours before, Iwan Setiawan described *Duyfken* as elegant, beautiful and mysterious. Now he faced a new reality, being battered and bruised as Peter tried to use his years of sailing experience to break free of the Banda Sea.

Year later, our 'refugee', Tom Goodman, remembers being confronted by the authenticity of the experience:

> *The day I boarded* Duyfken *was painful. Not emotionally; I felt so excited about the trip. My right foot had a small sore that wouldn't go away. It itched at first then got painful and puss filled during the journey. I learned later that it was a tropical ulcer common to such maritime regions of the world. It rained all the time in Banda, sometime in torrents all day. The sore never fully*

dried out. I put it out of my mind and focused on sailing on a real VOC ship. I would go on about how beautiful I found Duyfken. I saw the ship through the eyes of a historian and landlubber, both of which inform my memories. My first memory was the exhilaration of leaving Banda Neira like countless VOC ships before, laden with a cargo of spices and/or weapons of war. I got to the ship earlier than required and met most of the crew I hadn't met in town. A crew member explained my assigned duties for my upcoming night shift. One instruction caught my attention: never fall asleep on night watch. "If you fall overboard at night in the rough waters we will encounter, you are finished. Duyfken can't turn on a dime and the waves will prevent rescuers from seeing someone on the dark surface." Over 20 years later, I still remember that sobering advice. The trip to Tual was about to get real, really fast.

The first couple of hours I spent searching for my sea legs. Calm water in the protected bays around Banda Neira soon gave way to rougher seas. Shortly after passing Gunung Api, the waves reached two metres. Duyfken's bulbous shape made the boat pitch and turn in ways I'd never felt before. While the seasoned crew worked their pre-travel preparations like the sea didn't exist, I could barely remain standing without feeling dizzy. I remember moving slowly from the center of the boat toward the railings where I saw a few others hanging out. I felt eyes watching me, no doubt finalizing their bets on how soon I would deposit my breakfast into the Banda Sea. Whoever placed bets on a fast hurl, won big. Humiliating doesn't quite describe what I felt. That came later when I heard the laughing and clapping. No, I felt oddly calm, like I had gotten a difficult chore out of the way. I found my sea legs within 15 minutes and never lost them again.

The ship carried us north by northeast towards Seram Laut, the location of my first research in maritime East Seram. What a stroke of luck! I simply couldn't believe that I would see the those islands from the deck of a VOC era boat, as a crew member. It felt like hours of staring at the small gray shapes on the horizon as daylight slowly disappeared. It was the last time I saw Seram Laut. If you look at a map you might wonder why we took that route. A ship in theory could make a bee line to Tual from Banda Neira in about

20 hours. Unfortunately, Mother Nature had other plans for Duyfken. A stubborn storm lurked further east in the Banda Sea. The navigator decided to play it safe and head due north then make a right turn at Seram Laut, bypassing the storm from the north. Looking at the boat's elaborate rigging and dark clouds eastward I remembered the advice about sleeping on watch duty.

I can't remember the time line of the trip to Tual. It couldn't have been more than two or three days. Maybe five? Twenty years have distorted the memory. I do remember the squall. That memory will never leave me. Before I discuss those events, I will give a few impressions of life aboard the ship from an outsider's perspective. A few women worked on Duyfken, more than I had expected to see. One did most of the cooking; two or three others worked the rigging. The four hour shifts began the first day. The ship's cargo hold contained hammocks hung just below the ceiling and two or three inches thick bedding placed along the Duyfken's curved underbelly. No port holes allowed light in. Only one escape hatch permitted exit via a ladder. I didn't sleep particularly well. My foot still hurt and would get progressively worse in the coming days. The ship's strange movement in the rough water amplified sound in the hold. The wooden ship creaked and growled with each pounding wave. I slept on the floor bedding in the hull's curvature. My head rested on the upper curve mimicking a kind of pillow while my spine and legs adapted to the ship's angles. When a wave hit the hull it sounded like a dull sledge hammer. My mind eventually adapted to the assortment of hull sounds and allowed me to get some restless sleep. It reminded me of similar adaptations I had to make when I first arrived in East Java and heard the 4:00am Muslim call to prayer every morning. Eventually I actually enjoyed it as a reminder that I had four more hours of uninterrupted sleep. I wouldn't be so lucky on Duyfken. I also remember a most unusual feature of Duyfken, its whipstaff or steering pole, the precursor to the more popular ship's wheel. As a crew member I had the honor of manning the whipstaff for one night shift (or part of the shift). How often does a VOC era historian get to man the helm of a VOC era ship as a crew member? I was pinching my self that whole night as I guided tons of lumber through the night seas. Luckily for the rest of the crew, I'm sure the powers that be picked a calmer night for the landlubber's turn at the helm.

The squall hit Duyfken at the worst possible time; about 2 or 3 am. I was 'sleeping' below deck when I heard a loud bell ring multiple times, followed by a shout "All hands. On deck. Now." The command wasn't really necessary. When the hatch door was opened everyone in the hold heard the whistling screams of a violent wind and loose canvas sails snapping above the deck. I jumped to my feet, then fell as quickly as I stood up. I could hear the screaming of people trying to organize a response to the winds. I found my shoes, climbed the ladder and entered a maelstrom. Sheets of rain flew perpendicular into the boat. I only had a moment to gaze at the sails still in place high above the deck before a rope was placed in my hands. Fixed sails in a squall — even a landlubber understands that means trouble. Duyfken pitched to the right in a steep 45 degree angle, or perhaps less. Whatever the angle the pitch was not getting better with those sails in full position. Someone got mad at me: "Pull damnit. Put some strength into it." I pulled as hard as I could then held my ground and watched the crew. I assumed that the crew had practiced a squall drill or even experienced one or two on their journey to Banda. This squall put that training to the test. The ship felt like it would tip over if we couldn't find a quick solution to the sails. Someone had to climb the rigging in the pitch black night against horizontal rain and tie down heavy canvas sheets. And then climb down safely. From my position manning a single rope to something high above me it appeared that volunteers were few. I only knew that I would not raise my hand to offer my services. At 6'1", and a portly 240 lbs, I was not a good candidate for rapid mast ascents. I held fast to my rope. Who would scale the mast? Then I saw a female crew member starting to climb. She wasn't following an order; she volunteered with her hands and feet. To this day I think that I witnessed the greatest act of bravery I have ever seen. This female crew member climbed up the main mast with the ease of a gymnast and worked the sails until they were secure. Another female may have helped her. None of the men aboard ship assisted on the rigging. They helped stabilize the myriad of rope lines to allow the riggers to finish

> the dangerous job. Now that I think about it, maybe the women were the only people aboard quick and nimble enough to do it. And I can't really know how much danger the Duyfken faced. From my perspective, this woman, or women, saved the boat that night.

Peter and the crew were intent on sailing as much as possible but, with forecasts of 25 knot winds coming from the south-east and intimidating swells, the prospects did not look good for an easy passage. *Duyfken* was a tremendously uncomfortable ship when pushing into the wind under diesel power. The first two days out of Banda emphasised, however, that sometimes the engines were a great asset. Even though they were averaging three knots, they had made only 15nm of progress towards the Kei Islands in two-and-a-half days of sailing and it was disheartening that they could still see the commanding silhouette of the cone of Gunung Api in Banda on the horizon. For hours it was on the horizon on the port side, and then on the starboard side, and then back on the port side. Much to the frustration of the crew, the pattern repeated with no prospect of making headway. When the wind abated and the sea smoothed out, Peter decided to succumb to modernity and turn the engines on. When winds became more favourable, he planned to put the ship under sail again. He set course for the Kei Islands and the port of Tual.

At Tual, *Duyfken* trimmed down to just 13 crew for the run to Queensland. Iwan had enough for his feature article on *Duyfken* and our new American friend, Tom, was suffering. His leg infection worsened as time passed onboard ship. "I told a couple of crew members of my increasing pain and asked for any assistance they could render. None were doctors, of course, and the boat's stores of medicine were just enough for the regular crew. I needed antibiotics. The infection turned an ugly red color and leaked puss down my leg. I bandaged the wound as best I could and toughed out the remaining days to Tual. To me I wasn't really suffering on board such a beautiful ship and a talented crew. I diverted my mind by watching marine life off the ship's bow, or telling stories about life in war torn Ambon. Suffering happened elsewhere, not on *Duyfken*. I felt privileged beyond measure. When we finally landed in Tual, members of the crew quickly conveyed me to the PUSKESMAS, the Indonesian acronym for community health centre. There a team of emergency personal cleaned the wound and fed me antibiotics. I felt better in under an hour."

Paul Hough's work was done. He dived six times on one of the world's fastest growing and newest coral reefs, and he found 20 species of coral and 10 species of fish which he thought were new to science. He returned to Reef HQ with many specimens and much to study. Marcus Gillezeau and his camera operator, Geoff Longford, also left the ship. We would meet again at the Pennefather River. Marcus had enough of sixteenth century Dutch ships to last a lifetime. He told me in Banda that for him, sailing aboard *Duyfken* was a kind of hell — "Sleeping on a brick floor in the hold beneath a choir of snoring sailors was one of those life experiences that certainly hardens you," he said. "Seasickness for me was a nightmare and something that I never really overcame." And it was not just because of the living conditions. He found it difficult to cope with some of the personalities aboard. The feeling was mutual from some of the crew, too.

Even in the isolated Kei Islands, forgotten by the rest of the world, the violence plaguing Maluku was evident. The TNI naval compound at Tual was a camp for about 850 refugees which the crew were told were fleeing the violence in North Maluku. In fact, in May the previous year, 50 people died in fighting between Muslims and Christians. Then there were more deaths when the police and TNI started shooting into the crowds to try to stop the warring factions. The death count at Tual was reported to have reached 200, and 3,000 houses and 48 mosques and churches, as well as schools and health centres on the islands were destroyed. Amnesty reported that as many as 18,000 people sought refuge in police stations and local air and naval bases at this time when the 'foot soldiers of the Jihad' arrived.

The challenge for our crew was now clear. There were no passengers aboard, just 13 crew members. Up to this point, the longest passage was 12 days. If the previous few days from Banda had been tough, now they faced more of the same, but for weeks on end. They had a month to reach the Pennefather River with no scheduled stopover ports for rest and recuperation.

But this was not an immediate concern for the crew who had a trouble-free time in the Kei Islands. They cleared Indonesian customs and immigration and firmly set their gaze on the great southern land they called home. It was short-lived relief. Peter and his crew left Tual just in time. Nicole Gardner recounted hearing the radio news a few days later: "Jihadi troops and Indonesian Navy were boarding vessels at random in our area, and two-hundred Jihadi troops had arrived at Tual. Among the people killed were the harbourmaster and his staff who'd been so helpful to us barely a few days earlier. Our elation waned and we stared at the dark ocean in silence, wondering what would happen next."

Peter and I were in daily email contact, and I asked he and the crew to begin thinking about how they wanted to conduct themselves at the Pennefather River. For me it was an open book. All I knew was that we didn't want to play to the old play sheet: "a man dressed as a sea captain comes ashore with marines holding muskets and declares that he has discovered a new land and in this case it is (insert Australia here)." They then plant a flag on a pole and declare ownership of the real estate. Peter's logs had shown him to be a deep thinker about the meaning and significance of the Expedition. We all learned that the *Duyfken* story that came to the surface as we sailed through the archipelago of Indonesia was not quite as simple as we had thought when we were building the ship. The discussions became passionate with a free exchange raising issues of European colonialism and reconciliation, and what *Duyfken* represented.

On day 98 of the voyage, nine days out of Tual, Nicole Gardner described a day in the life of a crew member:

> *And the days roll on. Helm and lookout, pumps and weather reports mark the passage of time. Meals provide a distraction. The sight of a log in the water, a bird, a flying fish, unusual cloud is the subject for discussion. There is a sense of timelessness, of having been here forever: watch, helm trick, lookout being infinitely long, yet over in a flash. There is no way to explain to a person who has never been to sea what it is like; huddled on lookout in wet weather gear, trying to shelter from the wind behind the mast, drenched by spray with every pitch of the ship; hungry, after a meal of three pieces of bread, 13 people all staring at the last piece; holding the whipstaff against the roll of the ship; too tired to focus on the compass; pumping ship when you think you are too tired to stand, your muscles moving automatically; waking to the roar of "all hands, ready about!" after only an hour's sleep and stumbling out on a rainy night. They could never understand the sense of duty and comradeship that drives us to keep going, to do our fair share, no matter how tired and uncomfortable, and in not understanding this, they can never understand the beauty of a sunrise after a long, sleepless night; the sense of satisfaction of a job well done; the peace of a calm, clear night with a free breeze; the freedom of dolphins playing in the bow wave; the excitement of finding land. We can be content with simple things that they, in their socially acceptable lives, do not*

> appreciate. For us, a filling meal or a few hours of sleep are a privilege. A wash and a change of clothes a luxury. I believe we are the rich ones.

The course took the *Little Dove* along the south coast of West Papua in the Aru Sea. It was tough going for the crew who were battling illness and frustrating weather. A flu virus went through the crew, then in one day, a strong current took them 10nm backwards. They were heading away from Australia faster than toward it. "*Duyfken* laboriously climbs over each crest and tumbles with a jolt down into each trough," is how Peter described *Duyfken's* motion under engines while fighting the headwind. After 100 days from Fremantle, Nicole Gardner did some sums from the ship's log and estimated that the ship had been under sail for 1078.5 hours and under engines for 379.6 hours — most of that trying to make headway during the past few weeks. The ship consumed 5,400 litres of fuel during that time. This was not now a glorious re-enactment voyage but a hard slog.

After a few weeks at sea, supplies were running low: fresh food had run out, cooking gas was rationed. Hot drinks were out. Jane Doepel was cooking with a simplified menu of rice and dahl which left the crew short of vitamins. Tropical sores would not heal. The hand pumps were used every three hours to control the ingress of water into the bilge, rather than using precious fuel to drive the modern pumps.

There were now significant doubts whether the voyage could be accomplished. The ship had a fuel capacity of 2,724 litres. On an assumed daily generator use of two hours per day at five litres per hour then 550 litres was used for power generation. That left 2,174 litres. The most efficient speed to run the engines was 2200rpm. On a consumption of 25 litres/hour then 87 hours of steaming time at three knots would provide a range of 261nm. At more moderate headwinds enabling the ship to achieve four knots, the range was 348 nm, or at five knots the range was 435 nm. Two 200 litre drums of diesel were on deck. That gave an extra 16 hours steaming at 2200rpm. The wind was against them. The current was against them. A day of sailing gains could be negated by eight hours of adverse currents.

The fuel taken aboard in Indonesia was contaminated and it was causing problems for Mick Hemsley. The engines regularly lost power. He was continually working on them. Fuel filters were regularly replaced. With less than five days of fuel onboard, Peter and I discussed his options across Sat

C emails. He decided he had only one option: to visit the industrial port of Amamapare in West Papua for refuelling. It held some major risks. Amamapare was a closed port for general traffic. *Duyfken* had already cleared Indonesian customs and immigration and our permit specifically prohibited us from visiting any port in Irian Jaya. The Indonesian Government did not want any outsiders in this area. Amamapare is the port for the famous, perhaps infamous, Freeport mine which held the world's largest gold and third largest copper reserves. Freeport was an international pariah at this time, and ironically perhaps, Julius Tahija had a long association with the company since helping it get underway in its early days. The Free Papua Movement wanted self-determination for West Papua, and the Freeport mine was operated under the constant threat of attack by the insurgency. The roadside bombs, arson and protests resulted in what humans rights campaigners estimated to be a death toll of more than 160 people killed in clashes since 1975. The mine was able to continue thanks to massive payments to Indonesian generals and everyone else down the chain of command who provided what could only be called a protection racket. The gold royalties were substantial and former President Suharto turned a blind eye to the human rights abuses and the billions of tonnes of mine waste that was being dumped into the jungle rivers near the mine. One report asserted that enough waste had been dumped to fill the Panama Canal twice.

On day 100 of the voyage, 16 July 2000, Peter had to shut down the engines three times for Mick to attend to the fuel filters. By 5.30 the next morning, and after yet another engine shutdowen, they made it to the Amamapare harbour entrance. They were prohibited from entering the harbour, so Peter anchored at the mouth of the nearby Tipuka River. Several fishermen from Tual paddled over to the ship and told Peter and Greg that two weeks before the crew arrived at Tual they had seen severed heads of Christians hanging from the suspension bridge near where we anchored at the port. According to Sat C reports, after we left Tual a ship arrived with 200 jihadis and 28 people died in the resulting clashes. There was a feeling that *Duyfken* got out at just the right time. There was a sense of fear and trepidation amongst the crew. Robert Jefferson described the experience:

> We are awoken for breakfast amid disquiet, there is no motion of any kind except for the lapping of water alongside. After punching waves for the last few days, the silence is eerie. Duyfken *is lying off the mouth of a*

highland stream of water awaiting sufficient light to negotiate our way upstream. We are going to request fuel from the harbourmaster at the industrial port whose glow I saw last night. It is overcast and a low southeasterly swell continues. Before us in the distance all that is visible is an expanse of muddy water and a drab mangrove laden shore, an air of despondent defeat hangs over the scene. Some dugout canoes and larger perahus move sluggishly around the mouth of the Tipuka River. It feels spooky, very weird to be entering this river. A sense of dread and foreboding pervades as we move slowly into the moving stream of milky brown water. Because I continue to feel much pain from my injury last night and do not feel confident to handle lines or any weight I call off the depths to Peter as we go into the river mouth and beyond. My eyes do not move from the depth sounder except to time my readings to him, using my watch every 15 seconds or so. 13 metres…12 metres…nine metres.

The tangled growth of scraggy mangroves on each side seem malevolent in the early morning stillness and the monotone surrounds close in, swallowing us in its cloying and seemingly impenetrable thickness. I am so tired. Implicit in the tableaux is a feeling that Joseph Conrad was describing this place on his journey upriver to the unknown and that somehow we are contemporising Heart of Darkness. Simultaneous vistas of the human forces of the Jihad from which we have been fleeing are seemingly given tangible form in this unwelcoming and somnolent backdrop. And so, we travel on our mission in a crazy world of violence where even the environ seems to whisper unspeakable evil. Yet this is no sanctuary for us.

Nick Burningham thought of *Heart of Darkness,* too. He described the arrival in his diary: "We anchored between banks of dark mangrove forest, mysterious and unquiet as a Conrad novel. The whole coast is a maze of creeks and channels winding through thousands of square miles of mangrove swamp. We would never have been able to find fuel without the unstinting help of the local Indonesian coastguards station and Loi Trang, a Vietnamese Australian running a fishing operation there. Searching for a few drums of fuel I traveled in the coastguard launch through miles of channels and creeks. Occasionally we passed families of Melanesian people paddling slowly and quietly through that endless swampland, in huge dugout canoes — grandma and grandpa paddling at bow and stern, mother over a cooking fire midships, kids scrapping further forward and dad mending nets."

With millions of rupiah stuffed in his pockets, he later mused that at any time he could have been despatched by his new friends and dumped overboard and nobody would have been any the wiser. The fuel he was eventually able to purchase was dirty — but at least some was available.

The crew was once again confronted by the contradictions of life in Indonesia. They were at the port of one of the most profitable gold mines in the world made possible by modern mining methods but the most basic supplies weren't available. Mick Hemsley was frustrated and voiced his outrage and anger that Freeport would not supply the ship with any fuel.

"Some time later, a five metre unadorned dugout with an adult, two kids and a sorry looking, bedraggled pelican with a line attached to its leg pulls alongside to starboard," said Robert. "Items of our clothing are bartered for crabs and a search is made throughs the ship for more apparel. We have so little ready cash onboard that we are unable to pay much money for these victuals but the clothing seems much appreciated by these extremely poor people, their own garments are so threadbare. The crew happily give up shirts and shorts. I feel very moved and proud of their generosity."

Nick Burningham's experience in Indonesia and his ability to speak Bahasa was invaluable as the challenge of getting the fuel aboard was considered. Peter Manthorpe described the improvised state-of-the-art fuel delivery method:

> *At four in the afternoon the fuel boat finally arrives. They ask us to pass down our pump. We shake our heads. We have no pump. They have no pump either. We are back to syphon technology. Mick and Ben go down into the boat and syphon the fuel into 20 litre drums, then hand them up to us on the deck of* Duyfken. *We carry them to the filler pipe and pour them through a funnel, then pass the drums back down to the boat. A chain gang develops and the drums start to rotate more rapidly. All is going well, except that the fuel is very dirty. It is full of grit and scale. Mick doesn't want to put it in the tanks without straining it because of our short supply of filters, but the cloth we are straining it through keeps clogging up.*
> *After a lot of experimentation we hit on the following procedure. Each 200 litre drum is lifted onto the quarterdeck and the hose stuck inside. Mick stands underneath and sucks on the pipe until the diesel starts to flow. He spits out what he manages not to swallow and directs the hose into a bucket, over which Jane and*

> Gary hold a cloth as a filter. When the bucket is half full, Gary pours it into the tank through the funnel, over which Greg holds another cloth as a final filter. One of Jane's old sarongs has just the right porosity for the job. In this way, 10 litres at a time, we load 1000 litres of fuel. It takes us four and a half hours and by the time we are finished the entire ship, all the crew and all their clothes are covered in a greasy, slippery coating of diesel fuel.
>
> About a dozen of the locals have climbed onboard to watch the show. They are especially entertained when, half way through a pour, Jane's pants start falling down. She has no spare hands to pull them up again, so she calls out to Andrea who comes running to the rescue, holding them up until Jane has her hands free again. All in a day's work for the *Duyfken* crew.

With fuel bunkered, it was time to leave Amamapare. Peter asked the crew for any spare cash to contribute to buy food before they departed: "A scrabble through purses and wallets ensures a small amount of cash. We have only a small amount of petrol to power the Zodiac but John, Jane and Greg go ashore to procure what victuals they can obtain, beaching the runabout on a small fringe of brown silt between water and the tree line near some decrepit perahus which are being maintained by two languidly moving men. They return with lollies, biscuits, tinned meats, sardines and a bag of rice and describe the village where the people live in desperate subsistence. The shop was barricaded with bars within a mesh and razor wire compound and a number of people carrying guns observed them with quiet but alert scrutiny. Some of the locals helped cut and collect firewood which we have bagged and placed on deck – damp, evil smelling mud encased mangrove roots and branches," said Robert Jefferson. Jane Doepel noted that the locals couldn't afford to buy the rice at the kiosk. They were ageing prematurely and their teeth were falling out.

"Selling us their fish and crabs had been a small boon for these families," said Peter. "Strange, that such poverty can exist here while in the very next inlet in the mangroves thrives a busy port servicing the world's richest gold mine. Too strange for a simple sailor like me to fathom."

Without any cooking gas to buy, the barbecue was removed from the firebox at the forepeak and the crew began cooking for a few days with the firewood. Old technology rescued us again. At least they now had diesel fuel to burn as *Duyfken* set sail across the Arafura Sea. The crew was now focused on a timely arrival in Australia while also despairing over the futility of opposing the trade winds. With barely enough fuel, they had to sail as much as possible and they were under sail as they entered the Gulf of Carpentaria. Mick cleaned clogged fuel filters with an old toothbrush and reused them. It worked and the engines only stopped once. Fresh water was rationed as it required a lot of fuel to power the water making unit. When very heavy tropical rain showers came through, all of the crew came up to the main deck and stripped off into underwear, soaping up and having a guilt-free wash.

Ship's Cook Jane Doepel was utterly spent from the relentless grind of cooking 40 meals a day but she seemed indefatigable — but how long could she last?

Peter decided to call into Gove in Arnhem Land for more diesel as he expected to be ploughing into a headwind across the Gulf to Queensland. The stopover was a blessing. Unplanned or not, it was comforting to know that *Duyfken* was back in the safety of Australian waters and fresh food could be obtained.

Duyfken sailed past Cape Arnhem as they left Gove and we were reminded that we were back in a part of Australia explored by Dutch ships. Jan Carstensz lead a VOC trading expedition in 1623 when he named the cape after one of his two ships. The other was the *Pera*. He noted in his log that Willem Jansz and *Duyfken* had been in the area 17 years before and he probably had a copy of his chart. In a VOC report written in 1624 it was written: "Our men landed in sundry places, but found nothing but wild coasts, barren land and extremely cruel, savage and barbarous natives, who surprised and murdered nine of our men, partly owing to their own negligence; according to the report of the said coast, there would be nothing in particular to be got there." We were sailing in the wake of Jansz's *Duyfken*, too. However, almost four centuries had now passed. Some time after *Duyfken* and *Pera* sailed these waters but before Lieutenant James Cook navigated the east coast, the local Aboriginal people began the peaceful trading of trepang (sea cucumber) with the Makassarese who sailed down with the monsoon from Indonesia and then returned when the winds, which were blocking our ship, began to blow from the south east. Like the Indonesians, the Aboriginal people of the area call white people Belanda ('Hollander') which is a name they must have learnt from the Makassarese.

The restricted diet aboard the ship in Indonesia affected the crew. As Nicole described it "every cut, scratch and salt-water boil got infected" and refused to heal. Nick Burningham wrote: "By the time we reached Gove, some problems with vitamin deficiency were evident. I had a slight respiratory tract infection, and some others were sorely afflicted with ulcerations. Multi-vitamins, antibiotics, fresh salad, vegetables and bucketloads of red wine were prescribed or self-administered according to taste and we all recovered." The doctor at the hospital in Gove said that the crew members were showing the early signs of scurvy. This was not the sixteenth century sailing experience we'd dreamed about.

Meanwhile, the violence in Maluku dragged on until the Malino II Peace Agreement between the warring parties was signed in February 2002. We were incredibly fortunate to have avoided the troubles. It was only by a whisker at times. Several years later, a diplomat said to me in passing, "we always knew where you were". It was reassuring that both the Indonesian and Australian navies had us on their radar. I was relieved that we were in Australian waters. As the crew tackled the Gulf of Carpentaria, they now only had the singular challenge of getting to the Pennefather River on time. I no longer checked the daily travel advisories from the Australian Department of Foreign Affairs — just the Bureau of Meteorology wind charts! Thanks to our engines, we had almost achieved what the local seafarers wouldn't even dream of trying.

Chapter 21

In Search for Meaning

After Banda, the next time I would see the ship and her crew was at the Pennefather River. I returned to Perth to throw myself into planning for the arrival. *Duyfken* was only four weeks away from what we all saw as the defining moment in the life of the *Duyfken* Foundation. Six years of work had got us to this momentous occasion when a replica of the first known European ship in Australia's history would make landfall at the place where the original crew came ashore.

We had one opportunity to get it right. As an event organiser, I usually assembled a team and we put together a precise plan, every activity went onto a spreadsheet, every minute was accounted for, everyone had a script and knew what to say and when to take to the podium. Singers and dancers were choreographed to perform at just the right moment. I liked it that way. Risk of disaster and embarrassment was reduced. Everything was controlled. There were no surprises.

This was not going to be one of those events.

We had a blank sheet — even the location for the arrival was up for discussion. The Queensland Premier's Department favoured holding the event at the mining port of Weipa so more people could attend but we didn't like that idea. Our preferred location initially was along the coast at the Pennefather River. It is generally accepted that Jansz and his crew probably launched the ship's sloep and rowed it up the Pennefather River, naming it the Coen River. There is even an obvious place near the river mouth, a sandy strip of beach, where, in all likelihood, they could have actually set foot on Australian soil and gathered timber for the firebox on the ship. It is noted on Jansz' chart. When I flew over the Pennefather River while we were planning the Expedition, I saw that spot and we discounted it. It would have been too difficult to get anyone in from the land side. Instead, all the interested parties agreed on location at a beach near the river mouth which was accessible by a dirt track.

Naturally, the garrulous Queensland Premier Peter Beattie would say a few words. Now there was a man who had the gift of the gab! The CEO of Chevron Overseas, Peter Robertson, planned to fly in from San Ramone in California, the Australian chief executive John Gass planned to attend along with Dr John Powell from PNG Gas. They were our commercial sponsors and very important, however, the event would have less significance if the Aboriginal people of the area were not represented. I asked Cliff Leggoe from Chevron to whom I should talk to see whether they would like to attend the arrival. Cliff spent a long time in Cape York speaking to members of local communities about the PNG Gas concept and he knew the lay of the land. He said I should ring Noel Pearson.

Sure. Of course I could ring one of the most controversial men in Australia. Now I was way out of my depth. Noel Pearson was a 35 year old Bagaarrmugu man who grew up at the Lutheran Aboriginal Mission at Hope Vale near Cooktown. Noel was a national figure with a reputation as a firebrand and an outspoken and formidable leader in the Aboriginal community. He graduated from Sydney University with a degree in law and history, and returned to far north Queensland, helping lay the foundations for the Cape York Land Council in 1990. He successfully negotiated land claims up and down the Cape. Following the Mabo decision in the High Court of Australia in the early 1990s, he was a member of the Indigenous negotiating team for the Native Title Act of 1993. The preposterous idea of 'Terra Nullius', that Australia was occupied by heathens who were effectively 'non human' and who had no rights under Crown law, and that, therefore the country was empty and could be annexed on behalf of the British monarch, was a core part of the Mabo decision. His most controversial views described the impact of passive welfare on Aboriginal families and their communities. He generated a national debate but he stood by his views. How would he react to the concept of a re-enactment of the first time his people met Europeans? Would he see *Duyfken* as a symbol of the white 'invasion' of Australia? Cliff Leggoe explained that such was his influence on the Cape, if he supported the arrival at the Pennefather River, then it would happen. If he didn't, then I could forget it. I was nervous. I didn't want to stuff up this phone call.

So I steeled myself and dialled his number. A receptionist answered and kept me waiting for what seemed like 10 minutes. Eventually Noel came on the line and I gave him the potted history of the Project and the Expedition, and finally, that we intended to land at the Pennefather River and we would like to invite the local Aboriginal people to attend — but only if they wanted to come. If they didn't, I said, that was fine, as we understood the sensitivities involved.

"So you are going to dress up like clowns in a circus and come ashore and you want us to dress up and sing a few songs for the white man?" he said in an off-hand and sarcastic way. I could hear the aggression in his voice, like a criminal lawyer attacking a witness. I was on trial. He was clever. How I responded would be carefully assessed.

"Actually, no. We are not going to dress up in seventeenth century gear. We are modern people and we'll be dressed like modern people. We are Australians marking a point in history to help us fully understand how we came to be here. This is not some sort of costume drama. And I don't care what you dress like" I said. "That's up to you. We'll ask for permission to land. That's about all we have in mind. If you don't want to attend, then that's fine. It's up to you. If you don't want us to sail to the Pennefather River, then that is OK as well. We'll respect that," I said.

There was silence for a moment. Uh oh. I might have over-stepped the mark here. Then Noel spoke with a softer and more relaxed voice. "OK. I probably won't be able to attend but you can talk to my brother, Gerhard, who will help arrange things."

I have never met Noel Pearson, but from that moment on we had nothing but positive dealings with the people of Cape York.

Aboard *Duyfken*, the same question was being asked. How would they conduct themselves at the beach? As with the traditional owners, I had no interest in telling the crew what they were to do or say at the beach except in the broadest possible terms: Peter, as Master of the ship, should come ashore at a prescribed time. What he did was up to him. The inspiration for the arrival came from, perhaps, the most unexpected source. "During crew meetings, after the evening bowl of rice and lentils, we discussed how we should approach the landing at Pennefather River and our meeting with the Aboriginal people of Cape York. Mick, our Engineer, could be gruff and often sounded truculent, but it was Mick who stated simply that we'd been approaching people in Indonesia on the basis that it was their land, treating them with respect and friendship, and that had worked well; so we should approach the Aboriginal people of Cape York in the same spirit," said Nick Burningham. The stage was set.

Weipa was a rough tough mining town but unlike most remote

communities, it really was the end of the road. Comalco established the town in 1962 to exploit huge bauxite deposits which were destined for refineries in Japan. The new town caused severe disruption to the local Aboriginal communities which already had been relocated to missions. The 2000 people living in Weipa today are a resilient mob. They have to be. Roads are often cut off from the rest of the world during the summer wet season from January to April. The locals were incredibly hospitable and so excited that *Duyfken* was coming to town. Tracy McCullough had been working on the arrival details for months and we relocated to several rooms at a motel in Weipa to finalise the arrival details. She was stunned when she wandered over to the town supermarket just after she flew in and the local school kids had the word *Duyfken* written up their legs. It turned out that they were having a sports day and one of the school faction teams was called *Duyfken*. We'd come to *Duyfken*-land! Her room became the *Duyfken* Foundation office with computers and printers and stacks of files all over the place. Peggy Rogers was due to arrive closer to the actual arrival day. Tracy, Peggy and I worked well together. They both had an eye for detail. Tracy enjoyed the extended personal communication with local people which was necessary after I had painted the 'big picture'. We were a great team and much of the success of the voyages was down to their work behind the scenes.

Weipa was a service town for the Comalco bauxite mine (we planned to bring the ship to the town jetty after the arrival at the Pennefather River) and everything was going to be coordinated from the town. We were helped by many people in Weipa including Mark Payne, who had flown to Fremantle all the way from Weipa to come aboard the ship for our first sail the year before. Mark's other love was cranes (that was handy!) and he couldn't have been more helpful while we were in the area. Geoffrey Ewing from Comalco was our liaison person who opened every door that needed opening in the company-controlled mining town. Richie Ah Mat was an Aboriginal person working for Comalco and another Aboriginal person, Terry Piper, who had an Aboriginal liaison role with Chevron in Cairns, also helped us out.

This was a town of contrasts. I was invited one evening to participate in the cultural phenomenon of a local Hash House Harriers run. We were taken to a spot and then told that the beer was "in that direction" while pointing straight into the trackless bush. I thought these people are mad.

What if I tripped over a saltwater crocodile or a deadly taipan snake? It was hot, humid and horrible running through the bush. I just imagined getting lost overnight and the locals having to send a search party out in the morning. Fortunately I staggered to the finish — a barbecue trailer parked somewhere in the bush — and I had to be initiated by pouring an ice-cold beer over my own head. I must admit, it felt good, but wow, my hair was sticky afterwards! On another night, I attended the Croc Eisteddfod Festival, a gathering of hundreds of Aboriginal and Torres Strait Islander schoolchildren from schools all over the north. They came together to sing and dance just like a Rock Eisteddfod in the city, except it was a blend of traditional Aboriginal song and dance and modern music. Thousands of people filled the outdoor venue and it was an unexpected surprise and a joy to see.

It was emphasised to me that it wasn't the men who controlled the Pennefather River area but it was the woman who were the custodians of the land where the ship would arrive. It was important that we met these women. Tracy and I were introduced to three of the most charming people. Thancoupie, Aunty Flo and Aunty Ina were Pennefather area elders and great friends. The made us feel welcome immediately and they made us laugh with their remarks about the relaxed way things happened in the north. Thancoupie was a local legend. She came from the Napranum community and studied art in Sydney when she was in her mid-thirties. Her artworks, and her ceramics in particular, gave her an international reputation and she was known as a significant Australian contemporary artist. She exhibited widely around the world. They women were so positive about *Duyfken* and the arrival arrangements that we knew we were in good hands. We were immediately regarded as friends.

I asked Thancoupie if she knew about *Duyfken*. "Of course," she said. "We still talk about when the ship came here last time." Last time? She then proceeded to say how scared they were of the big sails and the white people on the big canoe. She said that some of the crew must have been at sea too long, and they were naught boys! Thancoupie began talking about how the stories were part of local lore and then I came to the realisation that she wasn't differentiating between the original ship and the replica. Our visit was just a continuation of what had happened 394 years before. Everything was connected. I was gobsmacked. I hadn't thought of it like that. When I asked about what they had planned at Pennefather River, Thancoupie told us not to worry. They'd organise something at the beach. And we left it at that having no idea what we were in for.

Thancoupie's positive view wasn't the only one in the local community. There was also outright hostility to our visit. This letter was published in the local Weipa community newsletter on July 28, 2000 — less than two weeks before we were due to arrive at the river:

> Dear Editor,
> As great Wimaranga-Andumakwithi and Bwilmi Tanikwith descendants of the people from the southern and eastern side of the Pennefather River may we remind our traditional peoples that this Duyfken boat is the same 'Little Dove' that came from Holland and turned into a 'Fire Breathing Dragon', this boat has the dubious record not only of landing on this land before Captain Cook, but also of slaughtering our peoples before other Europeans. Our so called 'savage' ancestors (as they called us) lived peaceful lives, providing for their families in their usual way, respecting laws of our lands, living within our set boundaries, and, of course, if our peoples broke laws, protocols and over-stepped set limits there were repercussions on a local and wider scale. However, on that fateful day when families were enjoying themselves, also respecting Ikwiggle Story of that area, saw these Nhighi-Mbu (strangers like ghosts), they knew there was trouble coming, not a peaceful 'dove'.
> To talk about reconciliation, you don't bring the gun, knife or whatever ('boat') that killed the loved ones to those that survived the carnage. Would Martin Bryant's (he massacred those people in Tasmania) family's sorrow be accepted if they went around showing everyone the automatic gun and gloat over being the first mass murderer! Why don't the Queensland Government, if we are considered as one and all Australians, help us put a plaque of remembrance to the first defenders of this great country and state! … That would truly be reconciliation at work!
> Who or what is this reconciliation for? That the Dutch won the race! Could someone please give them their long lost trophy (hidden in old Cookies cupboard) or didn't anybody tell them that Australians, white and black fought in Europe, North Africa and Asia for theirs and others freedom in World War II and again defending this land from invasion!
> Our traditional people of all these areas, our lands are being

disturbed as it is, now you mob want to disturb our old peoples spirit too, bringing and showing them the same boat that took their lives from them (how short our memories hey!) forgive ... but never forget.

And there are those so called traditional ones that don't really have our peoples interest at heart. You mob all gamin ones, only out for yourselves. "Look at me, I'm in the photo with important people", in it for what you can get and not what you's can give, that's you fella ways and you's can't change it! (If you's felt hurt, then you know it's you.)

As the white man saying goes "you can fool some of the people some of the time, but you can't fool all of the people all of the time!"

Sure, visit the Township, however this time this boat was built up until now, they never got permission and would never get permission to bring that boat to Tithani'arrenh due to the sensitivity, but they wormed their way through somehow. The American Indians would say they spoke with 'forked tongues'.

Anyway, you mob better do all them ceremonies properly because them dreaming stories, old people's spirit and Chivirri's spirit is proper strong you know. 'Trelim' was spilt on the beach area, walk carefully!

(Signed) Descendants of those who died fighting

We were unaware of this letter at the time and it was only handed to us later.

Meanwhile, *Duyfken*'s passage from Gove to the Pennefather River was both frustrating and pleasurable for the crew. Frustrating that they had to use the engines once more, but pleasurable that the wind gods soon smiled upon them and blew them across the Gulf of Carpentaria in double-quick time. After a four month passage, they were closing in on the Pennefather River five days early. I panicked and shot off a terse email to Peter directing him not to anchor at the Pennefather River. Even sailing up and down the coast would be OK but not stopping at the Pennefather River. I was blissfully unaware what effect this instruction would have on the Ship's Master and crew who were spent after a strenuous month sailing towards Australia in the wrong season. They had suffered days on end with the motors drumming and vibrating everything in the ship. The constant engine noise caused the most unpleasant living conditions possible. They almost ran out of food and most had been ill with some kind of flu which quickly spread through the crew and they had not been able to fully recover.

They were wondering why arriving on time was so important in a re-enactment voyage anyway.

Peter fired back with an email: "I can't believe it. We have travelled all this way, done absolutely everything in our power at considerable cost to our own comfort to make sure we are not late, and now, because of a lucky break in the weather, we have to traipse aimlessly about the sea for days. Don't we deserve a break? How am I going to tell this to the crew?"

Has he ignored my message? I was getting worried. I tell myself, "Mmmm, you could have over-stepped the mark on that one, Graeme. Maybe time to send another message to smooth the water?" So I wrote and pressed send: "Dear P, Congratulations on arriving at *Duyfken* Point. Well done to all. If you arrive now it will be an enormous letdown for everyone. I refer to my previous email that you cannot go ashore yet. The sensitivities here are extremely important and your arrival must be done in the proper way. A lot of people here have worked for a long time to make sure that next week's arrival is special."

Peter had already resolved to drop anchor at the Pennefather River after receiving the first email and my second email presented him with a quandary. He decided to talk to the crew about it. They were furious and it was a good thing that I was not on the ship at the time — I was the target.

They wanted to anchor rather than sail aimlessly up and down the coast. This message came back: "Hi G, Rcd your msg requesting us not to anchor. My intention was not to land, but to anchor north of the mouth, where *Duyfken* made landfall, about six miles north of the spot where the celebration will be. If this is too sensitive how about we anchor further north, away from the river? Understand we must not step ashore until the ceremony, but can't see the issue with anchoring. Isn't the issue with the land, and the ceremony to mark the landing? We are abeam of the Pennefather River now, so we have already arrived in that sense. *Duyfken*'s rigging is in serious need of setting up (Gary uses an uncouth simile to describe how slack it is) and we can't do it at sea. Standing by for yr reply. ATB (All the best) p"

Meanwhile, I'm on the phone to Weipa asking Mark Payne for his advice. He told me that there was a great spot about 65 km up the coast from the Pennefather River between the Jackson and Macdonald Rivers where *Duyfken* would "never be found". I send an email back to Peter. Done. Problem fixed but now I have a very annoyed crew on my hands. Mick, our Ship's Engineer who had put up with the worst job onboard (or maybe second worst — Ship's Cook Jane Doepel might argue with that) and performed it brilliantly was totally fed up. He'd had enough and said he was going to dive overboard and swim ashore. Not a good idea with the sharks and crocodiles in the area and he was later talked out of it — but it was a reflection of the mood aboard and the effect of my rash email.

I'd fallen into the same trap as *Endeavour*, which clinically arrived on time in every port. I'd temporarily forgotten our point of difference, which was the unpredictability of life at sea in an old square rigger, and how the lack of an arrival time was something we used to our advantage when promoting port arrivals. However, it went deeper than that. Even though the crew had been through some pretty hard times in the last three months, it hadn't exactly been a cakewalk for me, either. The *Duyfken* Foundation was just about broke. The Expedition was way over budget, and while I was trying to find a way out of the mess, every day I received emails talking about the other reality of life aboard the ship and the challenges of the difficult voyage they were undertaking. It was a clash of the pressures of life at sea, with the different pressures on land. On the day of our exchange of Sat C emails, I was about to jump on a plane from Perth to Weipa via Cairn. I had to find time to speak to eight media people, and then to sit down with the Croc Eisteddfod organiser in Weipa to find a way of bringing 27 school groups of six students each aboard the ship. In some ways, we were having similar personal dilemmas just in a different place. I had barely seen my family for months. When I was at home in Perth, I was often tucked away in my office until late at night. Peter was also torn between two loves. He had proposed to his girlfriend, Michelle, only a few weeks before the Expedition began and he, naturally, had to weigh up in his own mind the great opportunity *Duyfken*'s voyage presented with the desire to be with his loved one. It wouldn't be the only time when the Ship's Master and the boss clashed at times of high stress but it was the first time for Peter and me.

With only one day to go until the scheduled arrival, I had an offer I couldn't refuse. Lieutenant Commander Warren Bairstow of the Royal Australian Navy's patrol boat, HMAS *Gladstone*, invited us to be guests on his vessel as they scouted for *Duyfken*. This was my kind of voyage. Another Fremantle class patrol boat, HMAS *Geraldton*, was in Fremantle when our ship was launched. My mind flashed back to that day — it seemed like ancient history now. Boarding the patrol boat at Weipa, I was struck by the modernity of the vessel compared with our humble *Little Dove*. Even the bridge was air-conditioned. The crew were polished. Every sailor had a position as the ship left port. I commented about how officious and over-the-top all the orders, with their 'slick professionalism', were compared with the 'quiet professionalism' of my crew. The commanding officer explained that there were more officers than ships in the Royal Australian Navy. *Gladstone* was his first command and his naval career would end right there if he ran aground. Once we were in the open sea, he opened up the two 16-cylinder main engines and the ship easily ran up to 20 knots. I said I liked engines and the Chief Engineer invited me to the engine room to take a look at the MTU Maybach engines working hard. The two exhaust manifolds were glowing orange and the patrol boat still had a lot of power it could use — it peaked out at 30 knots. What a way to travel.

Meanwhile, *Duyfken* was happily trundling along the coast to the Pennefather River at 3.5 knots. Soon we closed on her. At this moment, I was immensely proud and excited. Then Mick Hemsley starts firing off water-filled balloons at us with an ingenious contraption made from rubber spear-gun cord. The fourth projectile finds its mark and splatters over the patrol boat, showering some of the Navy crew. Yep. That's my *Duyfken* crew! Pure professionals — every one of them! Fortunately the patrol boat sailors were more restrained and didn't return fire.

When the ammunition ran out, the Firelight film crew and I transferred to *Duyfken*. Peter wrote about our meeting:

> Graeme joins us for a while, slapping me on the back and congratulating us for getting here safely. All the tension of Day 119 is forgotten. He is jubilant. "Did you see the signal fires along the coast? The locals are passing the message down to Pennefather to say you are on your way." Of all the events of today this information affects me the most profoundly. These fires are not a re-enactment. They are a contemporary method of communication, a thousand-year-old survivor in a satellite age, like those who lit them.

My memory of our meeting was different. Sure, the crew was welcoming but I didn't feel much energy and it was a subdued reunion. *Duyfken* had become this crew's home and it was like I was setting foot in their house. But hang on a minute, it was my house, too. The crew who sailed the ship on the last leg from Banda to Pennefather were the professionals or the crew who saw themselves as future professional sailors. They had bonded. They had shared experiences which I had not. They could have no understanding of what I had been through to get the Project, rather than the ship, to this point. Didn't they understand what I had sacrificed and done so that they could be here? What I felt was nothing new. I was not the first to feel this way. It has always been — this gulf between life at sea and on land.

I began handing out the crew mail which had been accumulating in Perth for a month. Some took their letters immediately and found a quiet spot to open them. Others just put them in their back pocket. I was struck by the open sores on Ben Manthorpe's face, arms and legs. He was in agony. Gary Wilson looked thin. Peter showed me the white flag he made for tomorrow's arrival. It was made from ship's canvas. Thancoupie, Aunty Flo and Aunty Ina only asked us for one thing on the arrival day: that was for the Ship's Master to arrive with a white flag. It was a simple and profound request and we were happy to do it. There was no explanation of how it would be used except that it should be on a stick and planted into the sand on the beach.

There was the usual round of media enquiries to answer next morning and we were scheduled to leave Weipa and drive out to the Pennefather River to arrive by lunchtime. Premier Beattie was originally scheduled to reach the Pennefather River aboard HMAS *Gladstone* but the plans changed at the last minute and he arrived by helicopter. We gave him a lift from the clearing to the arrival beach. He fell asleep in the back seat of the car as we drove down the track. I thought to myself that I hoped he was awake for the ceremony. I am not being fair to Peter — he'd been unwell and he was determined to make it to the arrival. He did a good job when we arrived. The Tjungudji, Yuppungutti and Thnikwithi community members also soon arrived. They were excited and they gave the beach a happy atmosphere. *Duyfken* was laying at anchor, festooned with flags and bunting, the sea shimmering around her in the light breeze and sunshine. The Mapoon community put together a great spread of food for us under the trees behind the beach. We were all warned not to take any meat from one particular warmer tray. It was Dugong meat. They caught a Dugong a few days before to be eaten at the occasion. Only Aboriginal and Torres Strait Islander people were allowed to eat this tucker as it was an endangered species. Imagine the scandal if the Premier had polished off a plate of the delicacy.

An ABC reporter asked me for an interview and I obliged. Sure, I have answered questions about *Duyfken* thousands of times. She asks me what I thought the day meant. I am stunned. Suddenly I am taken back to the years we have taken to build the ship, Michael Kailis' death before the ship sailed for the first time, all the people who have been involved, the stress of sending the crew into Indonesia and the profound event which will shortly take place. My voice quivered and tears began to well up. I can't remember what I said but I now realise, at that point, that our little ship had found a place in my heart.

I won't describe the ceremony. It is captured best by Peter Manthorpe in the Captain's Log.

> *Day 124*
> *Pennefather River*
> *9 August, 2000*
> *'Yes'*
> *In an uncharacteristic moment of softheartedness Gary has told everyone they can sleep in till eight, but by half past seven, all hands are wandering about making breakfast for themselves. Is it force of habit that rouses them, or the knowledge that this is the final day of the re-enactment, the day we arrive on shore at the same place the crew of the original* Duyfken *landed in 1606, the day this four month voyage has been leading up to? I wonder.*
> *Taking advantage of the earlier than expected start to the day, Gary has the crew busy straight after breakfast festooning the ship with bunting. By 10,* Duyfken *has so many flags fluttering in the fresh breeze it's a wonder she doesn't drag her anchor.*
> *Looking over to the beach we can see folk milling about everywhere and the two canvas shelters are filling with people. Graeme comes out in a boat to brief us on the plan for the day's events. At 1300 two crew and I are to paddle in to the beach in the orembai, the boat we had built in Banda, followed by the rest of the crew in dinghies. I am to wait until told to come ashore before stepping out of the orembai. Then I am to follow the instructions of the traditional owners of the land who will guide us all through the proceedings. Only a few hours away and I still don't know all that is going to happen. This is a voyage into the unknown right to the end. I am probably going to have to say some words when we come ashore, so I try to find a few moments to think about a short speech. There is too much happening and I never get a chance. Lunch time already. We eat our lunch on deck waving to the constant stream of well wishers in tinnies. A sea rescue boat brings out a group of VIPs*

in life-jackets. Peter Beattie, Premier of Queensland, waves and calls his congratulations to us. We wave back between mouthfuls of spaghetti bolognaise.

You know how hard it is to eat spagbol without splattering your shirtfront? Try eating it in the downdraft of a hovering chopper.

The word comes over the radio from Graeme that we should make our way ashore. I am about to climb over the rail when someone shouts 'Have you got the message stick?' I don't believe it. I nearly forgot. Someone passes it to me with the white flag. I climb down with them into the orembai and start bailing out the water as Nic and Rachelle climb in and take up their paddles. We have two inches of freeboard and the choppy little waves are much bigger than that. Our craft has also dried out in the last weeks and the planks have shrunk. She leaks. Will we make it half a mile to the beach? I express my concerns to a man in a nearby tinnie and he laughs: 'He's brought a sixteenth century sailing ship thousands of miles, I think he can paddle a canoe a few yards.' I wish I had his confidence. I have a wet bum already.

We paddle in towards the tents. Nic and Rachelle do most of the paddling because I have to stop from time to time to bail out. When we are about half way in the crowd surges down the beach from the tents to the water's edge. The shore gets closer and closer until I can make out familiar faces in the crowd. There is Rupert, beaming. We haven't seen him since our emotional farewell in Broome. James Henderson, who has written a book on Duyfken, wades out waist deep in his moleskins for a photo. Too many friends to mention, but among them many faces I hope we can get to know in the coming weeks.

My paddle scrapes the sand under the orembai. I call softly to the others to stop paddling. The boat stops in the shallow water and three women on the beach raise a chant. When they finish one of them explains: 'That means you survived.'

The crowd parts and a man comes towards us with a spear. He signals us to come ashore. I collect the white flag and the message stick, step into the warm water and walk up onto dry sand. I plant the white flag in the sand and the man jabs his spear in right next to it. There is silence on the beach. No one moves, all eyes on the spear and the flag, flapping slowly in the sheltered breeze. It is hot.

The man goes to the edge of the sand and scoops up handfuls of water, pouring it over my head. Now the water feels cool in my hair, trickling down my shirt.

Three shell necklaces are placed around my neck. One of the women says: 'This means you are welcome here, and you can come back any time.'

I thank them and make a short speech: 'We have visited many ports, both in Australia and in Indonesia. Each place we visit we follow marine protocol that goes back centuries, which is to ask permission to arrive and come ashore. This is a courtesy, a sign of humility and respect, that has sadly been ignored too often by colonial powers in the past. We intend to follow this protocol here, like everywhere else we have visited. I have here a message stick from the Noongar people of Fremantle which is a question asked on our behalf: "MAY WE WHITEMAN WALK UPON YOUR GROUND? YES. NO." With this stick I would like to ask the traditional owners of this land for permission to be here.'

I am ushered to the tent where three women are sitting waiting for us. I hand over the message stick. In return one of the women hands me a timber plaque adorned with shells. It says 'Coen River, 2000'. I nearly drop it, it is so heavy. 'Wood from 'round here. Iron wood,' she says. (The two women were Margaret Note and her sister Hazel Miller from the Yupungutti tribe - Ed.)

Coen River, the old name for Pennefather River. It was named, probably by Carstensz, after the infamous Governor Coen of the VOC. I read out the message on the stick once again and wait for a reply. There is a pause. Everyone is smiling. A voice says 'It's a question. Yes or no?'

'Oh, yes, you're welcome to walk our ground. You're very welcome.'

I thank them. There are some more speeches. The Premier, the head of the overseas division of Chevron our sponsors, Graeme Cocks our Project Director, and the man with the spear whose name I learn is John Cockatoo. A rhythm starts up on a pair of sticks behind us. The crowd turns to watch a group of about a dozen dancers, their bodies daubed in dramatic stripes of white paint. Spears whirl, knees and elbows shake, feet stamp in the sand. Each dance segment ends with a whoop. In the background, small on the horizon, rides *Duyfken*, flags fluttering.

After the dancing a woman in a yellow dress, an elder I presume, stands and makes an impromptu speech. I can only remember snatches: 'The present is now we are living... The future is where we are looking ahead... The past is looking backwards. We must not dwell on the past. The past is a story we can tell our kids sometimes. .. but we must look ahead into the future.'

Her speech receives the loudest applause of the day.

The ceremony dissolves into interviews and photoshoots. I am a little envious of the crew, who are able to mingle among the locals. They are already making friends, learning names, laughing and swapping stories, while I am answering the same questions over and over and grinning endlessly into camera lenses.

We have arrived.

The open warmth of the locals towards us combined with the media attention are affecting me. It is not just salt spray from paddling the canoe that stings my eyes this afternoon. I can't help thinking what a special moment this is for so many people to be treating a group of simple sailors with so much generosity, so much attention.

How different is our arrival from Jansz's on the original *Duyfken*. His log does not survive so we don't know his version of the story, but I am told the local people here have stories that tell of the arrival of the Dutchmen and the trouble they caused. I am looking forward to hearing them. One thing we know is that Jansz sailed away from these shores disappointed. For us that would already be impossible. The people here have put on a welcome for us we will remember vividly for ever.

Peter Manthorpe
Master

It was Ina Thallo (Aunty Ina) who spoke about the future and not the past. That day belonged to her. Up to that point, I had no idea what reconciliation meant. I now appreciated that the Aboriginal people of Cape York owned the story of *Duyfken,* but by bringing *Duyfken* back all of us could now share the narrative. John Cockatoo from the Yupungutti tribe who challenged Peter Manthorpe at the shore looked out at the ship afterwards and I asked him what he thought of our replica ship. He said to me: "That IS *Duyfken*."

Chapter 22

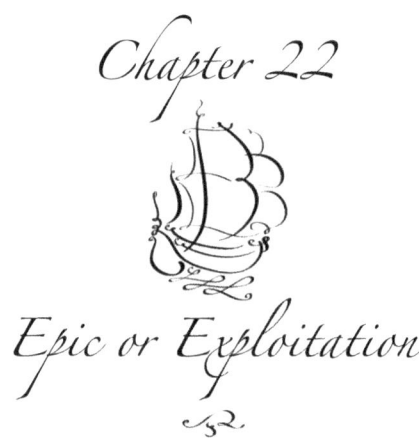

Epic or Exploitation

Duyfken quietly slipped into Weipa two days after the arrival at the Pennefather River. Our Engineer Mick Hemsley tendered his resignation at the Pennefather River. Keeping the engines alive while constantly battling dirty fuel and stifling conditions in the engine boxes was a mighty effort. He had done a great job. From Weipa, voyage crew would supplement the permanent crew and provide some much needed income.

It was time to show the ship to the whole community. After months at sea, *Duyfken* was placed into 'museum mode' as we called it. The crew packed away their gear and replaced it with the seventeenth century items which would have been found aboard a ship like this. Rupert arrived after his long drive from Broome with the ship's cannon, which were jettisoned before the voyage to Kupang and the ship's trailer shop, which Tina Driver and James Holdsworth would operate while we were in Queensland. I knew that the ship must pay her own way and I must stop the drain on the *Duyfken* Foundation's bank account or we would have to call an end to our voyage.

I had some serious discussions with Cliff Leggoe and his assistant Peppi Buetti on how Chevron might help us above and beyond its present commitment. I said funds were perilously low. While the oil giant would not directly support us with more sponsorship cash, they said it could conduct training programs in each port. They could pay for this out of other parts of their budget. I couldn't thank them enough. This was just the financial lifeline we needed in the coming months. We also began a major promotional campaign for voyage crew to supplement our income. The campaign opened with:

SOAKED TO THE SKIN,
SICK AS A DOG,
DEPRIVED OF SLEEP:
DO YOU HAVE THE RIGHT STUFF?

You will be soaked to the skin, tossed about the Pacific Ocean like a cork working more than 16 hours a day, eat on deck with a bowl between your legs, shower with a bucket and do things you never thought that you could do. You'll also have the adventure of your life sailing the world's most authentic sixteenth century sailing ship replica in the way that sailors of 1606 would have done.

Notwithstanding slipping into the previous century (*Duyfken* was an early seventeenth century ship) I thought it summed it up quite well — a real pleasure cruise — and we were flooded with applications.

When I had a chance to talk to the crew I found that both ship and crew were battered by the dreadful experience of the last month. One crew member lost 6.5 kg on the voyage. Three crew still had open pustulous tropical sores from the lack of fresh food combined with the dampness of the ship and the constant salt spray on deck. They went to the hospital in Weipa to see what could be done about it. A doctor wanted to admit them for treatment but none would have it. Ben Manthorpe clearly suffered the most and I couldn't believe my eyes when I saw him on his day off sailing a catamaran across the harbour to give us a wave. The ignorance of youth! He spent two days in hospital afterwards to have his infected open sores treated. When I visited him, I asked him whether I could get him anything. He said, "A Big Mac." A scar on his leg to this day is a permanent reminder of the *Duyfken* Voyage.

The ship's rig did not fare well. It had to be re-tensioned after the battering it had received. The crew ran out of pine tar and we needed some to seal the rig and prevent the rope from rotting. Mark Payne said that it wouldn't be a problem — he knew just where to find some. Pine tar was used to seal nuts and bolts on the big steel structures at the mine. It was duly delivered and used on the ship. Unfortunately, it was not real pine tar made from the resin of pine trees but a hydrocarbon equivalent made as a by-product of oil refining. It was smelly, dirty black horrible stuff which didn't provide the same level of protection on the rigging anyway. It was the only time we used it, but Mark had done a great job sourcing it for us.

The excitement we felt with the accomplishment of successfully navigating the Expedition from Fremantle to Cape York was tempered by some negative stories calling into question the motivations for the voyage. The most galling was from the Brisbane-based Courier Mail newspaper's writer Martin Thomas. He viewed the whole thing through a cynical lens of local politics – as a stunt. After making the point that *Duyfken*'s voyage was to highlight a historical reality lost on most Queenslanders that the Dutch arrived before Cook, he wrote: "But the reason is less to do with righting an historical wrong and more about exploiting the *Duyfken*'s role in our history to lure a new wave of European tourists. It is also being touted as an important opportunity to further Aboriginal reconciliation and hopefully heal some of the deep rifts in the north that threaten to bedevil Premier Peter Beattie's special business summit later this month in Weipa." He was deluded if he thought that many European tourists would venture to Weipa. Linking our efforts at reconciliation to a business summit made little sense and we were dismayed by his cynicism. Something completely different was occurring and he hadn't bothered to look very closely.

Thancoupie was keen to travel aboard *Duyfken* from Weipa to the Aboriginal community at Aurukun. When the ship arrived, Peter met the elder, Silas Wolmby, on the beach and he asked him for permission to come ashore. Silas responded: "Yes, you are welcome to come ashore. You can come here anytime." He placed his spear, tip first, into the sand. Then the Wik people danced and clapped and sang to acknowledge the ship's arrival. I had no part in these events along the coast but it was pleasing that *Duyfken*'s visit to Queensland was generating its own momentum. At the Pennefather River, I had the broadest control over the narrative but I had no idea what anyone would do. This welcome came straight from the people. I wasn't even there. The new stories were their stories.

For the first time, *Duyfken* was given an Aboriginal flag. Many times previously I had been asked why we did not fly an Aboriginal flag. It is a flag loaded with symbolism: black represents the Aboriginal people, yellow the sun and red the earth. I'd always thought it was a better flag for Australia than the southern cross with the Union Jack in the corner but it was not our flag. I responded that if an Aboriginal person gave us a flag to fly, then we would fly it. It was not up to us to fly it without asking. Silas gave Peter a woven basket, two spears, and an Aboriginal flag when they had lunch at the Aurukun Three Rivers Tavern. From then on, we flew it proudly.

Duyfken was continuing to be woven into the web of local storytelling. The farthest Jansz went south along the Gulf coast was Cape Keerweer. It means 'turn about' in Dutch. It marked the most southerly point for our voyage of discovery, too. Silas and his brother Ray joined the ship for the short run to the cape and he sat on the deck telling stories while the crew waited for a breeze to get them moving. He soon had the crew mesmerised. Peter was finding answers to the question he had posed when we left Fremantle. The big WHY of this Expedition. The artikelbrief he was given in Fremantle had vague words about the shared history of Australia, Indonesia and The Netherlands; and encouragement to build bonds of friendship between the peoples of the three countries. It was true: we hadn't thought about it a great deal deeper than that. Being compelled to write the Captain's Log each day gave all of us a window into how he was coalescing these thoughts:

> *Silas sits cross legged on the deck and talks. Slowly a small crowd of us gathers around to listen to him. His words emerge from his wiry white whiskers in a long circuitous stream, meandering from place to place and from time to time. At first he is hard to follow as he talks of events past and present without distinguishing the timeframe. After a while I understand. His words are a long continuous poem that has been going on so long that to talk of a beginning is meaningless. But imagine how I feel when Silas fixes me with his deep-set eyes and says: 'These stories have been passed down to me, from my father, from my grandfather, from my great grandfather... I must pass them down to my children. And I will tell them of the Dutch, coming here and meeting with us. And I will tell them about you people on the* Duyfken, *coming here and meeting with us. These are old stories, but they are new stories too.'*
>
> *Perhaps this is why these people like the idea of our re-enactment so much. They understand better than we do what we are up to. We are re-telling an old story, keeping it alive by living it, but at the same time making it a story of our own, of our own time.*
>
> *Silas explains the meaning of the dance we saw this morning. It is a dance for the spirits of the dead. Though they are long since buried, their spirits are still here. They come looking this way, then that way, as the Big Man sings. The people call out for the ghosts to stay. They are missing their dead ones, their ancestors. But the Big Man says: 'No. Stay away. Finished. Enough.' The ghosts go away*

> *again.*
> *The spirits have been evoked by the song, but they must remain where they belong.*
> *Silas tells us that the dance is for the spirits of all dead people, black and white. The dance today commemorates both the Wik ancestors and the Dutch who met in 1606 at Cape Keerweer.*
> *Silas and his ancestors have been telling the story of Jansz and the* Duyfken *all these hundreds of years while the rest of the world remained ignorant. Silas, sitting on the deck of* Duyfken, *his milky eyes moving between us and the sky, tells the story to us as though it were common knowledge. Now we are part of his story too.*
> *And he is part of ours at last.*
> *Two branches of the same story intersect. And the spirits look this way, then that way, while the Big Man speaks.*

There is no record of what Willem Jansz thought as he carefully made his way south. When James Henderson visited this spot, another Aboriginal elder, Clive Yunkaporta, told him a vivid story of conflict. When our ship arrived at Cape Keerweer and the crew went ashore, they were also told a story. Peter once again:

> *I think of Jansz sailing along here in the original* Duyfken, *dodging shoals and sand-bars with a crew member swinging the lead continuously to sound the depth. They would have been a weary crew of explorers by the time they got here… This is as far south as the original* Duyfken *came and, given the difficulties of negotiating these shoal waters, it's no wonder they turned here and headed back north.*
> *There are more than just navigational hazards in this area. Silas and Ray tell us that one of the reasons they wanted to come with us when they heard we planned to visit Cape Keerweer was that they wanted to protect us from spirits who might get angry with us for disturbing them. This area is highly charged for these people. It has a lot of stories attached to it and not all of them are happy.*
> *We shuttle people ashore in the rubber boat and we spread out across the open expanse of sand, revelling in the space and silence. I walk beside Silas as he leads me on a hunt for a well. As we walk along the narrow strip of beach between the Kirke River and the sea he*

tells me many stories over and over. His voice is hypnotic, easy to listen to, but his words are complex and difficult. It is hard work to follow the many threads of his stories as they weave back and forth between generations and from place to place. His stories fascinate me, but I'm exhausted piecing them together.

'The first mob, they came and anchored their ship way over there somewhere (off to the north-west). They came ashore in a smaller boat with three fellas on this side, three fellas on the other side, all with long paddles. The blackfellas, they were all watching from the trees over there. The Dutchies didn't know the language so they made signs with their hands: 'Water, water.'

'They must have had that fight back that way (back towards the trees on the other side of the river). That girl, she really wanted that Dutchie. He must have been a young fella. That girl was a nice, beautiful girl. She had hair down to here (right down her back) and she had breasts and she was really beautiful. The Dutch fella turned around all of a sudden and there's this beautiful girl. The first time he turned he didn't see anything. Then he looked and saw her. She looked... that was enough.

'That silly old fella my grandfather (ie ancestor) he hit him in the back of the neck. Maybe he is angry. Maybe he wants her for his wife, I don't know. Maybe he doesn't want the Dutchie taking the women-folk.

'That silly old fella he speared one fella. Then there were gunshots from the Dutchies: 'boom boom boom boom'. Then he tells the blackfellas: 'You go and kill them all.' They have to obey him. After the gunshots he says: 'You have to go and burn that boat.' The blackfellas killed nine of those Dutchies.'

'How many blackfellas were killed?' I ask.

'80 or 90 blackfellas killed, something like that.'

I ask Silas about the second mob. 'Did they come for water also?'

'This is the spot mate, in this hollow. Those trees came later. It was all clear then. The second mob. Not the first mob, they were all killed. That second mob, they dug this well. We never found this one. It belongs to them. They found this water.'

Silas and I are sitting under the shade of two big trees growing out of a slight indentation in the ground. Am I sitting at the site where Carstensz and the crew of the Arnhem and the Pera collected water

> *for their journey back to the Indies in 1623?*
> *Across the river, under those trees, was that the battleground where half* Duyfken's *crew lost their lives?*
> *'The* Duyfken *has come here twice now,' says Silas. 'This is an old story, but it's a new story as well. We will remember you fellas coming here. We will remember for ever.'*
> *Back aboard the ship we heave up the anchor, set sail and head back to the north. Silas and Ray get a bucket of water and ask us to gather around. They pass their hands under their arms and then rub their fingers over our heads, legs and feet. They blow over our heads, and rinse sea water through our hair.*
> *'The spirits can smell us on you now. They know you are our friends. They won't harm you now.'*
> *As we sail slowly northward in the dying sea-breeze we sit around on deck eating our dinner and watching the sun go down. Silas and Ray are silent now after a day of talking. The crew are quiet and contemplative as well. It is a powerful thing to know we are now incorporated into the same story as Jansz and his crew.*

The next day, Silas and Ray left the ship at Weipa.

> *We say farewell to our friends Ray and Silas Wolmby this morning. Rick from the volunteer rescue comes out from Weipa in a big cat as we go past, and picks them up. As we say our goodbyes Silas grasps my hand firmly in both of his. He looks me straight in the eye, unashamed that his eyes are moist. Mine aren't too dry either. He says: 'Peter, we will remember you fellas.* Duyfken *has come here twice now. We will remember you fellas coming here for ever.' I feel the cigarette packet in his shirt pocket crush against my chest as we embrace. He whispers in my ear: 'Thank you for coming here. You are my son now.'*
> *'I'm proud,' I reply. Silas reminds me of my dad too. Eyes that can see detail in the distance, a low but arresting voice, and those endless stories...*
> *So now he is gone from* Duyfken.

Willem Jansz, perhaps with a depleted crew, sailed to Torres Strait and then turned left back to Banda. I had always told the story of Willem Jansz's visit to Cape York blithely as a story of the Aboriginal people pushing back to the Dutch, beating them, and the Dutch never returning. In my interpretation the Indigenous people won: a win for the Australians. The Dutch found nothing they wanted and never settled the continent. It was left to the English to undertake that controversial act. The story was shown to be sadly wanting and more complex. Many stories are woven together, of Jansz and Carstensz, of *Duyfken* and *Pera*. Time is compressed. Four hundred years can seem like last year.

Duyfken's mission was to sail north along the coast, to visit Thursday Island in Torres Strait and then sail to Port Moresby. *Duyfken* tied up at the Engineer's Wharf on Thursday Island. A delegation of Kaurareg people (traditional owners of the inner island group of islands including Thursday Island) and local dignitaries met the crew. The ship now had another flag — the blue and white flag with the traditional Torres Strait island headdress, the Dari, in the middle. In only a couple of weeks since the arrival at the Pennefather River, *Duyfken* had hosted 1,500 school children aboard the ship. Peter had one last moment of self-awakening when the ship crossed the path of *Endeavour* and James Cook. It was at Possession Island in Torres Strait where Cook claimed the Great Southern Land for his King. Cook was Peter's boyhood hero and he found him to be no hero of the Torres Strait Islanders. They say he had no right to claim their land. Peter found it hard to disagree. As a seafarer, he was torn by the other side of the Cook story — his skill as a navigator.

Duyfken visited Port Moresby to participate in the silver anniversary celebrations of the nation's independence. When the original *Duyfken* sailed from Cape York, north along the western fringe of Torres Strait, and saw the shoals of Papua New Guinea ahead near Mare, her crew became the first Europeans recorded in history to sight the southern coast of the island. The voyage marked the beginning of the European exploration of eastern Indonesia and beyond, including the northern, western and southern coasts of the Great South Land. While *Duyfken* sailed along the western fringes of Torres Strait in early 1606, later in the same year, the *San Pedrico*, under the command of Luis Vaez de Torres sailed through the strait from east to west, missing the great land to the south. Our *Duyfken* diverted from Jansz's riskier northern passage and did what the Dutch sailors could not manage — sailing from west to east through Torres Strait. The ship anchored overnight at Cape Grenville and traversed Blackwood Passage on her way to Port Moresby. For the local promotion, the Chevron 2000 *Duyfken*

Expedition which had become the Chevron 2000 *Duyfken* Expedisi in Indonesia was now the Chevron 2000 Raun Bilong *Duyfken*. In Pidgin, of course!

In Port Moresby we were in the hands of the PNG Gas Project crew from Chevron. The *Duyfken* arrival was part of a bigger lobbying push to win the hearts and minds of the local decision makers to support the gas pipeline. I flew into Port Moresby early to finalise our arrival plans. I didn't expect a welcoming committee but I was met by three men at the airport. There was a driver and two security guards with machine guns. All just for me? I was honoured and a little bit worried. I was told in a routine way to follow them to a minivan. Where were they taking me? I needn't have worried. I was transferred to my hotel so that I could relax before my meeting. Later in the morning they returned and shuttled me to an office tower in the central business district. I was warmly welcomed at the Chevron office and then I was told that I should meet the distinguished executive, Moseley Moramoro, from their joint-venture partner Oil Search. His office was less than 200 metres away in another office block down the hill. "No problem," I said. "I'll walk down." The answer came back, a firm "No". Nobody walks in Port Moresby. Really? So I was escorted out of the building, into the minivan, for a 200 metre mini-drive down the road to another building.

Moseley was a highly respected businessman and had a great deal of influence. He was working with his government contacts to put on a memorable welcome for our ship. I told him how unusual I thought it was to have a machine gun escort, especially for a trip of only 200 metres. He then took me to the window of his office and began to tell me a story. It was in the lead up to Christmas the year before and he said that there was a stranger than usual atmosphere in town. Everyone knew something was up. The first sign of anything unusual was when a helicopter landed on the roof of the PNG Bank Building. The helicopter had been hijacked from Port Moresby airport and five 'raskols' (the pidgin name for criminals) dressed in military uniforms with all manner of weapons, including hand grenades, jumped out and stormed the bank. After the raskols fired a few shots to warn everyone off, undercover police officers who were strategically positioned in the building and dressed in plain clothes started returning fire. In retreat, the robbers got back into the chopper and took off. There were other police on the tops of buildings in the centre of the city who started shooting at the chopper. Moseley watched all this unfold from the panoramic windows in his office. He pointed out to me where the chopper took some hits and crashed in a nearby parking area. The police surrounded the disabled chopper and he had a bird's eye view of the ensuing gun battle. He said it finished when all five robbers were dead. He said that the police ensured there were no survivors to arrest. "It was just another day in Port Moresby", he said. "You can't be too careful." This was some crazy town!

I was assured, however, that *Duyfken* and the crew would be safe in this 'wild west' town. Tracy arranged for the crew to stay at a place called Ambers Inn at Boroko. It was way more expensive than anywhere we had billeted the crew in Australia or Indonesia but I thought I should take a quick look to see whether it was secure. Secure? It was surrounded by a steel fence and razor wire. It looked more like a prison. Chevron was very mindful of the risk and arranged for two security guards to be on the ship while she was at anchor at nearby Manubada overnight before arriving to a gala welcome the next day. A safe berth was set aside for us at the PNG Defence Force Landing Craft Base (Lancron) on the waterfront supervised by the relaxed Commander, Richard Amba, as there were no naval ships in Port Moresby during our visit.

Duyfken was fully dressed with every flag and pennant that could be flown from a yard or mast as she sailed into the bay. Under the blue sky and with a soft breeze rustling the pennants, she was a grand sight. The biggest welcoming flotilla since Fremantle turned out to greet us. Cliff Leggoe and his team wanted this welcome to be one for the ages, to show the locals what they could do for Papua New Guinea. It didn't disappoint.

PNG Gas arranged a traditional welcome involving the local high school and member of the Motu people who live along the southern coast. Young men and women in traditional dress performed a Hiri dance which celebrated the trading voyages which carried Motu cooking pots to the people of the Gulf of Papua in exchange for sago. The trade was performed in large sailing canoes called lagatois. The show was designed to make the point that the people of this country weren't averse to running a complex trading system of their own, long before people like Willem Jansz came along. It was a point well made. The Dutch thought they were exploring these seas but the local navigators knew their way around. Maybe all they needed to do was ask.

The fierce Motuan tribesmen, pointing spears at the crew, were to remonstrate like they were attacking the ship. The young women in grass skirts lined up along the edge of the wharf, placing themselves between the warriors and the ship. The tribesman were calling out "Aladia! Aladia! (Kill them! Kill them!). Umui daidia, Baia alamui! (Who are you? We will kill you!)."

Peter was then to respond with his choreographed lines: "Ai na tau namodia. Dia tuari bona henao taudia. Mai maino danu al mai" meaning "We are peaceful people, not fighters and not stealers. We come in peace."

Everyone on shore was waiting for Peter's big lines but he stood quietly, looking blankly at everyone. He had completely lost track of where to come in with his lines. Never mind. This is Papua New Guinea. The show must go on. The dancers sing "Namo Aoma, baita hebou" a traditional welcome song anyway.

The formalities began with Lady Kidu, the MP for South Moresby, welcoming us to the national capital. Born in Brisbane and adopted by the Motu tribe when she married Sir Buri Kidu (who later become Chief Justice), she had an affinity and understanding of the coastal people. She spoke with confidence about the extensive trading networks called Hiri which operated for millennia from the Gulf of Papua to the Arafura and Coral Seas. "Our people are also sailors. We have big sailing canoes and navigation is one of our arts. This voyage helps to re-rewrite the previous history of national self-interest, in an era of cooperation between independent people," she said.

It was not bad that we had not one, but two Prime Ministers on the wharf to meet us a well. Sir Michael Somare, the nation's first prime minister, welcomed *Duyfken* and declared open the celebration of PNG's 25th anniversary of independence. We were the first event in a fortnight of celebrations. Former Prime Minister, Sir Rabbie Namaliu, also greeted the crew. Looking around I soaked it all in. There were dancers on the wharf, and dancers on the ship. There was singing and a band playing. Some of the dancers are climbing the rigging. Our crew was dancing too — what great fun — what a joyous welcome.

Over the next few days, *Duyfken* was transformed into a floating classroom. More than 700 schoolchildren swarmed over the ship. It was a stunning success for Chevron and for *Duyfken*.

Cliff Leggoe insisted that Peter and I should be Chevron's guests at the Lake Kutubu oil and gas fields in the Southern Highlands near Moro, so while the crew were opening the ship to visitors the next day we were whisked by air, up through the clouds, to a lonely airfield in jungle covered mountains at the end of the deep blue Lake Kutubu. Once again, we'd been taken to another world but this time were 800m above sea level. This time it was in the clouds. We were treated as honoured guests and offered a canoe ride along a creek with the fantastical sight of Birds of Paradise criss-crossing from tree-to-tree above us. I remembered stories of the Birds of Paradise which were sent back to Europe from here for hundreds of years. The sellers cut off the legs so the plumage wouldn't be damaged in transit to Europe. The Europeans thought that the birds must have been legless. Willem Jansz probably visited the island of Dobo in January 1606 during his voyage to Australia to trade for the lucrative Birds of Paradise feathers. The first two dead birds came with the survivors of the Magellan circumnavigation to Europe in 1522, a gift from the Sultan of the Moluccan island of Bacan to the King of Spain. "We were told that those birds came from the earthly paradise, that is to say they were the birds of God," said Antonio Pigafetta who chronicled the Magellan voyage. The plumage became highly prized in Europe. We saw them alive in their earthly paradise.

I found it difficult to enjoy this extraordinary location. I stepped on a rusty nail at the naval jetty in Port Moresby and it went right through my shoe and pierced my foot. It would have healed quickly in a temperate climate, but in only a couple of days it become a deep, weeping tropical sore and I found it increasingly difficult to walk. I ended up in hospital. I was given the full admissions formalities at the company medical centre within the barbed wire enclosed camp (I was the only patient) and I was given the largest needle into my foot I had ever seen. The heavy duty antibiotic treatment was a total success. The swelling soon went down and I could keep my foot.

PNG Gas aimed to link these gas-rich fields in the highlands with a coastal processing facility and, ultimately, the gas markets of Queensland. This grand project never eventuated. Cheaper sources of gas were developed and the 'ribbon of steel' as Chevron described it has still not been built. Our timing was fortuitous. If our voyage had been only one season later, Chevron would have had no reason to sponsor us. The PNG Gas Project was moth-balled.

Upon our return to Port Moresby, it was time for Gary Wilson to take over as Ship's Master while Peter returned to South Australia for a break. It had been an arduous voyage and I could see that they were both worn out. Gary was a more than able replacement and the weight of responsibility was now on his shoulders. He had such passion for *Duyfken* that I had no doubt the ship was in good hands, but he needed a break, too. Five crew from

Papua New Guinea including two PNG navy men joined Gary and the crew for the voyage back to Australia. Gary was soon in the swing of things with the Captain's Log, providing an altogether different, but equally entertaining view of the Expedition. *Duyfken's* web pages received approximately 3,000 page reads per day from all over the world. From the start of the voyage until the second week of September 2000, people spent 16,686 hours looking at our web pages. Even the crew were reading them. Nicole Gardner once told me that she read the Captain's Logs at net cafés in port so she could find out what she had just done at sea.

A reminder how fortunate we had been to dodge the violence in Indonesia was brought home when I contacted Michael Young after reading news that three UN aid workers were murdered at Atambua near the town of Soe in West Timor. Michael, Robert and I visited Soe before the ship arrived in Kupang. Michael sent me an email on 12 September. He said that the violence in Kupang was escalating when he returned from Banda and he was forced to flee:

> *I managed to evacuate Kupang after some cat and mouse Keystone Cops stuff. Am now on route to East Java...the last white Balanda to exit Timor. Windows up but not cowed!!!! It's a great place and I love Timor, but has been mucked over greatly by the Tim Tim (East Timor) crises and politics as Indonesia skids along its tumultuous democratic revolution...hope it will recover. A heap of Jihad crazies are hiding in Kupang, too, from Ambon and Java hoping to somehow break this Christian bastion through the refugee crises in Kupang if the opportunity arises. Can't forget my crazy confrontation with that refugee mob after we left Soe just before* Duyfken *arrived.*
>
> *Had rocks thrown on my Kupang house last night in town — by crazy infiltrators from Atambua where the poor relief workers were murdered. The TNI have been trying to block a huge crazy Atambua mob coming to Kupang...everyone in Kupang wanted me to stay but the Aussie Embassy rep plus some aid workers evacuated to Jakarta had put real pressure on me. One Aussie mate copped a knife in his back from some militia in Kupang a month ago. Army and Police can't seem to do a thing. They are frightened and poorly trained and paid. Some are on the side of the troublemakers for their own political ends...Timor will be hurting now with no more tourist business. Can tell lots of more stories but 99 per cent of the*

> *Kupang people are great and are hurting too.*
>
> *Refugees can't get anything now that UN and all aid workers are out and I will try and help the four Dili refugees staying at my Kupang house (a bit ironic, no) who lost everything in Dili. Several families I was sponsoring with their artefacts and wood carving and weaving will suffer, too, now that I am not there to support their beautiful creative work. You met some of them in Soe — they are dirt poor and I could not even get Community Aid Abroad to buy their stuff. They can get cheaper copies from their agent in Java and I have had some ding dong battles with their gross behaviour.*
>
> *Hope my house in Kupang survives and that I can get my computer and other things back later.*

Michael Young was irrepressible and not easily discouraged. He soon re-established his art business in Bali.

The next leg of the voyage became the greatest nightmare for ship and crew — damnable out-of-season sailing. Difficult became almost impossible. Up against trade winds reaching force 7, Gary struggled to find a way to head south along Australia's east coast. Here is one day from the Captain's Log:

> *What follows is a day of slow progress. The south easterlies blew fresh all day, battling headwinds for the run south. Even modern yachts have trouble getting south along this coast, vessels much more weatherly than* Duyfken. *We do not have enough fuel to motor all the way to Cooktown nor do we have enough time to beat our way there. We could do it if we had a few weeks to spare. So we have to compromise. We sail on one tack, making as much ground to the south as possible and when we run out of room by being set inshore, it is hand all sail and motor up to windward. That is the slow, tedious bit, the poor little ship struggling to make two or three knots into the steep head sea, seas bursting against the bow and covering everything and everyone in salt. Not good for the rig, everything leaping about up there and not good for everyone's humour. It all changes dramatically when we get under sail each time though, the smiles come back, people snatch a few hours of lost sleep and the ship goes easily under her low sails. Slowly, slowly, we work our way south past reefs with such interesting names as Noddy, Magpie, Hedge and Grub. Who named these, a gardener?*

Gary sought refuge in Stokes Bay near Cape Melville, and the Melville Passage between the Great Barrier Reef and the Queensland coast, hoping that the weather would change. Everything was lashed down and the crew occupied the rest of the day catching hammerhead sharks.

The Sydney Olympics were underway. Back in 1994 we had great plans to be there alongside *Endeavour* and *Batavia*. Now we were stuck near the northern tip of Australia. In one 10 hour attempt to motor south, Gary returned the ship to the same spot to anchor — beaten. Every day I received Gary's update, I cursed this unseasonable voyage. The crew were totally demoralised and tired from the constant pounding. The ship was holding together, but for how long? The rig was not made to be flexed and whipped about in this way. We emailed constantly about contingency plans and workable options. Maybe we should just sail out into the Pacific, visit some island nations and sail a great arc back into Australia? Nothing I can see in the forecast indicated that there was any window we could use to get to Cooktown. The weather looked like it could set in for weeks and *Duyfken* would have to wait for a change of season to escape her prison-like anchorage. Then a saviour arrived in the form of Jardine Shipping's tug *Cairns Express* which was working her way south. For the grand towing fee of $1, lines were extended and *Duyfken* was underway, albeit not under her own power but had she ever done six knots into a strong breeze before? When *Duyfken* arrived in Cooktown there were cheers from spectators on the wharf. *Duyfken* was officially back in Australia but she had taken a hell of a pounding with cracks opening up in the planking toward the bow which would have to be repaired. Gary and I resolved that the next voyage would be trade winds sailing — just as the Dutch intended — and we began to hatch serious plans for a voyage from Australia to The Netherlands. Peter returned to the ship after his break and Gary's initiation by fire was over. He used every sailor's trick in the book in that passage south and it was a total credit to him that we were able to continue. The Expedition, however, was taking its toll on him and I would later discover just how big a toll it was.

The financial position of *Duyfken* was now dire. I hadn't drawn a salary since August and I was now the Foundation's largest creditor behind the Kailis debt. Some would say it was a self-inflicted wound as I was in charge. Other crew members also agreed that they would work under reduced wages until we could rustle up more funds. I was immensely grateful that they supported me. On 27 September, Rinze Brandsma was seriously considering finishing the voyage. He had no option, and I understood his position. The Board members were liable for all debts if the Foundation traded while it was insolvent. The visitor numbers in Cooktown were good but we were about to max out the $200,000 overdraft, and we still had the $300,000 debt to the MG Kailis Group which needed to be repaid when we could afford to do so. The head of the voyage committee, Charlie Welker, and I agreed that we should talk to the Australian National Maritime Museum in Sydney to secure a berth at Darling Harbour after *Batavia* was transported back to Lelystad. Charlie joined *Duyfken* at the same time as me. We had both been through thick and thin with the Project and we shared a desire to see this voyage through and to look beyond. If only we could get a deal up to take the ship to The Netherlands we'd be OK. A Board Meeting was called for 9 October 2000.

I was in Cairns when I got the call from Rinze. It went along the lines of: "I am sorry to say that we can't continue with the Expedition, you will have to tie the ship up in Cairns and we'll have to work out what to do next." It wasn't unexpected but it was the call I never wanted to take. I am not going to say that I had a sinking feeling. I was absolutely devastated.

I responded with a lie. "I can't do that," I said. Then I went on to say that *Duyfken* had already left Cairns and that she was sailing for Townsville. I asked Rinze for one more port to turn the finances around. He didn't really have a choice. I explained that we were at sea and it made no sense to turn around. He agreed. "Take her into Townsville and see how you go," he said. Rinze was right to call a halt to the Expedition but I was just being bloody-minded and I didn't want to accept failure. If I was rational, I should have agreed. I was still not receiving any pay and Cathy and I were getting by with her salary and our savings — but this couldn't become a permanent situation. The running cost of the ship was about $3,000 a day, every single day, while we were voyaging. Patricia Kailis had the most to lose. She could be stuck, not with a $300,000 problem which she already had, but with a $500,000 problem if we exceeded the overdraft limit with no capacity to pay it back. It was only my unwillingness to face the obvious and accept defeat which kept me pushing on. I was like an addicted gambler just wanting to put money on one more race to turn my fortunes around.

Rinze did not know that the ship had not yet left Cairns.

Friday 13 October, 2000 stands out for me as an important date in my *Duyfken* adventure. It is not because we made landfall in some amazing port. I was in Sydney ready to board *Batavia* for what could be loosely termed a 'sail' (*Batavia* never really sailed for any more than a few minutes).

After the day 'sail', I planned to discuss the possibility of striking a deal with the Australian National Maritime Museum for *Duyfken* to visit. But it wasn't for either of these activities that I remember this day. It was day 189 of the voyage, and on this day *Duyfken* arrived in Townsville after five days under sail from Cairns. It is the day that the people of that fair northern city embraced *Duyfken* and saved my skin. The response to *Duyfken* in Townsville was nothing short of amazing, awesome and any other superlative I can find to describe it. Townsville embraced *Duyfken* and the wharf was crowded with visitors. The thousands of people who paid a few dollars each to see the ship saved us. Money flowed into out bank account and we got on a financial roll which carried us all the way to Brisbane. We generated about $150,000 from entries, shops sales and day sails from Cairns on 30 September to Brisbane on 18 December. The crew ashore and aboard had done a brilliant job, but it had come at a cost. They were exhausted. Other funds came though. I was successful in a funding application to the Andrew Tyne Reid Charitable Trust for $50,000 to get the ship to Brisbane, and then they said that there was another $50,000 if we exhibited the ship all the way down the coast to Sydney. They also wanted us to head to Melbourne and the Trust could supply matching funding if I signed up another backer. If I could get to Melbourne, then Hobart and Adelaide were possibilities, and it was only a crossing of the Great Australian Bight and rounding Cape Leeuwin and we'd be home. However, I knocked on many doors in the Bleak City and I could not uncover any more benefactors. Stung by the near financial disaster, the Board resolved that in future, *Duyfken* would not depart on any voyage without it being fully funded. I couldn't disagree. It had been a nightmare managing the dwindling finances while the Expedition appeared from the outside to be a great achievement and a huge success.

Duyfken's exhibition tour of Queensland delivered everything we hoped. Enthusiastic visitors supported us everywhere we went, including some places such as Palm Island which were not on many ship's itineraries. We also got the hang of structuring a schedule in port so that there was less stress on the crew and the shore team. In Townsville, the official welcome happened three days after the ship arrived. When we left Fremantle, at what seemed like another time in another world, we travelled with the message sticks from the Noongar people. Since the arrival at the Pennefather River where Peter asked for permission to land, asking for this permission became an important part of what we saw as an act of reconciliation with the

Aboriginal people of Australia. It was a small gesture but hugely symbolic. We were coming to understand that the ship was a powerful symbol and how we behaved mattered. At Townsville's official welcome, Peter asked for permission to come ashore from Ralph Ross of the Bindal people and Bernie Johnson of the Wulgurukaba people. As Peter said at the time: "Was it righting past wrongs? Of course not, but it acknowledged that we understood some of the failings of the past." It contrasted with some of the insulting treatment of Aboriginal people at the time. When Queen Elizabeth and Prince Phillip visited Queensland 18 months later, the Prince surprised his Aboriginal hosts by asking them whether they still threw spears at each other.

In the following months, we repeatedly delivered on our promise to Peter Beattie to tell the story of the first time Aboriginal people met people from the outside world. The voyage down the coast had many highlights. The crew dropped anchor in the Whitsundays overnight and had 40 yachts discover a sixteenth century sailing ship in their midst when they opened their hatches and came on deck in the morning. At Airlie Beach, the ship took part in the 'Paddling Through History' cultural festival which reminded participants that the traditional people of the area, the Ngaro, had been visiting the Whitsundays for 6000 years since the islands were separated from the mainland. *Duyfken* joined a fleet of outrigger canoes and kayaks and the Ngaro gave Peter a message stick inscribed with 'Wadda Mullie', a traditional greeting.

After Mackay, the ship crossed the Tropic of Capricorn for the second time. It was 10 November 2000 and we had accomplished an 8,500 nm, 216 day tropical voyage to Indonesia and Papua New Guinea in the southern winter season, learning that perhaps it would have been just a little bit easier during the cyclone season. Compared with our professional crew of 13 toughing it out sailing east from Banda to Cape York, *Duyfken* was now a ship to be shared. The Queensland coast is not like the lonely leeshore of Western Australia. Large communities were in just about every safe anchorage or river mouth and there were many keen local sailors and holidaymakers who were tremendously enthusiastic about our little ship. Voyage crew came and went, adding their own energy and turning the professional crew into storytellers of their escapades. We never totalled overall visitor numbers but they numbered in the tens of thousands. Following on from the 700 school children who visited the ship in Port Moresby, another 8,000 students came aboard in regional Queensland.

Brisbane marked the symbolic end of the voyage. Peter Manthorpe was contracted until the ship arrived in the Queensland capital. He planned to have a break and spend more time with his fiancé. He was spent. Gary Wilson agreed to take over as Ship's Master and there was no question that he had the ability to be permanent captain of our ship and a fine ambassador for the Foundation. We were all running on a high and I had no appreciation of the toll that the responsibilities of leadership, the financial pressures and the relentless schedule were taking on him.

Duyfken sailed into the Brisbane River to be tied up at the old Customs House late in the afternoon. Thanks to David Franken at Channel Seven, the Brisbane station broadcast the whole arrival with live coverage from the ship. The one hour telecast recorded a 50 per cent increase in ratings at that time compared with regular programming. I'm embarrassed to talk about it now, but Channel Seven needed something to put into the telecast to liven it up. The ship made her way up the river during the time usually allocated to children's programming. A local re-enactment group, Prince Rupert's Bastards, agreed to raid the ship, tie up the Captain and provide a few minutes of good television. It was cringe-worthy, especially since a few months before I had told Noel Pearson that we didn't do that sort of stuff. I was always conflicted by the need to be true to ourselves and our mission and the ease of slipping into the pirate ship cliché for crass promotional purposes. I must also, however, defend Prince Rupert's Bastards. They were great people and they seemed to understand our passion. They became devoted friends of the ship while we were in Brisbane. Many of Prince Rupert's Bastards volunteered as guides and shipkeepers.

Needless to say, the arrival was a tour de force. Peter's log described it:

> *With the pirate raid over I am summoned to the forecastle for an interview. I extricate myself from bondage and obediently hop up on the forecastle. This is a very strange feeling. I am having trouble getting used to being told what to do next and where I have to stand onboard the ship I have been commanding for nearly a year. But there I go getting precious again.*
>
> Duyfken *passes beneath the Storey Bridge and is suddenly dwarfed by skyscrapers. I am startled to see the reflection of her masts and yards passing across the faces of the buildings.*
>
> *We tie up at the Customs House landing where a welcoming party has assembled. Three Aboriginal women stand at the front of the*

crowd. I ask them for permission to walk on their traditional lands. Maroochy Barambah responds on behalf of the Turrbal people with a short speech greeting Duyfken *and telling us we are welcome here. She starts a song and the Wakka Wakka dance group perform a welcome dance for us, their bodies elaborately painted and clothed in animal skins.*

Then a remarkable thing happens. Though we have had light winds all day and it has been nearly calm for an hour or more, at the moment the Wakka Wakka group start to dance a sudden wind springs up from the south, building rapidly until Duyfken's *topsails, still hanging loose after our arrival, are flogging a noisy accompaniment to the didgeridoo. The wind whistles around the buildings, shaking the branches of a tree overhanging* Duyfken's *foredeck as the dance continues. A young Aboriginal girl standing next to Maroochy says in a matter of fact tone: "There are the ancestors."*

The dance ends, the TV crew starts packing up their equipment, and the ship's crew climb Duyfken's *rigging to secure the flogging topsails. Within minutes the wind dies away to a flat calm again. And I'm smiling. I'm very content now with the way things have gone, today and for the whole year. That gust of wind has made me very happy. Some things are out of the control of TV crews and ship captains alike.*

There was a lot of back-slapping and congratulations. Chevron and the Queensland Government were pleased. Peter Manthorpe gave media interviews, one after another. He was now a celebrity. His Captain's Logs with their mix of sailing deeds and philosophical musings captured the imagination of thousands of readers. Our web pages receiving an average of 3,000 page hits per day from all over the world — a big number for those days. Total hits made on the server were 867,222 and people spent 18,052 hours looking at our web pages.

A writer from Chevron asked Peter to talk about his experience aboard and he re-iterated some of the themes from his Captain's Log:

For our re-enactment we changed the script, asking the locals for permission to walk on their ground. It was such a simple gesture, but it had a profound effect. The response we got was amazing and I will never forget it. I have never felt so welcome in my own

> country. All we had done was show a little respect, a bit of ordinary courtesy, and the next thing I knew tribal elder, Silas Wolmby, was embracing me and calling me his son. The battle should have ended 400 years ago but I think it's still going on across this country. Arriving on Cape York Peninsula in the modern Duyfken I had the feeling that a black hand is being held out to us white fellas and all we have to do is grasp it. It isn't all that difficult. And nobody loses anything by having more friends.

I was conflicted. I remember a feeling of being alone on that day. The crew were a tightly-knit family now and their charismatic leader was about to leave. It was an emotional time for them. My family was in Perth. The media were interviewing Peter and the crew as celebrities. One part of me was very happy about this. From the first days promoting the construction of the ship and then the voyages I knew that the media needed heroes. My background in the media and public relations taught me that to get *Duyfken* media attention, I had to make the story easy for the media to digest. To gain coverage, the media had to be fed the narrative. The former Queensland Premier, Joh Bjelke-Petersen, called it "feeding the chooks." In Fremantle, it was Michael Kailis, the self-made man with a passion for history, and Bill Leonard, the master craftsman, who I put to the forefront. On the Expedition it was the Ship's Masters. They had everything the media wanted: they were young and attractive, and they spoke well and made sense. There was always something exotic about captains of sailing ships which drew the media to them. But I still felt snubbed. Why didn't people want to talk to me? Did people not realise how much I had given to *Duyfken* to get to this point? How much of my children's lives I was missing? The birthdays, the school concerts? All the little things? Was I merely the administrator in the background? I crafted this Expedition. I had raised the funds. I had selected the Captain and crew. I had negotiated the passage from Australia to Indonesia and Papua New Guinea. I had promoted the voyage. It was my baby. When Peter leaves in a few days time, I will still be here. The ship will still have hundreds of thousands of dollars of debt. It will still have contractual commitments to complete with the Queensland Government and Chevron. It will still have staff and crew which have to be paid — and it will still have an uncertain future. I have an ego, too. "Forget it, Graeme", I tell myself. "Stop being precious. Premier Beattie is about to leave and you have to thank him for coming."

Chapter 23

Where to Next?

My diary of 8 December 2000 should be full of notes about the climactic arrival of *Duyfken* into Brisbane that day. It isn't. Instead, it has a voyage plan with days between ports and nautical miles listed for a seven month voyage beginning in Sydney and taking *Duyfken* to Darwin, Denpasar, Jakarta, Singapore, Melaka, Galle, Cochin, Mumbai, Oman, Djibouti, Suez, Malta, Cadiz, Lisbon, Portsmouth and Amsterdam.

We already knew that we had a berth in Sydney after completing our agreements in Queensland and Tracy assembled a very good exhibition schedule in northern New South Wales. We would be stranded in Sydney if I could not find more funding. This meant that I had no funded means of getting the ship back to Fremantle. My focus turned to the next 12 months. Despite exploring many avenues, I still couldn't generate a lot of interest for our ship in Melbourne, and without some champion in the Victorian capital, I could not see how I could justify sailing south. During my initial discussion in Jakarta with Enric Hessing from the VOC 2002 Jaar, he doubted the notion that *Duyfken* even had the ability to sail to Indonesia, let alone Europe. We discussed his preferred option of shipping her to Antwerp on a container ship, pontoon or dock ship from Fremantle and sailing for a couple of days to The Netherlands. After the last eight months of preparing the ship and voyaging to Indonesia I could not countenance such an idea. I offered an alternative: sailing from Fremantle to Jakarta, Singapore, Colombo, Goa, the Suez Canal, Gibraltar and Amsterdam. Everything was predicated on returning to our home port of Fremantle before the next voyage. The ship ended her present Expedition in Sydney, and Gary Wilson and I timed the voyage from Sydney via the Suez Canal at 15 months. A voyage from Fremantle to Amsterdam would take only 370 days at sea, not including port visits, but we had to get her home first.

We enlisted the help of Captain Kasper Kuiper, the ebullient honorary Dutch consul in Brisbane, who was a great friend of the Project. Born in The Netherlands and qualified as a sea captain, he had been involved in some of the world's largest port and underwater constructions in Saudi Arabia, Kuwait, India, Pakistan and The Netherlands. In 1980, he moved to Brisbane and worked on the construction of the Brisbane International Airport and the Woodside gas projects in Cape Lambert and Port Hedland in WA. He was always an enthusiastic supporter of the *Duyfken* Project from afar and he even flew over to Perth to witness Crown Prince Willem-Alexander lay the keel. He offered to help with anything we needed in Queensland. He was true to his word and we became firm friends after the ship was launched and the Expedition took shape. There wasn't anyone in the port business up the Queensland coast he didn't know or he couldn't ring for a favour.

Duyfken was now in Brisbane, Kasper's home port, and he offered the use of his office so that Gary Wilson (we'd appointed Gary to the Master's role until we arrived in Sydney) and I could plan the voyage in detail. Gary agreed to be the Ship's Master for our grand voyage to Europe but he understood it would be a relatively short tenure if we got no further than Sydney and we ran out of funds. We began to plan a voyage to The Netherlands which we could put to the VOC 2002 Committee. Kasper Kuiper's library was a great help. He had a couple of magnificent books in his office bookshelf which detailed the great sailing routes of the world. It was a thrill to plan a new voyage around the world on a clean sheet of paper with two men who had a combined 60 years at sea. We set ourselves some criteria. Our guiding principle when planning the voyage was to act on the key lesson learned from the Expedition into Indonesia and down the east coast of Australia. *Duyfken* was not designed to sail upwind. Even though 74 per cent of that voyage was under sail, we knew we could design a voyage route which could almost totally eliminate the need to use the engines at sea. The square-rigged VOC fleets were designed for downwind sailing on trade winds. The VOC fitted out 1,700 ships from 1602 to 1700 and there were 993 Dutch voyages from the East Indies to The Netherlands. These ships carried about 317,000 people from Europe to the Indies and only two or three per cent of these ships were lost. They knew how to sail and they knew the easiest and best sailing route. All we had to do, we reasoned, was to follow in their wake and nothing could possibly go wrong. Downwind sailing at all times if possible was our mantra. Avoiding cyclone seasons and foul weather areas was imperative. Ideally, by keeping to well-established traditional sailing routes, the ship would sail for the shortest time between ports and avoid crew fatigue. VOC ports were preferred so that we could appeal to our potential Dutch sponsors. We would use recognised ports of entry to minimise government fees. We would avoid piracy areas and war zones. This would be treated as a 'delivery' voyage designed to ensure that the ship arrived on time. Therefore, we only had one date to achieve and if the ship made quicker passage then she arrived earlier and left ports earlier than the schedule. We would gain time which may be required later.

Kasper occasionally dropped in to his own office, which we now occupied, to see how we were going. At the end of each day, he opened the liquor cabinet for some of his fine schnapps and a chat. Eventually, his long-suffering wife, Roberta, would butt in to break up the party and gently encourage us to leave — everyone else would have left the building and gone home hours before.

A voyage took shape over those days in that office. I always liked using historic links as a hook for funding. My initial thought was that we could latch onto the story of the famous Dutch explorer, Willem Barentsz, who prepared a major atlas of the Mediterranean Sea which was revolutionary at the time. This would mean we could sail through Suez, saving time by not rounding the Cape of Good Hope. However, practicality prevailed. There was a major obstacle. It became quite apparent that a voyage through the Suez Canal, while it looked to be quicker on the Mercator Projection in my diary, was longer and unworkable for a square-rigged sailing ship. We faced headwinds in the Eastern Mediterranean.

Returning to Fremantle to begin the voyage was also not feasible in the time we had to get to The Netherlands. We had two possible routes from Sydney. One was to head north then west and the other to go south then west. A passage south and then across the Great Australian Bight was out of the question. The only time which seemed possible under sail on this route was in February when easterlies could help us. The westerlies dominated for the rest of the year. A route north via Torres Strait gave us following winds until we turned south down the West Australian coast. The winds blowing hard from the south compelled us to head deep into the Indian Ocean so that we could sail all the way to Fremantle in a great arc, probably as far west as Mauritius. If we sailed close to the Western coast, there were headwinds to fight all the way south and we knew what a battle that would be.

The answer was to avoid returning to our home port and to go for the tried and true: trade winds sailing just like the Dutch, visiting Dutch East India Company ports in Indonesia and the Indian Ocean en-route. *Duyfken* was now a ship of the world.

The original *Duyfken* sailed from The Netherlands to the Indies twice, and returned once, in 1602, when she sailed in the fleet of Admiral Wolfert Harmensz. It was this voyage, with the ships *Gelderland*, *Zeeland* and *Duyfken*, that the proposed VOC 2002 Voyage most closely followed. Admiral Harmensz' log was fully translated into English by Adriaan de Jong and I arranged for it to be published by the *Duyfken* Foundation as a book entitled 'Spice Adventurers'. The log told of *Duyfken*'s role in battle with the Portuguese fleet and helping to end the dominance of the spice trade by the Iberians (Portuguese and Spanish). With *Duyfken*, Willem Schouten surveyed Jakarta Bay where the Dutch capital of Batavia (now Jakarta) was later built, and sailed to the spice islands of Ternate and Banda to load cloves and nutmeg for the company. He rejoined the fleet for the voyage home, setting out from Bantam to cross the Indian Ocean.

In November 1602, *Duyfken* was separated from the fleet in a storm off Cape Agulhas, the southernmost tip of Africa. She rounded the Cape of Good Hope and headed for St Helena which was used as a roadstead. After a one-month stay at St Helena, the ship sailed north and made landfall at the islands of Fernando de Noronha off the east coast of Brazil. From Fernando de Noronha, *Duyfken* sailed for The Netherlands and arrived at Vlissingen on the estuary of the Schelde River on 17 February 1603, where Schouten probably learnt that an exciting new enterprise called the United Dutch East India Company (VOC) had been formed in the previous year.

The aim of the VOC 2002 Voyage was primarily to re-locate the ship to The Netherlands in time for the commencement of the VOC celebrations on 30 April 2002 (Queen Beatrix's Birthday). The ability to highlight locations en-route which had significance to the VOC was a bonus. We proposed for *Duyfken* to become the Ambassador for the VOC celebrations. During the voyage, we planned to place the ship on exhibition in the same manner she had been shown in Australia, except that we would not have the dockside retail sales component of the operation. The Voyage was fundamentally different to the Expedition. The times in port were separated by much longer times at sea compared with our short hops in Indonesia and Australia. While the Expedition was set to rediscover a relatively short voyage from Indonesia to Australia, the VOC2002 *Duyfken* Voyagie was designed to recreate the return voyage of Dutch spice traders. The log of the *Gelderland* was our inspiration and an important historical template for the voyage. As *Duyfken* was part of this fleet, we were able to compare our progress in 2001 with the sea passages of 400 years ago, juxtaposing the sailing characteristics of the two ships and understanding the challenges of life aboard as a window to the past. The voyage was to begin in Sydney, then sail north up the east coast to Cairns and through Torres Strait to Jakarta. Our advice from the Dutch and Australian embassies was that we would probably be warmly welcomed in Jakarta this time around. Then we would sail to the former VOC port of Galle in Sri Lanka, then to Mauritius, Cape Town and to St Helena (which was a roadstead for the VOC fleets) and onto the Ascension Islands. From there, Flores in the Azores Islands was a perennial stopover for modern sailing ships coming from the South Atlantic and the last port of call before Amsterdam. It was an ideal staging post for us. Gary and I calculated that the ship would be at sea for 289 days and sail 18,200 nm at an average of 63 nm per day. To put it into perspective, Christopher Columbus' first voyage of discovery was 36 days and estimated to have covered about 3,066 nm.

Our voyage was to be a mammoth undertaking. The time at sea would be the greatest test of the crew. Perhaps the most famous return voyage from the East Indies to Europe was the return of the Magellan ships in 1522, 80 years before *Duyfken*. On the return from Tidore in Maluku, Spanish navigator Juan Sebastián Elcano's ship *Victoria* sailed (Ferdinand Magellan died in a battle in The Philippines) to Ambon and Timor, then to the Cape of Good Hope and the Cape Verde Islands off Africa before arriving in Europe and completing the circumnavigation. That voyage was 10 months. Reduced to a ration of rice and water, 21 crew members died between the Cape of Good Hope and Cape Verde. Of the five ships and 270 crew who left Spain, only 30 men and one ship returned after circumnavigating the world. Of course, we had no intention of reenacting this voyage, but even in the modern era, few long voyages in replica ships were tackled.

To put it into perspective, when Warwick Charlton built a replica of the *Mayflower* in the 1950s to replicate the 1620 voyage from Plymouth, UK to Plimouth Plantation, USA, they were at sea for a mere 55 days. For *Duyfken*'s crew, the longest single ocean passage would be from Ascension Island to the Azores where the crew would be at sea for 55 days if the wind was kind to us. The VOC voyage was the equivalent of 5¼ *Mayflower* voyages with only 39 days or 12 per cent of the voyage in port en-route to rest and re-supply. It was not enough time but I had to balance the total voyage duration with the fixed arrival date. This was the longest and most testing voyage for ship and crew ever contemplated in an 'Age of Discovery' replica ship.

The logistics of putting so many crew on a ship for long ocean passages was critical in the planning. Gary had an excellent understanding of the intricacies of planning a voyage. Just because the Dutch did it 400 years ago did not mean that it was a simple exercise. *Duyfken* was ill-equipped for passages of longer than a month. They must have had the same challenges in the 1600s. Water was one of the most basic necessities on *Duyfken*. It was required for drinking, cooking and occasional washing. We had quite small water storage aboard and we did not want to carry additional water if we could avoid it. The ship had a single desalination unit to handle crew requirements. At the early stages of the Expedition to Indonesia, the crew consumed up to 417 litres of water each day, however, as the voyage developed and fuel was in short supply, water usage had to be more carefully rationed. The longest anticipated passage of 55 days was used to assess total water production and storage needs. With the generator working for two hours per day, 240 litres per day was produced. Gary and I worked on a figure of 200 litres which amounted to 11,000 litres produced during the proposed voyage. Fresh water usage was 10 litres per person each day solely for drinking and cooking. The crew had to use water sparingly for personal hygiene. With 16 crew on a 55 day passage then 8800 litres was required. The ship was equipped with two 1000 litre tanks. We thought of adding two more 1000 litre flexible tanks which could be installed easily in the bilge area of the ship to give more flexibility with water use.

Fuel needs also had to be determined. Without engines, the original *Duyfken* only stowed firewood as fuel for its cooking requirements. We used gas in the galley. Our diesel engines were still new. They only had 1,000 hours on them by the time we reached Brisbane so they were in excellent condition. Without having to battle headwinds, we thought that the ship would be able to bunker enough diesel for the voyage.

We underestimated the challenge of sourcing enough food in Indonesia during the Expedition, so food storage was a critical issue for the longer passages ahead. There were several accepted formulae for crew nutrition at sea. Gary assumed that the average crew member would consume 1772 calories per day and if the crew was at sea for 55 days then 19.92 kilograms of shipped food (tinned and dry) would be required per person. The crew's diet wouldn't be as bad as the *Duyfken* of 1606 when salted meat rotting away in barrels was part of the sailor's diet. We could stow more than enough food to provide for the entire crew for the longest anticipated passage of 55 days at sea but refrigeration was limited and fresh food ran out quickly.

The modern fit out of the ship was a major concern. Gary's wish list included dozens of items which required attention with an estimated cost of $20,000. We would also need spare rope for the rig, another $6,440, and a second full suit of sails some time into the voyage — this was yet another $25,000. Our Sat C system had to be upgraded with an Icom 2000 HF system so we could use SailMail. It came with a $5000 cost but a great saving in satellite charges. Also a weatherfax was a useful addition to the on-board equipment, and cost approximately $5000.

Safety during the longer voyage was a primary concern. *Duyfken*'s safety equipment was to international standards and sufficient for the Australian and Indonesian temperate waters we'd been sailing through but we wanted to upgrade the gear for the long ocean passages. It had to be suitable for the cool waters the ship would encounter. The VOC Committee wanted some measure of assurance that we were totally professional and aware of the safety risks. New technology was available to equip the crew with personal EPIRBs (Emergency Position-Indicating Radio Beacons). These are considered essential today but in 2000 they were only ever used in extreme situations because of their cost. Self-inflating lifejackets with in-built harnesses from Stormy Seas in Tasmania were also on our shopping list. They could be worn at all times in heavy seas but they weren't cheap. The lifejackets and EPIRBs cost $10,000. We also had to consider the worst scenario: if *Duyfken* went down and everyone was floating in freezing Atlantic water. Immersion suits were not necessary for Australian conditions, however, they offered the best chance of survival in cold waters. It was $30,000 for a full crew fit out.

The cost of insurance sky-rocketed. With all the risks associated with our Expedition through Indonesia, we had paid $60,000 for insurance. For the voyage to The Netherlands, the quote was $102,000. Other costs surprised me, too. The sailing charts cost us just shy of $10,000. We estimated the total cost of the voyage to The Netherlands including a summer sailing season to be $1,263,795. I left out one crucial element out of the budget. The document did not mention what we were going to do after the summer season in The Netherlands was over. We were so focussed on the voyage itself that I had completely ignored making a medium term plan and it came back to haunt me 18 months later.

One of the reasons I had been so keen on the voyage was that it was the only way I could see that we could fund getting the ship back to Fremantle. It was a 30,000nm voyage in total distance to get to a port which was only 2,200nm away from Sydney! On the plus side, it would be the longest re-enactment voyage in an 'Age of Discovery' vessel ever undertaken. All we had to do was to convince the Dutch that it could be done, and to convince them to pay for it.

As we were preparing to sail from Fremantle in March 2000, I had received the first letter from Benno van Tilburg. He subsequently formed an organisation called the Stichting *Duyfken* VOC 2002 Nederland (*Duyfken* VOC 2002 Netherlands Foundation) to generate and raise funds for *Duyfken* to visit. Since meeting Enric Hessing in Jakarta, the Dutch politician had worked the corridors of power in the Dutch capital of Den Haag to sell them on the idea of *Duyfken* visiting in 2002. I wasn't aware that he had also secured a modest budget of about $4 million for the VOC celebrations. He contacted me and said that Benno van Tilburg was coming to Australia to discuss our ideas for the voyage. I hastily prepared a broad document with input from Gary Wilson and our financial controller, Michiel van Doorn, in September 2000, but I let Benno know that we had an exciting new, fully-costed plan to put to him. Meanwhile, Kasper Kuiper had been working his own contacts through the diplomatic service so that we were seen as a credible operation.

After I returned to Perth for Christmas, I caught up with our Board. Meanwhile, the crew was overwhelmed by the hospitality shown to them in Brisbane. Kasper and Roberta Kuiper and Dr John Powell, Cliff Leggoe and Peppi Buetti from Chevron's PNG Gas Project were flawless Christmas hosts. Gary gladly bid the Brisbane River farewell (it had always been a challenging berth with the strong tides). We conducted a very profitable, if exhausting, day sailing program at the Brisbane coastal suburb of Redcliffe which opened its heart to the ship. Never before, or since, has such an intense and successful series of day sails been conducted. Thanks to Gary and his hard-working crew, hundreds of passengers came aboard and the revenue gave us a financial buffer which helped us survive for the next six months.

Benno's visit in the new year coincided with the Sanctuary Cove International Boat Show, a big event which brought tens of thousands of people to the Gold Coast. It also marked the end of the Chevron 2000 *Duyfken* Expedition exhibition tour — 18 January 2001. The ship was the star attraction and we were accommodated in some luxurious accommodation nearby. If this was the life of the leisure boat fraternity, we could get used to it.

Gary and I had no idea what Benno and his wife Giulia Gerola-Van Tilburg would be like. Would we warm to them? Would they warm to us? Was he one of the tough, no-nonsense Dutchies we learnt to deal with? We planned their visit carefully and in great detail to give the impression of a first-class organisation. Kasper began as the perfect host, collecting them from Brisbane Airport in the early hours of the morning and taking them to a hotel in Brisbane to rest before driving them to Sanctuary Cove for a cocktail function aboard the ship. We invited all our Queensland supporters. Benno and Giulia were the guests of honour.

We needn't have worried about whether Mr and Ms Van Tilburg would be a challenge. They were the most delightful couple. Benno and I were a similar age and Giulia came from northern Italy, not far from where Cathy's family migrated to Australia 100 years before. Benno and Giulia both had a great sense of humour and an interesting set of life experiences. Benno was a 'Russia watcher' before he got a job running museums. Giulia was a professional translator and her English was impeccable.

The pleasantries over, the next morning it was time to get down to the job at hand: convincing Benno that we could deliver a voyage. As it turned out, Benno required little convincing. He had read the comprehensive proposal document I sent to him as a primer for the meeting and it answered most of his questions. He seemed confident that Gary and I knew what we were doing. I accompanied Benno and Giulia to Sydney to meet Max Dingle, the Deputy Director of the Australian National Maritime Museum and Ed Reitsma, the Consul General of The Netherlands, who were both great supporters of the Project, before flying to Perth. We wanted to introduce them to the Board of the Foundation. Benno and Giulia's visit went without a hitch, or so I thought at the time. Years later, Benno told me that he saw it differently.

"The most interesting meeting I had was with the Board of the *Duyfken* Foundation. Imagine this: me sitting with jet lag in a room filled with Australian speaking Board members. I do speak English but the Australian way of talking to say the least is sometimes not that easy to understand!" he said. "So there I was talking to this Board. They offered me a contract of 100 pages which, if we were going to do this Project together, I should sign and follow. This was maybe the Australian way of negotiation but I proposed a different one. I put on the table only one page where I wrote down the concept of an agreement. If they agreed to sign this one I said the payment and financing of this Project would be 100 per cent covered by the Dutch Ministry of Economics. Sign here, then I will try back in The Netherlands to get the green light for this Project."

Benno wasn't aware that the Dutch Government's VOC2002 committee asked us to prepare a comprehensive legal contract for the voyage. Rinze Brandsma simply asked his law firm to prepare a document in response to the brief. Clearly, there was a communications breakdown somewhere along the line. After a round of meetings and touring the city sights, Cathy and I hosted a dinner for the Tilburgs and *Duyfken* Board members at our home in Inglewood. I set up a table with objects from *Duyfken* and Benno remarked as he went past: "What's that — a *Duyfken* shrine?" I thought we were going to get on just fine. I flew back to the Gold Coast and Benno returned to The Netherlands to present his findings.

Peter Manthorpe once told me that, as a wooden sailing ship, *Duyfken* should be regarded as a constantly oxidising lump of organic matter. The role of the crew was to battle against the gradual decay of all this organic matter. How well they battled against the oxidation determined how long the ship would last. The ship had not been lifted since she went up the BHP slipway in Port Hedland in May. Then she had an eight month tropical voyage through Indonesia and Queensland where every marine organism seemed to see her timber as a good place to hitch a lift. The sparkling new Gold Coast City Marina near Sanctuary Cove agreed to help us out with a lift and a scrub. If anyone thinks that anti-fouling is a great protector of ship's hulls then the sight of *Duyfken* out of the water would be a surprise. When we lifted her, the hull was alive with marine organisms including pesky little worms that found ways to get through the coating and have many tasty meals of European Oak. They scampered in and out of their homes like they were living on the piers of a jetty. It became a massive job to clean the hull, cut out the woodworm and get some more anti-fouling onto the bare timber. Once again, the crew worked incredibly hard and for long hours. Everyone had to be off the ship during the refit and we stayed at a particularly cramped motel down the road which bore no comparison with the luxurious accommodation at the tourist resort of the previous week. It was basic but it was all our budget could afford. I was humbled during this period when we were teetering on the edge of a financial precipice that the crew and shore staff just kept giving to the ship and the Project. Without them, the *Duyfken* Project would have stalled under the weight of debt.

I was glad that Benno did not see *Duyfken* out of the water. We were very concerned with the state of the ship's stem (the large timber which forms the shape of the bow). It was the worst piece of timber on the ship. The dreaded teredo worm found its way deep into the timber and there was a constant and slightly depressing stream of water oozing from it as soon as the ship was lifted out of the water. Worm also found its way into the lower wale (the ship's rubbing strake) as a consequence of the ship coming up against all sorts of makeshift fenders whilst in tropical ports. The soft paint which was designed to stay attached to the part of the ship which is sometimes dry and sometimes wet, had been rubbed off creating an easy entry point for worms. On some of the Latvian oak on the deck, rust stains were starting to bleed out of the timber. While the ship was being built, shrapnel from World War II which had been embedded in the Latvian trees was found in some of the timber and it began to rust. Bill Leonard agreed to fly over from Fremantle and take a look at the decaying stem, and to supervise any fix that was necessary. He saw a very different ship to the one he waved goodbye in Fremantle. The rich honey-coloured oak timber which he wanted varnished to show off the woodworking skills of his shipwrights was long gone, replaced by Gary's wood oil mix which comprised one-third pine tar, beeswax and linseed oil. It sealed the wood and slowly turned a dark blue-black colour. It now looked just like a ship from an old masters oil painting. The deck planking was furry from being scrubbed every day — and it still leaked. The hemp rigging was heavily tarred to a deep black and the flax sails were grey rather than cream with many repairs. The ship, however, was shipshape and a credit to the crew who looked after her every day. He was shocked by what he saw with the teredo worm. It found its way into the good timber which was used to cover the repairs made to the curved oak tree trunk of the stem. When the oak log arrived in Fremantle from Latvia in the first shipment, it was found to have a rotten core. Bill Leonard did not want to use it but he had no option at the time other than to slice it longitudinally, cut out the rot and replace the rotting timber, finally sealing it all with a one inch oak lamination that was screwed and glued to the side of the stem. It was a massive job to save the one tonne piece of oak.

In Bill's usual no-nonsense approach, he immediately put on his work dungarees and set to work in the fierce Gold Coast sun, removing and replacing the (now worm-infested) lamination from the lower port side of the stem. The whole stem was then covered with a thin layer of micro-smooth (a filler with tiny glass beads in it) placed over the whole surface to ward off the little critters. The work was done quickly. We couldn't hang around the marina. Ships on the hard are a money pit. The more time they are out of the water the more ways are found to spend money. Bill got onto a flight back to Perth, and immediately nodded off to sleep — totally exhausted — but staggered at what we'd achieved in only a few days. The ship was placed back in the water, rigged and bound for New South Wales.

Chapter 24

Mountain Scaled

It is cold, wet and windy standing on the near-deserted Throsby Wharf in Newcastle. Thunderstorms battered the port overnight and now a south-easterly is coming in hard. The dark grey sky adds a threatening tone as the ropes and blocks on *Duyfken* rattle in the wind. Our crew come and go from the ship with last minute supplies. We have a safety briefing. Gary Wilson is not prepared to take the ship to sea with a Force 8 gale coming in from the direction we are planning to sail. That means we'd be pumping into a 5.5m swell with winds gusting to over 70kph. With our windage, we'd be lucky to make it past Nobby's Head at the harbour entrance. So, best that we wait for a couple of hours.

By late morning, the breeze is moderating to Force 5 (gusting to about 40kph with two metre swells) and Gary decides it's time to go. I have mixed feelings as the ship quietly motors out of the harbour. As Joseph Conrad said: "There is nothing more enticing, disenchanting, and enslaving than the life at sea." It's another day in the office for our professional crew who take to the task of setting sail like they have done it a thousand times, because they have. They cross the deck to take a line without a word, instinctively knowing what is required.

This was the leg I desperately wanted to sail. I had only occasionally travelled aboard *Duyfken* since we left Fremantle. I tried to be in every port when the ship arrived and to stay until after the ship departed to make sure we paid all our bills and thanked the people who helped us during the visit. Then I'd fly ahead of the ship to sit in the next round of port meetings. I'd fly back to Perth, catch up with my family, meet our head office team, have more meetings and then get ready for the next port visit. I envied our crew who didn't have to worry about the dwindling finances or what the future would hold beyond delivering the ship successfully to the next port. I thought they had it easy, and they thought I had it easy. Such is the chasm between landlubbers and sailors. Even if it was for only a few days, this trip from Newcastle was my time to be a crew member on my own ship, and to sail into the most famous harbour in Australia.

We had 19 people aboard. Gary ordered the lower sails be set, then the top sails to be raised to half-hoist. From my favourite spot way up in the stern, I saw Gary on the poop deck. This was his territory. The ore and coal bulk carriers we sailed by were the ships on which he built his career. He knew these waters well. Sydney was his home and he was excited to be able to fill an ambition he had harboured since he sailed aboard the brigantine *Eye of the Wind* in his youth. He wanted to be master aboard a square-rigger sailing through the Sydney Heads. His dream was about to come true. Jane Doepel, the Ship's Cook, was one of the heroes of the Expedition. She cheerfully cooked for 18 crew in a galley the size of a small wardrobe since leaving Fremantle. If she had thrown her bags on the wharf in Geraldton and said "enough of that", I couldn't have blamed her, but she stuck it out right to the end and Sydney was her final port.

Rupert Weller returned as a day worker aboard for the leg into Sydney. Everyone admired Rupert. His association with *Duyfken* began in the shipyard as a volunteer. He sailed as one of the original crew members. He suffered chronic sea-sickness, he toughed it out on the passage north to Broome until Peter Manthorpe said enough was enough. He still wanted to contribute so he towed our mobile shop and display items (such as the cannon which we didn't need for Indonesia) across the top to Weipa. As the Expedition was coming to a close, Rupert told a writer from Chevron: "I feel I have an intimate relationship with the ship — an extremely emotional attachment. I used to stand at the forward part of the ship during construction and think what a beautiful ship it was going to be when it was finished. I think the hull shape is attractive. Above the water line is not especially pretty but she has character. What people don't see is that lovely smooth flowing line which was generated by the plank-first construction technique. It probably sails a lot better than any of us ever envisaged." He wasn't the only one who felt such an intimate relationship with our collection of timber and rope but after his total commitment to the Project, I was delighted that he could be aboard as we sailed in Sydney.

Andrea Cicholas was in charge of the first watch which was currently sailing the ship. She had the quiet professionalism of someone who knew more about sailing *Duyfken* than most. Before the ship was completed, she hand-stitched many of the sails which were now powering us to Sydney. Already an experienced sailor before she left on the voyage, she was now an old hand at sailing a seventeenth century jacht. She told the same Chevron writer: "I like having nature make the rules to live by rather than someone in an office somewhere saying: 'You will do this or that — you will stop when the lights turn red!'"

Walter Walker was leading hand on Andrea's watch. He joined the ship in Queensland, getting the first taste of life under sail as one of the 40 young people who took part in the Chevron Leadership Program. When he had an opportunity to re-join the ship as a member of the crew, he jumped at it. Heidy Bontjer was a young Dutch woman, who had been living in Australia for several years, joined as voyage crew in Queensland and stayed. I was one of four voyage crew allocated to Andrea's watch.

Greg O'Byrne was in charge of the second watch. He had now fulfilled his ambition to circumnavigate Australia under sail. It was one of his motivations to join the ship in Fremantle. Like Andrea, Greg was a natural at sea and destined for a career afloat. Nicole Gardner was his leading hand and a pocket dynamo; feisty, too. She took the greatest of pleasure in showing her boss, me, how to coil a rope properly each time I sailed aboard. She gave me a bucket and broom one day and ordered me to swab the decks just for the sheer pleasure of being able to boss me around in her territory, where she was in charge. Nicole was the only person who could patiently and cheerfully explain to me how the rig worked and what each rope did in a way which I could understand. Unfortunately, she had to do it every time I came aboard as I had always forgotten from the last time. Nicole taught me how to coil and secure lines, and tried to make me into a useful hand. She was infuriating at times when she told me exactly how it was and what should be done to manage the Project even if I didn't ask. But besides all that, she was a fine sailor. She had grown in confidence and she was one of the most dependable crew members in a crisis. Tracy McCullough and her husband David Kerbey were voyage crew on Greg's watch. Tracy, along with Peggy Rodgers and Con Smit back in Fremantle, was part of the team which saved the *Duyfken* Foundation when it looked as if we'd have to tie up the ship in Cairns. She put together the arrangements for every port visit, the welcome events and coordinated the voyage crews. Crew from Australia, The Netherlands, Indonesia, Canada, USA, New Zealand and Papua New Guinea sailed aboard during the Expedition. Peg helped her coordinate school visits which drew more than 8,000 school children to the ship in four months, including one school whose students saw a ship and the sea for the first time.

I fancied myself as a modern day supercargo when I was aboard: watching operations, assessing the way the Master and crew worked, making carefully considered decisions, walking the deck at will, heading to bed after dinner and waking at a sensible hour in the morning as a gentleman would do. It was a fantasy I was never able to live. Everyone aboard *Duyfken* worked the passage. I was placed on Andrea's watch with all the duties of a sailor on the lowest rung of the ladder.

As I looked over the deck from the stern, slowly succumbing to mal-de-mer, I saw the true believers who had stuck with it and were now on board to finish the job. What a fine bunch. But soon it was time to stop the day-dreaming and to find a spot where I could quell the queasiness. After tasting the sailor's gravy too many times, Andrea saw the sad state I was in and dismissed me from my watch. I failed the sailor's duty again! Andrea wasn't too concerned about losing a crew member of my quality. We'd been on the same tack for hours anyway so there wasn't much need for someone as useless as me. It was best was to take her advice and lie down in the most stable spot, near the ship's centre of gravity, which is in the hold at the foot of the mainmast. That didn't work — it never worked for me. Then I took to my next favourite spot to sleep in the hold. This was on top of the starboard engine box. Eventually Gary came down and offered me his bunk in the Captain's cabin. Heaven. This thin slice of timber was the most comfortable place on the ship, although the serenity of a cabin made for two was constantly interrupted by the Watch Officer who came in to check the heading on the chart laid out on the table and then to make annotations in the ship's log. And so it was there that my water torture began and lasted all night. By morning, the weather moderated to a beautiful sunny day and *Duyfken* was under courses and topsails. Crackneck Point on the central coast was visible as Gary encouraged me to get out of the bunk and have something to eat and drink. I took some convincing but I dragged myself out on deck and sat down for breakfast. Everyone, even the most hardened sea-dog like Gary, has been sea-sick at one time or another so there is always sympathy for the sufferers. I spoke to one of the most decorated sailors in the Royal Australian Navy at a function in Sydney after we arrived. Rear Admiral Rothesay Swan was President of the Australian Sail Training Association and the function was to present sailing medals to Nicole

Gardner and Greg O'Byrne. I admitted that I had been horribly seasick. He smiled and said: "Don't feel bad about it. You know there wasn't a week since I went to sea at the age of 16 when I wasn't seasick." I don't know how he did it.

With the wind turning to east north east and a slight swell, and the ship rolling slightly, even I could enjoy the sailing. We made excellent time from Newcastle, 68nm in a day. We were well ahead of schedule and Gary had in mind some pleasure and pain. This is how he described our overnight interlude at Broken Bay in his log a few days later on day 330 of the voyage, 2 March 2001:

> *I decided to do a bit of a cruise up the bay before returning to our anchorage. We carried on up to the entrance to Cowan Creek under foresail and topsails and to give all the new crew some additional sail handling drill, I decided to put her on the wind and beat back up to the anchorage. The ship did really well, pointing up under this rig to about 60 degrees off the wind and making little leeway. The breeze proved a bit fluky close to shore though and she was a bit reluctant to tack, missing stays twice and forcing us to wear ship. I put the mizzen on her, that cured the problem, and we made great progress to windward, going about every 10 minutes or so. The port anchor was cleared away, fore topsail and mizzen handed and we fetched gently in to Flint and Steel Bay under fores'l and main topsail. A couple of cables offshore in about 10 metres of water, the helm was put down and the fores'l clewed up as she rounded up. Main yard squared and down goes the anchor as the way comes off her, veering cable as she comes astern under a backed tops'l and finally handing all sail as we bring up to four lengths of cable. Very satisfying to do it all without even putting the engines on standby. A very pleasant overnight anchorage in the middle of a national park, very peaceful with only the sounds of birds to keep us company.*

His description of 'additional sail handling drill' does not adequately describe what it required to tack, set up again, tack again and again and again, until we were scrambling across the deck like marathon runners trying to find the finishing line. Eventually Gary got bored with the game and sailed the ship gently to a most seductive anchorage at Flint and Steel Bay on the Hawkesbury River. It wasn't far from where Skippy was filmed at Ku-ring-gai Chase National Park. We were so close to Sydney, but so far from anyone in that secluded bay. Thick green bushland tumbled off the steep outcrops and came right down to the rocky shore. We didn't see a soul. James Holdsworth, our shop manager, found the ship and came aboard with Jenny, one of our volunteers from Sanctuary Cove. The crew went swimming and we sat around and yarned about the Expedition, about what crew members would do when the ship arrived in Sydney and what lay ahead for the *Little Dove*. Greg brought out his tin whistle, Gary his mandolin and Nicole sang some songs as the night descended upon us. This was the last night together for the remaining crew which had left Fremantle 11 months before. I admired them. They were happy but also a little sad that the spell would soon be broken. Eventually it was time to call it a day. I was also tired and emotional, yes, three sheets to the wind as a sailor would say. The evening was warm and humid and I didn't like the idea of finding a spot below. I put my sleeping bag near the firebox for'ard in the forecastle. I couldn't care less when a torrential downpour came through overnight and soaked me to the skin. We were all only hours from accomplishing our individual dreams.

Rinze and Jenny Brandsma, Michael and Janine Young and a new Board member, Marc Florey, joined the ship by Peninsula water taxi in the morning. It was particularly pleasing to see Rinze. He had taken on the poisoned chalice of Chair of the Board of the *Duyfken* Foundation after Michael Kailis passed away and the Board became like a game of musical chairs. With Board Members drifting away one by one, he held it all together with a refreshed group which took on a more conventional overseeing role rather than Michael Kailis's hands-on approach. He did a fine job. Entering his old home town of Sydney was yet another highlight for Michael Young who was now thinking about new challenges and a new life in Indonesia.

The joy we felt that day was universal. As Michael Day from The West Australian newspaper said, *Duyfken* became an ambassador for peace and an emissary for reconciliation. The ship had visited more than 30 ports. As some said, *Duyfken* was an old ship spreading new values. Everyone was stimulated to be a part of *Duyfken* in different ways but we all shared in the accomplishment. Without the crew, the shore crew and the Board of Management, we wouldn't be sailing into Sydney Harbour.

Gary always boasted that Sydney Harbour was the finest harbour in the world and on that day I couldn't disagree with him. I must give Gary the privilege of describing the day which unfolded in his home port.

> *Approaching the cliffs at North Head, we shut the engines off again and soon after have some media helicopters around getting footage of our arrival. We are also met by the ex-Customs vessel* ET Hall, *with a whole heap of my friends and family aboard who have come out to meet us. Sydney is my home port and I have to admit I had a bit of a lump in my throat as a long held dream of mine begins to be realised — to be in command of a square-rigged vessel and enter Sydney Harbour under sail. I knew that our arrival had been advertised but was not really prepared for the scale of welcome. The pilot comes aboard off North Head, some skilful handling of the cutter making the transfer look easy and we stand in. The spectator fleet grows around us, boats of all shapes and sizes including another little sloop named* Duyfken. *That raised a cheer from our crew. An escort of Waterways launches ensured enough sea room for us and the fire fighting tug* Shirley Smith *provides a spectacular water spray welcome as we enter the Western Channel. The hermaphrodite brig* Windeward Bound *is under sail with us, also coming in from sea to join the increasing parade; schooners* La Violante *and* Boomerang *meet us just inside the entrance, and the ex-RAN patrol boat HMAS* Advance, *with guests from the Australian National Maritime Museum, is there as well to see us in, making us welcome by closing in and giving us three cheers. The breeze does not serve as we head up the harbour and we clew up and proceed under power towards Bradleys Head. Rounding that headland with the prominent mast of HMAS* Sydney *in view, we get under sail again and with the weather becoming overcast and squally we run up the harbour at a good clip, nearly seven knots in bursts, dipping our ensign to the gun salute at Fort Denison and racing past the big crowd on the forecourt of the Opera House. Shortening sail as we sail under the famous arch of the Sydney Harbour Bridge, we give a long blast on the whistle, people waving back from both foreshores and all the escorting boats. We hand all sail as we begin the final run up Darling Harbour, the drizzle that has set in not diminishing in any way the smiles on the faces of all aboard. Passing close under the stern of the VOC replica* Batavia, *a cannon booms out in welcome, we dip our ensign in reply and I lead*

three cheers for our big sister. The spectator fleet drop back to give us manoeuvring room and we swing slowly past the famous World War II vessel Krait, *and into the berth opposite the destroyer* HMAS Vampire *to applause from the gathered crowd. Lines are made fast, fenders in position and the engines are shut down. We have arrived and I can't deny it is a little emotional for me to have brought her in to such a welcome. I thank all the crew, they have been superb, both the permanent crew — Andrea, Greg, Nic, Jane, Walter, Rupert, James, Trev, Heidy, and the voyage crew with us on this leg and am humbled when they give me three cheers. A big beaming smile from Jenny, the familiar cheeky grin from Trev and a heartfelt handshake from Graeme — I have to go and sit in my cabin for a few minutes.* Duyfken *has arrived in Sydney, the end of this voyage… The dove's wings are folded for but a while.*

So ends this 8,900nm voyage, the equivalent of two Atlantic crossings.

And Gary makes his last entry in the ship's log, Day 330, at 1836 on Saturday 3 March 2001. Days Run: 31 miles.

Chapter 25

The Big One

Wish you luck in your travels
Sail safe, suffer no harm
Our countries to prosper
May the Lord lend you his arm
Lead you, guide you
That everything will be right
Fine from start to finish
In good stead by his might
And have you some trouble
Ask him please attend
Remind yourself also
That day will follow night
Take heart to face contraries
From his word we send*

A farewell credo to the Admiral Wolfaert Haermans fleet of five ships, including Duyfken, *to the Indies in 1606, translated by Adriaan de Jong.

For those who were not paid off in Sydney, there was little time to reflect on our achievement. We planned to begin the longest voyage ever contemplated in an 'Age of Discovery' replica ship in a little over eight weeks (on 5 May, 2001) — and we didn't even have an agreement in place for the voyage to be funded.

Constant negotiations with the VOC 2002 Foundation in Den Haag which had begun in late January were dragging on. We were required to reach an agreement on a workable contract for the epic voyage and the summer exhibition tour of The Netherlands. It wasn't easy, however, dealing with the Dutch Government bureaucracy which was reluctant to accept any financial or operational risk. It was embroiled in a humiliating controversy over the return of the *Batavia* replica. *Batavia* was not the financial bonanza expected by the Australian-Netherlands Chamber of Commerce (ANCOC) during the Olympic Games. At the heart of the problem was that while West Australians were deeply invested in the stories of the 'Dutch coast' on the western side of the continent, people living in eastern Australia were more in tune with the stories of Cook and *Endeavour*. *Batavia* did not generate the public excitement they expected, or the patronage needed, to pay the bills and it was still moored near us at the Australian National Maritime Museum. ANCOC was unable to fund the return of the ship to Lelystad. There was a 2.7 million guilders (approx AUD2 million) invoice to transport the vessel and when it finally reached Antwerp, *Batavia* was chained to the wharf until the shipper had been paid. The Bataviawerf Foundation almost went bankrupt and never really recovered from this financial disaster. In 2022, the ship was still tied up at Lelystad with only the lower mainmast in place. Nobody wished for another national embarrassment arriving from Australia. On 3 April, 2001 with only a month to departure and a year since we left Fremantle, we announced that the go-ahead had been obtained from the VOC2002 committee. Our voyage would take 12 months and traverse 18,200 nm (33,700 km) — more than twice the distance of the Expedition into Indonesia.

The wording of an announcement was agreed and we declared that the VOC 2002 *Duyfken* Voyage marked the 400th anniversary of the establishment of the world's first multinational trading company, the United East India Company, which pioneered the Dutch spice trade. "It has been more than 300 years since a Dutch jacht sailed the spice route which brought cargoes of untold wealth back from East Asia to the markets of Europe," we said in our media material. We emphasised that this wealth from spices helped create the Dutch 'Golden Age' and resulted in a flowering of culture. Artists such as Rembrandt made an impact on European art and Dutch scientists made many discoveries, but we made no mention of the darker sides of the VOC. Instead, we focused on the maritime aspects of the voyage and our uniqueness; that *Duyfken* was the only fully-voyaging Dutch 'Age of Discovery' vessel sailing in the world, pre-dating Captain Cook's ship *Endeavour* (which is categorised as a pre-industrial revolution ship) by almost 170 years.

I told the media that the voyage was an opportunity which was only possible because of funding from The Netherlands. "The re-enactment of a spice trading voyage in an accurate replica of a Dutch VOC ship is an opportunity which may never be repeated in our lifetimes. *Duyfken* is in excellent condition, little more than one year old and she has been thoroughly trialled after 8,500nm of sailing through Australian and Indonesian waters on the Chevron 2000 *Duyfken* Expedition," I said. "There may not be another chance to sail an authentic 'Age of Discovery' ship on such a long voyage along one of the classic routes. . . we will be able to understand for the first time what it was really like for sailors 400 years ago." They were prophetic words.

"The voyage route has been meticulously evaluated to enable the *Duyfken* Foundation to be confident that the ship can meet a deadline to arrive in The Netherlands on 30 April 2002, Queen Beatrix's birthday. The VOC 2002 Voyage will fulfil a long held ambition of the *Duyfken* 1606 Replica Foundation for *Duyfken* to visit her 'spiritual' home in The Netherlands."

We were totally unaware that the whole concept of celebrating the formation of the Dutch East India Company was controversial in The Netherlands and, more particularly, in nations which had been subjected to Dutch colonialism. For us, the voyage was simply a technical challenge to sail an archaic ship over such a distance. We were absolutely confident that we could achieve what nobody else had done in modern times.

The confidence masked an enormous effort to deliver on the promise made to the VOC Committee. We had one deadline and we could only achieve it by leaving Sydney on time, but we were totally unprepared. We didn't even have any crew applications for the VOC voyage when we sailed into Sydney. Gary Wilson agreed to continue as Ship's Master and several crew members from the voyage expressed an interest in continuing to The Netherlands. Thankfully, they stayed with the ship for a month not knowing whether they would have a job or not. Everyone needed a long break from the ship but the announcement re-energised us all. We had a new challenge. The ship required a great deal of work to get her ready and time was running out. Trevor Smith, who joined the ship in Queensland as temporary Engineer, worked closely with Gary to access all the trades and services required in Sydney.

The crew for the Expedition into Indonesia was assembled over the best part of a year. Our objective had been to obtain the best sailors in Australia to fill the main positions and to find people who had some experience and a lot of enthusiasm to fill the rest of the positions. We did not have the luxury of time to select a new crew. Gary and I agreed that it was a 'delivery voyage' rather than a mix of Expedition and exhibition tour like our last journey. Almost every port we would visit was in a new country so signing up short term voyage crew would be time consuming and expensive. Instead, we resolved to pay the whole crew as professional seafarers so they had some money to spend in the layover ports. That way, they could enjoy the time away from the ship and come back refreshed — and hopefully they would be more likely to stay aboard for the whole voyage. For a year at sea we thought we should try to create a community of people on the ship. That would include a variety of skill levels; couples; older and younger crew members; male and female. Our thinking was that a mix of people which reflected a community ashore would help the tone aboard. To meet the tight budget for the voyage we could not afford to have crew members coming and going for the year. The cost of flying crew around the world and accommodating them during crew transfers would significantly drain our finances. Also, I thought that the voyage would have more significance if the people who embarked on the voyage in Sydney were the people who arrived in Texel. They would complete their own great personal achievement. As the year rolled on, I came to realise that my crew selection philosophy was a massive mistake.

The crew was settled as Gary Wilson, Ship's Master, and a new sailor to the ship, Glenn Williams, as First Mate. Born in New Zealand, Glenn moved with his family to Canada and the USA. His experience working on the South Australian ketch *Falie* was his introduction to traditional sailing vessels. He worked on a supply vessel for the oil industry and he applied for leave to participate in the voyage. Greg O'Byrne agreed to continue with the ship and to take on the Second Mate position. We appointed Alan Campbell as Ship's Engineer. At age 67, the Tasmanian was the oldest crew member and a steadying hand for the younger crew. The inimitable Nicole Gardner was as keen as ever and she relished her time at sea with us. She was leading hand alongside Walter Walker from Queensland who was keen to pursue a career at sea after joining as part of the Chevron Leadership Program. He was part-way through an apprenticeship as a diesel mechanic and we hoped that he would eventually be able to take over from Alan Campbell in the role of Engineer. Jane Doepel left the ship, and a couple joined. Julie Milne was keen to take on the formidable challenge of being

Ship's Cook for a year while her partner Mike Redding from Napier in New Zealand agreed to join as Ship's Carpenter. He was also an experienced photographer who wanted to film the voyage and take pictures. Greg O'Byrne's girlfriend, Alice Turnbull, was completing an environmental degree but she jumped at the chance to take a sabbatical. With previous experience as voyage crew, we knew that she was competent and she signed on for the year long odyssey. John Quigley was a late starter. While only 23 years of age, he was already an experienced square rig sailor.

It was made clear to us when we began negotiating with the VOC committee that it would like us to have some Dutch crew aboard. This was not difficult. The Dutch we met on our travels were all incredibly keen on the ship. Heidy Bontjer joined as voyage crew in Queensland and stayed on. One day I wandered down the wharf at Darling Harbour to meet a young Dutchman living with his parents aboard a magnificent topsail schooner, *La Violante*. The ship was built at Lekkerkerk shipyard in Rotterdam in 1922 as a private yacht and it was beautifully decorated throughout with art nouveau styled brass fittings. Only 19 years of age, Bob Looijschelder was cruising the Pacific with his parents and the possibility of a voyage on *Duyfken* back to The Netherlands appealed to him. We signed him up. He and Walter Walker became good friends.

Englishman Brett Torin Yates was young and inexperienced but he was incredibly keen to join the crew. His American girlfriend, Shannon McGuire, would later join the ship. A Dutch couple, Christine Henschien and Stijn Somers, worked on the *Batavia* Replica and were keen to join us. Stijn was a baker turned rigger and Christine lived in Australia for a couple of years after becoming disillusioned with her nursing studies. They would both make a great contribution to the crew. The only sticking point was that *Batavia* was now out of chains but there was a lot of rot in the hull which would require work. Fortunately for us, it was decided that *Batavia* would be dry-docked for repairs and the rig would have to wait, enabling Stijn and Christine to join our ship in Jakarta.

Shaun Piggin and Davina Taylor joined the crew for the departure from Sydney. James Holdsworth, who began as a volunteer guide in Fremantle when the ship was being built, also joined the crew. Nick Burningham came aboard once again.

With a week to go until departure, Gary Wilson asked if we could have a private chat. He was visibly upset. He explained that he was totally spent, both physically and mentally. The Expedition into Indonesia had been incredibly demanding, and then, without a break, the exhibition tour through Queensland was unrelenting. As soon as the voyage was completed in Sydney, we had launched immediately into a headlong rush to get the ship ready for the VOC voyage. He carried the responsibility admirably but it had taken its toll and he couldn't see himself carrying on at the same level for another 12 months. At first he agreed to take a break to regain his energy and re-join us en route at Cairns but eventually he decided that he would have to withdraw from the voyage entirely. I had underestimated the pressure he faced every day. At least, I could return to my home and family in Perth and recharge my batteries. While my role had pressures of its own, they couldn't really compare with being in charge of a ship 24 hours a day for months on end.

During this maelstrom of activity with *Duyfken*, my dear mother, Shirley, passed away. I was devastated. Of course, my father Jack was also shattered, and I asked him to come to Sydney to help us in the lead up to departure. I thought it would help him recover from his grief. The crew was tremendous, making him welcome and being very kind. I was very grateful with the way they welcomed him into the fold.

There was no time to look for another Ship's Master. Glenn Williams was the obvious choice to take over. Glenn did not have the high level of sailing qualifications enjoyed by Gary Wilson or Peter Manthorpe and his square rig experience could not be compared with the previous Masters. He hadn't sailed aboard the ship before and we selected him as First Mate so that he could gain experience and, if he warmed to the role, perhaps take over a leg or two of the voyage to give Gary a break. We assessed that he had the ability, enough experience and the required ticket to master the ship. I asked him whether he was prepared to take over and, hesitatingly, he agreed. Fortunately, he had been part of the build-up to departure so he could take over straight away but it left us with only one senior officer on board.

Steve Meacham from the Sydney Morning Herald newspaper interviewed Glenn on the day before departure. The first season of the Australian version of the reality television show created by John de Mol called Big Brother, was being aired on television at the time and the journalist equated sailing aboard a seventeenth century sailing ship with the popular television show. Big Brother had 14 people (*Duyfken* had a crew of 5 women and 11 men) locked into a large house for three months while *Duyfken,* about the floor area of a school bus, would be at sea for a year. The longest stretch out of sight of land was 55 days. We knew that it would be an extra-ordinary test of stamina for all the crew. Glenn said that the biggest trial for his crew would be living in a confined space with a small group of people for a long time without making enemies. "There's a strict difference between Big Brother and the *Duyfken*," he said. "They've picked people who will promote conflict whereas our crew has been picked for their ability to get on with people. Their sailing skills come on top of that." Then the journalist added: "Like reality-show wannabes, the crew — 14 Australians and two Dutch — have been hastily introduced to each other. The oldest is 67, the youngest, 18. As if to provide the obligatory sexual tension, three of the women have their partners aboard. Does Williams think it might cause problems? "Oh, I should think so," he says"."

When *Duyfken* sailed out of Darling Harbour on 5 May 2001, we still did not have a regular flow of funds from the VOC 2002 committee, but we were assured that they would be forthcoming. Rinze Brandsma wrote to Enric Hessing and stressed that the voyage budget was based on a break-even operation and we did not see the voyage as a business venture. We couldn't wait for the instalments to arrive at some indeterminate time in the future. He said that the "voluntary board resolved that under no circumstances would the ship risk leaving Cairns without absolute certainty that the funds for the voyage were in place." I still had not been paid by the *Duyfken* Foundation for months and I was awaiting my reimbursement, too. Whilst this excruciating tussle over funding was happening behind the scenes, we were racing to get everything in place for the ship to leave Sydney, otherwise there was no way we could make our Texel deadline in April 2002. I gathered the crew together for a day long meeting to go through the arrangements for the year ahead. I wanted to treat them like professionals. This came as a complete surprise to many of the crew who weren't used to my corporate approach. They'd rather be down at the ship preparing her for departure.

Duyfken was stowed with a bewildering array of gear for the voyage including bulky survival suits and wet weather gear. Julie Milne planned the crew's meals precisely so that their diet was adequate. Vitamin pills could supplement any deficiencies. For the initial passage, she ordered 400 kg of flour, 200 kg of pasta, 60 kg of rice, 112 kg of canned tuna and 60 kg of breakfast cereal. Fresh food was supplemented by new supplies in each port as it ran out after only two weeks at sea. It was a far cry from the original *Duyfken*'s voyage to the Indies. Each of the 16 crew members on that voyage was allocated four pounds and ten ounces of bread for every eight days at sea. This bread was more like a flat biscuit. Other provisions were pickled beef, fat bacon, pork and fish pickled in barrels as well as wine and vinegar. Yummy.

Hundreds, not thousands, of supporters gathered at the Australian National Maritime Museum jetty to farewell *Duyfken* on her monumental voyage. It was a disappointing turnout compared with our grand arrival some months before when many hundreds of spectator craft welcomed us to Sydney. Just the brigantine *Windeward Bound* and Fred Looijschelder's schooner *La Violante* escorted us out to the heads. Only the hard-core square-rig sailors of Sydney really understood the scale of our undertaking. I stayed aboard with my father, Jack, until the last possible moment but we misjudged the line and we crossed the range limit of the Sydney Harbour water taxis. Captain Sarah Parry on *Windeward Bound* saw our plight and so my father and I transferred across to her ship for our return to the Museum. Once again, I was seeing *Duyfken* sail into the distance on another voyage while I returned to the dock to confront the problems on shore rather than those at sea. It had been a whirlwind preparation phase and there were a lot of loose ends to tie up. Only a couple of weeks before, *Duyfken* was in dry dock getting her bottom scraped, and now she was sailing back into the tropics with a new crew.

Amongst the crew, the magnitude of the challenge now struck home. Julie Milne wrote in her diary: "In front of the cameras I fight back emotions of anxiety, frustration, stress, apprehension and a homesickness I have never felt before. The past few weeks have been full of anxiety and trepidation. A flotilla of yachts flank our little ship. Some friends cruise alongside in their yacht. All I want to do is to jump overboard. I have no sense of pride or belonging, I envy the day trippers and their known world, their cosy cabins, their eskies of champagne, bread and cheese lunches – and more where that came from. I hardly notice the gleaming Opera House, the imposing Sydney Harbour Bridge. I do notice houses dotted along the hills and inlets, the trees and blooms, the tall office buildings and the ferries. They are all symbols of a familiar city life that I now leave behind. For the next 12 months my life is aboard this little ship. My view of the world will be a 360 degree patch of horizon. These people are not my family and yet we must live as one. They will become more familiar yet there is a separateness between us that will not dissipate … I take a deep breath and hold out my hand to Glenn for a 'good luck' shake and disappear below deck to prepare lunch." Julie later said: "It was apparent to me, if not yet to the rest of the crew, that remarkable though this undertaking was, our challenge was not the sailing, nor even completing the voyage – our challenge was a personal one — of living together in such difficult circumstances."

I felt vindicated when *Duyfken* was set free from Sydney Harbour and flew north. The crew enjoyed exhilarating downwind sailing. They were settling into the daily routine and heading north into Queensland when Chris Blake, the Master of *Endeavour*, contacted Glenn over the radio. *Endeavour* was at Coolangatta and fancied making contact. *Endeavour* and *Duyfken* had never been in the same patch of water since *Duyfken* was launched and this would be the first opportunity for the two Fremantle-built replicas to sail in company. *Duyfken* had always been seen as the 'little sister' of the far larger and more well-known *Endeavour*. Even though both were built by the same hands, there was a constant rivalry and a debate about which ship was faster. Would a 170 year newer design be superior? On 9 May 2001, the argument was settled when Glenn sailed in company with *Endeavour*, and she made so much distance on the Whitby collier that he tacked across her and back to take up station alongside Cook's ship. Fair to say that Chris Blake responded with a cannon salvo but the point had been made. *Duyfken* was a fast little ship that could sail rings around a Whitby collier, even in light airs. I was told that Chris Blake's crew were made aware of his disgust.

With this major voyage leaving from Sydney, and crew coming from all over Australia and indeed, the world, *Duyfken* was now disconnected from her home port supporter base and the Board of Management in Fremantle. This had long term repercussions. To help address this, and for the Board Members to have a connection with the new crew, I budgeted for a different Board Member to join me each time I caught up with the crew during the voyage. Captain Chris Bourne joined me at Port Douglas in Far North Queensland to meet the crew and assess how the ship was being run. It had been an easy passage north although Mike Redding had a bad case of the flu and had to spend time ashore before rejoining at Thursday Island. We arrived at the ship with pizzas and drinks — a surefire way to be welcomed aboard. On the surface, our crew appeared to be in good spirits and we didn't have many issues to discuss. I did not read the changes in the crew dynamics and I thought everything was fine. Glenn was coming to grips with the demanding life at the top and he found the first weeks to be very exhausting. This was understandable. During watches, long term crew members were imposing their procedures on the new crew. I thought there was nothing unusual about that. They had the experience, but some of the new crew did not like to be lectured. Trouble was brewing.

A little further north at Cape Melville, the Chevron 2000 *Duyfken* Expedition almost came unstuck when Gary was faced with the wind blowing fiercely from the south. It was blowing again, but this time the ship was sailing north and making six to seven knots in the same breeze. What a difference sailing in season makes. A few days later, the crew set a new four-hour sailing record of 27.7 nm, then topped it with 32 nm covered in the same time.

Funds were once again becoming critically short and the VOC 2002 Committee continued to fob us off with promises of the funds coming 'soon'. We were easily making our voyage schedule and once we left Thursday Island in Torres Strait we would be totally committed to the passage to Jakarta. I didn't want to have to continually chase funds for the next 18 months. It wouldn't take long to run out of money again. Eventually, I had to put my foot down and get tough, declaring that the ship would not leave Australian waters until the second instalment of the funds was forthcoming. Rinze agreed on the resolute stance. The crew would be paid off at Thursday Island and we would not sail to The Netherlands. Finally on 29 May, two days before *Duyfken* was due to reach Thursday Island, Enric Hessing and Rinze Bradsma's signatures were on the agreement. The threat got the people who were responsible for activating the payment to do their job and now *Duyfken* was adequately funded from Den Haag for the first part of the voyage.

The new voyage seemed to be creating more hiccups than I had expected but they weren't from the ocean or the weather. Walter hadn't travelled outside Australia before and his passport still hadn't arrived. It didn't make it to Port Douglas then it was lost in the Government office at Thursday Island in Torres Strait (and later found) so a new one was applied for to be picked up in Darwin. This extra unplanned layover was just another unforeseen expense. The voyage was beginning to look like a bus tour of northern Australia. Influenza was working its way through the ship, too. The crew members who continued with the ship after the first expedition seemed jaded. The crew was just not coming together like we had hoped. In frustration, Glenn began airing the morale problems he had with the crew in his Captain's Log for the whole world to read. What didn't find its way into the log was a minor collision with a German yacht at Thursday Island after *Duyfken* dragged anchor. It caused an ongoing legal stoush for $12,500 in damages. We eventually had to pay up.

It wasn't all bad news. Working in our favour was that the ship was still ahead of schedule thanks to the extra time we had put in the program and the reliable south east trades which caused us so much trouble on the previous expedition. It had taken us a few years, but *Duyfken* finally made it to the Tanimbar Islands on 17 June 2001. This was where Julius Tahija fought the Japanese in the World War Two battle which made him a household name in wartime Australia. *Duyfken*'s crew were surprised by their treatment. As Nick Burningham described it:

> *Our reception in Saumlaki was reasonably courteous although we proved a disappointment to the townsfolk. Tanimbar is part of Indonesia's Maluku Province torn apart by a civil war incited by men using religion as a tool of evil. Islands where different religious communities have co-existed harmoniously for centuries are now totally partitioned. At Saumlaki the entire Muslim community had fled, though the fine timber-panelled houses built by the Bugis and Butonese traders remain easy to recognise. The beleaguered Christian community at Saumlaki was living in fear of invasion and retribution, and in the hope that the Christian Western World would come to their rescue.* Duyfken, *they hoped and believed, had brought them reinforcements and firearms. But we hadn't: the West is scarcely Christian and certainly not crusading (unless oil is involved). Our only slight help was to employ a bereft refugee from Ambon to make a set of hardwood heaving mallets for $10 each. With constant rigging maintenance, and lines being frequently unrove and re-rove for tarring, there never seemed to be enough heaving mallets onboard.*

From Saumlaki, *Duyfken* sailed north of Timor into the Java Sea and anchored at Karimun Jawa Island. It was a chance for the crew to relax and they benefited from the break.

Our most important port of call was Jakarta. I flew to Jakarta early to finalise arrangements for the visit. This was a pattern I repeated all the way to Texel. By arriving early, I could address any customs and immigration issues before the ship came over the horizon, make contacts for spares and services, talk to local media and then coordinate a welcome arranged remotely by Tracy in Perth. Jakarta is a massive city with a population of 8.5 million people. It was founded by our nemesis, Jan Pieterszoon Coen, in 1619 on the site of Sunda Kelapa, a port with coconuts established by the kingdom of Sunda Papajaran. In true Coen style, it was a bloody takeover of the kingdom. Coen used troops from Maluku to assert his authority and to build a fortress ringed by Dutch-style canals. He called it Batavia. Surrounded by rice and sugar cane fields, it was a notoriously unhealthy place to visit. In later years, people who could afford to get away from the malarial swamps moved inland to where the main business area of Jakarta is today.

Since we had been prohibited from visiting the city the previous year, the Indonesian/Australian relationship improved to such an extent that President Wahid (Gus Dur) was on his way to Canberra on the first state visit by an Indonesian President in more than 25 years. Indeed, Gus Dur made an impromptu visit to Darwin a week after *Duyfken* departed. His ageing Boeing 707 Presidential jet made the unscheduled landing due to mechanical problems and three Australian RAAF jets were despatched to transport his 50 strong entourage the rest of the way from Darwin to Canberra. Gus Dur's government was also on its last legs and it was only a matter of time until Megawati Sukarnoputri would be given the keys to the Presidential palace. Indonesia in peril: it seemed like the previous voyage all over again.

I was in constant communication with the Australian Embassy to divert the ship in case violence flared up. Once again, I engaged Tanya Alwi to help give some shape to our Jakarta visit. This was her home patch and she had quite a network across the city including Robert Silalahi who worked for the City of Jakarta. His view was that the visit would be beneficial to Jakarta since it would coincide with the celebration of the 474th Anniversary of Jakarta and the 56th Anniversary of Indonesian Independence. Some Indonesians I met knew about the VOC in terms of colonialism and suppression of the local culture by the Dutch, but most were not interested in the topic. Their needs were far more contemporary — modernising the economy, better government and an improved standard of living. The events of 400 years ago were most interesting to the academics and museum people I met in Jakarta. The Indonesian Government did not have the money to fund historical studies and the restoration of colonial buildings but the academic community saw Dutch colonial history as a source of income from international bodies which funded research projects. *Duyfken* was a useful tool to raise awareness of the need to study this part of their history, and nothing more. There didn't appear to be a great deal of passion for *Duyfken*'s visit one way or the other so I thought our time in Jakarta would be relatively uneventful.

Tanya arranged a meeting at the Jakarta Governor's palatial office to discuss some sort of official welcome. Governor Sutiyoso and the Mayor of North Jakarta, Subiago, wielded immense power in the Indonesian capital. Like most people in high positions after years of Suharto rule, they were both ex-generals. I was surprised when Tanya and I arrived at the meeting, and then more and more people filed in behind us. There were 12 or 14 people crowded into the boardroom. Several spoke just a little English, and I spoke virtually no Bahasa. The meeting began cordially enough and then turned into a massive debate across the table with everyone speaking loudly and almost shouting to make their points. I was oblivious to what they were talking about, unable to participate in the discussion. One faction did not want us to visit Jakarta at all. Tanya occasionally made an interjection, mentioning Jakarta's own birthday celebrations or something else the visit could be linked to, and then the discussion would fly off once again. She occasionally looked at me and gestured for me to keep calm. I had no inkling of what was being discussed, anyway. There weren't a lot of people smiling at me. After the meeting, I asked Tanya what it was all about and she explained that one person questioned why the Governor of Jakarta should welcome a ship representing the evils of colonialism. The discussion then centred upon whether this aspect of the past should be ignored so that Indonesia could have modern diplomatic relations or whether *Duyfken* should be boycotted to make their point. One view was that the VOC history of Jakarta was associated with the subjugation of the local leaders, and this led to the modern colonial era and its attendant problems. The arrival of the ship was a reminder of the negative events in Jakarta's history. Fair enough. At the other end of the scale were the people who saw the VOC history of the city as a useful lever to encourage urban renewal of the Sunda Kelapa area where many VOC buildings were still to be found. International aid funds would flow to the area, too. In her unerringly positive manner, Tanya almost flippantly said to me: "Don't worry about it. I'll sort it out later." And she did! Governor Sutiyoso and Mayor Subiago were soon committed. Economic pragmatism won through.

With the history of Jakarta centred around the old port of Sunda Kelapa, I was encouraged to berth the ship amongst the fleet of tall-masted Bugis trading ships called Pinisi rather than at the modern port or the yacht club. Certainly, *Duyfken* would look at home amongst the traditional trading vessels, and the recently renovated warehouse of the VOC was close by.

David Ramsay and Geoff Leach arranged for the Indonesian Navy's sail training ship KRI *Dewaruci* to escort *Duyfken* into port. It was a stunning sight to see *Duyfken* slowly move up the main canal at Sunda Kelapa with sometimes only a metre to spare and then berthing among dozens of Pinisi ships all unloading timber from other islands.

"*Duyfken* was much the smallest wooden ship crowded into the fetid canal. The timber-hulled vessels that carry sacks of cement from Jakarta to West Kalimantan, gravel thence to South Kalimantan, and construction timber back to Jakarta retain a standing gaff rig, mainly because motor-sailers enjoy cheaper registration and port fees than fully motorised vessels. The largest can load about 1000 tonnes … Sunda Kelapa is a dusty, dirty, smelly port," said Nick in his journal. Jakarta's sewers seem to overflow into the canal and it is not the place for anyone with a sensitive nose.

I arranged for the area where we were to berth to be cleaned up and an official welcome was arranged with the Governor and Mayor, Julius Tahija and his family, and officials from both the Australian and Dutch embassies attending. I never expected the President Gus Dur but I was delighted to meet Ali Alitas, the recently retired Indonesian foreign minister. With Australian Foreign Minister, Gareth Evans, he was well known in Australia for signing the now infamous Timor Gap Treaty to share oil and gas resources from East Timor in 1989. He was a skilled diplomat, and his presence showed the strong connections fostered by Australian diplomats in Jakarta, even if the actions by John Howard which accelerated East Timorese independence were unpopular in Indonesia at the time.

Glenn Williams and the new crew began to appreciate that they were now looked up to as celebrities. Everyone wanted to talk to them and to show them around. It was a new role for Glenn and it wasn't always comfortable for him but he grew in confidence as the port visits rolled on. The Governor's official welcome lunch was an honour bestowed on few visitors to Jakarta. The whole crew was invited. Glenn described his initiation into the world of pomp and splendour found in the top tier of Indonesian government:

> *This was going to be important and we were all dressed in our finery. Even so nothing had prepared us for the splendour of the*

place. For an office it was a building on its own, made with cut marble, very large, quite cold and clinical. We were paraded to the reception room where tables were laid out and were welcomed by the other guests, who were all important government officials. The Governor was late but after his arrival, which is much like the arrival of a mogul, we sat down and were put through the speeches and exchanging of gifts. I was caught short when they asked me to give a speech as I was in no way prepared but with what courage I could muster I stepped forward and introduced the crew and thanked all who were there (I think!). Then it was lunch and finally entertainment, which consisted of first Alan, Nic, Christine and James standing up and singing Waltzing Matilda and then all of us getting up for a song and finally all the guests getting up to sing and have a dance. If this was not crazy enough, the Governor then stepped up and sang two songs.

Without an appreciation of the sensitivity of Duyfken's ambassadorial role, he finished his report with: "Land of the Karaoke, pretty weird." It was an embarrassing sign-off to the report of a very important day for the *Duyfken* Project. The Captain's Logs were widely read and there was nothing to be gained mocking our hosts in such a way. Love it or hate it, singing politicians are a long-standing tradition in South East Asia.

While the crew were billeted at the Omni Hotel nearby, we required some crew aboard the ship all day and night. Every nasty bug in Jakarta was living in the fetid waters of Sunda Kelapa and one by one just about all the crew got sick. It was history repeating. When James Cook with *Endeavour* visited Batavia, 80 per cent of his crew came down with malaria and dysentery. When he sailed out, seven crew members had died and only about 50 crew were in any fit state to sail the ship. Fortunately all our crew survived.

Glenn had begun confiding his crew problems with me in our email correspondence as he sailed towards Jakarta. I said that I would deliver any warnings or directives to individuals in the crew as I was not aboard and the crew always saw 'head office' as an enemy anyway. I failed to appreciate the depth of feeling amongst the crew even at this early stage of the voyage. As soon as *Duyfken* arrived in Sunda Kelapa, I was the recipient of the crew's gripes about conditions aboard and people whingeing about other crew members. The ship was not a happy place. Heidi complained that the word 'privacy' was not in the *Duyfken* dictionary. She had a good point but everyone had to learn to adapt to the close living conditions aboard the ship. The crew had not gelled as a unit and it was deeply fractured. I thought that the best way to address the problems was to sit each crew member down and to run a performance interview. Having worked in the corporate sector, this was a standard way of addressing basic issues with staff. I thought it would help me understand what was going on and persuade each crew member to improve their behaviour. I hadn't foreseen that most people aboard had no idea about the concept of performance reviews and had no intention of being candid about what was happening. I was naive.

Glenn joined me for the reviews at the pleasant coffee shop adjacent to the ship. I reasoned that this would enable the crew to see that I was united with the Ship's Master even if a lot of their criticism had been directed at him (and me, it must be said, but I was used to it by this time!). It was obvious that cliques were developing aboard. I didn't understand it at that stage, but even the Ship's Master was developing his own circle of confidantes. The remaining crew from the previous expedition were prepared to share information on the intricacies of sailing this particular early seventeenth century ship with the Ship's Master and the new crew, but this was interpreted in different ways — welcomed by some and labelled as arrogance and a threat to their seniority by others. The older members of the crew tended to have more social skills and avoided conflict. Some younger members of the crew could not adapt to life in such close quarters for the long passages. This had not shown up in the shorter legs of the Expedition and the exhibition tour where people could get breaks ashore. Our desire to form a normal community on the ship was failing on a personal level, too. Singles saw other crew members sharing the highs and lows with their partners, while they were alone with nobody close to talk to. They felt isolated. With more men than women, there was jealousy, rivalry and disappointment. I naively thought that this would not come to the surface but it had begun even before the ship left Sydney. Added to all this was the tendency for the Dutch crew to speak Dutch to each other, raising suspicion from other crew members that things were being said behind their backs. I don't think it was the case but sometimes perception is reality. Glenn felt that he didn't have enough senior support aboard. He referred to Alan's sailing inexperience relative to his vast engineering knowledge and he was correct. Alan wasn't able to leave Walter to tend the engines. With the Ship's Master sitting in on my interviews, most of the crew didn't want to be totally frank about what was actually going on. It was a mess and I did not have the skills to deal with it. My response was inadequate. After hearing all the feedback, filtered at the reviews and unfiltered at other times, I could see difficulties ahead and before the crew departed Sunda Kelapa I got everyone together and re-iterated my support for the Ship's Master and basically told them all to get on together. This just added to the bitterness toward me from the crew members who thought I could help and didn't. I said I wasn't planning to send home anyone who other people wanted off the ship.

More of the *Duyfken* story came to light in Jakarta. An island in Jakarta Bay was called *Duyfken* Island on early charts, reflecting the role *Duyfken* played in charting the bay. It is now called Pulau Dapur (Kitchen Island) and is about six kilometres from Sunda Kelapa. The VOC island of Pulau Onrust (Restless Island) in Jakarta Bay has enjoyed some restoration work and was visited by *Duyfken* on a day trip while in Jakarta. VOC activities included service and repair of ships on the island. At that time, the shipyards supported 2,000 workers. Storehouses on the island contained trading goods such as copper, tin, brass, pepper and coffee.

Back in June, my advice from the Australian Embassy was for the ship to depart from Sunda Kelapa on the scheduled departure date and no later. They expected Gus Dur to be replaced as President of the world's fourth most populous country on the first day of August. They feared that the ship or the crew members could become embroiled in some way if protests spilled out into the streets. On 22 July, Gus Dur declared a state of emergency which was immediately opposed by the military. We slipped out of port on 25 July. Fortunately there was a peaceful transition of power to Megawati Sukarnoputri and the safety of our crew was never compromised.

Duyfken now had its first new sail and rope to replace some of the standing rigging. Glenn decided to drop anchor near Pulau Panjang, where the Battle of Bantam took place, to renew the rig before the ocean passage to Galle in Sri Lanka. In six days, *Duyfken* was completely re-rigged — an outstanding achievement. It was also a chance for the crew to recover from the bugs they collected in the filth of Sunda Kelapa.

After sailing from Pulau Panjang, *Duyfken* slowly sailed into the submerged caldera of Krakatau, past Anak Krakatau, the remains of the famous volcanic island which was occasionally spewing rocks and dust into the air. They used buckets to scoop up floating pumice stone. Many of the crew thought that sailing a seventeenth century ship through the Krakatau lagoon and then into the Sunda Strait was a highlight of their life.

Chapter 26

Into the Indian Ocean Again

For the sailor it is always about the sea; for me it was always the ports and the countries the ship visited which hold the greatest fascination and motivated me to plan the voyages.

Galle in Sri Lanka was an obvious port of call but it was a slight deviation from the route normally followed by most of the spice-laden VOC ships homeward-bound from the East Indies. The first Dutch ships to Sri Lanka arrived in 1602. A decisive battle took place in 1640 near Galle between the Dutch and Portuguese for control of Sri Lanka and the cinnamon trade. The Dutch won the battle and ruled the port until 1796. Galle became a major VOC port, an entrepôt for trade between Europe and the Indian sub-continent. Dutch jachts like *Duyfken* were the VOC's courier service, taking messages between the VOC outposts in the Indian Ocean and the East Indies. An impressive fort guarded the port and it is still intact. Inside the bastion, Galle has more buildings built by the Dutch than anywhere else in Sri Lanka. Among the Asian ports of the VOC, Galle was second in importance only to Batavia. With several VOC ships amongst the 26 shipwrecks in the harbour, it is now perhaps the most actively studied harbour for VOC ship remains. *Duyfken*'s visit was planned to highlight the progress made towards restoring Galle's historical assets.

The Dutch Ambassador to Sri Lanka was an enthusiastic supporter of the VOC 2002 celebrations and WA Maritime Museum archaeologists had done a lot of work on Dutch shipwrecks in the bay. I was hopeful that we could be free of the problems of civil war and political violence which we seemed to have been skipping around in Indonesia for 18 months. I was wrong. The Liberation Tigers of Tamil Eelam (known as the Tamil Tigers) had been fighting a guerrilla war to create an independent state in the north of the country for almost two decades and a unilateral cease fire was declared by the group in December 2000. We were told that Galle, in the south of the island nation, was far from the fighting and we would be out of danger. Sri Lanka's tourism industry was recovering and Europeans in particular were holidaying in increasing numbers at the beach resorts a long way away from the Tamil areas in the north. But things can change rapidly. Two weeks before we were due to sail from Sydney, the Tamil Tigers declared an end to the truce and began a new offensive. I was still assured that we would be safe in Galle.

As the Governor of Jakarta farewelled *Duyfken* at Sunda Kelapa, my thoughts immediately turned to paying bills and thanking everyone in Jakarta before getting on a plane back to Perth the next morning. The Tamil Tigers were in the news again for the boldest strike seen in the long-running civil war. In the early hours of 24 July 2001, they launched a brazen suicide attack on the Bandaranaike International Airport at Colombo and the adjacent military base. In five hours they damaged or destroyed 20 military aircraft, and completely destroyed three Airbus passenger jets and damaged another two. The 14 suicide commandos perished in the raid but they achieved their objective and effectively sabotaged the Sri Lankan economy. It was sent into recession for the first time since independence. The shocking footage went around the world, only to be eclipsed by an even more horrific attack a few months later in New York.

The news raised all the obvious questions: Should we divert the ship to an Indian port, maybe Goa, which had been on one of our early voyage plans? Perhaps we should sail to the safety of the Cocos Islands? I was in contact with the Sri Lankan marine archaeologist, Ltnt Cmdr Somasiri Devendra, who led the Australian/Sri Lankan Project in Galle Bay to survey the VOC ship *Avondster* (*Evening Star*). He assured me that Galle would be fine. The Australian High Commission in Colombo had initially been keen for us to visit the Sri Lankan capital but they said that they could not recommend Colombo. Galle was still the best option. I kept the port options open until the latest possible time so that we had total flexibility.

In heavy rain more than half way into the voyage to Sri Lanka, Christine fell a metre onto the deck landing on her back; then a day later, Heidy fell heavily, too. *Duyfken* was still two weeks out of Galle with two seriously incapacitated crew members. The whole crew were frustrated when they didn't have good sailing conditions. Everyone had a different experience of this part of the voyage. Nicole later wrote about her personal experience being aboard at this time.

I cursed and jerked the sail needle out of my thigh again. I pushed the thin canvas of the fore-topsail off my lap and rubbed my growing collection of puncture wounds. I was repairing the sail, but I was hot, tired, sweaty, and distracted. When I wasn't stabbing myself in the leg, I was sewing the sail to my shorts. I decided it was time for a break and headed up on deck where, predictably, nothing was happening.

"We were still drifting around in the Indian Ocean doldrums, which were living up to their name. We were heading for Galle in Sri Lanka, but the wind had other ideas. We'd been drifting in the same patch of ocean for so long that I once noticed a floating halo of food scraps from the last few days' dishwashing had surrounded us. Some days earlier, we'd actually made big oars to get the ship pointed in the right direction.

As the sailmaker, I was actually happy that there was no wind: a 40 knot squall a few days earlier blew out both topsails. Without topsails, we weren't going anywhere. The main problem with flax canvas is that it rots. By that time, our sails were several years old. Despite our best efforts, the canvas was rotten. Every time I patched a sail, it would tear around the edges of the patch. I'd patch that split, and the sail would tear around the new patch. At various times, we'd tried soaking the weak spots in linseed oil, pine tar and tallow to reinforce them, but it didn't help.

On the plus side, the patches formed an overlapping fish-scale pattern growing in from the corners and converging on the middle of the sail. Because we'd resorted to using old clothes for patches, it was quite pretty, if ineffective.

The doldrums are where the north-east and south-east trade winds meet at the Inter-Tropical Convergence Zone. They're a notoriously frustrating place to sail. The problem is, either there's no wind at all or there are squalls: sudden, sharp increases in wind and rain. If we put the rotten sails up and we're hit by a squall, the sail gets shredded. If we didn't put the rotten sails up, we wouldn't go anywhere and we'd never get to Sri Lanka. One of the crew pointed out, accurately, that the only times we went anywhere fast in the doldrums it was always in the wrong direction.

I'd been on lookout the day before, when a little fishing boat came over to gawp at the funny-looking sailing ship. One of the fishermen *had a half-eaten apple. We'd run out of fresh food a few weeks earlier so the sight of that apple made several mouths water. The fisherman saw us staring and held the apple up, a question on his face. Seeing our vigorous nodding, he threw it to us.*

We shared the remains of the apple between those of us who were awake. There was just enough for a small nibble each. While we were eating, someone had the presence of mind to retrieve our trade goods and start negotiating.

In exchange for several packets of Indonesian cigarettes, we acquired several apples, a pile of coconuts, and a large fish. Not long after that, life took a turn for the better. We had a memorable feast, repaired the topsails, and a few days later the wind changed. Little more than a week later, we were in Sri Lanka!

Christine improved a little as the ship closed on Galle but Heidy had more severe damage to her lower back. The injury was giving her much more trouble. On 28 August, with only days until the ship was due to make landfall in Sri Lanka, Maria Poulos from the High Commission gave us clearance that Galle would be fine for us to visit. I flew out to Colombo the next morning, destined to miss my daughter Louise's thirteenth birthday. This was the the second year in a row that her Dad had missed her birthday — a year before, I was in Port Moresby.

I flew into Colombo in the early hours of the morning and I was unprepared for the view outside the window as we taxied to a halt. The airport was littered with the shells of damaged military and civilian aircraft. It was a war zone. After passing through Customs and Immigration, I was whisked across town by taxi in the dead of night. The city was under curfew and there was nobody on the streets. There was barely even a street light left on. My destination was the ageing Galle Face Hotel near the beachfront. It was renowned for its famous guests including Emperor Hirohito, Richard Nixon, Sir Laurence Olivier and George Bernard Shaw. Every room had a plaque celebrating one guest or another. It is a bit disconcerting to have the names of people who have stayed in your room listed on a plaque near your bed. I planned to meet the Australian High Commission staff the next morning. I'd also arranged to meet two Perth expatriates, Lorraine and Bruce Fellsmith, in the evening. Their son, Scott, was one of the more experienced crew members aboard *Endeavour* and they wanted to extend their hospitality to another Fremantle ship's crew — and to find out from me what was happening in their home town. Bruce was an accomplished tropical home architect who had a thriving consultancy. Their house in Galle called Victoria (now called Ambalama Villa) won many international architecture awards, ensuring a long list of commissions. It was magnificently located on a beach with a matrix of coconut palms framing the ocean waves and an appealing mix of modern and sensible traditional architectural features. They were also renovating a colonial mansion in Colombo as their city residence and office. When I met Bruce and Lorraine in the morning, I told them about the ship's voyage and the terrible bad luck of having two crew members getting injured in the space of a few days. They gave me good advice on whom to contact and what to do but I had to wait until the ship arrived before I could do anything more.

I arranged a driver to take me from Colombo to Galle. The 116 km Colombo to Galle road has a reputation as one of the world's most dangerous stretches of tarmac — not because of any narrow mountain passes or difficult weather but because the locals who use the road are said to be crazy. I couldn't disagree. It was like a demolition derby, dodging trucks, buses, cars, bikes, horses and carts, cows, elephants, people, goats etc. My destination was the Closenberg Hotel in the old P&O agent's house on a promontory overlooking the port. It was not the most modern hotel, but it felt like I was sharing someone's rambling country house. The only other guests were the English coach of the local rugby team and a South African computer boffin who was introducing computers to the local women's underwear factories. He had a lot of good stories to tell about our future ports of call in Africa as he had served as a conscript in the South African Defence Force, fighting Swapo (South West African People's Organisation) in what is now Namibia. Inevitably, we'd spend evenings together enjoying Sri Lanka's fabulous curries.

Life on the road now followed a familiar pattern. To communicate with the ship and home required internet access. Mobile phones had not yet become mini-computers — they were still simply phones. The BlackBerry 5810 phone, which was the first smartphone, had not been released. I had a laptop to connect to a phone line but most hotels often didn't have the capacity to handle data on their old systems. It was easier to send a fax. Sometimes I'd get lucky and have a hotel with a business centre with computers connected to the new-fangled internet, but more often than not I'd have to find a net cafe. While the concept of surfing the internet and having a cup of coffee was not even 10 years old, it had spread around the world. They were often hip, alternative places attached to a computer shop where mostly young people dropped in to check emails, surf the net or download music. The telephone networks were often not set up to handle the ballooning demand for data transfer so I could waste hours as my connection dropped in and out or buffered longer emails.

While in Galle, I hired a local driver, Hashana, with his three-wheel taxi (called a tuk-tuk in other places) to get me around town while I waited for the ship to arrive. It was the only way to travel: no constant haggling over fares and no waiting for a driver to turn up. My day started at the local net cafe to check my emails. Hashana dropped me at the door and loitered around outside while I attempted to get a connection and read my messages. Then he took me to visit the Harbour Master or spend time with Somasiri Devendra. The old harbour proved to be too shallow for *Duyfken* and lacked the security the ship required. I was taken down to the new harbour to meet the Assistant Harbour Master, Captain Athula Hewavitharana, who showed me our proposed berth early in the morning. It looked fine. There was a small boat moving across the harbour entrance with a net. "What's he doing?" I asked. With a nod of the head, he replied, "No problem." Every afternoon the net was run across the harbour so that scuba divers couldn't enter. He told me to tell the crew not to be alarmed if they heard explosions in the evening. It was only the harbour guards tossing hand grenades into the harbour to discourage incursions by divers overnight.

Duyfken arrived in Galle with a friendly local welcome. After the dignitaries departed, I arranged for two ambulances to take our ailing crew members to the hotel. Unfortunately, they both looked to be in a sorry state. The local physiotherapist (who was also employed by the Sri Lankan cricket team) had a look at them and recommended for them to be taken to a private hospital in Colombo for treatment. Lorraine Fellsmith recommended the Nawaloka Hospital which was only 16 years old and had the most modern facilities in the Sri Lankan capital. I couldn't find an ambulance for the transfer so I arranged for a van (where Heidy could lie horizontally and Christine was able to sit up) for the trip back up the notorious road to Colombo. After being on the ship for a month, being in the back of the van was an altogether different experience. At one point, Heidy looked out the window to see an elephant walking next to the van and peering in at her. Welcome to Sri Lanka!

The hospital in Colombo was packed with patients as well as friends and family coming and going and bringing meals and other essentials. The entrance foyer was like a street market at peak hour. The decor was stark: the walls were covered with shiny white tiles and stainless steel. The nurses and staff were friendly and efficient and our two crew members had beds next to each other. I think they were terrified by the hospital environment. I had to visit every department and queue up to pre-pay in cash for all the tests such as x-rays. I also paid in advance to cover the costs of the rooms. Fortunately, Dr Panasami who handled both cases concluded that Christine was badly bruised but was otherwise fine. Heidy on the other hand had a ruptured disc (L4-5) and she would require time away from the ship for a treatment and rehabilitation program. There was no option but to repatriate her to Perth. The Fellsmiths generously offered to look after Heidy at their Colombo home until she could fly out. Then my battle began with airline staff to secure a seat on an aircraft for a person with a back injury. She travelled business class.

Tracy McCullough and Peggy Rogers were at Perth airport when she arrived. They had flowers and letters from home and Heidy knew she was amongst friends after a harrowing three weeks. Even though she'd been in a plane for 13 hours, she was still able to crack a smile. She was immediately transferred to St John of God Hospital in Subiaco. All her tests, and then some, were repeated in Perth and a course of hydrotherapy treatment was recommended. I talked the situation through with Cathy, to ask whether Heidy could stay at our home while she recovered. It was above and beyond the call of duty but she agreed and in the next couple of months, Heidy became part of our family. Heidy became 'Princess Heidy' for our children, Louise and Daniel, because she wasn't able to do too much except lie around for the first couple of weeks. As she began to recover, she was able to do more including helping to cook meals and buying Belgian beer from our local liquor store to share with Cathy. Every day she swam at Inglewood Pool to strengthen her back. She was grateful for the kindness shown by Cathy, Louise and Daniel and reciprocated with some beautiful gestures. Louise loved (and still does love) purple so Heidy painted her bedroom purple for her. With her sailor's rope skills, she spliced the ropes together on a very high swing hanging from a tree in our backyard. After she recovered and returned to the ship in Cape Town she left a special place in my family's heart.

The hand grenades thrown into the harbour at Galle to deter mischievous divers did, indeed, cause some alarm aboard *Duyfken*. The surge from the explosions caused the ship to rub against the dock, and to burst our inadequate fenders on the first evening. After that, it was a battle to find something in port to protect the ship against the wharf.

Some of the greatest fun I had during the port visits was sourcing materials for the ship. It usually meant exploring markets and shops in back alleyways and meeting interesting people. I found the old port areas endlessly fascinating. Something had to be done about our ageing sails. Glenn wanted some sails for light airs so he could get some movement out of the ship in the doldrums. It took some time to find light canvas and Nick Burningham suggested using plastic tarpaulins "like the little fishing boats in the harbour." It was a quirky practical solution and cheap. Fortunately, we didn't have to resort to plastic tarps, and local sailmakers put together a suite of light canvas sails for only a few hundred dollars. I agreed to the khaki green canvas on one condition: that no photographs would ever be taken with *Duyfken* sailing under these sails! With our commitment to authenticity, I thought that it would terrible to have images of the modern canvas sails circulating around the world. On the positive side, the sails worked a treat, and the ship could sail on in light airs.

There was huge interest in the ship at Galle. A staff writer from Sri Lanka's Sunday Observer newspaper, Asiff Hussein, wrote "Never since Thor Heyerdahl's famed *Kon-Tiki* expedition has a re-enactment voyage aroused such public interest as that of *Duyfken* which sailed into Galle Harbour last week…ever since then,'Age of Discovery' voyages undertaken on replica ships based on some old originals have captured the fancy of many an adventurer. But none surpasses the *Duyfken*." Frustratingly, with the harbour security arrangements, members of the public were not allowed to casually enter the port to see the ship. We enjoyed such overwhelming hospitality that I pushed the issue with the help of Somasiri, and the Harbour Master agreed to an arrangement where the port would allow visitors for a day. Every single person had to show their identity card and write their name on a list at the security gate. The people of Galle were tremendously excited to see the ship. Some dressed in traditional costume and others dressed like Dutch merchants for the occasion. More than 12,000 people visited the ship on that single day and it is a credit to the patience and good humour of the Sri Lankans that it was achieved at all.

Andrea Cicholas joined the ship in Galle, taking over as Mate and watch leader, with Alan Campbell returning to the role of Ship's Engineer. I hoped that Andrea would provide support for Glenn. Walter hadn't taken to the engineering job with as much enthusiasm as participating in the watches (he also flew out of Sri Lanka to make a speech at a youth forum in Canberra, returning in Mauritius) so Andrea agreed to stand in for a leg or two.

Discord continued among the crew so, before the ship was due to depart, once again I called a crew meeting. Up to this point, I had been comfortable to absorb criticism from the crew if it helped them get things off their chest but the ill-will was building up. I told the crew that I had seen some crew members working hard in port and getting on with it and others complaining about how hard the work was. I told the crew that this was the voyage they had signed on for, and if they didn't like it they could resign immediately and there would be no hard feelings. "At this time, like everyone else who has worked on the Project before, you ARE the *Duyfken*," I said. Only four of the crew had been with the ship in Fremantle and only Nick Burningham had been with the Project before it was pieces of lumber in a shipyard. I didn't see the driving passion for the Project in this crew which I saw in the crew from the year before. I told them that I made no apologies for making the tough decisions required to get the ship to The Netherlands and the Project was bigger than the individual. The three senior crew, Glenn, Andrea and Alan had my full support. "I will support to the end the people that support me and the ship. If you support me and *Duyfken*, I will support you." I was later told that some of the crew resented my speech because I had no real idea what was happening aboard. They felt like jumping ship — but they didn't.

Outwardly I expressed my solidarity with the Ship's Master, but I knew that he was unprepared for the magnitude of the task I had given him at late notice in Sydney. On the Expedition into Indonesia, we had two Master Class 1 professional sailors in the two key roles of Master and First Mate. Even though they took a while to gel, they became an excellent leadership team. Glenn did not have a First Mate with the same level of experience to support him. Also, the role as Ship's Master was not just the responsibility of sailing the ship safely from port to port but also as a psychologist to deal with the needs of the crew on the long passages at sea — it was not so important on the relatively short hops from Fremantle to Indonesia then to Sydney. This voyage which we had designed for trade winds sailing was proving to be boring for the sailors. Week could pass without sighting land. The ship regularly went through a watch without a change of tack. Without a shared challenge to focus upon, minds wandered and problems were created where none existed. It wasn't a new phenomenon — strict discipline was used on the long voyage to and from the Indies in the days of the VOC to counteract crew problems. The Master of *Duyfken* had unusual and demanding duties. The Captain's Logs required the Master to produce regular copy talking about life aboard. It was tough for a professional writer to keep up with the task, let alone a person who had never had to write creative copy probably since high school. *Duyfken* had now been afloat and worked hard for several years and it became like a new car coming up for a major service. Many things which were new in 1999 started to wear out and needed to be replaced. Every day, Glenn asked me to source something else in port. The master had to cope with all of these issues, plus the loneliness of leadership and its onerous responsibility of keep the crew out of harm's way.

I left Galle with warm memories of kind and gentle people who were genuinely enthusiastic about our visit. It was devastating to see the television images of a giant tsunami crash through Galle during Christmas in 2004. It left more than 35,000 dead and over a million people displaced as the wave pushed five kilometres inland along the Sri Lankan coast. Galle was only 1,600 km from the epicentre, and it was all but destroyed. I wondered what happened to my driver Hashana and his family? We became buddies during my stay. He showed me his home nestled amongst coconut palms in a village just outside the city. It almost certainly would have been washed away. Before I left, his three wheeler had become an 'official' *Duyfken* vehicle. I gave him a *Duyfken* poster. He had it plastic-coated and he mounted it to the inside of the passenger cabin of his taxi. He was very proud that he'd been part of the visit. Weeks after the tsunami and appalled by the homelessness, Bruce and Lorraine Fellsmith began a charity to help build homes for people who had lost everything in the tsunami. I heard that the charity was the first to complete houses in the ravaged hinterland of Galle and within a short time more than 50 homes had been constructed.

The crew pushed south across the equator to find the south-east trade winds for their passage to Mauritius. Julie Milne, the Ship's Cook, was now settled into a work pattern where she cooked for 12 to 13 hours a day. It was a tough, unrelenting job. Earlier in the voyage, she lamented, "Apparently today, there were dolphins, and streaks of lightning on the horizon, so I was told. I am a mole and I live in a hole!" With only two small refrigerators, fresh fruit and vegetables which were purchased in Galle only lasted between 10 to 18 days. Julie's challenge was to cook nourishing meals with tinned and dried food, and to "find 101 different ways to cook with lentils".

The day started early with four loaves of fresh bread baked in the small oven. A typical day's menu began with breakfast of porridge, muesli or flakes served with canned or stewed dried fruit, topped with pumpkin seeds and yoghurt. Morning tea was usually fresh coffee, tea and herb tea, biscuits (or crackers and jam, or muffins). Lunch was a daily highlight for the crew with the hot, steamy bread fresh from the oven. Everyone was rationed to four slices. Tuna, cheese, egg or canned ham was available for sandwiches. Sometimes pizza, damper or herb scones were baked. The previous night's leftovers, beetroot, asparagus, peanut butter, Vegemite, honey or pasta salad added variety. Dinner was typically salmon curry with rice, dahl and rice, corned-beef hash and mashed potato, pasta and spicy tomato, creamy pasta, tofu laksa and noodles, lentil lasagne, chilli beans and rice, or baked salmon and cous cous. To help alleviate Julie's fatigue, Shannon McGuire agreed to relieve her of the cook's duties for two days a week. It was a godsend. Julie had time to rest and she said it also helped Shannon, as it sometimes gave free rein to the 'stifled creativity' she felt as a deckhand. On weekends, she cooked scones, pancakes, pizzas – even ice cream – and 'wonderful variations' like toasted cheese sandwiches.

Duyfken enjoyed a good day's run on 11 September 2001. Nick Burningham finished stitching a new fore topsail made from the khaki green canvas I purchased in Galle, and once it was hoisted the ship gained a half-knot of speed, making 118nm in the day's run. The next day was Greg O'Byrne's 23rd birthday and the crew celebrated aboard with bread and butter pudding and coffee. A small wood screw jammed the bilge pump so Alan Campbell was hard at work fixing it so that the sullage tanks could be pumped. It was just another day at sea with *Duyfken* making an impressive 121nm in 24 hours.

After writing his Captain's Log and sending it on Sailmail, Glenn downloaded the day's emails. One of the emails he received read: "And last night the world trade centre in the US was hit by hijacked planes — it was a terrible sight watching the events unfold, with the first building on fire and then seeing the plane crash through the other, then the first building collapse, this does not bode well for the near future, either peace-wise or for air travel." Glenn thought that his friend was making a joke until he received an email from me:

> *Regards the terrorism in New York, it just occurred to me that you have probably not heard any news at all unless you have got SW*

> radio. The last 48 hours have been horrendous. I think a total of seven buildings are now destroyed in New York. The whole world is in shock. Up to 70 Australians have probably died when the towers collapsed after the passenger jets hit the towers. The jet which hit the Pentagon was probably aimed at the White House. I cannot describe the horror of seeing this on TV. Between three and five terrorists took over each plane as they left Boston for LA. They were fuelled up, and the terrorists must have killed the pilots and flown the planes themselves. They sped up as they flew into the buildings and it was captured live on CNN worldwide because the second plane to hit the World Trade Centre hit 18 minutes after the first. Just to give you an idea of the carnage, more than 50,000 people worked in the complex and 80,000 visit each day. The world saw the twin towers collapse on live TV. Even Colonel Gaddafi has condemned the insane act. The pilots were probably trained by a private flying school in Florida. I don't know how much more you want to know.

Glenn read out the email to the crew and said later that he had never seen the crew so quiet or stunned as when he read out that message. "This is a time when I regret that we do not have a better means of receiving news onboard. On a brighter note, thinking that the last time the USA mobilised its might against another, they shut down the GPS system, so I dusted off the sextant and took some sights. Amazingly my position came to within 8nm from our GPS position. Looks like the old skills are there just a bit rusty, so I will keep practising."

This event epitomised the massive disconnect between the crew's own internalised struggle to endure life aboard the ship during the VOC voyage, and the struggles I was having in the outside world. The consequences of the 9/11 attacks hit the insurance industry hard. It was a nervous time as the world watched to see how the United States would respond. Our brokers were concerned that the global insurance industry could go under. This could then mean that *Duyfken* would be in international waters and uninsurable. Already, a maritime insurance ban had been placed on a long list of countries including Sri Lanka. The *Duyfken* Board was extremely nervous. A condition of conducting the voyage was that the ship and the crew were to be fully insured. If they were uninsured then the Board Members were concerned that they could be personally liable and have to carry the cost of any catastrophic disaster. The issue of turning the ship back to Fremantle was considered a possibility. Fortunately, our fears were not realised. As the Global War on Terrorism was announced by President Bush, *Duyfken* sailed on, enjoying warm following breezes, starry nights and pods of dolphins playing around the ship.

Almost every day, I began receiving emails asking more about the crew and the people Glenn Williams mentioned in the daily log. I asked the crew to write about their experiences aboard so that we could place them on the website. Shannon McGuire was the first to contribute (and few others could be bothered) and I was stunned by what she had to say.

> *A letter from Shannon.*
> *Hello, Hello, Hello, I hope this finds you all well. Life has been full of its ups and downs, the* Duyfken *voyage continues to evolve, as do we. I have found the most recent leg of the journey exceedingly challenging as I confront an inward journey of my own.*
> *The sea is a strange place, fully alive with a magic and seduction all its own. At times it will thrill and enrapture one with its playful moods, but it can also bring one to the end of oneself. It can become a barren and lonely wilderness, with predictable patterns and motions that leave one with nothing but time. As the horizon stretches on and on, so does my reflection as I become aware of and face different aspects of myself not seen before. There is no escape or denying the essence of oneself and I have been facing, accepting, and changing many things. At times I think this aspect of sailing will drive me mad, but my deepest belief is that this is what will make me. When the voyage is long gone, a thing of the past, I will be left with the memories and the person I have become, the result of moulding and changing as I journeyed. I often think of the way waves erode rocks at the seashore, carving and forcing change. This is what I am experiencing. There is a raw reality in life at sea and as the pretences erode away, I am evolving with each tide.*
> *I write and share all of this with you because this is my deepest treasure, the best that I have gleaned from this journey so far. This is what makes me hang on thru hell and high water and this is what makes it worth it. I have determined that the purpose in life is in becoming the deepest, richest, passionate person of character one possibly can. That is why this is my treasure, that is why I sail,*

that is why as hard as it may be, I am happy and content. And although the reflection I see in the mirror is more ragged, feral, and filthy than ever, her eyes are bright and I like her more and more each day.

Now for the icing on top. Amidst the inward transitions, life has been full of magical and memorable surprises. Brett and I have thoroughly enjoyed our latest adventures in port. We both took time off together in Sri Lanka for a bit of R&R, and had a time of it indeed. We toured the hills and tea plantations, visited the local colourful markets, shopping till we dropped of course. We also went to a turtle hatchery and held the little babies, some just days old. My squeals of delight were a point of amusement for the locals as I adopted and named each one. I know it is gushy but they were soooo cute. I asked the captain if I could keep one but he said no. Blast. We also toured the Old Dutch fort in keeping with the nature of our voyage. Later we were captivated by a group of lace makers working along the road in the traditional manner, weaving each piece by hand with a series of threaded knobs and board cards. Amazing. But the best part was just being together away from the ship, remembering what it is like to laze over coffee or wine with a bit of wittering and a couple of good laughs. I still think that it is what we are best at. We spent many magical moments dining on the beachside and received some of the most incredible seafood plates known to man. One local offered freshly caught butternut fish and king prawns, and then proceeded to serve them in a garlic ginger marinade complete with a feast fit for a king. And royalty we have been as we are accepted, received, and spoiled by the locals, sharing our lives and becoming a part of theirs. So special.

Life at sea has been equally treasured as we rush to see the latest pod of dolphins and share each sunrise and set. The moon has been stunning rising late in an orange glow. Such beautiful pictures we each carry in our heart. One special delight was the visit of a Minke whale. As he played about the ship we clapped like little children running from one side to the other to see what he would do next. On one pass he turned on his side one flipper in the air to show us his handsome sheen tummy. My was he a proud fellow, and how we loved him for showing off. The phosphorescence continues to be a source of joy, crashing and flanking the sides of the ship with its

> *sparkles and luminescence. And yes — fair winds have met us as we sail our* Little Dove, *dancing over the waves quite happy in herself and pleasing us as well.*
> *I find life to be the utmost in extremes both high and low and would not trade a moment of this incredible journey. I am rich and blessed.*
> *Best Wishes,*
> *Shannon McGuire*

Even though *Duyfken* dodged many of the problems which beset the countries we visited, we were constantly reminded that we could set sail for another port and leave the problems behind. The people who had helped us would battle on with more important issues in their lives than a little ship and a difficult and fractious crew. In October 2001, Maria Poulos from the Australian High Commission in Colombo, with whom we had formed a great rapport, contacted me with news that Romanie from her office opened an envelope addressed to the High Commissioner. It contained a white powder. A terrorist group sent anthrax-laced letters to embassies in Argentina, Brazil and Kenya. The first letters were sent to media companies and congressional offices in the United States a week after the attack on the World Trade Centre and five people died. There was then a wave of copycat letters sent around the world. The US, French and Indian diplomatic missions in Colombo also received letters. Romanie was immediately admitted to the same hospital in Colombo that cared for Heidy and Christine. Fortunately the tests were negative and it was a hoax. The world seemed to be going crazy.

Chapter 27

Leave Nothing But Footprints

Duyfken was 150 days out from Sydney. I had looked forward to the ship's next port-of-call, the island of Diego Rodrigues, since I began planning the voyage with Gary Wilson at Kasper Kuiper's office in Brisbane. I had never heard of this speck on the ocean before Gary pointed it out on a chart. Diego Rodrigues in the Mascarene group of islands looked to me to be one of the loneliest islands on earth. It is 560 km from Mauritius, which itself is east of Madagascar and 6000 km from Fremantle. It was only 18 km long and 8 km wide.

Up to then, the story of *Duyfken* was intertwined with the story of the Dutch East India Company, trade, exploration, the tragic effects of colonialism and the first recorded contact between Aboriginal Australians and people from the outside world. Now we would see the ecological impact of our little jacht.

While Diego Rodrigues was probably visited by Arab seafarers in antiquity, it was named after the Portuguese sea captain, Diego Rodrigues, who sighted the uninhabited island in 1528.

It is disturbing to realise that Diego Rodrigues was once the Indian Ocean equivalent of the Galapagos Islands of the Pacific. One estimate is that there were as many as 300,000 giant tortoises on the island. As he was approaching this important island, I sent Glenn an email with a piece I had been sent:

> *The island's ecology has been on the losing end ever since the first prototype tourist. The impact of humans has been devastating and the naturalists' paradise that evolved in isolation for millions of years was destroyed in a relative blink. When early ships arrived, the*

> *slow-footed giant tortoise could be seen in herds that numbered thousands. The reptile's impressive two to three hundred year lifespan was drastically reduced by hungry sailors desperate for protein. An excerpt from a ship's log dated 1759 shows that in one haul 5,000 tortoise were carried away, only 1,035 of them survived the journey. The solitaire, a cousin of the ill-fated dodo, did no better. The unfortunate bird knew no predators and had evolved itself into an attractive meal. The flightless creature, weighing up to 20 kg, was soon hunted into extinction by the visiting seafarers.*

The original *Duyfken* was the first Dutch ship to sight the island. In 1601, she was a scout ship for the *Gelderland*, *Zeelandt*, *Utrecht* and another jacht, the *Wachter*. While our *Duyfken* was sailing towards Rodrigues, almost 400 years to the day, Willem Jansz had been doing the same. His crew sighted land on 20 September 1601. They stayed for three days before sailing west to Mauritius. It was their first landfall since leaving Texel 150 days before, and how they must have feasted on the bountiful animals living in this untouched paradise. *Duyfken's* arrival had marked the beginning of the tragic end for an array of local species.

I flew into Rodrigues Island from Mauritius with Peggy Rogers from our Perth team and it was immediately obvious to us that the island was no longer the paradise described in the early seafarers' logs. The airstrip was precariously located on the only relatively flat piece of land on the rocky island. Coming into Port Mathurin, I was told that the island was almost bare because the endemic forests had been cut down for fuel and had never been replaced.

In what became a unsurprising pattern on this voyage, much of my time in port was taken up with individual or small group chats mainly dealing with the often toxic human relations aboard. After five months, most crew members' minds were made up about who they liked and who they didn't and who they wanted me to remove from the ship. The issue was coming to a head and sooner or later I would be forced to act. I could have avoided this problem if I had not been so keen on having one crew for the whole voyage. I should have rotated all the crew members off the ship for breaks beginning with the Ship's Master and including everyone else. Even one month away from the confines of the ship would have refreshed the crew. The next leg was a relatively short hop to Mauritius so I undertook to deal with the problem there.

Like the voyage of 400 years earlier, we were also passing on our way to somewhere else. On 21 October 1602, the original *Duyfken* lost touch with the *Gelderlandt* and the *Zeelandt* and became separated from the fleet near Rodrigues Island on day 59 out of Bantam in Java. The crew kept heading for home and they sailed non-stop to Vlissingen in The Netherlands in 176 days. It was a fast passage. We allowed for 222 sailing days from Jakarta to Texel with visits to Cape Town, St Helena and Ascension Islands and the Azores en-route. There was a much more leisurely transit in front of our crew.

A short passage took *Duyfken* from Diego Rodrigues Island to Port Louis in Mauritius. We billeted the crew at a small resort hotel along the coast. They enjoyed the carefree atmosphere of the island which was such a contrast to the sometimes tense port visits of the previous few months. The niggles coming from crew members were becoming more difficult for me to handle. The range of complaints widened. Several crew members complained to me of lethargy and a general lack of interest in life aboard. It wasn't the food. The Ship's Cook, Julie Milne, consulted a dietician before we left Sydney and the diet was carefully constructed. Vitamin supplements were donated to ensure that everyone was able to maintain their health (of course, some of the younger crew members stowed their own health supplements in the form of Coke, Mars bars and other sweets in their sea chests). Nutrition was not a problem but several of the crew complained that they were losing weight, strength and fitness. Cathy was on the Board of Sports Medicine WA and our friend, Anne Johnston, was the Executive Officer of the organisation. They recommended that I talk to Dr Tim Ackland from the University of Western Australia. He was an Associate Professor and a recognised expert in functional anatomy and biomechanics in the School of Human Movement and Exercise Science. He was the Chair of the 5th IOC World Congress on Sport Sciences at the Sydney Olympics and a qualified sailing master in his own right. It was a long shot, but I thought he might be prepared to give me some advice. So I rang him and went to see him at his office in the hallowed halls of the university.

I explained to Tim that I had a crew with a mix of professional sailors and amateur expeditioners. While the voyage had moments of frantic activity and heavy work, most of the time the crew were lying down or sitting down as the ship was small and there was nowhere to go. We were now approaching the mid-point of the voyage but people complained of a lack of energy. Glenn was worried about the reduced performance of the crew when hard physical tasks were required and there was boredom and a 'general malaise'. Tim was immediately intrigued and quite excited to be able to help out in some way, although he cautioned me that he may not be able to solve all the problems aboard. He had never been asked to devise a fitness program for a crew of a seventeenth century ship before. We agreed that he would meet the crew in Cape Town and work up a program. Maybe this would help.

We knew that the sea passage from Mauritius to Cape Town would be the most difficult of the whole voyage. It included the need to avoid the notorious Agulhas Bank. The 'Cape of the Needles' (Cabo das Agulhas) was named by Portuguese seafarers because all their compass needles pointed to true north as they sailed by. The Portuguese ships had to confront two powerful ocean flows: the Agulhas and Benguela currents. The warm Agulhas current runs from south and west in the Indian Ocean and pushes against the cold waters coming up from Antarctica. Only the Gulf Stream is a faster ocean current. It meets the Benguela current off the Cape of Good Hope. It was an area to be avoided. The narrow passage between Madagascar and Mozambique created a trap for the current. Gale force winds of up to 180kph are found in spring, and this was the time when we planned to make the passage. If the winds blow from the west and south-west in the opposite direction from the current, massive rogue waves of up to 30 metres have been recorded.

The original *Duyfken* almost certainly would have had the book of charts and navigation produced by the Dutchman, Jan Huygen van Linschoten, who wrote about the Agulhas current in his 1595 work 'Reys-gheschrift vande navigatien der Portugaloysers in Orienten' (Travel Accounts of Portuguese Navigation in the Orient).

> *And because that about this Cape Das Agulhas, there is ground found, at the least 30 or 40 miles from the land, we knew we were past it: as also by the colour of the water, and the birds, which are always found in those countries: and the better to assure us thereof, the great and high sea left us, that had so long tormented us, and then we found a smoother water, much differing from the former: so that as there we seemed to be come out of hell into Paradise, with so great joy, that we thought we were within the sight of some haven, and withall had a good wind, though somewhat cold.*

Even in recent times, this part of the Indian Ocean is spoken about in hushed tones by those who have experienced its wrath. One of our Board members, Wim Alebeek, had a particularly frightening experience when he was caught on the Agulhas Bank while a member of a crew delivering a brand new ship. They were caught on one of the standing waves caused by the eddying currents and the ship ruptured in the middle. Fortunately it did not sink and it limped into a South African port. He did not want *Duyfken* to fall into the same trap, and indeed, our insurance was not valid if we did cross into the 'no go' zone marked on the charts.

The stopover at Mauritius proved to be a pressure release for the worsening morale of the crew. The resort accommodation and the support provided by the Australian and Dutch diplomats in Port Louis refreshed the crew. By the end of the stay, rather than looking inwardly at their own frustrations on board, they were now contemplating the challenge of the next ocean passage. If the weather turned against us, it could be the biggest test yet of ship and crew.

The clever work required by Glenn and his crew to get *Duyfken* through the next leg, however, took second place for me as our 10-year-old son Daniel came down with a nasty illness. Fortunately I was home from Mauritius for a couple of weeks between port visits. Daniel was covered head to toe and even in his mouth and throat with a distinctive raised red rash and he was admitted to Princess Margaret Children's Hospital in Subiaco. He was placed into full isolation until the illness could be determined. It was a worrying 24 hours. I missed my scheduled email communication with Glenn so I sent him a message the next day: "Sorry to be off air last night. Daniel has a mystery disease that they are now growing on a petrie dish at the hospital. They still do not know what it is but they talked about Scarlet Fever. In any case, he is improving rapidly and back home out of the isolation ward." It was promptly diagnosed as scarlet fever. Immersed in the challenge of running the *Duyfken*, I was missing so much of my family life. The day would come when I would make a choice between family and ship.

Meanwhile, the sailing had been intoxicating for the crew. Glenn ordered safety lines on deck and everyone was required to wear safety harnesses. They covered an incredible 100 nm in a 12 hour period and 170nm over 24 hours. We estimated a 40 day passage from Port Louis to Cape Town but 21 days seemed possible. They recorded a top speed through the water of nine knots – impressive – but more was to come. Glenn was rolling the dice, or as he announced in his Captain's Log, he had the 'tiger by the tail'. Then they were struck by a Force 7 gale: a portent of even worse weather ahead and waves continually splashed over the deck and the wind contantly battered anyone on the poop deck. The tips of the lower yards often touched the foaming sea. Sometimes visibility was down to a few metres in the driving rain and the spray kicked up by the gales swept across the deck and it was difficult to stand up. When *Duyfken* clipped the northern zone of the Agulhas Bank, everyone who had been tracking the course through *Duyfken*'s daily plots (both the ones on our website and via Omnistar) contacted me. Capt Chris Bourne sent a message asking basically "what in the hell are they doing?" I had no answer so I sent a message to the ship. The reply came: "just been hit by a force 8 wind from the WSW presently making seven knots at 190 degrees with just courses and spritsail. All is well and we are comfortable. Tell Chris, on the Board, that we do not need to worry about abnormal waves as we are south of the known limit. I think this will be over by tomorrow morning, mind you, I have been known to be wrong. . . Tell the builders that between 1630 yesterday and 1630 today we made 170nm between 0800 this morning to 1600 today we made 80nm!" An incredible 10 knot average!

Every day while the ship was at sea I plotted her progress and checked the weather charts. Things were not looking good for *Duyfken*. I was at home, preparing to get on a plane to South Africa, when the first messages came through from Glenn on my email. They were heading into the eye of a storm and there was absolutely nothing I could do to help. Today, I have put it to the back of my mind, but Cathy reminds me that I didn't sleep at all that night, checking emails, contantly updating online weather and wave charts and plotting the course of the ship. *Duyfken* was south of Port Elizabeth with Cape Agulhus far to the west. Glenn had a lot to write about:

> *We pay our dues to the weather gods.*
> *Days run. 85 nm.*
>
> *The watches during the night have a quiet time with very dark skies, so black in fact that the near full moon is unable to penetrate. The wind still holds in favour for the night and when I arise for the morning it is still light but is beginning to back.*
> *At 0800 I take the watch from Alan and the breeze has stiffened considerably, we are both glad that he did not set the foretops'l. At*

0830 the wind continues to back around to the west and I am considering the option of wearing ship but then all hell breaks loose. We are struck by a very strong gust of around 30 knots, which gives us a considerable heel until the foresail's tack parts. This is a 32 mm diameter rope, which is worn, but it parts like string. The foresail rides up being now only controlled on the weather side by the sheet. At this point there is nothing serious and I take a moment to assess the problem. First the wind is much too strong to wear ship with one watch, so I call all hands. With the extra hands, I order to square the main and Christine who is on the helm to bear away, so as to run with the wind as we square the main. Greg stands by her to give her a hand and ensure we do not round up. Then it became obvious that the weather was saving itself as we were set upon by some strong gusts in excess of 40 knots, this causes the port main sheet lead block to break its strop and the main becomes free. No choice but to get the sail down. The order is given and the crew jump to it. Within 10 minutes, the sail is down and we are furling it to the yard. Once the sail is furled we go to the fore, brace it square and then bring the vessel onto a port tack with the yard braced up sharp to port. The wind is too strong for the spritsail and I order it to be taken in, we bear away again to assist the team out on the beak. As soon as the spritsail is secured in the beak we bring the vessel back into the wind on the port tack. The wind really kicks in now and I gave it an estimate of about 55-plus knots. The water is white with foam and spray. It is too much for the rig to handle and so I order Christine to again bear away and for the rest of the team to take in the foresail. Again this was performed in a very seamanlike manner and we soon had it under control. Now we have no sails up, both course yards are lowered, and still we make four knots under bare poles. Nicko has the helm now and it is obvious that it is hard to steer, so I have Greg grab some crew and set the spritsail again to try and give the vessel some direction and help steer. It is still difficult to keep the vessel running before the wind, I also note that the sea is rising. My thoughts are towards heaving to soon as I think we will ride better and not risk broaching when the seas have really become very big. Stijn takes over from Nicko an hour later and he is having all sorts of trouble holding a course. Soon he loses control and the vessel rounds up into the sea, broaching. The spritsail is aback and starting to bang around. I order the spritsail to be braced to try and bring the ship's head off of the wind but the windage from our raised poop is too much to overcome. Admitting that we were committed to lying hove to, I order the spritsail to be brought in and secured in the beak. Again this was smartly done in trying circumstances, and in a very short time we have the vessel all squared away. We begin the task now of repairing the broken rigging and making things ready for when we want to set sail again.

At this point all crew are in harnesses, which are clipped on to lifelines, these run the full length of the deck. We are also wearing our inflatable life jackets as a precautionary measure as well, at this stage the vessel is only just rolling to the sea. Later on the sea will increase and the risk of someone being rolled off is very real but the crew take all of this in their stride, proper precautions are taken everywhere.

I think that Julie is the quiet hero of the day, without any fuss she prepares our meals, which are both hot and very filling. This job is performed with the vessel rolling and pitching about, I think we all would like to say good on you, Julie.

With the helm lashed hard to port, the only jobs that are required are lookouts and Greg rightly points out that we should have two with such very poor visibility. The rest of the crew mend gear and help with all of the odd duties that need to be performed.

As we continue through the day hoved to, it becomes obvious that we are making to windward along our desired course at a speed of three knots! The Agulhas current has got a good grip on us and is helping. In fact the dilemma comes when the wind drops, if the wind stays in the west then we would probably make better ground to Cape Town with the sails down!

As the day progresses, I begin to see hope with the gusts becoming further spaced apart and the cloud beginning to lift. I give this storm 24 hours before coming back to normal. The main thing for now is to maintain an air of confidence, which in a way I do feel but somehow I do not feel that I am projecting this very well. It is obvious that there are a few members of our crew who are nervous of the situation, which is hardly surprising. I try and instil into the group the feeling that the vessel is handling these conditions very *well, which it is. In fact the way the* Duyfken *rises to the sea is amazing. I feel very comfortable with the situation and personally feel no fear of any sort but I have seen many more storms than most of my combined crew, so even though I am tense I know we will be ok. By mid afternoon the weather has abated quite a bit, the seas have risen considerably, but the vessel is sitting quite at ease in all of this and I feel the worst is over. During the middle of my watch the wind drops out considerably and apart from the swell the storm is all over.*

The disconcerting factor is that now the visibility has improved we are seeing ships approaching. I wonder how many slipped past without either of us knowing we were in the area? The stars are out and though we are still rolling quite violently we are all much more relaxed, we now all know that we can survive a storm such as we have just had, and what's more, survive it well.

Compared with the description of man against the elements published in the Captain's Log, a description I received only when I asked former crew members for their experiences aboard gives a sense of what the crew was facing. Nicole Gardner described wind of between Force 9 and 10: "The noise is amazing — it is a combination of a roar and several high notes as it blows through the rig." She described one night as eternal rolling, blowing and freezing. Here is her personal account:

"All hands on deck!" I jerked awake and tumbled out of my hammock, cursing whatever had prompted me to take my wet clothes off.

There were two options if you were wet: sleep in your wet clothes, or sleep dry and put the wet clothes back on in four hours. I'd decided to try sleeping dry for a change, and there was no time to get dressed. I scrambled up onto the dark deck in shorts and a singlet, and flinched from the driving hail. The duty watch had taken in the main topsail, so my watch dropped the fore topsail, then two of us went aloft to furl it.

There's a barrier of cold and exhaustion where my brain disconnects from my body. All I can do when I hit it is focus on the next step, the next movement. The next few hours are just disconnected flashes in my memory.

I remember climbing aloft when my fingers were too numb and I was shivering too hard to hold on. Seeing smears of blood on the sail and not knowing where they came from. Gratitude that my hands were too cold to feel it when the yard squashed them. Panic as my numb foot slipped off the damp cross-trees, leaving me dangling by one hand. Fumbling to grasp the wet flax canvas as it flapped in the wind. Struggling to tie knots in the stiff hemp rope. Realising that I wasn't shivering any more, but not understanding the implications. Half-sliding, half-falling down the slick shrouds to the deck.

By the time we'd secured the sails, checked the lashings on the cannons, anchors, and rescue boat, tidied up the deck, and helped the duty watch pump most of the water out, the sky was light and we were wide awake. My watch was due back on watch in only two hours, so I put the rest of my wet clothes on, wrapped myself in my sleeping bag, and shivered in my hammock until the next call, wondering why on earth I'd signed up for this.

When we took the watch again at 08:00, the wind had dropped and veered, so we set the topsails and headed south. On sailing vessels, when the wind's coming from the direction you want to go, you have to zig-zag back and forth to try to make progress in the right direction. It's known as tacking. It's not too bad on a yacht because they can sail quite close to the wind; on any sort of square-rigged ship, it's a frustrating and demoralising exercise in futility.

One wonderful thing about the Agulhas Current, off the coast of South Africa (which is where we were at the time), is that the current pushes ships to the west. As long as that's the direction you want to go, you're set!

When we calculated the day's run at noon, we were delighted to learn that, despite the wind being from the wrong direction, we were making good progress because of the current. In daylight, the damage from the night before was more obvious. Once we'd got the pumping out of the way, we started repairs.

Falling asleep after lunch was easy. Waking up to another all-hands call three hours later was hard. The wind had increased to gale force, and the duty watch needed help.

Sailing ships are designed for the wind to push the masts and sails from behind (astern). If the wind hits the ship from ahead, it can *break the masts. With that in mind, we turned the ship and trimmed the sails to put the wind astern.*

As soon as we turned around, the wind increased and things started breaking. First was the main sheet, which is a rope that controls the biggest sail. Once we'd got that under control, we took in the spritsail, our smallest sail at the front of the ship. While we were doing that, the foresail tack snapped.

By this time, the wind had increased to a violent storm, but with no sails up it was difficult to steer. This was a serious problem: if a ship is going downwind and she goes off course, the waves can roll the ship over. It's known as broaching, and it can sink the ship. We put the spritsail back up. It worked for a while, but the sail wasn't going to last, so we took it down again. By this time we were soaking wet, exhausted, and running out of options, so the captain decided to heave-to.

Heaving-to is a fancy name for taking all of the sails down, turning into the wind, lashing the helm, and waiting to see what happens. There's more to it, but that's the gist of it. By the time the ship settled (by which I mean she was rolling violently, but in no immediate danger), my watch was back on duty. With no steering, all we had to do was look out, pumping, and fix the broken sails and rigging.

In amongst it all, we ate something. I have no idea how the cook managed to cook anything in those conditions, but she did, and we loved her for it. When I finally got there, I loved my hammock even more.

Nick Burningham was stunned to see the 'vertical waves' feared by seafarers. He said he saw one particularly large wave which stood with a crown almost like a cobra's head that seemed to break into the foretop (halfway up the foremast). He was sure that it would curl like a surfing wave over the ship but somehow *Duyfken* just rose over it. He described the exhilaration of the next day:

The storm passed and we got under way again, then we were becalmed, then beset by more strong wind from dead ahead, but on the 8th the wind went round to the south and in conditions where we would normally furl the topsails we started a race for Cape Town before the next depression came through. The wind went round to

> the east and increased but we held on to all our square sails, storming past Cape Agulhas at maximum speed, surfing down steep seas with the lion figurehead skimming the troughs. She steered beautifully in those circumstances. Every ship that saw us must have thought they'd come upon the Flying Dutchman, and indeed they had!"

Duyfken and her crew had survived their greatest test.

After the excitement of the storms and record 24 hour runs, Simonstown in South Africa was an anti-climax for the crew. Tracy and I had been working for months to arrange a refit in the dockyard. Its history went back to the VOC in the eighteenth century and the Royal Navy's famous battle cruiser, HMS *Hood,* was dry docked where we were lifted. Even with fresh anti-fouling applied in Sydney, the hull was still covered with barnacles and slime. The ship would have even more speed once it had a fresh coat of paint. I arranged for a painting contractor, Gary Brinkley, to clean and repaint the hull with anti-fouling but it was still up to us to prepare the surface. This was boring, hot and dirty work. Another contractor was engaged to kill the bugs which lived in our fuel tanks and to clean and filter the fuel. This probably was caused by the poor diesel we bought in Indonesia. Once again, teredo worm was in the hull and this time we engaged a couple of local shipwrights to help our Ship's Carpenter, Mike Redding, to chop it out and make a repair.

The crew was tired and the same old gripes surfaced again but some conflicts were getting very personal. It also was concerning that a routine check of the medical cabinet showed large quantities of some items missing, including 100 tablets which could not be accounted for. On a brighter note, hospitality shown by the members of the False Bay Yacht Club was heartwarming. One of the crew wrote: "Someone turned up on the dock when we arrived in Simonstown, cooked us a barbecue with meat while we waited for the formalities to finish, then took us home in turns for a shower and to check our email. I can't remember who he was, but I wish I could thank him. His wife said they did that for all the yachties who arrived in Simonstown. A local lady delivered lunch to us in the shipyard every day. For the first few days, she carefully made sandwiches, which we'd eat, then go out of the shipyard to the bakery and buy two meat pies each. When she realised, she took it well — and started providing us with meat pies rather than sandwiches, much to our relief."

Confident that the short run from Simonstown to Cape Town would not cause me too much pain, I went aboard the ship with Rinze Brandsma, Board Member David Kerbey, Tracy McCullough, James Holdsworth and Dr Tim Ackland. It was a beautiful run around the Cape of Good Hope. As the wind picked up in the afternoon, I was asked to steer the ship using the whipstaff. With Table Mountain in the background, *Duyfken* skated along at a superb 6.5 knots and I struggled to hold the ship while she ploughed through the white-capped waves. It was an exhilarating ride but I was happy to pass over the helm to someone more experienced and skilled when I couldn't keep her on course. I could imagine what the crew would say if we broached while I was steering.

Since 1503, when the Portuguese first entered Table Bay, the Cape of Good Hope was a place to re-supply European ships heading east and returning to Europe from Asia. The shipwreck of the VOC ship, *Nieuwe Haarlem,* in 1647 began the Dutch settlement in the Cape. The survivors built a small fort and named it 'Sand Fort of the Cape of Good Hope', seeking refuge for a year before being rescued by a fleet of VOC ships. In April 1652, Jan van Riebeeck established a permanent provision station for the VOC, supplying fresh water and produce for the large sailing ships. In 1795, the English seized the prosperous colony. We were unaware that, before we in Cape Town, protesters condemned the VOC year commemorations, citing the land theft they say was perpetrated by Van Riebeeck against the Khoikhoi and San peoples of the region. They demanded that his statue be pulled down and that it should be locked up in a prison, as a symbol of what should have been done to van Riebeeck for committing crimes against the people he subjugated.

Nick Malherbe, who had been such a great help in facilitating the port visit, put on quite a welcome for us. Nick was as eccentric a person as you would ever meet. He described himself as a cultural historian of Huguenot descent. The Huguenots arrived from France to the VOC colony to escape religious persecution in France. They left an indelible mark on the colonial society. The South African wine industry began when they planted the first vines near Table Mountain.

Nick loved the history of the Huguenots and the VOC and he was a stickler for historical authenticity. He was also incredibly racist. On the back window of his decrepit BMW car he had a picture of himself with a massive boa constrictor wrapped around his torso. The photograph had been taken at a wildlife park in Florida. It had the heading 'CAUTION: SNAKE HANDLER' above the image and then a few lines of text below warning that snakes were carried inside. I asked him why he had this on the back of the car and he said: "The blacks hate snakes, and my car has never been stolen since I put that sign on the window." When he briefed me on the welcome he planned for the ship at the Victoria and Alfred Waterfront, he told me that it would have a mix of "Cape white and coloured people" but no black Africans.

When I questioned Nick Malherbe about why he was not planning to involve any black people in the welcome, he replied: "At the time of the VOC to 1795, the black man had not been encountered at the Cape. The settlers moving north met the black people moving south, about 800 miles north of the Cape at the Kei River, between Durban and East London. Thus, historically, a Cape descendants welcome is correct." He gave no recognition to the Khoikhoi who were displaced by the VOC settlers at the Cape. The welcome was a delight, notwithstanding the complete lack of recognition of the majority of South Africa's population! Nick came dressed like a soldier straight out of a Rembrandt painting. He was very hospitable, but for people like him who relished the past, the times they were a changing, as the song goes. One afternoon he took me to a traditional braai (barbecue) with his friends. Late in the evening, when the red wine started to do the talking, he got into a short fist fight with a woman when he fronted up against her. She had the temerity to talk about a 'new' South Africa where everyone could live in harmony. By the time *Duyfken* set sail from Cape Town, 3,000 people had visited the ship. We'd hoped for more.

The simmering problems with the crew had come to a head on the passage from Mauritius to Simonstown and I had asked Rinze, as Chairman of the Foundation, to come to Cape Town specifically to help Glenn and I address the issue. We arranged a series of formal meetings with the individuals involved and one crew member left for Fremantle.

With the wisdom of hindsight, I should have made substantial changes to the crew in Cape Town. A fresh start was in order but I was still committed to this group finishing the journey to Texel. It was now an exercise in mental endurance but we believed that the remaining crew would stick it out. After discussing life aboard with the crew, Tim Ackland devised a self-paced exercise program. Some embraced his exercise program and others completely ignored it, regarding it as a ridiculous joke and blaming Glenn. It was not his idea, it was mine, but battle lines had been drawn aboard the ship. Those that persisted with the program found it increased the release of endorphins, they were more flexible and then had more stamina. They also said that they had improved decision-making after exercising. The exercise program survived on the ship for several months but ultimately, it was a failure. After the voyage, Tim reflected on his program and evaluated what had happened after the crew had effectively abandoned it: "The combination of bad weather, slow progress, sickness and the inability to exercise daily eventually began to take its toll on the crew during the long passage from Ascension Island to the Azores. Some of the crew began to suffer mental fatigue. It was noted that many could not focus on a job for more than 10 minutes, others became withdrawn and easily depressed, and tempers flared quickly at the slightest hint of aggression. These problems were lessened, however, when favourable winds sped them to their next landfall." It was another lesson learned on this long voyage.

Rinze Brandsma and I were keen to visit Mossel Bay which was a short distance up the coast. On 3 February 1488, Bartolomeu Dias was the first European to sail into the bay. It was also the first time recorded in history that southern African people encountered Europeans. Dias was trying to find a sea route to the east. The Portuguese built a caravel to re-enact his voyage from Lisbon in Portugal in 1987 and it was placed in a museum after the voyage. We thought the Museum's treatment of this point in history would be interesting. We wanted to see whether the idea worked as a tourist attraction and what we could learn about it. We wanted to begin working on a long term home for *Duyfken* in Fremantle. The building almost deserted when we arrived, and lacking any atmosphere. We flew back to Cape Town unimpressed and knowing that the *Duyfken* Seaport idea was a better option.

With the voyage ahead of schedule, we agreed to the VOC Committee's request to add another port to the Atlantic Ocean stopovers. With fatigue so evident in the crew, perhaps another port could help them survive the rigours of the longer passages ahead. VOC 2002 funded archaeological work on the 1747 wreck of the *Vlissingen* on Namibia's 'Skeleton Coast'. The ship of 1,000 tonnes (compared to the *Duyfken*'s 110 tons), made four successful journeys to the East and back before she perished on the treacherous shore. Our plan was to sail to the small port of Walvis Bay which serviced the offshore diamond mining industry.

Benno and Giulia van Tilburg saw that I was being drained by the constant problems with 'that schip' as they called it, and I needed a break. They persuaded me to take time away from *Duyfken* after she sailed from Cape Town. I agreed to drive with them from Cape Town to Namibia via

Springbok, visit the renowned Fish River Canyon near Keetmanshoop, and the national capital of Windhoek, before driving across the desert to Swakopmund to meeti the ship at Walvis Bay. It was a 1,700 km trip. Shannon McGuire found the last leg of the voyage very demanding and she had always wanted to see Africa since she was a child. She asked whether she could join us and re-board the ship at Walvis Bay. We agreed and we hired a car for four.

It turned out to be an epic road trip. With equal doses of ignorance and blissful over confidence, we decided to divert from the main road north and look for a more scenic coast road. Soon we were totally lost on a sandy track in the middle of the bush somewhere north of Lambert's Bay surrounded by a flock of ostriches which wasn't the least perturbed by our presence. Then my phone (which had been out of range almost since Cape Town) rang. It was Cathy calling from Perth saying that her handbag had been stolen and a hold had been placed on our shared credit card. I couldn't use my card. I told her that we also had a problem — we were lost on a bush track somewhere in Africa and surrounded by ostriches. The last thing I would be doing at this moment was using a credit card!

We stumbled onto the main road again and continued heading north towards Namibia, taking an overnight break at Springbok. The border was defined by the Orange River. It was named by Colonel Robert Gordon in 1779 when he was on an expedition from Cape Town. He was the VOC garrison commander and he named the river in honour of William V of Orange. It was hard to get away from VOC links even so far from the ocean.

As we were approaching the border, I asked for everyone to make sure they had their passports. Then Shannon offhandedly replied from the back seat, "I don't have one." We couldn't believe it. All she had was a debit card. She naively thought she could explain to the border officials that she had left it on the ship. I wasn't going to take an American to a border post in the wilds of Africa without identification. I had visions of her being arrested and ending up in a detention centre somewhere. There was no option but for her to leave us and return to the Cape by bus to get a temporary passport issued by the US Consul. If she could get one in time, she'd have to join us later in Windhoek or Walvis Bay.

With our car fading into the distance and 435 Rand (about US$36) in her pocket, Shannon decided that she would try to grease someone's palm to get across the border, reasoning that the passport was on the ship and once she was in Namibia, the problem would disappear. She could simply catch a bus to the next port of call at Walvis Bay. She approached the South African border guard. Incredibly, he let her cross the border without a passport, but with a warning that she wouldn't be able to get into Namibia and that if she returned to South Africa he would lock her up. She slipped the last remaining money she had between some papers and handed it to the Namibian border official who slipped the money into his pocket, gave her back the papers, and sent her back to the South African border post. True to his word, the South African border official put her in a holding cell and called the US Consulate to tell them that they had detained a US citizen.

Shannon could hear the response from the woman at the other end of the phone as she shouted to the border official, "She's an American citizen! Let her out now!" Eventually she was released and the border official issued her with a 24 hour pass. It was late afternoon, and it was soon dark as she walked into the small border town of Vioolsdrif. She was now penniless. "I saw a cash machine on a wall. I had a debit card from a US bank in my pocket but I knew it didn't have any money in it. I put the card in the machine, punched my code and it gave me 4,000 Rand (about $330) in one go. It was a miracle!" she said. "So I shoved the card in again, and it gave me another 4,000 Rand. I tried again but my luck ran out. It said: 'No Funds.'"

Then she walked across the street and knocked on a door with an illuminated 'Rooms for Let' sign above it. "A lovely elderly British woman in a bathrobe with an enormous dog by her side answered the door and let me in. She was very kind and she put a blanket on her couch and let me sleep the night. She made me breakfast in the morning and arranged for me to catch a mini-bus to Cape Town." It was an epic, 18-stop trip.

Our man in Cape Town, Nick Malherbe, came to Shannon's rescue. "When I needed to leg it back to get a new passport, he took me in for the night and what an adventure that was," she said. Nick was determined to give his hapless visitor a good time. "It was the first and only time I have ever posed as 'elbow candy' for a man but he and I played it up so greatly that the gents at his club would be toasting his successes with that pretty young sailor lass for years to come. It was again the stuff of legends, and in spite of my precarious situation, he was impeccable in his decorum and honour and shuttled me safely from embassy to airline so I could make it to Namibia at last." The miracle at the cash machine was later explained. A friend had been borrowing Shannon's Jeep while she was away, and making regular payments into her bank account to cover the loan repayments on the car. It was fortuitous that the monthly payment had been transferred into her account but it had not yet been transferred out by the bank to the loan account. It was, indeed, a miraculous stroke of luck.

While Shannon had been heading south again, we made it to the our destination. Compared with its rival, the Grand Canyon in the USA, the Fish River Canyon was deserted. We counted fewer than 20 tourists while we were there. We stayed in the spectacular Cañon Lodge in stone huts nestled amongst massive granite boulders. Windhoek struck me as a small but prosperous capital city. Unfortunately, Benno and Giulia ran out of time to make the final part of the trip from the mountains to Walvis Bay so we said our farewells and we agreed to meet in Amsterdam a few months later. It was back to work.

The prospect of driving on my own to the coast did not appeal to me and I was asked whether I could give a ride to a university student who was returning home to Walvis Bay for her Christmas holidays. She spoke a little English but her main language was Oshiwambo and, like many Namibians, she also spoke some German. It was a spectacular drive through the Gamsberg Nature Reserve down to the Namib-Naukluft National Park across a sandy desert landscape. There was almost no road, just wheel tracks across the compacted sand, and we could drive as fast as the car could go.

After driving for hours on the deserted track, way ahead in the distance we could see a car broken down and people waving madly in the middle of the road. It was the only car we'd seen for hours. I said I would stop to see if I could help them. My passenger started getting agitated and shouted "No. Don't stop. Speed up!" I could see they were white people and with my racist stereotyping, I thought that it would be OK. She kept shouting: "Speed up. Speed up!" So we raced past them as they shrugged their shoulders and nodded their heads. She then told me that nobody stops for anyone broken down out there. Too many people have been robbed and murdered when they thought they would do the right thing and be good samaritans. A few hours later, I dropped her off at her parent's fabulous brightly-painted house so typical of the old houses in Walvis Bay. I think she couldn't wait to get out of that foolish Australian's car.

Our hosts in Walvis Bay were Hans van der Veen, who was the First Secretary at the Dutch Embassy in Windhoek, and Gunter Kock, who was the Commodore of the Walvis Bay Yacht Club. I rang Gunter as soon as I arrived and he said that he would come around to the hotel and collect me. After living in Walvis Bay for 30 years, there was nobody he didn't know. Our first stop was the Yacht Club and just as we walked in the bell at the bar was rung. It was a member's birthday so everyone appeared from out of the woodwork and glasses were put in a long line and filled with schnapps. After a rousing German song it was cheers all round. How strange to be in Africa singing German beer drinking songs. That set the tone for my visit to Walvis Bay. It was a very hospitable town and they couldn't have been more welcoming. Unfortunately, the lee shore, which has trapped many seafarers in its thick sea mist, was not the crew's greatest problem. It was simply a lack of wind to drive them to the bay. They averaged barely more than three knots on a glassy sea and the crew amused themselves watching sea lions playing around the ship. I waited and waited. Hans, Gunter and I made plans, then changed plans. Then we waited some more. The days were ticking off before Christmas. I was becoming agitated by the delay. I was not about to lose this time at home with my family after missing so many birthdays and spending so much time travelling. Christmases were sacrosanct. I knew I'd spent too many months away. I got the message when I arrived home after one trip and when I walked through the front door expecting a hugs all round, the children wouldn't stop watching television. Once I returned home to find that we had a new puppy.

My problem was that the air route between Johannesburg and Perth was only served by South African Airways and Qantas, and at Christmas all the seats were booked months ahead. To get home in time, I had to drive back to Windhoek, then catch a connecting flight to Johannesburg to connect with one of the twice-weekly flights to Australia. The services were overbooked so there was no way of deferring the flight for a couple of days. I was in a quandary — family or ship? I chose family, and Glenn let me know that he wasn't happy that I wouldn't wait around for the ship to arrive. Really, it was hardly a problem. Shannon would be at Walvis Bay with her temporary US passport and she had everything in hand as my representative. I was made to feel like I had let everyone down. This mental assault only intensified as the months drew on.

When Shannon arrived at Walvis Bay, Gunter and his partner, Heidi, treated her as a VIP. "There in the heart of Africa, at a Swiss looking chalet complete with red geranium window boxes, we ate German bratwurst and borsch. Such a splendid and bizarre treat!" she said.

The ship eventually arrived on 11 December and, with help from her new friends, Shannon completed all the last minute arrangements for the visit. Nicole Gardner and Brett Yates were interviewed by a local newspaper called The Namibian Youthpaper. They were quite candid in their responses to questions about life aboard the ship: "After seven months onboard, 26-year-old Brett Yates of England still calls his boyhood dream come true 'an event of a lifetime'. Nicola (sic) Gardner of Australia has been onboard since the ship's maiden voyage two years ago and loves it. She plans to stay as long as possible. Her experience so far has taught her the most important lesson for survival: 'If you do not stick together you die'. . . He (Brett) says it is a life of extremes, recalling a storm they encountered while sailing around South Africa. 'The swell crashed over the side of the ship just like in the movies. The deck was like a swimming pool. Then there was the close encounter with a minke whale, about two-thirds the size of the ship, in the Indian Ocean. He dived underneath the ship and was so close we could see his eyes. An event Yates would never forget was the night somewhere between Sri Lanka and Mauritius when they were surrounded by phosphorence in the ocean. Dolphins were swimming around leaving a streak of light behind them."

Duyfken wouldn't have visited Walvis Bay without the VOC connection. On the Cape, the local Khoikhoi herders encountered the Dutch traders on their land in 1652, but Europeans visited much earlier. Bartolomeu Dias anchored his flagship *São Cristóvão* in Walvis Bay in 1487, but the first VOC ships to sail into the bay were the *Grundel* and the *Boode* which visited in 1670 and 1677. With the VOC well-established at the Cape, there was no need for a settlement further along the treacherous coastline.

The National Monuments Council of Namibia, the Namibian Underwater Federation and the Dutch Embassy in Windhoek were working on a project to locate the wreck of the VOC ship *Vlissingen*. A University of Namibia student, Martha Akawa, prepared an exhibition to coincide with our visit It documented the arrival of a VOC ship to Walvis Bay in 1793. The VOC wanted the crew to search for a fabled copper mine said to be an eight day ride from the coast. Martha Akawa said: "One of the crew walked for six hours over heavy sand hills and found a big, dry river that abounded in big game such as rhinoceros, elephants, wild horses and another animal unknown at the Cape of Good Hope". Over 12 days the sailors killed 20 rhinos and three elephants in the river bed. The captain of the ship commented that "whales are so abundant here ... for the whole shore is strewn with a great many carcasses of all possible shapes and sizes for a distance of three miles to the south of the bay up to the mouth of the Rhinoceros River". It must have been a fascinating place in those days.

Leaving Walvis Bay on 16 December 2001, Glenn sought the southeasterly winds of the great trade-wind belt that circles the southern hemisphere from the tropics to the temperate zone. His destination was lonely St Helena. Christmas was celebrated at sea and the ship arrived on Boxing Day. The crew found St Helena to be a beautiful, verdant island. It was a critical watering point for the VOC ships of old. It was often used to re-group the fleets. Like Cape Town, St Helena ended up in English hands. Now in the South Atlantic with pleasant sailing conditions, the crew could see that the end of the voyage was only months away. Morale improved for a few weeks. Our sailing passage northwards through the Atlantic had more port stopovers for re-provisioning than the VOC ships enjoyed. The next was the small island of Ascension, 750 miles north-west of St Helena. It was discovered by the Portuguese seafarer, Joao da Nova Castelia, in 1501, although this visit apparently went unrecorded. It was found again two years later on Ascension Day by the Spanish explorer, Alphonse d'Albuquerque, who gave the island its name.

We were now eight months into a 12 months voyage. *Duyfken* was 242 days out of Sydney and making five knots towards Ascension Island. The short stay in Ascension would be followed by *Duyfken*'s longest passage to date. Glenn was now reflecting on the time at sea:

> *I think now it is important to begin to emphasise to all of the crew what a remarkable feat that they are achieving and to take note of these last few months as it will be all over in a flash. One thing is for sure, this last leg, which will be the longest in the voyage, will certainly be the toughest challenge that most of our crew will have ever faced. The challenge will not be physical but mental. Everyone is showing signs of mental fatigue and mistakes are beginning to come to light. There is a lack of energy and enthusiasm as the long months of continuous work and living in a very small space begins to tell. Very few people in this world can handle the long hours, cramped space, lack of privacy and demanding discipline that is required to make a voyage such as this possible. I think when we have finished all of us will look back and be amazed that we achieved it. We will be both proud and disappointed with our roles and the way in which we conducted ourselves but we will all I think recognise that we have changed a bit in looks and a lot in our attitudes towards life. There is nothing like a really long and arduous adventure to change a person.*

This personal meditation did not speak to the far more disturbing reality most of the crew were experiencing. Individual crew members told me that they withdrew into a private zone. The Ship's Carpenter, Mike Redding, constructed partitions in the hold so that crew members could have a measure of privacy. Lit only by tiny globes strung across from cubicle to cubicle, this was where the crew members retreated between working on watch and eating meals. Even with a crew of only 16 aboard, cliques developed. Glenn spent hours behind the closed door of the Captain's Cabin with Heidy. Greg and Alice, Shannon and Brett, and Mike and Julie could share the experience with their partner. For the singles aboard, life was more difficult, and the loneliness more acute when they could see the partners providing each other with support. The singles were attracted to people of the same age and world experience with whom they could share time and talk. I can only imagine how difficult it must have been aboard for those without partners or close friendships. After the voyage, John Quigley was asked by The Age newspaper about the conflicts aboard: "Yes, there have been fights — verbal fights, and not everyone loves each other. But given the diverse range of personalities aboard and our confinement I'm surprised how well that it's gone." He was asked what qualities were required to be a crew member of *Duyfken*? "An insanely strong sense of adventure and a complete lack of forethought." And asked whether he would do it again, he said: "No way in Hell!"

Nicole Gardner reflected on life aboard:

> *Meals were the highlights of our lives, and our cook (Julie Milne) was a genius. She only had dry stores to work with, but she managed to make porridge, rice, beans and lentils taste like gourmet meals three times a day for months on end. The fact that we were always ravenous probably helped. The process of eating was more challenging than you'd expect: a few weeks into the voyage, a tired crew member tipped all of the cutlery and most of the bowls overboard with the washing up water. Porridge and dahl aren't designed to be eaten with fingers (But rice is! - Ed); belt knives are not a good substitute for spoons.*"
>
> "*Living in close quarters with 16 strangers is always challenging. Add in a chronic lack of sleep, relentless work, the total absence of home comforts, and the complete lack of meaningful communication with the outside world, and you'll understand the*

reason for the frequent and wide-ranging disagreements: everything from food rationing, to the correct way to secure a cannon in bad weather, to the relative benefits of beef tallow over mutton tallow as leather dressing were fodder for heated arguments. After a year onboard, one crew member observed, 'This ship treads a fine line between character-building and soul-destroying.' He was right. Despite that, we loved Duyfken.

"The *Duyfken* voyage was a challenge in many ways. The teachings and understandings it has paid out over these years have been gold," said Shannon. She only began to understand when reflecting on life aboard many years later. "I often think of sailing 'full and by' remembering to keep my nose into the wind but remaining vigilant so as not to luff the sail and be set aback. Keeping a course that is true and keeping my eye on the heading regardless of the swell or tack buffeting my way has also been a plumb line of remembrance. I also think of progress at times in miles gained beating it to windward only to lose the mileage and more over the next watches only to gain it again in the next go around. Cycles, seasons, gains, losses, mustering to bloom, all of these lesson plans unfolded for me in the extraordinary classroom *Duyfken* offered."

Up to this part of the voyage, the crew enjoyed mostly favourable winds but the winds became more fickle after crossing the equator. Perhaps being so close to the final destination and with thoughts moving to life after the VOC2002 *Duyfken* Expedition, people became more agitated. The pervading mood aboard was worse than at any other stage of the voyage. Nerves were frayed, minds wandered, and molehills become mountains. I became concerned that the crew would fall apart, so my emails to the ship became focused only on achieving the goal rather than critiquing the troubling stories I was being told about the crew dynamics.

Like the VOC ships of the past, *Duyfken* was forced to ghost through the doldrums and claw her way northwards against the north-east trade winds until she reached higher latitudes and westerly winds to carry her to Europe. The Azores Islands were the next port of call. The first regular visits to these mid-Atlantic islands were thought to have been by Flemish fishermen. In 1492, Christopher Columbus visited Santa Maria on his way back from the Caribbean. Vasco da Gama, returning from India in 1499, stopped over in Angra where he buried his deceased brother. In the 1600s, the Dutch and the Portuguese were great trading rivals. The Portuguese island of Faial was a useful re-provisioning stop for us, but out of bounds for the VOC ships of old. The popular cruising yacht port of Horta was our destination. It was accustomed to receiving modern square-rigged sailing ships as many European sail training ships used the port as a stopover. After the long ocean passage there would be a lot to do to in port make the ship presentable for her arrival at Texel. As usual, I arrived at Faial loaded down with supplies for the ship. The bulk of my baggage comprised large rubber ship's fenders which I purchased in The Netherlands before flying to Portugal.

The ship was only two years old but she required constant maintenance. The ocean placed enormous stresses on her. In the quest for authenticity, the ship had a range of natural fibres, hemp in the sails and flax for the rigging. Constant pounding flexed the standing rigging and it had to be re-tensioned often so that the masts would not come down. Unlike modern sailcloth and ropes, the hemp and flax rotted from exposure to rain water and sunlight. Large gasket seals were made from cow leather. The crew constantly applied a range of mixes using tallow, fish oil, pine tar, linseed oil, gum turpentine, beeswax and tallow. Eventually it washed off and it was reapplied. Despite outside appearances of dark timber and stained sails, the ship was in excellent condition with a crew aboard. There was always something to oil and natural products seemed to do a better job than modern petrochemical wonder coatings. In spite of the constant care of the crew, some lines rotted from the inside and simply broke apart. Bolt ropes on the sails often had to be sewn back on after parting ways, and the sails ripped in heavy winds requiring more repairs. As the sails aged, more time needed to be spent on repairs. The endless cycle of life aboard required the crew to be motivated. It was not just a question of keeping the ship in a good state of repair, it was also about safety aboard. A poorly maintained ship is a death trap.

The passage north in the Atlantic was hard going. Glenn was becoming more introspective: "Getting harder and harder to motivate people into action now, it is a chore to put all of the gear on to go out on deck. In fact most of the time it is a chore just to stay upright let alone move about."

Christine Henschien suffered stomach cramps for a month (most likely a stomach ulcer), then Stein came down with the flu and Shannon succumbed, too. The crew, already suffering from fatigue, were being kept awake by Christine's constant groaning in pain. Mike hurt his back, and on 17 February, Heidy hurt her back again. One crew member later said that the thing she wanted most on that long leg of the voyage was simply a fresh salad. Despite all this, the ship was three weeks ahead of the original schedule we had set. Outwardly, all appeared to be going well.

Marit van Huystee, the Dutch linguist who did such a splendid job determining the history of the original *Duyfken*, was now living in Amsterdam, and Benno van Tilburg asked her to coordinate the ship's summer exhibition season in The Netherlands for the VOC 2002 Foundation. She flew with me to Portugal to meet the ship. We booked into a hotel called the Estalagem de Santa Cruz. Set in a sixteenth century fort overlooking the port, it would give us a good view of *Duyfken* sailing into the bay set against the volcanic peak of Mt Pico on the adjacent island. That was, of course, if *Duyfken* was able to make it against the prevailing winds.

The 3,480 nm passage plan from Ascension Island to the Azores had the ship arriving to Faial Island on 21 February, but the arrival was set back a week to about 1 or 2 March. With no sign of the ship, Marit returned to Amsterdam on 4 March 2002 and I waited on my own. My time in Horta waiting for the ship turned into a daily routine. Firstly I took breakfast alone overlooking the harbour, then I left the hotel for a short walk to the famous Peter's Cafe Sport bar. This little nautical-themed bar is an institution amongst trans-Atlantic sailors, a meeting place and watering hole that has been serving travellers for a century. Tracy found it almost impossible to get accommodation for the crew on this small island and the owner of the cafe, Peter Azevedo, assisted us by sourcing homestay accommodation all over the small town.

Every morning I checked the faxed weather map on the pin-up board and lamented that the ship would not be arriving that day. Then I had a coffee while I checked my emails and walked down the road to see our shipping agent, Marco, to let him know that it would be at least another day until we sighted the vessel. The rest of the day was taken up with working on my laptop at Cafe Sport or another cafe, if I could find one open in the off-season. I filled in the time with many, many long walks. One day, I returned to the hotel and the manager asked whether she could have a quiet word. My credit card was frozen. She very kindly said that I could stay at the hotel but I had to sort out a payment as soon as possible. It didn't make any sense and I had neither cash nor an alternative card. It turned out that the bank froze my account automatically. It installed a new fraud alert program which flagged my account for buying thousands of euros worth of rubber fenders in The Netherlands and then spending large chunks of money in the Azores. It took hours of phone calls to Australia late in the evening to get the card freed up. The only person who could authorise the clearance worked 9 to 5 in Sydney.

I could think of a worse island to be trapped on. It was a beautiful, friendly place but I didn't fancy being stuck in Horta for longer than I needed. The fantasy romance of running a voyage around the world with a replica sailing ship was now replaced with the grim reality of fulfilling my commitment to deliver the ship and crew on time for the anniversary events and on budget. I was trapped in a story of my own making, a dream which had become an obsession. The loneliness of almost constant travel was beginning to take its toll. My life was lived through emails with home. I became increasingly isolated from everyone — my family, the crew, our staff and the Board of the Foundation. I was alone on an island in the Atlantic. My leadership was constantly being challenged by emails from the ship. I was the whipping boy. Oblique criticism of the decisions I had made were inserted into mundane messages. It was clear that the factions within the crew were becoming increasingly vocal and Glenn was struggling to keep the critics at bay. On the previous Expedition, Peter and Gary were two elite square-rig sailors with many years of experience between them. The crew looked up to them as masters of the craft. Glenn did not have a highly-credentialed first officer to share the responsibilities of leadership.

On 3 March, *Duyfken* had made only 14nm towards Faial and she still had 133nm to go. The strain onboard went to another level. They were running out of food with only tins of sardines and beans, pasta, and old flour to eat. Julie expected her food supplies to only last another week. Glenn contacted me to ask whether I could arrange a food drop by air but he was too far away from Faial for any available aircraft to make it. I told him that he would just have to plug on. One good day under sail would get the ship to the Azores.

Cold driving squalls and unsettled seas made ordinary work aboard the ship extremely difficult. Then the crew missed a change in wind direction and the ship lost position. The ocean was angry and intimidating. They ended the day further away from the Azores than where they had been 24 hours before. Crew morale by this stage had completely broken down. The patchwork of personal relationships was now causing deep dissent and there was even talk by a crew member about self-harm. Ed Biermans, the Dutch First Mate who joined in Cape Town to replace Andrea Cicholas, openly questioned the decision-making. It was crunch time. Glenn called a crew meeting on 5 March 2002 and what follows is his report of the day:

We continue northward with a slight trend towards the east. This keeps getting us closer to our goal but we are going to end up to the west of Horta and the winds are not going to be in our favour for the moment. Being closer is a good thing though it gives us confidence that we are going to make it.

As with all problems when you have a group of people you have a large source of expert advice on what to do when things get difficult. It is a bit like having a chess game in the park with onlookers giving continuous well-meaning advice that they are sure will be the winning move. The catch is when it goes wrong and who is responsible then? The hindsight debate is a big thing in the hold at present and I find it amazing as to what decisions I should have made, if only I could have known then. It is always the same so I never let it worry me, but I do find it an interesting part of human nature.

The new weather chart does not bode well for us as it stands, a high has formed to the NNE of us and looks to be giving us more easterlies, not good. On the up side the Sat 'C' forecast is predicting that this new high will move to the east, which could be just what we need. We continue on in hope of that favourable wind change, if we are close enough we may just make it.

It is a fine day today and clothes make their way out on deck to be dried. Brett has made the ultimate sacrifice and has decided to wash his clothes. I have to mention this classic statement from him 'it is not until you wash your clothes that you realise how smelly you actually are'. We have tried to tell him before but I think for some they have to experience it before they learn. On a good note both Brett and Shannon have been excellent with their positive attitude and easy going banter. It is a welcome distraction from other conversations and I must say I thank them both for their sunny disposition.

The midday crew meeting proved to be a very heated affair. After giving my talk about what we have done in the past 24 hours and what I am expecting the weather to do, I opened the meeting for questions and comments. Ed immediately asked if we will start motoring to Horta should the wind drop out again. I knew this was coming but was not pleased with the way it was brought up. I then found out why. Ed wanted to have a debate then a hidden ballot to decide whether we should motor or sail on, using the meeting as a means to force me to do what he thinks is the right thing. Unfortunately I had to remind him in public that there is only one person aboard who makes the decisions like this and that is myself. I hate leadership issues. Democratic choice stopped when everyone on their own, made the decision to join the ship. It obviously did not go down well and I feel sorry for him as he is becoming negative and depressed. Something is bothering him. Maybe it is in regard to our situation, but that is just what we do not want, as it affects everyone and leaders must lead. This question, however, had brought up the whole debate of what do the crew think we should do? Most would appear to want to sail all the way, after all we have stuck it out for the last 60 days, to motor would make a mockery of it. We are, however, all concerned about Christine who is still having stomach pains. While these are not life threatening, she is beginning to give up, having reached her limit of tolerance. As I am not trained medically, having only completed my shipmasters medical training (six days to learn how to be a first aider, paramedic, nurse, doctor and, of course, palliative care), I must take what she says as being serious. We are not likely to be sailing into Horta in the immediate future. This means I have little to no choice but to call in for help. I do not feel that this is the right thing to do, I would rather not draw upon the resources of the Portuguese Government and solve this our own way, but as I am in an area where I am not specifically trained I must take the safest course. The discussion then centred about should we motor? Most say no, as for all, one of the reasons to join the voyage was to avoid motoring and sail to Europe. This is all very well but, of course, most had forgotten that we cannot motor into this sort of weather. This is on top of the fact that earlier when the vessel was not rolling as much Alan had a look at our tanks and determined that we have 300 litres less than he reported last time. The final point, none of the people who want to sail all the way are ill. The debating really, I think, was more for the crew to let off steam as none of it was anything new to what I had already been debating within myself for the past week. My decision was that we keep sailing and find a way to have Christine, with Stijn accompanying her, taken off.

The obvious thing to do was to call Graeme who is in Horta and ask could he arrange a vessel to make the trip out but he came back and suggested we call the Marine Rescue Co-ordination Centre in

Delgada and have them conduct the operation. Contact has been made and we have started the proceedings. As with all of this, we are likely to sail in when the pick up vessel arrives. There are some alternatives, one is that we sail to Flores where there is an airport! Unfortunately while we would be able to send our invalid ashore we would also have added another 60 nm to our journey, the port is also open to easterlies but it could be the best option. I hope we could do this as it would be far less dramatic and so I am looking into this possibility. Need a few answers first.

As has been the case for the past week the wind is holding in the right direction for us if we were where we were three days ago ie. due south of Horta.

Where are the westerlies that we need or southerly or any wind except that which blows from the direction we wish to go?

At 2.30 in the afternoon of the midday crew meeting, I received an email from Glenn and he requested an evacuation of his sick crew members. I asked him to contact the Marine Rescue Co-ordination Centre (MRCC) directly (as the authorities required direct contact with the ship rather than an intermediary) then I went down to the naval police station at the port to report the incident and get things moving. Even though I can't speak more than a few words of Portuguese, I got by speaking Spanish and I explained the situation to them. Then I advised the Australian consul. Walking back from Peter's Cafe Sport, I saw Marco striding up towards me. News travels fast and we talked about what to do next. We fell into our crisis plan. Tracy in Australia contacted Christine's mother in The Netherlands and for the rest of the afternoon and late into the evening I made phone calls and worked up alternative ways to extract Christine from the ship. The news had already reached The Netherlands and the newspaper De Telegraaf ran a story headlined 'Food shortage Onboard VOC ship' and followed with: "Where the VOC's seamen died from scurvy hundreds of years ago, the crew of the *Duyfken*, the replica of the sixteenth-century VOC ship that is on its way from Australia to our country, is now also struggling with a lack of fresh food and medicine." The media also knew that one of my options was to call up a Puma rescue helicopter from Porta Delgada. Our efforts were obviously being closely followed now we were nearing Europe.

The difficulty of hoisting two crew members from a small sailing ship in heavy seas made helicopter evacuation an option only if it was a life threatening emergency. The helicopter crew could also only drop food if the ship was totally without supplies. I investigated arranging a drop-off with food and medical supplies from a trawler but none of the Portuguese trawlers fished in that area. I even asked the Dutch Navy whether they had a ship in the area which could assist but they couldn't help. By morning I found out that no communication has taken place between the MRCC and *Duyfken*. The rescue coordination centre had mis-typed the ship's address and hadn't cared to contact me when they hadn't heard from the ship. Meanwhile, Glenn considered his options:

> *Yesterday we had tacked to head back south. There is a hope that the high, which has formed to the north of the Azores will move east and give us southerlies. We want to be slightly SW of Horta to take advantage of this. I hope that this will work out as this is a losing tack but we have to keep trying.*
>
> *By morning we still have not heard from Delgada MRCC and we have reached as far south as I dare go with this wind. The wind still has not veered as we expected (nothing new there) and so at 0900 we come around again to head north once more. If MRCC Delgada is unable to help us then I will have to rethink this situation, I am sure I will have lots of advice to assist me.*
>
> *By midday it has become obvious that MRCC Delgada has decided that we are not worth the trouble of sending immediate help; which is fair enough I would probably think the same. So I make more inquires about the Flores option and mention this option to Christine and Stijn. If this is going to work I will also send Heidy ashore as well, as her back which gave trouble in Sri Lanka is also troubling her a bit out here and a rest with some proper exercise will do her a lot of good for the next leg.*
>
> *During the crew meeting I outline this option and let everyone be aware of what could happen.*
>
> *The wind is still not all that good for us. We are just making north and the sloppy sea is keeping us from pointing the bow up into the wind, each time we do so the vessel just stops, falls off the wind, and makes a lot of leeway. Progress is slow and we are all feeling the frustration of our lack of progress.*
>
> *At 1600 I take the watch, I had just received an email on the Sat C which was good news. The option of going to Flores has become a reality as Graeme in Horta has confirmed all that we want can be*

> achieved. Flores is at present 80 nm to the north and with the present wind we can just make it by tomorrow. What makes this decision difficult is that in the last two hours we have had the wind veering 20 degrees and our course for Horta has improved tremendously. Unfortunately despite the overwhelming desire to make Horta I have to defer and sail to Flores for humanitarian reasons. I have a special meeting after dinner to explain all of this to the crew, citing also that while we are making a better course for Horta, it is only at 1½ knots, and we do not know if it will last. Where we can make Flores at a speed of 3-4 knots, which I am confident we will make. The last factor is that if the wind is veering, it is slow, and hence the wind could be in a better quarter after we leave Flores. Everyone takes it well and the way Christine was jumping around you would swear she was on a high, I am glad we will be able to get her to a doctor and find out what the problem is. It has been quite a strain on all of us.
> I am glad we have gone for this option, even though it means for those of us who stay aboard we will have an extra 60 nm to sail. I was never very happy about calling in the rescue services. It is better that we solve this in our own way without making a big fuss over it. So we bear away from the wind and for the first time in ages the wind assists us to our destination. Let's hope this is a sign that the weather will turn in our favour. I certainly hope so. This leg from Ascension has cured me of ever wanting to sail a square-rigged vessel to windward.

Glenn and his crew had been at sea on this leg of the voyage for over two months but they were now making useful progress to Flores.

> The wind has eased a bit during the night as well as veering slightly to the south, which bodes well for our attempt to reach Horta. We have though one small duty to perform first and that is land three of our crew at Vila das Lajes, Flores.
> Approaching the island we see that it is quite rugged and very green with cloud low down on the hills. Water at this time of the year is obviously not a problem. As we begin to see the town we notice that red roof tiles must have been on special and that the whitewash salesman had a field day just recently. The town extends up through a small valley with the houses spaced well apart; everything looks

> clean and well ordered, a nice place.
>
> The port is a substantial affair of concrete, not large but built to withstand very serious weather. There is a breakwater/wharf extending out to make the harbour and as we close in we see the masts of a three-masted topsail schooner, which attracts our attention. Within a mile of the breakwater we begin taking in the sails. It is an all hands call and soon the deck is swarming with the crew busy bringing in sails furling hoisting yards and coiling down. It is a good effort and we are all squared away as we round the breakwater and enter the port proper.
>
> The tall ship is the Vida, a Swedish sail-training vessel, a good-looking example of her kind. It is a bit obvious on first glance that we will not be tying up to a mooring buoy and we wait about to see if the agent will contact us and let us know what the plan is. Eventually we find out by some long distance phone calls (mobiles come in handy some times) that the agent is at the wharf and when the Vida departs, which would be in 15 minutes, we would be able to come alongside. We were not quite ready for actually berthing, however, I decide that, as we are only transferring crew and taking on a few stores, we would only need to have a spring out and I would hold the vessel alongside with that.
>
> The transfer went as planned and within 10 minutes, of having our line ashore, we were pulling away and setting sails. I felt sorry for the people on the wharf, I am sure that they as much as I would have liked to stay and see their island. Flores looked very provincial but also very calming and after 61 days at sea, very attractive.

The crisis was averted. Christine, Stijn and Heidy were safely in port, and our agent, Marco Quadros, supplied enough food and drink for the ship. I could rest easier. Christine felt much better after a visit to hospital and Heidy was soon refreshed. Back at sea, the daily logs I received from Glenn showed the strain he was under and for the first time in two years, I decided not to place the Captain's Logs online. Right from the beginning of the first voyage, I never wanted to clean up or edit the master's musing, but these logs had more dirty washing than Brett's sea locker. They were windows into how crew unity had completely broken down. I wasn't looking forward to the ship's arrival in Horta when everyone else's dirty laundry was bound to come out as well.

The crew looked spent when I saw them after they tied up. They seemed to be walking around almost in a trance. Their eyes vacant. Nicole Gardner later re-counted the arrival: "I hadn't slept properly for several months, I hadn't washed or taken my wet weather gear off for about a month, my clothes were rancid and full of holes, and I was dreading having to deal with officials and the media while looking and smelling like a rotting garbage skip. My only clear memory of arrival is someone (the tourist department?) providing us with clean clothes that were too big and pointing us to some showers. I remember sharing half a bar of soap with Alice, Julie and Shannon, and not wanting to touch my dirty clothes afterwards because they stank."

My diary for Horta shows meetings with individual crew members and long discussions. I brought the crew together for one last time when the three crew members arrived from Flores. I had only one objective and it was a selfish ambition. It had to keep this crew together for the last push to Texel. I got tired of telling individual crew members that I would not fire any crew member at this stage of the voyage even though everyone seemed to want someone or other from the top down removed. My view was that whatever weaknesses individual crew members had shown and however disliked they were, it was their right to finish the voyage. I was in a situation where I couldn't satisfy the crew whatever I did. Everyone had a grievance, and no doubt many of them were valid. Glenn's sailing ability, however, had safely delivered the ship and crew to within striking distance of our goal. I felt an obligation to give him the opportunity to finish the job which he had taken after short notice in Sydney almost a year before.

While I didn't want to make wholesale changes to the crew, I asked Cian Pereira to join at Horta. An electrician by trade, Cian was a mature, positive, optimistic and enthusiastic sailor who first came aboard following a lead from Andrea, and stayed. He was a very good hand and sailed on *Duyfken* from Cape York through Queensland when we were struggling to keep the project afloat. He was coming to Europe and rang me to ask if we needed a hand. I said divert to Horta now! The remaining crew from the first voyage knew him very well and I thought he could help change the culture which had developed aboard. When he arrived at Horta, his immediate impression was that the crew were absolutely exhausted.

I also invited Ralph Dekkers from the popular Dutch newspaper De Telegraaf to join the ship, hoping that the crew would be on their best behaviour. "All of a sudden I was standing there in the Azores, no sailing experience whatsoever and only a pen in my pocket to describe how my

Dutch forefathers might have felt when they discovered the world hundreds of years ago," he said. "I was there for the last bit, the last stretch, which is always the hardest. Squeezing myself into a crew that already traveled for about a year, with bonds made and — sometimes — tensions boiling over was difficult. I told my newspaper I was going to be away for about a week, not realizing the wind doesn't conform to a schedule. In the end it took a bit more than a month, but it gave me an experience that lasted a lifetime."

We only had to keep it together for a short time and then we could all part ways and get on with the rest of our lives. So I told the crew that for every one of us, this voyage would probably be the greatest accomplishment of our lives. I was proud of the job they had done to this point and I now required one final effort from them. I told them that the plans for the ship in The Netherlands were now set and all the agreements made for the crew would be met. Individual crew members were welcome to talk to me about continuing on for the exhibition tour but their individual contracts would reflect the changed circumstances. Gary Wilson was refreshed after leaving the ship in Sydney and he was ready to take on the challenge of traversing the Dutch canal system. He would take over as Ship's Master when we arrived in The Netherlands. I said that Gary and I would work closely together as a management team. I wanted a positive group aboard as the summer sailing and exhibition program would be demanding. Most of the crew from the Master down told me that they just wanted to gather their gear as soon as possible after the ship arrived in Texel (not Amsterdam) and leave immediately. Certainly Glenn expressed his wish to get the job done and move on, and I respected that.

It would have been ideal to reward the crew with a bonus for the fine work they had done but, as usual, *Duyfken* was being run on the barest puff of wind in the sails. The refit in Horta and the high cost of accommodation put us $20,000 over-budget for that port alone. The ship was $65,000 over-budget for food and port accommodation expenses and I was still getting grief from the crew who thought they had been hard done by. When one of the crew sent me an email directly questioning why she hadn't had better accommodation in Horta, I replied tersely: "I think we have been pretty generous with accommodation and food arrangements this voyage — definitely better than last year's Expedition and definitely better than many other tall ships. Count your blessings." It was all getting to me, too.

While I farewelled the crew from Horta, Marit van Huystee was finalising plans for the summer tour and exhibition in The Netherlands. The tour comprised 86 days on exhibition and 46 days to re-locate the vessel from port to port. It was to be the most intense exhibition program ever undertaken by the *Duyfken* Foundation, with short transit times and short, sharp exhibition periods. It was important for the Foundation that *Duyfken* made a strong impact in the very competitive Dutch market of summer events. Anything less, and the *Duyfken* Foundation was doomed.

On 16 April 2002, Ralph Dekkers sent back a report to his newspaper editor for publication. Here is a translation of his outsider's view:

> *Life on board* Duyfken *is tough. The international crew of the replica of the sixteenth-century VOC ship, which departed Sydney last May, has already sailed 21,000 nautical miles. From the Azores it is only about 1600 miles to the end of the voyage at Texel, but it is the most gruelling stage. The Atlantic Ocean is rough and weather conditions are harsh.*
>
> *Before the departure of the Azores, 21-year-old Australian crew member Nicole Gardner warns: "The ship will make it. I'm just worried about the crew, which is overtired." The captain, 41-year-old New Zealander, Glenn Williams, agrees: "The crew has had it." How the crew got so tired quickly becomes clear at sea. The predominantly young crew members, including three Dutch people, run shifts of about four hours. If one half works, the other sleeps. And so it goes day and night, day in and day out. Washing hardly happens; the work clothes serve as pyjamas, and vice versa.*
>
> *The first few days everything is OK The wind is favourable and with an average of about 100 miles a day it looks like The Netherlands is easily reached on time. During the day there is time for numerous chores. For example, the rope (in total there is about 14 km of it on board), must be constantly smeared with tar, as protection against the water. There is also the refurbishment work to make* Duyfken *completely ready for the entry on Texel.*
>
> *"When we arrive in the Netherlands, the ship is actually only ready to leave Australia," says 47-year-old Ed Biermans from Hoorn. After a long day, catching sleep is not easy. The water of splashing waves seeps down the deck on the sleeping bags of the crew members. The cold continues to haunt everyone, from the deck to the hammock. But hardly anyone complains. Everyone realises that he or she is part of a unique experience. Just like at the time,* Duyfken *now has to deal with the vagaries of the weather. Fate strikes after the right start. The wind, with force 10, is coming from the wrong direction. The sails are rushed down. The crew of a luxury yacht in*

the neighbourhood (value: €8 million) decides to leave the ship under these dangerous conditions. Duyfken *is fighting back*, although the crew is having a terrifying night. After drifting a long way, it changes again. Now it is windless and Duyfken *floats aimlessly in the ocean again*. Meanwhile, the deadline is approaching, the crew is getting tense. The irritations arise. The mental challenge of the expedition may be even greater than the physical one. It's no fun to live together in such a small space for a year, without any form of privacy. "It's like Big Brother's house," says 20-year-old Dutchman Bob Looijschelder, "but without cameras." However, no one can be voted down, but a crew member has been sent away for aggressive behaviour.

"In a house of this size, you'd already go crazy," says 26-year-old Brett Yates from Britain. "And you can still get out of there."

The difference in characters also often plays a role. "I don't like a large part of the crew," Bob says. "That's the heaviest. But this trip has taken me past countries like Namibia, South Africa and Indonesia." Bob will stay on board The Netherlands for another five months with his 22-year-old Australian comrade Walter 'Wally' Walker. Wally also doesn't like part of the crew, but: "We're all here for the ship. If something needs to be done, we'll do it. Then all problems are put aside."

The love for the ship is present with everyone on board. However, since the departure of the Azores, the crew has had the idea that it is no longer their boat, their expedition. The 28 April arrival date looms daily. Numerous festivities have been organised and Prince Willem-Alexander will come on board. When the weather between the Azores and The Netherlands continues to be miserable, the Captain decides to use the engines under pressure from the approaching deadline. 'A huge setback,' as he himself puts it.

In a year, the engines have only been used for 97 hours, mainly to get in and out of the ports. The disappointment is great. Everyone would have liked to have completed the journey sailing, just like the sailors of the VOC did 400 years ago. Crew members also have a wry feeling about the use of the engines. "Commerce has taken over," Brett says. "It's not a journey anymore like they did at the time, it's become a delivery."

Spring gales made the last leg of the voyage the toughest for *Duyfken's* weary and dispirited crew. Sometimes they were hove to, being lashed by freezing seas. Cian Pereira said that he had never been so cold sailing on *Duyfken*.

Ralph Dekkers' reports were big news in The Netherlands. Another caused alarm when it was splashed in 'De Telegraaf'. *Duyfken* had been hove to for a day, with winds up to force 10 pushing the ship away from Europe. When the engines were started, they had little effect:

> *The oil tanker, which at first could only be followed by radar, can now be seen with the naked eye in the morning twilight. And what was feared is true: the immense colossus is on a collision course.*
> *Attempting to establish radio contact. Nobody responds.* Duyfken *cannot respond. The 22 metre long VOC ship has been a plaything of the ocean since Saturday afternoon. The wind suddenly changed direction and increased in strength. All sails had to be lowered to prevent damage to the ship and not to go completely off course. In the past 24 hours, only 25 miles have been travelled, in the wrong direction.*
> *The tanker is approaching within three miles.* Duyfken *has radio contact, but it turns out to be a ship 20 miles away that had received the signal. Two miles. The captain decides to start the engines, an extreme emergency measure given the nature of the expedition. However, the ocean is too rough, the storm too powerful. An evasive manoeuvre is impossible. One mile. The panic is increasing. An attempt is made in haste with light signals to attract the attention of the watch commander of the oil tanker.*
> *The desperate attempt also seems to fail, but after two minutes, and less than a mile away, the oil tanker changes course. A radio link is established. "Don't be afraid. Don't be afraid," says the drowsy guard commander in broken English and with a heavy Russian accent. "I'm scared", the captain of* Duyfken *responds. "We are in danger. You are on a collision course." The watch commander: "Don't be afraid. Don't be afraid." Radio contact is lost. The tanker passes the* Duyfken *in front.*

Tracy organised a last minute, expensive, un-budgeted stay at Lowestoft in the UK before The Netherlands. Despite the adverse weather, *Duyfken* was still ahead of schedule. More fuel had to be bunkered and Christine and

Heidy would re-join the ship for the last few days.

Communications were getting worse. I was receiving bizarre emails from the ship. One proposed visiting three ports along the English coast before arriving in The Netherlands. My emails in reply were left unanswered. I still had not received a voyage plan for the last leg. The anger aboard the ship was now being re-directed toward me. The journalist, Ralph Dekkers, contacted me from the ship in a panic intimating that I was forcing him to stay on the ship. It was not the case. I had to explain the actual circumstances. For months I had treated the Master's increasingly aggressive communications as positively as I could but I could only be pushed so far.

Adding to my unease, as Ralph Dekkers mentioned in his log, the highly credentialled skipper, Chris Sherlock, and his crew of six, had abandoned a 30m racing yacht called the *Leopard of London* in heavy seas 400nm from the Spanish coast while *Duyfken* was further east making her way to Falmouth in the UK. We saw the yacht while we were in Horta. If this weather could claim a modern racing yacht, how would we go? We were all feeling the pressure. A senior Dutch crew member committed the cardinal sin of smoking on board – a dumb idea on a wooden ship covered in oil and tar. Then he did it again — he just didn't care any more. The increased commercial traffic funnelling into Europe and the arrival date (which was the only deadline set in stone for the whole voyage) were placing added strain on master and crew. Glenn had to pick his way through the congested English Channel in rough seas with a vessel under sail — no mean feat.

I was at my wit's end to know how to deal with the situation. A wise head who had done a lot of long distance sailing told me I had to read a book called 'In the Mind of the Sailor' which had been released the year before and talked about why some sailors handled stress better than others, while adversity tore other crews apart. It was great advice but, yes, I should have read it a year before!

Duyfken did make it to Falmouth, bunkered fuel and Ralph Dekkers disembarked. It was then a matter of the crew surviving their last battering before the grand arrival in Texel. We were in sight of our goal, indeed, the ship was ahead of schedule, and the crew spent three days in harbour at Lowestoft on the east coast of England, only 155 nm from Texel.

The VOC 2002 organisation arranged for me to join them aboard the Dutch naval ship, the magnificent frigate HNLMS *Jacob van Heemskerck*, a veteran of Operation Desert Storm. The rendezvous with *Duyfken* was done with military precision. An Orion aircraft tracked down *Duyfken* and sent her position to the *Heemskerk*. The frigate then steered a course for *Duyfken*, and a helicopter with a film crew and photographers aboard lined up *Duyfken* and the naval ship to achieve an image contrasting 400 years of Dutch seafaring. I found it strange that the crew aboard *Duyfken* showed little interest in the rendezvous and barely acknowledged our presence. The occasional grey, ghostly, silhouetted figure could be seen crossing the deck but that was all. Was *Duyfken* now the Flying Dutchman?

Meanwhile, Marit van Huystee was working long hours to pull together a summer exhibition program. "It was a hell of a job to coordinate in advance the many ports and berths. I had to talk to the mayors of each small town, the directors of museums and other people involved. Where would the little ship attract the most visitors? What other activities should take place? How to get the ship at the right spot? Which locks and bridges, shallows and tides," she said. "What about the tickets, catering for the crew, where could the crew sleep? The list was endless."

"I had an incredible number of meetings sometime driving from Amsterdam where I lived, to the island Texel, and back to Den Haag in one day," said Marit. She did a fine job in difficult circumstances.

On 28 April 2002, day 359 of the voyage, Crown Prince Willem-Alexander travelled to Zuiderhaven, Texel to welcome *Duyfken* to The Netherlands. For the first time since we had begun planning the construction of the ship in 1994, the operation of the vessel was taken out of our hands and I had no say in any of the arrangements. The VOC2002 organisation was in charge of every detail of the welcome and we were simply the actors on a greater stage. I was amused when a Dutch person congratulated me on bringing *their* ship home. It was *our* ship, we were Australians, and we had built the ship to echo a Dutch design. Her home was Fremantle. How dare they.

The Texel roadstead, which had welcomed the return of the great VOC fleets for more than five centuries ago, now welcomed 'home' the *Little Dove*. The royal sailing yacht, *Groene Draeck*, arrived first and tied up so that Prince Willem-Alexander and his wife, Princess Máxima, could come ashore. Guns fired a salute. A local newspaper reported that 40,000 people crammed every vantage point to see the ship arrive. At 2pm, Glenn brought the ship up to a berth at the front of the Stoombootkoffiehuis (steamer coffee house) Restaurant where I had sat down with Benno many months before while it was snowing outside to devise a plan for the ship touring The Netherlands. The Oudeschild Fishermen's Choir sang from a fishing boat.

My father, Jack, and my sister, Sandra, were there to witness the arrival. Cathy, and our children, Louise and Daniel, were home in Perth. We couldn't afford the cost of a trip to The Netherlands.

The little ship and her crew had sailed three great oceans, visited four continents and delved back four centuries into VOC history. The final distance covered was 23,000 nm (42,600 km) with 500 nm using the engines. Nine of the 16 crew members who sailed from Sydney on 5 May the previous year were still aboard and most of the crew which had joined in Jakarta were still with us. The scene in the tiny little harbour was more like the return of a winning football team. The whole crew lined up along the wharf to be officially welcomed. Michael 'Barney' Barnett sang his 'Ballad of the *Duyfken*' and it brought a tear to my eye. It was a massive accomplishment for everyone involved: the shore team and the crew which sailed the voyage. The doubters were quiet now.

For the Dutch, it was the beginning of the year of 'celebrations' of the 400th anniversary of the formation of the VOC. Already the word 'celebrations' was controversial with people saying that commemoration would be a more appropriate way to describe the year. Australian Governor-General, Peter Hollingworth, spoke about the significance of the VOC to the European exploration of the Australian continent. Glenn presented the artikelbrief he was given in Sydney to Benno van Tilburg. I spoke of my pride in the achievement of my Master, the crew and my shore team who had worked so hard behind the scenes to make the port visits so memorable. I wanted the world to know what a great achievement it had been, but I allowed my hubris to cloud my judgement. Rinze Brandsma was clearly upset that he did not have the opportunity to speak, as a Dutch/Australian, on behalf of the Project. I was affected by the way I had been abused and manipulated for the last leg of the voyage, and I wanted everyone to know who was still in charge. I wanted the world to know who had conceived, fund-raised and organised this accursed voyage. I wanted the recognition. Today, I still regret my poor judgement in making that speech myself.

In the evening, Marit van Huystee arranged a final celebratory dinner for the crew, shore team, family and friends. It was a muted affair. Everyone was utterly drained. There was no great outpouring of emotion and not many laughs. For the crew, they were completing an obligation. As something of a *Duyfken* tradition, Rinze gave the Mayor of Texel, Joke Geldorp-Pantekoek, a large spun aluminium plate commemorating the arrival of the ship. "The 28th April 2002 here arrived the ship *Duyfken* of Fremantle to the island of Texel to commemorate the 400th Anniversary of the establishment of the Dutch East India Company (VOC). The VOC 2002 Voyage visited Indonesia; Sri Lanka; Mauritius; South Africa; Namibia; St Helena and Ascension Islands; Azores of Portugal and the United Kingdom." The plate then named everyone involved in the voyage and cheekily ended with the line: "Departed Texel bound for Amsterdam and further explorations." This time, the tables were turned and we were giving the Dutch a plate! Every crew member received a small personally engraved box as a token of the *Duyfken* Foundation's appreciation. It was symbolic of their existence lived out of a small sea chest for the last year. It was evident that excitement about the arrival was not shared by the whole crew. I hadn't understood the bitterness harboured by some of the crew now the voyage was over. Several boxes were simply left at the tables and gathered up by our shore team afterwards.

Next morning, I barely said a word to Glenn Williams, and I am sure the feeling was mutual. Any personal relationship we had was washed away by the events of the last few weeks. To his credit, he had accomplished the major goal of getting the ship to The Netherlands on time. The metrics were positive. We didn't lose any crew. The ship was in good condition. Our sponsors and supporters were pleased. This, however, had not been quite the triumphant voyage I had imagined when Gary and I planned it in Brisbane. In Texel, I did not see a crew united by their achievement, bonded like a sporting team which had won a grand final, celebrating the great accomplishment, punching the air and shouting: "We did it!" Rather, I saw a group of individuals, utterly exhausted in body but even more in mind, who wanted to simply move on.

The romance of sailing an early Dutch ship for months on end was obviously divorced from reality. True, the conditions aboard were nothing like those endured by the original crew of 1606, but they were by no means what a modern western person expected either. Sharing 12 months with 15 other people in a room barely larger than the average lounge room of a suburban house and eating meals made from ingredients which could be stored without refrigeration, prepared in a kitchen no bigger than a wardrobe, while sitting cross-legged on a heaving deck would test anyone. It was a psychological battle as much as a physical one. One of the crew later told me that she thought the crew's view aboard had become very limited and self-centred. "We lived in an insular society focused on our problems in our little world." Another said that by the time the crew arrived in The

Netherlands, the occasion was overshadowed by an overwhelming feeling of weariness. She said that she felt disturbed and angry by what she perceived as injustices on board. "I felt definitely 'done' with *Duyfken*," she said.

The sailors did not choose who they would be living with in close quarters for a year. Small disagreements became major issues when there was no way to let off steam. Every single decision made aboard the ship was discussed and evaluated. On *Duyfken*, you were either on deck or down below in the cramped hold where there were no windows to gaze on the outside world. There was no escape from the ocean's moods. It didn't care whether you were hungry, cold, lonely or tired. The VOC Voyagie also showed that ships of the sixteenth and seventeenth centuries which were sailed for such long periods faced a constant battle to slow the deterioration of everything on board. Sails rotted and tore. They needed constant repair. The rigging stretched and had to be repeatedly retensioned. The hull had to be oiled. The decks washed and scrubbed. There were hundreds of jobs for the crew. This was a sailor's life. It was tiring but it could also be dull and repetitive, and by the end of the voyage, the crew had nothing more to give. Looking back now, 20 years later, I can see that we pushed the crew to the limits of their human endurance for an ephemeral goal — to say that we could have a single crew sail the longest voyage in an 'Age of Discovery' replica ship. With the wisdom of hindsight, all members of the crew including the Master, should have been given shore leave for complete legs of the voyage. They would have returned refreshed. I should have done something about the flawed command structure and the personality issues aboard the ship when they first became in issue in Jakarta. I didn't, and the crew was fractious during the voyage.

It has taken me 20 years to write about it, and in contacting some of the crew to write this book they have not been so keen to talk. Amongst many of the crew, even today, there is a massive questioning of the voyage and how it changed them as individuals. They are still trying to come to understand the psychological effects of a year at sea in close quarters with people who they wouldn't have any desire to meet again. The response has been varied. One wrote to me, "20 years, man alive it is as palpable and living as if it were yesterday. I suppose touchstones of time are that way. I for one am delighted to reconnect with you as you have always and will always hold a place of indelible fondness in my heart. Port after port, your presence was the first thing that greeted us weary worn sailors and each time you were a beacon of hope, respite and safe haven; our Hero." Is that how some of the crew really felt? I never knew. I am sure others would disagree. With the passing of the decades, I have felt increasingly proud of the crew members who sailed on both the voyages and I accept that I sometimes asked too much of them.

The arrival in The Netherlands, however, was no time for reflection. Our great challenge was to make the ship pay her own way again. I knew that all eyes would be on our financial performance. I had been contacted in February 2002 out-of-the-blue by Patricia Kailis. The MG Kailis debt was still hanging over the ship and she strongly suggested that the *Duyfken* Foundation erred when it did not factor in the repayment of the debt in the budget supplied to VOC2002. She proposed that the *Duyfken* Foundation sell the ship once we reached The Netherlands or sell it immediately upon our return to Fremantle. She tersely said that she was Governing Director of the MG Kailis Group of Companies and she did not need the *Duyfken* debt on the books. Quite reasonably, the success or otherwise of the exhibition tour in The Netherlands was being looked at very closely. While it was underway, Patricia called Rinze and proposed that any profits from the tour should firstly be directed towards eliminating the *Duyfken* Foundation's debt to the MG Kailis Group before being used to cover the operating expenses of the Foundation. I couldn't fault the reasoning but Rinze outlined the difficulties with the plan. We had a contractual obligation with VOC2002. The funds would only be released to the *Duyfken* Foundation after completion of the summer season, subject to further negotiations.

I did not want to see the *Duyfken* sold. I was still just as keen as ever to progress the *Duyfken* Seaport concept that Michael Kailis and I had developed in 1999. I can see now that it was a lost cause. Quite understandably, in early 2002, Patricia had many issues to consider for the future of the MG Kailis Group. She never had the same passion for the ship as her husband but people change. She was at Texel when *Duyfken* arrived and she was able to share our pride in the achievement. In later years, it was gratifying to see her develop a genuine soft spot for the ship. She would often attend special events involving *Duyfken* and become quite emotional at times. *Duyfken* does that.

Chapter 28

A Fresh Start

Spring had not yet come to Texel. Force seven winds were blowing from the Arctic. It was cold, wet and windy for two days as *Duyfken*'s voyage crew spent the time gathering together their belongings and preparing to hand over to the team which would show the vessel for the next five months. Glenn Williams gave control of the ship to Gary Wilson.

Gary's first job was to relocate *Duyfken* to Amsterdam for the start of the public exhibition tour. Eight of the crew who sailed the last leg of the delivery voyage were keen to stay aboard for the final short hop to Amsterdam. It was only about 60nm from Texel with the new experience of our first opening bridge and our first lock. After an overnight stay tied up at Enkhuisen, we had another big ceremonial welcome planned in Amsterdam.

Benno told us to expect some protests, otherwise, with typical bullish optimism, all would be just fine. We weren't aware that a protest movement against the VOC2002 celebrations was gaining support. It was led by the Maluku Action Committee and a support group called Aksi Setiakawan which staged a picket line at the official opening of the VOC year at the 'Hall of Knights', the Ridderzaal in Den Haag. *Duyfken* was being denigrated by the protest movement as a 'theme park' version of history.

The official opening of the VOC year was controversial. The protestors had to be moved down the street so that visitors could enter the Ridderzaal. The Indonesian Government distanced itself from the VOC celebrations but the Indonesian Minister of National Development and Planning, Kwik Kian Gie, had close ties with The Netherlands and he agreed to speak at the reception. His wife was Dutch and he studied at The Netherlands School of Economics (now Erasmus University) in Rotterdam.

A FRESH START

With Queen Beatrix in attendance, he put a dampener on proceedings and was reported as saying: "The VOC has caused lasting damage in Indonesian society. It has not laid down a system of government from which participation, representation or participation for Indonesians could grow. On the contrary, the VOC has been instrumental in their oppression, exploitation and abuse of power." He urged the Queen, and all those attending to appreciate that, "the VOC was experienced by the inhabitants of the provinces as a 'sucking polyp' and a 'paternalistic monster'".

The ship entered Amsterdam with every flag flying and she was an impressive sight. There was one solitary protest ship called the *Papillon* (butterfly) which was attempting to get close to us and kept being turned away by the Police. They were sprayed with a water cannon by the harbour fire fighting boat which was there to give a ceremonial welcome spray ahead of us. The protest was arranged by a group called "Viering VOC? Nou nee!" which translates to "Celebration VOC? Well No!"

The protest craft banged out music and gave speeches through loud hailers — none of which we understood, but it annoyed the people in other boats who were there to see our grand arrival. *Papillon* was emblazoned with hastily scrawled protest statements. At one point, the protestors threw out some floral wreaths to commemorate the victims of the VOC era. The Police boarded their ship for a chat, and it all seemed like quite a well-mannered affair.

When we arrived at our berth at the Amsterdam Convention Centre, the protestors set up a small gathering further down the wharf and then the group moved up the wharf towards us. The protestors seemed to be a mix of people of Dutch and Indonesian descent. One of our young male crew members foolishly told a local journalist that he thought the protest was "dumb". I only learnt about it later when it was used to make a point about how ignorant we appeared to be. It should never have been said.

With the ship tied up, we stood around the wharf having a chat while the protestors seemed to be getting equally bored nearby. I remember smiling at one of them who was looking very curiously at the ship from the wharf. He appeared to be of Malukan descent. He was a little hesitant to talk to us but soon Gary Wilson and I struck up a conversation. We said that of course we were aware of the atrocities committed by the VOC in Maluku, particularly by the 'psychopath' Jan Pieterszoon Coen. We visited Banda and saw the place where it happened. He seemed surprised that we weren't defending the VOC. Then I explained that we had seen the reenactment expedition in 2000 as an important voyage of reconciliation with the Aboriginal people of Cape York. He was totally surprised, not quite believing it. I invited him to go aboard and take a look in the Captain's Cabin where John Cockatoo's spear given to Peter Manthorpe at the Pennefather River had been mounted above the chart table. I also said that he would see the mask and crocodile which had been given to the ship in Timor. I had no intention of escorting him onto the ship — I just pointed to the gangway and said he could go onto the ship alone. This also surprised him. Gary and I kept talking while I kept one eye on the protestor as he wandered about the deck, genuinely interested in what he was looking at. He came back from the ship and thanked me. I thought afterwards that we actually shared many sentiments. *Duyfken*'s presence was opening up old wounds which didn't sit comfortably with us, either. We built the ship to help tell a story of the early exploration of the Australian coastline by Europeans. This had quickly morphed into a narrative about Aboriginal people meeting people from the outside world for the first time.

James Henderson was the first person from the *Duyfken* Project to acknowledge and talk to the Aboriginal people of Cape York to get their side of the story. That began to change to the way we all viewed the encounter. When we were voyaging the ship, I began to tell people that as far as I was concerned, the Aboriginal people of Cape York actually owned the story, not us. It was their story. The drive to build the ship, however, had been to create the most exacting replica of an 'Age of Discovery' Dutch vessel. We had been very keen to replicate a jacht and learn why they were such highly regarded ships at the time. We called it an exercise in 'experimental archaeology'. Then we focused on the maritime and trading achievements of the Dutch, not even really addressing the symbolic choice of this vessel which participated in bloody encounters with Aboriginal people and was an instrument in crushing the traditional trading system of the Spice Islands and conquering the Indonesian archipelago. Indonesian scholars today talk about the Dutch 'Golden Age' being funded by the exploitation of the people of Indonesia and the rise of Amsterdam being built on this colonial economic system. *Duyfken* was an advanced ship for its time. It was a product of Dutch ingenuity which led to the Dutch maritime supremacy which made them a wealthy people. *Duyfken* was an enabler of this same 'Golden Age'. So many contradictions.

A month later we were on exhibition in the city of Hoorn where Jan Pieterszoon Coen was born in 1587. The local tourist literature described him as "equally famous and infamous". They got that right. The bookkeeper turned governor of the VOC in the Indies was regarded as a favoured son of the town and his statue was in a town square near our ship where Gary Wilson and I occasionally sat down for a quiet beer on a sunny day. There, in front of us, was the despicable Coen in all his finery. Then we noticed one day that someone had climbed the plinth of the statue and painted a red tear from one eye down his face. It was deeply moving and such a subtle but profound way to make a statement.

After the ship's arrival in Amsterdam, we ordered all the vestiges of the voyage crew to be removed from the ship. This wasn't for any other reason than I had been disappointed that the hold had become a labyrinth of plywood panelling and 12 volt wires strung across the ceiling. In a matter of hours everything was removed and unceremoniously dumped near some skip bins, and our seventeenth century display materials came aboard. For the exhibition season, we doubled the size of the dockside exhibition and purchased more reproduction ship ephemera to put on display. This included a dazzling number of new items such as buckets, an arquebus, helmet, musket and a captain's sword. Europe was full of original artefacts from the sixteenth century so we had to make sure that we offered something interesting for visitors who may have seen it all before in museums.

Duyfken was a heavily armed jacht with a prickly array of guns and the onboard exhibition reflected this. The Dutch loved the menacing sight of bristling guns on *Duyfken* as it conveyed the power of their merchant navy at this time. When I commissioned the guns in Fremantle, all but one was cast using aluminium and one from brass so it could be made to fire. The heavily armed nature of *Duyfken* seemed to jar with her name meaning *Little Dove* and the white dove as a symbol of peace. In view of the confrontations in Cape York and the history of the VOC in Indonesia I had no plans to make the brass weapon able to be fired and I always resisted the school-boyish desire to have a functioning weapon aboard.

The protest in Amsterdam was the only major physical demonstration against *Duyfken* which we experienced during our stay. For the most part, the people of The Netherlands embraced us and the ship with such enthusiasm that we became minor celebrities. Often I couldn't remain on the ship to do my work as people swarmed over her. I had to find a quiet café nearby to hide away. There was a sense of wonder that the ship sailed all the way from Australia and that Australians built such a fine and historically accurate vessel which had almost circumnavigated the world when the Dutch had been unable to build a similarly seaworthy craft. I am sure that *Duyfken* reinforced the Dutch national view of the glories of the 'Golden Age'. Despite the weather in Amsterdam, we enjoyed 2,000 visitors in two days. We moved the ship to the Scheepvart Museum (Maritime Museum) and a further 4,200 people came aboard. This was one of the biggest days ever for *Duyfken* as far as visitors go. The stage was set for a great summer.

Thanks to Marit van Huystee's months of work to pave the way for our visits, we began taking the ship to places which people deemed impossible. This began in Amsterdam on Sunday 5 May. The local publicist, Gert Tetteroo, suggested that it would be possible for *Duyfken* to make it through the city canals to the Amstel River. The voyage along the canals of Amsterdam was inspired by paintings of ships and canals in the Amsterdam Rijksmuseum. Dutch jachts similar to *Duyfken,* were often seen in 'Golden Age' paintings, moored close to the city centre where buildings and railways now dominate the landscape. He said that he could arrange dozens of sailors to run lines from the ship to the sides of the canal. The city authorities spent time bottom-trawling bikes and shopping trollies out of the canal so we could make it through. For the first time, a VOC vessel would enter the city centre itself. The trip began at 3pm from the Scheepvaartmuseum (Maritime Museum) then went via Kadijksplein and Nieuwe Herengracht to the river Amstel, in the heart of the old centre of Amsterdam between Waterlooplein and Rembrandtplein. *Duyfken* went past the Hortus botanical garden to which the VOC brought back the first coffee seeds to counter the Arab monopoly. These seeds were propagated and it was said that all the coffee plants in the New World were propagated from these plants. The last part of this spectacular trip was for *Duyfken* to be towed by singing sailors walking along either side of the canal. A naval band followed on a barge to play in between songs performed by the singing sailors. Once *Duyfken* entered the city canals, there was no space on either side of the vessel. One false move and the ship would be jammed. Each small street bridge (and there were six of them) had to be raised. People hung out of windows in the houses along the route for the first and probably last ever sight of a VOC ship coming by their window. Much of the canal trip was done in complete silence with everybody appreciating that it would not be pretty if things went wrong. There was only one mistake when a yard hit a bridge and a sickening sharp cracking sound rang out across Amsterdam. The end of the yard was completely snapped off, recovered and cheekily presented to Gary afterwards.

A FRESH START 433

The visit to Amsterdam was a triumph and it set the scene for a summer of successful exhibitions.

One of the most rewarding aspects of touring The Netherlands with the ship was that the Dutch had a creative flair which we hadn't seen in Australia. Most of our port locations became a theatre set with the ship and the wharf as the stage and a tribune assembled for the theatregoers. It was the creation of a Theatrical Director, Ab Gietelink, who formed Theatre Nomade in 1984 as a location group to stage plays in historic locations. Over the years, he had used 80 venues around The Netherlands and put on 350 performances. He said that rather than psychological drama, he preferred theatre with historical or political content. In 1996, he performed a play called 'Batavia' in museum spaces with museum artefacts as props. His next foray into VOC history was with a play called 'De Heeren Zeventien' (The Gentlemen 17) in original VOC locations. The location tour concept expanded over the years into a trademark of the company. The 'De Vliegende Hollander' (The Flying Dutchman) with *Duyfken* as the backdrop was the first time a ship had been used. Often the weather was terrible. "The play was performed with a lot of storms, sensations and setbacks in 10 Dutch ports," said Ab in his theatrical way. He described the play as musical theatre using the spectacle of *Duyfken*. His story began with Cornelis de Houtman's first voyage to the East Indies between 1595 and 1597 and then merged the myth of the Flying Dutchman into the story. "Houtman encounters the 'Flying Dutchman' and a story unfolds on the edge of reality and imagination. The legend of the 'Flying Dutchman' is probably Holland's most renowned myth. By sailing on Easter Sunday, the Dutch skipper Willem van der Decken is doomed to sail for eternity. In the howling wind, his black ship with blood-red sails races across oceans. After years of sailing, the devil gives the Dutchman a means of redemption. Once every seven years, the skipper is given the opportunity to go ashore to find peace and seek a wife who will be faithful to him for all eternity. One day on the Scottish coast, he goes ashore to find the woman who has been waiting for him for years. The 'Flying Dutchman' is delivered from his doom." I was determined to try this theatrical use of the ship when we returned to Australia. We had a much better climate for it and if the hardy Dutch could sit outside to see a performance then surely we could too. It was not to be.

Duyfken was also used as a prop for a television production concerning the 'Flying Dutchman' story. The ship was filmed under sail and then in post-production the sails were painted red and torn to shreds.

It would be wrong to assert that the Dutch were unable to look back at their own history with a critical eye. We were approached by an educational filmmaker, Willem A van der Spek, to hire the ship. He wanted to film scenes of slaves manacled on deck for a ground-breaking children's television series. About five per cent of all the African slaves taken to the West Indies were transported aboard Dutch ships.

The story for the series began in a busy Dutch street where two Dutch boys (one is descended from parents who came from the Amazonian Dutch colony of Suriname) read Asterix comics about the Roman Empire and dream about keeping slaves of their own. The film deals with slaves transported from Ghana in around 1780. The opening scene has a Dutch trader negotiating with an African head man about the sale of his slaves. They were being chained, branded and locked in dark cellars under a fortress near the sea. The rooms were packed with human cargo. The slaves were described by the film treatment as 'scared and aggressive'. Then *Duyfken* came into the picture. The slaves were taken aboard a Dutch ship. The voyage was described as having to reflect 'nothing less than hell. This perspective matched with some of our crew members who had been on the voyage from Australia. We thoroughly enjoyed the filming on the Ijsselmeer. All we had to do was occasionally come about when Gary ran out of sea room. The film series was broadcast to critical acclaim in 2003, and it won several major international awards. It was seen as dealing sensitively with the issues surrounding Dutch slave trading. The film broke the silence in Dutch school books about the slave trading era. In July 2002, while we were touring The Netherlands, Queen Beatrix unveiled a monument dealing with the slavery issue in a park in Amsterdam. A similar monument was not erected voicing regret over the ills of the VOC.

Perhaps our greatest opportunity to use *Duyfken* as a set for a major film came through the acclaimed Dutch film-maker, Paul Verhoeven. He is probably best known for his hit films 'Basic Instinct', 'Total Recall', 'Starship Troopers' and 'Robocop'. After a long contract with Sony in Hollywood, he was back in The Netherlands working on his own pet projects. He teamed up with an old friend, the screenwriter Gerard Soeteman, to produce a film based on Mike Dash's best-selling book '*Batavia's* Graveyard' which told the bloody story of the *Batavia* mutiny. I had a couple of meetings with his business manager who wanted to know whether we could provide *Duyfken* as the rescue ship *Saardam* which sailed from Batavia to rescue the survivors marooned on the Abrolhos Islands. The mutineer, Jeronimus Corneliusz, would be the evil figure in the story and naturally Wiebbe Hayes would be the hero. It had all the hallmarks of a Verhoeven film with lashings of sex and violence. It was a tremendous opportunity for *Duyfken* so we discussed spending a day sailing the Ijsselmeer with the director and a small team from his company. Our aim was to show him what life was really like aboard a ship of the era in which the film was set. It was a horrible windy day and Gary had quite a time getting off the wharf. Putting up any sail was out of the question. Such a chop was whipping up on the Ijsselmeer that there was sometimes no clearance under the hull and the ship seemed to be bouncing on the bottom. It was not at all pleasant but it seemed that the worse it got, the more they could see the possibilities of producing something very dramatic. Paul Verhoeven had a great time and it was quite a coup for us to have him aboard for a whole day. Lunch was a 'traditional VOC meal' cooked by Heidy. A volunteer, Ron, made a wood fire in the open metal firebox lined with bricks on deck. Then we returned to Bataviawerf at Lelystad and enjoyed a hot coffee out of the gale. Paul said that it had been his dream to make a film of the *Batavia* story for many years but he couldn't interest Hollywood in the idea. His best chance was to find investors in Europe. While the *Batavia* replica in Lelystad would be used for many scenes leading up to the shipwreck, it was proposed that one, or even two portions of *Batavia* would be constructed as set to be used for the grounding on the reef and the subsequent escape to the shore. He sought out locations in North Africa which looked like Australia. We proposed that the *Batavia* pieces could be built in Fremantle by our ex-*Duyfken* shipwrights and perhaps the film could be partially shot in Western Australia. I made contacts with the government film agency, Screenwest, in Perth to help facilitate the locations but in the end, '*Batavia*'s Graveyard' did not secure a major investor, and another project called 'Black Book' about The Netherlands during German occupation in World War II, got the funding and was made. The *Batavia* story has still not been moulded into a major motion picture, but the story deserves it.

During the spring and summer of 2002, *Duyfken* played a major role in the VOC2002 Jaar celebrations, visiting all of the original Dutch VOC ports and taking part in a host of maritime events. It was an exhausting schedule and Marit van Huystee was constantly having to make new arrangements as the program changed almost daily. For Marit, we were a very demanding client. "I found it an enormous challenge to balance the different demands and priorities of the Dutch and Australians during the exhibition tour," she said. I wanted visitor revenue and the towns wanted to provide a summer attraction.

Tina Driver operated the *Duyfken* Shop which sold tickets to come on board the ship and James Holdsworth coordinated local volunteer guides. They did a wonderful job in each port, especially when we were inundated with visitors. The Firelight documentary was completed and it was screened on Dutch television in prime time and on the Peter chanel in France and Germany to coincide with our arrival in Europe (it was also broadcast in Australia, Singapore and New Zealand). Marcus Gillezeau and Ellenor Cox enjoyed recognition around the world for their web publishing efforts. "Our micro-docs as we called the small online clips turned out to be the world's first web series," said Marcus. "It's something which makes us proud. The entire multi-platform project was also a world-first and significant on many levels. It was delivered as a TV documentary, Rich Media double DVD, and with Consultas, a narrowband website with rich media content (videos) and a broadband website."

"The *Little Dove* documentary was significant for me in career terms," said Marcus. "It put myself and producer Ellenor Cox at the forefront of multi-platform digital production and delivery. We went on to produce a highly successful digital multi-platform drama project 'Scorched' that went on to win the International Digital Emmy Award for Best Drama."

Robert Garvey's book was re-published in Dutch by National Geographic in Europe. The ship was featured in an article by the Dutch edition of the magazine. I was thrilled to walk into a bookstore in Den Haag and see stacks of Robert's books in the prime position at the front of the shop. They were walking out the door and selling like a JK Rowling novel.

We were regularly enjoying fabulous visitor days. In Delft, the ship recorded three amazing days: on 18 May we had revenue of €3085, then the next day it peaked at €8254 then €8047 on the third day. Some ports were also enticing us with an appearance fee which could be as much as €10,000.

At Zaanse Schans, *Duyfken* nestled amongst traditional Dutch windmills in a scene which could have been taken from a Vermeer painting. The nearby town of Zaandam and the river Zaan was a major shipbuilding centre at the time of *Duyfken*. Timber came from Norway, the Baltic lands, Hamburg, Bremen and the Rhine to create ships like *Duyfken* for the Dutch East India Company. Thanks to the invention of a vertical saw powered by the windmills, the time to produce ships could be drastically reduced. By 1630, there were 83 saw mills to the north of Amsterdam. Windmills would have stretched across the horizon — it must have been a magnificent sight and *Duyfken* looked right at home within it.

Sometimes we felt like rock stars. As we travelled down a canal to Middleburg on a sunny summer's day, dozens of cyclists followed the ship on the cycle path along the canal. The canal was higher than the surrounding countryside and we looked down at the cyclists and chatted with them as the ship traversed rich farmland on either side. Only in The Netherlands.

The VOC2002 Executive Officer, Laura van Deelan, worked out of Den Haag and she was a fine host, introducing me to fresh herring washed down with gin from the barrowmen in the streets of the capital and pointing out places rarely visited by tourists. We stayed in a lightship at Hellevoetsluis and in seamen's quarters in Rotterdam. We were billeted in the officers' quarters of the naval barracks in Amsterdam. After a day on exhibition, it was the perfect place to get away from the frenetic street life of the Dutch capital. One Sunday morning, I was tasked with finding some wood screws so I went to look for a hardware store. The only one which was open was in the red light district. It was a novel experience asking for a screw in Amsterdam on a Sunday morning and the joke followed me for months. It was still early days for email communications. In Amsterdam, rather than the small net cafes across Asia, the city had two massive net cafes. They had a sleazy vibe. One was attached to the Virgin Megastore and the other was called EasyEverything which was an entrepreneurial start-up from the man who began easyJet. They had hundreds of computer screens to feed the demand from tourists in the Dutch capital. The boom which created the barn-style net cafes was short-lived and the smartphone sounded the death knell for these facilities. They are long gone.

For some time I was exploring options to return the ship to Fremantle — kissing frogs to see whether one of them turned into a prince! Under our contract we were obliged to return the ship to Australia by the most economical possible means. This meant shipping her on a cargo vessel. The first option was to float the ship onto a Dockwise yacht carrier and return via Port Everglades in Florida. I thought that it was a most unsatisfactory outcome after sailing the equivalent of more than a global circumnavigation in the last three years. Laura van Deelan and Enric Hessing would happily release us from our contract if we had a viable alternative. I began working with the City of Hoorn to conduct a voyage from Hoorn around Cape Horn in the wake of Schouten and Le Maire who sailed from Hoorn in 1616. Schouten sailed aboard *Duyfken* so there were some nice links. The 1616 voyage was designed to upset the VOC spice monopoly. We intended visiting Uruguay and then Hawaii and the old Dutch trading post of Deshima in Japan. Afterwards we could visit Shanghai, Hong Kong, and Singapore and follow an easy track back to Fremantle. We needed €700,000 to accomplish the voyage. It also gave us time to purchase the *Endeavour* Shipyard in Fremantle for $1.1 million as a permanent home for the ship — *Duyfken* Seaport. I hadn't given up on this idea. I had many meetings about it. We commissioned a feasibility study which proved it would be viable. I saw the attraction as the only way the ship could generate enough revenue to be home-ported in Fremantle for the long term.

Another option was to sail the ship directly to Fremantle from Texel, once again rounding the Cape of Good Hope. Gary put together a voyage plan which allowed a six month passage with stops. There was more enthusiasm for this option compared with the ship being ignominiously shipped by freighter. One of our Dutch volunteers was so keen to see it happen that he contacted every large Dutch company trying to convince them of the value of the idea. I also investigated two other options including shipping *Duyfken* either to Singapore or Auckland and sailing back to Fremantle on a short hop. These hybrid options ended up being the worst of both worlds as they combined expenses for shipping and sailing. I even had a hair-brained idea for *Duyfken* to be the first sailing ship to sail the North-East Passage from Texel to the Pacific via the Arctic ports of Russia. It was technically possible then and now almost even practical! The Board let out a collective sigh when I mentioned it. Later, I looked at another option to sail in the wake of Willem Barentsz to the Arctic island of Nova Zembla controlled by Russia. This was the farthest point of his ill-fated expedition. He sailed with two jachts similar to *Duyfken*. I would like to see this one happen one day. All of these options remained unfunded as the year progressed, however, I was confident that I could raise the money if I had another 12 months to do it. I proposed that we winter the ship at Texel or the next island of Terschelling where Willem Barentsz was born in 1550. Benno could arrange shipkeepers for the winter months. The owners of Zaanse Schans also offered to winter the ship amongst the windmills and we received overtures from the *Vasa* Museum in Stockholm and the new Itsas Museum in Bilbao which thought we would complement its exhibition on

Juan Sebastián Elcano, another spice islands traveller. We could return in the spring with a new crew and then sail to Scandinavia where we had a long list of ports which wanted us to visit. This could give *Duyfken* another profitable summer season in Europe.

These schemes required the VOC2002 organisation to amend the repatriation clause in the contract, or simply, we could free them of the obligation of paying for the return cargo trip to Australia. My proposals were debated at *Duyfken* Board meetings and the Board Members never backed me. Nobody wanted to take the risk of financial failure. It was a very disheartening outcome. I knew it would be extremely difficult to set up a profitable operation in Western Australia, and this was a way to get some money in the bank. The only way I could see *Duyfken* paying her own way in Fremantle was with the *Duyfken* Seaport concept and that would require a major fundraising effort. We discussed mothballing the ship in Fremantle until we had a clear plan for the future. I knew I could make the extra season in Europe work and we could do very well in the Baltic ports. In the end, it was decided to bring *Duyfken* back to Fremantle on a specially fabricated cradle aboard a Spliethoff cargo ship. I accepted defeat.

Our final exhibition for the summer season was at Oude Haven in Rotterdam. Gary skilfully manoeuvred the ship into this tiny harbour in one of the oldest parts of Rotterdam. It was a fine, sunny afternoon and we were given a warm welcome. As we slowly passed by lines of house barges, the residents leaned out to hand us glasses of Dutch gin. Then they started handing us whole bottles. As we tied up and sat watching the sails dry in the warm sun, we repeatedly toasted the phenomenal summer we had enjoyed. It was a great release for us to have only one exhibition left before the ship was dismantled for her transition into deck cargo. I ordered takeaway pizzas and we sat on deck with beer and pizza. We began discussing how we'd go about stripping the ship. With the gin and beer talking, I proclaimed that if we could finish the packing in a week then I would take the whole crew to Stockholm to see the *Vasa*. The local laughed at me and said that I was crazy. I said that Australians were aren't afraid of long drives. I pulled out my diary and showed them that Stockholm was, indeed, quite close to Rotterdam. No problem at all — we'd drive there.

Laughing and chatting with our team, I was content for the first time in three years. Early in the spring, Gary and I had quickly worked out who we wanted to stay with us through the whole summer sailing season and who would have to find work elsewhere. Marit van Huystee worked hard to adapt to the needs of the ship on tour and she'd done a fantastic job coordinating the port visits. We had a happy team which worked well together and a very profitable exhibition season. The Dutch had been very good to us and we had enough money in the bank to re-establish the ship in Fremantle. My future was uncertain but I didn't care.

There was one day to go. Amsterdam was the only port where *Duyfken* had been the backdrop for a large physical protest. It was more subtle in some other locations. During our stay in Rotterdam, several people handed out pamphlets to visitors approaching the ship. Delfshaven in Rotterdam is home to many descendants of the Malukan refugees who came from Indonesia after independence. Even though they were primarily soldiers who had fought with the Dutch and their families, they were never well accepted into Dutch society and this fostered a range of civil protest movements. The Malukans also strongly believed that the Dutch colonial power promised them their own South Malukan nation independent of Indonesia and didn't deliver it. A series of terrorist acts in the 1970s highlighted their frustration. The Rotterdam Indonesia Solidarity Committee (RISK) was formed in 1996 to oppose the Suharto regime but with the Indonesian President's demise they widened their interest to a broad range of social justice issues. They joined with the Trotskyist leaning International Socialists and the Young Socialists of Rotterdam to protest *Duyfken*'s visit. A flyer read:

VOC
400 years of impoverishment of Indonesia
No reason to celebrate!

Thank you for coming to visit the beautiful ship 'het Duyfken*'. We would like to draw your attention to the importance of colonialism 400 years ago and we continue to do so to this day.*
In the Dutch shipyards, ships were built en-masse for the long voyages. Not that the workers saw any of the enormous profits, they had to work hard for a meagre wage. Child labour, long hours and hard work ensured that the average age barely exceeded thirty years. That was in the 'Golden Age'.
A visit to the Duyfken *will teach you that the sailors did not have an easy life. Here again long shifts and dangerous work and*

unhealthy food, resulting in scurvy and for many a frightful death. Dutch society did not enjoy the profits from a distant land. No, only a handful of merchants and high lords, including our royal family, made their fortunes.

The VOC, the first multinational, the first monopolist. Not much more than a bunch of rich gentlemen who sent pirate ships out to occupy and loot 'the Indies'. The inhabitants of that time were murdered, raped or turned into slaves for the greasy profits of the peppercorns and nutmeg. The VOC received from the Dutch Government the right to conclude treaties independently, build fortifications, wage war and make peace again.

Under the leadership of Jan Pieterszoon Coen, 15,000 people were murdered on the Banda Islands in the year 1620 because the population did not wish to submit to the VOC.

The pamphlet went on to highlight other eras of VOC and Dutch colonialism. We saw that most people did not take the pamphlets. The protests in The Netherlands were insignificant compared with the overwhelming support and enthusiasm for *Duyfken* we enjoyed. Once again, it exemplified the great contradiction which our ship represented. *Duyfken* had been an excellent choice to replicate. It linked Australia with Indonesia and The Netherlands. The Dutch jacht was one of the finest products of the Dutch 'Golden Age' and the 'Age of Discovery' — a fast, manoeuvrable little ship vastly superior to its European maritime rivals. But also this superb design expressed Dutch power and perceived cultural superiority around the globe. Through *Duyfken* we could see that the 'Golden Age' had a 'Dark Shadow' as some Dutch academics called it during the VOC year. To some, *Duyfken* was a 'ship of shame' and to others it was an example of the power of human invention. Maybe it can be both.

We were in Rotterdam as the feature ship for the world's biggest harbour festival called World Harbour Days. As honoured guests, we were invited to take part in a rowing race using traditional 'pulling boats' in the Haringvliet. Having been a member of the Fremantle Rowing Club for many years, I was keen to give it a red hot go. We were a motley crew with Phil Rose-Taylor as coxswain and James, Barney, Kirk, Cian, Gary and myself as oarsmen. Having the heavy weight of responsibility as the only person who had ever rowed a shell in a race, I gave the crew a bit of quick coaching and a pep talk. Fundamentally, all we had to do was put all the oars in the water at the same time, then pull, then get them out of the water at the same time. The boat would then sing along and victory would inevitably come not to the strongest but to the best co-ordinated crew. Gary described this important moment in international rowing competition.

> *Each heat consisted of three crews, in identical six oared steel boats and we watched the first two heats with interest. In the narrow waterway the boats often fell foul of each other, oars getting entangled, boats struggling to find clear water. The course was along the length of the Haringvliet, round a buoy and return, a distance of about four cables, the eventual result to be decided on times. The third heat arrives and we man our boat, only having a couple of minutes to practice our technique before the start. The gun goes, strong pulls from all gets us going but unfortunately in the congestion, we fell foul of the boat to starboard and we had difficulty getting clear. The third boat pulled ahead and when we finally got into clear water we were in last place. Undaunted, with Phil at the tiller urging us on, we gained ground, overhauling the first of our rivals just before the turn. Down goes the helm, hold water port; pull strongly starboard and we spin round the buoy. Give way together shouts Phil, the boat leaps ahead again, and the chase was on. Slowly gaining on the leader, we settle into a good rhythm, pulling long and strong, until a Herculean effort from Kirk snaps his oar and he is forced to toss it upright to get it out of the way. Winged somewhat we redouble our efforts and we catch the leader and cross the line a boat length or two ahead. 6 minutes 50 seconds — the best time so far despite the poor start and broken oar. What a team — Aussies on top again! A well-earned couple of beers as we watched the remaining heats, seeing some teams, obviously having had much more practice than our couple of minutes, edge us out. We then had a request from the Maritime Museum team for assistance. They were one man short for their boat and wanted to shanghai one of us to help. Our crew, only too willing to help, all pointed to me and I found myself in another shirt at another oar. More congestion in this race but sadly this team didn't have the comeback the* Duyfken *team did and we came in third in this heat. All good fun though. When the times were finalised we found* Duyfken *had managed a creditable seventh position out of 24*

teams. I think I will try and get the broken oar as a souvenir for the ship.

For me it was, and will forever be, my only win in an international rowing race.

At 5pm on Sunday 8 September 2002, on day 492 since leaving Sydney and having completed two major voyages totalling 882 days, a rope went across the gangway in Rotterdam. Tina and James closed the window of the ShipShop and we had one final function to complete our program. This one was the best of all as we thanked everyone who had made the summer such a success. I felt very proud of our whole crew but particularly happy for Gary. The pressure of the Expedition and the exhibition tour of Queensland and then the hectic months preparing the ship for the VOC2002 voyage broke him. However, he came back and I have no doubt that there was no other Ship's Master who could have threaded *Duyfken* so skilfully through the canals of The Netherlands. In summing up his experience he wrote:

> *We all felt a sense of accomplishment — this little ship of ours has made quite an impact in the Netherlands this year and I think we can all feel quite proud of what we have done. I personally am very happy in what my crew have achieved, proving wrong quite a few people who doubted the ability of the ship and her people. They said we would never be able to sail on the Ijsselmeer and we did. They said we would never be able to get up the canal to the Amstel River and we did. They said we would never get the ship up to Delft and we did. They said we would never get into Hoorn and although we nearly didn't, we did (three times!). They said we could not sail on the North Sea canal or the River Maas and we did. There was little expectation of doing much sailing this season, heavy use of the engines thought to be needed. In reality we took on fuel once, way back in the second week in Middleburg and we still have 700 litres of fuel left, some 35 per cent of our capacity. When the current crew joined, the previous crew told us that the old sails were worn out, but in fact they have done good service, carrying us through the season despite a few holes here and there. A few facts and figures to show the extent of the challenges we have faced. Since arriving at Texel in April, we have covered 1028 nautical miles, have entered port 30 times, (quite a few ports more than once), passed through*

> *32 locks and were on standby to pass through 94 bridges, many of them little wider than the ship.*

In 1995, Michael and Patricia Kailis attended the launch of *Batavia* 100km away from us at Lelystad. Michael came back with an idea to ship *Duyfken* to The Netherlands and sail her back, to build a ship which could sail the oceans of the world. He was now vindicated and we had accomplished more with the ship than even he had ever dreamt. Between the ship leaving Fremantle in 2000 and the end of the summer season in The Netherlands, *Duyfken* sailed more than 65,000 km across four oceans, visited 10 countries in four continents, more than 300,000 people came aboard the ship and more than an estimated million people visited her. We successfully undertook the longest re-enactment voyage in an 'Age of Discovery' ship without any loss of life or serious damage to the ship, and in doing so, proved many sceptics wrong.

However, there was no time for this sort of reflection. Next day, it was time to relocate the ship to our work berth in the main harbour of Rotterdam to strip the hull and prepare her to be deck cargo. More bridges were ahead of us. It was another busy day. We approached the Erasmus Bridge, our last opening bridge before the completion of the voyage. I was in the waist of the ship with a fender poised in case the ship moved across to the barriers after the bridge opened. Just as we were about to enter the bridge channel, my phone rang. It was an Australian number. With one hand on the fender and the other hand holding the phone I answered it. It was a Perth car collector, Peter Briggs, and he asked me whether I would like to run a new museum he was planning to open in Fremantle. "Sorry Peter, I am in the middle of Rotterdam, we are just about to pass through the Erasmus Bridge and I can't talk. Can you ring me back?"

With the remaining crew and our volunteers, *Duyfken* was stripped and prepared for lifting. Four shipping containers were packed ahead of schedule. True to my word, we drove to Stockholm to enjoy a collective break and to see the greatest surviving ship from the age when Dutch shipbuilders were without peer. Gary bid us farewell. His work was done and he was quite happy to rest for a day or two then fly back to Australia. For Tina, James, Cian, Barney and I, it was time for our road trip through Germany, Denmark, Norway and Sweden to Stockholm. We all felt free at last.

It was left to me to write the last ship's log in The Netherlands.

The Duyfken *crew is thinning as our visit to Europe is drawing to a close. Gary Wilson has departed for other shores, all but two of our crew members have left and now we are three; waiting for the ship to be lifted and transported back to Australia.*

It has not been my habit to write the daily logs, preferring to delegate the task to our Captains. However, Janine Oosterloo and James Holdsworth who will be accompanying Duyfken *to Australia, thought it a good idea that I write a log or two before they take over the task aboard the* Da Zhong.

So what has happened since the masts were removed, and the hold cleared of goods?

The daily maintenance never stops but it has been a regular routine for the crew and our loyal volunteers from De Delft *Shipyard who continue to shipkeep and assist with whatever needs to be done.*

Duyfken *is now bare and looks like she was in January 1999 when she was launched as a hull in Fremantle. The major difference, however, is that she has endured four years of the elements since then. The glistening varnish she had at launch is now replaced by darkening pine tar. The kevel posts now show the signs of wear from thousands of heaves on the rigging. The hatch coamings are stained from the hands of many people holding on as they climb above or below decks. The red paint of the scuppers is chipped from constantly rolling the cannon in and out as we go from lock to lock, berth to berth. Our little ship has done some hard work and she shows it.*

Duyfken *is clean, too. It has been an enormous effort to clean the ship from stem to stern. I'm sure that it has been years since some nooks and crannies were explored.*

We are continuing to improve the vessel. This does not mean that we are making her more modern, but we are constantly asking ourselves how we can make her more authentic to the period. Many people in The Netherlands have commented on our ballast bricks in the main hold, saying that they look far too modern. The museum at Hellevoetsluis took the lead and donated some handmade, 300 year old bricks. Since then we have sourced another 1500 bricks to replace our trusty Perth house bricks in the hold. The new old bricks are a delight. Some show the finger marks from the brick makers of 300 years ago as they extracted them from the mould and put them in the kiln. They will make a fine addition to the ship.

> *Hempels Paints also delivered to the ship this week paint to be used aboard during the journey to Australia. Hempels have been a great sponsor of* Duyfken *and Janine and James will have a lot of work to do while the ship is at sea. We are particularly keen to make sure our unwelcome passengers, the teredo worm in the hull are no longer enjoying a free ride. Forty days out of the water should kill the last of them and we can apply a new coat of Hempels Anti-fouling. A piece of European Oak was delivered to the ship today to replace the piece in the stern that was damaged by a careless yachtsman in Hellevoetsluis. With the skilled shipwrights available in Fremantle we will wait until we are there to effect the repair.*
>
> *The four containers which will be travelling with the ship aboard the* Da Zhong *are now almost full. Yesterday they were removed from the pontoon and put on the dock to be loaded.*
>
> *The new crane next to* Duyfken *has moved and our ship sits alone at her berth. She looks tiny and abandoned: it's a little sad to see her sitting here dismasted after being such an active, purposeful and proud sailing ship for so long. She is now just cargo for another ship. We'll be sitting next to industrial transformers and other heavy freight. It is the crews and the volunteers that bring her alive and now we must wait until Fremantle for her to be reinvigorated with fresh energy. She has always been self-reliant but now we are all in the hands of Spliethoff to make sure that she arrives home in one piece and structurally sound.*
>
> *Today is lift day. James and Janine are making the final packing of the containers. Our last* De Delft *shipkeeper from The Netherlands leaves and* Da Zhong *sits about 400 metres up the harbour loading heavy cargo into her hold. A tug master from the Port of Rotterdam pays a visit to wish us well. Shiny chrome tape which would look more at home on a space station marks the lifting points for the crane. Now we wait. Our turn to be lifted will come this afternoon.*

It was a most difficult year managing *Duyfken,* and even on the second last day, there was one last surprise in store.

Da Zhong was at the other end of the quay with cranes and forklifts arranging cargo for the hold. We were to be placed on deck so we were amongst the last cargo to be lifted aboard. Our turn would came after lunch, and the big steam driven crane Ajax was at the other end of the harbour to prepare for the lift.

Spliethoff's team leader, Joost Beuker, came striding down the wharf to tell us the latest news. The contract's requirement that two *Duyfken* crew would travel with the ship would not be honoured. The *Da Zhong* would only permit one of our crew to join the vessel for the voyage home. Janine or James would have to stay behind and as it was an all-male vessel, it would be Janine who would miss out.

For over a month we had been planning for two people to travel with our precious ship. Like a beached whale out of the water, *Duyfken* must be regularly kept wet with salt water to stop the deck and hull timbers drying out and shrinking so that the hull remains watertight. The rigging must be constantly tarred to prevent rot. The hull timbers and the masts and yards must be oiled too. With a tight schedule in Fremantle to make the ship ready to sail we also hoped to patch the anti-fouling ready for a final coat on arrival. Little of this could happen. It was too much for one person working alone.

Our two crew prepared well for six weeks at sea on a Chinese operated vessel. They were willing to accept that the Chinese crew could not speak English and they would have to be self reliant and talk to each other for the voyage. They had also packed enough equipment to get a lot of the work done.

For the remainder of the day, the mobile phone ran hot as I desperately tried to resolve the problem. We were placed in an impossible position: to either send the ship away under-crewed, or cancel the contract and miss the opportunity to have the ship in all her glory in Fremantle at the opening of the new Maritime Museum on 1 December. More Spliethoff staff arrived to move our pontoon a little closer to make it easier for the crane to get close to our ship.

Then the crane arrived under tug tow. Quite a crowd gathered to see the lift including past crew members and our ever faithful volunteers from *De Delft* Shipyard. Two of our greatest supporters, Enric Hessing and Dirk Dragt from VOC2002, were on hand to witness the spectacle. Everyone was called to disembark from *Duyfken* so that the Spliethoff team could begin the task of positioning the straps around the hull. Cian drained the fresh water tanks as Janine and James handled the lines. The straps went on easily, the divers gave the all-clear and in what felt like only a few minutes, the steam crane slowly began to lift *Duyfken* aloft. With seemingly little effort, *Duyfken* climbed skyward until she was maybe 20 or 30 metres above the water. The *Little Dove* wasn't quite flying but it was quite a sight to see *Duyfken* from below rather than from above.

Duyfken's last voyage in The Netherlands was at altitude 20 metres from one end of the Waalhaven harbour to the other. We all walked down to the *Da Zhong* as the crane carried *Duyfken* into position next to the heavy lift ship.

Joost's team worked busily aboard, positioning the steel supports and preparing the keel blocks. They knew exactly what to do and they set about the task very efficiently. He was sure the ship would slip adequately between the two deck cranes but he wasn't taking any chances. It was a precarious position. The *Da Zhong* moved up and down on the swell, and the crane moved out of sync with the ship. The hull swayed every time the crane moved. *Duyfken* was lifted yet further aloft before squeezing between the shipboard cranes and then gently landing on the deck of the ship. The crane straps were kept in place until the Spliethoff team ensured *Duyfken* had no chance of toppling over.

When the crane was finally removed, Joost Beuker remarked that he had never had so many pictures taken of him. For the first time since we began meeting with the Spliethoff team months ago, they could see the shape below the waterline of the unusual cargo they were to transport. The welders from Poland and the local carpenters had a tight schedule now to position all the supports and the wooden cradle before dark. Each support was individually shaped to fit the curve of the hull. By 7.30pm, most of the cradle was in position.

A close inspection of the hull was now possible. The anti-fouling applied in Simonstown, South Africa had peeled off in large strips like sunburn and we would have to strip the hull and repaint it in Fremantle. The Hempels anti-fouling underneath was still in good condition. The good news was that our feared passenger, the teredo worm, did not seem to have made much progress in the cold, fresh water of The Netherlands.

We finished the day happy with the lift but uncertain whether commonsense would prevail and we would be permitted two crew members for the long trip home. Janine was getting rather tired of people asking her whether she was THE crew member to be denied the opportunity to travel with the vessel. It seemed like everyone she met in Rotterdam heard of our predicament. Still, *Da Zhong* wasn't sailing until Monday so we still had three days to break the impasse. That was, until the departure time changed once again, and *Da Zhong* was rescheduled to leave on Saturday evening.

Janine re-packed her bags and took them off the ship. James prepared for an extremely busy 40 days.

I admired Janine and James' ability to cheerfully continue their work in a professional manner. Hopes were raised when a Chinese crew member asked James for the names of the two crew members joining the voyage. It was a false hope. By next morning, our four shipping containers were strapped on deck and the masts were lifted aboard and secured. The webbing straps began to be applied to hold down the ship to the deck. By the time all the bright yellow straps had been put in place, the ship looked like it had been visited by fluoro spiders overnight. The Spliethoff team worked quickly and efficiently to get *Duyfken* secured. Their job done, they left in mid-afternoon and we helped James with the last minute details required before departure. It was disappointing that our First Mate, who had worked so hard since she had arrived to work for us, could not complete the job.

When *Duyfken* arrived in The Netherlands, tens of thousands of people were there to welcome her. But arrivals are always different to farewells. This time, Janine, her boyfriend and I were the only people dockside to wish James well and to farewell *Duyfken*. For the first time since 1999, the ship was empty of people and cargo. Our incredible sequence of voyages around the world under our own power and resources was over.

With a glowing peach sunset, *Da Zhong* slipped from the berth, James climbed to the highest deck on the ship and waved farewell. We scrambled up a dockside crane but he still looked down upon us as the impressive heavy lift ship cruised by. In minutes, *Duyfken* and *Da Zhong* disappeared from view into the industrial maze of Rotterdam harbour. *Duyfken* was returning home at last.

As I drove back to the Zeemanshuis Hotel in Rotterdam, the leaves were beginning to fall from the trees, there was a cold wind blowing from the North Sea and the threat of rain again. The days were getting shorter and colder. It was time for me to go, too. Spring was coming in Perth and I knew where I would rather be. Leaving behind a family each time I flew to a new port to prepare for the ship's arrival placed enormous strain on my relationships. I didn't have the luxury of being able to simply close a door and disappear for months on end.

In the last three years, I had spent more than a year and a half travelling — finding sponsors, raising funds, organising port visits, waiting for the ship to arrive, listening to crew concerns, waving the ship and her crew away, then paying bills and ensuring that all our helpers in port had been thanked. It was a relentless and often lonely task. On top of that was the dangerous times in which we lived where I had to ensure that both the crew and the ship were kept safe while civil wars and terrorism swirled around us. I realised that maybe I had gone the same way as Gary and Glenn who had both been pushed beyond the point of total exhaustion. Now it was my turn. I decided it was also time for me to move on.

Epilogue

A handful of people were at North Wharf in Fremantle Harbour to see *Duyfken* unceremoniously lifted from the *Da Zhong*. The riggers got to work, and by December 2002, she sailed in home waters again.

It was the end of a personal odyssey which began for me with a casual conversation eight years before and led me to join a small group of dreamers drinking coffee on Saturday afternoons and talking about grand plans. Together we dared to dream of building the finest sixteenth/seventeenth century fully-sailing replica ship, and we did. When *Duyfken* sailed from the MG Kailis Dock in Fremantle Fishing Boat Harbour on 8 April 2000 bound for the troubled province of Maluku in Indonesia, I had no idea that in less than three years we would visit Indonesia twice and sail from Sydney to Europe on the longest re-enactment voyage conducted by any replica ship of the era. We proved that *Duyfken* was indeed a fine ship which sailed at least as well as her predecessors. Beyond the sailing accomplishments, we learnt to view the European age of exploration as a much more nuanced story than we were taught at school. Hopefully we played a small part in helping reconcile the often grim history of Australia, when Aboriginal people were forced to share their land with others.

With such an extraordinary few years and such great international success behind me, I felt I had nothing left to prove. I never had the appetite to run the ship as a tourist attraction in Fremantle. Setting up and running a private motor museum was my new job, and an easy challenge to accept after years of relentless pressure running the *Duyfken* Project.

Soon, however, the *Duyfken* nest egg we built in The Netherlands was gone and I was asked to return to the Board of *Duyfken* to help rescue the Project. I agreed, but only if my friend from the *Endeavour* days, John Longley, came aboard as well. He was now the Executive Officer of the

Fremantle Chamber of Commerce and he had roped me in to be the Chair of its tourism marketing committee. John agreed to join me on the *Duyfken* Foundation Board. Yes, he was a died-in-the-wool *Endeavour* man, but he had a soft spot for the *Little Dove*. We immediately planned to rustle up some national interest and perhaps stimulate a good measure of outrage for the predicament of the *Duyfken* Foundation. We did this in May 2003 by placing an advertisement in the national newspaper, The Australian, offering the ship for sale. Our most promising enquiry was from Hans Felser who operated the steam tugboat in Hoorn. More than once, he pulled us off a mud bank at the harbour entrance during the exhibition tour. Hoorn wanted to buy the ship. We could say quite openly that if Australia didn't want the ship then she would almost certainly return to The Netherlands.

With the prospect of Western Australia losing *Duyfken*, we sent a letter to the then WA Premier, Dr Geoff Gallop, highlighting that, in May 1995, our State Government agreed that after the ship's voyaging had been completed, the ship was to be gifted to the local Maritime Museum in perpetuity to become a part of the Historic Maritime Precinct in Fremantle. This was a condition of the Treasury funding of $500,000 provided to build the vessel and to use the facilities of the Western Australian Maritime Museum for the construction shipyard. "We have explored all options available to us in light of the Foundation's difficult trading conditions and this is believed to be the most responsible course of action. It ensures that the ship will remain in Western Australia. Certainly, the *Duyfken* Foundation would be reluctant to place itself into administration. Under this scenario, inevitably the ship would have to be placed on sale and it would be sold to interests in either Queensland or The Netherlands," said the letter from the Foundation's new Chairman, the high profile Fremantle Mayor Peter Tagliaferri. It met with silence and then total refusal. We were stunned by the response. The *Duyfken* Seaport concept which offered Fremantle an exciting new attraction for minimal cost also met a dead end at Geoff Gallop's office. I was wrong when I thought that a Premier who studied at Oxford and came from Geraldton would understand the importance of *Duyfken* remaining in our community to tell stories from our past.

I wrote a column for the Fremantle Herald newspaper asking readers what had happened in the old port since the days when we all thought nothing was impossible and we embarked on the crazy idea to build a seventeenth century Dutch ship? "It is important to recognise that community projects such as *Duyfken* work because the community makes them happen, and with government support along the way, very good projects can be done which would cost the government far more if it attempted to do it itself…My greatest fear is that Fremantle will just let *Duyfken* slip away, and another community, which has not made a contribution to *Duyfken*, will reap the benefits. Worse still, the ship might quietly rot away at the end of the wharf. It all came home to me when my young son Daniel asked me whether *Duyfken* would be scrapped. He was very sad and thought it would be a great shame for the ship to go down like this. It is our children who will be the poorer if they are not given the chance to be part of projects such as *Duyfken*. Are we all about to let it happen?" We organised a letter writing campaign amongst the *Duyfken* alumni. Letters from Gary Wilson and Benno van Tilburg appeared in local newspapers. The level of anger often surprised us. One letter from a Carlisle resident who visited Fremantle was particularly scathing: "As I left the Museum, I pondered on the fact that our State Government, in its infinite wisdom and totally ridiculous misjudgment, is prepared to let go of a piece of our long and proud nautical history. *Duyfken*, handcrafted in the oldest of traditions, built in the open air for all to see, is under the threat of being sold off interstate or overseas. What saddened me more, with the sheer amount of money flowing through this once great State, our knees buckling under the weight of an overtaxing and uncaring Labor Government, is that no other body was prepared to make an offer and keep history here in WA. Shame on you, Dr Gallop. Shame on you, millionaires of Perth. Shame on you, industry and business leaders. The future should always include the past. Don't let the *Duyfken* sail away without the opportunity of it returning to its proud home." This protest campaign created enough outrage in Perth to get local support and give us hope that *Duyfken* could be retained in WA even without Premier Gallop's support.

Duyfken was laid-up in Fremantle for 12 months as we desperately tried to find a way to keep the ship. The Foundation was converted back to a volunteer organisation, just like it was back in 1994. With the help of many volunteers from all walks of life led by Jenny Gibbs, *Duyfken* continued to operate in a low-key way in Fremantle and from the jetty at the Old Swan Brewery on the Swan River. Patricia Kailis and the Kailis family could see that we were committed, and they agreed to defer any immediate move to call in the Foundation's debt. Thanks to the persistence of Peter Tagliaferri and the new Board, a lifeline was thrown to our ship. After an 18 month effort, we bundled together $250,000 in funding to enable the ship to sail for a year under the banner of the *Duyfken* Traineeship Programme where 'youth-at-risk' were able to experience team work in a maritime environment. *Duyfken* was saved by the contribution of local government authorities, contributions from the private sector, and dozens of volunteers who came to the rescue.

We talked about the ship as a national treasure and the exposure of *Duyfken* at the Old Swan Brewery proved conclusively that West Australians expected the *Duyfken* Foundation, as the custodian of the vessel, to protect 'their' heritage. We said that we had that responsibility to the community who supported us so enthusiastically.

Meanwhile, the HM Bark *Endeavour* Foundation was also in financial trouble and its problems did not help us when we talked to bureaucrats and politicians. In 2005, a provision in the funding agreement with the Commonwealth Government which enabled the ship to be completed was enacted and ownership of *Endeavour* was transferred to the Government which, in turn, allocated the asset to the Australian National Maritime Museum at Darling Harbour. Our plan was to survive until 2006 so we could use the quatercentenary of *Duyfken*'s visit to Australia to drum up more national interest. We had an ally in Canberra in the form of Rupert Gerritsen who was born in Geraldton of Dutch migrant parents. He was a highly-respected historian. His research into the possibility that survivors of Dutch shipwrecks were absorbed into local Aboriginal groups was controversial, but also fascinating. He traced genetic similarities, and elements of language and social organisation which seemed to be derived from the earliest Europeans in Australia. With Peter Reynders, who was also passionate about early Australian maritime history, he formed a committee called 'Australia on the Map: 1606 – 2006' to give recognition to the quatercentenary of *Duyfken*'s visit to Cape York. He was determined and persuasive in his dealings with Canberra decision-makers, and his efforts to help us paid off.

We had an ally in WA Senator Ian Campbell, the Federal Minister for the Environment and Heritage. He announced in March 2006 that *Duyfken* would embark on a nine month, 12,000 km voyage in every state of Australia to mark the 400th anniversary of the first recorded European contact with the 'Unknown Southern Land'.

At the time, Senator Campbell said: "The chronology of that part of

Australia's history is not as well known as I think it should be, and I agree with the Prime Minister's (John Howard) view that we need to know our beginnings to understand ourselves." *Duyfken* and her crew were once again storytellers, giving life to history.

The success of the 'Australia on the Map' tour which touched 25 ports in 2006 was the catalyst for *Duyfken* to enter into a three year agreement with the Cairns Port Authority and the Queensland Government for the vessel to be home-ported in Cairns, and to sail between Queensland ports telling the story of the first Dutch visit to Queensland. We could see the ship alternating seasons in Queensland and Western Australia. Despite positive early signs, it was not a happy time for *Duyfken*. By June 2010, the Queensland Board of Directors of the Foundation which we had established to create a local support base was inactive. It hadn't met since November of the previous year and Cian Pereira, who was in charge of the vessel, was left with little support. The chair of the Queensland Board which was appointed to operate the vessel resigned. Our great friend from Brisbane, Kasper Kuiper, agreed to take on the role on a temporary basis and assume the responsibility for the ship in Queensland. He did a fine job in our hour of need. His daughter, Louisa Schmidt, took over the finances and kept a tight reign over what little money was flowing into the Project. We found that even though *Duyfken* was in tropical waters she had not been slipped for 18 months. *Duyfken*'s Queensland agreement ran its course and we ended where we had started a few years before, with little money in the bank and no immediate prospects.

Once again, I agreed to chair a governing body of *Duyfken*. It transpired that I spent twice as many years working for the *Duyfken* Foundation in a voluntary capacity as I had as an employee but I couldn't let go. Thanks to Kasper Kuiper's influence, *Duyfken* was allocated a berth at the Queensland Maritime Museum. The ship was at this berth in January 2011 when the Brisbane River flooded to 2.5 metres above high water mark. Working night and day, her shore crew secured *Duyfken* and she safely rode out the flood.

With our short term future in place in Queensland but the long term in doubt, we had to do some serious medium and long term planning. I had a personal long term objective to return *Duyfken* to Western Australia but we needed the State Government to help. We discussed it at the Board and we concluded that I needed a way to see the newly-elected Western Australian Premier, Colin Barnett, who was a great supporter of the Project. He launched the *Duyfken* 1606 Replica Foundation back in 1995. One of my

Board Members, Malcolm Hay, the indomitable founder of the sail training foundation with the operated STS *Leeuwin*, was a constituent in Colin Barnett's electorate of Cottesloe and greatly respected by the Premier. We had no hope of meeting the Premier in his St George's Terrace office, but he set aside time every week to meet local constituents at his electoral office. Malcolm rang and arranged a meeting on 18 December 2008, saying that his friend, Graeme, would accompany him. It was an enlightening meeting. He had only been Premier for a short time but he had big plans. He was toying with the idea of the redevelopment of the area between Perth and the river to include a small harbour. He wanted to extend the waterfront under the Narrows Bridge all the way to the old Swan Brewery building below Kings Park. Town planners call it 'activating' an area. I explained to the Premier that the City of Hoorn in The Netherlands wished to enter into a 10-year chartering arrangement for the ship to be incorporated into its new harbour project after the completion of our Queensland contract. However, we believed that the ship should be home-ported in our State, where she was built, and where the impetus for her construction came from. He agreed and embraced the idea. He thought that we should berth *Duyfken* at the new Perth port when it was completed.

Following a refit, *Duyfken* sailed from Brisbane in February 2011 to Cockle Bay in Sydney under a one-year contract with the Australian National Maritime Museum. *Duyfken* replaced *Endeavour* as a floating museum attraction until May 2012 while the Cook replica circumnavigated Australia. *Duyfken* was once again the centre of attention in Australia's biggest city. With revenue estimated at between $60,000 and $70,000 for the 14 month period, it was a far cry from the days of the ship's big exhibition tours. The *Duyfken* Foundation was once again short of funds and the ship was a long way from home.

We constantly sought options to keep *Duyfken* in Australia. In early 2010, we were prepared to hand over the ship permanently or on a long-term lease to the Australian National Maritime Museum. *Duyfken* was offered via my local member, Stephen Smith, the Minister for Foreign Affairs, and the Member for Fremantle, Melissa Parke, to the Australian National Maritime Museum to become a part of the national heritage collection. The proposal reached the desk of the Federal Heritage Minister, Peter Garrett, but the silence was deafening. The Museum did not want the financial burden of another replica ship in its collection and the Minister had little interest in advocating our case.

Meanwhile, there were still more ambitious options. Benno van Tilburg was at St Petersburg in Russia inspecting a piece of wood from Willem Barentsz' ship which was wrecked on the Russian Arctic island of Nova Zembla in 1595. He returned to The Netherlands and joined a steering committee to form a foundation to build a replica of the Barentsz' jacht on a wharf in Harlingen. Barnetsz' ship was, like *Duyfken*, 30 lasten (60 tonnes) cargo capacity, and the evidence being used to reconstruct the design included, like *Duyfken*, data from the shipwreck SO1 which was found in The Netherlands. Planning began in October 2010 and we discussed relocating *Duyfken* to The Netherlands under a lease agreement and sailing *Duyfken* and the new vessel to Nova Zembla in a re-enactment of the ill-fated voyage attempting to sail the North East Passage. It was a great option to keep *Duyfken* sailing but, once again, a backer was not found to get the ship to Europe.

It was not until early 2012 that the *Duyfken* 1606 Replica Foundation's commitment to the Australian National Maritime Museum, which followed the Queensland contact, was completed. I proposed to the Premier that *Duyfken* could sail back to Western Australia forthwith, visiting Queensland ports and Darwin along the way. *Duyfken* could return to a temporary berth at the Old Swan Brewery wharf in the Swan River where we had been in the past. It was not an ideal location as she would take a battering from the winter southerlies, but it was the best we had. It had the important benefit that the politicians in Parliament House would see the ship every day as they drove into Parliament. It could be a staging point for a permanent berth at what had now been dubbed the Perth Waterfront Development. I proposed that the State Government could provide sufficient funding so that *Duyfken* was available for educational visits by school groups on a free-of-charge basis. *Duyfken* would be on exhibition at Perth for the entire school year, and once a year she could be re-located to Fremantle for maintenance and a day sail programme. The ship could be available to the State Government for special events in regional ports and overseas including the 1616-2016 commemoration of Dirk Hartog's visit to Western Australia, and the 1915-2015 Gallipoli Convoy events in Albany. Negotiations with the Premier's office took months. The Government did not want to fund the full amount but a compromise was reached whereby the State Government provided a fixed level of funding and seconded two public servants to help run the vessel. Special events were not included in the funding agreement and would have to be funded separately. It wasn't a perfect solution, but the best I could negotiate.

It was six years since *Duyfken* was last in Western Australia. Acting Premier Kim Hames announced in February 2012 that the WA Government had entered into an agreement with the *Duyfken* Foundation for the ship to return to her home state. The 10-year grant agreement ensured that *Duyfken* would once again became part of the fabric of the Western Australian community. Importantly, the ship would be available for the Gallipoli Centenary in 2014/15 and the 400th Anniversary of Dirk Hartog's landfall on the western coast of Australia in 2016. With a 10 year buffer, I was confident that we could build up a legacy fund to ensure that the ship was financially self-sufficient. It would require a committed fundraising effort from the Board.

In April 2012, *Duyfken* set sail from Sydney to Fremantle via Brisbane, Mackay, Townsville, Port Douglas, Cooktown, Weipa, Darwin, Port Hedland and Geraldton to return home. *Duyfken* was once again operated in Fremantle by the *Duyfken* Foundation and open for schools and the general public to visit.

WA Premier Colin Barnett said in his media release: "To have a ship like that here in WA representing Australia's rich pre-colonial history and more-so directly connecting to WA's links with our amazing Dutch maritime history is a fantastic achievement and will provide a unique opportunity for tourists to visit a new attraction exuding massive educational appeal".

The ship arrived back in Fremantle in September 2012. It was a proud moment for me and the thousands of people who contributed to *Duyfken* since the first spark of an idea in 1993 caught the imagination of people from all walks of life and the incredible Project began. We aimed to revive the Friends of the *Duyfken* and to rekindle interest in the ship which had slipped since the halcyon days. With the ship back in Fremantle, I began looking at ways to mark the 400th anniversary of the Hartog voyage. My primary plan was to sail *Duyfken* from The Netherlands to Cape Inscription in Western Australia and then maybe finish the voyage, as Hartog did, in Macassar. It was a relatively straight-forward voyage sailing the Brouwer Route. We could ship *Duyfken* to somewhere in the north-east of the USA and sail her 3000nm across the Atlantic to begin the voyage in Texel.

It became obvious that many groups wanted their fingers in the Hartog pie, and like the Vlamingh Tercentenary of almost a decade before, the small amount of money allocated by the State Government would be spread around a wide range of events – of lot of activities but not much impact. It was not a time for big thinking. The great voyage was not endorsed, and then my request for $250,000 to conduct a modest voyage to Cape Inscription and a high profile tour of regional ports met with a stony silence. On top of this, the arrangement for State Government officers to work for the *Duyfken* Foundation turned into a nightmare, and I found that I was working one full day a week as a de-facto CEO of the Foundation. My long term aim of raising another $1.2 million to match the State Government's contribution was also going nowhere. Perhaps I was part of the problem? I knew that the Board simply did not have the horsepower to drive a major corporate funding program. I could not do it on my own. I was frustrated. I also thought that I had done enough, helping raise more than $7 million for the Project over the years.

The issue came to a head on 16 October 2013. I walked into the Board meeting and Ron Reddingius immediately asked me what was wrong? I sat down, declared the meeting open and resigned from the Board of the *Duyfken* 1606 Replica Foundation. I said that I had served *Duyfken* for 20 years. I explained that I was making no headway in any of the plans for the future and I had to move on with my life. John Longley agreed to take over as interim chair for a few months (which stretched into seven years).

The Hartog year which was announced with great excitement amounted to little in the end. The Foundation was offered a pittance to sail to Cape Inscription in 2016 and it accepted the offer. It was a low key affair compared with the grand voyages of the past. She motored back to Fremantle along the coast rather than taking a great arc under sail into the Indian Ocean. She punched into daunting headwinds which tormented the crew. It looked like her great voyaging days were over.

In November 2016, Prince Willem-Alexander of Orange was now His Majesty King Willem-Alexander of The Netherlands. Visiting Canberra, the new monarch was honoured with a state lunch where he reflected on his connection with *Duyfken* and the seafaring feats of his forebears:

> *For us, personally, Australia holds many fond memories, not least of our extensive visit 10 years ago. Then, as now, we followed in the wake of the Dutch mariners who mapped out Australia's coastline four centuries ago:*
> *Willem Janszoon, who set sail on the* Duyfken *in 1606.*
> *And Dirk Hartog who sailed on the* Eendracht *in 1616.*

> *Their explorations are traced on the great world map in the marble floor of Amsterdam's Royal Palace, which was built in the seventeenth century. The map shows only half of your great country, labelled 'Nova Hollandia'.*
>
> *Every time I walk across that marble floor, I'm struck by the presumptuousness of giving the continent that name. As if it hadn't been inhabited for thousands of years by a civilisation that deserves respect as the planet's oldest living culture. The fact is, Australia has always captured the Dutch imagination. For us it remains a land that 'abounds in nature's gifts of beauty rich and rare'. A beacon of freedom and independence. A permanent source of human enterprise and energy. In The Netherlands, just hearing the word 'Australia' brings a smile to our face.*

As Peter Manthorpe once said, *Duyfken* was a constantly oxidising lump of organic matter. She was now reaching middle age. The wretched leaking deck was replaced and oakum and tar was used to seal the seams in the traditional way. Equipment which was installed to accomplish the great voyages 20 years before was in urgent need of replacement. Funds were raised and the work was done. She looked like her old self again.

In 2017, the Barnett government was defeated in the General Election and Mark McGowan was elected Premier. He was the sixth Premier to serve the State since the *Duyfken* Project began. He made no secret of his desire to extricate the State Government from some initiatives which he saw as 'pet' projects of the previous government. *Duyfken* was one of those projects and he indicated that there would be no funding for the ship, asking why the private sector did not come to the ship's rescue? In fact, the private sector and the public had contributed millions of dollars to the ship over the years. He even wanted to 'renegotiate' the final years of the 10-year agreement citing a budget 'black hole' for his actions. The Premier's glib comments were an insult to the voluntary board of the *Duyfken* Foundation led by Vikki Baldwin, the staff and the volunteers from across the WA community who had worked hard to raise funds and to keep the Project afloat. Of course the *Duyfken* Foundation sought out corporate backing. It was nonsense to suggest otherwise, however, the Board was unable to find any high level corporate or private backers to supplement the State Government funds I raised in 2012.

With the agreement I negotiated due to expire and its money running

EPILOGUE 461

out, *Duyfken* once again faced a dire financial situation. I received a call from John Longley in 2020. He was no longer on the Board of *Duyfken* (although he maintained his interest in the Project) but he was now sitting on the Board of the Australian National Maritime Museum with Senator Campbell. They raised the possibility of the *Duyfken* Foundation gifting the ship to the Museum and he asked me for my opinion. He knew I was proud that we had maintained the *Duyfken* 1606 Replica Foundation as a totally independent, not-for-profit organisation for so many years. He and I had been through a lot with the ship during this time. We would meet at the Fremantle Motor Museum long into the evening after the doors had closed, strategising and formulating plans to keep the *Duyfken* Foundation alive. It was history repeating. He did not want to see the ship chained to a wharf in Fremantle. We had been there before. While more funding could probably be raised, I had to agree that it was probably time to find a long-term solution to the Foundation's constant funding nightmares.

I knew how to rattle the cage. I'd been lobbying behind the scenes and putting the case for more *Duyfken* support with a few strategically placed Letters to the Editor and letters to politicians over the past few years. John Longley sounded me out whether I would oppose the gifting proposition if it gained support. I told John that I thought the *Duyfken* Foundation did not have the sense of purpose which had inspired two great voyages and the circumnavigation. I felt the great days of *Duyfken* as a ship for great voyages and big thinking were over. The ship had largely been used for a small scale public exhibition and schools program, and for day sails. I had never liked that the ship had been conducting pirate days. I believed that this ran absolutely counter to our mission to tell the serious story of the first encounters between Aboriginal Australians and European seafarers. Why would a government or a private backer want to fund a ship like this? I said to John that my insightful secretary Peggy Rogers once told me "there is nothing more ex than the ex-Project Director". I would not publicly oppose the move.

I did, however, voice my disappointment to the State Government that it had effectively abandoned a great State asset. It could have worked with the *Duyfken* Foundation to find a solution which would keep the ship in our State. In reply, I received a most depressing letter from David Templeman, the Minister for Heritage, Culture and the Arts. He said:

The replica was built as you point out to raise awareness of Dutch

> *exploration of Australia in the 1600s and the first known European contact with Aboriginal and Torres Strait Islander people. The significance of the original* Duyfken *1606 voyage, as the first recorded European encounter with the Australian mainland is beyond question however this contact was with the western coastline of Cape York in northern Queensland. The original* Duyfken, *as far as we know, had neither contact with nor knowledge of what we now call Western Australia. The* Duyfken *1606 replica's relocation to the Australian National Maritime Museum will see it take centre stage in the heart of Sydney where this story can be told to a wider audience at the Australian National Maritime Museum, an excellent Museum which enjoys significant support from the Federal Government. It is a logical move that I believe is in the* Duyfken *1606 replica's best interests both for its future survival and so that its story can be told to all Australians. I am aware of your long association with the* Duyfken *1606 Replica Foundation, as well as the spiritual attachment of the replica vessel to Fremantle, however, I genuinely believe that the Australian National Maritime Museum is best placed to care for her and to tell this all Australian story.*

I was astounded by the Heritage Minister's appalling ignorance and nonsensical reply. For almost 30 years we had been talking about *Duyfken* as being the beginning of 164 years of Dutch maritime exploration, most of which had been along the western coast. The impetus to tell this story came from West Australians. It seemed incredible that a WA Government minister would be so provincial in his thinking, and happily acquiesce to a major local heritage asset being re-located to another state. If his logic was followed, then the ship should be in Queensland anyway. There had to be something more to it. So I placed a Freedom of Information request to the Premier's office. I mostly received vague memoranda still refusing to entertain the idea of the McGowan Government supporting the Project. Certainly the heavily redacted documents revealed under Freedom of Information showed that no competent and serious assessment of the value of the ship to the WA community was undertaken. It was an arbitrary decision based on vague budget principles — and not even the tired old excuses trotted out by the Minister in his letter. There was one document to which I was not allowed to examine: "access is denied on the basis that disclosure could reasonably be expected to damage relations between the Government and other governments." I appealed the decision and I was again refused access to the document. We will probably never know exactly why the WA Premier abandoned *Duyfken*. My curiosity for the decision-making process which went behind the Premier's decision was irrelevant. The deal had been done during the pandemic when the community's mind was on bigger short-term issues and the Premier was enjoying unprecedented popularity.

Patricia Kailis, who had grown very fond of the ship in later years, generously forgave the debt which the *Duyfken* 1606 Replica Foundation had carried on its books for more than 20 years. This cleared the way for the ship to be handed over to the Federal Government debt-free. The Australian National Maritime Museum insisted that three independent marine surveys and valuations of the ship had to be done prior to reaching an agreement. The ship passed with flying colours. She was in excellent condition. Asset valuations indicated that the ship was worth approximately $3.5 million.

Duyfken was shipped to Newcastle in New South Wales aboard a cargo vessel before Christmas 2020. She was rigged, and then sailed the last small stretch to Cockle Bay in Darling Harbour.

Duyfken has left many memories in Western Australia, but there are still small, more tangible traces of *Duyfken*. One of my last acts as Project Director in 2002 was to donate oak timber left over from *Duyfken*'s construction to a community group to help them build an eight metre replica of *Batavia*'s long boat in Geraldton. It was the boat which Captain Francois Pelsaert sailed 3,000 km to Batavia to seek help for the survivors of the *Batavia* shipwreck. He returned aboard the *Saardam*, a jacht not unlike *Duyfken*. The long boat replica is now tied up outside the Maritime Museum in Geraldton.

The dream of creating a replica shipbuilding industry in Fremantle based on the success of *Endeavour* and *Duyfken* never eventuated. No large scale replica ships have been built in Australia in the last 20 years, perhaps because it is now so difficult to navigate through the issues of colonialism and invasion which these ships can be seen to represent. It would be wrong, however, to suggest that the two ships haven't left a valuable legacy in the State. Many people who worked at the *Duyfken* yard had fine careers in ship construction afterwards. Some of the young shipwrights who couldn't see themselves working on fibreglass or aluminium craft took their skills and passion to other fields where a commitment to excellence and a strong work ethic was admired. The young sailors of *Duyfken* were drawn back to the sea and a number progressed to bigger ships and greater responsibilities, forging fine careers in the merchant navy. Closer to home, *Endeavour* and *Duyfken* also made West Australians proud that they could achieve anything if they set their minds to it.

So did we achieve what we set out to do in 1995? I am proud of what we achieved in many areas. The *Duyfken* Foundation's first constitution listed our aims which included building a ship and making more Australians aware of their earliest known maritime history. We also wanted to "encourage a greater understanding by Australians of the contribution and involvement by the Dutch to Australian and South East Asian culture and Australian history." We, and I include everyone who has been a part of the *Duyfken* story for the last 28 years, have done so much more than this. I soon realised that we did not own the *Duyfken* story. If anyone owns the story it is the people of the Pennefather River who saw those sails on the horizon and the ghostly apparitions on board. We never knew the story, but they never forgot it. I am embarrassed to think today that we did not include them in our original constitution. Yes, the Dutch story has 'Dark Shadows', too. We understand that now. Today, the story of *Duyfken* has its rightful place in the Australian National School Curriculum.

The last rites for the *Duyfken* 1606 Replica Foundation, which was formed in February 1995, were performed on 18 February 2021. The *Duyfken* Foundation was no more after 26 years of building and sailing the ship as an independent not-for-profit foundation. Only a few dozen people attended the final meeting compared with the hundreds of supporters who attended our early Friends of the *Duyfken* meetings in the exciting early days. It was a sombre occasion with several speeches painting the demise of the Foundation and the gifting of its major asset as a win for the long-term future of the ship. At the time, I didn't agree. I had conflicting emotions. I sat at the back of the room, keeping my thoughts to myself. I was saddened to see the end of our dream.

But maybe it wasn't the end. Our ship is being maintained and cherished. If funds are needed for her upkeep they will be found. There is now recognition in Australia's national museum of maritime history that the first recorded encounter by Aboriginal people with people from the outside world is a story which rates in national importance. We have done good.

As for me, I am still a landlubber. *Duyfken* represented a moment in time I will cherish but it did not make me yearn for a life at sea. I found other challenges. The *Duyfken* years showed me that there is a world of possibilities that we can make real by stubbornly chasing a goal and never giving up.

Duyfken is now a permanent part of Australia's National Heritage Collection, delighting everyone who sees her sailing on Sydney Harbour. Treat her well, Sydney, and never forget the marvellous adventures we had, the stories we told, the people who built her, cared for her and sailed the amazing *Little Dove*.

Have I mentioned a Barentsz voyage?

Life and Times

A Duyfken Album

Gillian Kaye-Peebles took this photograph (above) of Michael Young in his lounge room on the evening in 1993 when he decided to push for a replica of Duyfken *to be contructed. He is reading Priscilla Murdoch's 1974 book,* Duyfken and the first Discoveries of Australia, *which inspired him to find out more about the ship. He found a kindred spirit in retired journalist and author, James Henderson (right).*

An early visualisation by Adriaan de Jong of Duyfken *arriving at Ternate with the volcano, Mount Gamalama, in the background. The painting of the ship was inspired by Dr Cornelis (Cees) De Heer's scale model of the first* Duyfken *to sail to the Indies in 1595 and other jachts from this time. The ship has extravagant ornamentation, a prominent gallery at the stern and crows nests. The painting from 1994 was an essential part of early marketing of the Project. Subsequent ground-breaking research commissioned by the* Duyfken *Foundation showed that this ship was not the one which sailed to Cape York Peninsula. The final design of the* Duyfken *replica created a more accurate interpretation of the first ship recorded in history to visit Australia. By then, however, the painting had done its job – inspiring people to support the Project.*

470   THROUGH DARKEST SEAS

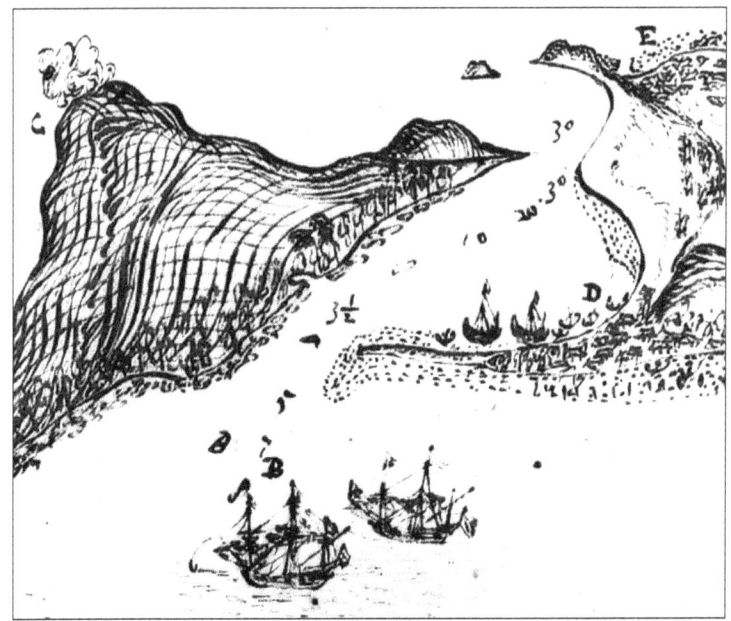

One of only two drawings taken from life. Duyfken *(right) moored at Banda. The drawing gave clues to the rigging of the vessel.*

An etching of Duyfken *(in the centre) at the Battle of Bantam. On Christmas Day 1601, five Dutch ships fought a fleet of Portuguese ships including eight galleons and twenty-two galleys. Skirmishing continued until New Years Day. The Portuguese retreated. The battle marked the emergence of The Netherlands as the rising power of the European spice trade.*

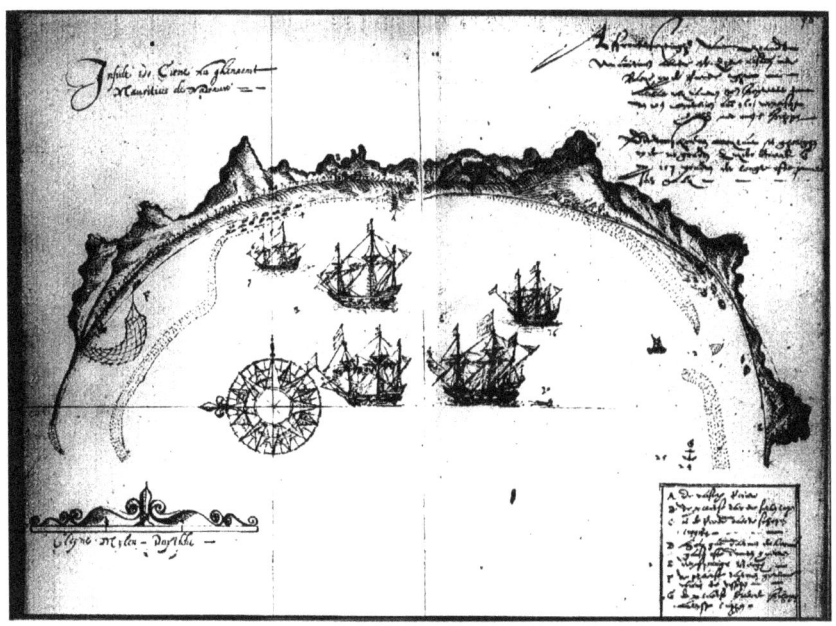

The second extant drawing. The Fleet of Admiral Wolfert Harmensz at anchor on the south west coast of Mauritius in October 1601. Duyfken was sketched at the top left in this chart (enlarged below) in the log book of the ship Gelderland. The fleet returned to The Netherlands in 1603.

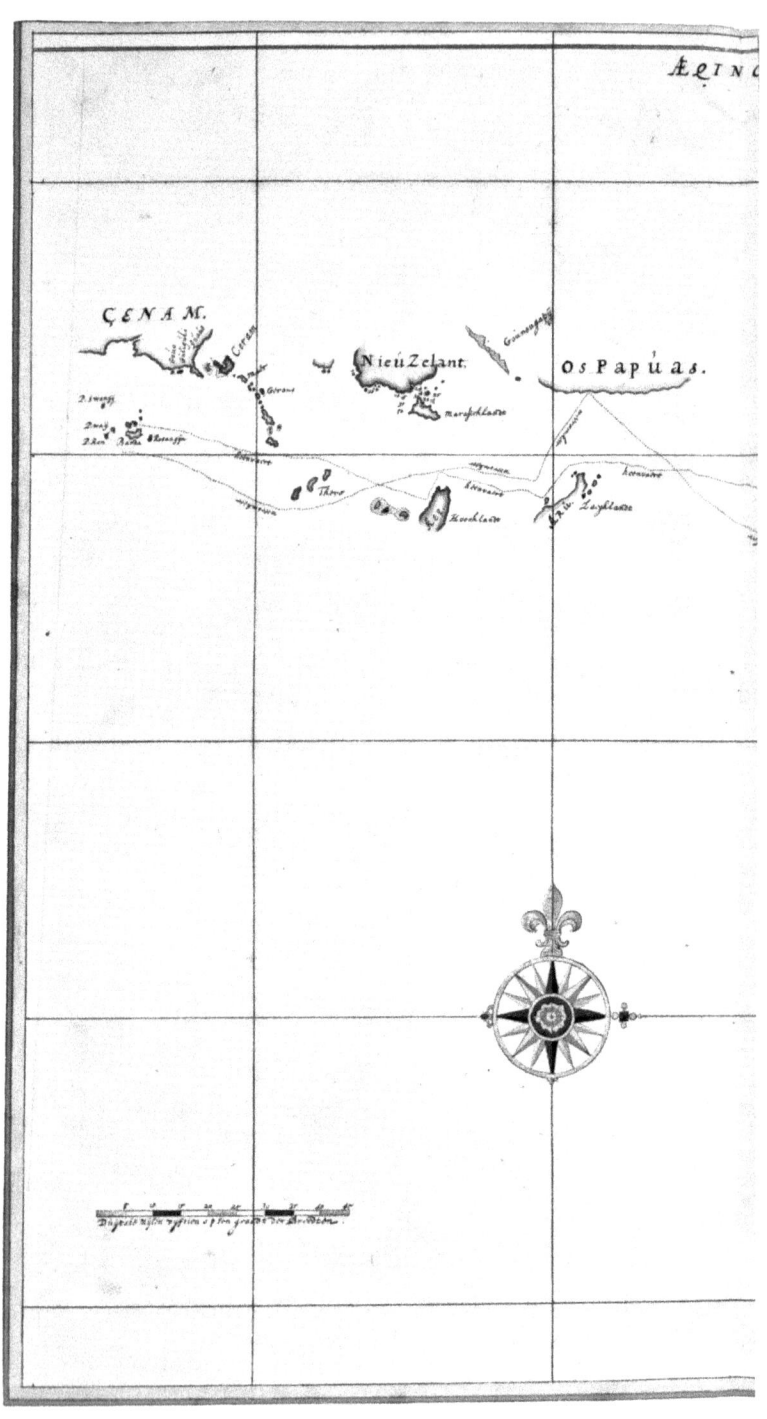

A copy of the original map drawn on board the Duyfken during her voyage of discovery along the Australian coast in 1606. It was contained in the secret atlas of the VOC. This copy is from

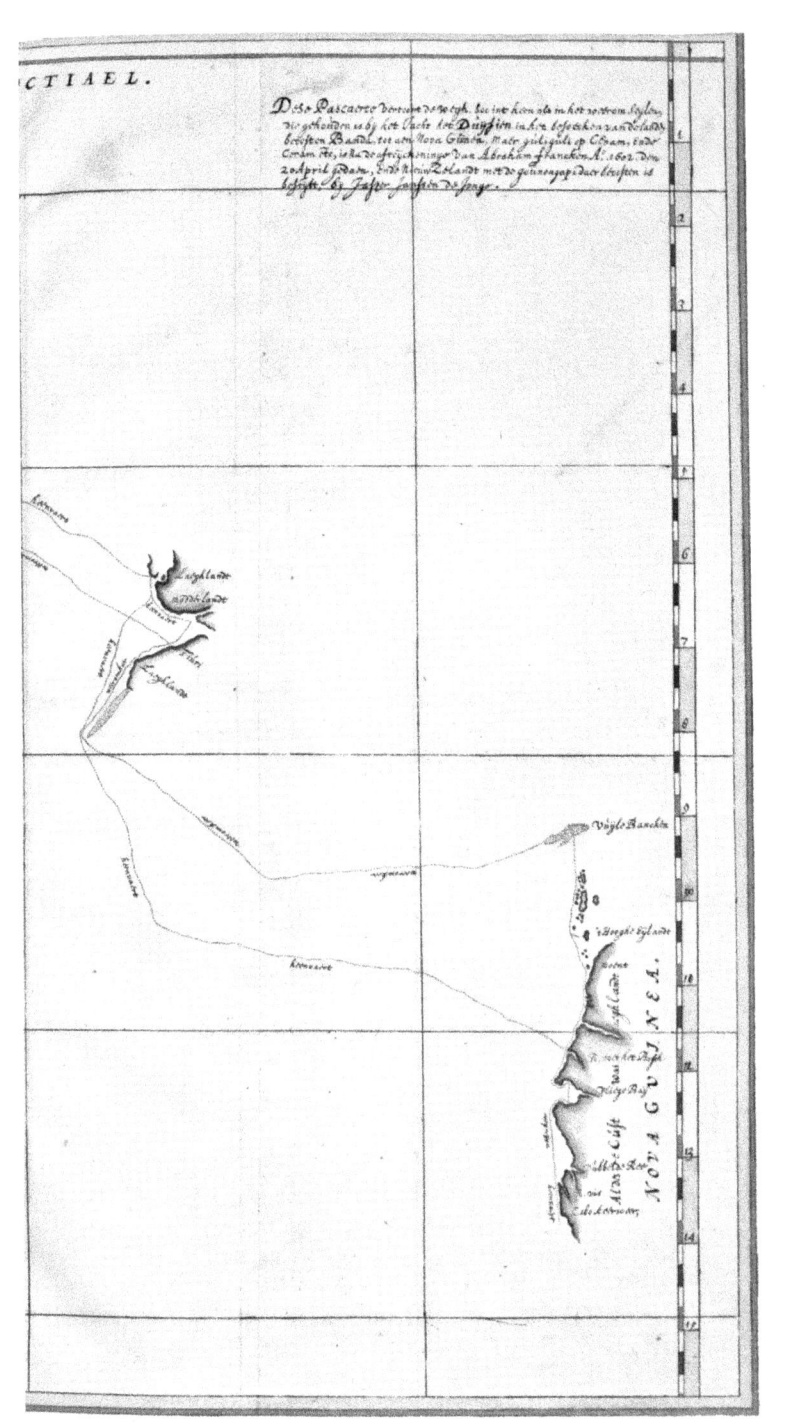

the Atlas Van der Hem printed in 1670, one of the treasures of the Österreichische Nationalbibliothek in Vienna, Austria. (Copied by State Library of Queensland)

Under the portico recovered from the wreck of the Batavia, Perth actor, James Sollis, playing Captain Willem Jansz gatecrashed the launch of the Duyfken 1606 Replica Foundation on 25 February 1995 by the Deputy Premier of Western Australia, Colin Barnett. Great fun! (Photo: Gonnie Bonda)

Michael G Kailis, Chairman of the Duyfken 1606 Replica Foundation, and one of the key figures in the formative years of the project.

Nick Burningham, with the assistance of Adriaan de Jong and Marit van Huystee, researched and designed Duyfken.

Project founder, Michael Young, and Ashley Haywood from the Noongar community with the traditional Boorn Wongkiny (stick talking) or message stick with a message written in Noongar to go with the ship from Fremantle and to be presented to the traditional owners of the Pennefather River area in Cape York, Queensland. (Photo: Klaus Schmechtig)

The Lotteries Duyfken *Village shipyard was built outside the Shipwreck Galleries of the Western Australian Maritime Museum in Fremantle. The building was temporary and later relocated to Albany for a whale boat project.*

Father Vincent Conroy was called to bless the keel on the eve of the keel laying ceremony. He used a ceramic Bellarmine jug from the Duyfken *era. (Photo: James Henderson)*

Crown Prince Willem-Alexander of The Netherlands lays the keel of Duyfken *on 11 January 1997 with Michael Kailis standing nearby.*

Three titans of the successful campaign to fund Duyfken*: (from left) Julius Tahija from Indonesia, Michael G Kailis and Sir James Cruthers.*

Master shipwright, Bill Leonard, with a highly skilled and motivated team of shipwrights and trades people applied traditional skills to build Duyfken. *(Photo: Richard Polden)*

Using fire, the same technology applied by Aboriginal people to straighten spear shafts, the hull planks were heated to just below the point of combustion. The cellulose becomes plastic at this temperature and substantial pieces of timber can be bent into remarkable shapes.

Bill Leonard and his team lift into place the keelson, a longitudinal beam above the floors and the keel. It adds strength and stiffness to the robust structure.

Duyfken's *stern rose to the ceiling of the shipyard. All the major oak timber (Quercus robur) was shipped from the forests of Latvia.*

The Duyfken *construction team in the days leading up to the launch of the ship. (Photo: Ria Sjerp)*

A major milestone. All hands to bring the tying strake to the hull.

The hull of Duyfken *is ready to be launched and the building around it is removed, exposing the hull to the West Australian summer sun for the first time.*

With a heritage-listed Moreton Bay fig tree blocking the shortest route, Duyfken was paraded through the streets of Fremantle on its way to the launch location. The parade stopped in Market Street and South Terrace, better known as the 'Cappuccino Strip'. Exemplifying the pride felt by the people of Fremantle, Mayor Richard Utting cheekily said the event proved that the old port city was, indeed, the 'centre of the universe'.

Duyfken *was launched with great fanfare at Fremantle Boatlifters in Fishing Boat Harbour on 24 January 1999 by Jo Court, the wife of the WA Premier.*

Duyfken's *first voyage was under tow from Fremantle up the Swan River to the Australia Day fireworks at Perth water. She was then returned to Fremantle for her fit-out. (Photo: Ria Sjerp)*

Duyfken *under sail for the first time during July 1999 in the waters of Gage Roads near Fremantle. The deep honey coloured oak enjoyed many coats of varnish and looked magnificent. The coating would only last a few weeks into the voyage to Indonesia. The hull would soon be oiled instead and it is now a deep blue-black colour. (Photo: Klaus Schmechtig)*

Ship's Master for the expedition, Peter Manthorpe, with the Boorn Wongkiny which was carefully stowed in his cabin for the voyage. (Photo: Klaus Schmechtig)

Cape Town, South Africa with Benno van Tilburg, chair of the Stichting Duyfken Nederland, the charitable foundation formed in The Netherlands to raise funds and coordinate the voyage and exhibition tour in 2002. (Photo: Author)

Volunteer guides and Friends of the Duyfken *farewell Duyfken and her crew on 8 April 2002 as the ship begins her expedition to Indonesia and Cape York. Symbolic of breaking ties with loved ones, for a moment,* Duyfken *was held back by hundreds of streamers connecting her to the wharf. (Photo: Klaus Schmechtig)*

An idyllic scene as Duyfken *rests at anchor at Menanga on the island of Solor between Kupang and Banda in Indonesia.*

Duyfken *First Mate, Gary Wilson, with the new whipstaff or kolderstok made of ironwood from Menanga and shaped in minutes by more than a dozen local boys with sandpaper — and tons of enthusiasm.*

(From right) Peter Manthorpe, Des Alwi and the author as the Malukan orembai boat is prepared for launching. We looked upon our new boat with amazement and then pure delight. (Photo: Robert Garvey)

Duyfken *at anchor, the crew drying the sails at Banda in Indonesia with the jungle covered slopes of the Gunung Api volcano in the background — an entrancing sight in the soft morning sun. (Photo: Author)*

The Pennefather River mouth near Weipa on Cape York. The starting point for the European relationship with the first Australians. (Photo: Author)

Almost four centuries later, a replica of the first ship recorded in Australia's history is anchored near the Pennefather River. The 1606 voyage of Duyfken was the first time recorded in history when Aboriginal people met people from the outside world. (Photo: Author)

History reinterpreted. Peter Manthorpe, in the orembai, is paddled ashore at the Pennefather River mouth and places a white flag into the beach sand and asks for permission to land. (Photo: Author)

John Cockatoo places a spear in the sand next to the flag, symbolically inviting Peter Manthorpe to come ashore peacefully. Ina Thallo (Aunty Ina) later said: "We must not dwell on the past. The past is a story we can tell our kids sometimes . .. but we must look ahead into the future." (Photo: Author)

Margaret Note and her sister Hazel Miller from the Yupungutti tribe represented the traditional custodians of the Pennefather River. Peter Manthorpe presented them with the Boorn Wongkiny (message stick) from Fremantle and he was given a plaque made from ironwood from the river banks. (Photo: Author)

Duyfken pounding through the waves in Moreton Bay, Queensland. The highly successful exhibition tour of Queensland ports rescued the Duyfken Foundation from financial disaster.

Duyfken *about to leave the Australian National Maritime Museum, Cockle Bay, Sydney on the VOC 2002* Duyfken *Voyagie which saw the crew sail four great oceans to Europe.*

Ship's Master on the VOC 2002 Duyfken *Voyagie, Glenn R Williams, with* Duyfken *on the hard standing at Simon's Town Naval Dockyard near Cape Town, South Africa in November 2001. (Photo: Author)*

Duyfken *at Sunda Kelapa in Jakarta, Indonesia passes the tall-masted Bugis trading ships called Pinisi to approach her berth. Only 12 months before it was unthinkable for the ship to visit the Indonesian capital. (Photo: Author)*

How others see us. At Galle in Sri Lanka, two students visited the ship with their faces painted white and dressed as Dutch spice traders, reminding us of just how strange Duyfken *and her crew must have seemed. (Photo: Author)*

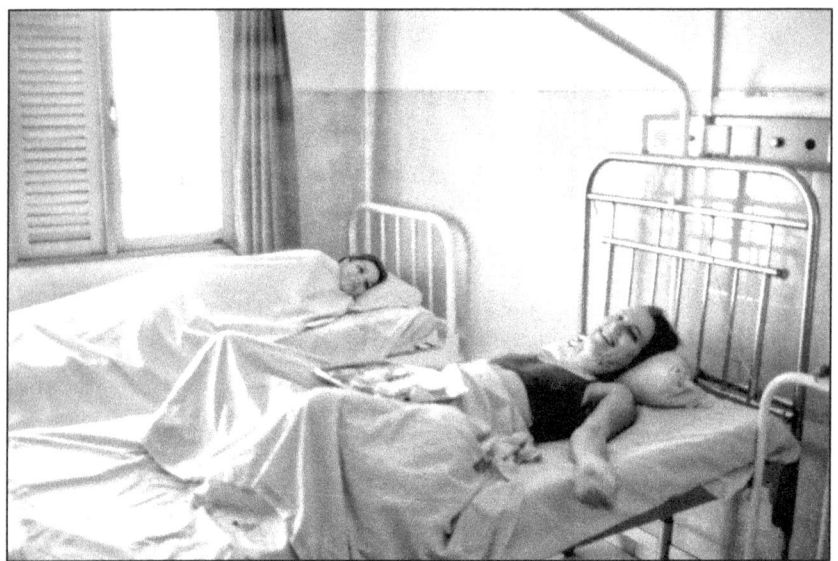

Christine Henschien (left) and Heidy Bontjer at the Nawaloka Hospital in Colombo, Sri Lanka after suffering injuries in heavy seas. Christine rejoined the ship and Heidy was flown to Perth for treatment. She stayed for several months with the author's family. (Photo: Author)

With the deck awash, crew member, Nicole Gardner, repairing a sail during a storm between Mauritius and South Africa.

In every port, school children came aboard and the author and crew members told the story of the ship and her place in history. These students came as part of a program of book distribution to local schools coordinated by the Dutch consulate in Cape Town, South Africa.

The Dutch Navy makes contact with Duyfken *in the North Sea near Texel during spring squalls. The crew had to dodge commercial shipping in the English Channel before a final push to the finish at Texel and ultimately Amsterdam. (Photo: Author)*

Duyfken approaching Texel after a year at sea. The ship is now a dark colour after two years of the crew applying wood oil to the hull planks. The flags represent the nations visited by the ship during the VOC2002 Voyagie. (Photo: Elly Spillekom)

Prince Willem-Alexander arrives at Texel to join about 20,000 people who flocked to the small island to welcome Duyfken *and her crew to The Netherlands after the year long voyage from Sydney, Australia. (Photo: Gonnie Bonda)*

28 April 2002, and an exhausted crew line up to be introduced to Crown Prince Willem-Alexander and the Australian Governor-General, Peter Hollingworth.(Photo: Gonnie Bonda).

Returning the compliment. Chair of the Duyfken *1606 Replica Foundation, Rinze Brandsma, presents Joke Geldorp-Pantekoek, the burgomasster of Texel, with an aluminium plate to celebrate the arrival of* Duyfken, *commenting that 400 years ago, the Dutch were in the habit of leaving plates in Western Australia - now they can have one back! (Photo: Gonnie Bonda)*

The best of times. True believers celebrating with the crew at Texel, 2002. From left, Ria Sjerp, John Quigley, Nicole Gardner, Gonnie Bonda and Peggy Rogers. (Photo: Gonnie Bonda)

A protest vessel approaches Duyfken *in Amsterdam. The vessel is soon to be cut off by the authorities and sprayed with water by a fire fighting boat. (Photo: Author)*

For the first time, a Dutch jacht traverses the canals of Amsterdam to connect with the Amstel River. (Photo: Sandra Tresidder)

Tens of thousands of visitors queued for hours to step aboard Duyfken *during the summer exhibition tour of The Netherlands. This is a typical day - at Middleburg. (Photo:Author)*

Duyken *is dwarfed by* Batavia *at Lelystad in Flevoland — but the mighty little ship and crew had just completed the longest voyage in an 'Age of Discovery' replica. Size doesn't matter so much. (Photo: Author)*

Duyfken *on the River Zaan at Zaanse Schaans near Amsterdam. Windmills generated power to operate saws which helped cut the timber used on the Dutch fleets. (Photo: Author)*

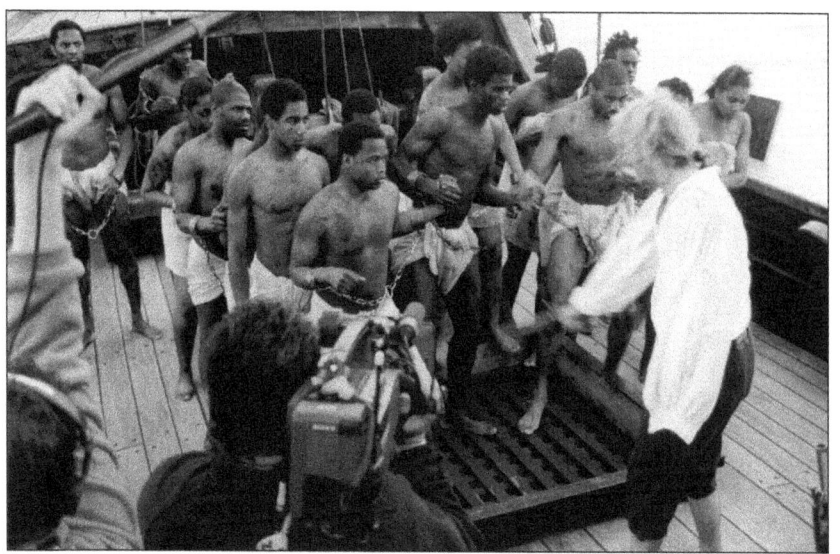

Disturbing scenes re-created. Filmmaker, Willem A van der Spek, hired Duyfken *to sail on the Ijsselmeer to film scenes for his ground-breaking children's television series, 'Slavery' on the Dutch involvement in the slave trade. (Photo: Author)*

Duyfken *was never allowed time to rest in The Netherlands. The wharf was converted into a theatre stage and a large tribune built facing the ship. Theatre Nomade performed a play, 'The Flying Dutchman', in the evenings. (Photo: Ab Gietelink)*

Unable to fund a return voyage or remain in Europe, Duyfken *is lifted aboard a ship bound for her home port of Fremantle. (Photo: Author)*

Strapped down and ready to leave. (From right) James Holdsworth, Janine Oosterloo and the author in Rotterdam with Duyfken *secured on the deck of the* Da Zhong. *In a cruel twist, our wonderful Mate, Janine, was prevented from accompanying James and the ship to Fremantle.*

Acknowledgements

A cascading series of events led to write this book. Principally, the loss of the ship to Western Australia announced in late 2020 caused me to reflect on the years of planning, construction and voyaging. I heard many stories of how *Duyfken* came about and what happened during her great years of voyaging the world. Many of them were wrong. I began to write as the coronavirus pandemic infiltrated our lives in Australia and the future became uncertain. Then, in early 2021, the *Duyfken* 1606 Replica Foundation which we formed two decades before, was wound up. I kept writing. Sadly, in February 2022, the founder of the project, Michael Young, passed away and shortly afterwards, our Master Shipwright, Bill Leonard, suffered a debilitating stroke. I realised that the remarkable story of the *Duyfken* Replica's origins may never be fully recorded. I resolved to redouble my efforts and to complete my manuscript and get it published.

Archive boxes I hadn't opened for years became rich sources of information. My old diaries provided information on long forgotten meetings, but the most enjoyment came from contacting old friends from my *Duyfken* days. Tracy McCullough and David Kerbey encouraged me. Ron Reddingius provided his usual insightful comments. Robert Jefferson, our Ship's Artist from the first voyage, bundled up some papers and posted them to me. What a delight they were to read. I spent many enjoyable hours talking to Bill Leonard and Nick Trulove. Nick Burningham reviewed the manuscript and corrected my historical slip ups. The drawing of *Duyfken* was completed by Nick in the early days. Benno van Tilburg, Marit Van Huystee and Ab Gietelink in The Netherlands helped me reconstruct the VOC2002 years. It was wonderful to once again talk about *Duyfken* with the ship's former Masters. I must especially thank Peter Manthorpe and Gary Wilson for giving me feedback. Crew members including Julie Milne (Dale), Jane Doepel, Ben Manthorpe, Shannon McGuire, Ralph Dekkers, Tom Goodman and Rupert Weller have helped me paint a picture of life aboard. I must especially thank Nicole Gardner who not only provided me with her thoughts, but also proofed the manuscript. Josh McLernon and Margaret Rapanaro have reminded me of the comings and goings in the shipyard. Graeme Henderson enabled me to fine tune my account of the competition to agree on which ship to build. A number of the stalwarts from the early days have reminded me of the good times we had and how the pieces fitted together: Janine Young, Margaret Rapanaro, Gonnie Bonda, Ria Sjerp and Gillian-Kaye Peebles.

Kathryn Daniels (nee Cartwright) helped me to gather my memories of the years with Michael Kailis, Sir James Cruthers and Syd Corser. Our resident musician, Michael (Barney) Barnett, will forever be an enthusiastic *Duyfken* supporter. From his time working in the shipyard to being part of the summer tour in The Netherlands, he was a great help.

John Longley and I share the singular experience of being in charge of the construction and voyaging of a replica ship and I valued his critique of my words, ideas and perspectives.

Robert Garvey and Richard Polden have generously allowed me to use their photographs. I apologise to photographers I have not been able to acknowledge.

Special thanks to my wife Cathy for proofing the manuscript — she knows more about *Duyfken* than she cares to remember!

Lastly, Elly Spillekom has constantly encouraged me every step of the way. Her enthusiasm is infectious and she has done more than anyone to ensure *Duyfken* is not forgotten in Western Australia.

This book was written from my perspective. I accept full responsibility for any errors or omissions. I hope that my story will stimulate more people associated with *Duyfken* to tell their story, even disagree with my assessment of some situations, and that it will bring back great memories for everyone whose lives have been touched by our ship.

I also hope that it will inspire others with big ideas to accomplish what naysayers condemn as impossible. Don't ever give up on your dreams.

Graeme Cocks
Perth, Western Australia
2023

Glossary

The story of building and sailing *Duyfken* has more than its fair share of obsolete and obscure words and sometimes confusing nautical expressions. The Project also straddled the worlds and words of Australia, The Netherlands and Indonesia. Here are some.

Admiralty model A model of a ship without planking so the interior structure of the ship can be seen
adze Similar to an axe except the blade is curved and a right angles to the handle. A traditional shipwright's tool for shaping timber
aftercastle The highest deck of the ship at the rear (stern)
aloft Above the lower yards and in the rigging of the ship
amidships In the middle of the ship
anchor fluke The wide part of the anchor which digs into the sea floor
anchor shank The long part of the anchor
anti-fouling A paint applied to the hull of a ship to prevent the growth of marine organisms
artikelbrief Orders for the Ship's Master from the owner of the vessel under command
Bajau Laut Nomadic seafarers of Indonesia sometimes called 'sea gypsies'
barquentine A sailing ship with only the foremast square-rigged and the remaining masts rigged fore and aft
baulk A roughly squared piece of timber
beak (head) The structure jutting forward of the bow of a ship
beam The width of a ship at its widest point
beating to windward Sailing as near to the direction of the wind as possible

Belanda (or Balanda)   A white person in South East Asian and northern Australian languages. Said to come from 'Hollander'
bilge pump   A pump used to extract water from inside the lowest part of a ship's hull
block   A single or multiple pulley
bonnet   An extension to a sail to add sail area
bosun   The crew member responsible for the maintenance of a vessel;
bosun's chair   A small wooden or rope seat used to hoist sailors aloft or over the side for maintenance
bowsprit   A spar pointing forward of the bow to carry the spritsail
breasthook   A v-shaped piece of timber connecting the port and starboard sides of the ship's hull at the bow
brigantine   A square-rigged sailing ship with two masts but without a square mainsail
broaching   When a sailing ship loses direction and points towards the wind
Bugis   The people of Sulawesi in Indonesia
Butonese   People from the islands of southwest Sulawesi including Buton Island
bulkhead   The walls of a ship separating rooms
burden   An old measure of the tonnage of a ship based on the number of tuns (casks) of wine that it could carry in its hold
capstan   A vertical drum on a ship used to raise anchor cables or ropes
carlines   Like the beams of a roof, carlines are fore and after timbers underneath the deck planks
carrack   A sturdy sailing vessel of Portuguese origin from the fourteenth to seventeenth century
ceiling   The roof inside a cabin of a ship
cleat   A wooden hook attached to the ship to hold a rope
coaming   A raised frame on the deck to stop the ingress of water into a hatch
coiling down   Arranging ropes in a spiral on deck
compass timber   Curved structural timber near the bow which creates the shape of the hull
corecore (Kora Kora)   Large open Indonesian canoes with dozens of paddlers, similar to dragon boats
course   A square sail set on the lowest yard on a mast
cross-tree   (and trestle-tree) Horizontal wooden beams between the top of the lower mast and top masts, used to spread rigging and for sailors to sit or stand, wrongley called a crow's nest

crow's nest A nineteenth century term used to describe the platform at the intersection of the lower mast and top mast where a sailor sat or stood. *Duyfken* did not have such a plaform (see cross-tree)
cutter A sailing boat with a single mast rigged fore and aft, carrying a mainsail and at least two headsails
dead-eye A flat wooden disk used as part of the rig
deadrise The angle formed between the horizontal plane and the hull surface
doubling A second layer over the hull
downwind Sailing with the wind aft of the ship
drawing The distance from the bottom of the hull to the waterline
Duradon Commercial product name for a modern synthetic sail material looking like flax
fairing To smooth the hull timbers so that planking can be attached
fashion piece The curved timbers which define the shape of the stern
flax A fibrous plant used to make linen
floor The lowest timber frames attached to the keel
forecastle The forward part of the upper deck of a ship
foremast The forward vertical mast
frigate A medium sized square rigged ship
furling To gather a sail into a roll on the spar
fusta A small ship powered by both sails and oars
gaff rig A sailing rig in which the sail is four-cornered, fore-and-aft rigged
galleon A large sailing ship of the fifteenth to the seventeenth centuries
galley (ship) A ship that is propelled mainly by oars
galley (on board) A ship's kitchen
galliot A small and fast Dutch sailing ship also propelled using oars
garboard strake The lowest plank of a ship's hull
greased ways The ramps on which a ship slides when it is launched
halliard A rope that is used to raise a sail
hard on the wind Sailing as close to the direction of the wind as possible
hawes piece (hawser pipe) The shape surround the hole that the anchor cable runs through on the hull
heads Ship's toilets
heaving mallet A sailors mallet with a round head used to strain a rope or twine
Heaving to See Hove to
hemp A tough natural fibre used for making rope

GLOSSARY

hermaphrodite brig A two-masted sailing ship which has square sails on the foremast combined with a schooner rig on the mainmast
hooker A cutter-rigged sailing boat
hove to Stopping the forward movement of the ship
jacht A fast, light sailing ship used by the Dutch from the sixteenth century
jihadi A fighter against the enemies of Islam
junk A typically flat-bottomed sailing vessel used in Chinese waters
ketch A two-masted, fore-and-aft rigged sailing boat with a small mizzen mast
kevel post Hooked timber cleat to which large ropes are attached
klass A large forked clamp to lever planks which have become flexible in a bending hearth
Kolderstok (see whipstaff)
knee (hanging knee) A right angled, curved piece of timber connecting the deck beams to the hull
lateen A triangular sailed attached to a yard, hanging at an angle to the mast on a sailing boat
leeward The direction opposite to the direction the wind is blowing
leeway The amount the ship drifts off course due to the sideward force of the wind
luffing To sail towards the direction of the wind, when the sails begin flapping
Makassarese The group of people who live in the southern coast of the South Peninsula, Sulawesi in Indonesia
manila A kind of hemp obtained from the abaca plant which is endemic to the Philippines
mate (First Mate) The highest rank on the ship behind the Ship's master.
mizzen The mast closest to the stern behind the mainmast
morion helmet An open faced combat helmet typical of the Kingdom of Castile in Spain
oakum Tarred fibre of old rope and animal hair used to caulk gaps between deck and hull planks
orembai A wooden planked boat from the Maluku province of Indonesia
payed To coat with waterproof material
Pelni Pelayaran Nasional Indonesia — the national cargo and passenger shipping company of Indonesia
Pinnasse A small speedy sailing boat
pine tar A tar made by distilling pine wood and used as a preservative on a wooden sailing ship, particularly on the rig

pinisi   Sailing ship used for trade by the people of South Sulawesi in Indonesia
pitch   Tar used to seal the seams of a wooden sailing ship
prahu   Sailing boat with outriggers used in the Maluku province of Indonesia
quarterdeck   A ship's upper deck near the stern
rabbet   An angular groove cut along the keel, stem, or sternpost
ribband   A long flexible piece of wood used to hold the hull framing together before planks are attached
Rijst Tafel   A feast of Indonesian dishes developed by the Dutch in Indonesia using local food traditions
rove   To fasten a rope through a block or loop
Satcom 'C'   Satellite communication used for ships at sea for email, weather forecast and small bundles of data
schooner   A sailing ship rigged with foreand aft sails on its two or more masts
scupper   A side opening in the side walls of a ship to allow water to flow off the deck into the sea
sheer   The curve of the deck
sheet   A rope used to control the setting of a ship's sails
Ship's Master   The most senior officer in charge of a ship
shoe   The protective planking on a ship's keel to save it from damage
shores   Props used to hold up the hull of a ship in a shipyard
sloop   A single-masted sailing boat with fore and aft rig
spar   A wooden pole used to hold a sail
spritsail   A square rigged sail carried on a yard below the bowsprit
square-rigged   A rig in which most of the sails are held on yards fastened to the masts horizontally
stanchion   Upright wooden post on a deck
standing rigging   The ropes which hold up the masts and stop them from falling over
stem   The most forward part of the ship's bow extending in a curve from the keel
stern-castle   (see quarter deck)
sternpost   The upright timber running up from the keel in the stern
stern tube   The holes through the hull which contain the propellor drive shafts
Stockholm tar   A highly refined pine tar used in the preservative mix on *Duyfken*
strake   (tying strake) The piece of timber running horizontally the full length of the ship from stem to stern

strop   A ring or grommet made of rope
supercargo   A person employed on board by the owner of the cargo carried on the ship
survival suit   A waterproof dry suit that protects sailors overboard in cold seas
tack   A sailing manoeuvre used to change a boat's direction to make progress into the wind
taffrail   The highly carved upper stern of the ship
tallow   Refined animal fat used as a preservative on board
transom   The flat timbers between the fashion timbers at the stern of the ship
trunnel   A wooden peg used to fasten planking to the hull
tumblehome   The narrowing of the hull above the waterline
under-canvassed   Not carrying enough sail area for maximum speed in the available wind
waist   The portion of the deck between the forecastle and quarterdeck
watch keeping   Rostering sailors to sail the ship at all times over 24 hours
wear ship   To change tack
wheelhouse   The room where the whipstaff or kolderstok is located on *Duyfken*
whipstaff   (kolderstok) A lever attached to the tiller which is then attached to the rudder

Index

A

911 Attacks 176, 381

Abidin, Sahran 265, 270
Aboriginal flag 315
Aboriginal people 19, 25, 32, 45, 52, 54, 90, 109, 130, 194, 200–201, 205, 267, 296, 299–302, 308, 312, 315, 317, 320, 329–332, 386, 431, 452, 455, 462, 477, 489
Abrolhos Islands, Western Australia 35, 47, 63, 110, 170, 205–206, 217
Abyssinia 75
Aceh, Indonesia 89, 175, 225
Ackland, Dr Tim 388, 397, 399
Adonara, Indonesia 245
Agulhas Bank 389–391
Agulhas Cape, South Africa 77, 337, 389, 396
Agulhas Current 389, 393, 395
Ah Mat, Richie 301
Airlie Beach, Queensland 330
Akawa, Martha 405
Aksi Setiakawan 429
Albany, Western Australia 122, 151, 458, 474
Albatross Bay, Queensland 280
Alebeek, Wim 217, 390
Alitas, Ali 367
Alston, Richard 88, 120
Alwi, Des 247–248, 254–256, 260–262, 264–266, 270–272, 273, 275, 487
Alwi, Ramon 248, 257
Alwi, Tanya 247–250, 264, 271, 273, 365–366
Amamapare, Indonesia 292, 295
Amba, Cmdr Richard 322
Ambalama (Victoria) Villa, Galle 375

Ambers Inn 322
Ambon, Indonesia 71, 74, 78, 123, 174–176, 186–187, 223, 225, 235, 247, 250, 252–260, 272, 273, 282, 325, 338, 364
Amcor Fibre Packaging 94
Amphitrite 87
Amstel River, Amsterdam 433, 499
Amsterdam Convention Centre 430
Amsterdam, The Netherlands 64–65, 82, 88, 97–98, 102, 118, 120, 122, 131–132, 141, 156, 164, 227, 229–230, 334, 338, 402, 409–410, 424, 426, 429–435, 438, 441, 460, 495, 498–500
Anak Krakatau, Indonesia 370
Anchor forge 157
Andrea 353
Andrew Tyne Reid Charitable Trust 329
Arafura Sea 130, 185, 279, 282, 295, 323
Ardika, Gede 249
Ardon, Rick 150
Arnhem Land, Northern Territory 47, 200, 279, 296
Arnhem ship 30, 130, 318

Arnison, Governor Peter 125
Artikelbrief 76, 200, 316, 425, 506
Aru Islands, Indonesia 222, 225, 279, 281, 291
Arung Samudera ship 220–222
Ascension Island 338, 388, 399, 405–406, 410, 416, 426
Atambua, West Timor, Indonesia 325
Atlas Blaeu Van der Hem 278
Atlas Van der Hem 471
Aunty Flo 302, 308
Aunty Ina (Ina Thallo) 302, 308, 312, 490
Aurukun community 201, 315
Aurukun Three Rivers Tavern 315
Australia Day 133, 149, 482
Australia II yacht 33, 67
Australia on the Map 455
Australian Maritime Safety Authority 120, 158–159, 187
Australian National Maritime Museum (ANMM) 21, 49, 181, 328, 352, 361, 455, 457–458, 461, 464
Australian National School Curriculum 465

Australian Sail Training Association 349
Australian-Netherlands Chamber of Commerce 355
Avondster ship 372
Azevedo, Peter 410
Azores Islands, Portugal 338, 388, 399, 408, 410–411, 415, 418, 420–421, 426, 546

B

Bacan Island, Indonesia 70, 187, 220, 225, 247, 324
Bairstow, Ltnt Cmdr Warren 306
Bajau Laut ('sea gypsies') 239, 244, 506
Baker, Matthew 102
Baker, Patrick 46, 278
Baldwin, Vikki 461
Bali, Indonesia 175, 186, 200, 237, 239, 279, 326
Ballad of the Duyfken 18, 146, 199, 425
Ballast 23, 125, 128, 149, 168–170, 446
Baltic 69, 96, 116, 119, 238, 437, 440
Banda Besar Island, Indonesia 255, 274
Banda, Indonesia 4, 8, 42, 65, 70, 74–75, 77–78, 80, 131, 175, 184, 185–187, 213, 220–225, 228, 247–250, 252–258, 261–264, 266, 268–272, 273–278, 279, 281–285, 288, 289, 298, 307, 309, 319, 325, 330, 337, 430, 442, 468, 485, 488
Bandaranaike International Airport 372, 374
Banks, Sir Joseph 22, 91, 180
BankWest 166
Bantam, Indonesia 73, 75–81, 82, 279, 337, 370, 388, 468
Barentsz, Willem 336, 439, 457–458, 465
Barnett, John 64
Barnett, Lorna 94
Barnett, Michael 'Barney' 17, 113, 169, 442, 445
Barnett, Premier (Minister) Colin 63–64, 67, 91, 456, 459, 461, 472
Barrow Island, Western Australia 214, 261
Batavia (Jakarta) Indonesia 34, 63, 205–206, 210, 212, 228, 275, 337, 364, 368, 371, 436, 464
Batavia long boat 464
Batavia River, Queensland 280
Batavia ship 24, 31, 33–35, 46–48, 57,

63–65, 73, 95–96, 102–103, 109–110, 121–122, 129, 151, 157, 170, 206–207, 229–230, 328, 352, 355, 358, 435, 436, 445, 464, 472, 500
Batavia's Graveyard book 435, 436
Bataviawerf Shipyard and Foundation 47, 355, 436
Bathurst Island, Northern Territory 35, 45–46, 90, 200
Battle for Surabaya 248
Battle of Bantam 76, 370, 468
Batu Gajah 258
Baudin, Nicolas 212
Beagle HMS, ship 33
Beales, Tracy 212
Beatrix, Queen of The Netherlands 47, 64, 108, 125, 337, 356, 429, 435
Beattie, Premier Peter 120, 125, 135–136, 264, 299, 308–309, 315, 330, 333
Beazley, Kim 68, 123, 238
Becu, Peter 39, 62, 134, 182
Beggs, Pam 33
Bellarmine jug 107, 139, 158, 474
Bellottie, Janita 212

Belu, Indonesia 225
Ben Manthorpe 18, 243, 307, 314, 504
Benedictine monastery, New Norcia 143
Bernstein, Else 110
Bertie 236, 238
Best, Lee 212
Beuker, Joost 448–449
BHP Transport 217
Bicentenary, Australia 25, 34
Bielken, Lawrence 157
Biermans, Ed 411–412, 420
Big Brother television program 359–360, 421
Bilge pump 114, 149, 169, 195, 207, 381, 507
Bindal people 329
Birds of Paradise 323–324
Bjelke-Petersen, Premier Sir Joh 33, 333
Bjorksten, Igor 118, 144, 152, 161, 164, 195, 204
Blackwood Passage, Papua New Guinea 320
Blake, Captain Chris 362
Bligh, Capt William 188, 237
Bolton, Prof Geoffrey 139
Bond Corporation 23, 54
Bond, Alan 23, 25–26, 33, 49

Bonda, Gonnie 39, 498, 505
Bontjer, Heidy 348, 353, 358, 372, 374, 377, 406, 409, 415, 417, 494
Boode ship 405
Boomerang ship 352
Borbidge, Premier Rob 120
Borneo, Indonesia 174
Boroko, Papua New Guinea 322
Bounty replica ship 119
Bounty ship 237
Bourne, Capt Chris 217, 362, 391
Bradleys Head, New South Wales 352
Bragg and Gill, Constables 137
Brambles Manford 134–135, 140
Brandsma, Rinze 44, 58, 61–62, 85, 116, 127, 182–183, 200, 202, 217, 327, 343, 351, 360, 363, 397, 399–400, 425, 428, 497
Brisbane River, Queensland 53, 187, 331, 341, 456
Brisbane, Queensland 135–136, 180, 235, 323, 329–331, 334–335, 339, 341–342, 386, 426, 456–457, 459

British Millerain Company 157
Broome, Western Australia 55, 186, 224, 231–235, 310, 313, 347
Brouwer Route 459
Buetti, Peppi 313, 341
Bukit Siguntang ferry 250, 252, 256, 277
Bunting, Heinrich 35
Bureau of Meteorology 185, 297
Burke, Premier Brian 34
Burningham, Nick 18, 34–35, 44, 47–48, 66, 68, 69, 73, 86, 89, 96–97, 107, 116, 120, 130, 138–139, 141–143, 151–152, 157, 159, 167, 170, 183, 185, 233–234, 236, 246, 257–258, 270, 278, 293–294, 296, 300, 358, 364, 378–379, 381, 392, 396, 473, 504
Burrup Peninsula, Western Australia 215
Bwilmi Tanikwith descendants 303

C

Cable Beach, Western Australia 235
Cairns City Council 456
Cairns Express tug 327
Cairns Port Authority 456

Cairns, Queensland 53, 151, 205, 301, 306, 328–329, 338, 348, 359–360, 456
Cakalele dance 274–275
Callao, Peru 31
Campbell, Alan 357, 368–369, 378–379, 381
Campbell, Senator Ian 93, 455, 461
Cape Agulhas, South Africa 77, 337, 396
Cape Arnhem, Northern Territory 296
Cape Grenville, Papua New Guinea 320
Cape Inscription 31, 36, 129, 211–212, 459–460
Cape Keerweer, Queensland 268, 280, 316–317
Cape Melville, Queensland 326, 362
Cape of Good Hope, South Africa 36, 71, 77, 336, 337–338, 389, 397–398, 405, 439
Cape Town, South Africa 188, 338, 377, 388–390, 393, 396–402, 405, 411, 492
Cape Verde Islands 77, 338
Cape Waios, Indonesia 279
Cape Wessel, Northern Territory 279
Cape York Land Council 299
Cape York Peninsula, Queensland 30, 32, 52, 65, 79, 109, 129–130, 179, 268, 280, 332
Captain's Log 207, 209, 215, 268, 308, 316, 324, 325–326, 332, 363, 368, 379, 381, 390, 394, 417
caravel ship type 159, 400
Carey, John 204, 206, 212–213
Carnarvon, Western Australia 213
Carrack ship type 76, 78, 507
Carrigg, Royce 33
Carruthers, Sherree 212
Carstensz, Jan 130, 311, 318
Cartwright, Bob 171
Cartwright, Kathryn 58–59, 161, 505
Castellorizo, Greece 54, 59
Casting Supplies 158
Catalpa ship 153
Celebes, Indonesia 81
Centenary of Federation, Australia 57, 93
Ceram, Indonesia 77
Ceylon 228

Charlton, Warwick 338
Chevron Leadership Program 348, 357
Chevron Petroleum Company 179–181, 187, 214, 281, 299, 301, 311, 313, 321–324, 332–333, 347–348
China 39, 70, 75, 81, 178, 228
Cicerello's Seafood Restaurant 137
Cicholas, Andrea 152, 156, 190, 194–195, 204, 212, 234, 347–349, 378–379, 411
Cinnamon 38, 78, 138, 228, 371
City of Fremantle 86
Claessen, Elisabeth 131
Clarke, Professor Adrienne 22
Cleland, Sam 185
Clough Engineering 51
    Entact Clough 87
Clough, Harold 51, 87
Cloves 66, 70–71, 78, 81, 187, 337
Coat of Arms of Fremantle 118, 141
Cockatoo, John 311–312, 431, 490
Cockle Bay, Darling Harbour, New South Wales 21, 457, 464, 492
Cockrell, Don 100, 106, 152

Cocks, Cathy 24, 43, 94, 125–126, 231, 328, 342–343, 377, 401, 424
Cocks, Daniel 7, 126, 231, 377, 390, 424, 454
Cocks, Jack 200, 359, 361, 424
Cocks, Louise 7, 126, 231, 235, 377, 424
Cocks, Rodney 158
Cocks, Shirley 359
Coen River (Pennefather River) 298, 311
Coen, Governor Jan Pieterszoon 268–270, 274–276, 311, 364, 430–432, 442
Colombo, Sri Lanka 334, 372, 374–375, 376–377, 385, 494
Columbus, Christopher 35, 79, 88, 131, 194, 266–267, 338, 408
Colvin, John 190, 204, 212, 214, 243
Comalco 301
Community Aid Abroad 326
Community Aid Abroad shop 170
Comoro Islands, Indian Ocean 78
Compagnie van Verre (Company from Far) 73

Compass Rose motor launch 121
Conroy, Father Vincent 107, 146, 474
Conservation and Land Management, Department of 117, 215
Constable, Dr Ian 90–91
Constable, Elizabeth 90
Consultas web designers 437
Cook, Ltnt (Captain) James 23, 31, 40, 91, 131, 268, 296, 320, 355, 368
Cooktown, Queensland 180–181, 299, 326–328, 459
Coral Sea 323
Corneliusz, Jeronimus 436
Cornell, John 153
Corser, Syd 60–61, 68, 85, 91, 121–123, 127, 182, 199, 505
Cortes, Hernan 79
Court, Billie 143
Court, Jo 482
Court, Premier Richard 33, 36, 52, 59, 63, 67, 84, 120, 145, 147, 154, 166, 178
Court, Premier Sir Charles 52, 67, 178
Cowan Creek, New South Wales 350
Cox, Ellenor 188, 250, 256, 261, 277, 437
Crackneck Point, New South Wales 349
Crean, Simon 68
Croc Eisteddfod Festival 302
Crusade yacht 101
Cruthers, Sir James 60, 67–68, 91, 94, 120, 122, 126, 135–136, 178, 181, 475, 505
Customs House, Brisbane 331

D

da Gama, Vasco 408
Da Zhong ship 446–450, 452, 503
Dampier, Western Australia 213–216, 224, 233
Dampier, William 31, 214
Dari headdress 320
Dark Shadows 227–228, 269, 442, 465
Darling Harbour, Sydney 21, 23, 49, 328, 352, 358, 360, 455, 464
Darwin, Charles 33, 235
Darwin, Northern Territory 46, 54, 90, 185–186, 200, 224, 239, 256, 334, 363, 365, 458–459
Day, Michael 351
Dayaks 174
De Delft shipkeeper 447
De Delft Shipyard 446
de Freycinet, Louis 212

De Hadleigh, Jonathon 119, 140

De Heer, Dr Cornelis (Cees) 41–42, 44

De Heeren Zeventien play 434

de Jong, Adriaan 44, 48, 65, 69, 73, 75, 86, 97–98, 120, 130, 135, 138, 141, 264, 278, 337, 354, 473

de Mendoça. Admiral Andrea Furtado 75

de Ruyter, Admiral Michiel 46, 147–148

De Vliegende Hollander 434

De Zon ship 74

Dekkers, Ralph 418, 420, 422–423, 505

Delfshaven, Rotterdam 441

Delft, The Netherlands 227, 230, 437

Delgada marine rescue (MRCC) 413, 414–415

Den Haag, The Netherlands 48, 88, 93, 230, 255, 341, 354, 363, 424, 429, 437–438

den Hartog, Barbara 111

Denham, Western Australia 129, 186, 211

Department of Transport, WA 159

Deshima, Japan 439

Devendra, Somasiri 378

Dewaruci KRI ship 221, 366

Dias, Bartolomeu 322, 400, 405

Diego Rodrigues Island 386–388

Dili, East Timor 174, 225, 242, 326

Dingle, Max 342

Dirk Hartog Island 31, 36, 211

Dobo, Indonesia 279, 281, 324

Doepel, Jane 191, 194, 204, 211–213, 252, 273, 291, 294, 296, 305, 347, 353, 357, 504

Dom Perignon 143

Downer, Alexander 93, 222, 224, 244

Dragt, Dirk 448

Driver, Tina 313, 437, 445

Dugong 215, 308

Duyfken 1606 Replica Foundation 17, 19, 42, 58, 61, 63–64, 69, 143, 163, 182, 200, 356, 456, 458, 460, 462–465, 472–473, 497, 504, 546

Duyfken Ale 138–139, 142

Duyfken Seaport 400, 428, 439–440, 453

E

Earl of Pembroke ship (Endeavour) 49, 91

East India Company (English) 79, 275
East Nusa Tenggara, Indonesia 236
East Timor 174–175, 185–186, 217, 222, 239–242, 253, 325, 367
EasyEverything 438
Edwards, Gregson 176, 219
Edwards, Hugh 31, 129
Edwards, Steve 113
Eendracht ship 31, 460
Elcano, Juan Sebastian 338, 440
Embassy, Australia 176–177, 217, 219, 223–226, 234, 237, 244, 247, 273, 325, 338, 365, 367, 370
Emery, Vaughan 145, 150
Endeavour replica 22, 23, 32, 51, 91, 101, 180–181, 189, 267, 269, 362, 374, 455, 457, 464, 546
Endeavour ship 49, 355, 368
Endeavour Shipyard 23–26, 34, 41, 111, 439
Endeavour Strait, Queensland 280
Endeavour yacht 101
Enkhuizen, The Netherlands 227, 230
Enterprize ship 33, 119, 191

EPIRB (Emergency Position-Indicating Radio Beacons) 340
Erédia, Manuel Godinho de 35–36
Estalagem de Santa Cruz Hotel, Azores 409
Evans, Gareth 367
Exmouth Gulf, Western Australia 55, 213
Exmouth, Western Australia 213
Eye of the Wind ship 189, 347

F

Fahey, John 88, 93, 161
Faial, Azores, Portugal 408, 410–411
Fairlie Yacht Yard 100
Falie ship 357
False Bay Yacht Club 397
False Cape, Indonesia 279, 281
Federal Government 23, 33
Fellsmith, Lorraine, Bruce and Scott 374–375, 376–377, 380
Felser, Hans 453
Fernando de Noronha Islands, Brazil 337
Firelight Productions 187–188, 207, 247, 250, 265, 271–272, 307, 437
First Fleet Re-enactment Voyage 267

Fish River Canyon, Namibia 400, 402
Fletcher, Bill 134–135
Flinders, Matthew 130
Flint and Steel Bay, New South Wales 350
Flores, Azores Islands, Portugal 338, 415–417
Flores, Indonesia 245
Florey, Marc 351
Fly Bay (Albatross Bay) 280
Flying Dutchman 396, 434–435, 501
Flying Foam Massacre 216
Forrest, Andrew 94
Fort Denison 352
Fort Henricus, Indonesia 245
Fort Nassau, Indonesia 269, 275
Fort São Sebastião, Mozambique 78
Foss, Minster for the Arts, Peter 36
Franken, David 331
Frederick Hendrik Island IPalau Yos Sudarsa) 279, 281
Free Aceh Movement 225
Free Papua Movement 175, 292
Freeport mine 292, 294
Fremantle Boatlifters 134, 137, 141, 145, 155, 160, 167, 197, 482
Fremantle Chamber of Commerce 452

Fremantle Crocodile Park 155–156
Fremantle Fishing Boat Harbour 22, 51, 92, 145, 149, 155, 160–161, 194, 197, 202, 452
Fremantle Herald 27, 38, 41, 140, 453
Fremantle Railway Bridge 150
Fremantle Rowing Club 150, 442
Freo Samba 140, 150
Friends of the Duyfken 42, 62, 69, 85, 94, 108, 110–112, 134, 142, 165, 183, 197, 199–200, 217, 459, 465, 485, 546
Fugro Survey 51, 207

G

Gaastra, Femme 98
Gage Roads 27, 33, 91, 138, 164–165, 191, 228, 261, 483
Gaines, Robin 87
Galapagos Islands 386
Galle, Sri Lanka 334, 338, 370–375, 376–378, 380–381, 493
Galley (kitchen) 28, 49, 159, 187, 194, 203, 339, 347, 508
Gallop, Dr Geoff, Premier 453–454
Gamsberg Nature Reserve 403
Gantheaume Point,

Western Australia 235
Gardner, Nicole 190, 204, 212, 214, 242, 244, 284, 289–291, 310, 325, 348–349, 351, 353, 357, 368, 372, 394, 404, 407, 417, 420, 494, 498, 505
Garvey, Robert 4, 250–251, 256, 261, 265, 273, 277, 437, 505
Gass, John 179, 299
Geelvinck ship 35
Gelderland ship 44, 74, 77, 81, 337–338, 387, 469
Geldorp-Pantekoek, Joke 425, 497
Géographe ship 212
Geraldton, Western Australia 158, 191, 203, 209–210, 212, 234, 347, 453, 459, 464
Gerola-Van Tilburg, Giulia 342, 400, 402
Gerritsen, Rupert 455
Gesner, Peter 53–54
Gibbs, Jenny 112, 140, 152
Gietelink, Ab 434, 504
Gillam, Brad 167
Gillezeau, Marcus 188, 204, 207, 261, 271–272, 274, 289, 437
Gillon, Ian 134, 149, 182
Gilt Dragon ship 46
Global Hire 134, 140

Gnangara Pine Plantation 117
Goa, India 75, 78, 334, 372
Gold Coast City Marina 343–344
Goodman, Tom 255, 258, 268, 273–274, 277, 284, 505
Gordon, Col Robert 401
Gove, Northern Territory 296–297, 304
Grange Hermitage Wine 23
Great Australian Bight 193, 329, 336
Great Barrier Reef Marine Parks Authority 235
Great Barrier Reef, Queensland 327
Great Sandy Island, Western Australia 214
Green, Jeremy 46, 48, 73, 84
Griffiths, Susan 87
Groene Draeck yacht 424
Groote Eylandt, Northern Territory 55
Grundel ship 405
Gulf of Carpentaria 30, 55, 130, 166, 187, 279, 282, 296–297, 304
Gun Island, Western Australia 205
Gunnick, Jan, Dutch Consul 41

Gunung Api, Indonesia 256–257, 261–262, 271, 273, 285, 288, 488

Guterres, Eurico 242

H

Habibie, President BJ 172–174, 185–186, 225, 238

Haermans, Admiral Wolfaert 354

Half Moon Reef, Western Australia 205, 209

Halmahera, Indonesia 223, 225

Halve Maen (Half Moon) ship 39

Hamelin, Capt Jacques 212

Hames, Kim 458

Hammocks 190, 194, 203, 394–396, 420

Harcourt Smith, John 204

Haringvliet, Rotterdam 443

Harlingen, The Netherlands 458

Harmensz, Admiral Wolfert 74–75, 337, 469

Harrison, Kevin 25–26

Hartog, Capt Dirk 31, 36, 110, 112, 129, 212, 459–460

Hash House Harriers 301

Hashana, driver, Galle 376, 380

Hati Marege ship 47

Hatta, President Mohammad 248

Hawke, Prime Minister Bob 88

Hawkesbury River, New South Wales 350

Hay, Malcolm 33, 456–457

Hayes, Wiebbe 436

Haywood, Ashley 473

Hellevoetsluis, The Netherlands 438, 446–447

Hempel Paints 89, 115, 233, 282, 447, 449

Hemsley, Michael (Mick) 191, 195, 204, 212, 214, 231–232, 252, 263, 291, 294, 307, 313

Henderson, Graeme 35, 41, 46, 57, 66, 101, 110, 128, 170, 505

Henderson, James 41–42, 48, 51–52, 54, 56, 58, 62, 130, 143, 147, 182, 267, 310, 317, 431

Henschien, Christine 358, 368, 374, 377, 392, 409, 413, 414–415, 417, 494

Herbert, George 118

Heritage Council of WA 86

Hessing, Enric 226, 229–230, 334, 341, 360, 363, 438, 448

Hewavitharana, Capt Athula 376
Hewitt, Terry 56, 167
Hewson, Dr John 27
Heyerdahl, Thor 88, 266, 378
Hicks, Robin 33
Hielscher, Sir Leo 179
Hilder, Renette 212
Hino diesel engines 11, 167, 282
Hiri network and dance 322–323
HM Bark Endeavour Foundation 23, 26, 45, 54, 91, 181, 455
HMAS Advance 352
HMAS Geraldton 147, 306
HMAS Gladstone 306, 308
HMAS Sydney 352
HMAS Vampire 353
HMS Hood 397
HMS Victory 158
HNLMS Jacob van Heemskerck 423
Hoare, Ralph 86
Hoedemaker, Bill 139, 156
Holdsworth, James 313, 351, 353, 358, 368, 397, 437, 442, 445–446, 448, 450, 503
Hollandia ship 131
Hollingworth, Peter 497
Hoorn ship 74

Hoorn, The Netherlands 74, 227, 229, 420, 431, 439, 444, 453, 457
Hope Vale, Queensland 299
Horgan, Dennis 61
Horta, Azores, Portugal 408, 410–413, 414–419, 423
Hortus Botanical Garden 433
Hough, Jan 62
Hough, Paul 235, 256, 272, 288
House of Orange 164
Houtman, Corneliz de 73–74, 78–79, 434
Hoving, Ab 98, 120, 282
Howard, Prime Minister John 87–88, 93, 174, 176, 186, 222, 367, 455
Hudson Bay Company 155
Hudson River, USA 39
Hudson, Henry 39
Huguenots 398
Hurd, Chris 125
Hussein, Asiff 378

I

l'Hermite, Jacque 82
Ijsselmeer, The Netherlands 228, 230, 435, 436, 444, 501
Indonesian Sail Training Federation 219

International Socialists 441
Irian Jaya, Indonesia 175
Islands of Angry Ghosts book 31, 129
Itsas Museum, Bilbao 439

J

Jackson River, Queensland 305
Jackson, Gloria 39, 62, 85
Jacobszoon, Lenaert 213
Jacquard, François 144
Jaeger, Werner 99
Jakarta Bay 370
Jakarta Post newspaper 172
Jakarta, Indonesia 91, 172–177, 186, 216–217, 219, 221, 224–226, 228, 234, 237, 244, 247–250, 255, 261, 264, 277, 325, 334, 338, 341, 358, 363–368, 370, 372, 388, 425, 427
Jansz (oon), Willem 32, 36, 46, 63, 74, 77–79, 82, 108, 110, 129–131, 136, 167, 184, 185, 201, 213, 245, 257, 267–269, 279–283, 298, 312, 316–317, 319, 322, 324, 387, 472
Jansz, Volckert 131
Jardine Shipping 327
Jarosek, Frank 159, 164

Java Sea 364
Jefferson, Robert 18, 204–205, 238, 243, 292, 295, 325, 504
Jemaah Islamiyah 176
Jihadi troops 273, 289, 292, 325, 509
Johannesburg, South Africa 404
Johns, Bob 24
Johnson, Bernie 329
Johnston, Adam 212
Johnston, Anne 388
Jones, Peter 178–179
Jones, Warren 120, 122
Joostenz, Jouris 75
Jorgen Jorgensen, viking longboat 33
Joseph Banks 91, 180

K

K Djartama ship 147
Kadir, Abdul 75
Kailis Broome Pearls 55
Kailis Fish Market & Cafe 56
Kailis, Alex 56
Kailis, Dr Patricia 55, 64, 92–93, 163, 166, 182, 188, 199, 328, 428, 445, 454, 464
Kailis, George 56
Kailis, Michael 54–57, 58–65, 67–68, 69, 85, 88–93, 94–96, 101, 107–110, 115, 119–124, 127, 134–135, 139, 141,

144–145, 147, 150–151, 154–155, 159–161, 163, 166, 173, 181, 199, 308, 333, 351, 428, 445, 473, 475, 505
Kailis, Victor 56, 154
Kalimantan, West and South, Indonesia 367
Karimun Jawa Island, Indonesia 364
KASAL (Indonesia Chief of Navy) 220–222
Kaurareg people 320
Kaye-Peebles, Gillian 40
Keating, Paul 27, 68, 87
Keel laying ceremony 11, 25, 66, 107–108, 110, 114
Keer Reef, Queensland 280
Keetmanshoop, Namibia 400
Kei Besar, Indonesia 281
Kei Islands, Indonesia 279, 281, 288, 289
Kei River, South Africa 399
Kennedy, Rear-Admiral Phillip GN 165
Kerbey, David 17, 348, 397, 504
Ketupat dance 242
Khoikhoi people 399, 405
Kidman, Nicole 87
Kidu, Lady 323
King Solomon 80
Kirke River, Queensland 317
Kleine Son ship 81
Knight, Alan 85, 128, 151
Kock, Gunter 403–404
Kok, Wim, Dutch Prime Minister 93
Kolderstok (whipstaff) 203, 246, 486, 509, 511
Komodo Island, Indonesia 175
Kon-Tiki boat 378
Koolinda, mv, ship 54
Kopassus, TNI 253–254
Kora Kora (corecore) boat 82, 132, 271–272, 273–275, 507
Kott Gunning solicitors 45, 61
Kouniali, Karim 195, 204
Krait boat 352
Kristal Hotel, Kupang, Indonesia 236, 238, 241
Ku-ring-gai Chase National Park 350
Kuiper, Kasper 108, 335, 341, 386, 456
Kuiper, Roberta 336, 341
Kulin Industries 150
Kupang, Indonesia 186, 217, 219–220, 225, 234–244, 246, 254, 257, 271, 313, 325–326, 485
Kutubu Lake, Papua New Guinea 323
Kwik Kian Gie 429

L

La Violante ship 352, 358, 361
Lach de Bere, Phillipe 73
Laha Airport, Ambon 259
Lahuyong, Indonesia 245
Laicos, Henry 153
Lam ship 131
Lamakera, Indonesia 245
Lambata, Indonesia 245
Lambert's Bay, South Africa 400
Lancaster, John 24
Larium anti-malarial 243
Laskar Jihad 217
Latvia 69, 95–96, 111, 113, 116, 153–154, 156, 264, 344, 478
Le Maire Strait 74
Le Maire, Isaäc 74, 439
Leach, Geoffrey 219–220, 222, 224–225, 244, 247, 249, 366
Leeuwin Estate Winery 171
Leeuwin, Sail Training Ship 33, 57, 152, 164, 191, 202, 207, 456
Lefroy, Mike 24, 119
Leggoe, Cliff 180, 299, 313, 322–323, 341
Leggoe, Ian 180
Lelystad, The Netherlands 33, 47, 64, 121, 230, 328, 355, 436, 445, 500
Leonard, Bill 22, 24–25, 35, 39, 41, 43, 97, 100–101, 106–108, 110, 112–115, 120, 138, 140–141, 143, 145, 151–152, 154, 156, 160, 166, 233, 333, 344, 476–477, 504
Lewotobi Strait, Indonesia 245
Linschoten, Jan Huygen van 71, 389
Lion of Orange figurehead 164
Lisbon, Portugal 334, 400
Little Creatures Brewery 156
Loi Trang 293
Lombardo's building 153
Longford, Geoff 289
Longley, John 22, 23, 25, 28, 38, 40–41, 54, 56, 91, 94, 119, 452, 460–462, 505
Longley, Richard 40
Looijschelder, Bob 358, 361, 421
Lords XVII 227, 434
Lotteries Commission of WA 66, 86, 122–123, 149
Lotteries Duyfken Village 66, 86, 97, 110, 112, 120, 123, 134, 139, 474
Lotteries Sailmaking Loft 123

Lotto Skyworks 149
Lucas, Jim 116
Ludlum, Scott 207

M

Maarleveld, Thijs 98
Maas River, The Netherlands 444
Macdonald River 305
Mace 66, 70–71, 78, 80, 187, 255, 270, 275
Mackay, Queensland 330, 459
Madagascar 386
Madura, Indonesia 47, 66, 174
Magellan, Ferdinand 80, 324, 338
Maher, Bob 152
Maio Island, Cape Verde group 77
Makassar (Ujung Pandang), Indonesia 250
Makassarese 296, 509
Makian Island, Indonesia 66, 70, 81, 82, 187, 220, 247
Malacari, Bob 158
Malherbe, Nick 398, 402
Malino II Peace Agreement 297
Maluku (Moluccas), Province and islands, Indonesia 55, 66, 70–71, 74–76, 79, 81, 82, 89, 174–175, 177, 184, 186, 217, 220–225, 237, 247–248, 250, 252, 254–255, 258–259, 262–263, 268, 272, 273, 278, 282, 284, 289, 297, 338, 364, 429–430, 452, 509–510
Maluku Action Committee 429
Manila, The Phillipines 81
Manitoba motor cruiser 123, 150, 155
Manthorpe, Pep 204
Manthorpe, Peter 188–189, 191, 193, 195–196, 200, 202–204, 208, 210, 212–213, 224, 234, 253, 256, 277, 281–282, 294, 304, 308, 312, 330, 332–333, 343, 347, 359, 431, 461, 484, 487, 490–491, 504
Manubada, Papua New Guinea 322
Marchant, Assoc Prof Leslie 35
Marcuson, Steven 35
Mare, Papua New Guinea 320
Maritiem & Jutters Museum 228–229
Maroochy Barambah 331
Martin, Rick 119
Mary Rose ship 171
Mascarene group of islands 386
Matelieff, Admiral 80–81

Matilda Bay Brewery 138
Matthew ship 33, 159
Maulana Hotel, Banda 256–257
Mauritius 75, 336, 338, 378, 380, 386–390, 399, 405, 426, 469, 494, 546
Mauritius ship 213
Maxsurf software 100
Mayflower ship 190, 338
McAlpine, Ken 128, 159, 167–168
McCarthy, John, Ambassador 176, 226
McCaskill, Em Prof Murray 35–36
McCullough, Tracy 17, 139, 209, 211, 301, 322, 334, 348, 364, 377, 397, 422, 504
McGowan, Premier Mark 461, 463
McGuire, Shannon 358, 380, 383–384, 400–401, 404, 406, 408–409, 412, 505
McLernon, Josh 100, 107, 113, 117, 505
Meacham, Steve 359
Megaw, Mike 68
Melaka (Malacca), Malaysia 71, 175, 177, 334
Melville Island, Northern Territory 35
Melville Passage, Queensland 326

Menanga, Indonesia 245–246, 485–486
Mendaña, Álvaro de 80
Mermaid ship 34, 47, 53
Mermaid, HM Cutter, ship 34, 47, 53
Mexico 79
MG Kailis Dock 91, 452
MG Kailis Engineering 161, 167
MG Kailis Group 42, 55, 161, 167, 169, 178, 182, 199, 217, 328, 428
Middelburg, The Netherlands 227, 230
Middleburg, The Netherlands 97, 438, 444, 499
Miller, Hazel 311, 491
Miller, Ray 114, 116–117
Milne (Dale), Julie 357, 360–361, 380, 388, 393, 406–407, 411, 504
Mitchell, Rick 17, 140, 152, 156
Moramoro, Moseley 321
Moreton Bay, Queensland 491
Morley Island, Western Australia 206
Moro, Papua New Guinea 323
Mosambique ship 78
Moss, Les, Shark Bay Shire 36, 129, 213

Mossel Bay, South Africa 400
Moti Island, Indonesia 70
Mottram, Jimmy 111
Motu people 322–323
Mozambique, Africa 78, 389
Mt Pico, Azores 410
Murdoch, Priscilla 45–46
Murdoch, Rupert 60
Murfitt, Rod 85
Murgatroyd, David 209

N

Namaliu, Sir Rabbie 323
Namib-Naukluft National Park 403
Namibia 375, 400–402, 405, 421, 426, 546
Namibian Underwater Federation 405
National Monuments Council of Namibia 405
Naturaliste ship 212
Nell Ottenhofff 110
Nemorin, Gaetan 87
New Holland 212
New Norcia 143
New York 911 attacks 176, 372, 381
Newcastle, New South Wales 20, 21, 45, 346–347, 350, 464
Newman, Geoff 143
Ngaro people 330
Nickol Bay, Western Australia 216

Nieuwe Haarlem ship 398
Nijptangh ship 35
Nina, Pinta and Santa Maria ships 266
Nine Network 26
Noah 143, 146
Nobby's Head, Newcastle, New South Wales 346
Nolin, Peter 139, 156
Nonsuch ship 155
Nooij, Albert, Dutch Ambassador 145
Noongar people 329
Noonkanbah Convoy 52–53
North Head, New South Wales 351–352
North West Cape, Western Australia 179, 213–214
North West Shelf Gas Project 178–179
Note, Margaret 311, 491
Notre Dame, University of 139, 141–142
Nova Guinea 77, 79–80, 268, 279
Nova Zembla, Russia 439, 457–458
Nusa Tenggara Timur 242, 260
Nusanive lighthouse, Indonesia 253
Nutmeg 66, 70–71, 78, 80, 187, 248, 255, 270, 275, 337, 442

O

O'Brien, Natalie 129
O'Byrne, Greg 190, 204–205, 210, 295, 348–349, 351, 353, 357, 392–393, 406
Oak, European 9, 11, 18, 20, 49–50, 65–66, 68, 69, 80, 92, 95–96, 100–101, 111–113, 115–117, 119, 138, 141, 144, 154, 156, 163, 166, 206, 217, 264, 343–344, 447, 464, 478, 483
Oil Search company 321
Old East India Company (Oude Oost-Indische Compagnie) 74
Old Swan Brewery, Perth 454–455, 458
Olympic Games, Sydney 2000 57, 65, 88, 109, 120–121, 151, 181, 355
Omni Hotel, Jakarta 368
On the Origin of the Species 235
Onkie 239
Onslow, Western Australia 214
Oosterloo, Janine 446, 448, 450, 503
Ophir 80
Orang Kaya 268–269, 275
Orange River, Namibia/South Africa 401
Orchard, Ltnt Commander Phil 147
Orembai boat 265–266, 270, 309–310, 487, 490, 509
Ortelius map 279
Os Papuas 268, 281
Österreichische Nationalbibliothek 278
Ottenhoff, Nell 62
Oude Haven, Rotterdam 440
Oudeschild Fishermen's Choir 424
Oudeschild, The Netherlands 228, 424
Ovens, HMAS, submarine 34, 128
Overijssel ship 73, 164
Ozols, Arvids 96

P

Palau Yos Sudarsa, Indonesia 279
Palm Island, Queensland 329
Palmer, Ken 161
Panasami, Dr 377
Papillon protest ship 430
Papua New Guinea 30, 55, 129–130, 179, 187, 191, 200, 268, 279, 281–282, 320, 322–324, 330, 333, 348, 546
Parke, Melissa 457
Parker King, Lt Phillip 34, 47

Parry, Captain Sarah 361
Parthesius, Robert 48, 73, 98, 282
Payne, Mark 166, 301, 305, 314
Peacock, Andrew 88, 176
Pearson, Noel 299–300, 331
Pegasus Bay ship 96
Pelni ferry 250, 254, 256–257, 259, 273, 509
Pelsaert, Capt Francois 464
Pennant House 164
Pennefather River, Queensland 18–19, 32, 44, 65, 130, 136, 187, 213, 264–266, 268, 278, 279–281, 289–290, 297–303, 304–305, 307–309, 311, 313, 315, 320, 329, 431, 465, 473, 489–491
Pepper 71, 75, 78–79, 370
Pera ship 30, 130, 296, 318
Perahu water craft 47
Pereira, Cian 418, 421, 442, 445, 456
Perintis line, 259
Peter's Cafe Sport bar, Azores 410, 414
Pett, Phineas 102
Philippines, The 338
Pierce, Gary 61
Pigafetta, Antonio 324

Piggin, Shaun 358
Pinisi ship type 366–367, 493, 509
Pinus pinaster tree 117
Pinus radiata tree 117
Piper, Terry 301
Piracy 178, 217, 224, 336
Playford, Dr Phillip 36, 60
Plimouth Plantation, USA 338
Plume, Michelle 212
Plymouth, United Kingdom 77, 338
PMFM radio station 149
PNG Defence Force Landing Craft Base 322
PNG Gas Project 179–181, 187, 299, 321–322, 324, 341
Polden, Richard 204, 209, 212, 476, 505
Pope, Nina 112
Port Douglas, Queensland 362–363, 459
Port Elizabeth, South Africa 391
Port Hamble Ltd 100
Port Hedland, Western Australia 217, 219, 224, 335, 343, 459
Port Louis, Mauritius 388, 390
Port Mathurin, Diego Rodrigues Island 387
Port Moresby, Papua

New Guinea 181, 187, 191, 281–282, 320–324, 330, 374
Portugal 117, 400, 408–409, 426
Poso, Indonesia 175
Possession Island, Queensland 320
Poulos, Maria 374, 385
Powell, Dr John 179–180, 299, 341
Powers, Dom Christopher 143
Prince of Orange 164
Prince Phillip 330
Prince Rupert's Bastards 331
Prince Willem-Alexander 107–110, 112, 125, 226, 229, 335, 421, 424, 460, 475, 497
Princess Máxima 424
PT Caltex Pacific Indonesia 90
PT Telekomunikasi Indonesia 263
Pulau Ai, Banda, Indonesia 270
Pulau Dapur (Kitchen Island) Jakarta 370
Pulau Keraka (Crab island), Indonesia 261
Pulau Onrust (Restless Island), Jakarta 370
Pulau Panjang, Indonesia 75, 370

Q

Qantas 28, 120, 167, 404
Quadros, Marco 417
Queen Elizabeth 330
Queensland Maritime Museum 456
Queirós, Pedro Fernandes de 31
Quigley, John 358, 407, 498

R

Raleigh, Sir Walter 78
Ram ship 131
Ramsay, Capt David 219–222, 224–225, 366
Randall, Don 93
Randall, Len 122
Rapanaro, Margaret 24, 111, 152, 192, 505
Redcliffe, Queensland 341
Redding, Mike 357, 362, 397, 406, 409
Reddingius, Ron 460, 504
Refugee Camps 186, 217, 238, 240–242, 257
Reid, Gavin 152, 156
Reid, Vern 23–24, 60
Reitsma, Ed 342
Reynders, Peter 455
Reynolds, Graham 94, 182, 184
Ridderschap van Holland ship 34
Ridderzaal, Den Haag 429
Riga, Latvia 95–96

INDEX 537

Rijksarchief, Den Haag 48
Rijksmuseum, Amsterdam 98, 120, 164, 433
Rijst Tafel 141–142, 510
Rinehart, Gina 94
Robertson, Peter 179
Robins, Noel 85–86, 89, 92, 117, 119, 121–122, 124, 127, 140, 151, 182
Roebourne, Western Australia 216
Roebuck Bay, Western Australia 55
Rogers, Peggy 85, 151–152, 301, 348, 377, 387, 462, 498
Rolfe, Graeme 84
Rose-Taylor, Phil 442–443
Rose, Andy 84
Ross, Ralph 329
Rossengin (supercargo) 280
Rothesay Swan, Rear Admiral 349
Roti Island, Indonesia 55, 256
Rotondella, Joe 51, 58, 65
Rotterdam Indonesia Solidarity Committee (RISK) 441
Rotterdam, The Netherlands 227, 230, 250, 358, 429, 438, 440–442, 444–445, 447, 449–450, 503
Rottnest Island, Western Australia 34, 44, 138, 193–194, 201
Roughan, Grey 51, 207
Rowe, Mike 152, 158
Royal Netherlands Embassy 57, 405
Rumphius, Georgius 235
Ryder, Dale 235

S

Saardam ship 436, 464
Sacrificial Keel 169
Safety Bay High School 158
Sago 76–77, 322
Sail & Anchor Pub 138, 141, 156
Sailing Permit, Indonesia 216, 219–222, 224–226, 231, 234, 292
SailMail 207, 340, 381
San Pedrico ship 320
Sanctuary Cove, Queensland 341–343, 351
São Cristóvão ship 405
Saris, Captain John 79–80, 279
Sarwono, Aji 220
Sarwono, Governor 239, 242
Sastrohandojo, Wiryono, Indonesian Ambassador 145
Sat C 340, 415

Satcom C 207, 412, 510
Saumlaki, Indonesia 90, 175, 225, 364
Savu Sea 237, 242
Scheepvaartmuseum 433
Schelde River, The Netherlands 337
Schmidt, Louisa 456
Schouten, Willem Cornelisz 74, 76–77, 337, 439
Scrayen, Jenny 117, 141, 156, 164, 170
Seelant (see Zeelandia) 76
Selamon village, Banda 274
Sent Forth a Dove book 143
Sentosa Island, Singapore 177–178
Seram, Indonesia 71, 76, 223, 259, 285–286
Setiawan, Iwan 277, 284
Seven Provinces ship 47
Seven Television Network 60, 88, 125, 142–143, 150, 188, 202, 331
Shark Bay, Western Australia 36–37, 151, 186, 193, 210–212
Shell company 51, 179
Shirley Smith tug 352
Silalahi, Robert 365
Simonstown, South Africa 397, 399, 449
Singapore 175, 177–178, 334, 437, 439

Sir Charles Gairdner Hospital 160–161
Sjerp, Ria and Nanne 39, 62, 110, 498, 505
Slaves 76, 275, 435, 442, 501
Smiltene, Latvia 96
Smit, Ambassador Roelof 36, 120–121
Smit, Con 85, 134, 151, 156, 217, 348
Smith, Andrew 27
Smith, Stephen 457
Smith, Trevor 353, 356
Snedden, Billy 88
SO1 Dutch archaeological site 99, 458
Soe, West Timor, Indonesia 239–240, 325–326
Sollis, James 63, 472
Solor, Indonesia 220, 225, 245, 485
Somare, Sir Michael 323
Somers, Stijn 358, 392, 413, 415, 417
South Africa 91, 126, 190, 375, 390–391, 395, 397–399, 404, 421, 426, 449, 492, 494, 546
Spain 79–80, 324, 338, 509
Spice Adventurers book 337
Spliethoff cargo ship 440, 448–450

INDEX 539

Springbok, Namibia 400
Sri Lanka 338, 370–375, 376, 378, 382–383, 405, 415, 426, 493–494, 546
St Helena 77, 337–338, 388, 405, 426
St John of God Hospital, Subiaco 377
Stannard, Bruce 23, 25
State Shipwrecks Act 170
Staten Generaal 226–227
States-General of the United Provinces 77
Stella Maris Seafarers Centre 107
Stichting 400 Jaar VOC 226
Stichting Duyfken VOC 2002 Nederland 341, 484
Stingray Creek, Western Australia 217
Stirling Marine 149
Stockholm tar 157, 233, 246, 510
Stokes Bay, Queensland 326
Stokes, Kerry 61, 67, 88, 121, 123, 199
Storey Bridge, Brisbane 331
Stormy Seas lifejackets 340
Straits of Magellan, South America 77
Subiago, Mayor of North Jakarta 365–366
Suez Canal 334, 336

Suharto, President 173–174, 237, 272, 292, 365, 441
Sukarno, President 248
Sukarnoputri, President Megawati 365, 370
Sularso, Capt Aji 219–220, 222, 224–225
Sulawasi, Indonesia 250
Sulawesi, Indonesia 46, 70, 175, 200, 507, 509
Sumatra, Indonesia 75, 175, 178, 225
Summi 238, 240–242
Sunda Kelapa, Jakarta, Indonesia 75, 364, 366–370, 372, 493
Sunda Strait, Indonesia 75, 370
Surabaya, Indonesia 89
Suriname 435
Sutiyoso, Governor 365–366
Sutjipto, Admiral Achmad 220
Swakopmund, Namibia 400
Swan Dock, Fremantle Harbour 51, 58, 123, 133
Swan River, Western Australia 33–34, 48, 110, 121, 124, 149, 201, 454, 458, 482, 546
Sydney Cove, New South Wales 31
Sydney Harbour 21,

121, 181, 267, 351–352, 361, 362, 465
Sydney Harbour Bridge 352
Sydney, New South Wales 21, 338, 350, 425
Szczerbanik, John 53

T

Table Bay, Cape Town 398
Tacoma, Eelco 68, 85–86
Tagliaferri, Peter 453–454
Tahija, George 90
Tahija, Jean Walters 89–90, 172
Tahija, Julius 89–91, 109, 160, 172, 176, 179, 181, 226, 234, 248, 292, 363, 367, 475
Tahija, Sjakon 90
Tall Ships Festival 1998 57
Tami lifter 134, 145, 148, 197
Tamil Tigers 371–372
Tanimbar Islands, Indonesia 90, 175, 222, 363–364
Tannock, Dr Peter 139
Tasman, Abel 151, 214
Taylor, Davina 358
Teddy's Bar, Kupang 239–240, 257
Templeman, David 462
Tempo magazine 277
Tenau Port, Indonesia 238, 242
Teredo navalis (Teredo worm) 82, 115, 217, 282, 344, 397, 447, 449
Ternate Island, Indonesia 56, 66, 70, 73–75, 80–81, 82, 97, 187, 220, 223, 225, 247, 268, 337
Terra Nullius 299
Terschelling, The Netherlands 439
Tetteroo, Gert 433
Texel, The Netherlands 73–74, 77, 120, 200, 228–229, 357, 360, 364, 387–388, 399, 408, 418–420, 423–426, 429, 439, 444, 459, 495–497
Thancoupie 302, 308, 315
Theatre Nomade 434, 501
Thnikwithi 308
Thomas, Martin 315
Throsby Wharf, Newcastle, New South Wales 346
Thursday Island, Queensland 320, 362–363
Tidore Island, Indonesia 70, 80, 187, 220, 223, 247, 338
Timor Sea 184, 219
Tipuka River, Indonesia 292–293

Tiuri village, Indonesia 281
Tjungudji 308
TNI (Tentara Nasional Indonesia) 220–221, 238, 241, 254, 273, 289, 325
Tonnison, Capt Greg 164–165
Torres Strait 30–31, 179, 191, 268, 280–281, 320, 336, 338, 363
Torres Strait Islanders 280, 320
Torres, Luís Vaz de 31, 320
Touwfabriek Langman 157
Towler, Marjolein 207
Townsville, Queensland 235, 328–329, 459
Traitors Island, Western Australia 206
Trathen, Susan 243
Treaty of Tordesillas 80
Tresidder, Sandra 424
Tricentennial Committee, Swan River and Rottnest Island 34–35
Trilling, Tony 69
Tropic of Capricorn 185, 282, 330
Trotter, George 112
Trulove, Nick 100, 106, 118, 138, 152, 156, 160, 164, 168, 504

Trunnel 105, 111, 113–114, 116, 511
Tual, Indonesia 277, 285–286, 288, 289–290, 292
Turnbull, Alice 358, 406
Turrbal people 331
Turtle Bay, Western Australia 207

U

Ujung Pandang, Indonesia 250, 253–254, 256, 277
Uniform Shipping Laws (USL) code 159, 185
Unimark Associates 69, 96
United Dutch East India Company (VOC) 19, 77, 337, 426
University of Western Australia 388
Unmack, Tony 153
Uranie ship 212
Utrecht ship 74, 76, 387
Utting, David 86
Utting, Mayor Richard 134, 140–141, 202, 481

V

Valentijn, Francois 131
van Caerden, Admiral Paulus 81, 82
van Deelan, Laura 438
van der Decken, Capt Willem 434
van der Haghen, Admiral Steven 74, 77, 79
Van der Hem, Laurens 278, 471

van der Spek, Willem 435, 501
van der Veen, Hans 403
van Doorn, Michiel 128, 151, 178, 217, 341
van Heemskerck, Admiral Jacob 74
van Heemstra, Baron Schelto 226
van Huystee, Marit 48, 69, 73, 98, 130, 139, 278, 409, 419, 424–425, 433, 436, 441, 473, 504
van Iterson, David 44, 52, 64, 226
van Neck, Jacob Cornelius 73, 131
van Raalte, Stewart 164
van Riebeeck, Jan 398
van Roosengijn, Jan Lodewijkszoon 78, 81, 82
van Tilburg, Benno 228–229, 341–344, 400, 402, 409, 425, 454, 457, 484, 504
Vasa ship 439–440
Vasco da Gama 36, 408
Vaughan, Allan 158
Vergulden Draak ship 31, 34
Verhoeven, Paul 435, 436
Victor Kailis 56, 154
Victoria and Alfred Waterfront, Cape Town 398
Victoria Quay,

Fremantle Harbour 23, 51, 91, 123, 152, 154, 156
Victoria ship 338
Vida ship 417
Viering VOC? group 430
Virgin Megastore 438
Vlaming Head, Western Australia 213
Vlamingh Tricentennial Year 93, 107, 110, 112, 459
Vlamingh, Capt Willem de 34–36, 48, 93, 107, 110, 112, 194, 212, 459
Vlissingen ship 400, 405
Vlissingen, The Netherlands 77, 337, 388
VOC 2002 226, 334, 371, 400, 424, 429, 436
VOC 2002 Committee 335, 360, 363, 440, 448
VOC 2002 Foundation 354
Vos, Willem 47, 64–65
Vosmer, Tom 69
Vroom, Hendrick Cornelisz 164

W

WA Maritime Heritage Association 34, 47
WA Maritime Museum 24, 35, 42, 46, 49–51, 63, 73, 84, 152, 157, 278, 371

WA Tourism Commission 25, 27, 34, 43, 139, 145, 546
   Eventscorp 34
   WA Development Corporation 34
Waalhaven, The Netherlands 449
Wachter ship 74, 76, 387
Wahid, President Abdurrahman (Gus Dur) 225, 272, 365, 367, 370
Wakka Wakka dance group 331–332
Walker, George 158
Walker, Rachelle 212, 243, 310
Walker, Walter 348, 353, 357–358, 363, 421
Wallabi Group, Western Australia 206–208
Wallace, Alfred 235, 237
Walton, Andrew 149
Walvis Bay Yacht Club 403
Walvis Bay, Namibia 400–405
WAPET 179, 214
Ward, Steve 101
Water Authority of WA 179
Watson, Chris 204, 207, 212, 261
Watubelus, Indonesia 281
Webb, James 145

Webbi Hayes 207
Weipa, Queensland 166, 298, 301–302, 305–306, 308, 313– 315, 319, 347, 459, 489
Weissenekker, Peter 243
Welker, Charlie 39, 43, 60, 124, 128, 186, 217, 224, 328
Weller, Arthur 54
Weller, Rupert 54, 156, 191, 204, 212, 231, 234, 243, 310, 313, 347, 353, 505
Weller, Sir Arthur 25
Wells, Dean 53
Weseltje ship 35, 194
West Irian 282
West Papua, Indonesia 70, 222, 258–259, 279, 281, 291–292
West Timor (Nusa Tenggara Timur) 186, 225
Whitsunday Islands, Queensland 330
Wieringa, Don 155
Wik people, Queensland 52, 54, 315, 317
Willems River, Western Australia 213
William Dampier 31, 214
William V of Orange 401
Williams, Glenn 357, 359–361, 362–363, 367–370, 378–382, 386, 388, 390–391, 399, 404–406, 409,

411, 414–420, 423–424, 426, 429, 451, 492

Wilson, Gary 21, 188–189, 203–204, 207, 209, 211–212, 233, 246, 282, 295, 307, 324, 330, 333–335, 341, 346, 356–359, 386, 419, 429–430, 432, 442, 444, 446, 451, 454, 486, 504

Wimaranga-Andumakwithi descendants 303

Windeward Bound ship 352, 361

Windhoek, Namibia 400–405

Witsen, Nicolaes 48

Wolmby, Ray 316–317, 319

Wolmby, Silas 315–319, 332

Wooded Island Passage, Western Australia 206

Woodside company 179, 335

Work for the Dole scheme 169–170

World Harbour Days, Rotterdam 442

World Trade Centre 382

Wulgurukaba people 329

Wymer, Rick 87

Y

Yamdena, Indonesia 90

Yapurarra people 216

Yardie Creek, Western Australia 213

Yates, Brett Torin 358, 404–406, 412, 421

Young Socialists of Rotterdam 441

Young, Gerald 158

Young, Janine 38, 40, 44–45, 62, 110, 138, 282, 351

Young, Michael 32–33, 38, 40, 42, 44–46, 48, 51, 53–57, 58, 60, 62, 65–66, 69, 73, 85, 87, 96, 110, 129, 137, 140, 147, 163, 182, 186, 200, 217, 228, 236, 238, 244, 257, 325–326, 351, 473, 504

Yungngora people, Western Australia 52

Yunkaporta, Clive 317

Yuppungutti 308, 311

Yupungutti 312

Z

Z Force 90

Zaan River, The Netherlands 437, 500

Zaanse Schans, The Netherlands 437, 439, 500

Zeeland Province, The Netherlands 97

Zeelandia ship 74, 337, 387

Zeemanshuis Hotel, Rotterdam 450

Zeewijk Channel,
Western Australia 206
Zeewijk ship 31, 205–206
Zmitko, Jiri 158
Zuiderhaven, Texel 424
Zuytdorp Cliffs,
Western Australia 210
Zuytdorp ship 31, 36, 60

About Graeme Cocks

Graeme Cocks was born in Perth, Western Australia. A child of the sixties, he grew up near the banks of the Swan River and on the beaches and islands along the coast first explored by Dutch seafarers in 1616. Fremantle was his home town, and rowing at the Fremantle Rowing Club was his sporting passion. He studied journalism at the WA Institute of Technology (now Curtin University) and after a brief foray into journalism and newspaper management, he spent a year backpacking through South America. It changed his life. The wanderlust never left him and he returned to write and edit travel magazines so he could keep travelling. He later ran the communications section of the WA Tourism Commission during the heady years of the post America's Cup tourism boom in the State. An opportunity to work at the *Endeavour* replica sailing ship project connected him with the world of wooden shipbuilding. A casual conversation over breakfast aboard Cook's ship, led him to meet the originator of the idea to build a replica of the first ship to chart Australian shores. Soon, he was enthralled by the idea and he became one of the founding members of the Friends of the *Duyfken* Project, later taking over the whole team as Project Director. He arranged the launch and final fit-out of the ship. He was responsible for the history-making Chevron 2000 *Duyfken* Expedition to Indonesia, Papua New Guinea and Queensland; and the VOC 2002 *Duyfken* Voyagie (sic) from Sydney to Indonesia, Sri Lanka, Mauritius, South Africa, Namibia, the Azores and The Netherlands. It remains the longest 'Age of Discovery' replica ship voyage ever undertaken. After 20 years involvement with *Duyfken*, including a number of years as Chair of the *Duyfken* 1606 Replica Foundation, he left to pursue another passion — historic racing cars. He has contributed to maritime books and is the author of many books on motoring history. Twice shortlisted for Book of the Year at the International Historic Motoring Awards in London (2015 and 2016), he's the only Australian writer to have achieved this honour. His book 'Red Dust Racers' also won the Gold Medal in the Transportation category of the International Independent Publishers Awards in New York in May 2017. His book, 'Claude Deane. Western Australia's Motor Dealer Extraordinaire' was short-listed for the Royal Automobile Club of the United Kingdom's Motoring Book of the Year Awards in 2020. It was also runner-up in the Royal WA Historical Society AE Williams Lee Steere 2020 Publication Prize. He was curator of the Fremantle and York motor museums. Today, he writes motoring history and assists owners to unearth the history of their early motor cars. He still gazes to the west at sunset in the hope of seeing square sails on the horizon.

www.ingramcontent.com/pod-product-compliance
Lightning Source LLC
Chambersburg PA
CBHW051541010526
44118CB00022B/2541